THE AMERICAN NOVEL

A The American Novel

CRITICISM AND BACKGROUND READINGS

SELECTED BY

Christof Wegelin

 THE FREE PRESS, NEW YORK

3/1972
Cont

For Tina and Jake

The Free Press
A Division of The Macmillan Company
866 Third Avenue, New York, New York 10022

Collier-Macmillan Canada Ltd., Toronto, Ontario

Library of Congress Catalog Card Number: 76-136274

printing number
1   2   3   4   5   6   7   8   9   10

PREFACE

The purpose of this anthology is to provide the student of the American novel with a convenient collection of background material and critical commentary on a substantial number of novels likely to be studied in college and university courses— a collection of items which in many college libraries may not be easily available or available only in a few copies. I have made no attempt to project or illustrate any one critical method or approach. The principle of selection has been eclectic. I have aimed at usefulness more than at uniformity of coverage and have thus chosen whatever material seemed most likely to develop the student's interest and sharpen his understanding of the individual novels: a note, a letter, an essay from the novelist's own pen, an interview, but mostly critical assessments and historical perspectives. The attempt to cover fourteen novels in some six hundred pages has imposed narrow limits on the space allowed to each, and if the reader is pained by omissions, let him take comfort in the thought that the compiler has been there before him. Two general sections (on "The American Novel and American Experience" and on "Romance, Realism, and Naturalism") are designed to extend the usefulness of the book.

I am grateful to Robert C. Albrecht for editorial advice, to Esther Anne Scherich for unwearied assistance in the library and at the desk, and to authors and publishers for permissions to reprint. Individual acknowledgements of the latter appear at appropriate places in the body of the collection.

C. W.

CONTENTS

▌▌ Romance, Realism, and Naturalism

▌▌▌ The Leatherstocking Tales (1823–1841) by James Fenimore Cooper

IV The Scarlet Letter (1850) by Nathaniel Hawthorne

V Moby Dick (1851) by Herman Melville

VI | The Adventures of Huckleberry Finn (1884) by Mark Twain

VII | The Rise of Silas Lapham (1885) by William Dean Howells

VIII The Red Badge of Courage (1895) by Stephen Crane

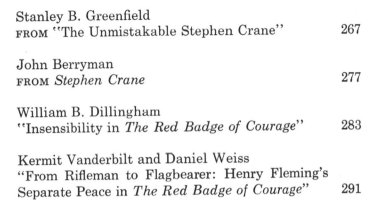

IX Sister Carrie (1900) by Theodore Dreiser

X The Ambassadors (1903) by Henry James

XI The House of Mirth (1905) by Edith Wharton

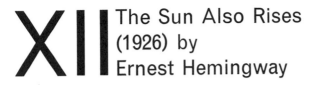

XII The Sun Also Rises (1926) by Ernest Hemingway

XIII Absalom, Absalom! (1936) by William Faulkner

XIV Invisible Man (1952) by Ralph Ellison

XV Go Tell It On The Mountain (1953) by James Baldwin

XVI The Assistant (1957) by Bernard Malamud

I

A
The
American
Novel
and
American
Experience

James Fenimore Cooper

⌒⋙⌒

from *Notions of the Americans* □

The literature of the United States has, indeed, two powerful obstacles to conquer before (to use a mercantile expression) it can ever enter the markets of its own country on terms
of perfect equality with that of England. Solitary and individual works of genius may, indeed, be occasionally brought
to light, under the impulses of the high feeling which has
conceived them; but, I fear, a good, wholesome, profitable,
and continued pecuniary support is the applause that talent
most craves. The fact, that an American publisher can get an
English work without money, must, for a few years longer
(unless legislative protection shall be extended to their own
authors), have a tendency to repress a national literature. No
man will pay a writer for an epic, a tragedy, a sonnet, a history, or a romance, when he can get a work of equal merit for
nothing. I have conversed with those who are conversant on
the subject, and, I confess, I have been astonished at the
information they imparted.

A capital American publisher has assured me that there
are not a dozen writers in this country, whose works he should
feel confidence in publishing at all, while he reprints hundreds
of English books without the least hesitation. This preference
is by no means so much owing to any difference in merit, as to

□ *Notions of the Americans: Picked Up by a Travelling Bachelor* (London:
Henry Colburn, 1828), II, 139–143.

All notes appear at the end of their respective selections.

the fact that, when the price of the original author is to be added to the uniform hazard which accompanies all literary speculations, the risk becomes too great. The general taste of the reading world in this country is better than that of England.[1] The fact is both proved and explained by the circumstance that thousands of works that are printed and read in the mother country, are not printed and read here. The publisher on this side of the Atlantic has the advantage of seeing the reviews of every book he wishes to print, and, what is of far more importance, he knows, with the exception of books that he is sure of selling, by means of a name, the decision of the English critics before he makes his choice. Nine times in ten, popularity, which is all he looks for, is a sufficient test of general merit. Thus, while you find every English work of character, or notoriety, on the shelves of an American book-store, you may ask in vain for most of the trash that is so greedily devoured in the circulating libraries of the mother country, and which would be just as eagerly devoured here, had not a better taste been created by a compelled abstinence. That taste must now be overcome before such works could be sold at all.

When I say that books are not rejected here, from any want of talent in the writers, perhaps I ought to explain. I wish to express something a little different. Talent is sure of too many avenues to wealth and honours, in America, to seek, unnecessarily, an unknown and hazardous path. It is better paid in the ordinary pursuits of life, than it would be likely to be paid by an adventure in which an extraordinary and skilful, because practised, foreign competition is certain. Perhaps high talent does not often make the trial with the American bookseller; but it is precisely for the reason I have named.

The second obstacle against which American literature has to contend is in the poverty of materials. There is scarcely an ore which contributes to the wealth of the author, that is found, here, in veins as rich as in Europe. There are no annals for the historian; no follies (beyond the most vulgar and common place) for the satirist; no manners for the dramatist; no obscure fictions for the writer of romance; no gross and hardy offences against decorum for the moralist; nor any of the rich artificial auxiliaries of poetry. The weakest hand can extract a spark from the flint, but it would baffle the strength of a giant to attempt kindling a flame with a pudding stone. I very well know there are theorists who assume that the society and institutions of this country are, or ought to be, particularly favourable to novelties and variety. But the experience of one month, in these states, is sufficient to show any observant man the falsity of their position. The effect of a promiscuous assemblage anywhere, is to create a standard of deportment; and great liberty permits every one to aim at its attainment. I have never seen a nation so much alike in my life, as the people of the United States, and what is more, they are not only like each other, but they are remarkably like that which common sense tells them they ought to resemble. No doubt, traits of character that are a little peculiar, without, however, being either very poetical, or very rich, are to be found in remote districts; but they are rare, and not always happy exceptions. In short, it is not possible to conceive a state of society in which more of the attributes of plain good sense, or fewer of the artificial absurdities of life, are to be found, than here. There is no costume for the peasant, (there is scarcely a peasant at all) no wig for the judge, no baton for the general, no diadem for the chief magistrate. The darkest ages of their history are illuminated by the light of truth; the utmost efforts of their chivalry are limited by the laws of God; and even the deeds of their sages and heroes are to be sung in a language that would differ but little from a version of the ten commandments. However useful and respectable all this may be in actual life, it indicates but one direction to the man of genius.

Notes

1   The writer does not mean that the best taste of America is better than that of England; perhaps it is not quite so good; but, as a whole, the American reading world requires better books than the whole of the English reading world.

Nathaniel Hawthorne

from the Preface to
The Marble Faun (1860)

Italy, as the site of his Romance, was chiefly valuable to him as affording a sort of poetic or fairy precinct, where actualities would not be so terribly insisted upon as they are, and must needs be, in America. No author, without a trial, can conceive of the difficulty of writing a romance about a country where there is no shadow, no antiquity, no mystery, no picturesque and gloomy wrong, nor anything but a commonplace prosperity in broad and simple daylight, as is the case with my dear native land. It will be very long, I trust, before romance-writers may find congenial and easily handled themes, either in the annals of our stalwart republic, or in any characteristic and probable events of our individual lives. Romance and poetry, ivy, lichens, and wall-flowers, need ruin to make them grow.

Henry James

from *Hawthorne* (1879)

For myself, as I turn the pages of his journals, I seem to see the image of the crude and simple society in which he lived. I use these epithets, of course, not invidiously, but descriptively; if one desires to enter as closely as possible into Hawthorne's situation, one must endeavour to reproduce his circumstances. We are struck with the large number of elements that were absent from them, and the coldness, the thinness, the blankness, to repeat my epithet, present themselves so vividly that our foremost feeling is that of compassion for a romancer looking for subjects in such a field. It takes so many things, as Hawthorne must have felt later in life, when he made the acquaintance of the denser, richer, warmer European spectacle—it takes such an accumulation of history and custom, such a complexity of manners and types, to form a fund of suggestion for a novelist. If Hawthorne had been a young Englishman, or a young Frenchman of the same degree of genius, the same cast of mind, the same habits, his consciousness of the world around him would have been a very different affair; however obscure, however reserved, his own personal life, his sense of the life of his fellow-mortals would have been almost infinitely more various. The negative side of the spectacle on which Hawthorne looked out, in his contemplative saunterings and reveries, might, indeed, with a little ingenuity, be made almost ludicrous; one might enumerate the items of high civilization, as it exists in other countries, which are absent from the texture of American life, until it should become a wonder to know what was left. No State, in the European sense of the word, and indeed barely a specific national name. No sovereign, no court, no personal loyalty, no aristocracy, no church, no clergy, no army, no diplomatic service, no country gentlemen, no palaces, no castles, nor manors, nor old country-houses, nor parsonages, nor thatched cottages nor ivied ruins; no cathedrals, nor abbeys, nor little Norman churches; no great Universities nor public schools—no Oxford, nor Eton, nor Harrow; no literature, no novels, no museums, no pictures, no political society, no sporting class—no Epsom nor Ascot! Some such list as that might be drawn up of the absent things in American life— especially in the American life of forty years ago, the effect of which, upon an English or a French imagination, would probably as a general thing be appalling. The natural remark, in the almost lurid light of such an indictment, would be that if these things are left out, everything is left out. The American knows that a good deal remains; what it is that remains— that is his secret, his joke, as one may say. It would be cruel, in this terrible denudation, to deny him the consolation of his national gift, that ''American humour'' of which of late years we have heard so much.

William Dean Howells

from *Criticism and Fiction,* ch. XXI□

In fact, the American who chooses to enjoy his birthright to the full, lives in a world wholly different from the Englishman's, and speaks (too often through his nose) another language: he breathes a rarefied and nimble air full of shining possibilities and radiant promises which the fog-and-soot-clogged lungs of those less-favoured islanders struggle in vain to fill themselves with. But he ought to be modest in his advantage, and patient with the coughing and sputtering of his cousin who complains of finding himself in an exhausted receiver on plunging into one of our novels. To be quite just to the poor fellow, I have had some such experience as that myself in the atmosphere of some of our more attenuated romances.

Yet every now and then I read a book with perfect comfort and much exhilaration, whose scenes the average Englishman would gasp in. Nothing happens; that is, nobody murders or debauches anybody else; there is no arson or pillage of any sort; there is not a ghost, or a ravening beast, or a hair-breadth escape, or a shipwreck, or a monster of self-sacrifice, or a lady five thousand years old in the whole course of the story; "no promenade, no band of music, nossing!" as Mr. Du Maurier's Frenchman said of the meet for a fox-hunt. Yet it is all alive with the keenest interest for those who enjoy the study of individual traits and general conditions as they make themselves known to American experience.

These conditions have been so favorable hitherto

□ First published in 1891.

(though they are becoming always less so) that they easily account for the optimistic faith of our novel which Mr. Hughes notices. It used to be one of the disadvantages of the practice of romance in America, which Hawthorne more or less whimsically lamented, that there were so few shadows and inequalities in our broad level of prosperity; and it is one of the reflections suggested by Dostoïevsky's novel, The Crime and the Punishment, that whoever struck a note so profoundly tragic in American fiction would do a false and mistaken thing—as false and as mistaken in its way as dealing in American fiction with certain nudities which the Latin peoples seem to find edifying. Whatever their deserts, very few American novelists have been led out to be shot, or finally exiled to the rigors of a winter at Duluth; and in a land where journeymen carpenters and plumbers strike for four dollars a day the sum of hunger and cold is comparatively small, and the wrong from class to class has been almost inappreciable, though all this is changing for the worse. Our novelists, therefore, concern themselves with the more smiling aspects of life, which are the more American, and seek the universal in the individual rather than the social interests. It is worth while, even at the risk of being called commonplace, to be true to our well-to-do actualities; the very passions themselves seem to be softened and modified by conditions which formerly at least could not be said to wrong any one, to cramp endeavor, or to cross lawful desire. Sin and suffering and shame there must always be in the world, I suppose, but I believe that in this new world of ours it is still mainly from one to another one, and oftener still from one to one's self. We have death too in America, and a great deal of disagreeable and painful disease, which the multiplicity of our patent medicines does not seem to cure; but this is tragedy that comes in the very nature of things, and is not peculiarly American, as the large, cheerful average of health and success and happy life is. It will not do to boast, but it is well to be true to the facts, and to see that, apart from these purely mortal troubles, the race here has enjoyed conditions in which most of the ills that have darkened its annals might be averted by honest work and unselfish behavior.

Richard Chase

⌒ᴡ⌒

from "A Culture of Contradictions"□

The imagination that has produced much of the best and most characteristic American fiction has been shaped by the contradictions and not by the unities and harmonies of our culture. In a sense this may be true of all literatures of whatever time and place. Nevertheless there are some literatures which take their form and tone from polarities, opposites, and irreconcilables, but are content to rest in and sustain them, or to resolve them into unities, if at all, only by special and limited means. The American novel tends to rest in contradictions and among extreme ranges of experience. When it attempts to resolve contradictions, it does so in oblique, morally equivocal ways. As a general rule it does so either in melodramatic actions or in pastoral idyls, although intermixed with both one may find the stirring instabilities of "American humor." These qualities constitute the uniqueness of that branch of the novelistic tradition which has flourished in this country. They help to account for the strong element of "romance" in the American "novel."

By contrast, the English novel has followed a middle way. It is notable for its great practical sanity, its powerful, engrossing composition of wide ranges of experience into a moral centrality and equability of judgment. Oddity, distortion of personality, dislocations of normal life, recklessness of behavior, malignancy of motive—these the English novel has included. Yet the profound poetry of disorder we find in the American novel is missing, with rare exceptions, from the English. Radical maladjustments and contradictions are reported but are seldom of the essence of form in the English novel, and although it is no stranger to suffering and defeat or to triumphant joy either, it gives the impression of absorbing all extremes, all maladjustments and contradictions into a normative view of life. In doing so, it shows itself to derive from the two great influences that stand behind it—classic tragedy and Christianity. The English novel has not, of course, always been strictly speaking tragic or Christian. Often it has been comic, but often, too, in that superior form of comedy which approaches tragedy. Usually it has been realistic or, in the philosophical sense of the word, "naturalistic." Yet even its peculiar kind of gross poetic naturalism has preserved something of the two great traditions that formed English literature. The English novel, that is, follows the tendency of tragic art and Christian art, which characteristically move through contradictions to forms of harmony, reconciliation, catharsis, and transfiguration.

Judging by our greatest novels, the American imagination, even when it wishes to assuage and reconcile the contradictions of life, has not been stirred by the possibility of catharsis or incarnation, by the tragic or Christian possibility. It has been stirred, rather, by the aesthetic possibilities of radical forms of alienation, contradiction, and disorder.

· · · ·

In *Democracy in America* Tocqueville tried to account for a number of related contradictions in American life. He noted a disparity between ideals and practice, a lack of connection between thought and experience, a tendency of the American mind to oscillate rather wildly between ideas that "are all either extremely minute and clear or extremely general and vague."

Tocqueville sought a genetic explanation for these disparities. He pointed out that in aristocratic societies there was a shared body of inherited habits, attitudes and institutions that stood in a mediating position between the individual and the state. This, he observed, was not true in a democracy, where "each citizen is habitually engaged in the contemplation of a very puny object: namely, himself. If he ever looks higher, he perceives only the immense form of society at large or the still more imposing aspect of mankind. . . . What lies between is a void." Tocqueville believed that this either/or habit of mind also owed much to the sharp distinctions made by Calvinism and its habit of opposing the individual to his God, with a minimum of mythic or ecclesiastical mediation. He found certain advantages in this "democratic" quality of mind, but he warned Americans that it might produce great confusion in philosophy, morals, and politics and a basic instability in literary and cultural values, and that consequently Americans should try to discover democratic equivalents for those traditional habits of mind which in aristocracies had moderated and reconciled extremes in thought and experience.

Tocqueville knew that the dualistic kind of thought of which he spoke was specifically American only in the peculiar quality of its origin and expression. He saw that with the probable exception of England, Europe would characteristically concern itself during the nineteenth century with grand intellectual oppositions, usually more or less of a Hegelian order. But even though the tendency of thought Tocqueville predicated belonged to Western culture generally, one is nevertheless struck by how often American writers conceive of human dilemmas according to his scheme, and how many make aesthetic capital out of what seemed to him a moral and intellectual shortcoming.

In his studies of the classic American writers, D. H. Lawrence presented his version of the contrariety, or, as he said, "duplicity" of the American literary mind by saying that he found in writers like Cooper, Melville, and Hawthorne "a tight mental allegiance to a morality which all their passion goes to destroy," a formulation which describes perfectly the inner contradiction of such products of the American imagination as the story of Natty Bumppo. In general Lawrence was thinking of an inherent conflict between "genteel" spirituality and a pragmatic experientialism which in its lower depths was sheer Dionysian or "Indian" energy and violence. Acute enough to see that the best American artistic achievements had depended in one way or another on this dualism, he seemed ready nevertheless to advocate, on moral grounds, a reconciliation of opposites, such as he thought he discerned in the poems of Whitman.

In short, like all the observers of American literature we are citing in these pages, Lawrence was trying to find out what was wrong with it. He is a sympathetic and resourceful reader—one of the best, surely, ever to turn his attention to the American novel. But he thinks that the American novel is sick, and he wants to cure it. Perhaps there is something wrong with it, perhaps it is sick—but a too exclusive preoccupation with the wrongness of the American novel has in some ways disqualified him for seeing what, right or wrong, it *is*.

Finally, there is the division of American culture into "highbrow" and "lowbrow" made by Van Wyck Brooks in 1915 in his *America's Coming-of-Age*. Brooks's essay is a great piece of writing; it is eloquent, incisive, and witty. But we have lived through enough history now to see its fundamental error—namely, the idea that it is the duty of our writers to heal the split and reconcile the contradictions in our culture by pursuing a middlebrow course. All the evidence shows that wherever American literature has pursued the middle way it has tended by a kind of native fatality not to reconcile but merely to deny or ignore the polarities of our culture. Our middlebrow literature—for example, the novels of Howells—has generally been dull and mediocre. In the face of Brooks's desire to unite the highbrow and the lowbrow on a middle ground, there remains the fact that our best novelists have been, not middlebrows, but either highbrows like James, lowbrows like Mark Twain, Frank Norris, Dreiser, and Sherwood Anderson, or combination highbrow-lowbrows like Melville, Faulkner, and Hemingway. Here again American fiction contrasts strongly with English. The English novel at its best is staunchly middlebrow. The cultural conditions within which English literature has evolved have allowed it to become a great middlebrow literature—the only one, it may be, in history.

Let us in all candor admit the limited, the merely instrumental value of the terms used in the last paragraph. They work very well, and are in fact indispensable, in making large cultural formulations. But in applying them to individual authors the terms must be constantly re-examined. We might ask, for example, whether from one point of view both Hawthorne and James performed the unlikely feat of becoming great middlebrow writers. Both of them, at any rate, achieve a kind of contemplative centrality of vision within the confines of which their minds work with great delicacy and equanimity. In so far as they do this, one certainly cannot chide them for shying away from some of the more extreme contradictions, the more drastic forms of alienation, the more violent, earthy, or sordid ranges of experience which engage the minds of Melville and Faulkner, and in fact most of our best writers. Yet to achieve a "contemplative centrality of vision" certainly requires an action of the mind; whereas the word "middlebrow," although suggesting centrality of vision, inevitably suggests, judging by our American literature, a view gained by no other means than passivity and the refusal of experience.

To conclude this brief account of the contradictions which have vivified and excited the American imagination, these contradictions seem traceable to certain historical facts. First, there is the solitary position man has been placed in in this country, a position very early enforced by the doctrines of Puritanism and later by frontier conditions and, as Tocqueville skillfully pointed out, by the very institutions of democracy as these evolved in the eighteenth and nineteenth centuries.

Second, the Manichaean quality of New England Puritanism, which, as Yvor Winters and others have shown, had so strong an effect on writers like Hawthorne and Melville and entered deeply into the national consciousness. From the historical point of view, this Puritanism was a backsliding in religion as momentous in shaping the imagination as the cultural reversion Cooper studied on the frontier. For, at least as apprehended by the literary imagination, New England Puritanism—with its grand metaphors of election and damnation, its opposition of the kingdom of light and the kingdom of darkness, its eternal and autonomous contraries of good and evil—seems to have recaptured the Manichaean sensibility. The American imagination, like the New England Puritan mind itself, seems less interested in redemption than in the melodrama of the eternal struggle of good and evil, less interested in incarnation and reconciliation than in alienation and disorder. If we may suppose ourselves correct in tracing to this origin the prevalence in American literature of the symbols of light and dark, we may doubtless suppose also that this sensibility has been enhanced by the racial composition of our people and by the Civil War that was fought, if more in legend than in fact, over the Negro.

More obviously, a third source of contradiction lies in the dual allegiance of the American, who in his intellectual culture belongs both to the Old World and the New.

Leslie A. Fiedler

from "The Novel and America"□

Between the novel and America there are peculiar and intimate connections. A new literary form and a new society, their beginnings coincide with the beginnings of the modern era and, indeed, help to define it. We are living not only in the Age of America but also in the Age of the Novel, at a moment when the literature of a country without a first-rate verse epic or a memorable verse tragedy has become the model of half the world. *The Age of the American Novel*, a French critic calls a book on contemporary writing; and everywhere in the West there are authors who quite deliberately turn from their own fictional traditions to pursue ours—or at least something they take for ours.

We have known for a long time, of course, that our national literary reputation depends largely upon the achievement of our novelists. The classical poetic genres revived by the Renaissance had lost their relevance to contemporary life before America entered the cultural scene; and even the lyric has provided us with occasions for few, and limited, triumphs. Whitman, Poe, and Dickinson—beyond these three, there are no major American poets before the twentieth century; and even about their merits we continue to wrangle. It is Melville and Hawthorne and James (together with such latter-day figures as Faulkner and Hemingway) who possess the imagination of a Europe already committed to the novel as the pre-vailing modern form. Not only in the United States, though pre-eminently there, literature has become for most readers quite simply prose fiction; and our endemic fantasy of writing "the Great American Novel" is only a local instance of a more general obsession. The notions of greatness once associated with the heroic poem have been transferred to the novel; and the shift is a part of that "Americanization of culture" which some European intellectuals continue ritually to deplore.

But is there, as certain continental critics have insisted, an "American novel," a specific sub-variety of the form? If we turn to these critics for a definition, we come on such terms as "neo-realist," "hard-boiled," "naive," and "anti-tradi-tional"—terms derived from a standard view of America as an "anti-culture," an eternally maintained preserve of primi-tivism. This view (notoriously exemplified by André Gide) ends by finding in Dashiell Hammett the same values as in William Faulkner, and is more a symptom of European cul-tural malaise than a useful critical distinction. While America is, in a very real sense, a constantly recreated fact of the European imagination, it is not only, or even pre-eminently, that. It is tempting to insist on the pat rebuttal that, far from being an anti-culture, we are merely a branch of Western culture; and that there is no "American novel," only local variants of standard European kinds of fiction: American sentimental, American gothic, American historical romance, etc. Certainly no single sub-genre of the novel was invented in the United States. Yet the peculiarities of our variants seem more interesting and important than their resemblances to the parent forms.

There is a real sense in which our prose fiction is im-mediately distinguishable from that of Europe, though this is a fact that is difficult for Americans (oddly defensive and flustered in its presence) to confess. In this sense, our novels seem not primitive, perhaps, but innocent, unfallen in a dis-turbing way, almost juvenile. The great works of American fiction are notoriously at home in the children's section of the library, their level of sentimentality precisely that of a pre-adolescent. This is part of what we mean when we talk about

the incapacity of the American novelist to develop; in a compulsive way he returns to a limited world of experience,
usually associated with his childhood, writing the same
book over and over again until he lapses into silence of self-
parody.

Merely finding a language, learning to talk in a land
where there are no conventions of conversation, no special
class idioms and no dialogue between classes, no continuing
literary language—this exhausts the American writer. He is
forever *beginning*, saying for the first time (without real
tradition there can never be a second time) what it is like to
stand alone before nature, or a city as appallingly lonely as
any virgin forest. He faces, moreover, another problem, which
has resulted in a failure of feeling and imagination perceptible
at the heart of even our most notable works. Our great novelists, though experts on indignity and assault, on loneliness
and terror, tend to avoid treating the passionate encounter of
a man and woman, which we expect at the center of a novel.
Indeed, they rather shy away from permitting in their fictions
the presence of any full-fledged, mature women, giving us
instead monsters of virtue or bitchery, symbols of the rejection or fear of sexuality.

To be sure, the theme of "love" in so simple a sense is
by no means necessary to all works of art. In the *Iliad*, for
instance, and in much Greek tragedy, it is conspicuously
absent; and in the heroic literature of the Middle Ages, it is
peripheral where it exists at all. The *"belle Aude"* of the
Chanson de Roland is a supernumerary, and the only female
we remember from *Beowulf* is a terror emerging from the
darkness at the bottom of the waters. The world of the epic
is a world of war, and its reigning sentimental relationship
is the loyalty of comrades in arms; but by the eighteenth
century the notion of a heroic poem without romance had
come to seem intolerable. The last pseudo-epics of the baroque
had been obsessed with the subject of love, and the rococo
had continued to elaborate that theme. Shakespeare himself
appeared to the English Augustans too little concerned with
the "reigning passion" to be quite interesting without
revision. Why, after all, should Cordelia not survive to marry

Edgar, they demanded of themselves—and they rewrote *King Lear* to prove that she should.

The novel, however, was precisely the product of the sentimentalizing taste of the eighteenth century; and a continuing tradition of prose fiction did not begin until the love affair of Lovelace and Clarissa (a demythicized Don Juan and a secularized goddess of Christian love) had been imagined. The subject par excellence of the novel is love, or, more precisely—in its beginnings at least—seduction and marriage; and in France, Italy, Germany, and Russia, even in England, spiritually so close to America, love in one form or another has remained the novel's central theme, as necessary and as expected as battle in Homer or revenge in the Renaissance drama. When the Romantic impulse led in Germany to a technical recasting of the novel form, even the wildest experimentalists did not desert this traditional theme; Schiller's *Lucille* is a dialogue on freedom and restraint in passion. But our great Romantic *Unroman*, our typical anti-novel, is the womanless *Moby Dick*.

Where is our *Madame Bovary*, our *Anna Karenina*, our *Pride and Prejudice* or *Vanity Fair*? Among our classic novels, at least those before Henry James, who stands so oddly between our own traditions and the European ones we rejected or recast, the best attempt at dealing with love is *The Scarlet Letter*, in which the physical consummation of adultery has occurred and all passion burned away before the novel proper begins. Our *Madame Bovary* is a novel about adultery with the adultery off-stage; and the child who is its product is so elfin and ethereal that it is hard to believe her engendered in the usual way. For the rest, there are *Moby Dick* and *Huckleberry Finn*, *The Last of the Mohicans*, *The Red Badge of Courage*, the stories of Edgar Allan Poe—books that turn from society to nature or nightmare out of a desperate need to avoid the facts of wooing, marriage, and child-bearing.

The figure of Rip Van Winkle presides over the birth of the American imagination; and it is fitting that our first successful homegrown legend should memorialize, however playfully, the flight of the dreamer from the shrew—into the mountains and out of time, away from the drab duties of home

and town toward the good companions and the magic keg of
beer. Ever since, the typical male protagonist of our fiction
has been a man on the run, harried into the forest and out to
sea, down the river or into combat—anywhere to avoid
"civilization," which is to say, the confrontation of a man
and woman which leads to the fall to sex, marriage, and responsibility. One of the factors that determine theme and form
in our great books is this strategy of evasion, this retreat to
nature and childhood, which makes our literature (and life!)
so charmingly and infuriatingly "boyish."

The child's world is not only asexual, it is terrible: a
world of fear and loneliness, a haunted world; and the American novel is pre-eminently a novel of terror. To "light out for
the territory" or seek refuge in the forest seems easy and
tempting from the vantage point of a chafing and restrictive
home; but civilization once disavowed and Christianity dis-
owned, the bulwark of woman left behind, the wanderer feels
himself without protection, more motherless child than free
man. To be sure, there is a substitute for wife or mother presumably waiting in the green heart of nature: the natural man,
the good companion, pagan and unashamed—Queequeg or
Chingachgook or Nigger Jim. But the figure of the natural
man is ambiguous, a dream and a nightmare at once. The other
face of Chingachgook is Injun Joe, the killer in the graveyard
and the haunter of caves; Nigger Jim is also the Babo of
Melville's "Benito Cereno," the humble servant whose name
means "papa" holding the razor to his master's throat; and
finally the dark-skinned companion becomes the "Black Man,"
which is a traditional American name for the Devil himself.

The enemy of society on the run toward "freedom" is
also the pariah in flight from his guilt, the guilt of that very
flight; and new phantoms arise to haunt him at every step.
American literature likes to pretend, of course, that its buga-
boos are all finally jokes: the headless horseman a hoax, every
manifestation of the supernatural capable of rational explanation on the last page—but we are never quite convinced.
Huckleberry Finn, that euphoric boys' book, begins with its
protagonist holding off at gun point his father driven half
mad by the D.T.'s and ends (after a lynching, a disinterment,

THE AMERICAN NOVEL AND AMERICAN EXPERIENCE

and a series of violent deaths relieved by such humorous incidents as soaking a dog in kerosene and setting him on fire) with the revelation of that father's sordid death. Nothing is spared; Pap, horrible enough in life, is found murdered brutally, abandoned to float down the river in a decaying house scrawled with obscenities. But it is all "humor," of course, a last desperate attempt to convince us of the innocence of violence, the good clean fun of horror. Our literature as a whole at times seems a chamber of horrors disguised as an amusement park "fun house," where we pay to play at terror and are confronted in the innermost chamber with a series of inter-reflecting mirrors which present us with a thousand versions of our own face.

In our most enduring books, the cheapjack machinery of the gothic novel is called on to represent the hidden blackness of the human soul and human society. No wonder our authors mock themselves as they use such devices; no wonder Mistress Hibbins in *The Scarlet Letter* and Fedallah in *Moby Dick* are treated half jocularly, half melodramatically, though each represents in his book the Faustian pact, the bargain with the Devil, which our authors have always felt as the essence of the American experience. However shoddily or ironically treated, horror is essential to our literature. It is not merely a matter of terror filling the vacuum left by the suppression of sex in our novels, of Thanatos standing in for Eros. Through these gothic images are projected certain obsessive concerns of our national life: the ambiguity of our relationship with Indian and Negro, the ambiguity of our encounter with nature, the guilt of the revolutionist who feels himself a parricide— and, not least of all, the uneasiness of the writer who cannot help believing that the very act of composing a book is Satanic revolt. "Hell-fired," Hawthorne called *The Scarlet Letter*, and Melville thought his own *Moby Dick* a "wicked book."

The American writer inhabits a country at once the dream of Europe and a fact of history; he lives on the last horizon of an endlessly retreating vision of innocence—on the "frontier," which is to say, the margin where the theory of original goodness and the fact of original sin come face to face. To express this "blackness ten times black" and to live by it in a society in which, since the decline of orthodox Puritanism, optimism has become the chief effective religion, is a complex and difficult task.

It was to the novel that the American writer turned most naturally, as the only *popular* form of sufficient magnitude for his vision. He was, perhaps, not sufficiently sophisticated to realize that such learned forms as epic and tragedy had already outlived their usefulness; but, working out of a cultural background at best sketchy and unsure, he felt insecure before them. His obligations urged him in the direction of tragedy, but traditional verse tragedy was forbidden him; indeed, a chief technical problem for American novelists has been the adaptation of nontragic forms to tragic ends. How could the dark vision of the American—his obsession with violence and his embarrassment before love—be expressed in the sentimental novel of analysis as developed by Samuel Richardson or the historical romance as practiced by Sir Walter Scott? These sub-genres of fiction, invented to satisfy the emotional needs of a merchant class in search of dignity or a Tory squirearchy consumed by nostalgia, could only by the most desperate expedients be tailored to fit American necessities. Throughout their writing lives, such writers as Charles Brockden Brown and James Fenimore Cooper devoted (with varying degrees of self-consciousness) all their ingenuity to this task, yet neither Brown nor Cooper finally proved capable of achieving high art; and the literary types invented by both have fallen since into the hands of mere entertainers—that is, novelists able and willing to attempt anything *except* the projection of the dark vision of America we have been describing. The Fielding novel, on the other hand, the pseudo-Shakespearean "comic epic" with its broad canvas, its emphasis upon reversals and recognitions, and its robust masculine sentimentality, turned out, oddly enough, to have no relevance to the American scene; in the United States it has remained an exotic, eternally being discovered by the widest audience and raised to best-sellerdom in its latest imported form, but seldom home-produced for home consumption.

It is the gothic form that has been most fruitful in the

hands of our best writers: the gothic *symbolically* understood, its machinery and décor translated into metaphors for a terror psychological, social, and metaphysical. Yet even treated as symbols, the machinery and décor of the gothic have continued to seem vulgar and contrived; symbolic gothicism threatens always to dissolve into its components, abstract morality and shoddy theater. A recurrent problem of our fiction has been the need of our novelists to find a mode of projecting their conflicts which would contain all the dusky horror of gothic romance and yet be palatable to discriminating readers, palatable first of all to themselves.

Such a mode can, of course, not be subsumed among any of those called "realism," and one of the chief confusions in our understanding of our own literature has arisen from our failure to recognize this fact clearly enough. Our fiction is essentially and at its best nonrealistic, even anti-realistic; long before *symbolisme* had been invented in France and exported to America, there was a full-fledged native tradition of symbolism. That tradition was born of the profound contradictions of our national life and sustained by the inheritance from Puritanism of a "typical" (even allegorical) way of regarding the sensible world—not as an ultimate reality but as a system of signs to be deciphered. For too long, historians of American fiction have mistakenly tried to impose on the course of a brief literary history a notion of artistic "progress" imported from France or, more precisely perhaps, from certain French literary critics. Such historians have been pleased to speak of "The Rise of Realism" or "The Triumph of Realism," as if the experiments of Hawthorne or Poe or Melville were half-misguided fumblings toward the final excellence of William Dean Howells!

But the moment at which Flaubert was dreaming *Madame Bovary* was the moment when Melville was finding *Moby Dick*, and considered as a "realistic" novel the latter is a scandalous botch. To speak of a counter-tradition to the novel, of the tradition of "the romance" as a force in our literature, is merely to repeat the rationalizations of our writers themselves; it is certainly to fail to be *specific* enough for real understanding. Our fiction is not merely in flight from the physical data of the actual world, in search of a (sexless and dim) Ideal; from Charles Brockden Brown to William Faulkner or Eudora Welty, Paul Bowles or John Hawkes, it is, bewilderingly and embarrassingly, a gothic fiction, nonrealistic and negative, sadist and melodramatic—a literature of darkness and the grotesque in a land of light and affirmation.

Moreover—and the final paradox is necessary to the full complexity of the case—ours is a literature of horror for boys. Truly shocking, frankly obscene authors we do not possess; Edgar Allan Poe is our closest approximation, a child playing at what Baudelaire was to live. A Baudelaire, a Marquis de Sade, a "Monk" Lewis, even a John Cleland is inconceivable in the United States. Our flowers of evil are culled for the small girl's bouquet, our novels of terror (*Moby Dick*, *The Scarlet Letter*, *Huckleberry Finn*, the tales of Poe) are placed on the approved book lists of Parents' Committees who nervously fuss over the latest comic books. If such censors do not flinch at necrophilia or shudder over the book whose secret motto is "I baptise you not in the name of the Father . . . but of the Devil," or fear the juvenile whose hero at his greatest moment cries out, "All right, I'll *go* to Hell," it is only another irony of life in a land where the writers believe in hell and the official guardians of morality do not. As long as there's no *sex!*

Yet our authors are as responsible as the P.T.A.'s for the confusion about the true nature of their books; though they may have whispered their secret to friends, or confessed it in private letters, in their actual works they assumed what camouflage prudence dictated. They *wanted* to be misunderstood. *Huckleberry Finn* is only the supreme instance of a subterfuge typical of our classic novelists. To this very day, it is heresy in some quarters to insist that this is not finally the jolliest, the *cleanest* of books; Twain's ironical warning to significance hunters, posted just before the title page, is taken quite literally, and the irreverent critic who explicates the book's levels of terror and evasion is regarded as a busybody and scandalmonger. It is at last hard to say which is more remarkable, the eccentricity of American books or our critics' conspiracy of silence in this regard. (Or is it the critics' *unawareness* of the fact?) Why, one is driven to ask, why the distortion and why the ignorance? But the critics, after all, are children of the same culture as the novelists they discuss; and if we answer one question we will have answered both.

Perhaps the whole odd shape of American fiction arises simply (as simplifying Europeans are always ready to assure us) because there is no real sexuality in American life and therefore there cannot very well be any in American art. What we cannot achieve in our relations with each other it would be vain to ask our writers to portray or even our critics to miss. Certainly many of our novelists have themselves believed, or pretended to believe, this. Through *The Scarlet Letter*, there is a constant mournful undercurrent, a series of asides in which Hawthorne deplores the sexual diminution of American women. Mark Twain in *1601* somewhat similarly contrasts the vigor of Elizabethan Englishwomen with their American descendants; contrasting the sexual utopia of pre-colonial England with a fallen America where the men copulate "but once in seven yeeres"; and his pornographic sketch, written to amuse a clergyman friend (for men only!), ends on the comic-pathetic image of an old man's impotent lust that "would not stand again." Such pseudo-nostalgia cannot be taken too seriously, however; it may, indeed, be the projection of mere personal weakness and fantasy. Certainly, outside their books, Hawthorne and Twain seem to have fled rather than sought the imaginary full-breasted, fully sexed woman from whom American ladies had presumably declined. Both married, late in life, pale hypochondriac spinsters, intellectual invalids—as if to assert publicly that they sought in marriage not sex, but culture!

Such considerations leave us trapped in the chicken-egg dilemma. How can one say whether the quality of passion in American life suffers because of a failure of the writer's imagination or vice versa? What is called "love" in literature is a rationalization, a way of coming to terms with the relationship between man and woman that does justice, on the one hand, to certain biological drives and, on the other, to certain generally accepted conventions of tenderness and courtesy; and literature, expressing and defining those conventions, tends to influence "real life" more than such life influences it. For better or for worse and for whatever reasons, the American novel is different from its European prototypes, and one of its essential differences arises from its chary treatment of woman and of sex.

To write, then, about the American novel is to write about the fate of certain European genres in a world of alien experience. It is not only a world where courtship and marriage have suffered a profound change, but also one in the process of losing the traditional distinctions of class; a world without a significant history or a substantial past; a world which had left behind the terror of Europe not for the innocence it dreamed of, but for new and special guilts associated with the rape of nature and the exploitation of dark-skinned people; a world doomed to play out the imaginary childhood of Europe. The American novel is only *finally* American; its appearance is an event in the history of the European spirit— as, indeed, is the very invention of America itself.

Marius Bewley

from "The Americanness of the American Novel"□

The American tradition differs from western European ones in that it is to some degree artificial. It was more or less legislated into existence in the beginning. I do not mean that it does not possess a life of its own, or is not an organic, growing thing. But like a new vegetable, it owes its existence to some artificial grafting. This factor, together with the provincialism and other conditions I discussed earlier, make it a particularly tractable field in which to study the interaction between creative activity and national existence at fairly inaccessible levels: I mean the levels below patriotic and personal expediency, below jingoism, below a nostalgic interest in native folklore and history, below the preachments and parables of literary axe-grinders and demagogues. I have tried to reach to that level at which the American artist confronts his own spiritual needs in all the terrible deprivation of his stark American condition, and struggles towards the resolution of those problems that only the artist of genuine fineness can ever *feel* as problems at all. It is a depth at which only the *great* American writers could exist, and for that reason I have dealt here with a very restricted number. At the same time it is a very *American* depth, an underworld of

□ Reprinted from *The Eccentric Design: Form in the Classic American Novel* (New York and London: Columbia University Press, 1963), pp. 289–294, by permission of the publisher.

complex tensions that are of specifically native growth. In my brief historical chapter I tried to suggest the intellectual and political grounding of these tensions. Simply because the American tradition is so circumscribed and, in a sense, concocted, I believe such a chapter to be far from irrelevant; but it would not be possible to write a similar chapter prefatory to a study of the major writers of any century in English literature without a sense of futility.

As each tension I have treated reflects only a facet of the total reality through which they are all related, so there are doubtless many others. But I think it demonstrable that the ones I have discussed are the ones which have shaped the creative impulses of the novelists considered here. I do not mean that this 'new American experience' levelled them to a common pattern, but through it they claim a recognizable fellowship among themselves. It is in this underworld of tensions that we find the common roots of those three great symbolic embodiments in American literature, the Scarlet Letter, Natty Bumppo, and the White Whale. The very diversity among these symbols should prove adequate protection against the charge of being too schematic. My attitude towards this simultaneous similarity and diversity is suggested by the two epigraphs from Wallace Stevens I have appended to this volume: the one in which he speaks of 'a law of inherent opposites, of essential unity,' and the lines,

> It was when the trees were leafless first in November
> And their blackness became apparent, that one first
> Knew the eccentric to be the base of design.

It is through what they have in common that the great American artists have always expressed their uniqueness; and it is perhaps because it is so often November in American art, because there is so little leafage of shared manners, inherited institutions, and traditional attitudes, that we tend to regard the singularity of the great American novelists as almost absolute. But to carry the tree image farther, they all draw their nourishment from one deep, dark soil.

The number in this select circle is necessarily small.

The only other American novelist in the nineteenth century who belongs with those I have treated is Mark Twain. But I have not discussed Twain because he is not a writer who comes to terms easily with literary analysis. When he is great it is with a purity that makes analysis irrelevant; and when his materials offer ground for analytic comment, his art is likely to be at such low ebb that discussion seems hardly worthwhile. What there is to say positively of his achievement has been registered by T. S. Eliot, F. R. Leavis, and Lionel Trilling in their respective introductions and essays, and there is no point in rephrasing it here. As for Mark Twain's 'case,' Van Wyck Brooks's classic analysis of it is definitive.

I have ended my 'tradition' of American novelists with Scott Fitzgerald simply because it seems to me to end with him. I believe Scott Fitzgerald *is* a great American writer, and fully deserves the company I put him in. He deals with 'the new American experience' more critically than anyone in this tradition since Cooper, and at times it seems to me that he has a finer sense of the inherent tragedy in the American experience than any of the others. The alcoholic haze in which he spent so much of his time has obscured for us how intelligent he really was in his best writing. If he had some of the characteristic weaknesses of his decade and his country, he knew them with a rare inwardness, and his writing is not a celebration of them but a judgement on them. His one great figure, Gatsby, is the only symbolic figure in American literature who descends to the depth of the American Dream and comes back to tell us it is a nightmare.

There is one final problem I should like to mention. This 'tradition' as I have set it up here has no room for the so-called realists and naturalists. I hardly suppose that anyone would think of advancing the claims of Dreiser anyway; but collectively the realist writers in American fiction carry some weight. I agree with D. H. Lawrence in finding a certain impressiveness in Frank Norris' *The Octopus*, and I think I can indicate very briefly why the realists cannot belong with the writers discussed here by a reference to this novel. Mr. Robert E. Spiller has written of *The Octopus*: 'Since *Moby*

Dick, by then virtually forgotten, there had been nothing like it in American literature.' Mr. Spiller may be only referring to the fact that Norris' book gives a detailed account of wheat growing and that *Moby Dick* gives us the whaling industry on an even more panoramic scale, but the remark reminds one that both are symbolic novels. The Octopus is the Railroad, whose tentacles squeeze the wheat growers to death, its killing force being the high rates for transport that it charges. The novel is heavily laden with symbolism throughout. The Railroad symbolizes our machine civilization; wheat, of course, symbolizes life. Typical of its technique is the rather effective and quite upsetting scene in which a locomotive, racing through the night with its headlight ablaze like a single eye, rips into a flock of sheep who have strayed through a broken fence on to the track. The destructive economic power of the Railroad over the wheat growers is dramatized effectively enough, but symbolism of this kind at best resembles Ibsen rather than Melville, and it is not often at its best. Norris' and Melville's symbolism point in quite different directions. Melville's symbols move inward, or downward, towards primordial depths of consciousness. Their meanings are not limited by the boundaries of the material world. But Norris' symbols, effective as they sometimes are within their small limits, are little more than marginal illustrations to his dramatized economics and sociology. The symbols explore nothing, discover nothing. They merely lend an obvious kind of structure and emphasis to the story and the meaning.

The extreme realists and naturalists among American writers are always concerned with these outside surfaces. Even their symbolism is an exterior frosting, and hence can hardly be considered symbolism at all. There is no point in speculating here about the reasons for this externality, whether it was because of the example of the French naturalists, or of Darwinism and the physical sciences, or was merely the effect of the gross materialism of America after the Civil War. 'The new American experience' that Cooper, Hawthorne, Melville, and James had dealt with had been, above all else, an inward thing: and it was inward, not with the professional curiosity of the Freudian, who came later, nor the impertinent inquisitiveness of the sociologist, but with the deeply humane recognition that the problems that tormented them as American artists had first to be confronted in the solitude of their own souls. They were all great moralists, great critics in their art, and, in their own way, metaphysicians; and the reality they sought to explore was where the sociological novelists, the naturalists and the documentarians, could never follow them.

I think it will be desirable to bring this account of the great American novelists to a close with a summary recapitulation of those characteristics I have sought to reveal in their work. *Great* artists everywhere are those who have been most seriously and intensely concerned with life. But the writers I have dealt with here suggest that 'life' for the serious American artist has a distinctive quality and set of interests of its own, and that these have traditionally been determined and conditioned by the deprivations and confinements of the American condition, and directed by a specific set of problems or tensions growing out of the historical circumstances of America's existence. Obviously no generalizations can be offered that will apply equally to all the novelists treated here, nor even to as many as two of them in the same way. But this much, at least, is worth hazarding: the novelists treated here are, as a group, extraordinarily non-sensuous. I do not mean that sensuous experience is closed to them, nor that they are inept at treating it when the occasion requires: but the occasion will almost always be for the sake of making an abstract point. Hawthorne handles Hester's and Dimmesdale's meeting in the forest with rare imaginative control, but he is not interested in their emotional natures nor their love except in so far as they illuminate a moral meaning that is essentially unrelated to them as individuals and as sexual beings. If one can imagine this great scene rewritten by D. H. Lawrence, one will begin to have some sense of the distance that lies between American and English fiction, for I take the genius of Lawrence to be the polar opposite of the artists I have dealt with. Sexual love as a subject carrying its own intrinsic interest is almost completely absent from their writing, and

when it is attempted, as it was with Poe, it is an embarrassment and a disease. Because the American tradition provided
its artists with abstractions and ideas rather than with manners, we have no great characters, but great symbolic per-
sonifications and mythic embodiments that go under the names
of Natty Bumppo, Jay Gatsby, Huckleberry Finn, Ahab,
Ishmael—all of whom are strangely unrelated to the world of
ordinary passions and longings, for the democrat is at last
the loneliest man in the universe. The great American novelists can, in their way, give us Lear, and make a decent attempt
at Hamlet; but Othello, and even Romeo, are beyond their
range. The urgencies that have always spurred them to their
greatest efforts have been less of the senses than of the spirit,
and less of the spirit than the mind. As artists they are
thinkers and a species of metaphysician: and a passion of
intelligence is the virtue we most often find in their work.
They analyse endlessly—not, indeed, the human psyche, but
the impersonal moral problems of men, and they analyse them
towards abstract ends. At the close of *The Scarlet Letter* we
have to sacrifice Hester and Dimmesdale for the sake of the
impersonal moral truth they illustrate and dramatize, and
Hawthorne expects us to rest in that truth with no backward
glance. If the European experience qualified all this in Henry
James, we still have to ask what other tradition on earth
could ever have produced the role of 'the restless analyst.'
The tensions I have spoken of are, in the end, merely so many
channels by which we are able, however stumblingly, to reach
the depth of meaning and the roots of creative impulse in
these writers. It was here that they sometimes encountered
problems that seemed insoluble, and which deflected them
towards despair, and hence those strangely nihilistic glooms
that sometimes darken the pages of America's greatest
novelists. Taken *en masse*, these problems that they coped
with were an attempt to discover, or perhaps create, a reality
beyond the aery speculativeness of their intellectual and
historical heritage which endowed them with ideas, but no
tangible vesture of manners, traditions, institutions, and
earthbound history by which their abstractions might live
with significant and personal meaning. James' famous list

of all the American novelists did not possess in the way of subject matter, in the end, a description of those conditions that gave rise to symbolism in American art. It is, then, in the light thrown by the tensions I have treated here that we can see what a different breed of artists these American novelists are in their deepest hearts and motives from their European fellows, but how, under their wide diversities, they all bear a resemblance to each other.

Ralph Ellison

∽⚭∾

from "Society, Morality, and the Novel"□

Enough of general definition; if the novel had not existed at the time the United States started becoming conscious of itself as a nation—a process still, fortunately, for ourselves and the world, unachieved—it would have been necessary for Americans to invent it. For in no other country was change such a given factor of existence; in no other country were the class lines so fluid and change so swift and continuous *and intentional*. In no other country were men so conscious of having defined their social aims nor so committed to working toward making that definition a reality. Indeed, a conscious awareness of values describes the condition of the American experiment, and very often much of our energy goes into finding ways of losing that consciousness. In the beginning was not only the word but its contradiction.

I would be on dangerous ground if I tried to trace too closely a connection between documents of state and literature, since in literature universality is an accepted aim; yet the novel is an art of the specific, and for my own working orientation that connection exists in the United States beyond all questions of cultural chauvinism. Certainly this is evident in our great nineteenth century novels. The moral imperatives of American life that are implicit in the Declaration of Independence, the Constitution, and the Bill of Rights

□ Reprinted with permission of The Macmillan Company from *The Living Novel: A Symposium,* edited by Granville Hicks. © by the Macmillan Company, 1957.

were a part of both the individual consciousness and the
conscience of those writers who created what we consider our
classic novels—Hawthorne, Melville, James, and Twain; and
for all the hooky-playing attitude of the twenties or the political rebelliousness of the thirties, and the reluctance of contemporary writers to deal explicitly with politics, they still
are. They are in fact the baffle against which Mr. Lionel
Trilling's "hum and buzz of implication" (his understandably
vague definition of manners in the novel) sound. These documents form the ground of assumptions upon which our social
values rest; they inform our language and our conduct with
public meaning, and they provide the broadest frame of
reference for our most private dramas. One might deliberately
overemphasize and say that most prose fiction in the United
States—even the most banal bedroom farce, or the most
rarefied, stylized, and understated comedy of manners—is
basically "about" the values and cost of living in a democracy. Being an American, wrote Henry James, is a complex
fate, but perhaps far more troublesome than the necessity of
guarding against superstitious overevaluation of Europe is
the problem of dealing with the explicitness of the omnipresent
American ideal. For out of the consciously experimental and
revolutionary origins of the country has grown the obsession
with defining the American experience; first in order to distinguish it from that of Europe and now to determine our
uniqueness as a civilization and our proper historical role
among the nations. The impetus was twofold, the need to
achieve national self-consciousness being, from the beginning,
a political goal springing from our rejection of European social
forms; and along with this was the pressure of our broad
cultural diversification brought about by the open character
of the society, the waves of immigration and the rapid expansion, horizontally along the frontier and then vertically
through the processes of urbanization and industrialization.
Out of this came our most urgent problem of identity, and who
and what is American are still perplexing questions even today. Many definitions are offered, in naturalistic art, in *Life*
picture portfolios of the American woman, in government
photographs of American workers (in which one seldom sees
a Negro), in the racial and aesthetic types of movie queens, in

works of sociology, in attempts to depict aspects of the American experience in novels—but few are acceptable without qualification, not even during wartime. All Americans are in this sense members of minority groups, even the Anglo-Saxons, whose image has from the beginning dominated all the rest—and one meaning of the social friction in American life is the struggle of each racial, cultural, and religious group to have its own contribution to the national image recognized and accepted. The novelist can bemoan this pressure, for it can be oppressive, but he cannot escape it; and indeed, in our time, it might be his road to a meaningful relationship to the community. "Who," asks Constance Rourke in her *American Humor*, "ever heard of a significant English novel called *The Englishman*, or an excellent French novel called *Le Français*? The simple aggressive stress belonged to an imagination perennially engaged by the problem of the national type. . . ."

Moreover, this national need gives us a clue to one of the enduring functions of the American novel, which is that of defining the national type as it evolves in the turbulence of change, and of giving the American experience, as it unfolds in its diverse parts and regions, imaginative integration and moral continuity. Thus it is bound up with our problem of nationhood. During the nineteenth century it was clearly recognized by those writers who speak meaningfully to us today, and it comes through novels which in their own times went, like *Moby Dick*, unread. *Moby Dick*, *The Adventures of Huckleberry Finn*, *The Bostonians*, and so on, are all "regional" novels, and each simultaneously projects an image of a specific phase of American life, and each is concerned with the moral predicament of the nation. For all the optimism of the early years, there was in this literature no easy affirmation, and for all its involvement with a common set of political and social assumptions, there was, as the list makes plain, no lack of variety of theme. It has been observed that modern American fiction is the only body of literature which is not the work of intellectuals, yet from the beginning our novelists have been consciously concerned with the form, technique, and content of the novel, not excluding ideas. What the observer (a Frenchman) missed was that the major ideas of our society were so alive in the minds of every reader that they could be stated implicitly in the contours of the form. For it is all grounded in a body of the most abstract and explicitly stated conceptions of human society and one which in the form of the great documents of state, constitutes a body of assumptions about human possibility which is shared by all Americans—even those who resist most violently any attempt to embody them in social action.

. . . .

One of the comic aspects to the current controversy over what a novel should be is the implicit assumption, held by Cooper, James, and Hawthorne, as well as several contemporary critics, that society was created mainly so that novelists could write about it. It is felt that society should be of such shape that the novelist can settle it neatly into prefabricated molds with the least spilling of rude life over the sides. The notion started when the forest was still being cleared, and it is understandable that a certain type of writer would have liked to deal with fine cabinetry instead of crude logs. Still, minds that were philosophically and politically most advanced and sophisticated conceived this society, but even they had nonetheless to deal with raw and rapidly moving materials. And so in the beginning did the American novel, and so today. We are not so crude now as during James' time but we have even less stability and there is no longer a stable England to which to withdraw for perspective. World War I, the Depression, World War II and Korea, the Cold War, the threat of the atom, our discovery of the reality of treason, and now Egypt and Hungary make us aware that reality, which during Dickens' time seemed fairly stable, has broken loose from its old historical base, and the Age of Anxiety is truly more than a poetic conceit. Closed societies are now the flimsy illusions, for all the outsiders are demanding in.

In fact there is no stability anywhere and there will not be for many years to come, and progress now insistently asserts its tragic side; the evil now stares out of the bright sunlight. New groups will ceaselessly emerge, class lines will continue to waver and break and re-form; great wealth there will be and a broader distribution of that wealth, and a broader distribution of ideas along with it. But the problem of what to do with the increased leisure which wealth makes possible will continue to plague us—as will the problem of deciding just what constitutes a truly human way of life. The fundamental problems of the American situation will repeat themselves again and again and will be faced more or less by peoples throughout the world: Where shall we draw the line upon our own freedom in a world in which culture, tradition, and even history have been shaken up? At how fast a pace should we move toward social ideals? What is worth having and what worth holding? Where and in what pattern of conduct does true value, at a given moment, lie? These questions will continue to press upon us even if the dream of world peace is achieved, for they are questions built into the core of modern experience.

For the novelist the existence of these questions creates a basic problem of rhetoric. How does one in the novel (the novel which is a work of art and not a disguised piece of sociology) persuade the American reader to identify that which is basic in man beyond all differences of class, race, wealth, or formal education? How does one not only make the illiterate and inarticulate eloquent enough so that the educated and more favorably situated will recognize wisdom and honor and charity, heroism and capacity for love when found in humble speech and dress? And conversely, how does one persuade readers with least knowledge of literature to recognize the broader values implicit in their lives? How, in a word, do we affirm that which *is* stable in human life beyond and despite all processes of social change? How give the reader that which we do have in abundance, all the countless untold and wonderful variations on the themes of identity and freedom and necessity, love and death, and with all the mystery of personality undergoing its endless metamorphosis?

Here are questions which cannot be answered by criticism; they call for the novel, many novels; and as long as there are writers willing to accept the challenge of reducing the reality in which they exist to living form there will be readers interested in their answers, and we need have no fear that the novel is moribund.

II

Romance, Realism, and Naturalism

Richard Chase

from "Novel Vs. Romance"□

Nothing will be gained by trying to define "novel" and "romance" too closely. One of their chief advantages is that, as literary forms go, they are relatively loose and flexible. But especially in discussing American literature, these terms have to be defined closely enough to distinguish between them, even though the distinction itself may sometimes be meaningless as applied to a given book and even though, following usage, one ordinarily uses the word "novel" to describe a book like Cooper's *The Prairie* which might more accurately be called a "romance" or a "romance-novel."

Doubtless the main difference between the novel and the romance is in the way in which they view reality. The novel renders reality closely and in comprehensive detail. It takes a group of people and sets them going about the business of life. We come to see these people in their real complexity of temperament and motive. They are in explicable relation to nature, to each other, to their social class, to their own past. Character is more important than action and plot, and probably the tragic or comic actions of the narrative will have the primary purpose of enhancing our knowledge of and feeling for an important character, a group of characters, or a way of life. The events that occur will usually be plausible, given the circumstances, and if the novelist in-

□ Reprinted from *The American Novel and Its Tradition*, by Richard Chase. Copyright © 1957 by Richard Chase. Reprinted by permission of Doubleday & Company, Inc.

cludes a violent or sensational occurrence in his plot, he will introduce it only into such scenes as have been (in the words of Percy Lubbock) "already prepared to vouch for it." Historically, as it has often been said, the novel has served the interests and aspirations of an insurgent middle class.

By contrast the romance, following distantly the medieval example, feels free to render reality in less volume and detail. It tends to prefer action to character, and action will be freer in a romance than in a novel, encountering, as it were, less resistance from reality. (This is not always true, as we see in what might be called the static romances of Hawthorne, in which the author uses the allegorical and moral, rather than the dramatic, possibilities of the form.) The romance can flourish without providing much intricacy of relation. The characters, probably rather two-dimensional types, will not be related to each other or to society or to the past. Human beings will on the whole be shown in ideal relation—that is, they will share emotions only after these have become abstract or symbolic. To be sure, characters may become profoundly involved in some way, as in Hawthorne or Melville, but it will be a deep and narrow, an obsessive, involvement. In American romances it will not matter much what class people come from, and where the novelist would arouse our interest in a character by exploring his origin, the romancer will probably do so by enveloping it in mystery. Character itself becomes, then, somewhat abstract and ideal, so much so in some romances that it seems to be merely a function of plot. The plot we may expect to be highly colored. Astonishing events may occur, and these are likely to have a symbolic or ideological, rather than a realistic, plausibility. Being less committed to the immediate rendition of reality than the novel, the romance will more freely veer toward mythic, allegorical, and symbolistic forms.

The Historical View

Although some of the best works of American fiction have to be called, for purposes of criticism, romances rather than novels, we would be pursuing a chimera if we tried, except provisionally, to isolate a literary form known as the American prose romance, as distinguished from the European or the American novel. In actuality the romances of our literature, like European prose romances, are literary hybrids, unique only in their peculiar but widely differing amalgamation of novelistic and romance elements. The greatest American fiction has tended toward the romance more often than the greatest European fiction. Still, our fiction is historically a branch of the European tradition of the novel. And it is the better part of valor in the critic to understand our American romances as adaptations of traditional novelistic procedures to new cultural conditions and new aesthetic aspirations. It will not damage our appreciation of the originality and value of *Moby Dick* or *The Blithedale Romance* to say that they both seem to begin as novels but then veer off into the province of romance, in the one case making a supreme triumph, in the other, a somewhat dubious but interesting medley of genres and intentions.

Inevitably we look to the writings of James Fenimore Cooper, for it was he who first fully exemplified and formulated the situation of the novelist in the New World. His first book, *Precaution*, was a novel of manners, somewhat in the style of Jane Austen. Considering this a failure, he wrote *The Spy*, a story of the Revolution, in which, following Scott, he put his characters in a borderland (in this case between the American and British armies) where the institutions and manners of society did not obtain. He sketched out in Harvey Birch the semi-legendary hero who would find his full development in Natty Bumppo. As for characterization and realism of presentation, he contented himself with what he called in *Notions of the Americans* "the general picture" and "the delineation of principles"—this being, as he said, all that could be expected of the American writer, given the "poverty of materials" and the uniformity of behavior and public opinion. He introduced an element of melodrama, believing that this might be suitable to scenes set in the American forest, even though we had no mysterious castles, dungeons, or monasteries. He introduced also a certain "elevation" of style and a freedom in arranging events and attributing moral qualities to his characters. It is thus apparent that if American conditions had forced Cooper to be content with "the general picture" and "the delineation of principles" this was, if a step away from the novel form proper, a step *toward* the successful mythic qualities of the Leather-Stocking tales. Here was proof of Tocqueville's idea that although the abstractness and generality of the democratic imagination would make unavailable some of the traditional sources of fiction, this abstractness would in itself be a new source of mythic ideality.

In Cooper's books we see what was to be the main drift of American fiction. Responding to various pressures, it would depart markedly from the novelistic tradition. When it did so, it would—with variations that may be observed in such writers as Hawthorne, Melville, Mark Twain, Faulkner, and Hemingway—became either melodrama or pastoral idyl, often both.

Although Cooper gave an indubitably American tone to romance he did so without ceasing to be, in many ways, a disciple of Scott. Another disciple of Scott, and to a lesser extent of Godwin, was Cooper's near contemporary, the South Carolina journalist and romancer William Gilmore Simms. This author is no less convinced than Cooper that romance is the form of fiction called for by American conditions. Historical romance was his particular *forte*, and his *Views and Reviews* (1845) contains an interesting investigation of the materials available to the American romancer. In his prefatory letter to *The Yemassee*, his most popular tale of Indian warfare (first published in 1835), Simms defines the romance as the modern version of epic:

> You will note that I call *The Yemassee* a romance, and not a novel. You will permit me to insist on the distinction . . . What are the standards of the modern Romance? What is the modern Romance itself? The reply is immediate. The modern Romance is the substitute which the people of the present day offer for the ancient epic. The form is changed; the matter is very much the same; at all events, it differs much more seriously from the English novel than it does from the epic and the drama, because the dif-

ference is one of material, even more than of fabrication. The
reader who, reading *Ivanhoe*, keeps Richardson and Fielding
beside him, will be at fault in every step of his progress. The
domestic novel of those writers, confined to the felicitous narration
of common and daily occurring events, and the grouping and
delineation of characters in the ordinary conditions of society, is
altogether a different sort of composition; and if, in a strange
doggedness or simplicity of spirit, such a reader happens to pin
his faith to such writers alone, circumscribing the boundless
horizon of art to the domestic circle, the Romances of Maturin,
Scott, Bulwer, and others of the present day, will be little better
than rhapsodical and intolerable nonsense.

When I say that our Romance is the substitute of modern
times for the epic or the drama, I do not mean to say that they are
exactly the same things, and yet, examined thoroughly . . . the
differences between them are very slight. These differences depend
upon the material employed, rather than upon the particular mode
in which it is used. The Romance is of loftier origin than the Novel.
It approximates the poem. It may be described as an amalgam of the
two. It is only with those who are apt to insist upon poetry as verse,
and to confound rhyme with poetry, that the resemblance is un-
apparent. The standards of the Romance . . . are very much those
of the epic. It invests individuals with an absorbing interest—it
hurries them rapidly through crowding and exacting events, in a
narrow space of time—it requires the same unities of plan, of
purpose, and harmony of parts, and it seeks for its adventures
among the wild and wonderful. It does not confine itself to what is
known, or even what is probable. It grasps at the possible; and,
placing a human agent in hitherto untried situations, it exercises
its ingenuity in extricating him from them, while describing his
feelings and his fortunes in the process.

Loosely written as it is, this statement, with its echoes
of Aristotle's *Poetics*, remains something of a classic in the
history of American criticism, its general purport being one
which so many of our prose fictionists have accepted. American fiction has been notable for its poetic quality, which is not
the poetry of verse nor yet the domestic or naturalistic poetry
of the novel but the poetry of romance. In allying romance to
epic Simms was reflecting his own preoccupation with
panoramic settings, battles, and heroic deeds; doubtless he
had also in mind, vociferous nationalist that he was, the

power of epic to mirror the soul of a people. There are many American fictions besides *The Yemassee* which remind us of epics, large and small: Cooper's *Prairie*, *Moby-Dick*, *The Adventures of Huckleberry Finn*, Faulkner's *As I Lay Dying*, for example. Yet on the whole, American fiction has approximated the poetry of idyl and of melodrama more often than of epic.

Not all of Simms' own romances have the epic quality. *Confession: or the Blind Heart* (1841), *Beauchampe* (1842), and *Charlemont* (1856) are "tales of passion" and have to do with seduction, murder, revenge, and domestic cruelty. They are dark studies in psychology that reflect Godwin and the Gothic tradition at the same time that in their pictures of town life, lawyers, court trials, and local customs they forecast later Southern writers, such as Faulkner and Robert Penn Warren. Simms' tales of passion, however, are fatally marred by the carelessness and crudity with which they are thrown together, and it was in the work of Hawthorne that for the first time the psychological possibilities of romance were realized.

As we see from the prefaces to his longer fictions, particularly *The Marble Faun*, Hawthorne was no less convinced than Cooper and Simms that romance, rather than the novel, was the predestined form of American narrative. In distinguishing between forms, his Preface to *The House of the Seven Gables* makes some of the same points Simms had made:

> When a writer calls his work a romance, it need hardly be observed that he wishes to claim a certain latitude, both as to its fashion and material, which he would not have felt himself entitled to assume, had he professed to be writing a novel. The latter form of composition is presumed to aim at a very minute fidelity, not merely to the possible, but to the probable and ordinary course of man's experience. The former—while, as a work of art, it must rigidly subject itself to laws, and while it sins unpardonably so far as it may swerve aside from the truth of the human heart—has fairly a right to present that truth under circumstances, to a great extent, of the writer's own choosing or creation. If he think fit, also, he may so manage his atmospherical medium as to bring out or

mellow the lights, and deepen and enrich the shadows, of the picture. He will be wise, no doubt, to make a very moderate use of the privileges here stated, and especially, to mingle the marvellous rather as a slight, delicate, and evanescent flavor, than as any portion of the actual substance of the dish offered to the public. He can hardly be said, however, to commit a literary crime, even if he disregards this caution.

As Hawthorne sees the problem confronting the American author, it consists in the necessity of finding (in the words of the Introduction to *The Scarlet Letter*) "a neutral territory, somewhere between the real world and fairy-land, where the Actual and the Imaginary may meet, and each imbue itself with the nature of the other." Romance is, as we see, a kind of "border" fiction, whether the field of action is in the neutral territory between civilization and the wilderness, as in the adventure tales of Cooper and Simms, or whether, as in Hawthorne and later romancers, the field of action is conceived not so much as a place as a state of mind—the borderland of the human mind where the actual and the imaginary intermingle. Romance does not plant itself, like the novel, solidly in the midst of the actual. Nor when it is memorable, does it escape into the purely imaginary.

In saying that no matter what its extravagances romance must not "swerve aside from the truth of the human heart," Hawthorne was in effect announcing the definitive adaptation of romance to America. To keep fiction in touch with the human heart is to give it a universal human significance. But this cannot be done memorably in prose fiction, even in the relatively loose form of the romance, without giving it a local significance. The truth of the heart as pictured in romance may be more generic or archetypal than in the novel; it may be rendered less concretely; but it must still be made to belong to a time and a place. Surely Hawthorne's romances do. In his writings romance was made for the first time to respond to the particular demands of an American imagination and to mirror, in certain limited ways, the American mind. In order to accomplish this Hawthorne had to bring into play his considerable talent for psychology. Cooper was not a psychologist of any subtlety and outside of the striking conception of the stoic inner life of Natty Bumppo, he gave to romance no psychological quality that might not find a close analogue in Scott. Although no one would mistake a fiction of Simms for one of Scott, Simms' originality was circumscribed by his apparent belief, as stated in the quotation above, that American romance would differ from earlier forms only because it has different material rather than a "particular mode" of rendering this material. His claim to originality was severely limited by the crudity and indecision of his literary form and of his psychological insights.

In the writings of Brockden Brown, Cooper, and Simms we have the first difficult steps in the adaptation of English romance to American conditions and needs. Following these pioneers we have had, ever since, two streams of romance in our literary history. The first is the stream that makes the main subject of this book and includes Hawthorne, Melville, James, Mark Twain, Frank Norris, Faulkner, Hemingway, and others who have found that romance offers certain qualities of thought and imagination which the American fiction writer needs but which are outside the province of the novel proper. These are writers who each in his own way have followed Hawthorne both in thinking the imagination of romance necessary and in knowing that it must not "swerve aside from the truth of the human heart."

The other stream of romance, justly contemned by Mark Twain and James, is one which also descends from Scott, and includes John Esten Cooke's *Surry of Eagle's Nest* (1886), Lew Wallace's *Ben Hur* (1880), Charles Major's *When Knighthood Was In Flower* (1899), and later books like *Gone with the Wind* and the historical tales of Kenneth Roberts. Although these works may have their points, according to the taste of the reader, they are, historically considered, the tag-end of a European tradition that begins in the Middle Ages and has come down into our own literature without responding to the forms of imagination which the actualities of American life have inspired. Romances of this sort are sometimes defended because "they tell a good story"—as opposed to the fictions of, say, Faulkner and Melville, which allegedly don't. People who make this complaint have a real point; yet they put themselves in the position of defending books which have a fatal inner falsity.

The fact is that the word "romance" begins to take on its inevitable meaning, for the historically minded American reader, in the writing of Hawthorne. Ever since his use of the word to describe his own fiction, it has appropriately signified the peculiar narrow profundity and rich interplay of lights and darks which one associates with the best American writing. It has also signified, to be sure, that common trait shared by the American romances which are discussed in this book and all other romances whatsoever—namely, the penchant for the marvelous, the sensational, the legendary, and in general the heightened effect. But the critical question is always: To what purpose have these amiable tricks of romance been used? To falsify reality and the human heart or to bring us round to a new, significant and perhaps startling relation to them?

Henry James

from Preface to *The American*□

(. . . The real represents to my perception the things we cannot possibly *not* know, sooner or later, in one way or another; it being but one of the accidents of our hampered state, and one of the incidents of their quantity and number, that particular instances have not yet come our way. The romantic stands, on the other hand, for the things that, with all the facilities in the world, all the wealth and all the courage and all the wit and all the adventure, we never *can* directly know; the things that can reach us only through the beautiful circuit and subterfuge of our thought and our desire.) There have been, I gather, many definitions of romance, as a matter indispensably of boats, or of caravans, or of tigers, or of "historical characters," or of ghosts, or of forgers, or of detectives, or of beautiful wicked women, or of pistols and knives, but they appear for the most part reducible to the idea of the facing of danger, the acceptance of great risks for the fascination, the very love, of their uncertainty, the joy of success if possible and of battle in any case. This would be a fine formula if it bore examination; but it strikes me as weak and inadequate, as by no means covering the true ground and yet as landing us in strange confusions.

The panting pursuit of danger is the pursuit of life itself. . . .

.   .   .   .

□ Reprinted from *The Art of the Novel*, by Henry James, with permission of Charles Scribner's Sons.

The only *general* attribute of projected romance that I can see, the only one that fits all its cases, is the fact of the kind of experience with which it deals—experience liberated, so to speak; experience disengaged, disembroiled, disencumbered, exempt from the conditions that we usually know to attach to it and, if we wish so to put the matter, drag upon it, and operating in a medium which relieves it, in a particular interest, of the inconvenience of a *related*, a measurable state, a state subject to all our vulgar communities. The greatest intensity may so be arrived at evidently—when the sacrifice of community, of the "related" sides of situations, has not been too rash. It must to this end not flagrantly betray itself; we must even be kept if possible, for our illusion, from suspecting any sacrifice at all. The balloon of experience is in fact of course tied to the earth, and under that necessity we swing, thanks to a rope of remarkable length, in the more or less commodious car of the imagination; but it is by the rope we know where we are, and from the moment that cable is cut we are at large and unrelated: we only swing apart from the globe—though remaining as exhilarated, naturally, as we like, especially when all goes well. The art of the romancer is, "for the fun of it," insidiously to cut the cable, to cut it without our detecting him.

William Dean Howells

Criticism and Fiction, ch. II □

I should, indeed, prefer another line of Keats', if I were to profess any formulated creed, and should feel much safer with his "Beauty is Truth, Truth Beauty," than even with my friend's reformation of the more quoted verse. It brings us back to the solid ground taken by Mr. Symonds, which is not essentially different from that taken in the great Mr. Burke's Essay on the Sublime and the Beautiful—a singularly modern book, considering how long ago it was wrote (as the great Mr. Steele would have written the participle a little longer ago), and full of a certain well-mannered and agreeable instruction. In some things it is of that droll little eighteenth-century world, when philosophy had got the neat little universe into the hollow of its hand, and knew just what it was, and what it was for; but it is quite without arrogance. "As for those called critics," the author says, "they have generally sought the rule of the arts in the wrong place; they have sought among poems, pictures, engravings, statues, and buildings; but art can never give the rules that make an art. This is, I believe, the reason why artists in general, and poets principally, have been confined in so narrow a circle; they have been rather imitators of one another than of nature. Critics follow them, and therefore can do little as guides. I can judge but poorly of anything while I measure it by no other standard than itself. The true standard of the arts is in every man's power; and an easy observation of the most common,

□ First published in 1891.

sometimes of the meanest things, in nature will give the truest lights, where the greatest sagacity and industry that slights such observation must leave us in the dark, or, what is worse, amuse and mislead us by false lights."

If this should happen to be true—and it certainly commends itself to acceptance—it might portend an immediate danger to the vested interests of criticism, only that it was written a hundred years ago; and we shall probably have the "sagacity and industry that slights the observation" of nature long enough yet to allow most critics the time to learn some more useful trade than criticism as they pursue it. Nevertheless, I am in hopes that the communistic era in taste foreshadowed by Burke is approaching, and that it will occur within the lives of men now overawed by the foolish old superstition that literature and art are anything but the expression of life, and are to be judged by any other test than that of their fidelity to it. The time is coming, I hope, when each new author, each new artist, will be considered, not in his proportion to any other author or artist, but in his relation to the human nature, known to us all, which it is his privilege, his high duty, to interpret. "The true standard of the artist is in every man's power" already, as Burke says; Michelangelo's "light of the piazza," the glance of the common eye, is and always was the best light on a statue; Goethe's "boys and blackbirds" have in all ages been the real connoisseurs of berries; but hitherto the mass of common men have been afraid to apply their own simplicity, naturalness, and honesty to the appreciation of the beautiful. They have always cast about for the instruction of someone who professed to know better, and who browbeat wholesome common-sense into the self-distrust that ends in sophistication. They have fallen generally to the worst of this bad species, and have been "amused and misled" (how pretty that quaint old use of amuse is!) "by false lights" of critical vanity and self-righteousness. They have been taught to compare what they see and what they read, not with the things that they have observed and known, but with the things that some other artist or writer has done. Especially if they have themselves the artistic impulse in any direction they are taught to form themselves, not upon life, but upon the masters who became masters only by forming themselves upon life. The seeds of death are planted in them, and they can produce only the still-born, the academic. They are not told to take their work into the public square and see if it seems true to the chance passer, but to test it by the work of the very men who refused and decried any other test of their own work. The young writer who attempts to report the phrase and carriage of every-day life, who tries to tell just how he has heard men talk and seen them look, is made to feel guilty of something low and unworthy by the stupid people who would like to have him show how Shakespeare's men talked and looked, or Scott's, or Thackeray's, or Balzac's, or Hawthorne's, or Dickens'; he is instructed to idealize his personages, that is, to take the life-likeness out of them, and put the book-likeness into them. He is approached in the spirit of wretched pedantry into which learning, much or little, always decays when it withdraws itself and stands apart from experience in an attitude or imagined superiority, and which would say with the same confidence to the scientist: "I see that you are looking at a grasshopper there which you have found in the grass, and I suppose you intend to describe it. Now don't waste your time and sin against culture in that way. I've got a grasshopper here, which has been evolved at considerable pains and expense out of the grasshopper in general; in fact, it's a type. It's made up of wire and card-board, very prettily painted in a conventional tint, and it's perfectly indestructible. It isn't very much like a real grasshopper, but it's a great deal nicer, and it's served to represent the notion of a grasshopper ever since man emerged from barbarism. You may say that it's artificial. Well, it is artificial; but then it's ideal too; and what you want to do is to cultivate the ideal. You'll find the books full of my kind of grasshopper, and scarcely a trace of yours in any of them. The thing that you are proposing to do is commonplace; but if you say that it isn't commonplace, for the very reason that it hasn't been done before, you'll have to admit that it's photographic."

As I said, I hope the time is coming when not only the artist, but the common, average man, who always "has the standard of the arts in his power," will have also the courage to apply it, and will reject the ideal grasshopper wherever he finds it, in science, in literature, in art, because it is not "simple, natural, and honest," because it is not like a real grasshopper. But I will own that I think the time is yet far off, and that the people who have been brought up on the ideal grasshopper, the heroic grasshopper, the impassioned grasshopper, the self-devoted, adventureful, good old romantic card-board grasshopper, must die out before the simple, honest, and natural grasshopper can have a fair field. I am in no haste to compass the end of these good people, whom I find in the mean time very amusing. It is delightful to meet one of them, either in print or out of it—some sweet elderly lady or excellent gentleman whose youth was pastured on the literature of thirty or forty years ago—and to witness the confidence with which they preach their favorite authors as all the law and the prophets. They have commonly read little or nothing since, or, if they have, they have judged it by a standard taken from these authors, and never dreamed of judging it by nature; they are destitute of the documents in the case of the later writers; they suppose that Balzac was the beginning of realism, and that Zola is its wicked end; they are quite ignorant, but they are ready to talk you down, if you differ from them, with an assumption of knowledge sufficient for any occasion. The horror, the resentment, with which they receive any question of their literary saints is genuine; you descend at once very far in the moral and social scale, and anything short of offensive personality is too good for you; it is expressed to you that you are one to be avoided, and put down even a little lower than you have naturally fallen.

These worthy persons are not to blame; it is part of their intellectual mission to represent the petrifaction of taste, and to preserve an image of a smaller and cruder and emptier world than we now live in, a world which was feeling its way towards the simple, the natural, the honest, but was a good deal "amused and misled" by lights now no longer mistakable for heavenly luminaries. They belong to a time, just passing away, when certain authors were considered authorities in certain kinds, when they must be accepted entire and not questioned in any particular. Now we are beginning to see and to say that no author is an authority except in those moments when he held his ear close to Nature's lips and caught her very accent. These moments are not continuous with any authors in the past, and they are rare with all. Therefore I am not afraid to say now that the greatest classics are sometimes not at all great, and that we can profit by them only when we hold them, like our meanest contemporaries, to a strict accounting, and verify their work by the standard of the arts which we all have in our power, the simple, the natural, and the honest.

Those good people, those curious and interesting if somewhat musty back-numbers, must always have a hero, an idol of some sort, and it is droll to find Balzac, who suffered from their sort such bitter scorn and hate for his realism while he was alive, now become a fetich in his turn, to be shaken in the faces of those who will not blindly worship him. But it is no new thing in the history of literature: whatever is established is sacred with those who do not think. At the beginning of the century, when romance was making the same fight against effete classicism which realism is making to-day against effete romanticism, the Italian poet Monti declared that "the romantic was the cold grave of the Beautiful," just as the realistic is now supposed to be. The romantic of that day and the real of this are in certain degree the same. Romanticism then sought, as realism seeks now, to widen the bounds of sympathy, to level every barrier against aesthetic freedom, to escape from the paralysis of tradition. It exhausted itself in this impulse; and it remained for realism to assert that fidelity to experience and probability of motive are essential conditions of a great imaginative literature. It is not a new theory, but it has never before universally characterized literary endeavor. When realism becomes false to itself, when it heaps up facts merely, and maps life instead of picturing it, realism will perish too. Every true realist instinctively knows this, and it is perhaps the reason why he is careful of every fact, and feels himself bound to express or to indicate its meaning at the risk of over-moralizing. In life he finds nothing insignificant; all tells for destiny and character; nothing that God has made is contemptible. He cannot look upon human life and declare this thing or that thing unworthy of notice, any more than the scientist can declare a fact of the material world beneath the dignity of his inquiry. He feels in every nerve the equality of things and the unity of men; his soul is exalted, not by vain shows and shadows and ideals, but by realities, in which alone the truth lives. In criticism it is his business to break the images of false gods and misshapen heroes, to take away the poor silly toys that many grown people would still like to play with. He cannot keep terms with Jack the Giantkiller or Puss in Boots, under any name or in any place, even when they reappear as the convict Vautrec, or the Marquis de Montrivaut, or the Sworn Thirteen Noblemen. He must say to himself that Balzac, when he imagined these monsters, was not Balzac, he was Dumas; he was not realistic, he was romantic.

Philip Rahv

"Notes on the Decline of Naturalism"□

Quite a few protests have been aired in recent years against the sway of the naturalist method in fiction. It is charged that this method treats material in a manner so flat and external as to inhibit the search for value and meaning, and that in any case, whatever its past record, it is now exhausted. Dissimilar as they are, both the work of Franz Kafka and the works of the surrealist school are frequently cited as examples of release from the routines of naturalist realism, from its endless book-keeping of existence. Supporting this indictment are mostly those writers of the younger group who are devoted to experimentation and who look to symbolism, the fable, and the myth.

The younger writers are stirred by the ambition to create a new type of imaginative prose into which the recognizably real enters as one component rather than as the total substance. They want to break the novel of its objective habits; some want to introduce into it philosophical ideas; others are not so much drawn to expressing ideas as to expressing the motley strivings of the inner self—dreams, visions, and fantasies. Manifestly the failure of the political movement in the literature of the past decade has resulted in a revival of religio-esthetic attitudes. The young men of

□ Reprinted from *Literature and the Sixth Sense*. Copyright © 1969 by Philip Rahv. Reprinted by permission of the publisher, Houghton Mifflin Company.

letters are once again watching their own image in the mirror and listening to inner promptings. Theirs is a program calling for the adoption of techniques of planned derangement as a means of cracking open the certified structure of reality and turning loose its latent energies. And surely one cannot dispose of such a program merely by uncovering the element of mystification in it. For the truth is that the artist of the avant-garde has never hesitated to lay hold of the instruments of mystification when it suited his purpose, especially in an age such as ours, when the life about him belies more and more the rational ideals of the cultural tradition.

It has been remarked that in the long run the issue between naturalism and its opponents resolves itself into a philosophical dispute concerning the nature of reality. Obviously those who reject naturalism in philosophy will also object to its namesake in literature. But it seems to me that when faced with a problem such as that of naturalist fiction, the critic will do well not to mix in ontological maneuvres. From the standpoint of critical method it is impermissible to replace a concrete literary analysis with arguments derived from some general theory of the real. For it is plainly a case of the critic not being able to afford metaphysical commitments if he is to apply himself without preconceived ideas to the works of art that constitute his material. The art-object is from first to last the one certain datum at his disposal; and in succumbing to metaphysical leanings—either of the spiritualist or materialist variety—he runs the risk of freezing his insights in some kind of ideational schema, the relevance of which to the task in hand is hardly more than speculative. The act of critical evaluation is best performed in a state of *ideal aloofness* from abstract systems. Its practitioner is not concerned with making up his mind about the ultimate character of reality but with observing and measuring its actual proportions and combinations within a given form. The presence of the real affects him directly, with an immediate force contingent upon the degree of interest, concreteness, and intensity in the impression of life conveyed by the literary artist. The philosopher can take such impressions or leave them, but luckily the critic has no such choice.

Imaginative writing cannot include fixed and systematic definitions of reality without violating its own existential character. Yet in any imaginative effort that which we mean by the real remains the basic criterion of viability, the crucial test of relevance, even if its specific features can hardly be determined in advance but must be *felt anew* in each given instance. And so far as the medium of fiction is concerned, one cannot but agree with Henry James that it gains its "air of reality"—which he considers to be its "supreme virtue"—through "its immense and exquisite correspondence with life." Note that James' formulation allows both for analogical and realistic techniques of representation. He speaks not of copies or reports or transcripts of life but of relations of equivalence, of a "correspondence" which he identifies with the "illusion of life." The ability to produce this illusion he regards as the storyteller's inalienable gift, "the merit on which all other merits . . . helplessly and submissively depend." This insight is of an elementary nature and scarcely peculiar to James alone, but it seems that its truth has been lost on some of our recent catch-as-catch-can innovators in the writing of fiction.

It is intrinsically from this point of view that one can criticise the imitations of Kafka that have been turning up of late as being one-sided and even inept. Perhaps Kafka is too idiosyncratic a genius to serve as a model for others, but still it is easy to see where his imitators go wrong. It is necessary to say to them: To know how to take apart the recognizable world is not enough, is in fact merely a way of letting oneself go and of striving for originality at all costs. But originality of this sort is nothing more than a professional mannerism of the avant-garde. The genuine innovator is always trying to make us actually experience his creative contradictions. He therefore employs means that are subtler and more complex: *At the very same time that he takes the world apart he puts it together again.* For to proceed otherwise is to dissipate rather than alter our sense of reality, to weaken and compromise rather than change in any significant fashion our feeling of relatedness to the world. After all, what impressed us most in Kafka is precisely this power of his to achieve a simultaneity of contrary effects, to fit the known into the unknown, the actual into the mythic and vice versa, to combine within one framework a conscientiously empirical account of the visibly real with a dream-like and magical dissolution of it. In this paradox lies the pathos of his approach to human existence.

A modern poetess has written that the power of the visible derives from the invisible; but the reverse of this formula is also true. Thus the visible and the invisible might be said to stand to each other in an ironic relation of inner dependence and of mutual skepticism mixed with solicitude. It is a superb form of doubletalk; and if we are accustomed to its exclusion from naturalistic writing, it is all the more disappointing to find that the newly-evolved 'fantastic' style of the experimentalists likewise excludes it. But there is another consideration, of a more formal nature. It seems to me a profound error to conceive of reality as merely a species of material that the fiction-writer can either use or dispense with as he sees fit. It is a species of material, of course, and something else besides: it also functions as the *discipline of fiction*, much in the same sense that syllabic structure functions as the discipline of verse. This seeming identity of the formal and substantial means of narrative-prose is due, I think, to the altogether free and open character of the medium, which prevents it from developing such distinctly technical controls as poetry has acquired. Hence even the dream, when told in a story, must partake of some of the qualities of the real.

Whereas the surrealist represents man as immured in dreams, the naturalist represents him in a continuous waking state of prosaic daily living, in effect as never dreaming. But both the surrealist and the naturalist go to extremes in simplifying the human condition. J. M. Synge once said that the artist displays at once the difficulty and the triumph of his art when picturing the dreamer leaning out to reality or the man of real life lifted out of it. "In all the poets," he wrote, and this test is by no means limited to poetry alone, "the greatest have both these elements, that is they are supremely engrossed with life, and yet with the wildness of their fancy they are always passing out of what is simple and plain."

The old egocentric formula, "Man's fate is his character" has been altered by the novelists of the naturalist school
to read, "Man's fate is his environment." (Zola, the organizer
and champion of the school, drew his ideas from physiology
and medicine, but in later years his disciples cast the natural
sciences aside in favor of the social sciences.) To the naturalist, human behaviour is a function of its social environment;
the individual is the live register of its qualities; he exists in it
as animals exist in nature.[1] Due to this emphasis the naturalist
mode has evolved historically in two main directions. On the
one hand it has tended towards passive documentation
(milieu-panoramas, local-color stories, reportorial studies of
a given region or industry, etc.), and on the other towards the
exposure of socio-economic conditions (muckraking). American fiction of the past decade teems with examples of both
tendencies, usually in combination. The work of James T.
Farrell, for instance, is mostly a genre-record, the material of
which is in its very nature operative in producing social
feeling, while such novels as *The Grapes of Wrath* and *Native
Son* are exposure-literature, as is the greater part of the fiction
of social protest. Dos Passos' trilogy, *U. S. A.*, is thoroughly
political in intention but has the tone and gloss of the methodical genre-painter in the page by page texture of its prose.

I know of no hard and fast rules that can be used to
distinguish the naturalist method from the methods of realism
generally. It is certainly incorrect to say that the difference is
marked by the relative density of detail. Henry James observes in his essay *The Art of Fiction* that it is above all
"solidity of specification" that makes for the illusion of life—
the air of reality—in a novel; and the truth of this dictum is
borne out by the practice of the foremost modern innovators
in this medium, such as Proust, Joyce, and Kafka. It is not,
then, primarily the means employed to establish verisimilitude
that fix the naturalist imprint upon a work of fiction. A more
conclusive test, to my mind, is its treatment of the relation of
character to background. I would classify as naturalistic that
type of realism in which the individual is portrayed not merely
as subordinate to his background but as wholly determined by
it—that type of realism, in other words, in which the environ-

ment displaces its inhabitants in the role of the hero. Theodore Dreiser, for example, comes as close as any American writer to plotting the careers of his characters strictly within a determinative process. The financier Frank Cowperwood masters his world and emerges as its hero, while the "little man" Clyde Griffiths is the victim whom it grinds to pieces; yet hero and victim alike are essentially implements of environmental force, the carriers of its contradictions upon whom it stamps success or failure—not entirely at will, to be sure, for people are marked biologically from birth—but with sufficient autonomy to shape their fate.

In such a closed world there is patently no room for the singular, the unique, for anything in fact which cannot be represented plausibly as the product of a particular social and historical complex. Of necessity the naturalist must deal with experience almost exclusively in terms of the broadly typical. He analyses characters in such a way as to reduce them to standard types. His method of construction is that of accretion and enumeration rather than of analysis or storytelling; and this is so because the quantitative development of themes, the massing of detail and specification, serves his purpose best. He builds his structures out of literal fact and precisely documented circumstance, thus severely limiting the variety of creative means at the disposal of the artist.

This quasi-scientific approach not only permits but, in theory at least, actually prescribes a neutral attitude in the sphere of values. In practice, however, most naturalists are not sufficiently detached or logical to stay put in such an ultra-objective position. Their detractors are wrong in denying them a moral content; the most that can be said is that theirs is strictly functional morality, bare of any elements of gratuity or transcendence and devoid of the sense of personal freedom.[2] Clearly such a perspective allows for very little self-awareness on the part of characters. It also removes the possibility of a tragic resolution of experience. The world of naturalist fiction is much too big, too inert, too hardened by social habit and material necessity, to allow for that tenacious self-assertion of the human by means of which tragedy justifies and ennobles its protagonists. The only grandeur naturalism

knows is the grandeur of its own methodological achievement
in making available a vast inventory of minutely described
phenomena, in assembling an enormous quantity of data and
arranging them in a rough figuration of reality. *Les Rougon-
Macquart* stands to this day as the most imposing monument
to this achievement.

But in the main it is the pure naturalist—that monstrous offspring of the logic of a method—that I have been
describing here. Actually no such literary animal exists. Life
always triumphs over methods, over formulas and theories.
There is scarcely a single novelist of any importance wearing
the badge of naturalism who is all of a piece, who fails to
compensate in some way for what we miss in his fundamental
conception. Let us call the roll of the leading names among the
French and American naturalists and see wherein each is saved.

The Goncourts, it is true, come off rather badly, but
even so, to quote a French critic, they manage "to escape
from the crude painting of the naked truth by their impressionistic mobility" and, one might add, by their mobile
intelligence. Zola's case does not rest solely on our judgment
of his naturalist dogmas. There are entire volumes by him—
the best, I think, is *Germinal*—and parts of volumes besides,
in which his naturalism, fed by an epic imagination, takes on
a mythic cast. Thomas Mann associates him with Wagner in a
common drive toward an epic mythicism:

They belong together. The kinship of spirit, method, and aims is
most striking. This lies not only in the ambition to achieve size,
the propensity to the grandiose and the lavish; nor is it the Homeric
leitmotiv alone that is common to them; it is first and foremost a
special kind of naturalism, which develops into the mythical. . . .
In Zola's epic . . . the characters themselves are raised up to a
plane above that of every day. And is that Astarte of the Second
Empire, called Nana, not symbol and myth?" (*The Sufferings and
Greatness of Richard Wagner*)

Zola's prose, though not controlled by an artistic conscience,
overcomes our resistance through sheer positiveness and
expressive energy—qualities engendered by his novelistic
ardor and avidity for recreating life in all its multiple forms.[3]

As for Huysmans, even in his naturalist period he was more
concerned with style than with subject-matter. Maupassant is
a naturalist mainly by alliance, i.e. by virtue of his official
membership in the School of Médan; actually he follows a line
of his own, which takes off from naturalism never to return to
it. There are few militant naturalists among latter-day French
writers. Jules Romains is sometimes spoken of as one, but the
truth is that he is an epigone of all literary doctrines, including his own. Dreiser is still unsurpassed so far as American
naturalism goes, though just at present he may well be the
least readable. He has traits that make for survival—a
Balzacian grip on the machinery of money and power; a
prosiness so primary in texture that if taken in bulk it affects
us as a kind of poetry of the commonplace and ill-favored; and
an emphatic eroticism which is the real climate of existence in
his fictions—Eros hovering over the shambles. Sinclair Lewis
was never a novelist in the proper sense that Zola and Dreiser
are novelists, and, given his gift for exhaustive reporting,
naturalism did him more good than harm by providing him
with a ready literary technique. In Farrell's chronicles there
is an underlying moral code which, despite his explicit rejection of the Church, seems to me indisputably orthodox and
Catholic; and his Studs Lonigan—a product of those unsightly
urban neighborhoods where youth prowls and fights to live up
to the folk-ideal of the "regular guy"—is no mere character
but an archetype, an eponymous hero of the street-myths that
prevail in our big cities. The naturalism of Dos Passos is most
completely manifested in *U. S. A.*, tagged by the critics as a
"collective" novel recording the "decline of our business
civilization." But what distinguishes Dos Passos from other
novelists of the same political animus is a sense of justice so
pure as to be almost instinctive, as well as a deeply elegiac
feeling for the intimate features of American life and for its
precipitant moments. Also, *U. S. A.* is one of the very few
naturalist novels in which there is a controlled use of language, in which a major effect is produced by the interplay
between story and style. It is necessary to add, however, that
the faults of Dos Passos' work have been obscured by its vivid
contemporaneity and vital political appeal. In the future, I

think, it will be seen more clearly than now that it dramatizes social symptoms rather than lives and that it fails to preserve the integrity of personal experience. As for Faulkner, Hemingway, and Caldwell, I do not quite see on what grounds some critics and literary historians include them in the naturalist school. I should think that Faulkner is exempted by his prodigious inventiveness and fantastic humor. Hemingway is a realist on one level, in his attempts to catch the "real thing, the sequence of motion and fact which made the emotion"; but he is also subjective, given to self-portraiture and to playing games with his ego; there is very little study of background in his work, a minimum of documentation. In his best novels Caldwell is a writer of rural abandon—and comedy. His *Tobacco Road* is a sociological area only in patches; most of it is exotic landscape.

It is not hard to demonstrate the weakness of the naturalist method by abstracting it, first, from the uses to which individual authors put it and, second, from its function in the history of modern literature. The traditionalist critics judge it much too one-sidedly in professing to see in its rise nothing but spiritual loss—an invasion of the arcanum of art by arid scientific ideas. The point is that this scientific bias of naturalism was historically productive of contradictory results. Its effect was certainly depressive insofar as it brought mechanistic notions and procedures into writing. But it should be kept in mind that it also enlivened and, in fact, revolutionized writing by liquidating the last assets of "romance" in fiction and by purging it once and for all of the idealism of the "beautiful lie"—of the long-standing inhibitions against dealing with the underside of life, with those inescapable day-by-day actualities traditionally regarded as too "sordid" and "ugly" for inclusion within an aesthetic framework. If it were not for the service thus rendered in vastly increasing the store of literary material, it is doubtful whether such works as *Ulysses* and even *Remembrance of Things Past* could have been written. This is not clearly understood in the English speaking countries, where naturalism, never quite forming itself into a "movement," was at most only an extreme emphasis in the general onset of realistic fiction and drama.

One must study, rather, the Continental writers of the last quarter of the 19th Century in order to grasp its historical role. In discussing the German naturalist school of the 1880's, the historian Hans Naumann has this to say, for instance:

Generally it can be said that to its early exponents the doctrine of naturalism held quite as many diverse and confusing meanings as the doctrine of expressionism seemed to hold in the period just past. Imaginative writers who at bottom were pure idealists united with the dry-as-dust advocates of a philistine natural-scientific program on the one hand and with the shameless exploiters of erotic themes on the other. All met under the banner of naturalism —friends today and enemies tomorrow. . . . But there was an element of historical necessity in all this. The fact is that the time had come for an assault, executed with glowing enthusiasm, against the epigones . . . that it was finally possible to fling aside with disdain and anger the pretty falsehoods of life and art (*Die Deutsche Dichtung der Gegenwart, Stuttgart,* 1930, p. 144).

And he adds that the naturalism of certain writers consisted simply in their "speaking honestly of things that had heretofore been suppressed."

But to establish the historical credit of naturalism is not to refute the charges that have been brought against it in recent years. For whatever its past accomplishments, it cannot be denied that its present condition is one of utter debility. What was once a means of treating material truthfully has been turned, through a long process of depreciation, into a mere convention of truthfulness, devoid of any significant or even clearly definable literary purpose or design. The spirit of discovery has withdrawn from naturalism; it has now become the common denominator of realism, available in like measure to the producers of literature and to the producers of kitsch. One might sum up the objections to it simply by saying that it is no longer possible to use this method *without taking reality for granted.* This means that it has lost the power to cope with the ever-growing element of the problematical in modern life, which is precisely the element that is magnetizing the imagination of the true artists of our epoch. Such artists are no longer content merely to question particular habits or situations or even institutions; it is reality itself which they bring into question. Reality to them is like that "open wound" of which Kierkegaard speaks in his *Journals*: "A healthy open wound; sometimes it is healthier to keep a wound open; sometimes it is worse when it closes."

There are also certain long-range factors that make for the decline of naturalism. One such factor is the growth of psychological science and, particularly, of psychoanalysis. Through the influence of psychology literature recovers its inwardness, devising such forms as the interior monologue, which combines the naturalistic in its minute description of the mental process with the anti-naturalistic in its disclosure of the subjective and the irrational. Still another factor is the tendency of naturalism, as Thomas Mann observes in his remarks on Zola, to turn into the mythic through sheer immersion in the typical. This dialectical negation of the typical is apparent in a work like *Ulysses*, where "the myth of the *Odyssey*," to quote from Harry Levin's study of Joyce, "is superimposed upon the map of Dublin" because only a myth could "lend shape or meaning to a slice of life so broad and banal." And from a social-historical point of view this much can be said, that naturalism cannot hope to survive the world of 19th century science and industry of which it is the product. For what is the crisis of reality in contemporary art if not at bottom the crisis of the dissolution of this familiar world? Naturalism, which exhausted itself in taking an inventory of this world while it was still relatively stable, cannot possibly do justice to the phenomena of its disruption.

One must protest, however against the easy assumption of some avant-gardist writers that to finish with naturalism is the same as finishing with the principle of realism generally. It is one thing to dissect the real, to penetrate beneath its faceless surface and transpose it into terms of symbol and image; but the attempt to be done with it altogether is sheer regression or escape. Of the principle of realism it can be said that it is the most valuable acquisition of the modern mind. It has taught literature how to take in, how to grasp and encompass, the ordinary facts of human existence; and I mean this in the simplest sense conceivable. Least of all can the novelist dispense with it, as his medium knows of no other principle of coherence. In Gide's *Les Faux-Monnayeurs* there is a famous passage in which the novelist Edouard enumerates the faults of the naturalist school. "The great defect of that school is that it always cuts a slice of life in the same direction: in time, lengthwise. Why not in breadth? Or in depth? As for me, I should like not to cut at all. Please understand: I should like to put everything into my novel." "But I thought" his interlocutor remarks, "that you want to abandon reality." Yes, replies Edouard, "my novelist wants to abandon it; but I shall continually bring him back to it. In fact that will be the subject; the struggle between the facts presented by reality and the ideal reality."

Notes

1 Balzac, to whom naturalism is enormously indebted, explains in his preface to the *Comédie Humaine* that the idea of that work came to him in consequence of a "comparison between the human and animal kingdoms." "Does not society," he asks, "make of man, in accordance with the environment in which he lives and moves, as many different kinds of man as there are different zoological species? . . . There have, therefore, existed and always will exist social species, just as there are zoological species."
   Zola argues along the same lines: "All things hang together: it is necessary to start from the determination of inanimate bodies in order to arrive at the determination of living beings; and since savants like Claude Bernard demonstrate now that fixed laws govern the human body, we can easily proclaim . . . the hour in which the laws of thought and passion will be formulated in their turn. A like determination will govern the stones of the roadway and the brain of man. . . . We have experimental chemistry and medicine and physiology, and later on an experimental novel. It is an inevitable evolution." (*The Experimental Novel*)
2 Chekhov remarks in one of his stories that "the sense of personal freedom is the chief constituent of creative genius."
3 Moreover, it should be evident that Zola's many faults are not rectified but merely inverted in much of the writing—so languidly allusive and decorative—of the literary generations that turned their backs on him.

III

The Leatherstocking Tales (1823-1841) by James Fenimore Cooper

Roy Harvey Pearce
"*The Leatherstocking Tales* Re-Examined"□

Of the two Coopers whom Parrington succeeded in making out of one, recent students of our literature have been more interested in the second, the Cooper of the Antirent novels, the social treatises, and the travel books. The Cooper of *The Leatherstocking Tales* has been taken for granted as the great romancer, the *improvvisatore*, the myth-maker. Certainly no one has really forgotten this Cooper; but no one has sufficiently remembered him. We have been given a life-size portrait of Cooper the political and social theorist; but we hear little nowadays of Cooper the novelist, involved in the problems of writing a novel. Yet the Cooper who is most significant in our literature is the Cooper of the *Leatherstocking Tales*. Here—to put it baldly—he succeeds or fails as his art succeeds or fails. And if for the great part he fails, it is important that we know the basis of his failure. Only then can we judge him and his masterwork.

In any case, we have had sufficient analyzing and dichotomizing and are in a position to view the two Coopers as one. Our knowledge of Cooper's social and political interests and of contemporary theories concerning the nature of frontier and savage society should enable us to gauge the success or failure of the *Leatherstocking Tales* in relation to their proper

□ *South Atlantic Quarterly*, XLVI, (October 1947), 4524–536. Reprinted by permission of Duke University Press and Roy Harvey Pearce.

background and to Cooper's total intent in terms of that background. For he was, we must remind ourselves, a man who at once had deep social interests and was moved to write a novel, then a series of novels. In the end, like it or not, one is forced to judge those novels as works of art. We can do so now because, with the work of students of Cooper in particular and of early national cultural and intellectual history in general, we are able fully to realize the nature and impact of the ideas from which the novels derive so much of their substance. Having understood and judged the novels, we shall be able to comprehend more satisfactorily the nature of Cooper's problems as an artist (if only of sorts) and to chart more adequately the depths and limits of his art.

Two elements inform the *Leatherstocking Tales*, Cooper's political and social ideals (that is to say, his own theory of the good life) and more general contemporary theories of the nature of frontier and savage society. Cooper was a firm believer in a conservative, evolutionary, eighteenth-century kind of progress. Throughout his career, even as his specific political alignment changed, he held to a belief that society must progress toward the (perhaps unattainable) goodness of complex (i.e., civilized) forms and usages. In many ways he was one with Jefferson, being concerned that American life be dominated by an intelligent, educated, benevolent *aristoi*. Civilization meant a devotion to higher cultural forms, never a turning away from those forms to a rude, down-to-earth egalitarianism. Specifically, the frontier, as he points out in *Home as Found*, represents one stage in our movement toward the best life, that stage at which the totality of man's intellectual and social proclivities might be realized. More specifically for our purposes, the frontier of the *Leatherstocking Tales* is not something to which Cooper would recommend that men retreat; the good life of an agrarian, aristocratically dominated, intellectually developed society was not to be retreated from. It was a goal which Americans, above all, might achieve.

The second of these two informing elements consists of a complex of more general contemporary theories of the nature of frontier and savage society. Certainly, Cooper himself was not concerned with expositing those theories as such. Yet an understanding of them is essential for anything which would approach complete understanding of the *Tales*. They amount to what historians of ideas would term implicit assumptions. They are something which Cooper and his contemporary readers would take for granted—as though they were the equivalent of widely used words, the definition of which anyone would know.

That the frontiersman occupied an anomalous position in American life is a commonplace in much eighteenth- and early nineteenth-century travel writing. Travel writers were continually being amazed to find living on the frontier raw, powerful, savage white men who seemed to have dissociated themselves almost entirely from civilized life. For the most part such writers were contented merely with observing. Yet Cooper in his portrait of Natty Bumppo went beyond this, to picture his frontiersman as the essential frontiersman, to make use of what writers on the "theoretical" aspects of society had said would be true of men living the hard life of the far frontier. These men were savages, Indians to be precise. And in Natty we have Cooper's portrait of the white man with all savage virtues and limitations conditioned by his white birth.

The eighteenth- and early nineteenth-century picture of the savage seems to us drastically oversimplified. He lived, so writers on his society insisted, in a hunting and warring culture, struggling for his existence, hardening himself day by day, seeing the future only in terms of the present, making intuitive, instinctive judgments; he was essentially an individualist, yet a believer in the man-to-man friendships and loyalties which he might form. His life was limited by the pattern of the society in which he lived. Further, both his virtues and his vices were fixed by such limits. He was a being who acted, not thought. His society and its milieu prevented his being genuinely civilized. A deep frontier life was essentially a life of what was called "savagism."

This view was such a commonplace in the late eighteenth and early nineteenth centuries that it was developed in great detail by Jedidiah Morse (the new England divine and historian) in his article on "America" in the American version of the *Encyclopedia Britannica* (1790) and was presented as a matter of course in most early writings on American history. It is in the light of such a view that Cooper conceives of his Indians and, more important here, that he conceives of Natty Bumppo. Natty's is a simpler than civilized life, a life the dynamic forces of which derive from those factors in savage life which would be considered virtuous even by civilized standards—physical courage, instinctive action, unthinking trust in the individual as individual, and the driving need for "elbow room." If he is not the frontiersman whom Americans actually encountered, he is a frontiersman in whom they could whole-heartedly believe, simply because he is the frontiersman as he theoretically could and should be. Thus the second of the two informing elements gave life to Cooper's frontiersman even as the first fixed the pattern and the values of the society for which he was to clear the way.

II

And so the *Leatherstocking Tales* are to be read as essentially the story of Natty Bumppo—as the beau ideal of the frontiersman—in the context of the frontier, with what was for Cooper and his fellows a tension of civilization and non-civilization. Bumppo is the superman in a milieu in which such could develop. But even this frontiersman in all his perfection—and this was Cooper's major insight—could not last; he was to be swept over by the very civilization for which he had cleared the way and to which in some respects he was superior. Hence his story is to be a kind of tragic story—made even more so by the essential rightness and necessity of it all. Cooper could never be on Bumppo's side: Never would he intend to suggest that the civilization which sent Bumppo to a death on the prairie was thereby an evil force. Yet, for all his devotion to the idea that men must realize their social, civil qualities, Cooper could see the mythic potentialities for good in a Bumppo. More important—and this is part of that major insight—he could see that westward expansion and progress in crushing such a man as Bumppo would crush something heroic in American life. If, as in the Preface to *The Pathfinder*, Cooper could speak of "the wonderful means by which Providence is clearing the way for the advancement of civilization across the whole American continent," still he knew too that Progress meant suffering as well as triumph.

Significantly, the very first Bumppo whom Cooper portrayed was the Bumppo of *The Pioneers* (1823). Here Bumppo was to be defeated once and for all. We see him at the beginning of the novel with an "air of sullen dissatisfaction" complaining bitterly of Temple's "clearings and betterments," which have more and more restricted his freedom. He is gnarled and hardy; he lives with Chingachgook, no longer Big Serpent but Indian John, a chief whom liquor and the white man's ways have made old and useless. Over against them is set Judge Temple, the civilizer, who wishes to conserve the land for a better and richer life. He is clearing the wilderness, and Natty is part of it. Temple is all-powerful. He brings with him law, the law of societies, not of individuals. And, as Natty tells Grant, the minister, ". . . might makes right, and the law is stronger than an old man. . . ."

It is inevitable that Natty try to oppose might and the law. The poaching incident, Natty's resisting search and arrest, his conviction—these are symbolic of the more bitter aspects of the progress in which Temple (and Cooper) so dearly believed. That Temple should be indebted to Natty for saving his daughter's life points up only more the sad necessity of his sentencing Natty to the stocks and to prison. Hence Natty's speech at the ruins of the hut, which he has burned rather than allow it to be broken into, expresses the motif of *The Pioneers* and, indeed, of all the *Tales:*

> What would ye have with an old and helpless man? . . . You've driven God's creaters from the wilderness, where his providence had put them for his own pleasure; and you've brought in the troubles and divilties of the law, where no man was ever known to disturb another. You have driven me, that have lived forty long years of my appointed time in this very spot, from my home and the shelter of my head, lest you should put your wicked feet and wasty ways in my cabin. You've driven me to burn these

logs, under which I've eaten and drunk—the first of Heaven's gifts, and the other of the pure springs—for the half of a hundred years; and to mourn the ashes under my feet, as a man would weep and mourn for the children of his body. . . .

If the rest of the novel is awkwardly and obviously managed, it is managed for a purpose—to set against Bumppo's heroic stand the power of the civilization which drives him westward. For westward he must go, even after the Temples and Effinghams have been united, even after the Judge has offered to care for him for the rest of his days. Cooper's civilization is a kindly, strength-giving force, if only one yields to it intelligently. But Natty can have none of civilization, as he can comprehend none of its ways. Being of the frontier, of an heroic age, he must perforce preserve himself in his own ways as long as he lives.

Around the motif set in *The Pioneers* Cooper built the rest of the *Leatherstocking Tales.* As he wrote them—*The Last of the Mohicans* (1826), *The Prairie* (1827), *The Pathfinder* (1840), and *The Deerslayer* (1841)—he described the stages of Natty Bumppo's mythic, heroic development, always setting him against persons and actions which represented the civilized world of which he could never be part. It is true that the particular details of Cooper's conception of Natty changed as he returned to him again and again. Most important, Natty became less and less the "real" frontiersman and more and more the beau ideal; the crudeness of the Natty of *The Pioneers* is hardly the freshness and naïveté of the Natty of *The Deerslayer.* However, these are strictly matters of detail, which condition the whole only incidentally. For Cooper was a busy man and—as we shall see—an unsure and sadly insensitive artist. Yet, even if at times he might falter in detailed execution, he never faltered—if we read his novels with attention to implicit assumptions—in total conception.

To glance briefly at the *Tales* according to Bumppo's chronology: In *The Deerslayer*, Bumppo is young, uncertain of himself, not yet having killed his first Mingo. With him we see Hutter and Hurry Harry, "real" frontiersmen in all their crudity, and the young Chingachgook and his beloved. More important, there is Judith Hutter, drawn to Bumppo, who will have none of her. He must be free of the complexities of a kind of passion which he does not comprehend and therefore does not trust. For, while he has not an Indian's "gifts," he has not those of white civilization.

And so it goes in *The Last of the Mohicans*, where Natty is entirely above the life of Alice and Cora Munro and young Heyward. Here it is Uncas, the son of Chingachgook, who, like his blood enemy, Magua, is brought to his death by his passion for Cora Munro. That the Indian and Cora should be united would be impossible in Cooper's world of civilization and progress; hence, temporizing the issue by making Cora's ancestry somewhat dubious, he must do away with them both. And so there remain only Bumppo and Chingachgook and their deep, heroic friendship.

In *The Pathfinder* Natty is in love, in love with a woman who represents the security and peace of the settler's cottage. He lives his adventurous life, killing Mingos, making rescues, winning victories; yet he cannot win Mabel. Realizing that this failure is only right, he tells Jasper Western (who is, as a matter of course, young and handsome and who does win Mabel) that he hasn't "idees enough" for her. She is of civilization, complex and thinking. He is of the frontier. Once more, it is the heroic concept which matters here. One can see in Cooper's picture of this and the other Bumppos all that contemporary historians and writers on society were saying about what the Indian (and the white man who might live an Indian life) should be as the product of a free, hunting, warring life—a man of action, not of "idees," a man whose hard life gave him time and means only to act and to intuit, not to think. And civilized men (Cooper, for example) thought.

Then there is *The Pioneers*, the first written and, as we have seen, the key volume in the series. And finally, *The Prairie*, with the end we have expected. Here is Natty Bumppo as spectator, as one whose age and accomplishments have set him above Ishmael Bush and his squatter family, Middleton, Paul, Inez, Ellen, and the naturalist, Obed Battius. Even though Natty is in the end to fight the Bushes, at the very first he realizes that he has something in common with them.

When he tries to make Ishmael understand that the Sioux have attacked the squatter and his family because the Indians think of themselves as owners of the prairie, Ishmael cannot understand:

"Owners!" echoed the squatter, "I am as rightful an owner of the land I stand on, as any governor in the States! Can you tell me, stranger, where the law or the reason, is to be found, which says, that one man shall have a section, or a town, or perhaps a county to his use, and another have to beg for earth to make his grave in? This is not nature, and I deny that it is law. That is, your legal law."

"I cannot say that you are wrong," returned the trapper, whose opinions on this important topic, though drawn from very different premises, were in singular accordance with those of his companion, "and I have often thought and said as much, when and where I have believed my voice could be heard. . . ."

Here is a strange thing. The squatter, as Cooper had made abundantly clear in *The Pioneers* and was to make even clearer in the Littlepage series, was an evil, noncivilizing force on the frontier. Yet he can make Natty agree with Ishmael, if on different grounds. Natty was to be as isolated as Ishmael. For, as Cooper points out *in propria persona* a few pages later, civil society was moving westward:

The gradations of society, from that state which is called refined to that which approaches as near barbarity as connection with an intelligent people will readily allow, are to be traced from the bosom of the States, where wealth, luxury and the arts are beginning to seat themselves, to those distant, and ever-receding borders which mark the skirts, and announce the approach, of the nation, as moving mists precede the signs of day.

In *The Prairie* Natty is most of all Leatherstocking *philosophe*. Here more than in any of the other novels he comments on the evil of perverted man-made institutions and on the assurance of moral order which he finds self-evident in God's Nature. (If his early training among the Moravians is recalled here, as elsewhere, it is only as something auxiliary to this pre-orthodox natural religion.) Here he is set against the caricatured naturalist Battius and his hope that science can "eradicate the evil principle" from the world. This Bumppo is, once more, essentially the primitive man of the

eighteenth-century rationalist historians and their nineteenth-century followers, who, even as they proclaimed the
total superiority of civilized to savage institutions, insisted
that the natural man could "philosophize," if only at a relatively low, intuitive level. Thus for Cooper and his fellows
Natty can partake in alarums and excursions and can face
death with the contentment and complacency of one who
serenely lives in the least complex and most directly comprehended of worlds, that untouched by civilized man.

Natty dies as he has lived. He is ready for death because
there is nothing left for him in a world of Middletons. It is
significant that Middleton is the grandson of Duncan Heyward, in whom Natty had first found the strengths and weaknesses of the civilized life that was to give order to the frontier.
The central motif of the *Tales* is stated explicitly. Middleton
tells Natty just what his grandfather had said of the Leatherstocking of the fifties: "In short he was a noble shoot from the
stock of human nature, which never could attain its proper
elevation and importance, for no other reason, than because
it grew in the forest." If there is to be a sorrow at Natty's
death, it is sorrow at the inevitability of change, at the passing
of one good, felt wholly, with the coming of another.

III

Such a reading of the *Leatherstocking Tales*, it must be
evident, requires more attention to implicit assumptions than
one should have to give. Such a reading is too much between-
the-lines, too much one-sided. For, whatever was Cooper's total
intent, he could not make it come alive in his five novels. And
such a reading, in its one-sidedness, emphasizes Cooper's
great creation, Natty Bumppo, and neglects those over against
whom he and his kind are set—the creatures of Cooper's
civilization and the life he invented for them. Only if we look
closely at Cooper's managing of them and their life in relation
to that total intent can we see clearly where and how he failed.

Cooper's general problem was to give artistic dimensions to his insight into the triumph and tragedy that was the
story of Natty Bumppo. He had to give artistic reality not

only to Bumppo but to those representatives of civilized life
and usages whom Bumppo meets and who ultimately shape his
life. Now Bumppo was to be conceived as a figure whose proper
realm was taken to be that of the heroic society of the savage.
And those civilized persons were to be conceived as living in
another realm, a realm intrinsically better than that savage
realm, heroic as it might have been. Thus the very elements of
the novel—characterization, situation, setting, and plotting—
had to be given existence on these two levels. One can best
classify the two as Cooper did—as the levels of action and of
ideas. (It will be recalled that Natty continually objects to
that in civilized life which he cannot understand and which he
finds to be misused—"idees.") The one is simple; it calls for a
narrative structure built in terms of adventurous activity and
intuitive insights. The other is complex; it calls for a narrative
structure built in terms of self-analysis, thought, and emo-
tionality.

The first level Cooper could handle like a master. Natty
and the Indians are "real" in terms of their adventures and
their intuitions. Natty himself as the frontiersman is ideally
heroic. Shooting at targets, deer, or Mingos; standing up
under the threat of torture; battling hand to hand; picking up
a trail; making direct, intuitive moral judgments; finding his
God in the Nature about him—in all these does he live in the
context of Cooper's fiction. It is of this Natty that adolescents
read with delight, for in a great sense Natty is conceived of as
a child—as in Cooper's time primitive, savage life was conceived of as childlike, as the life of action, not of thought. It is
in fact this very childishness which Cooper felt must give way
to the maturity of civilized life.

Natty, the Indians, and the frontier, then, Cooper
succeeds in drawing successfully—and this in spite of a certain
obvious carelessness and crudity which one comes to take for
granted. Elsewhere, of course, Cooper fails entirely. To say
this is perhaps to be guilty of gravely announcing a commonplace, of giving the *coup de grace* to a dead issue. But it is
essential that we see just what this failure means in relation
to the intent of this first important achievement in American
fiction.

Even if the *Leatherstocking Tales* are at bottom Natty Bumppo's story, still he exists in relation to more than the frontier. This we have seen. It is all-important that the characterizations and situations which exist on the level of civilization and thought and social maturity (or what were taken to be such in the eighteenth and early nineteenth centuries) be given existence too—not necessarily independent existence, but existence which will have artistic reality in direct proportion to Bumppo's reality. We do not have to be made to realize directly the glories of society and civilization; such we must grant Cooper as given. But we must believe in the nonfrontiersmen in the *Tales* precisely as we must believe in Natty Bumppo—in the context of the fiction. This is a beginning rule for the writer, certainly. But just as certainly Cooper was too little conscious of its existence.

Here *The Deerslayer* will serve as a suitable case-in-point. Natty (in this phase called Hawkeye) is first set against Harry and Hutter, and the leading motif of the novel is established. Young, heroic Natty is contrasted with the vicious, crude, "real" frontiersmen. Then Judith Hutter appears— "touched" by the iniquities of the garrison—a much more complex being than Natty, her father, or her suitor, Harry. She is drawn to Natty, and she is supposed to be struggling with herself. We are told of this. We hardly see it. She is not up to Natty, as she realizes; but this, for Cooper, is a matter of hush-hush sentimentality. In their last frozen conversation, during which she learns finally that Natty will have none of her, she is said to be broken by what Cooper deigns to call "the consciousness of undeserving." And that is all. This amounts to a kind of imputed characterization; we get an indirect treatment of Judith's injured sensibilities; we see ends but not means to ends. Certainly Judith is not supposed to "symbolize" civilization as it first touches Natty; to say this would be to read too much into Cooper and to focus the novel on her, not on Natty. But she represents Natty's first important close contact with a life different from that which he has known with the Delaware. And that contact is not real.

Likewise, Hetty Hutter, Cooper's idiot girl, exists for

no reason except to furnish pathos (that Cooper thought much of this is evidenced in his Preface to *The Deerslayer*) and a convenient plot link. Her presence finds no proper motivation in terms of Natty's relation to his forest and the settlers who were bringing a new life to that forest. And Natty himself somehow is not effectively portrayed when he comes into contact with Judith and Hetty. He is the same Leatherstocking; but there is here a change, a new complexity in the matter of the narrative. Here, further, that matter does not come alive. Infectious, it kills off Natty too.

Such is Cooper's treatment of those who live at the complex, civilized level in his pattern of culture. For the most part it is the women: Cora and Alice Munro, Mabel Dunham, Elizabeth Temple, Ellen Wade, and Inez Middleton. So far as the novels are concerned, it does no good to explain away their deadness by pointing out that these were the sort of women Cooper knew, or at least would have liked to know; this is the biographical fallacy. And the men of Cooper's civilized world—from Heyward through Middleton—also suffer thus. There is lacking in them the abundance of fresh, concrete detail which makes Bumppo and the Indians come alive. Cooper's method is to characterize his "civilized" men by establishing them as types in situations which are for the most part unmotivated, by summarizing and analyzing their actions, or the results of their actions, and by giving them set speeches. He has little to say of their thoughts, emotions, or judgments, of that very "civilizing" influence. In short, he tends artistically to treat them on the level of action, when conceptually he intends them to exist on the level of thought.

It was pointed out long ago that the plots of all the *Leatherstocking Tales,* taken in large, are almost identical. Further, this "identity" has been cited as a prime example of Cooper's lack of invention. The fact of the matter, as we have seen, is that there was a certain necessity that the plots of all the novels be conceived of in closely parallel patterns. Natty was to be portrayed at various stages in his life, coming into close contact with a kind of life of which he could not be part. We have observed how on the whole Cooper's portrayal of this life is a failure. The failure is owing not to his repeating narrative patterns, but rather to his inability to treat of the "higher" level as effectively as he did of the "lower."

Such considerations lead us back to the total problem here involved. In any strict sense of the word, the raw data of Natty's life could not for Cooper be termed "romantic"— if we take the word in its common meaning: desirable because of distance, strangeness, and uniqueness. Actually—so Cooper felt—the frontier, for all its terror and beauty, was once and for all part of the life of early nineteenth-century America, yet was something away from which America must grow. That is, Natty's life was an artistic imaging of what was taken as a cultural reality, a representation of a force which was at once vital in, yet inferior to, the life of any happily civilized American. The problem was to make the integral relationship between frontier and nonfrontier—a potentially tragic relationship between the known and the unknown, between the complex and the simple, between the heroic-savage and the civilized—artistically realizable. The problem was enormously difficult. And its difficulty was increased because received literary forms and methods gave no direct indication of how it was to be solved. That solution required an originally creative artist—a pioneer, so to speak. And Cooper was not.

Here, then, is the crux of the matter. Cooper had that special kind of insight with which art seems to begin. He wanted to write a novel, then a series of novels, which would give artistic life to that insight. Natty's story was a kind of tragic story—the story of a hero of mythic proportions being cut down by a better kind of life than he could know or comprehend. As the pattern for his fiction, Cooper, as we know, took the novels of Scott—novels in which action, individuality, and the adventurous and unusual predominate, novels in which character as observed in one's day-to-day existence is not too important. Such a pattern was well fitted to Natty's own sort of life—a life which by definition, an eighteenth-century definition, was a life of action. But Cooper was forced or, more likely, preferred, to conceive of his more complex characters, characters who were by their very natures closer to his day-to-day existence than was Natty, after the manner of Scott too. These characters were conceived of in terms of adventure, or as conventionalized, standardized, melodramatic types. And they fail to come alive. They can have no proper existence in terms which are so alien to their proper natures. What we have left are the fragments of pure adventure and action and intuition, of life lived at an ideally simple level.

Certainly this is a great deal. But it might have been more if Cooper had been more of an artist. We can understand the feelings of the friend of Dana who, so Dana wrote Cooper, wanted to go away with the Natty of *The Pioneers*, the Natty who no longer could endure the rigors and restrictions of civilized living. This is pathos and romantic yearning; and Cooper was sufficiently insensitive artistically to be satisfied with pathos and romantic yearning. Yet neither of these effects did he ultimately (at the point of the conceptual origin of his novels) intend. We *should* feel that Natty is a tragic figure, that there is a terrible rightness in the westward sweep of American life.

In the end, of course, Cooper's failure in the *Leatherstocking Tales* can be explained only by saying that he was not artist enough to succeed. But, as we discover precisely what he was trying to do, we can describe that failure. What is important here, then, is that, even while recognizing Cooper's fragmentary accomplishment in the *Leatherstocking Tales,* we see clearly wherein his art was not comparable to his intent.

Henry Nash Smith

"Leatherstocking and the Problem of Social Order"

Although Boone was not exactly the prototype of Cooper's Leatherstocking, there is a haunting similarity between the two figures. Cooper based a part of chapters X and XII of *The Last of the Mohicans* on a well-known exploit of Boone in conducting the rescue of Betsey and Fanny Callaway and Jemima Boone, his daughter, from the Cherokees.[1] Betsey Callaway, like Cora Munro in Cooper's novel, tried to aid her rescuers by breaking twigs to mark the trail, and was detected by her Indian guards.[2] The rescue also furnished Cooper with several other details for his story.[3]

Near the opening of *The Prairie* Cooper sets his stage by describing the migration of Americans from Ohio and Kentucky across the Mississippi immediately after the Louisiana Purchase. Although Boone actually settled in Missouri in 1799, Cooper names him among the emigrants of 1804:

This adventurous and venerable patriarch was now seen making his last remove; placing the "endless river" between him and the multitude, his own success had drawn around him, and seeking for the renewal of enjoyments which were rendered worthless in his eyes, when trammelled by the forms of human institutions.[4]

In a footnote added to the revised edition, Cooper elaborates this passage with the remark that Boone emigrated beyond the Mississippi "because he found a population of ten to the square mile, inconvenient."[5] The aged Leatherstocking has likewise "been driven by the increasing and unparalleled advance of population, to seek a final refuge against society in the broad and tenantless plains of the west. . . ."[6]

The similarities between Boone and Leatherstocking were analyzed at length by a perceptive writer in *Niles' Register* in 1825, when Leatherstocking had appeared in only one novel, *The Pioneers*. The critic points out that both these heroes love the freedom of the forest, both take a passionate delight in hunting, and both dislike the ordinary pursuits of civilized men. As testimony to the fidelity of Cooper's characterization, the writer quotes a letter from a traveler through the Pennsylvania mountains who came upon herdsmen and hunters reminiscent both of Boone and of Leatherstocking. One of their number, celebrated throughout the West as having once been a companion of Boone, had set out for Arkansas when he was almost a hundred years old, and was reported to be still alive, a solitary hunter in the forest. A nephew of the emigrant who remained in Pennsylvania, himself athletic and vigorous at the age of seventy, shared Leatherstocking's love of hunting and his antipathy for "clearings" to such a marked degree that the traveler felt he must have sat as a model for Cooper.[7] A similar point was made by the poet Albert Pike, who after graduating from Harvard went out the Santa Fé Trail and later settled in a very primitive Arkansas. "I cannot wonder that many men have chosen to pass their life in the woods," wrote Pike in 1834, "and I see nothing overdrawn or exaggerated in the character of Hawkeye and Bushfield." He listed as the prime attractions of the lonely hunter's life its independence, its freedom from law and restraint, its lack of ceremony.[8]

For at least one section of the reading public, then, Leatherstocking, like Boone, was a symbol of anarchic freedom, an enemy of law and order. Did this interpretation conform to Cooper's intention in drawing the character?

The original hunter of *The Pioneers* (1823) clearly expresses subversive impulses. The character was conceived in terms of the antithesis between nature and civilization, between freedom and law, that has governed most American interpretations of the westward movement. Cooper was able to speak for his people on this theme because the forces at work within him closely reproduced the patterns of thought and feeling that prevailed in the society at large. But he felt the problem more deeply than his contemporaries: He was at once more strongly devoted to the principle of social order and more vividly responsive to the ideas of nature and freedom in the Western forest than they were. His conflict of allegiances was truly ironic, and if he had been able—as he was not—to explore to the end the contradictions in his ideas and emotions, the Leatherstocking series might have become a major work of art. Despite Cooper's failures, the character of Leatherstocking is by far the most important symbol of the national experience of adventure across the continent.[9] The similarities that link Leatherstocking to both the actual Boone and the various Boones of popular legend are not merely fortuitous.

The Pioneers illustrates these aspects of Cooper's work with almost naïve directness. After a negligible first novel, *Precaution*, he had turned to the matter of the American Revolution in *The Spy*, which had had a sensational success. The Preface to *The Pioneers*, his next book, has a jaunty air bespeaking the apprentice novelist's growing confidence. Cooper announces that he is now writing to please himself alone.[10] We may well believe him, for the scene is the Cooperstown of his childhood, and the character of Judge Marmaduke Temple, patron of the infant community, landed proprietor, justice of the peace, and virtual lord of the manor, has much in common with that of the novelist's father William Cooper. Not only did both William Cooper and Judge Temple buy land on the New York frontier and oversee the planting of a town on the shores of Lake Otsego; they resemble one another even in the minor detail of springing from Quaker forebears but having given up formal membership in the sect.[11] When an author turns to autobiographical material of this sort and introduces a central character resembling his father, one does not have to be very much of a Freudian to conclude that the imagination is working on a deeper level than usual. This is certainly the case in *The Pioneers*. Still very much an amateur in the externals of his craft, Cooper contrived for his story of Cooperstown a flimsy plot that hinges upon a childish misunderstanding about Judge Temple's administration of the property of his old friend Major Effingham, but the plot is merely a framework to hold together a narrative focussed about an entirely different problem. The emotional and literary center of the story is a conflict between Judge Temple and the old hunter Leatherstocking which symbolizes the issues raised by the advance of agricultural settlement into the wilderness. In the management of this theme Cooper is at his best. From the opening scene, when Judge Temple claims as his own a deer that Leatherstocking's young companion has shot, until the moment when the Judge sentences the old hunter to a fine and imprisonment because of his resistance to the new game laws, the narrative turns constantly about the central issue of the old forest freedom versus the new needs of a community which must establish the sovereignty of law over the individual.[12] One aspect of the conflict is of course the question of a primitive free access to the bounty of nature—whether in the form of game or of land—versus individual appropriation and the whole notion of inviolable property rights. Not far in the background are the further issues of the rough equality of all men in a state of nature as against social stratification based on unequal distribution of property; and of formal institutional religion versus the natural, intuitive theology of Leatherstocking, who has little regard for theological niceties or the minutiæ of ritual.

The profundity of the symbol of Leatherstocking springs from the fact that Cooper displays a genuine ambivalence toward all these issues, although in every case his strongest commitment is to the forces of order. The social compact, with all its consequences, is vividly and freshly realized, as it had to be realized with every new community planted in the wilderness. And all the aspects of authority—institutional stability, organized religion, class stratification, property—are exhibited as radiating from the symbol of the father. But if the father rules, and rules justly, it is still true that in this remembered world of his childhood Cooper figures as the son. Thus he is able to impart real energy to the statement of the case for defiance and revolt.

But we are not concerned with Cooper's personal relation to his materials so much as with his treatment of the themes arising from the advance of the agricultural frontier. The broader setting for the story is indicated in an exclamation of Elizabeth Temple: "The enterprise of Judge Temple is taming the very forests! How rapidly is civilization treading on the footsteps of nature!"[13] When Elizabeth, with a burst of womanly sympathy for the imprisoned Leatherstocking, declares he must be innocent because of his inherent good ness, her father makes a crucial distinction: "Thou hast reason Bess, and much of it too, but thy heart lies too near thy head." The Judge himself means to pay Leatherstocking's fine, but he cannot brush aside the sentence of imprisonment which he imposed as the spokesman of necessary justice. He sends Elizabeth with a purse to visit the hunter and comfort him: ". . . say what thou wilt to the poor old man; give scope to the feelings of thy warm heart; but try to remember, Elizabeth, that the laws alone remove us from the condition of the savages; that he has been criminal, and that his judge was thy father."[14]

Another interesting scene occurs when the sonless Judge Temple invites Oliver Effingham to enter his household as a secretary. Oliver hesitates. Richard, the Judge's pompous factotum, says in an aside to Elizabeth, "This, you see, cousin Bess, is the natural reluctance of a half-breed to leave the savage state. Their attachment to a wandering life is, I verily believe, unconquerable." The Judge remarks that the unsettled life of a hunter "is of vast disadvantage for temporal purposes, and it totally removes one from within the influences of more sacred things." But this rouses Leatherstocking, who bursts out:

> No, no, Judge . . . take him into your shanty in welcome but tell him the real thing. I have lived in the woods for forty long years, and have spent five years at a time without seeing the light of a clearing, bigger than a wind-row in the trees, and I should like

to know where you'll find a man, in his sixty-eighth year, who can get an easier living, for all your betterments, and your deer-laws: and, as for honesty, or doing what's right between man and man, I'll not turn my back to the longest winded deacon on your patent.

This states the issue as succinctly as possible. Cooper is unable to solve it, and resorts to a compromise statement that represents exactly his unwillingness or inability to accept the full implications of the conflict he has stated. The Judge answers, "nodding good-naturedly at the hunter": "Thou art an exception, Leatherstocking; for thou hast a temperance unusual in thy class, and a hardihood exceeding thy years. But this youth is made of materials too precious to be wasted in the forest."[15]

The Judge's reply expresses the unfailing regard for status which qualified Cooper's attitude toward the idea of nature as a norm. Leatherstocking, noble child of the forest, is nevertheless of inferior social status; whereas even in disguise, Oliver's gentle birth is palpable to the Judge's Falstaffian instinct. Leatherstocking began life as a servant of Major Effingham, and he is wholly illiterate. The fact that he speaks in dialect is a constant reminder of his lowly origin. It is true that the social status of the old hunter was not to prove significant during the long passages of adventure in *The Last of the Mohicans* and *The Prairie*, which deal with Indian warfare and the rescue of Cooper's distressed heroines from their captors. Here Leatherstocking's prowess with the rifle, his talents as a strategist, and his skill in following trails could be exploited with little regard for gradations in rank. But the problem of the hunter's status could not be permanently ignored. The response of readers to this symbol of forest freedom and virtue created a predicament for the novelist by revealing to him that his most vital character occupied a technically inferior position both in the social system and in the form of the sentimental novel as he was using it. The store of emotion associated with the vast wilderness in the minds of both Cooper and his audience was strikingly inharmonious with the literary framework he had adopted.

A more self-conscious or experimentally inclined writer might have found in this situation a challenge to devise a new

form proceeding functionally from the materials. But Cooper
was not the man to undertake a revolution, either in life or in
literature. He chose a different course of action; he set about
modifying the traditional form of the novel as far as he could
without actually shattering it, and at the same time altering
his materials as much as possible to make them fit.

Cooper's efforts to solve his problem can be traced in
the last two novels of the Leatherstocking series, *The Pathfinder* and *The Deerslayer*, which appeared in 1840 and 1841.
In *The Prairie*, published thirteen years before, he had described the death of Leatherstocking, and had at that time
meant to abandon the character forever. This decision seems
to have been due in part to the technical difficulty mentioned
above, for in later years Cooper told his daughter he wished
he had left out of *The Prairie* the genteel hero and heroine,
Inez de Certavallos and Captain Middleton, retaining only
those characters who properly belonged to the locale.[16] But
if the upper-class hero and heroine were to be omitted, and
Leatherstocking was to be promoted to the post of official hero,
how was the plot to be managed? It is at this point that
Cooper's reluctance to break with the conventions of the
sentimental novel becomes most glaringly apparent. A novel,
according to canons which he considered binding, was a
love story. The hero of the novel was the man who played the
male lead in the courtship. If Leatherstocking was to be
promoted to this rank, he must be made to fall in love with a
heroine. In *The Pathfinder*, Cooper accordingly sets to work
with great good will to exhibit Leatherstocking in love. The
problem was to construct a female character, sufficiently refined and genteel to pass muster as a heroine, but sufficiently low
in social status to receive the addresses of the hunter and scout
without a shocking and indecent violation of the proprieties.

The object of Leatherstocking's affection, Mabel
Dunham, is the daughter of a sergeant—not an officer—in the
British army. When she is first introduced in the company of
Cap, her seafaring uncle, who occupies "a station little, if
any, above that of a common mariner," Cooper is careful to
point out that Mabel is "a maiden of a class in no great degree
superior to his own."[17] She is, therefore, technically acces-

sible to the lower-class Leatherstocking. But before she can qualify as a heroine Mabel has to be given some of the attributes of gentility. Cooper explains elaborately that upon the death of her mother Mabel had been taken in charge by the widow of a field-officer of her father's regiment. Under the care of this lady Mabel had acquired "some tastes, and many ideas, which otherwise might always have remained strangers to her." The results of this association

were quite apparent in her attire, her language, her sentiments, and even in her feelings, though neither, perhaps, rose to the level of those which would properly characterize a lady. She had lost the coarser and less refined habits and manners of one in her original position, without having quite reached a point that disqualified her for the situation in life that the accidents of birth and fortune would probably compel her to fill.[18]

In particular, Mabel had acquired a degree of sensibility that caused her to respond in approved fashion to the beauty of landscape—an index in Cooper almost as infallible as that of language for distinguishing the upper classes from the lower.

Ironically enough, the novelist's care in refining Mabel creates a fresh problem for him. The modifications of her character that qualify her for the role of heroine raise her somewhat above the actual range of Leatherstocking's manners and tastes. When Mabel's father proposes the marriage Leatherstocking is timid about it. He fears that a "poor ignorant woodsman" cannot hope to win the girl's affection. The sergeant compels the scout to admit that he is a man of experience in the wilderness, well able to provide for a wife; a veteran of proved courage in the wars; a loyal subject of the King. But Leatherstocking still demurs: "I'm afeard I'm too rude, and too old, and too wild like, to suit the fancy of such a young and delicate girl, as Mabel, who has been unused to our wilderness ways, and may think the settlements better suited to her gifts and inclinations." Pressed still further, Leatherstocking makes an avowal that throws a flood of light on Cooper's conception of the social relationships prevailing within his standard tableau of a captured heroine in the process of being rescued by Leatherstocking and a genteel hero:

I have travelled with some as fair, and have guided them through
the forest, and seen them in their perils and in their gladness; but
they were always too much above me, to make me think of them as
more than so many feeble ones I was bound to protect and defend.
The case is now different. Mabel and I are so nearly alike, that I
feel weighed down with a load that is hard to bear, at finding us so
unlike. I do wish, serjeant, that I was ten years younger [the scout
was then presumably in his early thirties], more comely to look at,
and better suited to please a handsome young woman's fancy!

In short, "I am but a poor hunter, and Mabel, I see, is fit to be
an officer's lady."[19] She is indeed, as appears in the course of
the story when the regimental quartermaster wants to marry
her: or is she? Cooper subsequently causes this officer to
prove a traitor, perhaps because of an unconscious impulse to
punish him for his subversive disregard of class lines. In any
event, when the actual moment of Leatherstocking's proposal arrives, Mabel's superior refinement is so unmistakable
that it decides the issue. One of Cooper's very few valid comic
inventions causes her, in her confusion, to use a more and
more involved rhetoric that Leatherstocking cannot follow
at all. He has to resort to his characteristic query, "Anan?"[20]
The match is quite unsuitable and in the end Leatherstocking
has the exquisite masochistic pleasure of giving his blessing
to her union with Jasper Western, the young, handsome, and
worthy Great Lakes sailor.[21]

   If Leatherstocking could hardly be imagined as married,
however, a feeling for symmetry would suggest that he at
least might be shown as himself hopelessly beloved. This is the
formula of the last novel of the series, *The Deerslayer*, which
removes the obstacle of the hero's age by going back to the
period of his early youth and thus represents the utmost
possible development of Leatherstocking into a hero of
romance. In this story he is loved by Judith Hutter, beautiful
daughter of a somewhat coarse backwoodsman. But Judith's
reputation is stained by past coquetries: She is obviously not
an appropriate mate for the chaste Leatherstocking, and
eventually is consigned to an offstage marriage with a British
officer.

   Despite these late experiments in depicting Leatherstocking in his youth, the persistent image of the hunter was that of his first appearance, as a man of venerable age. This trait of Leatherstocking was strengthened by whatever parallels were felt to exist between him and Daniel Boone. When John Filson's biography of Boone appeared in 1784, the Kentuckian, at fifty, already seemed a patriarchal figure, his active days of fighting in the past. The folk cult of Boone that developed after 1815 emphasized the picturesque conception of an octogenarian huntsman. Cooper himself gives testimony to the popular tendency to exaggerate Boone's age when he remarks in a note to the revised edition of *The Prairie* that the famous hunter emigrated to Missouri "in his ninety-second year."[22] Boone was actually sixty-five when that event occurred. The many Western hunters created in the image of Leatherstocking who people Western fiction through most of the nineteenth century are characteristically of advanced age.

If Leatherstocking was, so to speak, intrinsically aged, this fact hindered his transformation into a hero of romance as seriously as did his low social status. Cooper was thus led to experiment with younger heroes who had Leatherstocking's vital relation to the forest, but were more easily converted into lovers. The character of Oliver Effingham in *The Pioneers* had early suggested the idea of a younger hunter, wearing the garb and following the vocation of Leatherstocking. In *The Prairie* the impulse to double the role of the hunter in this fashion yields the character of Paul Hover, who, like Oliver, appears as an associate of Leatherstocking but is a real instead of merely a pretended child of the backwoods. Paul is a native of Kentucky and has a dialect that is the unmistakable badge of lowly status. It is true that he is merely a bee hunter rather than a hunter of deer and bear, but his sentiments concerning the rifle and his skill at marksmanship arouse Leatherstocking's enthusiastic approval. The most interesting thing about Paul is that, despite the presence in this novel of the official genteel hero and heroine, he is treated as an embryonic hero himself. He is young and handsome and virtuous, and in the end is allowed to marry Ellen Wade, who has carefully been given appearance, manners, speech, and sensibility superior to those of her crude companions—a distinct foreshadowing of Mabel Dunham's status and character in *The Pathfinder*. The Paul–Ellen love affair in *The Prairie*, in fact, seems to have furnished Cooper with the germ of his experiments in the two later novels.

Near the end of his life the novelist made a final effort to construct a story with a Western hero in *The Oak Openings* (1848). Like Paul Hover twenty years earlier, Ben Boden is a bee hunter of admirable character. In the absence of a genteel hero, however, he has to be refined somewhat beyond Paul Hover's level. This process is indicated in terms of the significant criterion of language. We are told twice in the first chapter that he used surprisingly pure English for one in his social class, and he has the further genteel trait of highly moral views concerning whiskey.[23] Margaret Waring, the heroine, like Ellen Wade, is related to a coarse frontiersman, but is made as refined as possible within the iron limits of her status. Although *The Oak Openings* is one of Cooper's weakest novels, the fault lies in his uncontrollable tendency to preach on any current topic that happens to come into his mind. The basic conception is very promising.

The novel begins as if Cooper were determined to see what might have been made of *The Prairie* if he had carried out his project of omitting the genteel hero and heroine. If this conjecture is valid, then Ben Boden represents Cooper's ultimate achievement in trying to use a man of the wilderness as a technical hero. After the dangers of Indian warfare in early Michigan have been endured by the young lovers, the novelist feels compelled to add an epilogue that exhibits Ben Boden in his old age as a substantial farmer, a man of influence in the community, and a state senator. This career "shows the power of man when left free to make his own exertions."[24] But if Boden's Jacksonian rise in the world gives retroactive sanction to Cooper's choice of him as a hero, it dissolves whatever imaginative connection he may have had with the mysterious and brooding wilderness.

Cooper's twenty-five years' struggle to devise a Wild Western hero capable of taking the leading role in a novel yielded the following results: (1) Since the basic image of Leatherstocking was too old for the purposes of romance, the novelist doubled the character to produce a young hunter sharing the old man's habits, tastes, skills, and, to some extent, his virtues. (2) The earliest of the young hunter companions of Leatherstocking, Oliver Effingham, could be a hero because he was revealed as a gentleman temporarily disguised as a hunter. That is, the hero retained all his genteel prerogatives by hereditary right, and at the same time claimed the imaginative values clustering about Leatherstocking by wearing a mask, a *persona* fashioned in the image of the old hunter. But this was so flagrant a begging of the question that Cooper could not be satisfied with it. He therefore undertook further development of the young hunter produced by doubling the character of Leatherstocking, and this process yielded (3) the Paul Hover–Ben Boden type of hero, a young and handsome denizen of the wilderness, following the gentler calling of a bee hunter and thus free from even the justifiable taint of bloodshed involved in Leatherstocking's vocation. This young Western hero is given a dialect less pronounced than that of Leatherstocking except in Leatherstocking's most exalted moments. His actual origin is left vague. He is not a member of the upper class, but he is nowhere specifically described as having once been a servant. Finally, the young hero has none of the theoretical hostility to civilization that is so conspicuous in Leatherstocking. These changes make it technically possible for a Wild Westerner to be a hero of romance, but they destroy the subversive overtones that had given Leatherstocking so much of his emotional depth.

Notes

1   Bakeless, *Daniel Boone*, p. 139. The reviewer of *The Pioneers* in the *Port Folio* (Fourth [Fifth] Series, XV, 232, March, 1823) remarked that Leatherstocking had been "modelled from the effigies of old Daniel Boone."
2   *The Last of the Mohicans: A Narrative of 1757*, 2 vols. (Philadelphia, 1826), I, p. 146.
3   Bakeless, *Daniel Boone*, pp. 133–139; *Mohicans*, I, pp. 166–174.
4   *The Prairie: A Tale*, 2 vols. (Philadelphia, 1827), I, pp. 14–15.
5   *The Prairie*, Red Rover ed. (New York, n. d.), p. 3n. Cooper has adopted Jefferson's estimate of the point at which density of population makes Americans "uneasy."

6   *The Prairie*, I, x.

7   *Niles' Register*, XXIX, p. 217 (December 3, 1825). The roving propensities of Leatherstocking had impressed an anonymous writer for *Niles' Register* within a few months after the publication of *The Pioneers*: "A settlement at the mouth of the *Columbia* has been seriously advocated in Congress, and will soon be made under the sanction of government; and, in a few years, we may expect that some persons *there*, feeling themselves too much crowded, like 'Leather Stocking' in the 'Pioneers,' will seek a country more *west*—Japan, perhaps, if good hunting could be expected therein!" (XXIV, p. 71, April 5, 1823).

8   *Prose Sketches and Poems, Written in the Western Country* (Boston, 1834), p. 60. Bushfield was a Kentucky hunter in James K. Paulding's novel *Westward Ho!* (1832).

9   Although critics often objected to the Indians of the Leatherstocking tales, they were enthusiastic about the old hunter from his first appearance. A reviewer in the generally unsympathetic *North American Review* called Leatherstocking "a bold and original conception . . . upon the whole, the best piece of invention our author has ever produced; one, we may say, which deserves to be ranked in the first class of the creations of genius" (XXIII, p. 172, July, 1826). A later reviewer in this periodical, on the other hand, was cool toward the character (XXXII, p. 517, April, 1831). The *United States Review and Literary Gazette* said in 1827 that Cooper must mainly depend on Leatherstocking for his future fame (II, p. 307, July). Four years after Cooper had described the death of the hunter in *The Prairie*, the *American Monthly Magazine* of Boston declared, "in the whole range of fictitious writing, you will not find anything finer than Long Tom and Natty Bumpo [*sic*]" (II, p. 696, January, 1831).—The suggestion that the Leatherstocking series should be read in terms of "a tension between civilization and noncivilization" is interestingly set forth in Roy Harvey Pearce's article, "The Leatherstocking Tales Re-examined" (*South Atlantic Quarterly*, XLVI, pp. 524–536, October, 1947). I have profited greatly in my discussion of Cooper from Mr. Pearce's observations.

10   *The Pioneers, or The Sources of the Susquehanna; A Descriptive Tale*, 2 vols. (New York, 1823), I, viii.

11   *Ibid.*, I, pp. 21, 27.

12   *Ibid.*, I, pp. 8–20; II, 206–215.

13   *Ibid.*, I, p. 269.

14   *Ibid.*, II, p. 228.

15   *Ibid.*, I, pp. 254–255.

16   Susan Fenimore Cooper, *Pages and Pictures, from the Writings of James Fenimore Cooper, with Notes* (New York, 1861), p. 157.

17   *The Pathfinder; or, The Inland Sea*, 2 vols. (Philadelphia, 1840), I, p. 14.

18   *Ibid.*, I, p. 114.

19   *Ibid.*, I, pp. 135–136.

20   *Ibid.*, II, pp. 34–40.

21   *Ibid.*, II, pp. 214–225.

22   *The Prairie*, Red Rover ed., p. 3n.

23   *The Oak Openings; or, The Bee-Hunter*, 2 vols. (New York, 1848), I, pp. 14, 18, 30–31.

24   *Ibid.*, II, p. 227.

David W. Noble

"Cooper, Leatherstocking, and the Death of the American Adam"□

Since the publication of *Virgin Land* in 1950, all students of American culture have been forced to begin their consideration of nineteenth-century America by taking into account the myth of the West. Henry Nash Smith has conclusively demonstrated that the imagination of Americans after 1800 was dominated by the belief that the American West represented a redemptive nature which would provide spiritual salvation for the men who settled upon it. European man, corrupted by civilization, was reborn, made innocent, when he abandoned old world history for new world nature; he was then that new man, the American.

In 1955, R. W. B. Lewis published his book, *The American Adam*, which brought the perspective of the American belief in a rebirth of innocence through the redemptive influence of physical nature to an analysis of nineteenth-century American literature. Professor Lewis found that the uniqueness of the American novel was based squarely on its acceptance of the myth of the West. European novelists placed their heroes within the confines of historical culture, within time. But the American novelist, beginning with

□ *American Quarterly*, Vol. XVI, no. 3, pp. 419–431, (Fall 1964). Copyright, 1964, Trustees of the University of Pennsylvania. Reprinted by permission of the publisher and the author.

James Fenimore Cooper, evoked heroes who had escaped from traditional society, from history, and lived freely in harmony with nature:

"If there was a fictional Adamic hero unambiguously treated—celebrated in his very Adamism—it was the hero of Cooper's *The Deerslayer*: a self-reliant young man who does seem to have sprung from nowhere and whose characteristic pose . . . was the solitary stance in the presence of nature and God. . . . The evolution of the hero as Adam in the fiction of the New World . . . begins rightly with Natty Bumppo. I call such a figure the hero in space, in two senses of the word. First, the hero seems to take his start outside time . . . and, second, his initial habitat is space as spaciousness, as the unbounded, the area of total possibility. . . . I agree with Lawrence in seeing the novel as the culmination of a process which exemplifies the American myth. Lawrence's words seem to me at once exact, poetic, and inimitable: 'The Leather-stocking novels . . . go backwards from old age to golden youth. That is the true myth of America. She starts old, old, wrinkled and writhing in an old skin. And there is a gradual sloughing off of the old skin, towards a new youth. It is the myth of America.' "

I would like to suggest, however, another way of reading the Leatherstocking series that leads to an absolute contradiction of Professor Lewis' position. I believe that if one reads the series beginning with *Deerslayer* and follows the aging Leatherstocking through his life cycle in *The Last of the Mohicans*, *The Pathfinder*, *The Pioneers* and *The Prairie*, one becomes aware that Cooper is indeed writing about the American myth but with the purpose of destroying rather than celebrating the American Adam.[1]

Let me begin my analysis by recalling that, according to the myth of the American West, the American Adam was to be the archetype of a new society; the myth was to become reality. The European, becoming American, was to live freely in space and in harmony with nature. The ultimate success of the myth depended upon its earthly fulfillment. Now, as Professor Lewis has declared, the figure of Deer-slayer is presented at the beginning of the novel as such an earthly fulfillment of the myth. He is the American Adam. He exists freely in space and in harmony with nature. He is outside of time and society. But *The Deerslayer* is a novel that is filled with drama. And we can ask how drama can enter the life of the new Adam in the new Eden for drama depends on disharmony. How, then, does Cooper introduce disharmony into Eden?

If Deerslayer represents the perfect expression of the Adamic myth, Cooper immediately calls our attention to the fact that the human Adam and Eve, dwelling within the supposedly redemptive bosom of nature, are not innocents. Hurry Harry and Judith are magnificent human specimens but their hearts are full of disharmony. And surely Cooper tells us that no amount of living with nature will abolish that disharmony. Cooper then reveals that the only one of these first settlers on the frontier who shares Deerslayer's innocence is Judith's sister, Hetty, a girl who transcends humanity because her mind has never reached maturity. I believe, therefore, that Cooper has asked the reader to distinguish between the myth of the West, Deerslayer, and the reality of the West, the Hutter family and Hurry Harry. And I believe that Cooper deliberately goes on to take Deerslayer out of those very qualities of timelessness and unbounded spaciousness which Professor Lewis sees as the necessary qualities of the American Adam.

Deerslayer is a white man living outside of society in harmony with nature. Chingachgook is an Indian living outside of society in harmony with nature. Deerslayer and Chingachgook are brothers. In a mythical West that has sprung from the imagination of Europeans, the American as natural man can live in harmony with his brother, the Indian, as natural man. But what happens when the Europeans, as men of history, come to take the West away from Indians who are also men of history? Then there will be wars, the inevitable clash between two historical cultures. And Deerslayer and Chingachgook must lose their freedom and innocence in these wars. Cooper, it would appear, is aware that the myth is of European origin and he is aware that the myth must change in response to historical events. The myth is a prisoner of time; it is a prisoner of the historical culture which gave it birth.

The action of the novel takes place at the beginning of

the great struggle between England and France for the control of the West. English pioneers are wresting the frontier from the French and the Indian. Since the myth is a product of English culture, it will be used by Englishmen in their war of conquest. Deerslayer is caught in time; he does not dwell in the free space of total possibility. He has no choice but to fight for Anglo-Americans against the French and Indians. The dramatic turning point in the novel is reached, therefore, when Deerslayer loses his innocence by killing a man—an Indian—for the first time, in defense of the Hutter family. Vainly he tries to avoid conflict but he has to keep the canoe, which is the key to the safety of the family on the lake, out of the hands of the attacking Indians. Finally, the fulfillment of this act of social commitment forces him to kill the Indian who threatens to capture the canoe. It is the dying Indian who informs Deerslayer that he has lost his innocence. Deerslayer, he says, "That good name for boy—poor name for warrior . . . eye sartain—finger lightning—aim, death—great warrior soon. No Deerslayer—Hawkeye—Hawkeye—Hawkeye." Here the man and the myth have lost their innocence. The myth must abandon nature and become a man as Hawkeye fights for English culture against the Indian.

We meet Leatherstocking next in *The Last of the Mohicans.* He is a soldier of the king. He is without innocence. The Deerslayer who could bring himself to kill a man only with the greatest reluctance is now Hawkeye, efficient, methodical, terrible killer of Indians. At the opening of the novel when Major Heyward brings an Indian scout into camp who is a Huron in background, Hawkeye warns against the Indian.

" 'Think you so?' said Heyward, 'I confess I have not been without my own suspicions.'

" 'I knew he was one of the cheats as soon as I laid eyes on him!' returned the scout, 'This thief is leaning against the foot of the sugar sapling that you can see over them bushes; his right leg is in line with the bark of the tree, and . . . I can take him from where I stand between the ankle and the knee.'

" 'It will not do.' [said Heyward] 'He may be innocent, and I dislike the act.' "

Hawkeye is the coldblooded frontier fighter who will shoot first and ask questions later. The English professional soldier supplies the restraint and innocence in the scene.

The purpose of this novel, as the sequel of the first, is to demonstrate the continued destruction of the myth by the demands of history. The first novel dramatized Deerslayer's loss of innocence. *The Last of the Mohicans* dramatized the death of the myth as it found symbolic expression in the noble savage. Chingachgook, the Indian as myth, like Deerslayer, has been forced to fight for the English culture which has created him. His son, Uncas, now carries the mythical mantle of innocence which his father has surrendered in joining Hawkeye as a hardened soldier. Uncas and the white girl, Cora, fall in love. If the myth of the American Adam, stripped of the burden of history and standing in that unbounded space which offers boundless possibilities, obtained as reality, then there should be no barrier to the marriage of these two children of nature. But Cooper does present a barrier, that of history.

Englishmen are not the children of nature; they are conquerors who will impose their culture on the continent. And the Indians are not the children of nature; they are the defenders of their own culture, of their own way of life. When the English will have defeated the French, then the only barrier between them and the West will be the Indian. When the Indian is seen as the last barrier to the conquest and exploitation of the frontier, white men will no longer be able to believe in the myth of the noble savage. It is only right, therefore, that Uncas, the last of the Mohicans, the last of the noble savages, shall die with the defeat of the French. And it is only right that he should be killed by Magua. Magua is an Indian of history; he hates the white men for destroying the Indian culture. When he desires Cora, he does so like an Indian; he wants her as an Indian squaw, as the subservient, obedient female of the Indian way of life. Dramatically, Cooper reveals the way in which Anglo-American culture will define the Indian after the French and Indian War. The Indian will be Magua, the eternally defiant Magua, who will fling his curses and his tomahawk at the white man who crosses the mountains into the Garden of the World. After 1760, the Indian can only be defined as the barbaric opponent of the spread of Anglo-American civilization westward. The defeat of France has opened the Ohio and Mississippi valleys to Anglo-American culture. Continuing to place the Adamic myth within the development of history, Cooper now presents Leatherstocking as the Pathfinder who will lead the Europeans into the Garden of the World. According to the Americans of 1830, this area of the Midwest presented a different kind of nature than that of the east coast. For Cooper's contemporaries, European culture had been able to make a beachhead along the Atlantic. The virgin land of the coastal colonies had not been able to redeem Europeans and to make them into that new man, the innocent American. But for the Jacksonians, when settlers went across the Appalachian Mountains, geography mastered and destroyed their heritage of European civilization and left them free from history to live in harmony with nature.

And as Cooper presents Leatherstocking in *The Pathfinder*, the man as myth makes his great effort to escape from the Anglo-American culture which has robbed him of his freedom. Pathfinder dreams of giving up his life as a soldier to return to innocence. But the myth is still being defined by history. It is here in the Mississippi Valley that people are to live in harmony in a new kind of society, a society without the complexities and weaknesses of civilization, a natural society. Such a society demanded the union of Adam with an Eve in domesticity surrounded by descendants.

Pathfinder, who is now specifically identified as Adam by Cooper, is willing to accept this responsibility to marry and become the archetypical father for a uniquely natural community. Cooper demonstrates, however, that Pathfinder has led human beings committed to historical society into the new West. There is no mythical Eve to complement the willing Adam. Pathfinder falls in love with Mabel but Mabel will not, indeed, she cannot give up civilization to marry the frontiersman. It is Pathfinder himself who tells the reader that the match should not take place because he recognizes that he

is not like other human beings, that he is a species apart.
When Mabel finally says, "Pathfinder—dear Pathfinder,
understand me . . . a match like that would be unwise—
unnatural, perhaps," Leatherstocking immediately agrees,
"Yes, unnat'ral—agin natur."

And Cooper obviously hopes that he is driving home a
moral to the American people. He has Pathfinder cry out,
"What a creature is a mortal man! Never satisfied with his
own gifts, but forever craving that which Providence denies!"
The American people long to escape history and live with
nature like the Pathfinder. But Cooper presents the Leatherstocking as an incomplete being; nature is no substitute for
what God has given man: the possibility of love and families
and civilization. The utter loneliness of Pathfinder, his longing for the society in which he can never dwell, is given beautiful expression by Cooper in Pathfinder's dream where he tries
to exchange physical nature for human companionship: "I
imagined I had a cabin in a grove of sugar maples, and at the
root of every tree was a Mabel Dunham, while the birds sang
ballads, instead of the notes that natur' gave."

Clearly the moral of this novel is that Americans need
humility, that they need to accept their humanity and frailty.
Cooper wanted to teach them that they could never escape
from history.

The next novel in the life cycle of Leatherstocking,
The Pioneers, is an extended elaboration of this point that
Americans can never escape from history. With the establishment of an independent nation, free from political connection
with the British Empire, it was possible for the people of the
United States to assert that they had cut their cultural ties
with the parent nation. It was possible for Americans to
claim that, while England was connected to history, America
was built on nature. It was possible to believe that a new kind
of civilization, one without historical roots, had been established in the new world.

Deerslayer was the mythical embodiment of this philosophy which described Europe in terms of historical time and
America in terms of physical space. But, Cooper was to argue,
how can Americans justify their cultural independence from

England on the strength of a myth that is English in origin?
The dramatic role of Leatherstocking in *The Pioneers*,
therefore, is to unite American and English culture and
Cooper reminds his readers that Leatherstocking, the man as
myth, is loyal to the historical culture which gave him his
identity.

Approaching Cooper from the traditional viewpoint
that he is celebrating, not criticizing, the myth of virgin
land, Henry Nash Smith has noted an element of ambiguity in
The Pioneers. Cooper, he declares, is presenting a case in
favor of civilization when he has Judge Temple speak philosophically to his daughter who has come to the defense of
Leatherstocking, guilty of hunting out of season, "Thou
hast reason, Bess, and much of it, too, but thy heart lies too
near thy head. . . . Say what thou wilt to the poor old man;
give scope to the feelings of thy warm heart; but try to remember, Elizabeth, that the laws alone remove us from the condition of the savage; that he has been criminal, and that his
judge was thy father."

Professor Smith has interpreted the drama of the novel
then as the ambiguity between Cooper's commitment to the
values of nature symbolized by Leatherstocking and the
values of civilization symbolized by Judge Temple. But the
drama of the novel revolves around the reconciliation of the
American, Judge Temple, and the Englishman, Major Effingham, a reconciliation which reaches fulfillment in the marriage of Oliver Effingham and Elizabeth Temple. There seems
little doubt in Cooper's mind that the values of Judge Temple
are superior to those of Leatherstocking. Indeed, the old man
is presented as a decrepit myth which survives only through
the indulgence of the Judge.

If Leatherstocking as Pathfinder has failed to become
the archetype of the pioneers, Judge Temple is so represented
here in *The Pioneers.* Leatherstocking was the myth which
promised that the American pioneers would be Adams and
Eves who might step out of time to live in nature's unbounded
spaciousness. But in place of the Utopian settlement which
Pathfinder could not establish is that which Judge Temple has

built. And Judge Temple is a man of civilization who is bringing complex culture, an historical heritage to the frontier. He is the man of law because the men and women who came west to live in his community are frail and imperfect human beings who need the law to control their evil and their selfishness. Nature cannot redeem them; indeed, these people would quickly destroy nature if the law did not restrain them and in turn give protection to nature.

Judge Temple and Leatherstocking debate this issue. Natty Bumppo, still the embodiment of the myth, argues that man can live in harmony with nature only if he can approach it in a completely free and spontaneous way without the interference of law. Judge Temple makes the counter-argument that given a human nature which is always self-seeking and avaricious, men will quickly ravage physical nature if it is not protected by law. For Cooper, society on the frontier is like all societies, self-destructive unless restrained and governed by enlightened and disinterested men who uphold the law.

Understanding that Leatherstocking represents an ideal of nature which, although it is erroneous, has dignity, Judge Temple tolerates and even protects the aging myth. It is not the Judge's upholding of the law which ultimately drives Natty Bumppo out of the community, rather it is the lawless mob which has no respect for Leatherstocking's need for privacy and isolation. It is as if the people must mock and harry the fading myth which has failed to redeem them. Indeed, the lingering presence of Leatherstocking with his superior virtue and purity infuriates the people who cannot rise to his level of behavior.

But the most important role of Leatherstocking in *The Pioneers* is to facilitate the reconciliation of Judge Temple and Major Effingham, to facilitate the reconciliation of American and English culture, to facilitate the understanding of Americans for their historical traditions.

The novel begins with Leatherstocking living in isolation with Chingachgook and a mysterious young man, Oliver Edwards. Together they carry on still more mysterious activities on a nearby mountain. Finally, we are to learn that

Leatherstocking and Oliver have been caring for an old man who has been dwelling underground in a cave; an old man who is Major Effingham, Natty Bumppo's English commander from the French and Indian wars. Major Effingham, who had purchased extensive lands on the frontier, had remained loyal to the Crown when the Revolution began. He had then put his lands into trust with Judge Temple, an American patriot. At the conclusion of the Revolution, Effingham assumed that with independence Americans had repudiated all ties with those who had remained loyal to England and that the legal right to his lands was in jeopardy. He assumed that Judge Temple would be motivated by lawless self-interest. The Judge, however, as a conservator of civilization had preserved his trust and is searching for Effingham or his heirs.

Out of the purging flames of a fire which sweeps over the mountain, there comes the reconciliation of patriot and loyalist as Oliver Edwards, the Major's grandson, and Elizabeth Temple discover their love and the dying Major and Judge Temple are brought together.

Cooper does not trust, however, to the subtlety of his contemporaries to understand the symbolism of reunion and continuity with the past. He will become even more explicit about the role of Natty Bumppo in bringing together American and English culture. Did the readers understand that Deerslayer had become a soldier of the king? That the myth had been used by Englishmen to steel the nerve and arms of their invading force? Now even as Major Effingham, the last direct symbol of English culture, lies dying in America, so Leatherstocking, who has served the English conquerors so well, has lost his vitality and is withering away. His final constructive achievement is to keep his commander alive until his rightful claim to be a part of the American frontier is recognized. And Cooper will not merely suggest the commander and follower relationship, he will spell it out in literal form, graven in the granite of Major Effingham's tombstone for all future Americans to see as the evidence of the relationship of the myth to the English heritage.

The weeping Leatherstocking is led to the grave where

his finger eagerly traces the letters as Oliver Effingham reads
to the illiterate frontiersman:

" 'Sacred to the memory of Oliver Effingham, Esquire,
formerly a major in his B. Majesty's 60th Foot; a soldier of
tried valor; a subject of chivalrous loyalty; and a man of
honesty. To these virtues he added the graces of a Christian.
The morning of his life was spent in honor, wealth, and power;
but its evening was obscured by poverty, neglect, and disease,
which were alleviated only by the tender care of his old,
faithful, and upright friend and attendant, Nathaniel Bumppo.
His descendants rear this stone to the virtues of the master,
and to the enduring gratitude of the servant.'

"The Leatherstocking stared at the sound of his own
name, and a smile of joy illumined his wrinkled features, as
he said—

" 'And did ye say it, lad? Have you then got the old
man's name cut in the stone, by the side of his master's? God
bless ye, children! 'Twas a kind thought, and kindness goes to
the heart as life shortens.' "

Leatherstocking now leaves at the end of the novel for
the unsettled frontier. On his first trip to the area of virgin
land as the Pathfinder, he had turned back because he could
not serve as the father of settlement. The myth had failed to
fulfill itself; it could not separate itself from the historical
culture which had brought it into existence. And so Leatherstocking returned to the real father of settlement, Judge
Temple. Here he could play the constructive role of illuminating the relationship of American and English society. If the
myth could not separate itself from historical culture, it
could clarify its relationship to that history and demonstrate
that it was a tradition which united America to the past.
Having revealed, however, that America was to be defined in
terms of history and time and not in terms of unbounded space,
what future and function did the myth now have?

When Leatherstocking set out for the unsettled areas
of the West as an old and withered figure in the 1790s, he
could not go hoping for fulfillment. That hope had been
crushed a generation before in *The Pathfinder*. Leatherstocking, alone, might still find harmony with nature but

he could not found a new society. And any harmony which he found with nature must be temporary because Leatherstocking was a prisoner of time. Human settlement constantly overran the virgin land which had given him strength and as the area of unspoiled nature shrank, Leatherstocking, in turn, withered away. But as long as there was an unsettled area, Americans would continue to believe in the myth that they might escape history to live with nature. Leatherstocking could not perish as long as there was a last frontier.

It is with sadness and resignation then that the old man sets out for the West to spend his last few remaining days. He knows that these days are numbered because inevitably settlers will come to the virgin land and when there was no more land without human habitation, there would be no more myth. The stage is carefully set for the final novel of the series, *The Prairie*.

The myth, for Cooper, must end with settlement because the settlers will be human; they will carry disharmony engraved indelibly in their hearts; they will have all the human weakness that the first frontier Adam and Eve, Hurry Harry and Judith, had demonstrated in *Deerslayer*. It is difficult to visualize how Cooper could have provided greater dramatic emphasis to this point than by painting the picture of the Ishmael Bush family which is the first invader of Leatherstocking's last refuge. Here is vulgarity and brutality in its most exaggerated form.

Cooper's literary art reaches its highest level when he brings the Bush family and Leatherstocking to their first confrontation which has the dramatic implication of Leatherstocking's doom and the death of the myth. Bursting with crude vitality, the Bush family is pushing westward toward their evening camp when suddenly out of the setting sun there grew a fantastic apparition: "The sun had fallen below the crest of the nearest wave of the prairie, leaving the usual rich and glowing train on its track. In the center of this flood of fiery light, a human form appeared, drawn against the gilded background as distinctly, and, seemingly as palpable, as though it would come within the grasp of any extended hand.

The figure was colossal; the attitude musing and melancholy, and the situation directly in the route of the travellers. But imbedded, as it was, in its setting of garish light, it was impossible to distinguish its just proportions or true character."

Brilliantly, Cooper has captured the situation of the myth. Only in the setting sun of the western prairie does Leatherstocking promise to be larger than life. And when the family comes to see the reality as the sun sets and shadows creep across the prairie, all they find is a peculiarly withered, almost mummified, old man.

If the myth has come to the final frontier to accept its fate, it is, nevertheless, no longer innocent. It is as if Leatherstocking, through his human suffering in the death of Major Effingham, has achieved a bond of understanding and sympathy with mankind that makes him a spokesman for the superiority of civilization to nature. A myth that embodies nature, he cannot choose to live in civilization. But he can warn those who would attempt to flee from civilization to turn back to accept their human responsibility. He can demonstrate, in the withering of his own body, the fallacy of the American belief in the unrestricted possibilities for men in the unbounded spaciousness of nature. There is no escape from the cycle of life and death, no escape from the ravages of time.

Again Cooper has skillfully used imagery to drive home his point. The action of this final novel takes place during Jefferson's administrations. The President has dispatched Lewis and Clark to explore the vast territories acquired in the Louisiana Purchase. The nation has hopes that this tremendous area will guarantee redemptive contact with nature for generations to come. But Cooper has placed the aging Leatherstocking on this new land, which the author describes as a dry and almost lifeless desert, the perfect physical complement of the desiccated hunter.

And Leatherstocking, who in *The Pioneers* still argued against Judge Temple's advocacy of conservation, of the use of law to preserve nature, now thinks back in agony to the irresponsible rape of the virgin land:

"What the world of America is coming to, and where the

machinations and inventions of its people are to have an end,
the Lord, He only knows. . . . How much has the beauty of
the wilderness been deformed in two short lives. . . . I often
think the Lord has placed this barren belt of prairie behind the
States, to warn men to what their folly may yet bring the
land."

Leatherstocking now realizes that harmony, whatever
harmony exists, comes not spontaneously from nature; it
comes painfully from human effort; it is imposed by human
law. "The law—'tis bad to have it, but, I sometimes think,
it is worse to be entirely without it. . . . yes—yes, the law is
needed."

To dramatize this point, Cooper returns to the first
settlers of this last frontier. The family of Ishmael Bush,
coarse, disharmonious, evil, has come to the West to escape
the law. As with Hurry Harry and Judith, as with all settlers,
they will not be spontaneously redeemed by nature; they will
not have a rebirth; they will not become innocent. But
Ishmael Bush does grow in moral stature. Gradually, he
comes to accept the moral implications of his role as head of
this first family. He is the head of a new society and that
society cannot exist without human justice and human law.
Ishmael Bush begins to be transformed when he accepts the
necessity of punishing the murderer who is part of his family.
Even in the middle of an unsettled desert, man achieves dignity only through the law.

As the last days of Leatherstocking grow near, there
has appeared on the prairie Lt. Duncan Uncas Middleton, a
representative of the eastern aristocracy; he is the last link
between the fading myth and its parent culture; he will make
it possible for Leatherstocking to perish in peace, secure in
the knowledge that his memory will be honored.

It was true, as Leatherstocking remarked: "I am without kith or kin in the wide world . . . when I am gone, there
will be an end of my race."

The myth could not find embodiment in society and now,
with the end of the frontier, it must disappear. But the myth
would find after-life among the eastern aristocracy; tradition

within an historical society does not die. The ancient hunter had been brought to tears of happiness as Lt. Middleton had recounted how his grandfather, Major Middleton of the British Army, had taught his children to revere the memory of the noble savage, as represented by Uncas, and the frontiersman, Hawkeye. Our grandfather, Duncan related, taught us that " 'Unlike most of those who live a border life, he [Leatherstocking] united the better, instead of the worst, qualities. . . . He was a man endowed with the choicest and perhaps rarest gift of nature; that of distinguishing good from evil. His virtues were those of simplicity. . . . In short, he was a noble shoot from the stock of human nature, which never could attain its proper elevation and importance, for no other reason than because it grew in the forest; such, old hunter, were the very words of my grandfather . . . . there are already three among us who have also names derived from that scout.'

" 'A name, did you say?' exclaimed the old man, 'what, the name of the solitary, unl'arned hunter? Do the great, and the rich, and the honored, and, what is better still, the just, do they bear his very, actual name?' "

Assured that his memory will be preserved in living tradition, Leatherstocking can die happily. Here is the final evidence that Cooper did not intend his hero to exist outside of time. Leatherstocking is happy because he will be embedded in time forever, his name will be passed from one generation to another.

As befitting a myth of nature, Leatherstocking does not die as a man. The rituals of Christian civilization have no meaning in his last hours. The spirit of the myth will leave its earthly abode to follow the setting sun westward forever:

"The trapper was placed on a rude seat, which had been made, with studied care, to support his frame in an upright and easy attitude. . . . His body was placed so as to let the light of the setting sun fall full upon the solemn features. . . . The trapper had remained nearly motionless for an hour. His eyes alone had occasionally opened and shut. When opened, his gaze seemed fastened on the clouds which hung around the western horizon. . . . Suddenly . . . Middleton felt the hand which he held grasp his own with incredible

power, and the old man, supported on either side by his friends,
rose upright to his feet. For a moment he looked about him
. . . and then . . . he pronounced the word—'Here!' "

For Cooper it was here on the great plains, during
Jefferson's administrations, that the myth of the frontier
perished because of the penetration of the last unknown
territories by human beings who, by their very presence,
destroyed the mysterious potential of the virgin land. In the
words of Professor Lewis, there no longer existed "space as
spaciousness, as the unbounded, the area of total possibility." And from the first moment when Deerslayer was forced
to participate in the disharmony of history, Cooper had prepared for this moment. The five Leatherstocking novels are a
sustained argument against the autonomous existence of an
American Adam. Inexorably, Cooper has forced the myth to
live within the historical rhythm of the Anglo-American
culture which had created it. Just as this society has a history
from 1740 to 1800, so Leatherstocking has a parallel history.

We must disagree, therefore, with the agreement of
Professor Lewis with D. H. Lawrence. It is true that Cooper
wrote *Deerslayer* after the four other novels of the series. But
surely the theme of these five novels is the absolute opposite
of Lawrence's contention that "The Leatherstocking novels
. . . go backwards from old age to golden youth. That is the
true myth of America. She starts old, old, wrinkled and
writhing in an old skin. And there is a gradual sloughing off
of the old skin, towards a new youth. It is the myth of
America."

It is indeed the myth of America. And we must conclude, therefore, that Cooper intended, deliberately intended, to destroy the myth of America, to take it from the
freshness of youth to its end, old, old and wrinkled on the last
American frontier.

Notes

1   The sequence in which Cooper wrote the Leatherstocking series is *The
Pioneers* (1823), *The Last of the Mohicans* (1826), *The Prairie* (1827), *The*

Pathfinder (1840) and *The Deerslayer* (1841). From this chronology, it is obvious that Cooper did not have a unifying conception for the five novels in mind when he wrote *The Pioneers*. But it is my argument that Cooper was aware of the myth of the West and that he set about self-consciously criticizing it in *The Pioneers*. I would argue that as his criticism of the myth continued, he pursued it back to its origins in the first half of the eighteenth century and thus concluded the series with *The Deerslayer*.

IV

The Scarlet Letter (1850) by Nathaniel Hawthorne

Richard Harter Fogle

from "*The Scarlet Letter*"□

nterpretations of *The Scarlet Letter* have been almost startlingly various. This is not surprising, for Hawthorne has himself pointed the way to a wide range of speculations. The concluding words of *The Scarlet Letter*, however, summarily dismiss the more cheerful readings, of which there are a number. In describing the heraldic device on the common tombstone of Hester and Dimmesdale, they describe "our now concluded legend; so sombre is it, and relieved only by one ever-glowing point of light gloomier than the shadow:—

'On A Field, Sable, The Letter A, Gules.' "

These words alone, in my opinion, are sufficient evidence for disproving the notion that *The Scarlet Letter* is "about" Hester Prynne the advanced feminist, or that the story can be satisfactorily summarized either by the moral which Hawthorne attaches to Dimmesdale, " 'Show freely to the world, if not your worst, yet some trait whereby the worst may be inferred!' " or by the doctrine of *felix culpa*, "the fortunate fall," that out of sin and evil comes good and that Hester is educated and refined by her wrongdoing. The sentiment is too darkly tragic to be appropriate to any of these conclusions, though Hawthorne at one place and another in *The Scarlet Letter* has suggested the possibility of all of them. The true conclusion of *The Scarlet Letter* is an unresolved contradiction—unresolved not from indecision or lack of thought but from honesty of imagination. Hawthorne gives the only answer that his formulation of the terms permits. If we consider that the problem of *The Scarlet Letter* is primarily the problem of Hester Prynne, the verdict is at best suspension of judgment after full examination of the evidence. And, as we know, Hester emerges from trial in better condition than her co-defendants Dimmesdale and Chillingworth.

This is the contradiction, and a very widely representative contradiction it is: the sin of *The Scarlet Letter* is a symbol of the original sin, by which no man is untouched. All mortals commit the sin in one form or another, which is perhaps the meaning of "your worst" in the exhortation occasioned by the death of Dimmesdale. Hester, having sinned, makes the best possible recovery; and the crime itself is of all crimes the most excusable, coming of passionate love and having "a consecration of its own." Yet the sin remains real and inescapable, and she spends her life in retribution, the death of her lover Dimmesdale having finally taught her that this is the only way. This is the dilemma: human beings by their natures must fall into error—and yet it would be better if they did not.

The letter, an "ever-glowing point of light," is gloomier than the shadow of its background. The shadow, the "Field, Sable," is roughly the atmosphere of Puritanism, the "Letter A, Gules" the atmosphere of the sin. These are at odds, and no absolute superiority is granted to either. The Puritan doctors are no fit judges of a woman's heart; nor, on the other hand, is Hester to be absolved. The letter is glowing, positive, vital, the product of genuine passion, while the sable may certainly be taken as the negation of everything alive. Yet the letter is gloomier.

These shades are both of hell, and there is no hue of heaven in *The Scarlet Letter* which really offsets them. Sunlight is the nearest approach to it, and its sway is too fleeting to have any great effect. In the forest scene of chapters XVI–XIX sunshine, "as with a sudden smile of heaven," bursts over Hester and Dimmesdale, but this is merely a momentary relief. The hope which accompanies it is short-lived, delusory, and dangerous. A more steadfast light, "The sun, but little past its meridian," shines down upon Dimmesdale as he stands on the scaffold to confess his guilt. This is triumph, indeed, but little to counterbalance the continual power of the "bale fire" and "lurid gleam" of the letter. Hope and regeneration are sometimes symbolized in Hawthorne by the celestial colors of dawn, transfigured by light: blues, greens, and golds. In "Ethan Brand" the tender hues of the twilight sky are overpowered by night and the red and black of Brand's Unpardonable Sin, but they are revivified by the atmosphere of dawn. So the storm in *The House of the Seven Gables*, which accompanies the crisis and blows itself out with the death of Judge Pyncheon, gives way to a world made new and bathed in morning sunshine. There is no such scene in *The Scarlet Letter*.

The problem of *The Scarlet Letter* can be solved only by introducing the supernatural level of heaven, the sphere of absolute knowledge and justice and—hesitantly—of complete fulfillment. This may seem to be another paradox, and perhaps a disappointing one. Without doubt *The Scarlet Letter* pushes *towards* the limit of moral judgment, suggesting many possible conclusions. It is even relentless in its search in the depths of its characters. There is yet, however, a point beyond which Hawthorne will not go; ultimate solutions are not appropriate in the merely human world. His sympathy with Hester and Dimmesdale is clear enough, but he allows them only to escape the irrevocable spiritual ruin which befalls Chillingworth. Figuratively his good wishes pursue them beyond life, but he does not presume himself to absolve them. Even in the carefully staged scene of Dimmesdale's death, where every impulse of both author and reader demands complete forgiveness, Hawthorne refuses to grant it. With his "bright dying eyes" Dimmesdale looks into eternity, but nothing he sees there permits him to comfort Hester. To her questions, " 'Shall we not meet again? . . . Shall we not spend our immortal life together?' " he can answer only, " 'The law we broke! —the sin here so awfully revealed!—let these alone be in thy thoughts! I fear! I fear!' " A grim and unflinching con-

clusion, considering everything. Dimmesdale is not of course
Hawthorne, but the very preservation of dramatic propriety
at this crucial point is significant.

There are four states of being in Hawthorne: one subhuman, two human, and one superhuman. The first is Nature,
which comes to our attention in *The Scarlet Letter* twice. It
appears first in the opening chapter, in the wild rosebush
which stands outside the blackbrowed Puritan jail, and whose
blossoms

might be imagined to offer their fragrance and fragile beauty to the
prisoner as he went in, and to the condemned criminal as he came
forth to his doom, in token that the deep heart of Nature could pity
and be kind to him.

The second entrance of Nature comes in the forest scene,
where it sympathizes with the forlorn lovers and gives them
hope. "Such was the sympathy of Nature—that wild, heathen
Nature of the forest, never subjugated by human law, nor
illumined by higher truth. . . ." The sentence epitomizes both
the virtues of Nature and its inadequacy. In itself good,
Nature is not a sufficient support for human beings.

The human levels are represented by Hawthorne's
distinction between Heart and Head. The heart is closer to
nature, the head to the supernatural. The heart may err by
lapsing into nature, which means, since it has not the innocence of nature, into corruption. The danger of the head lies
in the opposite direction. It aspires to be superhuman, and is
likely to dehumanize itself in the attempt by violating the
human limit. Dimmesdale, despite his considerable intellect,
is predominantly a heart character, and it is through the
heart that sin has assailed him, in a burst of passion which
overpowered both religion and reason. The demoniac Chillingworth is of the head, a cold experimenter and thinker. It is
fully representative of Hawthorne's general emphasis that
Chillingworth's spiritual ruin is complete. Hester Prynne is a
combination of head and heart, with a preponderance of head.
Her original sin is of passion, but its consequences expose her
to the danger of absolute mental isolation. The centrifugal
urge of the intellect is counteracted in her by her duty to her

daughter Pearl, the product of the sin, and by her latent love for Dimmesdale. Pearl herself is a creature of nature, most at home in the wild forest: ". . . the mother-forest, and these wild things which it nourished, all recognized a kindred wildness in the human child." She is made human by Dimmesdale's confession and death: "The great scene of grief, in which the wild infant bore a part, had developed all her sympathies. . . ."

The fourth level, the superhuman or heavenly, will perhaps merely be confused by elaborate definition. It is the sphere of absolute insight, justice, and mercy. Few of Hawthorne's tales and romances can be adequately considered without taking it into account. As Mark Van Doren has recently emphasized, it is well to remember Hawthorne's belief in immortality. It is because of the very presence of the superhuman in Hawthorne's thinking that the destinies of his chief characters are finally veiled in ambiguity. He respects them as he would have respected any real person by refusing to pass the last judgment, by leaving a residue of mysterious individuality untouched. The whole truth is not for a fellow human to declare.

These four states are not mutually exclusive. Without the touch of nature human life would be too bleak. The Puritans of *The Scarlet Letter* are deficient in nature, and they are consequently dour and overrighteous. Something of the part that nature might play in the best human life is suggested in the early chapters of *The Marble Faun*, particularly through the character Donatello. The defects of either Heart or Head in a state of isolation have already been mentioned. And without some infusion of superhuman meaning into the spheres of the human, life would be worse than bestial. Perhaps only one important character in all of Hawthorne's works finds it possible to dispense completely with heaven— Westervelt, of *The Blithedale Romance*—and he is essentially diabolic. In some respects, the highest and the lowest of these levels are most closely akin, as if their relationship were as points of a circle. The innocence of nature is like the innocence of heaven. It is at times, when compared to the human, like the Garden before the serpent, like heaven free of the taint of evil. Like infancy, however, nature is a stage which man must pass through, whereas his destination is heaven. The juxtaposition of highest and lowest nevertheless involves difficulties, when perfect goodness seems equivalent to mere deprivation and virtue seems less a matter of choosing than of being untempted.

The intensity of *The Scarlet Letter*, at which Hawthorne himself was dismayed, comes from concentration, selection, and dramatic irony. The concentration upon the central theme is unremitting. The tension is lessened only once, in the scene in the forest, and then only delusively, since the hope of freedom which brings it about is quickly shown to be false and even sinful. The characters play out their tragic action against a background in itself oppressive—the somber atmosphere of Puritanism. Hawthorne calls the progression of the story "the darkening close of a tale of human frailty and sorrow." Dark to begin with, it grows steadily deeper in gloom. The method is almost unprecedentedly selective. Almost every image has a symbolic function; no scene is superfluous. One would perhaps at times welcome a loosening of the structure, a moment of wandering from the path. The weedy grassplot in front of the prison; the distorting reflection of Hester in a breastplate, where the Scarlet Letter appears gigantic; the tapestry of David and Bathsheba on the wall of the minister's chamber; the little brook in the forest; the slight malformation of Chillingworth's shoulder; the ceremonial procession on election day—in every instance more is meant than meets the eye.

The intensity of *The Scarlet Letter* comes in part from a sustained and rigorous dramatic irony, or irony of situation. This irony arises naturally from the theme of "secret sin," or concealment. "Show freely of your worst," says Hawthorne; the action of *The Scarlet Letter* arises from the failure of Dimmesdale and Chillingworth to do so. The minister hides his sin, and Chillingworth hides his identity. This concealment affords a constant drama. There is the irony of Chapter III, "The Recognition," in which Chillingworth's ignorance is suddenly and blindingly reversed. Separated from his wife by many vicissitudes, he comes upon her as she is dramatically exposed to public infamy. From his instantaneous decision, symbolized by the lifting of his finger to his lips to hide his tie to her, he precipitates the further irony of his sustained hypocrisy.

In the same chapter Hester is confronted with her fellow-adulterer, who is publicly called upon to persuade her as her spiritual guide to reveal his identity. Under the circumstances the situation is highly charged, and his words have a double meaning—one to the onlookers, another far different to Hester and the speaker himself. " 'If thou feelest it to be for thy soul's peace, and that thy earthly punishment will therefore be made more effectual to salvation, I charge thee to speak out the name of thy fellow-sinner and fellow-sufferer!' "

From this scene onward Chillingworth, by living a lie, arouses a constant irony, which is also an ambiguity. With a slight shift in emphasis all his actions can be given a very different interpretation. Seen purely from without, it would be possible to regard him as completely blameless. Hester expresses this ambiguity in Chapter IV, after he has ministered to her sick baby, the product of her faithlessness, with tenderness and skill. " 'Thy acts are like mercy,' said Hester, bewildered and appalled. 'But thy words interpret thee as a terror!' " Masquerading as a physician, he becomes to Dimmesdale a kind of attendant fiend, racking the minister's soul with constant anguish. Yet outwardly he has done him nothing but good. " 'What evil have I done the man?' asked Roger Chillingworth again. 'I tell thee, Hester Prynne, the richest fee that ever physician earned from monarch could not have bought such care as I have wasted on this miserable priest!' " Even when he closes the way to escape by proposing to take passage on the same ship with the fleeing lovers, it is possible to consider the action merely friendly. His endeavor at the end to hold Dimmesdale back from the saving scaffold is from one point of view reasonable and friendlike, although he is a devil struggling to snatch back an escaping soul. " 'All shall be well! Do not blacken your fame, and perish in dishonor! I can yet save you! Would you bring infamy on your sacred profession?' " Only when Dimmesdale has successfully resisted does Chillingworth openly reveal his purposes. With the physician the culminating irony is that in seeking to damn Dimmesdale he has himself fallen into damnation. As he says in a moment of terrible self-knowledge, " 'A mortal man, with once a human heart, has become a fiend for his especial torment!' " The effect is of an Aristotelian reversal, where a conscious and deep-laid purpose brings about totally unforeseen and opposite results. Chillingworth's relations with Dimmesdale have the persistent fascination of an almost absolute knowledge and power working their will with a helpless victim, a fascination which is heightened by the minister's awareness of an evil close beside him which he cannot place. "All this was accomplished with a subtlety so perfect that the minister, though he had constantly a dim perception of some evil influence watching over him, could never gain a knowledge of its actual nature." It is a classic situation wrought out to its fullest potentialities, in which the reader cannot help sharing the perverse pleasure of the villain.

From the victim's point of view the irony is still deeper, perhaps because we can participate still more fully in his response to it. Dimmesdale, a "remorseful hypocrite," is forced to live a perpetual lie in public. His own considerable talents for self-torture are supplemented by the situation as well as by the devoted efforts of Chillingworth. His knowledge is an agony. His conviction of sin is in exact relationship to the reverence in which his parishioners hold him. He grows pale and meager—it is the asceticism of a saint on earth; his effectiveness as a minister grows with his despair; he confesses the truth in his sermons, but transforms it "into the veriest falsehood" by the generality of his avowal and merely increases the adoration of his flock; every effort deepens his plight, since he will not—until the end—make the effort of complete self-revelation. His great election-day sermon prevails through anguish of heart; to his listeners divinely inspired, its power comes from its undertone of suffering, "the complaint of a human heart, sorrow-laden, perchance guilty, telling its secret, whether of guilt or sorrow, to the great heart of mankind. . . ." While Chillingworth at last reveals himself fully, Dimmesdale's secret is too great to be wholly laid bare. His utmost efforts are still partially misunderstood, and "highly respectable witnesses" interpret his death as a culminating act of holiness and humility.

Along with this steady irony of situation there is the omnipresent irony of the hidden meaning. The author and the reader know what the characters do not. Hawthorne consistently pretends that the coincidence of the action or the image with its significance is merely fortuitous, not planned, lest the effect be spoiled by overinsistence. In other words, he attempts to combine the sufficiently probable with the maximum of arrangement. Thus the waxing and waning of sunlight in the forest scene symbolize the emotions of Hester and Dimmesdale, but we accept this coincidence most easily if we can receive it as chance. Hawthorne's own almost amused awareness of his problem helps us to do so. Yet despite the element of play and the deliberate self-deception demanded, the total effect is one of intensity. Hawthorne is performing a difficult feat with sustained virtuosity in reconciling a constant stress between naturally divergent qualities.

The character of Pearl illuminates this point. Pearl is pure symbol, the living emblem of the sin, a human embodiment of the Scarlet Letter. Her mission is to keep Hester's adultery always before her eyes, to prevent her from attempting to escape its moral consequences. Pearl's childish questions are fiendishly apt; in speech and in action she never strays from the control of her symbolic function; her dress and her looks are related to the letter. When Hester casts the letter away in the forest, Pearl forces her to reassume it by flying into an uncontrollable rage. Yet despite the undeviating arrangement of every circumstance which surrounds her, no single action of hers is ever incredible or inconsistent with the conceivable actions of any child under the same conditions. Given the central improbability of her undeviating purposiveness, she is as lifelike as the brilliantly drawn children of Richard Hughes' *The Innocent Voyage*.

These qualities of concentration, selectivity, and irony, which are responsible for the intensity of *The Scarlet Letter*, tend at their extreme toward excessive regularity and a sense of over-manipulation, although irony is also a counter-agent against them. This tendency toward regularity is balanced by Hawthorne's use of ambiguity. The distancing of the story in the past has the effect of ambiguity. Hawthorne so employs the element of time as to warn us that he cannot guarantee the literal truth of his narrative and at the same time to suggest that the essential truth is the clearer; as facts shade off into the background, meaning is left in the foreground unshadowed and disencumbered. The years, he pretends, have winnowed his material, leaving only what is enduring. Tradition and superstition, while he disclaims belief in them, have a way of pointing to truth.

Thus the imagery of hell-fire which occurs throughout *The Scarlet Letter* is dramatically proper to the Puritan background and is attributed to the influence of superstitious legend. It works as relief from more serious concerns and still functions as a symbol of psychological and religious truth. In Chapter III, as Hester is returned from the scaffold to the prison, "It was whispered, by those who peered after her, that the scarlet letter threw a lurid gleam along the dark passage-way of the interior." The imagery of the letter may be summarized by quoting a later passage:

> The vulgar, who, in those dreary old times, were always contributing a grotesque horror to what interested their imaginations, had a story about the scarlet letter which we might readily work up into a terrific legend. They averred, that the symbol was not mere scarlet cloth, tinged in an earthly dyepot, but was red-hot with infernal fire, and could be seen glowing all alight, whenever Hester Pyrnne walked abroad in the nighttime. And we must needs say, it seared Hester's bosom so deeply, that perhaps there was more truth in the rumour than our modern incredulity may be inclined to admit.

The lightness of Hawthorne's tone lends relief and variety, while it nevertheless reveals the function of the superstition. "The vulgar," "dreary old times," "grotesque horror," "work up into a terrific legend"—his scorn is so heavily accented that it discounts itself and satirizes the "modern incredulity" of his affected attitude. The playful extravagance of "red-hot with infernal fire" has the same effect. And the

apparent begrudging of the concession in the final sentence—
"And we must needs say"—lends weight to a truth so reluctantly admitted. Puritan demonology is in general used with the same
effect. It has the pathos and simplicity of an old wives' tale
and yet contains a deep subterranean power which reaches
into daylight from the dark caverns of the mind. The Black
Man of the unhallowed forest—a useful counterbalance to
any too-optimistic picture of nature—and the witchwoman
Mistress Hibbins are cases in point. The latter is a concrete
example of the mingled elements of the superstitious legend.
Matter-of-factly, she is a Puritan lady of high rank, whose
ominous reputation is accounted for by bad temper combined
with insanity. As a witch, she is a figure from a child's
storybook, an object of delighted fear and mockery. Yet her
fanciful extravagance covers a real malignity, and because of
it she has an insight into the secret of the letter. With one
stroke she lays bare the disease in Dimmesdale, as one who
sees evil alone but sees it with unmatched acuteness: " 'When
the Black Man sees one of his own servants, signed and
sealed, so shy of owning to the bond as is the Reverend
Mr. Dimmesdale, he hath a way of ordering matters so that
the mark shall be disclosed to the eyes of all the world.' "
    This use of the past merges into a deep-seated ambiguity
of moral meaning. Moral complexity and freedom of speculation, like the lighter ambiguity of literal fact, temper the
almost excessive unity and symmetry of *The Scarlet Letter* and
avoid a directed verdict. In my opinion the judgment of Hawthorne upon his characters is entirely clear, although deliberately limited in its jurisdiction. But he permits the
possibility of other interpretations to appear, so that the
consistent clarity of his own emphasis is disguised. Let us
take for example the consideration of the heroine in Chapter
XIII, "Another View of Hester." After seven years of disgrace, Hester has won the unwilling respect of her fellow-
townsmen by her good works and respectability of conduct.
From one point of view she is clearly their moral superior:
she has met rigorous cruelty with kindness, arrogance with
humility. Furthermore, living as she has in enforced isolation

has greatly developed her mind. In her breadth of intellectual speculation she has freed herself from any dependence upon the laws of Puritan society. "She cast away the fragments of a broken chain." She pays outward obedience to a system which has no further power upon her spirit. Under other conditions, Hawthorne suggests, she might at this juncture have become another Anne Hutchinson, the foundress of a religious sect, or a great early feminist. The author's conclusions about these possibilities, however, are specifically stated: "The scarlet letter had not done its office." Hester is wounded and led astray, not improved, by her situation. Hawthorne permits his reader, if he wishes, to take his character from his control, to say that Hester Prynne is a great woman unhappily born before her time, or that she is a good woman wronged by her fellow men. But Hawthorne is less confident.

Malcom Cowley

from "Five Acts of *The Scarlet Letter*"□

There was, however, another technical problem that required a more radical solution, arising as it did from the author's special experience and cast of mind. Until that time, the novel in all its forms had been essentially a chronicle of events and Hawthorne had no great talent or practice as a chronicler. As a very young man he had written a short and artlessly romantic novel called *Fanshawe*, which demonstrated not very much except that its author admired Sir Walter Scott and, in pure story-telling, could never hope to equal him. Feeling ashamed of the little book, Hawthorne had withdrawn it from circulation and had destroyed every copy on which he could lay his hands. In the twenty years since *Fanshawe* he had written nothing else of equal length, but he had published nearly a hundred tales or sketches, and these had given a special direction to his thinking. What he had learned from writing them was, among other lessons, how to work intensively in smaller forms and how to present his subjects as moral essays or allegorical pictures rather than as continually moving narratives.

His final problem, then, was to devise some method by which a larger theme could be adjusted to his training and personality as a writer. It was the solution he found, whether

□ *College English*, XIX (October 1957), 11–16. Reprinted with the permission of the National Council of Teachers of English and Malcolm Cowley.

by reason or instinct, that became the truly important technical innovation in *The Scarlet Letter.* Instead of conceiving the novel as a single or double narrative moving ahead in a straight or zigzag line and revealing the social landscape as if to the eyes of a traveler on horseback, Hawthorne approached it dramatistically, almost as if his characters were appearing on a stage. Instead of dividing his book into narrative episodes—now the hero falls in love, now he fights a duel, now he escapes from prison—Hawthorne divided it into scenes, each of which is a posed tableau or a dramatic confrontation.

The advantage of the method for this particular author was that it enabled him to work on each scene intensively, as if it were a separate tale. Although there was little movement within the separate scenes, he could create a general sense of movement by passing rapidly from one scene to another, for example, from the marketplace at night to the seashore and thence to the forest. Unity of mood was not one of his problems—that had already been achieved by his years of brooding over the central symbol—but the method enabled him to give the book architectural unity as well, by balancing one scene against another and by ending the story where it really began, on the scaffold of the pillory.

This dramatistic method followed by Hawthorne was also, in effect, the "divine principle" that Henry James would rediscover in 1895, when he went back to writing fiction after the failure of his career as a playwright. "Has a *part* of all this wasted passion and squandered time (of the last 5 years)," James would ask in his notebook shortly after having been hissed from the stage at the first night of *Guy Domville*—has part of it "been simply the precious lesson, taught me in that roundabout and devious, that cruelly expensive, way, *of the singular value for a narrative plan too* of the (I don't know *what* adequately to call it) divine principle of the Scenario?"

It was the principle that enabled him to achieve what he called his *big* effects—"scenic, constructive, 'architectural' "—and he would follow it in all the novels of his later years. "Yes, I *see* thus, I think, my little *act* of my little drama here," he said in his notebook when he was working on *What*

Maisie Knew. "Ah," he continued, "this *divine* conception of one's little masses and periods in the scenic light, as rounded ACTS: this patient, pious, nobly 'vindicative' application of the scenic philosophy and method—I feel as if it *still* (above all, YET) had a great deal to give me and might carry me as far as I dream!"

It carried him in a nobly vindicative fashion through *The Wings of the Dove* and *The Golden Bowl*, and it has carried later novelists through hundreds of more or less distinguished works. But Hawthorne in his solitude had discovered the "divine principle" almost fifty years before the first night of *Guy Domville*, and the discovery seems more amazing when we reflect that, unlike James, he had never tried to write for the stage. As a matter of fact, he had never even engaged in amateur theatricals, having shown little talent or taste for mimicry. Although he liked going to the Boston theatres, and sometimes reviewed the performances for a Salem newspaper, he seems to have had no consuming interest in acted plays; at most they may have confirmed him in his taste for conveying moods by visual effects.

Hawthorne's knowledge of the drama came mostly from his reading, which—according to the records of the Salem Athenaeum—included all of Racine, besides other classical French dramatists; he had been familiar with Shakespeare's works since boyhood. It might well be argued that his cast of mind was not Shakespearean, as Melville thought, but Racinian. The fact is that *The Scarlet Letter* can be read, and gains a new dimension from being read, as a Racinian drama of dark necessity.

II

It is a novel in twenty-four chapters, but, considered as a tragic drama, it is divided into the usual five acts and subdivided into eight scenes. (One principle of division would be that an act may include two scenes if the second follows without any great lapse of time.) There are of course some chapters that fall outside the dramatic framework, since each of them deals with a single character (Chapter V with Hester,

VI with Pearl, IX with Chillingworth, XI with Dimmesdale, XIII with Hester again, XX with Dimmesdale, and XXIV, the epilogue, chiefly with Hester), and since the method they follow is narrative or expository. These seven chapters serve as interludes in the dramatic action—or in one case as a postlude —and they provide some additional information about the characters that would have been difficult to incorporate into the dialogue. The essential chapters, however, are the other seventeen, in which Hawthorne is applying the scenic philosophy and method. Here is how they arrange themselves into rounded acts and scenes:

Act I, Scene 1 (Chapters I to III) is laid in the marketplace of Boston, fifteen or twenty years after the founding of the city. On the right, rear, is the enormous nail-studded door of the prison, with a wild rosebush growing beside it. On the left is the meeting house, with a balcony projecting over the stage. Under the balcony is the scaffold of the pillory, which will be the effective center of the drama. Hester Prynne emerges from the blackness of the prison, with the child on her arm not hiding the letter A in scarlet cloth pinned to her breast; in the whole scene it is the one touch of brilliant color. She moves through the gray crowd and climbs the scaffold. From the balcony overhead the Reverend Mr. Dimmesdale adjures her to reveal the father of her child. "Believe me, Hester," he says, "though he were to step down from a high place and stand beside thee, on thy pedestal of shame, yet better were it so than to hide a guilty heart through life." Hester shakes her head. Looking down at the crowd she recognizes her wronged husband, who had been missing for two years, but he puts a finger on his lips to show that she must not reveal his identity. All the named characters of the drama— including Governor Bellingham, John Wilson, and Mistress Hibbins—appear in this first scene; and there is also the Boston crowd, which speaks in strophe and antistrophe like a Greek chorus.

Scene 2 of the first act (Chapter IV) is a room in the prison that same June evening. Here, after the public tableau of the first scene, comes a private confrontation. Hester and the child have fallen ill, a leech is summoned to care for them,

and the leech is Chillingworth, the betrayed husband. He
tells her that the scarlet letter is a more effective punishment
than any he might have imagined. "Live, therefore," he
says, "and bear about thy doom with thee." After revealing
his determination to find the lover and be revenged on him,
Chillingworth extracts one promise from Hester: that just as
she has kept the lover's identity a secret, so she must keep the
husband's.

Act II, Scene 1 (Chapters VII and VIII) is laid in the
governor's hall, three years after the events of the first act.
Little Pearl is thought to be such a strange and willful child
that there has been talk among the Puritan magistrates of
taking her away from her sinful mother. When Hester, now a
seamstress, comes to deliver a pair of embroidered gloves to
Governor Bellingham he holds an informal trial of her case.
Chillingworth plays an ambiguous part in it, but Dimmesdale
—when Hester demands that he speak—makes such an
eloquent plea that she is allowed to keep the child. All the
named characters are again present—down to Mistress Hibbins, who, at the end of the scene, invites Hester to attend
a witches' sabbath in the forest. Hester refuses with a
triumphant smile:

"I must tarry at home," she says, "to keep watch over
my little Pearl. Had they taken her from me, I would willingly
have gone with thee into the forest, and signed my name in the
Black Man's book, and that with mine own blood!"

This tableau and its brief epilogue are followed once
more by a private confrontation. *Scene 2* of the second act
(Chapter X) is set in Chillingworth's laboratory, among the
retorts and crucibles. The old leech suspects Dimmesdale and
has taken up residence in the same house, to continue all
through the scene his relentless probing of Dimmesdale's
heart. The minister will not confess, but, at the curtain,
Chillingworth accidentally finds proof that he is indeed the
guilty man.

Act III (Chapter XII) has only one scene, the scaffold of
the pillory. Four years have passed since the second act.
Subtly tortured by Chillingworth and finally driven half-
insane, Dimmesdale has dressed in his ministerial robes and

left his room at midnight, hoping to find relief in a private mimicry of public confession. Standing on the scaffold he shrieks aloud, but nobody recognizes his voice. Governor Bellingham and Mistress Hibbins both open their windows to peer into the night. On his way home from Governor Winthrop's deathbed, good John Wilson walks through the marketplace in a halo of lantern-light; he does not look up at the pillory. Then, coming from the same deathbed, Hester appears with little Pearl, and Dimmesdale invites them to join him. Holding one another's hands on the scaffold, they form what Hawthorne calls "an electric chain," and Dimmesdale feels a new life, not his own, pouring like a torrent into his heart.

"Minister!" Pearl whispers. "Wilt thou stand here with mother and me, tomorrow noontide?"

When Dimmesdale refuses, she tries to pull her hand away. At this moment a meteor gleams through a cloud, forming a scarlet A in the heavens while it also reveals the little group on the scaffold. It is another of Hawthorne's many lighting effects, based partly on his Emersonian belief that the outer world is a visible manifestation of the inner world, but also based partly on his instinct for theatre; one might almost speak of his staginess. While the meteor is still glowing, Chillingworth appears to lead the minister back to his torture chamber. This tableau, occurring at the exact center of the drama, is the turning point of *The Scarlet Letter*; from now the tempo will be quicker. The first half of the story has covered a space of seven years; the second half will cover no more than fifteen days.

Act IV is in two intimate scenes, the second of which is the longest in the drama. *Scene 1* (Chapters XIV and XV) is laid on the seashore, where Chillingworth is gathering herbs to concoct his medicines. While Pearl goes wading in a tidal pool, Hester accosts the old leech and begs him to release her from her promise not to tell Dimmesdale that he is the wronged husband. Chillingworth answers in a speech that reveals not only his own heart but the other side of Hawthorne's philosophy. The Emersonian side contributed to his stage effects, but it was his surviving Calvinism (in some ways close to Racine's Jansenism) that enabled him to conceive a tragic drama.

"Peace, Hester, peace!" the old man says. "It is not granted me to pardon. . . . My old faith, long forgotten, comes back to me, and explains all that we do, and all we suffer. By thy first step awry thou didst plant the germ of evil; but since that moment, it has all been a dark necessity. Ye that have wronged me are not sinful, save in a kind of typical illusion; neither am I fiend-like, who have snatched a fiend's office from his hands. It is our fate. Let the black flower blossom as it may! Now go thy ways, and deal as thou wilt with yonder man."

He goes back to gathering herbs. Hester calls to Pearl, who, as they leave the stage, keeps asking her, "Mother!— Why does the minister keep his hand over his heart?"

Scene 2 of the fourth act (including four chapters, XVI to XIX) is set in the forest, which forms another contrast with the marketplace and helps to reveal the moral background of Hawthorne's drama. The forest, he tells us in what might almost be a stage direction, is an image of the moral wilderness in which Hester has long been wandering. But it was more than that for Hawthorne himself, and a close reading shows that the forest is the meeting place of those who follow their passions and revolt against the community. In this sense little Pearl, the natural child, is a daughter of the forest, and we observe in this scene that she is perfectly at home there. Witches like Mistress Hibbins go into the forest to dance with Indian powwows and Lapland wizards, and Hester has been tempted to join them. When she meets Dimmesdale in the forest, although she intends only to warn him against Chillingworth, it is natural in this setting that she should also urge him to defy the laws of the tribe and flee with her to a foreign country. The minister agrees; they will take passage on a Bristol cruiser then moored in the harbor. For a moment Hester unpins the scarlet A from her dress and lets down her long black glossy hair; but Pearl, who has been called back from playing at the brookside, sulks until she pins the letter on her breast again.

On his way back to Boston (in Chapter XX) Dimmesdale meets Mistress Hibbins. "So, reverend Sir, you have made a visit into the forest," says the witchlady, nodding her high headdress at him. "The next time, I pray you to allow me only a fair warning, and I shall be proud to bear you company."

Act V, in a single scene (Chapters XXI to XXIII), takes place three days after the meeting in the forest and is the culmination toward which the drama has been moving. Once again it is laid in the marketplace, with all the named characters present, as well as the Bristol shipmaster and the Boston crowd that speaks with the voices of the tribe. Dimmesdale preaches the Election Sermon, the climax of his ministerial career, while Hester listens outside the meeting house. The shipmaster tells her that Chillingworth has taken passage on the same vessel; there will be no escape. Then Dimmesdale appears in a great procession of Puritan worthies and, instead of marching with them to the official banquet, he totters up the steps of the scaffold after calling on Hester to support him. At last they are standing together, in public, on the pedestal of shame.

"Is not this better," Dimmesdale murmurs, "than what we dreamed of in the forest?" Facing the crowd he tears open his ministerial band and shows that there is a scarlet A imprinted on his own flesh. He has made his public confession and now, at the point of death, he feels reconciled with the community. As he sinks to the scaffold, Chillingworth kneels over him repeating, "Thou hast escaped me." Pearl kisses her father on the lips, and the tears that she lets fall are the pledge that she will cease to be an outcast, an embodiment of the scarlet letter, a daughter of the forest, and instead will grow up among human joys and sorrows.

I spoke of Hawthorne's kinship with Racine, but at this point, if not before, one begins to feel that his drama might have another ancestry as well, even though the author was not conscious of it. He has presented us with distinguished, even noble, characters who are inevitably brought to grief for having violated the laws of heaven and the tribe. He has presented "an action that is serious and also, as having magnitude, complete in itself . . . with incidents arousing pity and fear, wherewith to accomplish its catharsis of such emotions." The familiar quotation from Aristotle seems appropriate in a discussion of *The Scarlet Letter*. In telling his story by a new method, Hawthorne had done more than to extend the unity and economy of the brief tale into the realm of the novel; and more than to discover a new architectural form that would be rediscovered by Henry James and copied by scores of respectably talented novelists after him. It is not too much to say that he had recaptured, for his New England, the essence of Greek tragedy.

Seymour L. Gross

~~~

from " 'Solitude, and Love, and Anguish': The Tragic Design of *The Scarlet Letter*"□

I believe that *The Scarlet Letter*, like all great novels, enriches our sense of human experience and complicates and humanizes our approach to it. It does not try to convince us— or at least that is not its central or distinctive purpose—of the validity of this or that particular moral precept. The inadequacy of a didactic reading of *The Scarlet Letter*, whether it posits for Hawthorne an orthodox or romantic point of view, can be most clearly seen in the fact that neither of these positions has been able to take into account Hester's deep sense of having committed a sin and her feelings of guilt, even though Hawthorne insists upon our considering them. For example, of her continued stay in Boston she thinks, "Here had been the scene of her guilt, and here should be the scene of her earthly punishment . . ." (ch. V). And when Pearl strikes her scarlet letter with flowers, Hester refrains from covering her bosom "that her penance might be best wrought out by this unutterable pain" (ch. VI). In answer to Pearl's persistent questions about the significance of the letter, Hester finally tells her that "once in my lifetime I met the Black Man [and] this scarlet letter is his mark" (ch. XVI). Even more explicitly,

□ *CLA Journal,* III (March, 1960), pp. 154–165. Reprinted by permission of the College Language Association and the author Seymour L. Gross.

we are told that "she knew that her deed had been evil; she
had no faith, therefore, that its result [Pearl] would be good,"
and that "It appalled her to discern in [Pearl] a shadowy
reflection of the evil that had existed in herself" (ch. VI). For
obvious reasons the critics have paid little or no attention to
these remarks: they cannot be made to fit into any moralistic
reading of the novel: for whether Hester is seen as the glorious
incarnation of the transcendental soul or as the damnable
spirit of romantic self-indulgence, these guilt-laden comments
are equally out of character. If, on the other hand, these are
the legitimate marks of an orthodox repentance, then how can
Hester say after seven (supposedly) purgatorial years that her
adultery "had a consecration of its own?" John C. Gerber,
one of the best of the novel's critics, both presents the problem of Hester's guilt feelings most clearly and indicates, without solving, the central difficulty. "From the first it is plain
that Hester does not consider her act of adultery as a sin
against God or against any law of her own nature. Nor does
she feel that she has sinned against the community. Yet
clearly she knows that her deed has been wrong and that,
somehow, the result cannot be good." It is the purpose of this
paper to fix the nature of Professor Gerber's "somehow," and
to show how this shapes the tragic design of the book.

The "A" which Hester wears on her bosom does not, of
course, signify adultery in her eyes: its ornate embroidery
(which Hawthorne mentions three times) is an implicit rejection of the community's view of her act; it is, in fact, a symbolic foreshadowing of her "consecration" assertion seven
years later. But Hawthorne does not imply that Hester is
therefore an irresponsible libertine: it is simply that she cannot imagine any law as taking precedence over the law of love
between a man and a woman. For her, marriage *in se* is not a
sacramental union—only love can truly sacramentalize it.
In this she is not, like, say, Ivan Karamazov or Ahab, posing
her will against God's, as some recent critics assert; it is
rather that she, like Anne Hutchinson, with whom she is
twice linked in the novel, is convinced through an "Inner
Light" that her way is not a violation of God's law. This, I
take it, is what Hester means when in the "Conclusion" she

tells the troubled women who come to her for counsel "of her
firm belief, that, at some brighter period, when the world
should have grown ripe for it, in Heaven's own time, a new
truth would be revealed, in order to establish the whole relation between man and woman on a surer ground of mutual
happiness." Having arrived at this conviction through the
experience of love, Hester considers her marriage with
Chillingworth as invalid, for, as she reminds him, "I felt no
love [for you], nor feigned any" (ch. IV). Indeed, from the
vantage point of a "consecrated" marriage, she looks back
upon her loveless union with her legal husband with horror:
"She deemed it her crime most to be repented of that she had
ever endured, and reciprocated, the lukewarm grasp of his
hand . . ." (ch. XV). Though she talks of hands, what sickens
Hester is, I believe, clear. That Hawthorne does not present
Hester's position as either romantically irresponsible or
gloriously liberated is evidenced in Chillingworth's quiet
reply: "We have wronged each other . . . Mine was the first
wrong, when I betrayed thy budding youth into a false and
unnatural relation with my decay" (ch. IV). This scene, like
most of the novel, is the product of a deliberately controlled
balance of sympathies—the balance that is tragic not didactic.
I do not mean to imply that Hawthorne had no convictions
personally about the responsibilities and nature of marriage—
of course he did; it would not be difficult to isolate from his life
and letters a body of doctrine to which we can be fairly certain
he personally subscribed. The point is that abstract conviction
does not represent his total attitude towards the problem, for
it neglects the context of concrete experience, which for the
artist, as opposed to the theologian, is an essential element in
its definition. Therefore, what is significant in *The Scarlet
Letter* is not that Hester is right or wrong in an absolute sense,
but rather that she has integrity in her own terms, that she
has fallen in love with a minister who has integrity in different
terms, and that therefore their love is condemned to be
mangled in the clash of their ultimately irreconcilable moralities.

It is this conflict of moralities which is the source of
Hester's sense of sin: the guilt which she suffers can only be

related to what Hester has done to her lover. In Hester's view, as we have already said, she has not sinned against community, husband, or God; but she *has* sinned against Dimmesdale (it is a convenient coincidence that the "A" she wears is the initial of her lover's first name). Although she has committed no evil in terms of her own morality, she has been, nevertheless, the instrument of Dimmesdale's having committed a horrible sin against his: it is she who has caused the physical and spiritual desiccation of her lover, and for this she suffers her sense of guilt. It is beside the point that she has destroyed him unwittingly: the knowledge of what she has done to him is her own form of "bloody scourge." It is this tragic paradox—that out of love she has violated love—which accounts for Hester's painful awareness that "her deed had been evil." Her "impulsive and passionate nature" is neither romantically exalted nor moralistically condemned: it is simply presented as tragic because it was its fate to intersect with Dimmesdale's equally passionate desire for renunciation. In the iron world of *The Scarlet Letter*, passion, whether human or divine, is its own cross.

Hester's refusal to leave Boston—which has confused some critics—and her withdrawal from Dimmesdale are the necessary results of this tragic conflict. Roy Male's assertion that Hester stays in Boston to be close to her lover and that this shows that "her ideas about expiating her guilt are partly rationalization" misses the point I believe. Hester cannot go into Dimmesdale's world, where both might find peace of soul in an orthodox submission to the Calvinistic God; and he cannot come into hers, where both might find joy in a free submission to human love. They are both doomed to their own private purgatories, their own parallel agonies. But their release from the "sin and sorrow" of their lives must come from different sources. For whereas Dimmesdale must struggle to make himself a fit receptacle for God's grace before his "A" can be purged, Hester's purgation can only be effected by Dimmesdale himself—only he can take the stigma from her breast. That Hester's absolution can come only from Dimmesdale is made quite clear early in the novel. When the Reverend Mr. Wilson offers Hester the removal of the letter

in return for the name of Pearl's father, Hester answers,
" 'Never!' . . . looking, not at Mr. Wilson, but into the deep
and troubled eyes of the younger clergyman [Dimmesdale].
'It is too deeply branded. Ye cannot take it off. And would that
I might endure his agony as well as mine!' " (ch. III). Here,
quite explicitly, we are shown that Hester feels that her sin is
only against her lover and that, consequently, only he can
ease her of her pain. In the same vein she later tells Chillingworth, when he assures her that the community will allow her
to remove her stigma, "It lies not in the pleasure of the magistrates to take off this badge . . . Were I worthy to be quit of it,
it would fall away of its own nature or be transformed into
something which speaks a different purport" (ch. XIV). But it
has *already* been transformed into something which speaks a
different purport—the community now interprets the letter as
standing for Able (ch. XIII). The point is that forgiveness has
come from an irrelevant source. The theocratic society of
seventeenth century Boston would have the right to remove
the letter or transform its meaning only if Hester's sin were
that of adultery; but since she herself conceives of her sin
in different terms, the attitude of magistrate or minister (save
one) is beside the point. Only Dimmesdale has the power to
remove the letter—which is precisely what happens several
chapters later in the forest scene.

It is the index of Hester's love for Dimmesdale and her
consciousness of having violated him that at no time during
the seven years leading up to the climactic forest scene does
she try to save Dimmesdale (and herself) within the context of
her own beliefs. She leaves him, instead, to try to work out his
release in terms of his own orthodox world, even though such
a release can bring her no happiness; that is, if Dimmesdale
is able to resolve his spiritual agony with God, the painful
image of what she had caused would dissolve. But there would
be no radiant joy in its stead. Dimmesdale's peace would still
leave Hester alone in her world. The absence of pain is not
happiness, yet the absence of pain is all she allows herself
to hope for. Hester accepts this life of "no hope, and seemingly
no wish, of gaining anything" for herself because she loves the
man she ruined.

It would be a mistake to minimize the extent of her ordeal. For all the moral and psychological toughness she has achieved in the seven years, her life has been as drab and grey as the garb she wears. When Dimmesdale asks her in the forest, "Art thou in life?" she can only find it in herself to answer, "In such life as has been mine these seven years past!" But so deeply rooted is her sense of sin and her acceptance of its tragic consequences that even in the second scaffold scene, when years of unnatural asceticism have all but effaced the natural richness of her being, she still refrains from any attempt at intimate contact with the minister. It is Pearl who talks to him and it is she whose hand he holds. It is only when she has to face the "shuddering terror" of what was once her lover, with his "nerve . . . destroyed" and his "moral force abased" (ch. XIII), that she decides to break out of her penitential isolation; but her daring to intersect with Dimmesdale's life again has no personal element of hope in it. She is not going to attempt a resurrection of both their lives with the vitality of her love; she is merely going to rectify her error in judgment in having sworn to Chillingworth not to disclose his identity—an understandable concession when we remember that it was exacted from her when she had just undergone a mind-shattering experience.

Those critics who see the forest scene as the Second Temptation surely miss the fineness of Hawthorne's tragic vision. Hester is not a seventeenth century Sadie Thompson: she goes into the forest only to give Dimmesdale information (his tormentor's identity) which will strengthen him in his private struggle with God, and then to return to her own isolated world. That it becomes for Dimmesdale a Second Temptation is a consequence of his own terrible sense of defeat, not of Hester's guile. Indeed, at the outset, Hester tries to lift the burden of Dimmesdale's miserable suffering and wretched despair with the comforting words of *religion*, not love:

" 'You wrong yourself in this,' said Hester, gently. 'You have deeply and sorely repented. Your sin is left behind you, in the days long past. Your present life is not less holy, in very truth, than it seems in people's eyes. Is there no reality in the penitence thus sealed and witnessed by good works? And wherefore should it not bring you peace?' " (ch. XVII)

This is hardly the language of a woman who has been accused by various critics of "desperate recklessness," "romantic self-indulgence," "unyokable paganism," "foolish and fatuous arrogance."

What is usually missed in the forest scene is that Hester's final offer to go away with Dimmesdale is the result of a gradual interaction of his agony and her love—*in that sequence*. It is only when a spiritually shattered Dimmesdale, "crushed under this seven years' weight of misery," begs her "Resolve for me . . . be strong for me," that Hester dares to advise him to run away to a new *religious* life ("Preach! Write! Act!") before "the torments that have so gnawed into thy life . . . leave thee powerless even to repent!" It is only then that she dares to intimate that his orthodoxy has enslaved him needlessly: "what hast thou to do with all these iron men, and their opinions? They have kept thy better part in bondage too long already." Malcolm Cowley's comment that Hester *urges* Dimmesdale to "flee with her to a foreign country" is not a fair description of what happens in the forest, and Hugh Maclean's assertion that "Hester's continual harping on the 'happiness' she can win for them both would be almost comic, were it not such a pathetic effort to escape the will of God" is a gross distortion of it. It is only when Dimmesdale himself (and this is always overlooked) covertly begs her to go with him with his pathetically repeated "Alone, Hester!" that she allows her deepest desire to escape from its self-imposed penitential prison into the joy of consent. Hawthorne makes it quite explicit that she has not seduced him— she has merely articulated "what he vaguely hinted at but dared not speak" (ch. XVIII). Orthodoxy in her view, and, for the moment, in his too, has had its chance—and failed! Now human love—exalted and consecrated—is to have its chance at resurrecting their shattered world.

And for a pathetically brief moment, in the appropriately entitled chapter, "A Flood of Sunshine," it does. But unlike the Graham Greene character who hopelessly and despondently gives himself over to human love when

God seems gone, here human love is "transvalued" into religious exaltation, "Do I feel joy again!" Dimmesdale cries out ecstatically.

"'Methought the germ of it was dead in me! O Hester, thou art my better angel! I seem to have flung myself—sick, sin-stained, and sorrow-blackened—down upon these forest leaves, and to have risen up all made anew, *and with new powers to glorify Him that hath been merciful!* This is already the better life! Why did we not find it sooner?'" (ch. XVIII; my italics.)

It is at this moment, when Hester's love has freed Dimmesdale from the slough of despond into which it had cast him, that Hester can at last unclasp the scarlet letter from her bosom and cast it away "among the withered leaves." Dimmesdale's having "risen up all made anew" is the absolution of her sin: his rebirth is her forgiveness: *he* has taken off the letter. Free at last from her burden of "sin and sorrow," Hester, in a breath-taking movement, loosens her abundantly rich and dark hair from the nun-like cap in which she has encased it for seven years, releasing her "sex, her youth, and the whole richness of her beauty." This is not, however, an image of sexual potency to be admired or condemned according to the critic's point of view: it is a moment of fruition, a moment paid for with humiliation, isolation, forbearance, and pain.

But the "magic" of this hour in the forest is doomed to be dispelled in the resurgence of Dimmesdale's Pauline Christianity, as is symbolically foreshadowed in the failure of the brook (a baptismal image) to carry away the discarded letter and in Pearl's washing off of her father's kiss in the same brook. It is inevitable that Dimmesdale, being the kind of man he is, should shortly realize that, "Tempted by a dream of happiness, . . . he had yielded himself, with deliberate choice, as he had never done before, to what he knew was deadly sin," and should therefore renounce his human love. Customarily, Dimmesdale's final release in the spiritual embrace of his Orthodoxy is viewed either as a wretched betrayal of Hester's love or as an implicit condemnation of her misguided "presumption" which would have resulted in the loss

of both their salvations. In its final effect it is neither. In the
tragic conflict of moralities, it is inevitable that Hester
should try—after Orthodoxy seemed to have failed—to save
the man she loves and ruined in the only way she can; and it is
equally inevitable that this "polluted priest" should ultimately
save himself—even at the expense of his mortal lover—in the
only way he can. Had Hawthorne wished for Hester to appear
as erring romantic irresponsibility, he could have shown her
as bitterly and frantically attempting to recall Dimmesdale
from his beatific escape, in the manner of Paphnutius in
Anatole France's *Thais*. (It is the demonic Chillingworth, by
the way, who plays this role in the novel; it is he who tries
"to snatch back [Dimmesdale] from what he sought to do!")
Or had he wished Hester to appear as the glowing spirit of
romantic freedom and love, he would not have given to
Dimmesdale's final moments the sincere accents of mystical
joy. What Hawthorne has given us instead is a marvelously
poised and powerful vision of tragic separation: an excru-
ciating sense of division pervades the final scene from the
moment of Dimmesdale's entry until his death. As the minister, energized by his spiritual resolve, arrives to give his
Election Sermon, Hester suddenly realizes what she had
allowed herself in the forest to forget—that their lives could
never really mesh:

"She thought of the dim forest, with its little dell of solitude, and
love, and anguish, and the mossy tree-trunk, where sitting hand
in hand, they had mingled their sad and passionate talk with the
melancholy murmur of the brook. How deeply had they known each
other then! And was this the man? She hardly knew him now!
He, moving proudly past . . . he, so unattainable in his . . . un-
sympathizing thoughts, through which she now beheld him! Her
spirit sank with the idea that all must have been a delusion, and
that . . . there could be no real bond betwixt the clergyman and
herself."

Though it is Hester's strength that Dimmesdale asks
for in his ascent to the public confessional, though it is in her
arms that he dies, both pursue their separate destinies to the
end. When the clergyman asks her the rhetorical question,
"Is this not better . . . than what we dreamed of in the

forest?," she can only answer, "I know not! I know not! . . .
Better? Yea; so we may both die. . . ." And when Hester
pleadingly asks Dimmesdale, "Shall we not meet again? . . .
Shall we not spend our immortal life together? Surely, surely,
we have ransomed one another with all this woe!" all he can
say is, "Hush, Hester, hush. . . . The law we broke—the
sin here so awfully revealed—let these alone be in thy
thoughts!"

Hawthorne tells us that he suffered a "great diversity
and severity of emotion" while writing *The Scarlet Letter* and
that when he finished it he was in a "very nervous state." I
find it difficult to believe that such emotional upset could have
come from an intention that was merely moralistic or didactic. But the novel itself, as I have tried to show, is the best
proof of Hawthorne's tragic design. As I read the novel, it does
not matter who was "right." What matters is that Dimmesdale is dead and that Hester is alone; that a love that should
have flourished in the sunlight had but one moment of stolen
light and seven years of darkness. What matters is that in
The Scarlet Letter the color of adultery was the color of roses
and the color of death.

V

M oby Dick (1851) by Herman Melville

Herman Melville

Letter to Nathaniel Hawthorne, 1 June 1851 □

My Dear Hawthorne,—I should have been rumbling down to you in my pine-board chariot a long time ago, were it not that for some weeks past I have been more busy than you can well imagine,—out of doors,—building and patching and tinkering away in all directions. Besides, I had my crops to get in—corn and potatoes (I hope to show you some famous ones by and by)—and many other things to attend to, all accumulating upon this one particular season. I work myself; and at night my bodily sensations are akin to those I have so often felt before, when a hired man, doing my day's work from sun to sun. But I mean to continue visiting you until you tell me that my visits are both supererogatory and superfluous. With no son of man do I stand upon any etiquette or ceremony, except the Christian ones of charity and honesty. I am told, my fellow-man, that there is an aristocracy of the brain. Some men have boldly advocated and asserted it. Schiller seems to have done so, though I don't know much about him.[1] At any rate, it is true that there have been those who, while earnest in behalf of political equality, still accept the intellectual estates. And I can well perceive, I think, how a man of superior mind can, by its intense cultivation, bring

himself, as it were, into a certain spontaneous aristocracy
of feeling—exceedingly nice and fastidious—similar to that
which, in an English Howard, conveys a torpedo-fish thrill at
the slightest contact with a social plebeian.[2] So, when you see
or hear of my ruthless democracy on all sides, you may possibly feel a touch of a shrink, or something of that sort. It is
but nature to be shy of a mortal who boldly declares that a
thief in jail is as honorable a personage as Gen. George
Washington. This is ludicrous. But Truth is the silliest thing
under the sun. Try to get a living by the Truth—and go to the
Soup Societies. Heavens! Let any clergyman try to preach the
Truth from its very stronghold, the pulpit, and they would
ride him out of his church on his own pulpit bannister. It
can hardly be doubted that all Reformers are bottomed upon
the truth, more or less; and to the world at large are not
reformers almost universally laughingstocks? Why so?
Truth is ridiculous to men. Thus easily in my room here do I,
conceited and garrulous, reverse the test of my Lord Shaftesbury.[3]

It seems an inconsistency to assert unconditional
democracy in all things, and yet confess a dislike to all mankind—in the mass. But not so—But it's an endless sermon—
no more of it. I began by saying that the reason I have not
been to Lenox is this—in the evening I feel completely done up,
as the phrase is, and incapable of the long jolting to get to
your house and back. In a week or so, I go to New York, to
bury myself in a third-story room, and work and slave on my
"Whale" while it is driving through the press. *That* is the
only way I can finish it now—I am so pulled hither and
thither by circumstances. The calm, the coolness, the silent
grass-growing mood in which a man *ought* always to compose
—that, I fear, can seldom be mine. Dollars damn me; and the
malicious Devil is forever grinning in upon me, holding the
door ajar. My dear Sir, a presentiment is on me—I shall at
last be worn out and perish, like an old nutmeg-grater,
grated to pieces by the constant attrition of the wood, that is,
the nutmeg. What I feel most moved to write, that is banned
—it will not pay. Yet, altogether, write the *other* way I
cannot. So the product is a final hash, and all my books are

botches. I'm rather sore, perhaps, in this letter; but see my hand!—four blisters on this palm, made by hoes and hammers within the last few days. It is a rainy morning; so I am indoors, and all work suspended. I feel cheerfully disposed, and therefore I write a little bluely. Would the Gin were here! If ever, my dear Hawthorne, in the eternal times that are to come, you and I shall sit down in Paradise, in some little shady corner by ourselves; and if we shall by any means be able to smuggle a basket of champagne there (I won't believe in a Temperance Heaven), and if we shall then cross our celestial legs in the celestial grass that is forever tropical, and strike our glasses and our heads together, till both musically ring in concert— then, O my dear fellow-mortal, how shall we pleasantly discourse of all the things manifold which now so distress us— when all the earth shall be but a reminiscence, yea, its final dissolution an antiquity. Then shall songs be composed as when wars are over; humorous, comic songs—"Oh, when I lived in that queer little hole called the world," or, "Oh, when I toiled and sweated below," or, "Oh, when I knocked and was knocked in the fight"—yes, let us look forward to such things. Let us swear that, though now we sweat, yet it is because of the dry heat which is indispensable to the nourishment of the vine which is to bear the grapes that are to give us the champagne hereafter.

But I was talking about the "Whale." As the fishermen say, "he's in his flurry" when I left him some three weeks ago. I'm going to take him by his jaw, however, before long, and finish him up in some fashion or other. What's the use of elaborating what, in its very essence, is so short-lived as a modern book? Though I wrote the Gospels in this century, I should die in the gutter—I talk all about myself, and this is selfishness and egotism. Granted. But how help it? I am writing to you; I know little about you, but something about myself. So I write about myself—at least, to you. Don't trouble yourself, though, about writing; and don't trouble yourself about visiting; and when you *do* visit, don't trouble yourself about talking. I will do all the writing and visiting and talking myself—By the way, in the last "Dollar Magazine" I read "The Unpardonable Sin."[4] He was a sad fellow,

that Ethan Brand. I have no doubt you are by this time responsible for many a shake and tremor of the tribe of "general
readers." It is a frightful poetical creed that the cultivation of
the brain eats out the heart. But it's my *prose* opinion that in
most cases, in those men who have fine brains and work them
well, the heart extends down to hams. And though you smoke
them with the fire of tribulation, yet, like veritable hams, the
head only gives the richer and the better flavor. I stand for the
heart. To the dogs with the head! I had rather be a fool with a
heart, than Jupiter Olympus with his head. The reason the
mass of men fear God, and *at bottom dislike* Him, is because
they rather distrust His heart, and fancy Him all brain like a
watch. (You perceive I employ a capital initial in the pro-
noun referring to the Deity; don't you think there is a slight
dash of flunkeyism in that usage?) Another thing. I was in
New York for four-and-twenty hours the other day, and saw a
portrait of N.H. And I have seen and heard many flattering
(in a publisher's point of view) allusions to the "Seven
Gables." And I have seen "Tales," and "A New Volume"
announced, by N.H.[5] So upon the whole, I say to myself, this
N.H. is in the ascendant. My dear Sir, they begin to patronize.
All Fame is patronage. Let me be infamous: there is no
patronage in *that*. What "reputation" H.M. has is horrible.
Think of it! To go down to posterity is bad enough, any way;
but to go down as a "man who lived among the cannibals!"
When I speak of posterity, in reference to myself, I only mean
the babies who will probably be born in the moment immediately ensuing upon my giving up the ghost. I shall go down to
some of them, in all likelihood. "Typee" will be given to
them, perhaps, with their gingerbread. I have come to regard
this matter of Fame as the most transparent of all vanities.
I read Solomon more and more, and every time see deeper and
deeper and unspeakable meanings in him.[6] I did not think of
Fame, a year ago, as I do now. My development has been all
within a few years past. I am like one of those seeds taken out
of the Egyptian Pyramids, which, after being three thousand
years a seed and nothing but a seed, being planted in English
soil, it developed itself, grew to greenness, and then fell to
mould.[7] So I. Until I was twenty-five, I had no development at

all. From my twenty-fifth year I date my life. Three weeks
have scarcely passed, at any time between then and now, that
I have not unfolded within myself. But I feel that I am now
come to the inmost leaf of the bulb, and that shortly the
flower must fall to the mould. It seems to me now that Solomon was the truest man who ever spoke, and yet that he a
little *managed* the truth with a view to popular conservatism;
or else there have been many corruptions and interpolations
of the text—In reading some of Goethe's sayings, so worshipped by his votaries, I came across this, *"Live in the all."*[8] That
is to say, your separate identity is but a wretched one—
good; but get out of yourself, spread and expand yourself, and
bring to yourself the tinglings of life that are felt in the
flowers and the woods, that are felt in the planets Saturn and
Venus, and the Fixed Stars. What nonsense! Here is a fellow
with a raging toothache. "My dear boy," Goethe says to him,
"you are sorely afflicted with that tooth; but you must *live*
in the all, and then you will be happy!" As with all great
genius, there is an immense deal of flummery in Goethe, and
in proportion to my own contact with him, a monstrous deal
of it in me.

H. Melville.

P.S. "Amen!" saith Hawthorne.

N.B. This "all" feeling, though, there is some truth in.
You must often have felt it, lying on the grass on a warm
summer's day. Your legs seem to send out shoots into the
earth. Your hair feels like leaves upon your head. This is the
all feeling. But what plays the mischief with the truth is that
men will insist upon the universal application of a temporary
feeling or opinion.

P.S. You must not fail to admire my discretion in paying the postage on this letter.

Notes

1   Melville seems to have had in mind the quality pointed out in Menzel's
criticism of Schiller as quoted by Longfellow in *The Poets and Poetry of
Europe* (Philadelphia, 1845), p. 308: "We turn now to the second secret of
the beauty belonging to Schiller's ideal characters. This is their nobleness,

—their honorableness. His heroes and heroines never discredit the pride and dignity which announce a loftier nature; and all their outward acts bear the stamp of magnanimity and inborn nobleness. Its perfect opposite is the vulgar character, and that conventional spirit which serves for a bridle and leading-strings to the vulgar nature." "Elevation of mind" was called typical of Schiller's characters in "Aeschylus, Shakespeare, and Schiller," *Blackwood's Edinburgh Magazine, 32* (June, 1851), p. 651.

2 Melville may have meant any one of a number of members of the English Howard family, like Charles, the commander-in-chief of the fleet that destroyed the Spanish Armada, or Henry, collaborator with Wyatt and others in the songs and sonnets that achieved fame when published as *Tottel's Miscellany.* This family, which held the earldoms of Surrey, Effingham, and Carlisle, was a symbol of the English aristocracy.

3 Julian Hawthorne prints "revere the test of my Lord Shaftesbury." Shaftesbury maintained that one test of truth was its power to survive ridicule. "Truth," he wrote in "An Essay on the Freedom of Wit and Humour," " 'tis supposed, may bear *all* Lights: and *one* of those principal Lights or natural Mediums, by which Things are to be view'd, in order to a thorow Recognition, is *Ridicule* it-self, or that Manner of Proof by which we discern whatever is liable to just Raillery in any Subject. So much, at least, is allow'd by All, who at any time appeal to this *Criterion.* The gravest Gentlemen, even in the gravest Subjects, are suppos'd to acknowledge this: and can have no Right, 'tis thought, to deny others the Freedom of this Appeal; whilst they are free to censure like other Men, and in their gravest Arguments make no scruple to ask, *Is it not ridiculous?" Characteristicks of Men, Manners, Opinions, Times* (6th ed., 1737), V. *1,* p. 161. He cites, too, the fact that Socrates' character and doctrines seemed only the more "solid and just" after they had "stood the Proof" of Aristophanes' ridicule (V. *1,* p. 31). But whereas Shaftesbury is saying that you can know a thing is true if it survives ridicule, Melville is saying that you can know a thing is true because it is considered ridiculous. Melville may have revered Shaftesbury's test, but here he is reversing it.

4 Hawthorne's story was reprinted in *Holden's Dollar Magazine* for May 1851.

5 Melville might have seen some such announcement as early as 10 May in the *Literary World,* when the "Publisher's Circular," an editor's column, noted that "Ticknor, Reed & Fields have in Press . . . [a] New Volume of Stories by Hawthorne" and "a new volume by Hawthorne." A Ticknor, Reed and Fields advertisement containing these two items ran from 17 May to 9 August.

6 See *Moby Dick:* "The truest of all men was the Man of Sorrows, and the truest of all books is Solomon's, and Ecclesiastes is the fine hammered steel of woe. 'All is vanity.' ·ALL. This wilful world hath not got hold of un-christian Solomon's wisdom yet." (Mansfield–Vincent, 42).

7 At about this time, G. P. R. James carried on an experiment at Stockbridge south of Pittsfield of planting some Egyptian wheat seed taken from the inside of a mummy case. His son, Charles Leigh James describes the planting, saw it come up, and observed that "it did not seed 'worth a continental.' " See S. M. Ellis, *The Solitary Horseman, or the Life and Adventures of G. P. R. James,* as cited in *American Notes and Queries,* 7 (December, 1947), p. 41.

8 Melville's exact source remains to be discovered. The idea is general in

Goethe; the particular thought is doubtless a translation of a phrase in stanza four of "Generalbeichte:"

> Willst du Absolution
> Deinen Treuen geben,
> Wollen wir nach deinem Wink
> Unablässlich streben,
> Uns von Halben zu entwohnen
> Und im Ganzen, Guten, Schönen
> Resolut zu leben,

Carlyle, in whom Melville was well read, translates it "To live . . . in the Whole. . . ."—"Death of Goethe," *Critical and Miscellaneous Essays* (Boston, 1839), V. *3*, p. 205, and John S. Dwight renders it ". . . living." "In the Whole . . ."—George Ripley, ed., *Specimens of Foreign Standard Literature*, Vol. *3* . . . *Select Minor Poems from the German of Goethe and Schiller* (Boston, 1839), p. 48. One of Ripley's notes on Goethe may have helped give currency to the idea Melville was lampooning: "Total occupation of himself, heart and soul, in the subject nearest him—living *in* it, and identifying himself with it for the time— left no room for sick yearnings, made each little sphere a world, each moment an eternity. This is evidently what he meant by 'Living in the Whole,' by finding 'All in One, and One in All' " (ibid., p. 365).

Newton Arvin

⌒ᴡᴄ⌒

from *Herman Melville: A Critical Biography*□

To speak of the structure and the texture of *Moby Dick* is to embark upon a series of paradoxes that are soberly truthful and precise. Few books of its dimensions have owed so much to books that have preceded them, and few have owed so little; not many imaginative works have so strong and strict a unity, and not many are composed of such various and even discordant materials; few great novels have been comparably concrete, factual, and prosaic, and few of course have been so large and comprehensive in their generality, so poetic both in their surface fabric and in their central nature. In form alone *Moby Dick* is unique in its period, and that too in a sense more special than the sense in which every fully achieved work of literature is unique. Such a book could only have been written by an American, and an American of Melville's generation, working as he did in a kind of isolation from the central current of European writing in his time—an isolation quite consistent with his keeping abreast of it intellectually—and, while losing something in consequence, gaining something indispensable he could not otherwise have had.

Given his kind of creative power, Melville was wholly fortunate in his literary derivations and development. As we have seen, his springboard had never been the English or

□ From *Herman Melville* by Newton Arvin. Published by William Sloane Associates, Inc. Reprinted by permission of William Morrow and Company, Inc. Copyright © 1950 by William Sloane Associates, Inc.

European novel, not at any rate in its great characteristic
mode, the mode of the social novel, the novel of manners, the
novel of "real life." He belonged to a society that was in some
of its aspects too archaic to find a natural place for forms so
advanced as these, and his own origins, as if he belonged to
the Bronze Age or at least to the Age of Migrations, were
partly in oral story-telling, the story-telling of sailors and
travelers, and partly in forms that were either subliterary or
at the best on a modestly and hesitantly literary level. He had
begun as a writer of reportorial travel books, books that were
simply further examples of the "journal" or "narrative," and
in a certain sense he continued to be such a writer in *Moby
Dick*. It is wholly natural that Owen Chase's *Narrative*
should have been so vital to him, and that one pole of *Moby
Dick* should be constituted by the informative chapters on
whales and whaling. Melville's need as an artist was to take
the small, prosy, and terribly circumscribed form he had inherited, and somehow make it a vehicle capable of bearing a
great imaginative weight, of expressing a great visionary
theme. His problem was to find the bridge between J. Ross
Browne and Camoëns. He had quite failed to find it in *Mardi*;
he had run away from his true matter in pursuit of an allegorical will-o'-the-wisp, and the result had been fiasco. A
better wisdom had come to him in consequence; a better sense
of his own right path. His own right path was, as Emerson
would say, to "ask the fact for the form": to remain faithful to
his own crass, coarse, unideal, and yet grandiose material—
the life of American whalers—and to make of its unpromising
images his symbols, of its hardly malleable substance his myth.

It is what he does in *Moby Dick*. There is no question
here of chimerical priests and maidens, of symbolic blooms
and allegorical isles and Spenserian bowers; no question of
symbols wilfully imposed upon the meaning from without; no
question of what Melville himself now calls "a hideous and
intolerable allegory." In their stead one finds a fable almost
bare in its simplicity and, on the surface, journalistic in its
realism; the fable of a whaling vessel that sets out from
Nantucket and, like some actual whaling vessels, comes to a
disastrous end on the cruising-grounds near the Line. This

tale is launched in pages so homely in their substance, despite
their intensity of expression, that its earliest readers might
almost have doubted whether they had to do with a "novel"
or only with another and rather more dashing "narrative." It
comes to a close in pages in which we are still encountering
men like the bereaved Captain Gardiner and vessels like the
Rachel of Nantucket. The skipper and the mates of the
Pequod hail from Nantucket or the Cape or the Vineyard; all
the characters, including the pagan harpooneers, and even
perhaps the Parsees, are such men as might have been found,
though some of them rarely, on an actual whaler of the
'forties. In their company we sail over well-known whaling
routes, past familiar capes and headlands, giving chase not to
fabulous monsters but to Sperm Whales and Right Whales of
the sort that men had taken by the thousands, and having
glimpses as we do so of other creatures—sharks, squid, swordfish, seahawks—such as Owen and Cuvier had classified. In
short, with one or two great exceptions, the substance of
Moby Dick is as faithful to sober fact as that of Owen Chase's
or Ross Browne's book; if the impress on the imagination is
that of a high poetic form it is not because the poetry is
"allegorically" imposed on the stuff, but because the stuff is
allowed to render up its own poetic essences.

It does so partly because the organizing structure of the
fable—the Voyage, with its clear beginning and its predestined
catastrophe—is at once so firm and simple and so large and
free in its elasticity: like the structure of the *Odyssey* or the
Lusiads, it is both strict and pliable. It is a fable, moreover,
which, though it took shape in the most natural way out of a
set of dense facts and tough, unromantic conditions, could
nevertheless be made concrete and dramatic through a group
of basic, primary symbols (the sea, the quest, the great "fish,"
the ship, the watery tomb) and of incidental or secondary
symbols (the sword-mat, the monkey-rope, the sharks, and
others) that are both immediate and primordial, both local
and archetypal, both journalistic and mythopoeic. They are,
moreover, at the same time wonderfully various and powerfully interrelated, so that the balance, as Coleridge would say,
between "sameness" and "difference" is all but perfect. In

any composition less completely integrated there might seem to be a hopeless incongruity between Ahab's pipe and the mystic Spirit-Spout, as between the jolly, unimaginative Stubb and the satanic Fedallah: in the setting of *Moby Dick* they are no more incongruous than, in the *Odyssey*, the swine of Eumaeus and the magic veil that Ino bestows on Odysseus.

Such analogies are inescapable because, after every necessary thing has been said about Melville's homely and prosaic derivations, in the bookish sense, one has to go on to say that the design and the texture of *Moby Dick*, both of them so unlike those of the classical novel of the age, abound in reminiscences of forms that are somewhat, or even very, remote from the nineteenth century. There is no doubt that this is in part the result of a conscious and artful process. There is no doubt that Melville deliberately undertook to intensify, to elevate the narration of his tale—to express the strangeness and the grandeur that were latent in it—by resorting, at one point or another, to traditional styles that had no association in anyone's mind with the Novel. The most evident examples of this, familiar to every reader of the book, are the stylistic devices that came to him from his reading of Shakespeare and other Elizabethan playwrights. Everyone is struck at once, of course, by the stage directions that accompany some of the chapters (*"Enter Ahab: Then all"*); by the soliloquies that Ahab or Stubb or Starbuck, like Macbeth or Timon, delivers; by the chapters indeed (*"Midnight, Forecastle"* or *"The Deck"*), which are literally in theatrical form or in a form but one degree removed from it.

Some of these passages, just in themselves, are far from being very successful in execution; Melville, one feels, would have written badly for the stage, whenever he had lived. His imagination was profoundly nondramatic. Yet even so, and however oddly, the book as a whole gains something vital from these chapters, including the weaker ones, as other books have been strengthened by their imperfections. It gains as a musical composition does by shifts of rhythm and modulations of key: the total structure is by so much the more various, complex, and irregular as a result, and the threatening monotony of movement, in this as in other ways, is fore-stalled. Moreover, the peculiar immediacy that the dramatic style always produces is achieved, especially in such tense chapters as "Ahab and the Carpenter" and "The Deck to-wards the End of the First Night Watch."

This is so true, and the verbal echoes of Shakespeare are sometimes so striking, that certain writers have argued that the book has a structural rise and fall like that of Eliza-bethan tragedy, and a movement from scene to scene that ends by producing the five familiar "acts"; a movement that is marked thus by the great scene on the quarter-deck, by the meeting with the *Jeroboam*, the meeting with the *Samuel Enderby*, the "fourth-act" climax of "The Candles," and lastly the catastrophe itself. Scenes such as these are certainly among the moments of highest tension in *Moby Dick*, but they are dramatic only in a loose and metaphorical sense, as the scene of Dido's suicide in the *Aeneid* might be said to be dramatic; and the fact is that the structure of the book has only a superficial analogy with that of tragedy or of drama in general. The vital character of dramatic structure, as one need hardly say, is concentration; the vital character of this book's structure is expansiveness. A tragedy, in form, is ideally close, swift, and undivertible; *Moby Dick*, on the contrary, though in its own sense firm and unwasteful, is structurally open, loose, slow-paced, and ample. There are certainly tragedies that look in this direction—*Lear* and *Antony* do, and they made a great impression on Melville—but such tragedies, like some other Elizabethan plays, strain beyond the limits of that form.

If one must look for analogies that will do a little to express the effect *Moby Dick* has on us in form—and they can do no more than that at the very most—it is not to tragedy that one should turn but to heroic poetry, to the epic. And this for reasons that are not narrowly literary. The kind of life Mel-ville was raising to the fictive level in this book was not the kind that has ever furnished, or could furnish, the stuff of plays or novels; it was a life in some of its aspects reminiscent of that led by the Achaean peoples in the days of their folk-wanderings or by the Germanic peoples in the days of theirs;

the whole of American life at the time, with all its differences, was something like that. European migrants, from the sixteenth to the nineteenth century, had reverted in the Western world to a state of things that had much in common with an archaic, an "heroic" age. Here there had reappeared, as in the Bronze Age and the Age of the Vikings, a population of brawlers, boasters, and bullies, as well as of proud, touchy, self-reliant, heroic individuals; and among them there had reappeared a habit of story-telling, of recitation and legendary reminiscence, shot through with a love of the grandiose and never wholly free from an undercurrent of superstitious fear—fear of the hostile and mysterious powers in savage nature, in forests and seas, in wild animals. The life of trappers, hunters, and frontiersmen was of that sort, and the life of whalers equally so. This is part of the complex truth to which Fedallah points when he riddlingly says that the wood of Ahab's hearse "must be grown in America."

If any aspect of this world, and specifically that of whale-hunting, was to be embodied in a mighty book that would really render its essential character, such a book would inevitably take on some of the qualities of epic poetry. And so *Moby Dick* does, both in structure and in more intangible ways. In sober fact, of course, the book is not a heroic poem but a work of its own age; yet it genuinely helps to define the formal quality of *Moby Dick* if one says that what he feels in its spacious narrative movement is not unlike what he feels in the narrative movement of the *Iliad*, of the *Odyssey*, and even of the more "literary" poems that derive from them, the *Aeneid*, the *Lusiads*. It is quite true that there is no curving back upon itself of the narrative line as there is in all but the first of these; the line in *Moby Dick* is straight ahead and undeviating, like that in the *Iliad* or in *Beowulf*. Yet the movement forward, as in all such poems, is not from climax to climax in the sharp dramatic sense, but from one wave-crest to another, from one chase or encounter to another, from cruising-ground to cruising-ground, from departure to arrival, from storm to calm. It is in short an undulant, not a peaked and valleyed line, and as a result the book has an epic-like pattern that, at least in quality, cannot be mistaken; it suggests the threefold design of the *Iliad*, or the sixfold design of the *Odyssey*, or the fivefold design of the *Lusiads*.

Exactly what the pattern is no two readers would probably agree, and in a certain sense it does not matter: what matters is the stylistic principle itself. Some readers, however, would doubtless concur in feeling that the narrative of *Moby Dick* is conducted through a series of four basic "movements," one of which is disproportionate to the others in mere bulk. All the introductory chapters, up to the sailing of the *Pequod* on that bleak Christmas day, form a clear and defined movement, like that of the first four books of the *Odyssey*. A second unmistakable wave is the one that comes to its crest in the scene on the quarter-deck, when Ahab nails the doubloon to the mainmast. The whole central portion of the book, from the sunset scene in Ahab's cabin to the encounter with the bitterly misnamed craft, the *Delight*, forms a third movement; in this there are surely no breaks so marked as the first two. The fourth movement naturally begins with "The Symphony" and comes to a close with the catastrophe itself—the Epilogue forming a kind of musical coda, not wholly unlike the burning of Hector's body on the funeral pyre in the last few lines of the *Iliad*. It is certainly true that within the long third section one is conscious of other crests and troughs; the section occupies more than two-thirds of the whole book, and of course it is not written along an unvarying line. The crests are simply less high and the troughs less deep than the others; but they are there, and they are not very disproportionate among themselves. To one reader's feeling there are six of these lesser crests: the "first lowering" for a whale, the encounter with the *Jeroboam*, the passage of the *Pequod* through the Straits of Sunda and its emergence upon the Java Sea ("The Grand Armada"), the typhoon and the corposants, and finally the meeting with the *Delight*.

Meanwhile the principle of variety is observed and its effect achieved not in pitch only but in pace and key also. For surely what the descriptive and expository chapters on whales and whaling do is partly to slow down the tempo and partly to provide for a change of key. They suggest the passages of deliberate quietness and even dullness in all very large poems, and they are placed and spaced with beautiful compositional tact—the first of them ("The Advocate") appearing at the very opening of the second main movement, and the last of them ("Does the Whale Diminish?"), very near the opening of the fifth section of the third movement. The "intense *Pequod*" is now sailing northward through the China Sea; it is about to head eastward and sail through the Bashee Channel into the open Pacific; it is drawing nearer and nearer to its doom, and from this point on there can be no retardation of the narrative speed and no distraction from the spectacle of the fated cruise.

In the strictest sense Melville had no great model for the introduction of these magnificent non-narrative chapters; they sprang from his own creative feeling for composition and chiaroscuro; their only model was his own practice in his earlier books, especially *White Jacket*. In its formal wholeness indeed, as one has to repeat, *Moby Dick* is unprecedented and unique. No great poet has ever, before or since, brought zoology and poetry together in an even comparable way. Other great poets, however, have brought poetry together with the tangible facts of armament or equipment in a manner that *Moby Dick* does suggest, and again not for merely literary reasons. It is not Bronze Age warfare or hunting that is Melville's subject, as it was Homer's and the others', but it is an industry that had some of the aspects of warfare and certainly of the archaic hunt; and in the loving manner in which Melville lingers over his imagery of lances, harpoons, and cutting-spades, of whaleboats, whale-lines, and blubber-hooks, of cutting-in and trying-out and stowing-down, there is a shade of feeling that carries one far out of the nineteenth century and recalls again the epic minstrel and the way he lingered over his imagery of javelin and sword, shield and breastplate, chariot and ship, and such practical activities as sailing, hunting, plowing, and the performance of obligatory rites.

Of all this Melville cannot have been wholly unaware, and in the chapters in which the *Pequod* buffets its way around the Cape of Good Hope, it is hard not to feel that there is a conscious recollection of Gama and his men, in the

Lusiads, heading eastward around the same howling Cape.
From time to time, moreover, Melville launches upon the kind
of sustained and formal similes that everyone recognizes as
Homeric or Virgilian, and that have in *Moby Dick*, as in the
Iliad or the *Aeneid*, an effect either of aggrandizement or of
peaceful relief. The homeliest and most unexpected of these is
the simile in which the whaleman's trained capacity to predict the route of the whale he is chasing is compared to the
ordinary citizen's capacity to predict the arrival of a train on
"the mighty iron Leviathan of the modern railway." More
pastoral and more traditional than this is the familiar passage
that brings together the picture of a school of Right Whales,
sluggishly moving through a field of brit, and that of "morning mowers" slowly advancing their scythes through the wet
grass of a marshy meadow. And the noblest, surely, of Melville's "epic" similes is that in which, in the chapter on
"The Grand Armada," the great school of Sperm Whales
hurrying through the Straits of Sunda is likened to an army
accelerating its march through an unfriendly defile in the
mountains, "all eagerness to place that perilous passage in
their rear."

The imagery of armies and of warfare in fact is recurrent in *Moby Dick*, and for evident reasons. It keeps us
from forgetting that butchery and carnage are close to the
center of the theme, yet it lifts even them to a level on which
the imagination can accept them. In general, however, the
metaphors—and the allusions that have a quasi-metaphorical
role—point in two opposite directions and, as a result, en-
hance the duality of tone that is so profound an aspect of the
book's character. There are the metaphors that, like some of
the similes, ennoble and aggrandize the texture of the narrative; and there are those that, like others, diminish or subdue
it or even make it humorous. On the one hand, we are repeatedly put in mind of royalty or imperial dignity, of Czars
and Sultans, or of the great figures of legend or history
(Perseus, Alexander, the Crusaders, Tamerlane) or of Biblical
story. Some of the most profound intuitions, moreover, are
embodied in metaphors of architectural or monumental
grandeur (the ruins of Lima, "the great dome of St. Peter's,"

the halls of Thermes below the Hôtel de Cluny) or in metaphors of naturalistic power and beauty ("the unabated
Hudson," "one insular Tahiti," "the flame Baltic of Hell,"
or, perhaps most memorably of all, the meadows under the
slopes of the Andes). All this is true, but it is also true that
there is a constant contrapuntal play of shrunken or diminish-
ing metaphors, and that these have a decidedly Shakespearean,
or at any rate Elizabethan, rather than an epic quality, as
when Ahab hoots at the gods as mere pugilists and cricket-
players, or "Death himself" is likened to a postboy, or a
Sperm Whale and his spout are compared to a portly burgher
smoking his pipe of a warm afternoon. Close to these in feeling
are the images that come from nineteenth-century industry or
technology, the images of drilling and blasting, of mining, of
cogged wheels and mechanical looms and magnetic wires,
and even the "Leyden jar" of Ahab's "own magnetic life."

These latter metaphors are not without a suggestion of
some of the metaphysical poets or of twentieth-century poetry;
at other points in *Moby Dick* one is reminded, by the constant
recurrence of imagery from animal life, of *Lear* and *Timon* on
the one hand and on the other of Melville's contemporaries,
the naturalistic novelists, Balzac and Zola. The Sperm Whale
of course is one of the great primary symbols, and actual
creatures of the sea, squid and sharks and swordfish, appear
not as metaphors but as secondary symbols. In addition to
these, however, which are given by the very subject, almost
the whole range of animal life, wild and domestic, seems to
have been scoured for images. Ahab himself is likened to a
tiger, to a grizzly bear, to a wolf, a moose, a sealion, a walrus;
and Pip even calls him "that anaconda of an old man." There
is a steady, stately parade of elephants throughout the book;
these greatest of land beasts are deliberately evoked as
attendants, so to say, upon the greatest animal of the sea. The
pagan harpooneers and the Parsees are sometimes, like Ahab,
compared to tigers, and in the famous chapter on "The
Whiteness of the Whale" everyone will remember the polar
bear, the unspottedly white albatross, the sacred White Dog
of the Iroquois, and the spectral White Steed of the Prairies.
And indeed, as these allusions suggest, there is both a likeness

and a difference between Melville's animal metaphors and
either Shakespeare's or Balzac's. It is true that, like those
writers (in their wholly dissimilar ways), he sometimes intends to suggest an analogy between the ferocity or the bestiality of men and that of beasts; but Melville's intention is
more ambiguous than theirs, and it is quite as much for the
sake of imparting to his theme a certain majesty, a certain
grandeur, a certain strangeness of beauty, that he introduces
his often splendid animals and birds.

Certainly nothing could be more eloquent of the incan-
descence out of which *Moby Dick* was written than the variety
and the idiosyncrasy of the metaphors with which it is
animated; nothing, perhaps, except the equally extraordinary
resourcefulness and inventiveness of Melville's language. For
this there is nothing in his earlier books to prepare us fully,
though there are hints of it in the best passages of *Redburn*
and *White-Jacket*. In general, however, the diction in those
books is the current diction of good prose in Melville's time;
it has a hardly definable personal quality. Now, in *Moby Dick*,
it takes on abruptly an idiosyncrasy of the most unmistakable
sort; it is a question now of Melvillean language in the same
intense and special sense in which one speaks of Virgilian
language, or Shakespearean, or Miltonic. It is a creation,
verbally speaking; a great artifice; a particular characterizing
idiom; without it the book would not exist. One of its hall-
marks, as in all the other cases, is the "signature" furnished
by favorite words; the favorite nouns, adjectives, and adverbs that end by coloring the fabric of the book as strongly
as the use of a favorite range of hues affects the manner of a
painter. Like Virgil, with his *pius*, *ingens*, and *immanis*, or
Shakespeare, with his *rich*, *brave*, *sweet*, and *gentle*, Melville
has his own verbal palette: it is chiefly made up of the words
wild, *wildly*, and *wildness*, *moody* and *moodiness* ("moody
Ahab," especially), *mystic* and *mystical*, *subtle*, *subtly*, and
subtlety, *wondrous* ("most wondrous philosophies"), *nameless*,
intense, and *malicious* ("malicious agencies"). One has only
to cite these words to suggest how intimately expressive they
are of *Moby Dick's* dark, violent, and enigmatic theme.

It is a matter, however, not only of characteristic

words, familiar in themselves to readers of Melville's time and
ours, but of characteristic *kinds* of words and of words that
are again and again his own coinages or at least of a great
rarity. One feels, as in all such cases, that the limits of even
the English vocabulary have suddenly begun to seem too
strict, too penurious, and that the difficult things Melville has
to say can be adequately said only by reaching beyond those
limits. He does so, perhaps most strikingly, in the constant use
he makes of verbal nouns, mostly in the plural, and usually
his own inventions; such nouns, for example, as *regardings*,
allurings, *intercedings*, *wanings*, *coincidings*, and the nouns
one gets in the strangely connotative phrases, "nameless
invisible *domineerings*" and "such lovely *leewardings*."
Almost unanalyzable is the effect these have of uniting the
dynamism of the verb and the stasis of the substantive. And so
of the other abstract nouns Melville loves to use in the plural
—*defilements*, *tranquillities*, *unfulfilments*, "sorrow's *tech-*
nicals," and "unshored, harborless *immensities*." In their
very unliteral pluralized form these characteristic abstractions become an elusive kind of inverted metaphor. Very
different and less metaphorical, but almost as special in their
effect, are the nouns Melville habitually constructs with the
suffix -*ness* (*localness*, *landlessness*, *aborigalness*, *inter-*
indebtedness) or -*ism* (*footmanism*, *sultanism*, *Titanism*, and
the Carlylean *vultureism*).

Quite as abundant as the unfamiliar nouns are the
unfamiliar adjectives and adverbs that do so much to give the
style of *Moby Dick* its particular unconformable character.
And again, just as verbal nouns are Melville's most characteristic substantives, so adjectives and adverbs based on
present or past participles are his most characteristic modifiers; participial adjectives such as *officered*, *cymballed*,
omnitooled, *unensanguined*, *uncatastrophied*, "last, *cindered*
apple" and "*stumped* and *paupered* arm," and participial
adverbs such as *invokingly*, *intermixingly*, *gallopingly*,
suckingly, *postponedly*, and *uninterpenetratingly*. These however are only the most characteristic of his modifiers; a complete list would have to include such rarities as *unsmoothable*,
familyless, *spermy*, *flavorish*, *leviathanic*, and *unexempt*

(which might have echoed in his mind from *Comus*) or (for
adverbs) *diagonically, Spanishly, Venetianly,* and *sultanically.*
And even beyond these one would have to glance at the sometimes odd, sometimes magnificent compounds, almost always
adjectival, that give so vibrating a life to the pages of the book
"a *valor-ruined* man," "the *message-carrying* air," "the
circus-running sun," "*teeth-tired* sharks," and "*god-bullied*
hull." There is an energy of verbal inventiveness here that it
is hardly too much to call Aeschylean or Shakesperean.

It does not, curiously, express itself in the formation of
unfamiliar verbs so typically as in these other ways; this is a
kind of anomaly in a style of which the capacity to evoke
movement, action, and all kinds of kinaesthetic sensations is
so great. Melville, indeed, uses familiar or not unfamiliar
verbs, again and again, with beautiful force; yet the impulsion
of some of his finest passages of vehement action depends only
partly on these; it depends at least as much on other parts of
speech. . . .

. . . .

There is a passage in *Moby Dick* in which Melville
deprecates the possibility that some ignorant landsmen will
scout at the White Whale as "a monstrous fable, or still worse
and more detestable, a hideous and intolerable allegory." It
is quite plain that the remark has two edges and is meant to be
ironical; it is plain, too, however, that Melville was in fact
earnestly avoiding what we should now call allegory, in the
sense in which we would use it of *Mardi.* The word "symbolism," in its literary bearing, had not come into use at the
time *Moby Dick* was written; it was nearly twenty years before it did so, although Emerson had already dwelt with
extraordinary eloquence and subtlety, in the essay on "The
Poet," on the role of symbols both in experience and in art. If
Melville had had the word, no doubt he would have used it in
his own thinking about the book; as it was, he was limited to
the older and less suitable one. As almost always happens
in literary history, the *thing* had come before the term for it;
and so, when Melville answered an appreciative letter of

Sophia Hawthorne's, a month or two after *Moby Dick* had appeared, he expressed himself in this manner: "I had some vague idea while writing it, that the whole book was susceptible of an allegorical construction, and also that *parts* of it were—but the speciality of many of the particular subordinate allegories, were first revealed to me, after reading Mr. Hawthorne's letter which, without citing any particular examples, yet intimated the part-and-parcel allegoricalness of the whole."

There is a little touch here of the serious artist's particular sort of frivolity and disingenuousness, as one is pleased to find; it was the right tone for Melville to take, now that his book was well behind him. But of course he had had much more than a "vague idea" while writing *Moby Dick* that his fable, his images, his personages were the bearers of complex and unstatable meanings that no prosaic apprehension of them, even one that would be appropriate to other literary forms, could account for. Emerson's remarks had been highly symptomatic, as some of Carlyle's had also been, and the poetic mind in America was already symbolist in everything but the program, as Poe's and Hawthorne's work had shown and as Whitman's was soon to show. Unlike these others as he was in the special grain of his mind, Melville was at one with them in the conviction they all shared, the conviction that "objects gross" are only provisionally real, and that the eventual reality is the "unseen soul" they embody. In that familiar sense they were all "transcendentalists": their assumptions were those of romantic idealism, and their literary practice was in entire keeping with these. Ahab of course is only putting it all in his own manner when he speaks to Starbuck in a familiar passage thus: "All visible objects, man, are but as pasteboard masks. But in each event—in the living act, the undoubted deed—there, some unknown but still reasoning thing puts forth the mouldings of its features from behind the unreasoning mask." Or later, apostrophically: "O Nature, and O soul of man! how far beyond all utterance are your linked analogies! not the smallest atom stirs or lives on matter, but has its cunning duplicate in mind."

Such is Melville's personal version of the doctrine of

Correspondences that lay below so much romantic and symbolist writing, as a similar doctrine of analogies lay below
medieval allegory. That he entertained some such view has
long been a familiar fact, and there is nothing remarkable now
in saying that *Moby Dick*, in a sense that does not quite hold
for any other American book, is a symbolist prose romance. Its
leading images are symbols in the strict sense, not allegorical
devices or emblems; symbols in the sense that their primal
origins are in the unconscious, however consciously they have
been organized and controlled; that on this account they
transcend the personal and local and become archetypal in
their range and depth; that they are inexplicit, polysemantic,
and never quite exhaustible in their meanings. "The profounder emanations of the human mind," said Melville himself a little later in *Pierre*, "never unravel their own intricacies"; and he cannot have been unaware that his own book
would present difficulties to the unraveler. Many of these have
long since been disentangled, yet something always remains
to be added, however slight, to any cluster of interpretations,
however rich. It may be useful here to speak of *Moby Dick* and
its meanings by adopting our own version of Dante's "four-
fold interpretation" (which is of course inapplicable) and
suggesting that the intricacies of the book may be reduced to
four planes of significance; that these may be called the literal,
the oneiric or psychological, the moral and the mythic.

Of the first of these, the literal, not much (by definition)
demands saying. What is chiefly important is not to allow
ourselves to forget that it is there, just as it is in Dante's poem,
and that the literary critic, like the Biblical exegete, must
remember Pascal's salutary warning against two errors:
"1. To take everything literally. 2. To take everything spiritually." Taking everything in *Moby Dick* "spiritually" means
not taking it spiritually enough; the intangible meanings of
the romance would not be so wide-reaching and deep-plunging
as they are if they were not embodied in a fable of which
virtually every detail has a hard, concrete, prosaic, and even
naturalistic substantiality. There are some exceptions to this,
as the principle of contrast demands; the Spirit-Spout is one
of them, and the actual make-up of the crew is another.

Miscellaneous as the real crews of the whalers were, we are not intended to suppose literal-mindedly that any one of them ever included as harpooneers a Gayhead Indian, a Negro, and a Polynesian, as well as a boat's crew of Parsees, and along with them a Maltese sailor, a Tahitian sailor, an Icelandic, a Chinese, a Danish sailor, and so on. Yet all these freedoms with realism are dilatations of fact, not pure fantasies; even the Spirit-Spout doubtless had its origin in the surely quite breath-taking sight, at sea, of a Sperm Whale's jetting spout beheld at some distance on a moonlight night. The mere *scaffolding* of *Moby Dick*, as hundreds of readers have felt, would remain firm and stable if there were no question of symbols whatever.

The literalness of the book has another facet, however, to which justice has not been done. It is the facet provided largely by the factual chapters about whales and whaling. The true purpose of these chapters is to provide the book with an even intenser literalness than it otherwise has, and this on a serious intellectual level. This literalness, not of course stylistically but in substance, is that of systematic and exact knowledge; it is the literalness of the natural and especially the biological sciences. It is all, or much of it, translated into imaginative or humorous terms, and Melville insists on having his joke by arguing that the whale is not a mammal but "*a spouting fish with a horizontal tail.*" Yet the motive behind these chapters remains a serious one. Transcendentalist though he was at the center of his mentality, Melville had too tough and too capacious a mind to fall willingly into mere vaporous and subjective idealism. He was a romantic idealist with a passion for actuality, for precise knowledge, for facts; he was an intuitionalist who wished, in his essential reliance on the nonrational and the superrational, not to fall a victim to mindlessness; not to forswear the sanctions of the intellect. "Undeniably," says Bardianna in *Mardi*, "reason was the first revelation; and so far as it tests all others, it has precedence over them . . . so far as it goes, for us, it is reliable."

A passage like this, one hurriedly notes, must be seen in the context of Melville's whole work; taken by itself it is misleading: the fact is of course that Melville was no simple-minded idolater of what Wordsworth had called "our meddling intellect." There was a painful division in his mind, as in the minds of many of his contemporaries, between his distrust of the discursive reason and his respect for it; he suffered deeply from the inner dissociations of his age. Yet his aspiration, like Thoreau's for example, was to triumph over them; to do justice both to "visible objects," masks as they are, and to the immaterial reality that, as he believed, lies behind them. It was an impossible task, so profoundly split, so dualized was the mind of his time, and his own as representative of it. But it was a task of which Melville intuitively felt the momentousness, and as a result *Moby Dick*, symbolist romance that it is, draws close at one pole to the bias of naturalism. The White Whale is a symbol, certainly, and even some of the details of his anatomy contribute to what he symbolizes; but their literal value is there all the while, and we must know how to give the proper, prosaic attention even to a half-humorous classification (the Folio Whale, the Octavo Whale, and so on), to the measurement of the whale's skeleton, to the facts about his blubber, his sense-organs, his spermaceti, and his flukes. We are in the company, and should recognize it, not only of Coleridge and Carlyle and Emerson but of Linnaeus and Cuvier.

We leave their company abruptly, however, when we move beyond the reading of *Moby Dick* as literal narrative and exposition, and begin to read it as what, on one plane, it is, an oneiric or dreamlike projection of Melville's unconscious wishes and obscure inward contests. *On one plane* the book is this, and on that plane only; for of course *Moby Dick* is not a dream but a work of imaginative art, and this means that it is the product of a complex creative process of which a great part has been conscious, deliberate, reflective: the formless spontaneity of an actual dream, along with much else, has been transcended. It shares with a dream, however, its sources in the unconscious, its dependence on irrational symbols, and its power to give expression to deep, instinctive, irrational fears and desires. How much of the sway it exercises over us depends on this!

·   ·   ·   ·

Deep as are the psychological meanings, and serious as are the moral meanings, of *Moby Dick*, they by no means exhaust between them the richness of its interest or the scope of its significance. In the end, as one reflects on the book, one is aware that one must reckon with the most comprehensive of all its qualities, the quality that can only be called mythic. Few words even in our time have been used more glibly than the word "myth"; it has ended by taking on some of the hollow sanctity of the mystic syllable Óm in the mouths of the unenlightened. When one uses it, however, in association with *Moby Dick*, it means something precise and indispensable; and it is used here in the sense of an imagined narrative in which the leading roles are played by divine or god-like personages, engaged in symbolic actions and amid symbolic objects; which embodies some form of the conflict between human wishes and nonhuman forces, and which has its roots in a philosophically serious desire to comprehend the meaning of nature and the destiny of man. The literary expression toward which myth in this sense typically moves is the epic or some closely comparable form.

If *Moby Dick* has a strongly mythic character, it is partly because the human setting out of which it emerged, as we have repeatedly seen, reproduced many of the conditions of a myth-making phase of culture. There was much in Melville's own experience too—his life among the Taipis and Tahitians, as well as much else—that, along with the bias of his own creative faculty, led straight in the mythic direction. There was a mingling in his nature, as in that of every greatly endowed poet, of the primitive and the highly civilized; of the naive and the literate, even the bookish; of the primitive capacity to "think" in symbols and the cultivated capacity to deal in abstractions. He was unique, moreover among American writers of his time in the particular quality of his intellectual and moral seriousness; unique in his troubled preoccupation with problems that Emerson and Thoreau simply passed by, and that Hawthorne was intellectually too incurious to consider deeply. Like a truly myth-making poet's, Melville's imagination was obsessed by the spectacle of a natural and human scene in which the instinctive need for order and meaning seems mainly to be confronted by meaning-lessness and disorder; in which the human will seems some-times to be sustained but oftener to be thwarted by the forces of physical nature, and even by agencies that lie behind it; in which goodness and evil, beneficence and destructiveness, light and darkness, seem bafflingly intermixed. In none of the great formulations that were available to him, neither in Calvinist Christianity nor in romantic optimism, could Melville discover a myth that for him was adequate to the lighting up of these obscurities.

Moby Dick is his endeavor to construct his own myth. The personages of the fable, ordinary as they begin by seem-ing, very soon take on the large outlines and the poetic typicality of figures in legend or edda. They are engaged, moreover, in an action that is profoundly archetypal—that is, in a voyage by sea that is also a hunt or a quest, and that reaches its culmination in an all but complete catastrophe. As they do so they move among primordial forces in which their destinies seem involved almost as if they were Greek or Norse or Polynesian demigods or heroes—forces such as the sea that is both the source of life and the extinction of it, the solid land that is both safety and peril, the spires of flame that must be defied but also worshipped, the wind that is sometimes "glorious and gracious" and sometimes tainted and cowardly, the sun "like a royal czar and king," and the moonlight or starlight that serves to irradiate the mystic Spirit Spout. So intense is the animation, so nearly personal is the vitality, of these elemental forces that hardly a step would be needed to transform them into actual deities. Melville himself indeed remarks that the Greeks gave the sea a deity of its own; he calls the northeast wind by its Greek name, Euroclydon, and Ahab defies the fire of the corposants in language that leaves no doubt of its mythic deification. Nowhere, however, is Melville's myth-making power at work in a more truly primordial sense than in the creation of the White Whale himself.

Here chiefly, in the aggrandizement of a huge and fear-some animal to deiform proportions, does Melville surpass all other poets of his century in the rejuvenation of myth. On this ground he is quite incomparable; no other writer of the century can be set beside him. He himself could not wholly have realized how deep a descent he was making into the quarry of the past by penetrating so far as he did into the region of animal existence. He had some sense of this, but it was a flickering one: Unavailable to him in his generation was the knowledge of primitive thought and belief that enables us now to see Moby Dick for the deeply primordial symbol he is. Only a man who had himself been a hunter of wild beasts —only a man who had been in at the kill of a tormented Sperm Whale—could have re-entered so far into the intense and complex feelings with which the primitive hunter regards the animals about him and especially his chief prey; into that lost, archaic mingling of fear and gratitude, of resentment and veneration, in which all the savage's emotions toward the animal are steeped, and which leads him again and again to endow it with an awful divinity. Of all this Melville had little or no "knowledge" but a penetrating intuition. The three pagan harpooneers on the *Pequod*, Queequeg, Tashtego, and Daggoo, have all seen Moby Dick before; when Ahab speaks for the first time of the White Whale to his crew, they and they alone are at once aware what creature it is that he means.

"Your true whale-hunter is as much a savage as an Iroquois," Melville himself says, and he adds: "I myself am a savage." Certainly in his half-fearful, half-worshipful attitude toward the Sperm Whale he was closer to the primitive than to the civilized mind; and he gives us his own clues to this when he identifies the Whale with the dragons of Perseus and St. George, or recalls that the Hindu god Vishnu was incarnate in a whale. Yet he probably did not know, literally, that for many primitive peoples—for peoples as remote from one another as the Annamese, the Tongans, and the Unalit Eskimos—the whale is, or once was, the object of a solemn cult, a sacred animal as truly as the cow or the bear was elsewhere. He probably had not heard that some of these peoples prepared themselves for a whale-hunt by fasting for days beforehand, by bathing themselves repeatedly, and by other rites; that some of them, after a whale's life had been taken, propitiated his ghost by holding a communal festival; and that others, when a dead whale was washed ashore, accorded it solemn burial and preserved its bones in a small pagoda near the sea.

Melville knew that whiteness in animals had often been a mark of special sanctity; he alludes to the sacred White Dog of the Iroquois and the White Elephant of Pegu; did he know, however, that the White Whale itself was so superstitiously regarded by the Eskimos of Bering Strait that a hunter who had helped to kill one was forbidden to do any work for four days thereafter, and that the shore where a dead White Whale had been beached was thenceforth tabu? It is of no real importance whether he knew of these things or not; in the contemplation of the great white monster and its mystic ways, he could rely upon a deeper and more primeval knowledge than any he could have acquired from Tylor or Frazer. His imagination ran before the anthropologists; he forefelt, as other poets have done, what the savants would later confirm.

He could rely, in all this, upon the aboriginal myth-making fancy, still strong in his own nature, for which birds and beasts were not simply "lower animals" but creatures somehow identifiable with the beneficent or the malignant potencies of all nature; the fancy that again and again transformed these creatures into gods—eagle-gods, bear-gods, fish-gods, and the like. Even among nineteenth-century whalers generally there may have survived, obscurely and dumbly, much more of this fearful and worshipful emotion than has ever been supposed, and Melville may be pointing to this when he makes Starbuck say of the heathen crew of the *Pequod* that the White Whale is their "demigorgon"— Demogorgon, as he should have said if he meant the mysterious infernal deity to whom Milton and Shelley allude, but he may well have been confusing Demogorgon with the creative Demiurgos of Platonic or Gnostic thought. In any case, there can be no doubt about Moby Dick's deific attributes. There is something godlike in the mere crude fact of his physical magnitude, his "majestic bulk." Physically he is the greatest of all animals that have ever existed, and in proportion to his vast magnitude is his potency, the potency that

exhibits itself in his terrific speed, in the dreadful strength of
his great jaw, and in the "Titanism of power" with which he
wields his massive tail. He is not only physically huge and
appallingly powerful, but—as one realizes when one reflects
on the problem of his spout—there is in his whole being a
"great inherent dignity and sublimity." Moby Dick is godlike
in his beauty too, and when, after so many months of search,
we at last sight him, gliding swiftly and mildly through the
sea, he seems more beautiful even than Zeus himself swimming
in the shape of a white bull, with Europa, toward his nuptial
bower in Crete: "not Jove, not that great majesty Supreme!
did surpass the glorified White Whale as he so divinely swam."

Beautiful he may be, yet to the whalemen who have
encountered him, or even to those who have only heard of such
encounters, there is something so terrible, so mysterious, in
the ferocity and the apparently intelligent malignity with
which Moby Dick has rounded upon his attackers, that they
have ended by refusing to believe that such a creature is fit
prey for mortal man. Some of them have persuaded themselves that he is actually ubiquitous; that he has been sighted
in opposite latitudes at the same instant of time; and not only
so, but that he is immortal, and that no lance forged of earthly
iron can ever destroy him.

Certainly the penalty for attacking him seems always
to have been death and destruction in some frightful form, yet
Moby Dick appears never to have sought these encounters
himself, and to have dealt out ruin only when provoked by
his pursuers. Demoniac as he can be when hunted and har-
pooned, he himself seems rather to evade than to seek these
meetings, and perhaps, as the commonsensical English ship-
surgeon, Dr. Bunger, suggests, what Ahab takes for the White
Whale's malice is only his awkwardness. In any case, if we
regard Moby Dick not as an individual but as representative
of a species, as an archetypal Sperm Whale, it is not mainly of
his malice that we are reminded but of his unintentional
beneficence. On occasion he may have been the apparently
conscious cause of much evil and suffering, but certainly he is
also the source of great and even priceless goods. For many
men, both primitive and civilized, his flesh and his spermaceti

have served as food. When ambergris is found in his bowels, ignoble as that derivation is, the Sperm Whale becomes the bestower upon mankind of the precious sweetness of perfume. His chief gift to them, however, has not been sweetness but light: it is of spermaceti that the best candles are made, and with sperm-oil that the best lamps are lighted. Illumination, not darkness and terror, is Moby Dick's great boon to humanity. And when we meditate on this fact, we are less sure than we would otherwise be that the mad Gabriel of the *Jeroboam* is as mad as he seems when he warns Captain Mayhew that Moby Dick is the Shaker God incarnated.

However this may be, he is certainly not the God of orthodox or even of modernist Christianity. That is the meaning of his whiteness, of that "visible absence of color" which is at the same time "the concrete of all colors," and hence is the symbol of " a colorless, all-color of atheism from which we shrink." That beautiful and frightful whiteness appeals to our souls so powerfully because it may symbolize both the most spiritual of things, even the Christian Deity, and also the things most appalling to mankind. It cannot, and in Moby Dick it does not, reassuringly and finally symbolize the Christian God, transcendent and absolute, and, however mysterious in His workings, a God of absolute love and justice and truth. A cosmic scene lorded over by the White Whale is one from which the soul-freezing possibility of an ultimate atheism is never wholly absent, and of course it was terribly present to Melville's spirit when he wrote the book. Moby Dick's whiteness, however, may and does symbolize not only negation and denial but "all colors"; all positive goods, fulfillments, benefits. It is a symbol of profound and irreducible ambiguity, but that ambiguity has a pole of lightness as well as a pole of darkness.

The White Whale is a grandiose mythic presentation of what is godlike in the cosmos as this could be intuited by a painfully meditative and passionately honest poetic mind in the heart of the American nineteenth century. Moby Dick is an Animal God such as only the imagination of that century in the Western world could have conceived and projected; a god in Nature, not beyond it; an immanent god in some sense, not

a transcendent one; an emergent deity, not an Absolute; a
deity that embodies the physical vastness of the cosmos in
space and time as astronomy and geology have exhibited it;
a deity that represents not transcendent purpose and conscious design but *mana*; energy; power—the half-conscious,
half-unconscious power of blind, restless, perhaps purposeless,
but always overbearing and unconquerable force. There is
terror in such a conception, as indeed there is, on one side, in
the Calvinist conception of a transcendently powerful and
justly wrathful God; and Moby Dick owes something to the
deity of Calvin and Edwards. He is not that deity, however, if
only because nothing assures us that he is capable of loving
man as Calvin's God loved him despite his sinfulness; we
cannot imagine Moby Dick as conferring upon mankind the
ultimate gift of free and unmerited grace. Yet terrible though
Moby Dick is in his apparent and perhaps real indifference to
men, he is also sublime, sublime as the cosmos itself is, in its
unimaginable magnitude, its appalling beauty, and the de-
miurgic creativity of power that seems everywhere to be at
work and alive within it.

This is a nature myth such as only a nineteenth-
century imagination, obsessed with the spectacle of impersonal force and ceaseless physical change, could have created,
though Melville had unconsciously drawn, in creating it, on a
whole complex of thoughts that had come to him from reading,
or reading about, Job, the Stoics, the Gnostics and Mani-
cheans, Spinoza, and the men of science. It is a myth such as
other minds of the nineteenth century were groping toward,
and one can see dim analogies to Moby Dick in Schopenhauer's
blind irrational Will, in Herbert Spencer's Unknowable, and
still more truly in Hardy's Immanent Will or Urging Imma-
nence. In the traditional Christian God, the omniscient and
loving Father, Melville had now lost all confident belief; *that*
God survived in his mind, when he wrote *Moby Dick*, only as
a symbol of human fraternity and the quasi-religious sense of
equality: "The great God absolute! The centre and circum-
ference of all democracy! His omnipresence, our divine
equality!" The language here seems traditional enough, but it
is unsupported by anything else in the action or the imagery of

the book, and the truth is that the God of Melville's fathers has yielded place, at every other point, to the godlike and portentous White Whale. .

The mating of romantic idealism with the masculine sense of reality in Melville's mind has begotten here a myth that approaches, if it does not quite overtake, a naturalistic theism. The question remains: If Moby Dick embodies the deific principle in nature, what spiritual meaning can he have for mankind as an object of worship? The answer would have to be that, in the fullest sense of worship, he could have a very uncertain one, if he could have one at all. It is evident that, like Spinoza's God, Moby Dick cannot be imagined as, strictly speaking, either loving man or hating him; and, conversely, he is hardly conceived as sustainedly and satisfyingly inspiring that "intellectual love" which, according to Spinoza, the free man himself can feel toward God. A positive attitude he does nevertheless inspire, though certainly it is in the end a more austere and far less solacing attitude than that of happy and confident worship. The great clue to this, again, is the symbolism of the doubloon that Ahab nails to the mainmast. This coin was minted in the republic of Ecuador, "a country planted in the middle of the world, and beneath the great equator, and named after it; and it had been cast midway up the Andes, in the unwaning clime that knows no autumn." Arching over the mountain peaks stamped on it, one sees a segment of the zodiac and "the keystone sun entering the equinoctial point at Libra."

Obsessed with his proud and impious interpretation of the symbols on the coin, Ahab quite fails to understand its still deeper significance, quite fails to see that the coin he himself has nailed up is an emblem, not, to be sure, of ethical moderation in the Greek sense, but of the Double Vision; the vision, so to say, of the equatorial line from which one may look out on both North and South with equal comprehensiveness; the balanced vision of the sun itself as it enters the constellation of Libra or the Scales. This is the vision, surely, with which a wise man would contemplate Moby Dick, stoically accepting the fact that the White Whale, the cosmic force, has again and again unconsciously wrought havoc and destruction, and will doubtless continue to do so; but recognizing too that Moby Dick is, or may be made to be, the source of much genuine good—of nourishment, of fragrance, of light—and that, though "I know him not, and never will," one can glory in the spectacle of his sublimity.

That is what Ishmael has revealed a capacity to do, and it is the deepest reason for his rebirth from the sea. Ahab, on the other hand, has shown no such capacity; on the contrary, he has persisted in identifying Moby Dick with "all evil," and piling upon the whale's white hump "all the general rage and hate felt by his whole race from Adam down." But this is both madness and wickedness. Evil exists, it is true; essential Evil; it is no illusion, as Emerson would have it, but a dense and unexorcisable reality. So far as the reality of Evil is that of suffering, Moby Dick is indeed the source of much of it; but that is only one aspect of his dual nature, and moreover, so far as the reality of Evil is moral, so far as Evil connotes an evil will, then Moby Dick does not embody this at all: the one who does embody it is Ahab's own harpooneer, the diabolic Fedallah, to whom Ahab has surrendered his moral freedom, and whom Stubb quite properly identifies as the devil in disguise. "One cannot sustain an indifferent air concerning Fedallah." One cannot, indeed, for he is a principle of pure negation, of hatred instead of love, vindictiveness instead of charity, destruction instead of creativeness. Ahab has sold his soul to the fire-worshipping Parsee, the Parsee who, in this case, worships fire not as a symbol of light and truth but as a symbol of raging and destructive Evil. Moby Dick, however, is indestructible, and the upshot of their impious onslaught upon him is not his but their destruction.

There would be a religious solace in this thought if one could believe that Moby Dick, with his immunity and immortality, were in conscious, benevolent collaboration with the forces of love in their struggle against the forces of hate. As it is, one must be content with the consolations of philosophy in *Moby Dick*, or rather with those of a philosophical mythology; one cannot avert one's eyes from the fact that good and innocent men—Starbuck, Queequeg, and others— are involved in Ahab's doom. One can tell oneself that mad and wicked men inevitably wreak their own destruction in attempting to thwart the workings of "nature"; one cannot tell oneself that wise and virtuous men are preserved from suffering and fatality. They only *may* be, as Ishmael is.

Something else, however, is suggested in the book, though only obscurely, and this is something that takes us closer, if not to religion in the fullest sense, at any rate to a certain form of natural piety. Some years after he had written *Moby Dick*, Melville was sufficiently struck by a sentence of Spinoza's, quoted by Matthew Arnold, to mark the passage in his copy of Arnold's essays. The sentence is this: "Our desire is not that nature may obey us, but, on the contrary, that we may obey nature." Already in *Moby Dick* there had been an intimation of this cosmic submissiveness. The desire to understand, to fathom, the whole truth about the White Whale—the desire that is manifest at every turn in the explanatory and meditative passages—this is at least the true beginning of wisdom. The willingness to submit, to accept, to "obey," in that sense, would naturally follow. Father Mapple, indeed, in his sermon—employing, of course, the familiar language of faith—makes provision for this when he says that "all the things that God would have us do are hard for us to do. . . . And if we obey God, we must disobey ourselves; and it is in this disobeying ourselves, wherein the hardness of obeying God consists." The "will" of nature, even if there is something godlike in it, is hardly synonymous with God's will in the Christian sense. Yet *Moby Dick* seems to say that one might arrive at a kind of peace by obeying it.

James E. Miller

from "Moby Dick: The Grand Hooded Phantom" □

Resembling none of its predecessors, *Moby Dick* (1851) borrowed from all of them. The most obvious ingredients are the realism of the early tales of adventure fused with some of the allegory of *Mardi* and more of the symbolism of *Redburn* and *White Jacket*. *Moby Dick* has frequently been called an epic, and it is surely one metaphorically if not in fact. It memorializes the fabulous industry of whaling as well as embodies a good share of the complex metaphysical myth of nineteenth-century America, the "myth" born of the collision of the retreating world of puritan Calvinism and the emerging world of industrial materialism.

Moby Dick has also been called a tragedy—a classification which has its justification. Ahab is a heroic figure of impressive stature who seizes and by sheer force paralyzes the imagination. His awesome sway over the souls of his crew extends to the reader too who must bear witness in fascination mixed with dread and even horror. Finally, however, the question remains how to judge the cause of Ahab's downfall. Can it be tragic in any valid sense when it is precipitated ultimately by such a determined devotion to an evil purpose? Ahab's "flaw" is, finally, a chasm in his Soul that all the waters of the ocean cannot fill. But whether a tragic epic or an epic tragedy, or a sea yarn with fragments of both, *Moby Dick* is universally recognized as Melville's leviathan and masterpiece. Melville's technique is ideally suited to encourage controversy in the interpretation of *Moby Dick*. Melville chose for his narrator one Ishmael, a young vagabond out to see the world and revitalize his soul. But before the book is far along, Captain Ahab takes center stage, and it seems at times that Melville has forgotten his narrator, especially when characters are presented alone, in meditation or reciting soliloquies. At the end of the book, when only Ishmael survives the catastrophe that concludes the three-day chase of the great white whale, the reader is reminded that his endurance had to be assured in order to save someone to tell the tale. Only then, and in retrospect, is the average reader likely to raise a question about the consistency of Melville's technical point of view. It is to the credit of his narrative genius that in the vast solid center of the book, he simply takes the freedom he needs to advance his plot both metaphysically and realistically without resorting to ingenious or awkward devices to maintain Ishmael as narrator—and without violating outrageously the reader's sense of verisimilitude.

However well adapted the point may be to the philosophical substance and technical bulk of the novel, Melville's technique is perfectly suited to underscore many of the book's ambiguities. Is Melville to be identified with Ishmael, or are his feelings to be found in Ahab? Or does Melville divide himself between his narrator and hero, putting a bit of himself in each? Is it possible that Melville effaces himself, remaining aloof from his work, his own voice hidden and his vision sealed? All of these approaches have been elaborately defended, and it sometimes seems that *Moby Dick* has as many and various interpretations as it has readers.

The interpretation that has had the most thorough and prolonged defense identifies Ahab with Melville, making the captain's quarrel with God and his rage against the universe the author's as well. But many critics have split Melville between Ishmael and Ahab and have seen in the split a manifestation of a tension in the author that drove him to conceive *Moby Dick*, and filled him with the fury to finish it, but which remained unresolved when the Herculean task was completed, with Ahab swallowed by the sea and Ishmael plucked from it, drenched but alive. Some critics have seen in Ishmael's survival a kind of death and resurrection that provides the key to the novel, with Melville's affirmative theme complexly interwoven with Ishmael's developing insight and mellowing spirit, both of which run like strong but rarely glimpsed undercurrents thoughout the work.

As enigmatic as the chief characters has been the book's chief symbol, Moby Dick. Critics have stared at that huge expanse of whiteness and have, as though hypnotized by the brightness of the glare, found in it everything under the sun, and more. The glistening of the whale's shiny surface has provided a mirror in which readers have found reflected their own deepest fears and desires, their heart's delight and their private horror. Some critics have asserted that the whale was created to serve just such a purpose, an open-ended symbol with its meaning to be supplied by each reader in turn, no one meaning to supplant another. Of course, some readers have said that Moby Dick is a whale—and a whale is nothing more than a whale, mainly blubber and oil. Others have been quick to see Moby Dick as Ahab sees him—as all evil from the beginning of time made living and visible in a single monstrous creature. And if some have seen Moby Dick as the devil incarnate, others have seen him as God Himself, all-powerful and indestructible. Some readers have thought the whiteness to be innocence, while others have identified it with terror. Still others have read the blankness as the essential indifference of the universe. And at least one critic has said that Moby Dick is civilized man's deepest phallic consciousness which he is trying utterly to destroy.

John D. Seelye

from "The Ironic Diagram"□

According to Hawthorne, who knew him as well as any man ever did, it was Melville's curse never to rest "until he gets hold of a definite belief. It is strange how he persists—and has persisted ever since I knew him, and probably long before —in wandering to-and-fro over these deserts." An Ishmael in a wilderness of doubt, Melville could "neither believe, nor be comfortable in his unbelief; and [was] too honest and courageous not to try to do one or the other."[1] It is this uncertainty, compounded with Melville's deep desire to rid himself of it, which accounts for the ambiguity pervading his work.

It is not so much that Melville's art was hampered by his confusion, but rather that it was inspired by it: always a primitive artist in the sense that creation was for him an intense, subjective investment in the materials of his art, Melville was impelled by his psychological and philosophical uncertainties to create forms which would encompass them. "Swayed to universality of thought," like his artist-hero, Pierre, Melville felt that "most grand productions of the best human intellects ever are built round a circle, as atolls . . . digestively including the whole range of all that can be known or dreamed" (p. 333).[2] He regarded a work of art as all-inclusive, like "Lombardo's 'Koztanza' " in *Mardi*, a unity of

□ Reprinted from *The Recognition of Herman Melville*, edited by Hershel Parker (Ann Arbor: University of Michigan Press, © 1967). This material appears in revised form in Seelye's *Melville: The Ironic Diagram*, published by Northwestern University Press, 1970. By permission of Northwestern University Press and John D. Seelye.

totalness, an organic composite given order by the artist's "crowned and sceptered instinct" (V. II, p. 320). Much that is baffling about his work becomes clear if the reader understands that Melville regarded his art as a system of tensions produced by diagrammatic contrasts, a paradoxical structure which would accommodate his search for belief and express his capacity for doubt.

Take, for example, the problem of the double-consciousness in *Moby Dick*. There, two "voices" demand our attention: the heroic God-hatred of Ahab and the companionable, "cowardly" skepticism of Ishmael. The two attitudes meet on the common ground that there is a "wisdom that is woe," but whereas Ahab has carried his woe to an extreme, has hardened his heart against man, beast, and God, Ishmael realizes that there is also "a woe that is madness," and warns the reader against staring too long into the hell-fire of deepest doubt: "Give not thyself up, then, to fire, lest it invert thee, deaden thee" (p. 422). Fire is Ahab's portion, sunlight is Ishmael's. Both voices are invested with a deep weight of subjectiveness—the one through soliloquy, the other through a first-person address to the reader—and both have had their advocates among readers and critics who have imposed an absolute interpretation on Melville's ambiguities.

Writing to Hawthorne, Melville championed the man "who declares himself a sovereign nature (in himself) amid the powers of heaven, hell, and earth. He may perish; but so long as he exists, he insists upon treating with all Powers upon an equal basis. If any of those other Powers choose to withhold certain secrets, let them; that does not impair my sovereignty in myself, that does not make me tributary." This was written in 1851, as *Moby Dick* was being rushed towards completion, and it seems obvious that the Faustian "he" (Hawthorne) and "me" (Melville) reflect the "he-and-I" of Ahab, whose sovereign self dominates Melville's greatest book. But in another letter to Hawthorne, Melville noted that "what plays the mischief with the truth is that all men will insist upon the universal application of a temporary feeling or opinion." Ahab, plainly, is an absolutist, a "universal applicator," while Ishmael tempers his doubts with a saving skepticism. Both are important spokesmen for a troubled consciousness—both, moving in opposite directions, search for belief. Melville created in Ahab a figure to express his most profound doubts about the goodness of divine purpose; in Ishmael, he created a more complex vehicle, one which varies from sage appreciation of the wisdom of Solomon to a smug recommendation of home and hearth as Man's best felicity. Melville could not be completely an Ahab, nor could he subscribe to the excesses of Ishmael's kind regard for the sunnier aspects of life, but both voices serve as instruments to express his wanderings between those antipodes of light and shadow.

Notes

1   *The English Notebooks*, ed. Randall Stewart (New York: Russell & Russell, 1962), pp. 432–33. Though familiar, the full passage is herewith quoted: "He stayed with us [in Liverpool] from Tuesday till Thursday; and on the intervening day, we took a pretty long walk together, and sat down in a hollow among the sand hills (sheltering ourselves from the high, cool wind) and smoked a cigar. Melville, as he always does, began to reason of Providence and futurity, and of everything that lies beyond human ken, and informed me that he had 'pretty much made up his mind to be annihilated'; but still he does not seem to rest in that anticipation; and, I think, will never rest until he gets hold of a definite belief. It is strange how he persists—and has persisted ever since I knew him, and probably long before —in wandering to-and-fro over these deserts, as dismal and monotonous as the sand hills amid which we were sitting. He can neither believe, nor be comfortable in his unbelief; and he is too honest and courageous not to try to do one or the other. If he were a religious man, he would be one of the most truly religious and reverential; he has a very high and noble nature, and better worth immortality than most of us."
2   Page references to *Moby Dick*, *Pierre*, and *The Confidence-Man* are to the Hendricks House editions and are given in parentheses in the text. Page references to *Mardi* are to the first American edition (1849).

VI

A The Adventures of Huckleberry Finn (1884) by Mark Twain

Two Accounts of the Banning of *Huckleberry Finn* from the Public Library of Concord, Massachusetts

The Concord (Mass.) Public Library committee has decided to exclude Mark Twain's latest book from the library. One member of the committee says that, while he does not wish to call it immoral, he thinks it contains but little humor, and that of a very coarse type. He regards it as the veriest trash. The librarian and the other members of the committee entertain similar views, characterizing it as rough, coarse and inelegant, dealing with a series of experiences not elevating, the whole book being more suited to the slums than to intelligent, respectable people.

The Boston Transcript, March 17, 1885.

The Concord public library committee deserves well of the public by their action in banishing Mark Twain's new book, "Huckleberry Finn," on the ground that it is trashy and vicious. It is time that this influential pseudonym should cease to carry into homes and libraries unworthy productions. Mr. Clemens is a genuine and powerful humorist, with a bitter vein of satire on the weaknesses of humanity which is sometimes wholesome, sometimes only grotesque, but in certain of his works degenerates into a gross trifling with every fine feeling. . . . They are no better in tone than the dime novels which flood the blood-and-thunder reading population. Mr. Clemens has made them smarter, for he has an inexhaustible fund of 'quips and cranks and wanton wiles,' and his literary skill is, of course, superior; but their moral level is low, and their perusal cannot be anything less than harmful.

The Springfield *Republican*, as quoted in *The Critic*, III n.s., March 28, 1885.

Ralph Ellison

from "Twentieth-Century Fiction and the Black Mask of Humanity"□

Huck Finn has struggled with the problem poised by
the clash between property rights and human rights, between
what the community considered to be the proper attitude
toward an escaped slave and his knowledge of Jim's humanity,
gained through their adventures as fugitives together. He has
made his decision on the side of humanity. In this passage
Twain has stated the basic moral issue centering around
Negroes and the white American's democratic ethics. It
dramatizes as well the highest point of tension generated by
the clash between the direct, human relationships of the
frontier and the abstract, inhuman, market-dominated relationships fostered by the rising middle class—which in Twain's
day was already compromising dangerously with the most
inhuman aspects of the defeated slave system. And just as
politically these forces reached their sharpest tension in the
outbreak of the Civil War, in *Huckleberry Finn* (both the boy
and the novel) their human implications come to sharpest
focus around the figure of the Negro.

Huckleberry Finn knew, as did Mark Twain, that Jim
was not only a slave but a human being, a man who in some
ways was to be envied, and who expressed his essential
humanity in his desire for freedom, his will to possess his

own labor, in his loyalty and capacity for friendship and in his
love for his wife and child. Yet Twain, though guilty of the
sentimentality common to humorists, does not idealize the
slave. Jim is drawn in all his ignorance and superstition, with
his good traits and his bad. He, like all men, is ambiguous,
limited in circumstance but not in possibility. And it will be
noted that when Huck makes his decision he identifies himself with Jim and accepts the judgment of his super-ego—that
internalized representative of the community—that his action
is evil. Like Prometheus, who for mankind stole fire from the
gods, he embraces the evil implicit in his act in order to affirm
his belief in humanity. Jim, therefore, is not simply a slave, he
is a symbol of humanity, and in freeing Jim, Huck makes a bid
to free himself of the conventionalized evil taken for civilization by the town.

This conception of the Negro as a symbol of Man—the
reversal of what he represents in most contemporary thought
—was organic to nineteenth-century literature. It occurs not
only in Twain but in Emerson, Thoreau, Whitman and Melville (whose symbol of evil, incidentally, was white), all of
whom were men publicly involved in various forms of deeply
personal rebellion. And while the Negro and the color black
were associated with the concept of evil and ugliness far back
in the Christian era, the Negro's emergence as a symbol of
value came, I believe, with Rationalism and the rise of the
romantic individual of the eighteenth century. This, perhaps,
because the romantic was in revolt against the old moral
authority, and if he suffered a sense of guilt, his passion for
personal freedom was such that he was willing to accept evil
(a tragic attitude) even to identifying himself with the "noble
slave"—who symbolized the darker, unknown potential side
of his personality, that underground side, turgid with possibility, which might, if given a chance, toss a fistful of mud
into the sky and create a "shining star."
Even that prototype of the bourgeois, Robinson Crusoe,
stopped to speculate as to his slave's humanity. And the rising
American industrialists of the late nineteenth century were to
rediscover what their European counterparts had learned a

century before: that the good man Friday was as sound an investment for Crusoe morally as he was economically, for not only did Friday allow Crusoe to achieve himself by working for him, but by functioning as a living scapegoat to contain Crusoe's guilt over breaking with the institutions and authority of the past, he made it possible to exploit even his guilt economically. The man was one of the first missionaries. Mark Twain was alive to this irony and refused such an easy (and dangerous) way out. Huck Finn's acceptance of the evil implicit in his "emancipation" of Jim represents Twain's acceptance of his personal responsibility in the condition of society. This was the tragic face behind his comic mask.

But by the twentieth century this attitude of tragic responsibility had disappeared from our literature along with that broad conception of democracy which vitalized the work of our greatest writers. After Twain's compelling image of black and white fraternity the Negro generally disappears from fiction as a rounded human being. And if already in Twain's time a novel which was optimistic concerning a democracy which would include all men could not escape being banned from public libraries, by our day his great drama of inter-racial fraternity had become, for most Americans at least, an amusing boy's story and nothing more. But, while a boy, Huck Finn has become by the somersault motion of what William Empson terms "pastoral," an embodiment of the heroic, and an exponent of humanism. Indeed, the historical and artistic justification for his adolescence lies in the fact that Twain was depicting a transitional period of American life; its artistic justification is that adolescence is the time of the "great confusion" during which both individuals and nations flounder between accepting and rejecting the responsibilities of adulthood. Accordingly, Huck's relationship to Jim, the river, and all they symbolize, is that of a humanist; in his relation to the community he is an individualist. He embodies the two major conflicting drives operating in nineteenth-century America. And if humanism is man's basic attitude toward a social order which he accepts, and individualism his basic attitude toward one he rejects, one might say that Twain, by allowing these two attitudes to argue dialectically in his work of art, was as highly moral an artist as he was a believer in democracy, and vice versa.

History, however, was to bring an ironic reversal to the direction which Huckleberry Finn chose, and by our day the divided ethic of the community had won out. In contrast with Twain's humanism, individualism was thought to be the only tenable attitude for the artist.

Thus we come to Ernest Hemingway, one of the two writers whose art is based most solidly upon Mark Twain's language, and one who perhaps has done most to extend Twain's technical influence upon our fiction. It was Hemingway who pointed out that all modern American writing springs from *Huckleberry Finn*. (One might add here that equally as much of it derives from Hemingway himself.) But by the twenties the element of rejection implicit in Twain had become so dominant an attitude of the American writer that Hemingway goes on to warn us to "stop where the Nigger Jim is stolen from the boys. That is the real end. The rest is just cheating."

So thoroughly had the Negro, both as man and as a symbol of man, been pushed into the underground of the American conscience that Hemingway missed completely the structural, symbolic and moral necessity for that part of the plot in which the boys rescue Jim. Yet it is precisely this part which gives the novel its significance. Without it, except as a boy's tale, the novel is meaningless. Yet Hemingway, a great artist in his own right, speaks as a victim of that culture of which he is himself so critical, for by his time that growing rift in the ethical fabric pointed out by Twain had become completely sundered—snagged upon the irrepressible moral reality of the Negro. Instead of the single democratic ethic for every man, there now existed two: one, the idealized ethic of the Constitution and the Declaration of Independence, reserved for white men; and the other, the pragmatic ethic designed for Negroes and other minorities, which took the form of discrimination. Twain had dramatized the conflict leading to this division in its earlier historical form, but what

was new here was that such a moral division, always a threat
to the sensitive man, was ignored by the artist in the most
general terms, as when Hemingway rails against the rhetoric
of the First World War.

Hemingway's blindness to the moral values of *Huckleberry Finn* despite his sensitivity to its technical aspects
duplicated the one-sided vision of the twenties. Where Twain,
seeking for what Melville called "the common continent of
man," drew upon the rich folklore of the frontier (not omitting the Negro's) in order to "Americanize" his idiom, thus
broadening his stylistic appeal, Hemingway was alert only to
Twain's technical discoveries—the flexible colloquial language, the sharp naturalism, the thematic potentialities of
adolescence. Thus what for Twain was a means to a moral end
became for Hemingway an end in itself. And just as the trend
toward technique for the sake of technique and production for
the sake of the market lead to the neglect of the human need
out of which they spring, so do they lead in literature to a
marvelous technical virtuosity won at the expense of a gross
insensitivity to fraternal values.

Lauriat Lane, Jr.

"Why *Huckleberry Finn* Is a Great World Novel"□

O f all forms of literature, the novel is in many ways the hardest to describe with any precision. Its relative newness as a form and its varied and complex nature combine to make this so. Whenever we try to view such a full and living book as *The Adventures of Huckleberry Finn*, some of it always escapes our gaze. In fact, apart from its mere physical presence, paper, ink, glue, covers, and so forth, it is often easiest to assume that the novel does not exist at all, but only the experience of reading it. Each time we read *Huckleberry Finn* we read a certain book, and each time we read it we read a different book. No one of these books is the real *Huckleberry Finn*; in a sense, they all are.

At the heart of *Huckleberry Finn* lies a story about real human figures with genuine moral and ethical problems and decisions, figures placed in a society which we recognize as having everywhere in it the flavor of authenticity—the whole combination treated, for the most part, as directly and realistically as possible. I would like to move beyond this primary description or definition of *Huckleberry Finn*, however, and suggest that the novel may contain other elements equally important to a full appreciation. I would like

□ From *College English*, XVII (October, 1955), pp. 1–5. Reprinted with the permission of the National Council of Teachers of English and Lauriat Lane, Jr.

to extend the novel in three directions, in space, in time, and in degree: in space, by considering some of the ways in which the book extends beyond its position as one of the master-works of American fiction and becomes, if the term be allowed, a world novel; in time, by considering how much *Huckleberry Finn* resembles a literary form much older than the novel, the epic poem; and in degree, by considering just how much *Huckleberry Finn* transcends its position as a realistic novel and takes on the forms and qualities of allegory.

I

A world novel may be defined as that kind of novel whose importance in its own literature is so great, and whose impact on its readers is so profound and far-reaching, that it has achieved world-wide distinction. In the total picture of world literature, such a novel stands out as a work always to be reckoned with. The world novel, however, achieves its posi-tion not only through its importance but also because of its essential nature. And in discussing *Huckleberry Finn* as a world novel I shall deal not so much with this importance, as measured by permanent popularity and influence, as with the special qualities *Huckleberry Finn* has in common with certain other world novels.

The first real novel and the first world novel is, by almost universal consent, Cervantes' *The Adventures of Don Quixote*. The most important thing which *Don Quixote* has bequeathed to the novels after it (apart of course from the all-important fact of there being such a thing as a novel at all) is the theme which is central to *Don Quixote* and to almost every great novel since, the theme of appearance versus reality. This theme is also central to *Huckleberry Finn*.

Even on the simplest plot level the world of *Huckleberry Finn* is one of deception. The very existence of Huck at all is a continual deception—he is supposed to be dead. This falseness in his relations with the world at large merely reflects the difference between his standards and those of the outside world. Huck's truth and the truth of the world are diametri-cally opposed. Throughout the novel his truth is always cutting through the surfaces of the world's appearance and learning the contrary reality beneath. At the climax Huck tells himself, "You can't pray a lie—I found that out." That is to say, the lie of appearance is always far different from the truth of reality, and to the truly heroic and individual conscience no amount of self-delusion can ever bridge the gap lying between.

In the final section of the book, the theme of appearance versus reality reaches almost philosophical proportions. Both because of the way in which Jim's escape is carried out and because of the underlying fact of there being no need for him to escape at all, the situation is one of total dramatic and moral irony. At the end, however, Twain relaxes the tone, straightens out the plot complications, and lets the moral issue fade away. He avoids, in fact, the logical conclusion to the kind of disorder he has introduced into his world-in-fiction, a world in which the distinction between appearance and reality has, from the reader's point of view, been lost forever. For if we cannot tell appearance from reality, if the two do become totally confused and impossible to distinguish, the only answer can be the one Twain eventually came to in his most pessimistic work, *The Mysterious Stranger*; that all is illusion, and nothing really exists. In *Huckleberry Finn*, Twain does not yet reach this point of despair. By centering his action within the essentially balanced mind of the boy, Huck, he keeps his hold on reality and manages to convey this hold to the reader. But the main issue of the novel, between the way things seem and the way they are, is neverthess one that trembles in the balance almost up to the final page.

Huckleberry Finn also gains its place as a world novel by its treatment of one of the most important events of life, the passage from youth into maturity. The novel is a novel of education. Its school is the school of life rather than of books, but Huck's education is all the more complete for that reason. Huck, like so many other great heroes of fiction—Candide, Tom Jones, Stephen Dedalus, to mention only a few—goes forth into life that he may learn. One of the central patterns of the novel is the progress of his learning.

Yet another theme which *Huckleberry Finn* shares with

most of the world's great novels is that of man's obsession with the symbols of material wealth. The book opens with an account of the six thousand dollars Huck got from the robbers' hoard and ends on the same note. Throughout the intervening pages gold is shown to be not only the mainspring of most human action, but usually the only remedy mankind can offer to atone for the many hurts they are forever inflicting on one another. And as Mr. Lionel Trilling has remarked, in a certain sense all fiction is ultimately about money.

The world novel may also convey a total vision of the nation or people from which it takes its origin. It not only addresses the world in a language which is uniquely the language of that nation or people, but it brings before the view of the world at large many character types which are especially national. In *Huckleberry Finn* we recognize in Jim, in the Duke and the Dauphin, in Aunt Sally, and in Huck himself, typically American figures whom Twain has presented for inspection by the world's eye. *Huckleberry Finn* gains much of its justification as a world novel from the fact that it is an intensely American novel as well.

II

In his essay on "The Poetic Principle" Poe remarks that "no very long poem will ever be popular again." In part, no doubt, Poe bases this remark on his own special definition of poetry. But he is also recognizing that during the eighteenth and nineteenth centuries the epic poem was gradually dying out as a literary form. Or, to be more precise, it was gradually merging with another form, the novel. Much of the poetic form of the epic came from the requirements of oral rendition; with the invention of printing, these requirements vanished. More and more writers gradually turned to prose fiction as the appropriate form to accomplish what had once been accomplished in the epic poem. Some novelists, such as Fielding or Scott, drew quite consciously on epic tradition; other novelists and novels, by a more indirect drawing on tradition, took over some of the qualities originally associated with epic poetry.

One quality of the epic poem is simply scope. Some novels confine themselves to treating exhaustively and analytically a limited segment of life. But others seem to be constantly trying to gather all life into their pages and to say, within a single story, all the important things that need to be said. Such novels derive much of their strength from the epic tradition, and *Huckleberry Finn* is such a novel. It has geographical scope. It ranges down the length of the great river and cuts through the center of a whole nation. As it does so, it gains further scope by embracing all levels of society, from the lowest to the highest. And it has the added scope of its own varying qualities, ranging from high comedy to low farce, from the poetic tranquility of life on the raft to the mob violence and human depravity always waiting on the shore.

Epic poetry gives literary form to the national destiny of the people for whom it is written. *Huckleberry Finn* gives literary form to many aspects of the national destiny of the American people. The theme of travel and adventure is characteristically American, and in Twain's day it was still a reality of everyday life. The country was still very much on the move, and during the novel Huck is moving with it. Huck's movements also embody a desire to escape from the constrictions of civilized society. Such a desire is of course not uniquely American, but during the nineteenth century Americans took it and made it their own. The American of that time could always say, as did Huck at the very end of the story, "I reckon I got to light out for the territory ahead of the rest, because Aunt Sally she's going to adopt me and sivilize me, and I can't stand it. I been there before." Another specially American theme is that of the Negro, and Huck is faced with this problem throughout the story. Starting with the typically American prejudices and easy generalizations about Jim, he is gradually shocked into an increasingly complex awareness of Jim as a human being. And although Huck's relations with Jim do not so much embody a national attitude as suggest how the nation may purge itself of one, the theme of the Negro is still one which achieves epic stature in *Huckleberry Finn*.

The epic hero is usually an embodiment of some virtue or virtues valued highly by the society from which he has sprung. Huck has many such virtues. He holds a vast store of practical knowledge which makes itself felt everywhere in the story. He knows the river and how to deal with it; and he knows mankind and how to deal with it. And he has the supreme American virtue of never being at a loss for words. In fact Huck, though he still keeps some of the innocence and naïveté of youth, has much in common with one of the greatest of epic heroes, Odysseus, the practical man. Jim also has some of the qualities of an epic hero. He has strength and courage, and he possesses the supreme virtue of epic poetry, loyalty. It is part of Twain's irony that in Huck and Jim we have, in one sense, the two halves of an epic hero. In Huck, the skill and canniness; in Jim, the strength and simple loyalty.

In the society along the shore we see traces of other epic values, values which have survived from a more primitive world. The Grangerford-Shepherdson feud strikes the modern reader as a senseless mess, but as Buck says, "There ain't a coward amongst them Shepherdsons—not a one. And there ain't no cowards amongst the Grangerfords either." Huck sees the essential folly behind this courage, but the reader, one degree further removed from the harsh reality, is allowed the luxury of a double vision. Similarly, Colonel Sherburn, destroying a lynching mob merely by the courage of his presence, illustrates another epic theme, the bravery of one against many.

One final quality which *Huckleberry Finn* derives from its epic ancestry is its poetry. The novel is full of poetry. Not just the passages of lyric description, which mark a pause between the main actions and give a heightened and more literary tone just as they often did in the traditional epic, but also the many similes and turns of speech Huck uses, which, if they are not quite Homeric, are certainly unforgettable. And much of the exaggerated language of the frontier world, one not far removed in kind from that of the primitive migrations, is also a natural part of the epic style.

III

Allegory may be defined simply as the representation of one thing in the form of another. A second definition, more germane to literature, is that allegory is a process by which the spiritual is embodied in the physical. To go one step further, the main purpose of allegory is somehow to embody a spiritual action in a physical action. By making a suitable physical object stand for some metaphysical one, or at least for one which cannot be contained in the terms of normal, everyday life, the writer carries out one of the main purposes of all art, which is to bring to its audience, through the representation of real objects, an awareness and knowledge which transcend the limitations of such reality. Allegory, that is, deals primarily with matters of the spirit.

This assumption helps to explain why the great allegories deal either with a physical journey or a physical conflict or both. For a spiritual change, when embodied allegorically, will take the form of a meaningful physical journey through symbolic space. And a spiritual conflict, when embodied allegorically, will take the form of a real physical conflict between significant forces, each of them representing some metaphysical quality.

Although all novels are in a certain sense descended from *Don Quixote*, it is also true that in another sense all novels, and especially English ones, are descended from Bunyan's *Pilgrim's Progress*. The main difference between the allegorical novel as we know it today and Bunyan's narrative of the human soul is that whereas in *Pilgrim's Progress* we have an allegory that tends to turn into a novel, in most modern instances we have a novel that tends to turn into an allegory. As the author, whether he be Melville or Mann or Twain, develops and elaborates his original materials, he may become aware of certain meaningful connections which are tending to establish themselves between the physical objects and the physical narrative he is describing and the related spiritual values and conflicts. Drawing on a tradition which has existed for a long time in literature and which is a natural part of the artistic process in any form, the author finds himself writing allegory. And this is what happened to Mark Twain. Writing as he was a great novel, his masterpiece in fact, he organized and related certain physical materials to certain metaphysical conditions so that their relationship became meaningful in a special way—became, in short, allegory.

Huckleberry Finn is the story of a journey, a real journey. If we are to find any meaning in Huck's journey beyond the literal level, we must seek it first in the medium through which Huck journeys, in the great river down which he drifts during much of the story. And Huck's movements take on at least the external form of a basic symbolic pattern, one seen in such poems as Shelley's *Alastor*, Arnold's *The Future*, and Rimbaud's *Bateau Ivre*, a pattern stated most directly in *Prometheus Unbound*, "My soul is an enchanted boat." Implicit in this pattern is the suggestion that the river journey can have a distinctly metaphysical quality, that it can be, in fact, a journey of the soul as well as of the body. This suggestion is not at all arbitrary. Of all forms of physical progression, that of drifting downstream in a boat, or on a raft, is the most passive one possible. The mind under such conditions is lulled, as Huck's mind is, into the illusion that it has lost all contact with reality and is drifting bodilessly through a world of sleep and of dreams. Thus the nakedness of Huck and Jim when they are alone on the raft becomes a symbol of how they have shucked off the excrescences of the real world, their clothes, and have come as close as possible to the world of the spirit.

All journeys, even allegorical ones, must have a goal. What is the goal of Huck's journey? We find the answer in what happens while Huck and Jim float down the river. The pattern is, very simply, one of an ever-increasing engagement of the world of the raft, of the spirit, with the world of the shore, of reality. As the book progresses, more and more Huck tells about events that take place on the banks, and less and less he tells about those that take place out on the river. No matter how hard Huck and Jim try to escape, the real world is always drawing them back into it. Finally, in the Duke and the Dauphin, themselves fleeing for the moment from the harsh reality of the river's shores, the real world invades the world of the raft, and the latter loses forever the dream-like and idyllic quality it has often had for the two voyagers. The climax of Huck's lyric praise of the river comes significantly just before this mood is shattered forever by the arrival of the Duke and the Dauphin.

Parallel to this pattern of the ever increasing engagement of the world of the shore with that of the raft is a pattern which begins with Huck's pretended death, a death which is actual to all the world but Huck and Jim. The symbolic fact of his death accomplished, Huck must find an identity with which he can face the real world. His assumption of various such identities forms a significant pattern. The various masks he assumes, starting with that of a girl, as far removed from the reality as possible, gradually draw back nearer the truth. Huck's final disguise, as Tom Sawyer, is only slightly removed from his real self. When he is about to reveal this real self and is instead taken for Tom, Huck almost recognizes the meaning of his journey. For he says to himself, "But if they was joyful it warn't nothing to what I was; for it was like being born again, I was so glad to find out who I was."

This, then is the allegory of *Huckleberry Finn*. Dying symbolically almost at the opening of the novel, Huck journeys through the world of the spirit, ever working out a pattern of increasing involvement with the world of reality and with his own self, both cast aside at the beginning of the journey. Only when he is finally forced to assume this real self in the eyes of the world, through the sudden arrival of Aunt Polly, is he allowed to learn the all-important truth Jim has kept from him throughout the novel, that his Pap "ain't comin back no mo." We cannot say that Huck has undergone a total initiation and is now fully prepared to take on adulthood, but neither can we doubt that he has undergone a knowledgeful and maturing experience. And at the end of the story he is about to undertake another journey, this time to the west, in search of further experience and further knowledge.

Tony Tanner

from "Huck Finn and the Reflections of a Saphead" □

'You don't ever reflect, Huck Finn, and I reckon you really haven't got anything to reflect with.'

Tom Sawyer in *Tom Sawyer Abroad*[1]

'Shucks, it ain't no use to talk to you, Huck Finn. You don't seem to know anything, somehow—perfect sap-head.'

Tom Sawyer in *Huckleberry Finn*[2]

'Huck, you don't ever seem to want to do anything that's regular; you want to be starting something fresh all the time.'

Tom Sawyer in *Huckleberry Finn*[3]

Tom Sawyer stands for 'style'.[4] He always consults 'the books',[5] he believes in 'the rules'.[6] He does not believe that anyone can improve on the romantic precedents of the past. He prefers fantasticating 'enchantment'[7] to a crisp assessment of the unadorned facts. No matter what his adventures he is more interested in the scope they offer for 'fancy touches'[8] than the salvation of the innocent or the redressing of an injustice. He scorns Huck's simple and humanely based plan for helping Jim to escape, and substitutes for it a complicated and 'romantical'[9] insane parody of romantic adventure. As he himself boasts, he 'invents *all* the difficulties.'[10] To make Jim's confinement seem like a prison such as 'the books' prescribe he plans to introduce rats and rattlesnakes to torment the bewildered slave. And it is the simple Jim who raises the one consideration beyond Tom's mental scope—'what kine er time is Jim havin'?'[11] He takes his stand on the rules—'I wouldn't stand by and see the rules broke'[12]—and justifies his tissue of idiocies by maintaining that they provide him with 'intellectural'[13] fun.

□ From Tony Tanner, *The Reign of Wonder* (Cambridge University Press, 1965). Reprinted by permission of the publisher and the author.

The manner in which Tom reappears at the end of *Huckleberry Finn* and so changes the whole tone of the book has stimulated a variety of critical explanations.[14] Some defend it by saying that Clemens cleverly reasserts the 'boy's story' atmosphere, others explain it by saying that Clemens found himself with a more serious theme on the hands than he could manage—i.e. what happens to Jim and Huck's search for freedom—and reverted to the style of *Tom Sawyer* as a sort of subconscious evasion of the implications of the issues he had half wittingly roused. That Clemens did not know how to finish *Huckleberry Finn* is more clearly suggested by the fact that he did not know what to do with Huck after he had created him, as we shall see. It remains undoubtedly an unsatisfactory ending, yet an ending rich in innuendos and occasional significance. For it demonstrates at length the perverse folly of Tom's ideal of 'style.' Against those who would suggest that Clemens only intended us to read Tom's plans for Jim's escape as an extended prank I would put up this one fact. That the meanest action of the book is when the Duke and the King having used and abused Huck and Tom for their own selfish ends finally sell Jim—'for forty dirty dollars.'[15] Huck himself, antipathetic to the whole cash-nexus of society (he gets rid of the money he and Tom find), too sensitive to human suffering to be affected by profit motives, always sees straight to the core of human need in any situation. But Tom? For the sake of his conception of 'style' and 'romance' he subjects Jim to a series of indignities and dangers (even to the point of a lynching), and then announces that Jim was free all the time (Jim's freedom was the only thing Huck could think of—in his ignorance of 'the books'). But he offers some recompense to Jim for his prolonged misery—he offers him forty dollars. That the sums are meant to echo each other seems to me certain; perhaps there is even a hint of the Judas betrayal. Tom's sense of the human has been utterly corrupted by his addiction to 'the gaudy,'[16] his devotion to style, the books, the rules. I am convinced that Clemens was uncertain of his intentions and tone at the end of *Huckleberry Finn*, but Tom's treatment of Jim can easily be seen as a clumsily emerging comment on the South's treatment of the negro. In his classic study, *The Mind of the South*, W. J. Cash has a good deal to say about the contribution made by romantic illusions to the 'tragic descent into unreality'[17] which he diagnoses as one of the root troubles with Southern society, and Clemens himself held Walter Scott responsible for the Civil War because he provided a hegemony of romantic images in which the South could posture and with which it could delude itself. We have examined his struggle to escape the aesthetic falsehoods condoned and encouraged by romantic rhetoric: in this book we can see him probing the ethical mendacity lurking in everything that 'style' meant to society. For it is important to remember that Tom Sawyer is basically a social conformist: the style, romance and book-rules he believes in, in no way threaten society—in fact they consort with it. And the implications of 'style' are not restricted to Tom's hypertrophied imagination and its consequences for Jim. For instance when Huck stays at the Grangerford household he naively admires the style of the place. 'I hadn't seen no house out in the country before that was so nice and had so much style.'[18] Yet in his naivety he reveals the element of sham involved in the Grangerford style:

On a table in the middle of the room was a kind of a lovely crockery basket that had apples and oranges and peaches and grapes piled up in it which was much redder and yellower and prettier than real ones is, but they warn't real because you could see where pieces had got chipped off and showed the white chalk, or whatever it was, underneath.[19]

Huck's naive eye unconsciously, and unerringly, finds the truthful flaw in the stylistic flamboyance and offers us a quick and telling glimpse of a society both gaudy and chipped. How fatally flawed emerges, of course, in the folly of the feud, the logic of which Huck is at a loss to understand but, we may be sure, Tom would have readily taken to. Buck, defending the romantic idea of feuding, reveals a comparable corruption by romantic notions. After Buck has taken a shot at one of the Shepherdsons Huck questions him.

'Did you want to kill him, Buck?'
'Well, I bet I did.'

'What did he do to you?'
'Him? He never done nothing to me.'
'Well, then, what did you want to kill him for?'
'Why nothing—only it's on account of the feud.'
'What's a feud?'
'Why, where was you raised? Don't you know what a feud is?'
'Never heard of it before—tell me about it.'[20]

Huck was raised somewhere where ideas of 'style' had no currency: his naive standards of humanity are unapt for romantic distortion. And his naive admiration of the 'quality'[21] —who bring their guns to church to listen to a sermon on brotherly love—only underlines his own inability to fully comprehend the extent of the folly of the society in which he finds himself. And interestingly enough when he is forced to play the part of an English valet in the Duke and King's plot to rob Mary Jane and her sisters, and the girls ask him to outline English social customs, he has desperate recourse to the word 'style'[22] to explain the society of idle parsons and ill-treated servants which his imagination provides him with. It is the word which seems to explain the nonsense in Tom's head and the illogicalities and pointless cruelties in society at large. Style meant the paint over the chalk fruit, the romance of feuding over the madness of murder, the myth of feudalism over the cruelty of slavery. Style was how society dressed up its conscience. It is interesting at this point to note two entries in Clemens' notebooks for 1897 and 1899. In the latter he writes: 'Civilisation is the root of all evil'[23] while in the former he includes this meditation: 'What is civilisation? Clothes. . . . Strip the human race absolutely naked, & it would be a real democracy. But the introduction of even a rag of tiger skin or a cowtail would make a badge of distinction & be the beginning of a monarchy.'[24] This is worth mentioning because on the river Jim and Huck always go naked, and practise a perfect democracy devoid of all style. Tyranny and a minor hierarchy enter with the burlesque royalty of the Duke and King, and Huck's wistful lament—'Sometimes I wish we could hear of a country that's out of kings'[25]—indicates his, and Clemens', longing for some extra-civilized territory in which there would be no clothes, no degree, no gaudy concealments of evil—no style. For just as Clemens was after a written manner which eschewed romantic adjectival adornment and broke down Ciceronian hypotactic syntax into nude paratactic simple statements—so he yearned for a society rid of style and hierarchy. The two things are of course related. An excess of conventional epithets conceals and colours the empirical facts just as paint hides false fruit and such romantic conventions as feuding give a false dignity and colour to meaningless murder. Similarly a complex syntax which could subsume and organize the variety of the world according to a mental system of references and priorities reflected a society which kept everyone in place by imposing a hierarchy which found a proper station for all and true equality for none. Complex syntax could be autocratic. So Clemens broke it down. Romantic epithets tended to favour the mendacities of social 'style,' so Clemens tried to strip his writing bare. All of which, in turn, explain why Huck prefers to go naked, is happiest on the river, and talks in a manner which shows no evidence of having been taught the graces and complexities of 'style.' As he himself says, he was not 'brung up to it.'[26] In a very profound sense he does not belong on the society of the shore. Whenever he ventures into it he always invents a false history for himself, he sometimes dresses up, he adopts any name he can think of and—and this really is significant—he usually forgets what identity he has adopted. Early on having prepared his act as a girl and going into town as Sarah Williams he soon forgets his name, but quite readily slides into the part of a George Peters, 'runaway prentice.' When he arrives at the Grangerfords after the raft crashes with a riverboat he becomes George Jackson and settles in very well as the orphan from an Arkansas farm: but 'when I waked up in the morning, drat it all, I had forgot what my name was.'[27] As Adolphus, the English valet, he is less successful since it is a part imposed on him by the Duke, but it adds to our feeling that Huck cannot adopt and maintain a consistent authentic role in society. In the marvellous 'Raft Passage' which Clemens foolishly tore out of *Huckleberry Finn* to animate a chapter of *Life on the Mississippi*, Huck hides on a raft to try and discover from the raftsmen's talk where they are. He hears instead a long dismal story about an abandoned child who is thrown into a barrel on the river and then pursues his murdering father on every trip he takes: the child's name is Charles William Albright. When one of the men finds Huck and drags him forward and asks him who he is, Huck, with true inspiration and suggestive identification with the outcast child, says 'Charles William Albright.'[28] And at the end of the book when he arrives at the Phelps' and finds himself welcomed as an expected visitor he tells us: 'I had my mind on the children all the time; I wanted to get them out to one side and pump them a little, and find out who I was.'[29] Huck really has no authentic identity in society: the final irony of his being taken for Tom Sawyer underlines the fact that Tom is distinctly the kind of boy who does have a name, place and identity in society. As long as Huck forces himself to be like Tom he too can stay—as at the end of *Tom Sawyer*—but when his real nature asserts itself he seems to move centrifugally away from society quite automatically. Ideally he sheds his clothes and moves on. By instinct he is a loner. When he plans to escape from both Pap and the widow his programme comes to him quite naturally. 'I guessed I wouldn't stay in one place, but just tramp right across the country, mostly night times, and hunt and fish to keep alive. . . .'[30] It is because he is really in continual instinctive flight—from all societies— that he finds his only true companion in the runaway slave. Both belong on the raft, because 'it doan' *make* no track.'[31] After any involvement with the shore they are both 'mighty glad to get aboard'[32] the raft. 'We said there warn't no home like a raft, after all. Other places do seem so cramped up and smothery, but a raft don't. You feel mighty free and easy and comfortable on a raft.'[33] Whenever Huck is involved in shore life of one kind or another his inevitable comment is 'I wished I was out of there!'[34] He is always 'sorry I come':[35] when the feud is on 'then I clumb up into the forks of a cotton-wood that was out of reach, and watched.'[36] When he smells trouble, and he has an experienced nose for it, he tries to slide out. Involved in the King's plot to rob the girls he finds sleep impossible because 'I was in such a sweat to get through with the business';[37] and more than once he wishes he had just left things alone, though his instincts, as we shall see, always drive him to brave attempts to right human wrongs. When he thinks he has given the Duke and the King the slip—'the way I lit out and shinned for the road in the dark, there ain't nobody can tell.'[38] And this brings him back to the raft. 'So, in two seconds, away he went, a-sliding down the river, and it *did* seem so good to be free again and all by ourselves on the big river and nobody to bother us.'[39] Unlike Tom, neither he nor Jim have any taste for 'adventures' but much prefer to 'lazy around.' 'We laid off and lazied'[40] he says in one languorous reminiscence: or again:

And afterwards we could watch the lonesomeness of the river, and kind of lazy along, and by and by lazy off to sleep . . . we let her alone, and let her float wherever the current wanted her to . . . we was always naked, day and night, whenever the mosquitoes would let us, the new clothes Buck's folks make for me was too good to be comfortable, and besides I didn't go much on clothes, nohow.[41]

The fact that Huck, in his ignorance, can take a word describing a passive state of mind—'lazy'—and make it into a verb, a complete activity, is very important to our understanding of him (just as loafing and sauntering shed central light on Whitman and Thoreau). The preference for nakedness and the raft is related to this, and before attempting to explain this syndrome of predilections I want to quote some passages from *A Tramp Abroad*—written in the same years that Clemens was working on *Huckleberry Finn*. Clemens took a raft trip in Germany and reported it in a curiously lyrical vein, forgetting, absolutely, to be funny.

The motion of a raft is the needful motion . . . it is gentle, and gliding, and smooth and noiseless; it calms down all feverish activities, it soothes to sleep all nervous hurry and impatience; under its restful influence all the troubles and vexations and sorrows that harass the mind vanish away, and existence becomes a dream, a charm, a deep and tranquil ecstasy. How it contrasts with hot and perspiring pedestrianism, and dusty and deafening railroad rush, and tedious jolting behind tired horses over blinding white roads.[42]

Comparable idyllic yearnings are generated by the Alps:
all frets and worries and chafings sank to sleep in the presence of
the benignant serenity of the Alps; the Great Spirit of the Mountains breathed his own peace upon their hurt minds and sore
hearts, and healed them; they could not think base thoughts or do
mean and sordid things there, before the visible throne of God.[43]

Even the Kandersteg Valley stimulates this sort of desire for
peaceful self-obliteration. 'The spirit of the place was a sense
of deep pervading peace; one might dream his life tranquilly
away there, and not miss it or mind it when it was gone.'[44]
Huck too has an almost pagan sense of the benign moral
potency of nature—though, unlike Emerson, he had an acute
sense of its concealed threats and unpredictable hostilities.

To get at the root significance of this feeling for the
raft, for lazying, for nakedness and relaxation it is worth
recalling the import of the symbolism of the Sabbath Ritual.
The ban on all forms of work not only celebrates God's day of
rest after the labour of creation, it symbolizes a state of
harmony between man and nature, that paradisaical state
which existed before Adam brought sin and work into the
world. Work disturbs the man-nature equilibrium and reveals
the extent of our immersion and imprisonment; the almost
immobile 'rest' of the Sabbath is a temporary escape from time
and process, an anticipation of the Messianic time (which is
called the time of 'continuous Sabbath') of true freedom,
peace and harmony. Huck hates to interfere with the world
(he lets the raft go with the current) and all his instincts are
towards the establishing of a precarious preindividualistic
harmony. He likes to 'smooth people's roads' and he is endlessly patient of the Duke and King though he can see through
their posturing—'it would 'a' been a miserable business to
have any unfriendliness on the raft; for what you want,
above all things, on a raft, is for everybody to be satisfied,
and feel right and kind towards the others. It didn't take me
long to make up my mind that these liars warn't no kings nor
dukes, at all, but just low-down humbugs and frauds. But I
never said nothing, never let on; kept it to myself; it's the best
way; then you don't have no quarrels, and don't get into no
trouble.'[45]

'Peace in the family'[46] is what he is after, and this no
mere timidity: rather it is the result of an instinctive hunger
for the conditions of 'the continuous Sabbath.' (Interestingly
enough in one of his Sandwich Islands lectures Clemens had
described the place in this way: 'It is Sunday land. The land of
indolence and dreams, where the air is drowsy and things tend
to repose and peace, and to emancipation from the labor, and
turmoil, and weariness, and anxiety of life.'[47] Late in his life
Clemens was to write a story of a nightmare experience of
being lost and becalmed—and he called it 'The Everlasting
Sunday.' The 'continuous Sabbath' became an ambivalent
image for him.) When he and Jim are alone he indeed has
intimations of such a state of continuous peace with nature,
of a radical unconscious harmony with its pace. 'We had
mighty good weather, as a general thing, and nothing ever
happened to us at all that night, nor the next, nor the next.'[48]
Such is the even uninterrupted peace which Huck's inner
being craves for. He prefers to shed the insignia of 'sivilisa-
tion' (clothes) and immerse himself in nature's rhythms by
'lazying' on the raft. But—and this is why *Huckleberry Finn*
is in many ways a more probing work than any of the exercises
in nostalgia for a lost rapport with nature indulged by
Emerson and Thoreau and even Whitman—Huck is forcibly
involved with society, thrust into its mire and friction. He
seeks to extricate himself from the social mess, but not before
he has unwittingly delivered himself of some profound critic-
isms of it. For as Jim correctly predicts (and Jim and Huck's
superstition and belief in signs and portents indicates a
reverence and respect for nature) when he interprets the tow-
heads:

The lot of tow-heads was troubles we was going to get into with
quarrelsome people and all kinds of mean folks, but if we minded
our business and didn't talk back and aggravate them, we would
pull through and get out of the fog and into the big clear river,
which was the free states, and wouldn't have no more trouble.[49]

The second half of the prophecy is wishful thinking. For 'the
big clear river, which was the free states' is another way of
describing that mythical paradise of freedom, peace and

human harmony which Jim and Huck never find: which
Clemens (and it broke his heart to discover this) came to see
could never be found. It is this basic yearning for a lost
paradise which is responsible for various related themes
which recur in Clemens's work: the idealization of far away
and savage places of youth and the past, the endless moving on,
and the recurring sense of exile. Thus in an early manuscript
about Sandwich Islands he starts to transfigure reality into
myth by hypnotic superlatives—'the peacefulest, restfulest,
sunniest, balmiest, dreamiest haven of refuge for a worn and
weary spirit the surface of the earth can offer.'[50] Hence his
deliquescent recollection of Jackass Gulch as 'that serene
and reposeful and dreamy and delicious sylvan paradise.'[51]
He even brought his longing for paradise to Europe with him
and thought he caught occasional glimpses of it, in Switzer-
land for example. Inevitable disillusion leads to endless movement and the continual question 'what to do next?'[52]—with
which he significantly starts part two of *Roughing It* after the
paradisaical moment of the West had turned sour. After
returning from the Sandwich Islands he wrote in his *Notebook*
(1866): 'Home again. No—not home again—in prison again,
and all the wild sense of freedom gone. City seems so cramped
and so dreary with toil and care and business anxieties. God
help me, I wish I were at sea again.'[53] Water—the element
which moves, which is not built on, which cannot lastingly
be interfered with by men; the *uncivilizable* element. It is
interesting to note that Clemens's friend Twichell wrote in a
letter to a friend: 'Mark is a queer fellow. There is nothing he
so delights in as a swift strong stream.'[54] These aspects of
Clemens require full-length studies of their own but I wish to
point out their relevance to the figure of Huck Finn. For Huck,
water—the raft and the river—means more than just an escape from momentary threats. We have said that Huck is
forcibly involved with society from time to time, but his most
dangerous involvement is an internal affair. Certain social
mores have invaded, pervaded his mind; have corrupted his
conscience to use Clemens's own formulation. Whenever he
stops to think rationally, *socially*, he feels the only goodness
lies in betraying Jim. This is a most dramatic metaphor which

highlights Huck's midway position between two worlds: the world of men (the shore) and the world of nature (the river —and Jim), and his dilemma of being torn between inculcated morality and instinctive humanity. Clemens himself was obsessed by the curses of conscience and revealingly he writes in one letter of the peace to be found on a raft: 'a conscience in a state of coma, and lazy comfort, solid happiness. In fact there's *nothing* that's so lovely.'[55] The movement of the water could put the conscience in a coma: that was a virtue indeed. And how fruitfully this idea works itself out in *Huckleberry Finn*. It is well known that Huck risks social and religious damnation to save his friend, but it is less often noticed how he arrives at this heroic decision. Listen to him after he has written the betraying letter to Miss Watson and is deliberating whether to send it off:

But I didn't do it straight off, but laid the paper down and set there thinking—thinking how good it was all this happened so and how near I come to being lost and going to hell. And went on thinking. And got to thinking over our trip down the river; and I see Jim before me all the time; in the day and in the night time, sometimes moonlight, sometimes storms, and we a-floating along, talking, and singing and laughing. But somehow I couldn't seem to strike no places to harden me against him, but only the other kind. I'd see him standing my watch on top of his'n, stead of calling me, so I could go on sleeping; and see him how glad he was when I come back out of the fog; and when I come to him again in the swamp, up there where the feud was; and such-like times; and would always call me honey, and pet me, and do everything he could think of for me, and how good he always was; and at last I struck the time I saved him by telling the men we had small-pox abroad, and he was so grateful, and said I was the best friend old Jim ever had in the world, and the *only* one he's got now; and then I happened to look around, and see that paper.[56]

Of course he tears it up; because his whole being has been flooded with a logic superior to that of his social conscience. The flowing mellifluous reminiscence, the abdication of syntax so that he only pauses to let one feelingful memory glide into another, the almost hypnotic harmony which the rhythm and tone of the reminiscences recreate—these are all the result, not of hierarchical, social, rational thought which consults rules and precedents, but of the wayward unhindered currents of 'the sound heart.' Huck's heart has picked up the rhythm of the river, he is attuned to the pulses of nature which he so intimately understands. That is to say that a presocial order of being is feeling through him which melts and dissolves all rational obstructions, asserting instead echoes of a harmonious ideal world which is not based on degree (white man superior to negro) and property (man owning negro, *selling* negro), but on pre-individualistic harmony in which people and days flow into each other in peace and concord. Tom—stuffed with style—thinks Huck has nothing to reflect with. But Huck reflects with something bigger than Tom or his society could understand: he reflects with the river, with nature. It is because of this basic allegiance—which society tries to break but cannot—that Huck seems to have a distant origin, a remote destination, and to move inside a halo of isolation and lonesomeness. (He fits almost perfectly Thoreau's description of the Indian, that figure he spent so many years trying to trace, recapture, and turn into fruitful history and image: 'By the wary independence and aloofness of his dim forest life he preserves his intercourse with his native gods, and is admitted from time to time to a rare and peculiar society with nature.')[57] His basic wildness makes his assimilation by society impossible and any interruption of the balance between himself and nature makes him appear to us with some of the pathetic, though resilient and resourceful reactions, of a trapped animal. His melancholy sensitivity to the moods of nature seems to preclude forever his adoption by society. For instance when the widow has locked him in his bedroom, nature starts to exert its weird potency over him:

I felt so lonesome I most wished I was dead. The stars were shining, and the leaves rustled in the woods ever so mournful; and I heard an owl, away off, who-whooing about somebody that was dead, and a whippowill and a dog crying about somebody that was going to die; and the wind was trying to whisper something to me, and I couldn't make out what it was, and so it made the cold shivers run over me.[58]

Huck's response has nothing in common with Tom's itch to play hookey on a sunny afternoon; it reveals a profoundly felt emotional contagion between himself and nature. His sympathetic reactions to the suggestivity of nature are of a piece with his tender melancholy in the world of men (lights at night, as Lionel Trilling noted, immediately suggest sick rooms to Huck). He seems, in some uncanny way, to tap the sadness of a race and continent. His reaction after he has lost Jim is little short of cosmic:

When I got there it was still and Sunday-like, and hot and sun-shiny; the hands was gone to the fields; and there was them kind of faint dronings of bugs and flies in the air that makes it seem so lonesome and like everybody's dead and gone, and if a breeze fans along and quivers the leaves it makes you feel mournful, because you feel like its spirits whispering—spirits that's been dead ever so many years—and you always think they're talking about *you*. As a general thing it makes a body wish *he* was dead, too, and done with it all.[59]

Such passages, where the naivety becomes the means of transmitting an authentic awe complete the diapason of Huck's total sensitivity to nature, since elsewhere he exhibits a rich, wild, almost voluptuous joy in communing with the more benign moods of nature. His constant attitude towards nature is one of sensitive sustained reverence (a reverence heightened by the colloquial ease with which he talks about it—it makes him seem such a familiar, an intimate). This is what I mean by saying that he reflects with nature. His speech with its wistful or joyful cadences, its haunting evocative rhythms, cannot owe anything to the syntax and categories of society—indeed owes everything to its apparent ability to recall a more primitive manner of speech when man's capacity for wonder was more marked. It is the naive vision which enables Clemens to achieve this. A response not founded on reflection but nourished by natural impulse, a naivety which testifies to an unimpaired heart. As we have seen (as any reading of Clemens's letters, notebooks and works will readily reveal) the notion of the good heart was fundamental to Clemens' thought, at least until the black despair of age

overtook him. Rousseauistic though it sounds it was his
firm belief in this which enabled him to challenge the corrupt
social mentality of his time. It is important to recall that Huck
never arrives at a rational repudiation of the idea of slavery:
when he tries to think logically society's moral imperatives
invade his mind, so much so that he can say of Jim: 'I do
believe he cared just as much for his people as White folks
does for their'n. It don't seem natural, but I reckon it's so.'[60]
The *false* concept of the 'natural' that society has constructed
to hide its evil abuse of a minority is stuck in Huck's head;
and of course it is just because society's 'nature' is in his
head, and real nature is in his heart that his naive bewilderment at his own inner contradictions is so telling. When he
grudgingly concedes his heart the victory he immediately
relegates himself to a status inferior to society: and for us his
humble apologetic self-damnation turns into an excoriating
indictment of whatever it was that so corrupted his head. A
rational well-argued confrontation of social evil can be argued
against: but when Huck damns himself for having the virtue
of compassion society just seems to cave in like a card-house.
Because the whole point about compassion—as opposed to
organized charity—is that it is not legalized or ratiocinative:
by definition it is impulsive, antinomian, a spontaneous
moment of empathy with and sympathy for any suffering
thing. And it is because Clemens has made Huck's instinctive
compassion such a convincing affair that in his presence we
are prepared to believe in the potential natural goodness of
man. Huck's authentic, apologetic, unselfconscious habit of
compassion banishes incredulity. He is that rare thing in
fiction: the convincing embodiment of an ideal. His compassion strays out over the world: it takes in not only Jim, but a
drunk at a circus (while others laugh), murderers, animals,
the misguided victims of the feud, the victims of the Duke and
King's swindle, and then—marvellously—the swindlers
themselves when they get their deserts. His instinct is to help
anybody in trouble, no matter how they have mistreated him,
and any display of human cruelty sickens him, no matter
what the putative rights and wrongs of the matter. As he says
when he sees the Duke and King being run out of town,

'Well, it made me sick to see it; and I was sorry for them poor pitiful rascals, it seemed like I couldn't feel any hardness against them any more in the world. It was a dreadful thing to see. Human beings *can* be so awful cruel to one another.'[61] Just as he couldn't find anything hard in his heart against Jim, so he cannot find anything hard in his heart for the whole world. Indeed, and this is a daring stroke which is completely convincing, Clemens makes him feel vaguely to blame for a cruelty which in fact he had only sought to prevent. 'So we poked along back home, and I warn't feeling so brash as I was before, but kind of ornery, and humble, and to blame, somehow—though *I* hadn't done nothing.'[62] That is not quite sentimental, as it would have been if any vague allusions to a Christ-like taking-the-sins-of-the-world-on-his-own-head had been allowed to intrude: it is simply the unbearable ache which a sensitive heart feels for the unnecessary pain of the world. Huck continually feels ashamed of the human race because to the uncorrupted eye it appears all too often as a shameful thing. If Huck reflected, moralized, and sermonized we would weary of him very soon: but this of course, as Tom Sawyer points out, is the one thing Huck cannot do. But he is almost the only person who cannot. For there is another kind of 'style' ubiquitous on the shore, a style of pulpit oratory which seems to be available as a strategy of verbal deceit to every kind of rogue in the book. Henry Nash Smith has pointed out that 'any character can resort to this pompous language on occasion, even Huck's pap.'[63] Like the stereotyped aesthetic rhetoric we saw Clemens 'reducing,' this was a spurious mode of talk, impregnated with religiose clichés, which was used for morally imposing on people: and Huck reduces it in his story, not by any sophisticated arguments or by invoking critical standards of taste, but by an instinctive disaffiliation from it whenever he hears it which is as convincing (and damaging to society) as his compassion. In the last analysis it is Huck's linguistic sincerity which convinces the reader of his complete truth. He can lie and steal—in the world in which he finds himself these are necessary strategies of survival—but he seems quite without the inner equipment which can construct emotional untruths. And this very incapacity makes him an unusually sensitive register of any falseness in the words of the people he is surrounded by. He cannot help it—he winces at the spurious: it is a natural not a conditioned reflex. This instinct ranges from a refusal to accept Tom's 'enchantment' of the facts, to a disgust at the King's grotesque pious fabrications. The naive empiric eye will not see the Emperor's clothes. Huck says 'I couldn't see no profit in it'[64] when Tom suggests his romantic make-believe, and with a simple gesture of repudiating the fictitious he goes on to tell that 'there warn't no Spaniards and A-rabs, and there warn't no camels nor no elephants.'[65] And a more significant rejection of Tom's 'stylizing' of life really marks Huck's crucial separation from Tom's mental habitation. 'So then I judged that all that stuff was only just one of Tom Sawyer's lies. I reckoned he believed in the A-rabs and the elephants, but as for me I think different. It had all the marks of a Sunday school.'[66]

That the Sunday-school type of upbringing was quite inadequate for confronting the realities of the lived-in world is one of Huck's earliest instinctive realizations. Lies. A strong word. Tom's lies are perhaps harmless and trivial (there will always be disagreement about the end of the novel) but Huck is constantly coming up against the adult results of the 'Sunday-school' culture. His Pap's repentance, for instance—tears, confession and new resolutions—takes in the judge: 'the judge said it was the holiest time on record, or something like that.'[67] But that kind of empty, attitudinizing holiness cuts no ice with Huck: his offhand dismissal is marvellously summary. Similarly the sermon he hears with the Granger-ford's leaves him unmoved—'It was pretty ornery preaching—all about brotherly love, and such-like tiresomeness'[68]—yet he himself has more genuine love for his fellow men than any one else in the book, Jim excepted. His cool, contemptuous account of the fanatical prayer-meeting where the King makes his killing reveals how utterly unmoved he was by all the plangent rhetoric. When the King and the Duke set to work to deceive the Wilks girls and their friends they soon have the whole population weeping empty tears ('the place was that damp I never see anything like it'): [69] but for Huck it appears

as 'all that kind of rot and slush'[70] and, in a memorable
phrase, 'soul-butter and hogwash.'[71] Even the excessive
politeness in the house tires him—'all that kind of humbug
talky-talk'[72] just as he gets impatient with Tom's final fictional exploitation of Jim's real predicament—'Confound it,
it's foolish, Tom.'[73] Huck is the focal point of genuine feelings
and words in the book: his disavowal of the false is immediate
and subjective, never rationalized. An extension of this which
is worth remarking is Huck's suspicion of what Miss Watson
calls 'spiritual gifts'[74] and his lack of interest in the biblical
stories of Moses and such like because 'I don't take no stock
in dead people.'[75] Only the concrete here and now, only what
Emerson called 'the nearest and next,' the palpable immediacy
of the living engaging moment involves his attention and
feelings. But for that he is supremely alert, his senses and
heart unsullied by Sunday-school rhetoric and holy abstractions, unwarped by considerations of 'style.' Certainly he
'knows' nothing in Tom's terms; his is another form of cog-
nition; and just as certainly he wants 'to be starting something fresh,' though in a more profound way than Tom could
guess or Huck himself realizes. He wants a society scoured of
deceit and hypocrisy, of inequality and cruelty, a land where
the sound heart dominates the perversities of the mind, a
language unclouded by misleading accretions of rhetoric and
romance and capable of an honest unpretentious to-the-
pointness which his own way of speaking—such is Clemens's
skill—comes close to exemplifying to perfection. We have
seen this in his descriptions of nature: one might also with
profit compare the operatic burlesque of 'grief' which the
King and Duke stage over their dead 'brother' in front of the
Wilks' (which works so quickly on the people receptive to
rhetorical clichés) and Huck's own elegy over Buck as he
performs the touchingly simple last rites on the dead Grangerfords:

When I got down out of the tree I crept along down the river bank a
piece, and found the two bodies laying in the edge of the water, and
tugged at them till I got them ashore; then I covered up their faces,
and got away as quick as I could. I cried a little when I was covering
up Buck's face, for he was mighty good to me.[76]

The mass expenditure of aroused sentiment at the Wilks' is merely crass: Huck's quiet understating withholding of grief has the ring of true deep feeling. Clemens as Twain had made the discovery—better few words and clean than many and false: and Huck himself seems to bring back a lost form of honesty into language. The naive narrator is unquestionably veridical: that the forms of truth to which he might have access are definitely limited was only to appear in subsequent adoptions of the strategy, for Huck's kind of insight and response are exactly adequate to his particular environment and moral predicament. In this case the naive eye saw precisely what needed to be seen. And having seen it, and having found a way of saying what he has seen, what else could he do but abandon literature, abandon society, and light out for the unattainable paradise whose non-existence is the ultimate horror for the naive hero: '. . . so there ain't nothing more to write about, and I am rotten glad of it, because if I'd 'a' knowed what a trouble it was to make a book I wouldn't a tackled it and ain't agoing to no more.'[77]

That deserves to be ranked as one of the worst kept promises in literature. Huck made several more attempts to articulate under his own name: and subsequent incarnations have been numerous. What it is necessary to stress is that having perfected the strategy and the language Clemens was never again able to use them to discover new subjects, to produce important art. Since my book so far has concentrated on trying to reveal the gradual emergence of the naive vernacular narrator, the strange fact that this figure produced only one great book—for Huck has relations and descendants but no peers—deserves some careful consideration.

Notes

1   *Works*, vol. xix, p. 49.
2   *Ibid.* vol. xiii, p. 20. (Unless otherwise stated all references to *Works* in this chapter will be to vol. xiii and only the page number will be given.)
3   p. 333.
4   pp. 93, 324, etc.
5   pp. 12, 337, etc.
6   p. 341.
7   p. 18.

8 p. 46.
9 p. 326.
10 pp. 330–1.
11 p. 364.
12 p. 341.
13 p. 345.
14 See Leo Mark, 'Mr Eliot, Mr Trilling and Huckleberry Finn', *American Scholar*, XXII (Autumn 1953).
15 p. 294.
16 p. 332.
17 W. J. Cash, *The Mind of the South* (Vintage Books, New York, 1960), p. 50.
18 p. 138.
19 p. 139.
20 p. 150.
21 p. 148.
22 p. 241.
23 Notebook 32b (II), 24 Sept. 1897–Aug. 1899, MTP TS, p. 63. Copyright © 1963 by the Mark Twain Company.
24 Notebook 32b (I), 22 June 1897–24 Sept. 1897, MTP TS, p. 28. Copyright © 1963 by the Mark Twain Company.
25 p. 215.
26 p. 270.
27 p. 138.
28 *Works*, vol. XII, p. 30.
29 p. 308.
30 p. 36.
31 p. 61.
32 p. 100.
33 p. 162.
34 p. 81.
35 p. 95.
36 p. 158.
37 p. 247.
38 p. 282.
39 p. 283.
40 p. 59.
41 pp. 164–5.
42 *Works*, vol. IX, p. 107.
43 *Ibid*. vol. X, pp. 41–2.
44 *Ibid*. vol. X, p. 48.
45 p. 174.
46 p. 174.
47 Walter Francis Frear, *Mark Twain and Hawaii* (Chicago, 1947), see Appendix D2, Sandwich Islands Lecture, p. 436.
48 p. 90.
49 pp. 118–19.
50 MTP DV 111. Copyright © 1963 by the Mark Twain Company.
51 *The Autobiography of Mark Twain*, ed. Charles Neider, p. 139.
52 *Works*, vol. IV, p. 1.
53 Quoted by Paine in his Biography: *Works*, vol. XXX, p. 289.
54 *Works*, vol. XXXIV, p. 337 (see footnote).

55 *Ibid.* vol. xxxv, p. 558.
56 pp. 296–7.
57 Thoreau, *Works*, vol. 1, p. 55.
58 p. 17.
59 p. 303.
60 p. 215.
61 p. 321.
62 p. 322.
63 H. N. Smith, Introduction to *Huckleberry Finn* (Riverside Press, Cambridge, Mass., 1958), p. xxiv.
64 p. 17.
65 p. 18.
66 p. 20.
67 p. 31.
68 p. 152.
69 p. 227.
70 p. 228.
71 p. 228.
72 p. 238.
73 p. 337.
74 p. 15.
75 p. 2.
76 p. 160.
77 p. 80.

VII

The Rise of Silas Lapham (1885) by William Dean Howells

Two Reviews of *The Rise of Silas Lapham*

Anonymous

ᘓᕖᕃ

from "Novel-Writing as a Science"□

H e studies men and women as a naturalist does insects. We read his book on the manners, habits, sensations, nerves of a certain set of people as we might a treatise on the coleoptera. And he investigates and expounds his theme with the same soullessness and absence of all emotion. Even Mr. Henry James, beside this chilly *savant*, appears quite a child of sentiment. He is capable of receiving "impressions"— which, in Mr. Howells' eyes, would be a most unscientific weakness—and he manages to retain some smack of art about the work he does.

Is this kind of novel-writing an elevating pursuit? and is the reading of it beneficial? To these two queries the answer must be emphatically, No.

Novels like *Silas Lapham* mark a descent, a degradation. Of course art is debased when it has fallen so low into realism. Art is ever pointing upward, and the influence of true art upon man is to make him look upward, too, to that vast where his Ideal sits,

"—pinnacled in the lofty ether dim,"
where all is beautiful, but where all is immeasurable by him

□ *The Catholic World*, XLII (November, 1885).

until he beholds it with his glorified intelligence. Science points downward, and when science is unguided by religion it leads its followers lower and lower into the mud beneath their feet. And even as we see some scientists making a distinct "progress" downward from the study of the higher to that of the lower forms of animal life, so in the novel-writing of Mr. Howells we can already mark this scientific decadence. He began with people who were not quite commonplace, whose motives and acts and ideas were a little bit above the common. He now declares that nothing is worthy to be studied but the common feelings of common people; and having begun *Silas Lapham* with people who were inoffensively commonplace, he was unable to finish the book without falling a stage lower. Towards the end he introduces a young woman who speaks thus of her husband: "If I could get rid of Hen I could manage well enough with mother. Mr. Wemmel would marry me if I could get the divorce. He said so over and over again." He introduces a scene in which this young woman, her tipsy sailor-husband, her drunken mother, and Silas Lapham as the family benefactor, figure—a scene that, for hopeless depravity both in the author and subject, out-Zolas Zola. The old woman, who has a bottle in her hand, complains of her son-in-law not giving the daughter an opportunity to obtain a divorce. " 'Why don't you go off on some them long v'y'ges?' s'd I. It's pretty hard when Mr. Wemmel stands ready to marry Z'rilla and provide a comfortable home for us both—I han't got a great many years more to live, and I *should* like to get more satisfaction out of 'em and not be beholden and dependent all my days—to have Hen, here, blockin' the way. I tell him there'd be more money for him in the end; but he can't seem to make up his mind to it." Again says this old harridan: "Say, Colonel, what should you advise Z'rilla do about Mr. Wemmel? I tell her there an't any use goin' to the trouble to git a divorce without she's sure about him. Don't you think we'd ought to git him to sign a paper, or something, that he'll marry her if she gits it? I don't like to have things goin' at loose ends the way they are. It an't sense. It an't right." Before Mr. Howells reaches the end of the book he makes even the worthy Mrs. Lapham suspect her husband of infidelity and make a scene, accusing him, in the hearing of her children. It has seldom been our duty to read a book whose moral tone was so unpleasantly, so hopelessly bad; it is a book without heart or soul, neither illumined by religion nor warmed by human sympathy. This is all the more astonishing that Mr. Howells seems convinced that he is fulfilling a high moral purpose in writing it. It might be explicable on the theory that it was the legitimate outcome of the doctrine of total depravity; but it is more probably the logic of the downward progress of godless science. We shall not be surprised if the next book of Mr. Howells deal with characters and feelings that shall be so far below the commonplace from which he has already fallen that even M. de Goncourt will not enjoy reading about them. It is the progress from man to the apes, from the apes to the worms, from the worms to bacteria, from bacteria to—mud. It is the descent to dirt.

Hamilton Wright Mabie

from "A Typical Novel"□

In "The Rise of Silas Lapham" Mr. Howells has made a study of social conditions and contrasts everywhere present in society in this country; not, perhaps, so sharply defined elsewhere as in Boston, but to be discovered with more or less definiteness of outline in all our older communities. His quick instinct has fastened upon a stage of social evolution with which everybody is familiar and in which everybody is interested. The aspect of social life presented in this story is well-nigh universal; it is real, it is vital, and it is not without deep significance; in dealing with it Mr. Howells has approached actual life more nearly, touched it more deeply, and expressed it more strongly than in any of his previous stories. The skill of his earliest work loses nothing in his latest; it is less evident because it is more unconscious and, therefore, more genuine and effective. There is the same humor, restrained and held in check by the major interests of the story, but touching here and there an idiosyncrasy, an inconsistency, a weakness, with all the old pugnency and charm; a humor which is, in fact, the most real and the most distinctive of all Mr. Howells' gifts. There is, also, stronger grasp of situations, bolder portraiture of character, more rapid and dramatic movement of narrative. Still more important is the fact that in this novel life is presented with more

□ *Andover Review*, IV (November, 1885).

of dramatic dignity and completeness than in any of Mr. Howells' other stories; there is a truer and nobler movement of human nature in it; and the characters are far less superficial, inconsequential, and unimportant than their predecessors; if not the highest types, they have a certain force and dignity which make us respect them, and make it worth while to write about them. Add to these characterizations of "The Rise of Silas Lapham" the statement that Mr. Howells has never shown more complete mastery of his art in dealing with his materials; that his style has never had more simplicity and directness, more solidity and substance, and it will be conceded that the sum total of excellence which even a reader who dissents from its underlying conception and method discovers in this story is by no means inconsiderable; is, indeed, such as to entitle it to very high praise, and to give added permanence and expansion to a literary reputation which, from the standpoint of popularity at least, stood in small need of these things.

And yet, when all this has been said, and said heartily, it must be added that "The Rise of Silas Lapham" is an unsatisfactory story; defective in power, in reality, and in the vitalizing atmosphere of imagination. No one is absorbed by it, nor moved by it; one takes it up with pleasure, reads it with interest, and lays it down without regret. It throws no spell over us; creates no illusion for us, leaves us indifferent spectators of an entertaining drama of social life. The novelist wrote it in a cool, deliberate mood, and it leaves the reader cold when he has finished it. The appearance and action of life are in it, but not the warmth; the frame, the organism, are admirable, but the divine inbreathing which would have given the body a soul has been withheld. Everything that art could do has been done, but the vital spark has not been transmitted. Mr. Howells never identifies himself with his characters; never becomes one with them in the vital fellowship and communion of the imagination; he constructs them with infinite patience and skill, but he never, for a moment, loses consciousness of his own individuality. He is cool and collected in all the emotional crises of his stories; indeed, it is often at such moments that one feels the presence of a diffused satire, as if the weakness of the men and women whom he is describing excited a little scorn in the critical mind of the novelist. The severest penalty of the persistent analytic mood is borne by the writer in the slight paralysis of feeling which comes upon him at the very moment when the pulse should beat a little faster of its own motion; in the subtle skepticism which pervades his work, unconsciously to himself, and like a slight frost takes the bloom off all fine emotions and actions. There are passages in Mr. Howells' stories in reading which one cannot repress a feeling of honest indignation at what is nothing more nor less than refined parody of genuine feeling, sometimes of the most pathetic experience. Is Mr. Howells ashamed of life in its outcries of pain and regret? Does he shrink from these unpremeditated and unconventional revelations of character as vulgar, provincial, inartistic; or does he fail to comprehend them? Certainly the cool, skillful hand which lifts the curtain upon Silas Lapham's weakness and sorrows does not tremble for an instant with any contagious emotion; and whenever the reader begins to warm a little, a slight turn of satire, a cool phrase or two of analysis, a faint suggestion that the writer doubts whether it is worth while, clears the air again. Perhaps nothing more decisive on this point could be said of Mr. Howells' stories than that one can read them aloud without faltering at the most pathetic passages; the latent distrust of all strong feeling in them makes one a little shy of his own emotion.

Edwin H. Cady

from *The Road to Realism: The Early Years 1837-1885 of William Dean Howells* □

O n the surface of *The Rise of Silas Lapham* things seem rather tame. The main plot concerns an up-country farm boy come to Boston as an incipient millionaire from his devoted exploitation of a paint mine on the ancestral farm. In the struggle between his conscience and the immoral requirements of competitive success in the business world of the Gilded Age (the novel's time is 1874), Silas at first succumbs to the strong romanticism of the Business Mind and devours a partner. Ultimately, however, he is able to fight and suffer triumphantly against a series of temptations to save his wealth and business by still shoddier practices. In restoring his conscience he loses his million—and this is the (moral) rise of Silas Lapham, Horatio Alger upside down.

The subplot, yet another variation on the conventional-unconventional conflict, shows Howells' lover's quarrel with Boston-Under-the-Scalpel again. The energetic son of an otherwise decadent Brahmin-Proper Boston family, Tom Corey, comes to work for Lapham. This introduces him to Penelope and Irene Lapham, Silas' daughters, and he falls in love with Penelope. This, in turn, introduces the families, bringing the New Man, the Business Man and his wife, into

□ Edwin H. Cady, *The Road to Realism: The Early Years 1837–1885 of William Dean Howells* (Syracuse, N.Y., 1956). Copyright © 1956 by Syracuse University Press. Reprinted by permission of the publisher.

polite conflict with the Bostonians, and giving new dimensions
to the familiar conflict. "Make Lapham vulgar but not sordid," Howells advised his notebook; and again, "Make sure
of the fact that the Laphams don't know what to do with their
money." Since Irene is blonde and pretty and Penelope dark
and bookish, the Laphams make the unBostonian assumption
that Tom has come courting the blonde rather than the brain,
and this provides Howells with another go at a romanticism
he had already hammered in *Indian Summer*—the sentimental
feminine quixotism of self-sacrifice.

The Rise of Silas Lapham was a big and a controversial
book because it spoke directly to the condition of its time. In
creating the first important literary projection of the American business man, his mind and his morality, Howells provided symbols of the greatest importance for minds seeking
to grasp the new culture. His picture challenged the comfortable optimisms of the Gospel of Wealth and of Social
Darwinism—which made it the more important. While un-
settling readers with its challenge to the new, however, the
book also made its contribution to the advance of the newness.
Its author was openly out to demolish what he regarded as the
false emotions and outworn clichés of the obsolescent and
irrelevant romanticistic past. "The most fiercely debated
question in many clubs," reported Garland, was " 'Are
Howells's heroines true to life or are they merely satiric types?'
and most of his feminine critics were fiercely indignant over
his 'injustice to women.' 'He never depicts a noble woman,' "
they declared.

" 'Well,' retorted his male admirers, 'he's just as hard
on us. He is not concerned with nobly perfect individuals—he
is depicting men and women as they are.' "

Indeed, nothing about Howells seems to have stirred up
quite as much dust in his own time as his effort to shatter the
"chivalric" fiction of woman's helpless nobility and set
women free to become simple, equal participants in modern
culture. His enemies rejoiced in the chance to express their
"positive resentment" of his "libels . . . upon American
womanhood"—and mainly on the ground that "there is not
a *noble* woman among" all his many feminine characters. It

did Howells little good to explain, even when he did so in good humor.

"What have you to say to the charge that you create no noble women?" a reporter asked him.

"This criticism always seems to me extremely comical. I once said to a lady who asked me, 'Why don't you give us a grand, noble, perfect woman?' that I was waiting for the Almighty to begin."

Then he pointed out that, as he saw it, the portraiture of "ideal" characters was artistically "offensive"—"and as far as morality goes I believe that when an artist tries to create an ideal he mixes some truth up with a vast deal of sentimentality and produces something . . . extremely noxious as well as nauseous." But the people who clamored for the ideal females of the sentimental-chivalric tradition ("sappy as maples and flat as the prairies," as Lowell said of Cooper's women) were also the opponents of realism in general. They went on damning Howells' "curiously and indeed exasperatingly inadequate portraiture of American womanhood." Noble American ladies pictured as "only one remove from idiocy . . . silly and flighty"—why, the man was guilty of "treason to American woman!" And even those who sympathized with realism and granted the healthfulness of Howells' criticism were sometimes appalled. J. W. De Forest, who had suffered much from the unwillingness of the public to accept his portraits of women wrote:

'I admire . . . your honesty and courage. How dare you speak out your beliefs as you do? You spare neither manhood nor womanhood, and especially not the latter, though it furnishes four-fifths of *our* novel-reading public. It is a wonder that the females of America . . . do not stone you in the streets.'

Henry James and many others admired the originality and force of Howells' presentation of "the delicate, nervous, emancipated young woman begotten of our institutions and our climate, and equipped with a lovely face and an irritable moral consciousness." Each in his own way, Howells and James made the American girl internationally famous. But the impact of Howells' early heroines and then of "Daisy

Millerism" died away and left both men with a commercially dangerous reaction to avoid as they went about developing maturer phases of their careers. Instead of slacking off his criticism of American women, however, Howells intensified it, as we have seen, in *A Modern Instance* and *Indian Summer*. In *The Rise of Silas Lapham* he brought it one step further. He studied the marriages of the Laphams and of the Coreys carefully, drawing out in each case the strengths and weaknesses of the wives to show what contribution they made to Silas' fall and rise. Even more carefully he worked over the courtship to reveal the tangle of love, egotism, feminine logic, and quixotism which contributed so much unnecessary agony to it.

Profoundly aided by his extraordinary partnership with keen-witted Elinor Howells, he was fascinated by the feminine psyche and the (from a male point of view) illogical but often sagacious processes of feminine thought. He believed women to be morally and esthetically superior to men and very much wanted them, in every aspect of life, to be stimulated to give the best of their gifts to a sorrowfully needy world. Bad education and foolish romances encouraged women to be childish, he thought, and he aimed to use his access to the feminine novel-reading audience to correct that. A feminist in the best of all senses, he wished to help women become freer psychologically and intellectually, more honest, more mature, more realistic, healthier.

What seems to have worried Howells most about women was their susceptibility, when their nervous intuitiveness was childishly undisciplined, to quixotism, especially the quixotism of self-sacrifice. Naturally enough, he took marriage very seriously; he "might almost be called the apostle to the married," said one critic. And he hoped for the emergence of a modern ideal of marriage which would forever displace the ancient notion of Patient Griselda—who nobly triumphed over every evil and spite from her husband by an unutterably sweet and passionately passive endurance. His new ideal would be "that of a sort of Impatient Grizzle, who achieves through a fine, rebellious self-sacrifice all the best results of the old Patient one's subjection. It is the wife who has her will only the better to walk in the husband's way."

The key word, the dangerous word, there was "self-sacrifice." Howells became permanently concerned about that state of "emotional anarchy" in America, as one of his keenest contemporary appreciators put it, in which "an emotion is so sacred a thing that not only no outsider but not even its possessor may presume to undertake its regulation," leaving us thus "a society without an emotional code." From Swedenborg by way of his father, Howells believed that the sacrifice of self to moral right and the good of others was essential. All good came from self-abnegation, all evil from selfishness. But the clarity of his moral vision perceived that, in a state of emotional anarchy, a sentimental quixotism of self-sacrifice was a peculiarly insidious and destructive form of egotism. The roots of this kind of self-abnegation were subjective emotional debauchery and ego-loving pride. Evidently, he thought American women susceptible to that vice, for he portrayed them suffering in its toils and threatening to destroy the lives of others with it repeatedly, and established the Rev. Mr. Sewell in *The Rise of Silas Lapham* apparently mostly for the purpose of preaching against it.

Thus Howells' mind was becoming thoroughly and seriously, not merely literarily, antiromantic. And the freshest part of *The Rise of Silas Lapham*, the criticism of business, showed the effect of that change. Seeking to grasp the psychological meaning of the emergence of the business mind, Howells concluded that it was founded on a new kind of romanticism. "Money," says Bromfield Corey, ". . . is the romance, the poetry of our age. It's the thing that chiefly strikes the imagination." Nothing is clearer about Silas Lapham than the fact that only his business has romance in life for him. Mrs. Lapham charges him bitterly with having made his paint his god, but she, as usual, has only half understood him. His paint business and his success are much realer to Silas than God. Only when he is living and talking paint does Silas truly come alive. There his treasure is and his heart also, and he is even more deeply in need of a cleansing shower of cool, moral realism than the most quixotic of women.

The Rise of Silas Lapham is the testament of a realist

who wishes his reader to see directly the moral confusion
into which the new times have fallen. He also insists that the
reader see critically how false, feeble, or irrelevant are the
moral resources of the past, especially when those resources
are obsoletely romantic. In doing this he is renewing and
extending the insights of *A Modern Instance*. And much as
Marcia Gaylord was a kind of Maine Medea, Silas is a busi-
nessman Faust. Wealth, and more meaningfully the pride of
power in life which comes from money success in the Gilded
Age, have poured in on him. By trampling under his partner
Rogers, Silas has elevated himself at the opening of the book
to a position of sinful pride. Then the question becomes: what
shall it profit a man to gain the whole world and lose his own
soul? But with it goes the question: what kind of world—
American world—was it through which Silas moved to his
victory-in-defeat? The moral-spiritual rise of Silas Lapham
was a worldly descent from arrogance to doubt to struggle
and at last to repentance. There can be little question that
Swedenborgian-trained Howells knew from the start what his
conclusion was going to be; but the intensities and the implications of some of the insights Howells discovered within
his own mind day by day, as he worked out the dramatic
presentation of Lapham's rise-fall, shocked him.

   Lapham is not really either a comedy or a tragedy—
insofar as analogies from the techniques of the drama are
useful in understanding it—but a mixed form, what play
analysts of Howells' time called a *drame*, a free mingling of
the comic and tragic. In one sense *Lapham* is a comedy in
that there are striking and sometimes very funny satiric and
ironic scenes and moments throughout it. In a different sense
it is "comic" like Dante's *Divina Commedia*. It ends well: as
Christian faith has always insisted the cosmic drama and the
drama of human history will end—in victory for God and
goodness; or as the drama of any individual life may end—in
the hard-won triumph of grace and conscience over sin. In a
striking image Howells failed to transfer from his notebook
into the novel, he once envisaged the final situation as analo-
gous to "the young trees growing out of the falling logs in the
forest—the new life out of the old. Apply to Lapham's fall."

But in other ways *Lapham* is tragic. Like Christianity, it intimates that man's love of his prideful ego, its immunities and power, its aggressiveness and treachery, must lead to destruction. Either it will harry him into disaster, or it must be self-suppressed and humiliated. Even more, Howells' theoretical, Swedenborgian "knowledge" of the self-damnation—the worldliness—of the world became acutely real as it was dramatized in the texture of his novel. Who would have supposed the worlds of Boston—all of them and therefore the contemporary world everywhere—were so undone?

In his book, Silas Lapham moves through a series of morality plays, meeting persons clothed in the realistic texture of commonplace life, all of whom tend to corrupt rather than save him, in all of whom moral deficiencies and cultural inadequacies are organically united. In himself there is Colonel Sellers' irresponsible business romanticism united with what John Woolman called "the spirit of fierceness," the arrogant economic individualism which says: you shall serve and suffer; I shall take, exult, and perhaps enjoy. This was the root of the Business Mind, the essence of the System: Every man for himself, and the devil take the hindmost. Root, hog, or die! Stronger and fiercer as well as luckier than many, Silas was able to crowd out his rather vague partner, Rogers, and then to know in the face of the predatory Railroad later on what it was like to be under the wheel.

The Lapham daughters and, for much of the time, Mrs. Lapham are so caught in the meshes of female quixotism on the one hand and social competition on the other that they simply obscure Silas' vision and confuse his mind even more. That aside, however, there are two other large movements in this rich book which profoundly reveal the deficiencies of Silas' world. One of these centers on Mrs. Lapham, the other on Bromfield Corey and his family. Taken together in their major implications, these constitute a sweeping criticism of the New England of Howells' day—and therefore of the civilized world.

At first blush Mrs. Lapham might be taken as the moral *raisonneur* of the novel, Howells' spokeswoman. She sees and condemns Silas' treachery to Rogers; she understands and

condemns his motives and emotions. She represents the stern
Puritan tradition of the Vermont countryside from which the
Laphams have come. For a long time she is Silas' conscience,
unsparing, caustic, pessimistic. But the country culture from
which her Puritan hang-over comes Howells had long seen to
be riddled with dry rot. All the Lapham boys had gone West,
Silas only returning to the farm for a few years before the War
and his exodus to the city. The vitality of cultural relevance is
gone from Persis Lapham's morality (no longer rooted in
religion) as surely as it was gone from Marcia Gaylord's
Equity, Maine, or from the old farms going back to brush in
Private Theatricals. Consequently, Persis cannot avoid
becoming trapped in the sins of conspicuous consumption and
yearning to help Silas and her daughters compete with the
Coreys. She cannot avoid giving in to the code of respectability and so forcing Silas to be secretive in helping the wife
and daughter of his old comrade-at-arms and so betraying both
herself and him in flying into a fury of misguided wifely outrage when a malicious note intimates that Silas is really
keeping Zerilla as a mistress rather than a typist. Consequently she falters and fails Silas completely when the crisis
of his struggle for righteousness comes. In that crisis he is
left entirely alone, deserted by the dry-rotted culture of his
past as by the wife who embodies it.

The least well-digested part of *Lapham*, indeed, is
Howells' vision of slum Boston, given briefly and more or less
incidentally in glimpses of Zerilla (Millon) Dewey and her
plight. Obviously, Howells' concern for "the other half"
was deepening. Silas' refusal to deny help to Zerilla for the
sake of respectability and his insistence on taking personal
responsibility for keeping her from being lost in the morass of
Boston slum life make him morally superior to his wife as well
as to the frivolous Lady Bountiful humanitarianism of Clara
Kingsbury and her ilk. But it is also clear that Howells
himself, though troubled, was not yet ready to come to grips
with that problem.

He understood much better how to handle Bromfield
Corey, the perfect blend of Brahmin and Proper Boston, who

had made a failure of being a painter and a great success of "gentlemaning as a profession." One could take the four houses in *Lapham*—the Vermont farmhouse where Silas begins and ends, the Lapham's vulgar Nankeen Square house, their fine but doomed, architect-built, Beacon Street house, and Bromfield Corey's home—as the organizing centers for an understanding of the esthetic-cultural (as on the whole distinct from the moral-cultural) core of the book. Corey is a gentleman *par excellence*. He is utterly cultivated and all but utterly civilized. He knows how to appreciate the best in Silas, and he has, at least potentially, the resources to teach Silas how to enjoy his wealth through beauty. Corey has the generosity and even the imagination to see where he, his family, and his son really stand in modern society and therefore the magnanimity to encourage Tom to go into business with Silas, even to marry Penelope Lapham if he really wants to. He sees that it is good for Tom, since he honestly can, to throw himself into the mainstream of modern life and restore the living relationship to it which Bromfield's "India Merchant" father had enjoyed and dilettante Bromfield lost. He knows, but cannot himself overcome, his own "sterile elegance."

Bromfield Corey can rise above the snobbish hostility which makes Penelope say, as she drives away with Tom on the way to live in Mexico after her marriage: "I don't think I shall feel strange amongst the Mexicans now." But his condemnation and that of his class is that they can offer Silas no help in his moral warfare. Their elegance is better than his vulgarity, but they and their culture also leave him isolated in his struggle with good and evil.

At the crucial moment in the novel, Silas can still save himself and his wealth if he will connive at a deal cooked up by his old partner Rogers. A pair of rascally Englishmen will buy Silas' Western property, paying a large sum by way of defrauding a wealthy British humanitarian fund, regardless of the fact that the property will shortly be squeezed out of all value by the tyranny of the Great Lacustrine and Polar Railroad. Silas has only to wink. Rogers and the Englishmen will do the dirty work. In two quick, deliberately underwritten scenes of great emotional power and moral implication, Howells then achieves the climax of his novel. Silas has shut the door upon Rogers after Mrs. Lapham has failed him completely:

'His wife called down to him from above as he approached the room again, "Well?"

"I've told him I'd let him know in the morning."

"Want I should come down and talk with you?"

"No," answered Lapham, in the proud bitterness which his isolation brought, "you couldn't do any good." He went in and shut the door, and by and by his wife heard him begin walking up and down; and then the rest of the night she lay awake and listened to him walking up and down. But when the first light whitened the window, the words of the Scripture came into her mind: "And there wrestled a man with him until the breaking of the day. . . . And he said, Let me go, for the day breaketh. And he said, I will not let thee go, except thou bless me."

She could not ask him anything when they met, but he raised his dull eyes after the first silence, and said, "I don't know what I'm going to say to Rogers."

She could not speak; she did not know what to say, and she saw her husband, when she followed him with her eyes from the window, drag heavily towards the corner, where he was to take the horse-car.

He arrived rather later than usual at his office, and he found his letters already on his table. There was one, long and official-looking, with a printed letter-heading on the outside, and Lapham had no need to open it in order to know that it was the offer of the Great Lacustrine & Polar Railroad for his mills. But he went mechanically through the verification of his prophetic fear, which was also his sole hope, and then sat looking blankly at it.

Rogers came promptly at the appointed time, and Lapham handed him the letter. He must have taken it all in at a glance, and seen the impossibility of negotiating any further now, even with victims so pliant and willing as those Englishmen.

"You've ruined me!" Rogers broke out. "I haven't a cent left in the world! God help my poor wife!"

He went out, and Lapham remained staring at the door which closed upon him. This was his reward for standing firm for right and justice to his own destruction: to feel like a thief and a murderer.'

The Jacob image, so natural to Persis Lapham's Puritan heritage, functions very richly as a symbol in this context. Jacob, a far from attractive man, became the father of his people after wrestling all night with an angel and refusing to let him go "except thou bless me." Whereupon the angel both blessed him and crippled him for life. The popular clichés—all too popular in the best-selling fiction of Howells' day—demanded that chimes of blessing resound in this world and the next at a deed of moral heroism. Silas' deed is stumbling, not dramatically clean-cut, and it is heroic mainly in the consequences he has to bear. No heavenly music warms his lacerated spirit. He is crippled, and in worldly terms his blessing seems negative. He relinquishes the material gain, the loot, of his sin. He rises—but only out of the pit—up to the heights of humiliation, left there to work out the rest of his salvation with the blessing of the clarified vision his victory has won him. This is the way an agnostic moralist and literary realist will have us see the world. He has not written a novel against business, but against a world in the bonds of selfishness. The modern world had left behind such anomalies as feudal classes and slavery, but Howells wished to make it see that it had reclothed the spirit of fierceness in the business mind and in the gospel of wealth. *The Rise of Silas Lapham* remains important to us as one of its age's supremely suggestive aids to the historical imagination in its vivid presentation of the life of a lost era. As drama of the moral imagination, however, it is relevant now, at least as meaningful to an American of the second half of the twentieth century as to one of the nineteenth.

It is fruitless to argue that *Lapham* is or is not the best of Howells' novels. That the question is arguable is high tribute to the excellence of the comparable works, for this one is unchallengeably major. It has endured with great vitality the decades of ignorant and often malicious anti-Howells prejudice, and it may be expected to prosper further in readers' attention now that prejudice has begun to subside. Many of the reasons which favor that expectation were summed up by Hippolyte Taine in recommending the translation of *Lapham* to a French publisher:

'Je l'ai lu en anglais avec le plus grand plaisir et avec beaucoup d'admiration; c'est le meilleur roman écrit par un américain, le plus semblable à ceux de Balzac, le plus profond, et le plus compréhensif. Silas, sa femme et ses deux filles sont des types et nouveaux par nous, très solides et très complets.'

William R. Manierre II

"*The Rise of Silas Lapham*: Retrospective Discussion as Dramatic Technique"□

H owells' awareness of the benefits deriving from properly managed narrative perspective and of the dangers of inappropriate authorial intrusion is evidenced not only by his critical writings but by the dramatic rendering of incident in his fiction. If, as is generally granted, *The Rise of Silas Lapham* is his masterpiece, the fact is owing, at least in part, to Howells' discovery of and reliance on a dramatic formula perfectly suited to this particular novel. It is the threefold purpose of this paper to define the formula, demonstrate the extent of its use in *Lapham*, and suggest its relationship to the novel's structure of ideas.

The device, though open to an almost infinite variety of application, is basically simple, consisting of the discussion in retrospect by various interested characters of specific incidents which have already been presented in staged, set scenes. These incidents, in turn, will usually have been foreshadowed by the generous use of anticipatory detail. Following the occurrence of the anticipated action, whether it be an interview, for instance, or a dinner, or a proposal of marriage, everybody involved, both those actually present and those

□ *College English*, XXIII (February, 1962), pp. 357–361. Reprinted with the permission of the National Council of Teaching of English and William R. Manierre, II.

who, though absent, are in any way interested, are shown discussing what happened—in short, separate scenes linked rather by dramatic relevance and contrast than by authorial commentary or transition. This sequence of foreshadowing followed by incident and retrospective discussion occurs so often in *Lapham* as to create a kind of double anticipation in the reader who, caught up by the specific patterning, looks forward not only to the foreshadowed scene but with equal interest to the ironic counterpoint of the subsequent discussions.

The first three chapters, in their dependence on veiled or explicit reference to previous occurrences, adumbrate the importance to Howells' methodology of retrospective allusion. The interview between Silas and Bartley Hubbard (Ch. I) provides a convenient means of giving the reader an account of Silas' past and of characterizing him by contrast with the flippant reporter. Chapter Two furthers the exposition, introduces other members of the Lapham family directly and, by reference to a meeting between "the Lapham ladies" and "a mother and two daughters" at a "Canadian watering place," introduces indirectly certain members of the Corey group. Another important part of the action gets under way in Chapter Three with the appearance of Rogers. At this point Howells begins to develop his theme of business morality by stressing the conflict between Persis and her husband on the subject of Silas' treatment of his former partner. Exposition accomplished, Howells at once resorts to the formula with which this paper is concerned.

In Chapter Four Tom Corey meets Silas and family at the Beacon Street site; an amusing scene develops (Rinehart edition, pp. 53–59) in which Irene is alternately embarrassed by the terrible intimacy of references to the "girls' room" and by her father's bragging in Tom's presence. Following this fully developed episode is a series of five separate scenes in which the encounter is variously discussed from contrasting points of view. Silas, driving his family home, airs his views on young men who do not work for a living (p. 59)—a subject to which he "recurred seriously . . . that night" when alone with Persis (p. 60). This is at once followed by the more ex-

tended discussion of Irene and Penelope who, in the privacy of
their bedroom, shudder at their father's gaucherie, parody
his talk, and gigglingly evaluate Corey's appearance and
behavior (pp. 61–63).

The next two chapters view the meeting from the Corey
perspective. Tom's mention of the encounter to his father
Bromfield leads to various comments on Boston standards
("there can *be* no standard but ours"), the nouveaux riches
generally, the Lapham syntax, the vulgarity of Silas' advertising campaign ("rivalling the hues of nature in her
wildest haunts with the tints of his mineral paint") aristocratic and plebeian mores, and the recurrent theme of Silas'
bragging which differs from that of the Corey circle in being
"personal" and "about money" (pp. 67 ff.). When, in Chapter
Six, Tom tells his mother that he has met the Laphams at their
new house, her only comment is—"It is getting very common
down there" (p. 76).

Later in the same chapter, a less extended instance of
the technique may be noted. Tom goes to Silas' office and asks
to be taken into the business. This occurrence is then discussed alternately by Silas and Persis (pp. 88 ff.), by Tom, his
mother and sisters (pp. 106–107), and by his mother and father
(pp. 107 ff.).

Chapter Nine contains a more fully developed example.
Once again Tom has met Irene at the new house. This encounter, delightfully presented, proves largely responsible for
the misunderstanding of his amatory motives and, as well,
portrays Irene's literary ignorance. Tom's later discussion
with Bromfield (pp. 124–126) leads to comments on "the average
literature of non-cultivated people . . . the bestial darkness
. . . [of whom those] . . . who have the habit of reading . . .
can [scarcely] imagine." At least the young ladies "in certain
ways—to a certain degree . . . had knowledge enough to be
ashamed of their ignorance." But Tom's defense of the Laphams as "not unintelligent, as very quick, . . . shrewd and
sensible" calls forth the paternal remark, "I have no doubt
that some of the Sioux are so. But that is not saying that they
are civilized."

Having viewed this second meeting between Tom and

Irene from the lofty perspective of Bromfield's social and literary preoccupations, Howells now subjects it to Lapham scrutiny. First, Silas and his wife hold the floor (pp. 126–129). In contrasting Persis' dawning perception of the essential differences between Laphams and Coreys with Silas' blunt refusal to recognize their significance ("Does that make him any better? . . . My note of hand would be worth ten times what Bromfield Corey's is on the street today"), Howells begins the explicit development of his theme of social education during the course of which Silas comes to realize, albeit dimly, what Persis already suspects—that not quite everything is automatically available to the man with a large bank account.

Next, Penelope and Irene sentimentalize over Tom's offer of a wood shaving ("O Pen, what do you suppose he meant by it?") (pp. 129–132). Finally, on the next morning, Penelope ("with the quaint modern American fatalism") and her mother ("with the grim antique Yankee submission") estimate with greater coolness the difficulties of the relationship. Not until the conclusion of this scene can the dramatic presentation of Tom's encounter with Irene really be said to be over.

The sequential patterning recurs again and again in *Lapham*. Howells devotes three separate scenes to retrospective discussions of Bromfield's visit to Silas' office; four to Mrs. Corey's visit to the Lapham residence; five to Tom's declaration of love to Penelope; and three to Tom's offer to put money into Silas' business.

Surprisingly, the technique, so fundamental to this book, almost never appears in Howells' other fiction. (I find but one really striking instance: the sequence beginning with Mrs. Horn's musicale in *A Hazard of New Fortunes*.) Moreover, although the first 262 pages of *Lapham* contain at least seven clear-cut instances, the final 132 pages (Chapters XX ff.) contain but one—the sequence beginning with Tom's offer of financial aid. In his introduction to the Rinehart edition, George Arms maintains that it is precisely this latter portion that "lags" partly because "Howells became too pre-occupied with his characters as potentially tragic figures." And Donald Pizer maintains that it is precisely from this point that

Howells, having "solved . . . the subplot, . . . [turns his attention to the] . . . full exposition of Lapham's business crisis."[1] In short, one might argue that Howells becomes more involved, less objective and impartial; that, in so doing, he rejects the dramatic device which not only had helped him to maintain a rather strict impartiality in presenting his comedy of manners but had also been at least partly responsible for giving that comedy some of its life and vigor. Clearly, the appropriateness and serviceability of a method better suited to the presentation of a number of ironically juxtaposed viewpoints than to that of a single center of perception decline proportionately as the social panorama recedes into the background, as Silas' moral problem comes to dominate the action, and as, consequently, his perspective becomes central.

I believe that these changes are neither arbitrary nor reflective of altered focus. Accepting the world depicted in Chapters One through Nineteen as given, the narrowed world of the concluding chapters is both logical and inevitable. Undoubtedly there is a "slowing up" in the conclusion, a decrease in tempo that is partly owing to the relative absence of what might be called Howells' dramatic kaleidoscope. In the first nineteen chapters, the succession and multiplicity of brief, ironically contrasting scenes—momentary glimpses from altered perspectives—create an impression of speed, hurried movement, sudden change. This impression is precisely right. Laphams and Coreys both are acutely conscious of the rush of events. Silas and family in their social rise unexpectedly confront a world of new and unfamiliar standards, tastes, and taboos with all of which they must conjure. But from the Corey perspective—that of established Boston society—it is the Laphams themselves who represent change and difference. The very haste of their rise constitutes a charge against them.

A sense of hurry is, then, entirely appropriate to the first two-thirds of the book, and the dramatic method under discussion helps provide it. The reverse, however, is true of the last third. Quite properly, Howells stresses the slowness of Lapham's financial decline. Its gradual and grinding nature, its painful sequence of renewed hope followed by new loss of hope, helps to define the full meaning of Silas' temptation and of his victory over it. Explicit statement underscores the decrease in tempo as well as its significance. Pen refers to the slowness with which "the Colonel has gone to ruin" (p. 327), and elsewhere we learn that "the days were going by in a monotony of adversity to him, from which he could no longer escape, even at home" (p. 318). Here, as elsewhere in the novel, tempo reinforces theme.

In still another way, the method under discussion helps to suggest and reinforce meaning. Superficially considered, Howells' treatment of American society appears, in this book, basically complacent, his satire of a stratified Boston, gentle and good humored. On closer inspection, however, one notes that the repeated sequence of dramatically rendered incident followed by series of brief scenes of retrospective discussion, usually critical in nature, implies lack of cohesion, stability, solidarity. The initial episode has been fractured—atomized as it were—by being broken into a number of isolated, more or less fragmentary worlds from the perspective of each of which it is subsequently revaluated. Dramatic fragmentation reveals social fragmentation: a world at odds with itself, characterized by isolation, cross purposes, and misunderstandings.

Opposed reactions to Silas' generosity suggest discord in the Hubbard family even "before [Bartley's] troubles with Marcia had seriously begun." "The old fool's sent it to you as a present." But Marcia "sighed . . . from the bottom of her soul, . . . 'Oh, what a good man!' " Marital and family discord—the keynote to discord elsewhere in the social structure—is a dominant theme from the very first chapter. Mrs. Corey spends her summers in Bar Harbor while her husband remains in Boston. For selfish reasons, Penelope is delighted when she first hears of her father's troubles. Tom, too, is pleased. Persis thanks the "merciful Lord" that the demolished mansion is not covered by insurance. Nanny Corey is pleased that Pen is "going to Mexico. At that distance we can— correspond." And Pen, after spending a week with her new husband's family, knows that now she won't "feel strange among the Mexicans." Persis is quite incapable of helping her

husband when he most needs help. Zerrilla Dewey is anxious
to have Mr. Wemmel support her—but first she must get a
divorce. In one form or another, and in various degrees of
seriousness, separation or antagonism of interest undercuts
almost every human relationship in the book.

What Howells has done in the first nineteen chapters is
to create a world of fragments which hold together only by
adherence to arbitrary, external, and relative standards.
Absolute principles are largely irrelevant to its functioning.
What happens in the last third of the book is that a man comes
face to face with a moral problem requiring a choice based
squarely on absolute principles. Society has already abdi-
cated, and the man—this particular fragment—is thrown
entirely on his own resources. The meaningful Christianity of
an earlier New England might have helped, but America has
"outgrown" that. It lives on in Persis as a degraded Puritanism, which, though it enables Silas to recognize the nature
of the moral problem involved, lacks the spiritual strength
and vitality necessary to give him effective help in making his
decision.

And, according to the novel's entire structural and
thematic patterning, the social and business worlds of nineteenth-century America have no guidance to offer him. Clearly
the world of big business would consider Silas' scruples
ridiculous. Is there ever any question in anybody's mind as to
precisely what the Great Lacustrine & Polar Railroad will do if
it should want Silas' mill? It will simply steal it from him.
Everybody expects this, but nobody even suggests that there
is anything remotely unethical about such behavior. The
larger the corporation the less the conscience. And as the
individual's relationship with the organization becomes more
abstracted, his sense of moral responsibility dissipates. A
similar abstraction from the potential victims of Rogers' plot
constitutes part of Silas' temptation. That, legally, he would
be perfectly safe underscores the lack of society's moral
commitment. Silas' remark that "the day of small things was
past, and I don't suppose it will ever come again in this
country" (p. 16) is not without its significance.

At no point does Howells depict Lapham as a saint.

Certain things, however—such as caring for Jim Millon's daughter—or rejecting the Rogers deal—or telling the man from New York all the facts about the business—he has simply "*got*" to "do." And by stressing Silas' isolation in each of these instances, Howells rams home the point that the only source of morally responsible action in a fragmented society is the individual human being. Silas "stood in the isolation to which adversity so often seems to bring men." "It was for him alone to commit this rascality—if it was a rascality—or not." Persis "was helpless now in the crucial moment, when he had the utmost need for her insight." He keeps from Persis for "dread" of her "blame" his kindnesses to Zerrilla. He conceals from Bellingham his behavior with regard to Rogers and the Englishmen. "He believed that he had acted right in that matter, and he was satisfied; but he did not care to have Bellingham, or anybody, perhaps, think he had been a fool" (p. 379).

Silas' fear of being considered a fool carries right back to the method of dramatic fragmentation, in accordance with which each action receives judgment from multiple points of view, the totality of which constitutes social sanction. But the sanction of a society such as that depicted in *The Rise of Silas Lapham* is morally irrelevant, and will remain so until its members become aware of the principle that each is ultimately responsible for all. In his sermon on complicity in *The Minister's Charge*, Mr. Sewell asserts, "you can have a righteous public only by the slow process of having righteous men and women. . . . If a community was corrupt, if an age was immoral, it was not because of the vicious, but the virtuous who fancied themselves indifferent spectators."

Note

1   "The Ethical Unity of *The Rise of Silas Lapham*," *American Literature*, Vol. 32, No. 3 (1960), p. 324.

William M. Gibson

from *William D. Howells*□

T

he Rise of Silas Lapham (1885) opens dramatically with an interview between Bartley Hubbard, still a struggling reporter, and the newly rich paint-king of Boston, on the perennially fascinating subject of how he had made his million. The novel has always been popular, partly because it presents Lapham's financial and social failure as "consciously and deliberately chosen" when he has to decide whether he shall cheat and stay on top in business, or tell the truth and fail irrecoverably. Lapham's true rise is therefore moral, and all the more dramatic in the context of the elastic business codes of the Gilded Age and his own business failure.

How much the novelist had learned of his art by the age of forty-eight appears in the complexities of the plot. Lapham's physical strength and bulk and country speech indicate that he is still the son of a hard-scrabble Vermont farmer. He is vigorous, raw, naive, uneducated, and socially ambitious for his wife and two daughters—a man who had risen fast as a competent soldier and officer in the Civil War. In sharp contrast, Bromfield Corey is physically slight, well-educated, once fought under Garibaldi and has lived much abroad, lives moderately on family money, and plays at painting. In wit and ancestry he represents the Boston Brahmin type par excellence. Howells's device for bringing the two families into

□ William M. Gibson, *William D. Howells*. Pamphlets on American Writers, No. 63 (Minneapolis: University of Minnesota Press, 1967). Reprinted by permission of the publisher.

contact and conflict is chiefly the confused triangle of Tom
Corey, the son, and Irene and Penelope Lapham, the
daughters. Tom's polite attention to both girls and Irene's
charming but nitwit egotism lead the Laphams to believe that
he loves Irene, so that Tom's eventual proposal to witty,
reserved Penelope precipitates a period of harsh learning of
"the economy of pain," as the Reverend Mr. Sewell calls it,
before Tom and Penelope marry—and leave for Mexico.

But the heart motive of the novel, as Howells' original
synopsis shows, is Lapham's determination to emulate Boston
society and to make his family a part of it. The first clear sign
that he will fail occurs in the dinner party scene at the Coreys',
midway in the novel, when Lapham becomes boastfully tipsy
—the result of his being unused to wine and of Corey's lapse
of tact as he fails to note this fact. The vividest symbolic
indication of Lapham's determination is Silas' "letting out"
his mare and cutter one winter afternoon on the Longwood
road. Driving with iron control and unmolested by the moun-
ted policemen, he passes a "hundred rival sledges" with
little apparent risk. The effective symbol of Lapham's desire
is his building a new house on the Back Bay—a handsome,
airy structure, with library and music room, to be decorated
in white and gold. It is the product of an architect's taste,
chiefly: Lapham contributes only money. The impression of
this new house is strengthened by contrast to the ugly farmhouse of Lapham's childhood; the dark, overheated, over-
finished house in Nankeen Square; Mrs. Corey's "old-
fashioned" house with a classic portico and "bare" interior;
and Bromfield Corey's "ancestral halls" in Salem, presumably of the seventeenth century. When the new house burns to
the ground, the insurance on it lapsed, Lapham must confess
that he had set it on fire himself, carelessly, trying out his new
fireplace. In the end, Lapham wrestles, like Jacob, with an
angel and achieves an unhappy victory with his conscience;
he tells Sewell that if "the thing was to do over again, right
in the same way, I guess I should have to do it." Howells
presents the larger conflict of Laphams and Coreys more
stringently, however, and despite the marriage of the most
businesslike Corey and the most cultured Lapham, the couple

cannot remain in Boston. Of this conflict, Howells says: "It is certain that our manners and customs go for more in life than our qualities. The price that we pay for civilisation is the fine yet impassable differentiation of these. Perhaps we pay too much; but it will not be possible to persuade those who have the difference in their favour that this is so."

The Rise of Silas Lapham is more finely proportioned at the beginning than in the last third. This may be due to Howells' need to foreshorten Lapham's slow business decline; but it also stems from his inability to make business loss as interesting as social climbing, or even as Irene's error in love and her hardening into maturity. James' comment on his *Roderick Hudson*, that its head was too big for its body, applies equally here. But in terms of style, the novel deserves its reputation. Bromfield Corey's wit and Penelope's tartness gain from contrast with Colonel Lapham's boastful speech, in the idioms and rhythms of his New England vernacular. Howells' narrative prose is equally functional, concrete, and clear. This was the style that both James and Twain, themselves stylists, found so distinctive and took so much pleasure in.

VIII

The Red Badge of Courage (1895) by Stephen Crane

Stanley B. Greenfield

from "The Unmistakable Stephen Crane"□

The nature of heroic behavior and the state of mind of the courageous man lie at the heart of *The Red Badge of Courage*. The majority of critics accept the point of view that the novel is a study in growth, whether that growth be spiritual, social, or philosophic. These critics "concede" that the novel, especially in its earlier parts, has a strong naturalistic bias which tends to vitiate, most of them feel, its aesthetic integrity, though Berryman, a believer in Henry's ultimate heroism, asserts that it is the end of the novel that is deficient, since it fails to sustain the irony (p. 107).[1] Two critics, notably, depart from this opinion. Shroeder sees evidence of growth but feels it is inconsequential: he complains that the novel fails because Henry's heroism is largely accidental and because the pretty picture at the end "smacks too strongly of the youth's early impressions of the haunted forest; Crane seems to have forgotten everything that has gone before in his own book" (p. 126). Walcutt, on the other hand, claims that Henry, at the end of the novel, *is* back where he started from, naturalistic man still swelling with his ignorant self-importance (pp. 81–82).[2] I submit that neither interpretation of the novel—the heroic, with or without qualifications, or the antiheroic—gives proper credit to Crane's aesthetic

□ Reprinted by permission of the Modern Language Association of America; *PMLA*, LXXIII (December, 1958), pp. 568–572.

vision. For though earlier than "The Open Boat" and "The Blue Hotel," *The Red Badge of Courage* exhibits the same interplay of deterministic and volitional forces as the two short stories, and the same pervasive irony binding the heroic and the anti-heroic themes. It reveals the same ultimate refusal to guarantee the effectiveness of moral behavior or the validity of man's interpretative processes, while simultaneously approving of the moral act and the attempt to gain insight into the meaning of experience.

To understand the novel, then, we must analyze Crane's handling of *behavior* and *attitude*. We may begin with the former. Its deterministic side has so often been commented on that a brief summary will suffice. It is enough to note that, like Scully's presumptuous behavior in "The Blue Hotel," Henry's presumption to patriotic motivation and ethical choice, in the guise of enlistment in the army, is ironically punctured by the circumstance of his enlistment, the "twisted news of a great battle";[3] to observe that Henry moves from tradition-conditioned behavior ("the moving box" of "tradition and law") to instinct-conditioned behavior as the atmosphere of battle overwhelms him; and to recall that Henry *awakes* to find himself a *knight* because he had gone on "loading and firing and cursing without the proper intermission," and had acted like "a barbarian, a beast."

The use of animal imagery to reinforce the determinism of the novel and to deflate man's pretensions to heroic conduct has also often been noted. The similar use of eating and drinking, both in deed and in imagery, has not, however, been given sufficient attention. What is most interesting is the variety of ways in which Crane stresses the survival theme by his handling of food and drink.

When Henry returns home with the news of his enlistment, his mother is milking the brindle cow, and when he departs, "she . . . doggedly [peels] potatoes." Here, food and drink are shown on the simple level of existence, as staples of life, and they point up by understatement the contrast between normality and the excited Henry's impressions of war. As the men march along, they shed all superfluous equipment: " 'You can now eat and shoot,' said the tall soldier to the youth. 'That's all you want to do.'" Here, war as an eat-or-be-eaten affair is stated explicitly. When Jim Conklin and Wilson dispute about the running of the army, the former eats sandwiches "as if taking poison in despair. But gradually, as he chewed, his face became again quiet and contented. He would not rage in fierce argument in the presence of such sandwiches. During his meals he always wore an air of blissful contemplation of the food he had swallowed. His spirit seemed then to be communing with the viands." This passage is almost pure comedy, with its emphasis on the power of food to condition man's frame of mind. In contrast is the tragedy in the description of Jim Conklin's death: "As the flap of the blue jacket fell away from the body, he [Henry] could see that the side looked as if it had been chewed by wolves." According to Stallman, this wound is supposed to be an unmistakable hint, among others, that Jim Conklin is Jesus Christ, but clearly it is part of the same eat-or-be-eaten concept that pervades "The Open Boat" and that we find in the melon image in the description of the Swede's death. Still another way in which food and drink contribute to meaning is found in the scene in which Henry and Wilson, at a significant lull in the battle after Henry has awakened a knight, go looking for water. Instead of finding water, which is only an illusion on Wilson's part, they discover their own insignificance. Finally, at the end of the novel, Henry turns "with a lover's thirst" to images of peace. An evaluation of this image must be saved for later.

If Henry's and the other soldiers' behavior is conditioned by tradition and the instinct for survival, their fate, unlike Maggie's in Crane's earlier novel, is not the product of circumstance and the cumulative effect of other people's behavior. Their destiny involves other elements.[4]

For one thing, there is Nature or the Universe. Henry visualizes Nature as being most concerned with his fate. She sympathizes or is hostile according to his mood and circumstance; and this impression is part of the philosophy and aesthetic of the novel. But Nature's involvement in the affairs of man is really, as in the two stories, noninvolvement, though in *The Red Badge of Courage* she is not flatly indifferent as in

"The Open Boat," or malevolently indifferent as in "The Blue Hotel," but cheerfully so. Regularly throughout the book Crane provides glimpses of this cheerful reality, so that the reader does not lose sight of the illusions and delusions of Henry's limited perspective. The reader of the novel will recall the surprising "fairy blue" of the sky and the references to Nature's "golden process" and "golden ray" of the sun.[5] Henry sees this indifference, but he does not understand it.

Another element is man's will. Jim Conklin, for one, demonstrates that man has and makes ethical choices. Before the battle, he states that he will probably act like the other soldiers; but when many of them run, he nonetheless stands his ground. Wilson, too, feeling as the battle joins that it will be his death, does not run. And there is a decided growth in Henry's moral behavior as the novel progresses. From running away and rationalizing his cowardice as superior insight, Henry moves through a series of actions in which he does the right thing. When he and Wilson, on their mistaken expedition for water, overhear the officer say that not many of the "mule-drivers" will get back, both keep the secret and do not hesitate to make the charge. When the two friends grab the flag from the dead colorbearer, Henry pushes Wilson away to declare "his willingness to further risk himself." And in the final charge, Henry "saw that to be firm soldiers they must go forward. It would be death to stay in the present place, and with all the circumstances to go backward would exalt too many others." Henry at these moments is more than an animal.

Ethical choice, then, is part of the novel's pattern: the moral act is admired. Yet Crane refuses to guarantee the effectiveness of moral behavior, even as he refuses in the two short stories. For there is the element of chance, finally, as in those stories, that makes the outcome unpredictable. Jim Conklin, for all his bravery, is killed. The tattered man, who watches with Henry Jim's death struggle and who is concerned over Henry's "wound," has acted morally, but he is dying and is, additionally, deserted for his pains. Wilson, on the other hand, who has also done the right thing, is rewarded by chance with life and praise; but Henry's immoral behavior, not only in running but later in lying about his head wound, is equally rewarded.

The complexity and withal the simplicity in the nature of man's behavior and its effect upon his destiny is crystallized, it seems to me, in the figure of the cheery soldier. This man, before whom obstacles melt away, guides Henry back to his regiment after Henry has received a "red badge" from the rifle butt of one of his own men. As they move along, he talks blithely of the mixup in the battle and of another's death; he comes out of nowhere but takes Henry "firmly by the arm"; and as he leaves, whistling audaciously, the youth realizes that he has not once seen his face. This disembodied jovial voice is, like Nature, cheerfully indifferent. His materialization out of the blue seems to be an element of chance. His bringing Henry back to his regiment willy nilly suggests a deterministic pattern. Finally, he seems to represent Henry's own will, arriving as he does at that point in the action when Henry really desires to return to his regiment.

Man's behavior, then, as viewed in *The Red Badge of Courage*, is a combination of conditioned and volitional motivation. Man has a freedom of choice, and it is proper for him to choose the right way; at the same time, much of his apparent choice is, in reality, conditioned. But even acting morally or immorally does not guarantee one's fate, for the Universe is indifferent and chance too has scope to operate. Crane is interested, however, in more than man's public deeds. He probes in addition the state of mind of the heroic man and the possibility of his interpreting experience. Again, as in the short stories, the light of his irony plays over the presentation of man's attitude toward life.

The heroic attitude is given to us in the early part of the novel at a relatively simple level. Jim Conklin, the tall soldier, exhibits a serene faith in himself and his opinions, even when he is wrong. He will not run like Henry's squirrel. If the other soldiers stand firm, he will. Self-confidence, that is the keynote of the heroic temperament. The reader is made to admire Jim's attitude and subsequent bravery, to approve his calm acceptance of the incomprehensible movements of the army forcing him to build and then abandon three breast-works, "each of which had been an engineering feat worthy of being made sacred to the name of his grandmother." At the same time, however, as this last quotation reveals, Jim's self-confidence is slightly pretentious. We first see Jim developing virtues by washing a shirt, and he is "swelled with a tale he had heard from a reliable friend, who had heard it from a truthful cavalryman, who had heard it from his trust-worthy brother." When this rumor is proved false the follow-ing morning, Jim feels called upon to beat severely a man from Chatfield Corners. And in a passage I have cited above, we see there is comic deflation in Jim's blissful and righteous eating of sandwiches.[6]

Wilson demonstrates this confidence in a somewhat different key. The loud soldier is brash, first in his optimism, then in his pessimism. But whether he is supremely confident that he will not be killed or, raising "his limp hand in a pro-phetic manner," that he will, his is the attitude of the hero. The bravura deflation involved in Wilson's switch from one kind of brashness to another is obvious. Even later, however, when Wilson has become nonassertive and more humbly and quietly confident, when we feel for him, as we did earlier for Jim, a warm approval, there is something a little too self-humiliating, at first, in his new relationship with Henry.

The tattered man furnishes a third glimpse of the heroic attitude. Although he has just seen Jim Conklin die, and he himself is badly wounded, he is very sure of his own destiny: "Oh, I'm not goin' t'die yit! There's too much dependin' on me fer me t'die yit. No sir! Nary die! I *can't!*" He is more con-cerned over Henry's "wound" than over his own. But his mind wanders and we know he is going to die as Henry deserts him in the fields. Again we find a mixture of admiration for and ironic puncturing of this state of mind, though the ultimate effect in this scene is one of pathos.

In these characters, however, we do not see develop-ment of attitude, and hence the possibility of understanding experience. Even Wilson, who undergoes a metamorphosis, is not developed; we are merely shown the results of his change. It is through Henry, of course, that Crane shows us growth.

To see it, we have only to compare Chapter ii, where Henry fails to understand what a box of cigars has to do with war, with the "mule-driver" scene, where Henry overhears the officer speak of his regiment "as if he referred to a broom. Some part of the woods needed sweeping, perhaps, and he merely indicated a broom in a tone properly indifferent to its fate. It was war, no doubt, but it appeared strange." The word *properly* and the phrase "no doubt," which give us Henry's point of view, as well as Crane's explicit statement that Henry learns here that he is very insignificant, leave no room for doubt of the growth in Henry's insight and attitude. Indeed, by the time of this later scene, Henry is no longer worried about running away or pondering the question of death. Even when he reverts in the crises of action to illusions about himself and the nature of his accomplishments, his thoughts reveal the confidence that Jim, Wilson, and the tattered man had before him. To mention but one instance: when he is holding the colors, Henry resolves not to budge. "It was clear to him that his final and absolute revenge was to be achieved by his dead body lying, torn and glittering, upon the field. This was to be a poignant retaliation upon the officer who had said 'mule drivers,' and later 'mud diggers.'" The fact that he does not recall Jim Conklin's torn body and that he has, in fact, only once thought about or alluded to Jim's death is not only ironic but an indication of self-confidence in the extreme.

There would seem to be, then, despite the naturalistic light in which Henry's behavior and attitude are bathed, growth and development on both counts. Most of the critics of this novel, as I have observed, note a fading away of the irony as the novel draws to an end. But Walcutt, in his dissenting theory, claims that if we take Henry's thoughts about his new manhood in the context of the whole novel, we see that his motives always have been and still are vain; that he "has never been able to evaluate his conduct," and he is still deluded about himself (pp. 81–82). There *is* irony in the end of the novel; in fact, if one examines the longer version in the earlier manuscript of *The Red Badge of Courage*, he can have no doubt that there is. For there are long passages there, later excised by Crane, which clearly reveal a delusion in Henry's thoughts. For example, a passage which Crane later omitted has Henry musing that "Fate had in truth been kind to him; she had stabbed him with benign purpose and diligently cudgelled him for his own sake"; another passage has Henry feeling that though he is insignificant, he is "not inconsequent to the sun. In the space-wide whirl of events no grain like him would be lost"; and a third reveals him thinking, "He had been to touch the great death, and found that, after all, it was but the great death, and was for others." In his revision of this last sentence, Crane excised the telltale "and was for others." These pretentious thoughts about his role in the universe, coupled with the image of Henry turning "with a lover's thirst [to] an existence of soft and eternal peace" and the enigmatic last sentence, "Over the river a golden ray of sun came through the hosts of leaden rain clouds," reveal an irony similar to that in the endings of "The Open Boat" and "The Blue Hotel."

But at what is this final irony directed? Not, as Walcutt would have it, at Henry's evaluation of his conduct, but at the presumption in his false impressions of Nature and the Universe; at his *philosophical* self-confidence. Just as earlier Jim Conklin's, Wilson's, and the tattered man's supreme confidence in themselves had been held up to ironic scrutiny, so here is Henry's, only on a befittingly larger scale. But even as the minor characters' confidence has its approbation from Crane, even as in "The Blue Hotel" man's conceit was shown to be the very engine of life, so has Henry's. It seems to me that what Crane was trying to do in his revision was to eliminate the too obvious irony and redress the tonal balance of the novel.

This tonal balance is seen in Crane's handling of Henry's final evaluation of his conduct. Shifting from the apparency of things to positive statement in Henry's recapitulation of his conduct, Crane abandons the word *seems*, so pervasive in the novel. "His mind was undergoing a subtle change. . . . Gradually his brain emerged from the clogged clouds, and at last he was enabled to more closely comprehend himself and circumstance." As Henry reviews his deeds,

Crane writes: "From his present viewpoint he was enabled to look upon them in spectator fashion and to criticize them with some correctness, for his new condition had already defeated certain sympathies." No *seems* here; the tone is entirely sympathetic, though the refusal to guarantee interpretation is still here with "to more closely comprehend" and "with some correctness." There is no vain delusion about the past. As for the future—well, that is a different matter, highly ambiguous: "at last his eyes *seemed* to open to some new ways," and he "thirsts" for the obviously impossible, unchanging, "eternal peace." But however insecure the basis of Henry's thoughts about his future actions may be, Henry still has emerged from his experience with a new assurance of which Crane obviously approves: "He felt a quiet manhood, non-assertive but of sturdy and strong blood."[7]

The achievement of Crane in *The Red Badge of Courage* may be likened, it seems to me, to Chaucer's in *Troilus and Criseyde*, despite the lesser stature of the novel. Both works are infused with an irony which neatly balances two major views of human life—in *Troilus and Criseyde*, the value of courtly love versus heavenly love; in *The Red Badge of Courage*, ethical motivation and behavior versus deterministic and naturalistic actions. Both pose the problem, "Is there care in Heaven?" One is concerned with human values in a caring Universe, the other in an indifferent Universe. It is the age-old question of human values appearing in both, though the context varies. Too many critics of both works have suffered from an inability to see the validity of both of the conflicting sets of values. Chaucer shows us earthly love at its best. Alas that it is ephemeral against the backdrop of eternity and Christ's love for us and ours for Him: the perdurable quality of the poem that teases us out of our senses (and provokes so much critical commentary) is precisely the interplay throughout the poem of the two sets of values, so that even though Chaucer "guarantees" in his palinode that the love of "thou oon and two and three eterne on lyve" is ultimately more rewarding, the lovely though perishable quality of human love is not effaced. Crane's magnum opus shows up the nature and value of courage. The heroic ideal is not what it has been claimed to be: so largely is it the product of instinctive responses to biological and traditional forces. But man does have will, and he has the ability to reflect, and though these do not guarantee that he can effect his own destiny, they do enable him to become responsible to some degree for the honesty of his personal vision. It is this duality of view, like Chaucer's, that is the secret of the unmistakable Crane's art.

Notes

1   Berryman's interpretation of Crane as a whole is vitiated by his peculiar psychoanalytical view of Crane.

2   It is interesting to observe that Stallman, after examining the earlier manuscripts of *The Red Badge of Courage*, seems to have had a change of mind about Henry's "salvation." He sees the "images of tranquil skies" at the end of the novel as flatly sentimental and feels that they are given an ironic turn by the sun-through-clouds image: "[Henry] has undergone no change, no real spiritual development" (*Omnibus*, p. 221). I'm not sure where this "conversion" leaves the rest of Stallman's theory about Henry's rebirth when the rival colorbearer dies, but he himself has let it stand.

3   Cf. Walcutt, pp. 76–77.

4   That Crane developed and matured in his art from *Maggie* to "The Five White Mice" is, I think, indisputable, but a demonstration of this maturation is beyond the scope of this paper.

5   As for the hotly-debated wafer image, although it cannot be said to be cheerful, it seems to me that Scott C. Osborn is perfectly right when he suggests that it is the seal of Nature's indifference to Jim's (and man's) fate ("Stephen Crane's Imagery: Pasted like a Wafer," *AL*, xxiii, 1951, p. 362). I believe it was to insure this meaning that Crane deleted the "fierce" from his final revision of this passage.

6   Stallman sees this shirt washing as a sign of the right way to achieve spiritual salvation, by immersion in the flux of things; but surely the context renders this interpretation invalid. Crane's ironic attitude toward Jim Conklin in the instances I have cited certainly militates against our seeing him as a Christ figure.

7   I must dispute Walcutt's interpretation of this famous passage: "With all these facts [the juxtaposition of courage, ignorance, vainglory, etc.] in mind we can examine the Henry Fleming who emerges from the battle and sets about marshaling all his acts. He is gleeful over his courage. Remembering his desertion of the wounded Jim Conklin, he is ashamed of the possible disgrace, but, as Crane tells with supreme irony, 'gradually he mustered force to put the sin at a distance,' and to dwell upon his 'quiet manhood' " (p. 81). The mistaken identification of character is negligible. But two points are, I think, crucial: Henry is not gleeful about his courage, but "He was gleeful when he discovered that he now despised [the brass and bombast] of his earlier gospels." And Henry doesn't *dwell* upon his quiet manhood (the word is, I feel, prejudicial): "He felt a quiet manhood . . ."

John Berryman

from *Stephen Crane* □

*T*he *Red Badge of Courage* is the story of the mind of a
new young Northern soldier as it accustoms itself to war
during two days in and out of his first battle. There is a preliminary debate with himself as to whether he will run away
or not. When his regiment is charged a second time, he does;
and hides resentfully in a wood, where he meets a rotting
corpse in a chapel-like place. He joins the march of wounded
away from the battle, and comes on a friend hurt horribly, a
tall soldier, whom he accompanies to his extraordinary death.
A tattered man has befriended him on the march; this man,
whose plight is very bad, his mind wandering, the youth
deserts in shame, on the question, reiterated, of *where* he is
wounded. Then in a flight of the troops he is clubbed with a
rifle when he tries to ask a panic-stricken man a question. An
unseen man finally helps him back to his regiment. Since it
has got scattered during the battle, his shame is unknown; he
says he was shot and is cared for by a friend, a loud youth,
who bandages his bloody head. He sleeps. Next morning he
feels no remorse, and is full of "self-pride" even, when the
loud youth reluctantly and shamefacedly has to ask for the
return of a packet of papers given the youth, in fear, before the
battle. "He had been possessed of much fear of his friend, for
he saw how easily questionings could make holes in his

feelings." Now "his heart grew more strong and stout. He had never been compelled to blush in such manner for his acts; he was an individual of extraordinary virtues." In the battle of this second day he is a war devil. During the charge, when the color-bearer is killed, he wrenches the flag free and bears it. In hard new fighting he and the loud youth are commended. The regiment takes a fence and a flag, and rests. "He had been to touch the great death, and found that, after all, it was but the great death. He was a man. . . . Scars faded as flowers.

"It rained. . . . Yet the youth smiled, for he saw that the world was a world for him, though many discovered it to be made of oaths and walking sticks. He had rid himself of the red sickness of battle. . . ."

Though the major circumstantial irony survives in this account, Crane's sympathy as he dances near and behind his hero's mind does not, nor does, of course, the imagination of fear and war in the book; together, these produced a thing that was new in literature. It is produced with awful simplicity. Henry Fleming, the meditative, panic-stricken farm boy, is the one character to whom we attend; the tall soldier Jim Conklin and the loud one Wilson are scarcely developed, and the others are mere vignettes, sometimes admirable. Critics have not failed to ask *how* it was produced. Garland, who read the manuscript with amazement, was the first: How did Crane know about war? and "in his succinct, self-derisive way, he candidly confessed that all his knowledge of battle had been gained on the football field! 'The psychology is the same. The opposite team is an enemy tribe!' "

Football was more instructive, probably, than Zola; and some other roots of *The Red Badge* may be mentioned. A relative of Crane's in Port Jervis had told him war stories, veterans had, his brother William was a student of the strategy of Gettysburg and Chancellorsville. The battle is obviously modeled on Chancellorsville (the encampment until April on the Rappahannock with sentries across the river friendly, the pontoon bridges of Chapter III, the character of the Southern attacks—all this he could find in the *Century*, for instance in 1886, xxxii 770 ff.). Henry Fleming, in a later story, is a veteran specifically of Chancellorsville. But the

battle is not eagerly geographical and Lyndon Upson Pratt
must be right in suggesting that Antietam has influenced it.
The conception of the rout, the color-sergeant killed and the
colors saved, the loss of more than half the regiment (end of
Chapter XIV), and then its slow overnight reassembling,
show the marks of Van Petten's Claverack tales of the 34th
New York at Antietam. Crane's regiment is a (nonexistent)
304th New York; and this will appear, when we come to
examine his practices with names, to have constituted a
proof—he simply made the number imaginary by enlarging it,
and reduced the regiment to inexperience in order to have
Fleming *part* of an ordeal. He may, too, have glanced through
an enormous, banal chronicle of 1887, *Corporal Si Klegg and
His "Pard"* by Wilbur F. Hinman, though few of the correspondences rehearsed by H. T. Webster look anything but
inevitable in two stories, however different, dealing with a
recruit's experiences in the Civil War. If he saw the book—
which must not be regarded as probable—the brindle cow that
Henry Fleming's mother milks may be a memory of it, and
another detail or so; but brindle cows occur in nature. More
interesting is Crane's Civil War slang. This does not resemble
Colonel Hinman's (which is mostly midwestern), but an
investigator finds it authentic; evidently the young writer got
it from veterans, modified by contemporary rural speech in
New Jersey and New York State. Crane had an ear like a
trap. Aesthetic influences are more interesting still. Tolstoy's
is clearer, naturally, here than in *Maggie*, and as little accounts for most of the book. About Zola it is again hard to say.
If Crane had seen Ambrose Bierce's recent, comparatively
"realistic" images of the war, they may have encouraged him.
This author's whole inhuman, slight way of working is
unlike the felt, majestic, *humanly* dreadful art of Stephen
Crane. Perhaps the book took its origin really from Mark
Twain's young pilot in *Life on the Mississippi*, who hid during
his maiden engagement and then was acclaimed.[1] Who knows
how many origins a deep work has? An advance is perceptible
at any rate from the fully developed style of Crane's first book
to a style much better capable of registering degrees of
variation of feeling. The grotesquerie as well is better knitted

into narrative, and when let loose, in the great ninth chapter, this gave him a scene decisively beyond anything he had done before, as well as one of the major scenes in American writing.

Thomas Beer's account, however, which Crane could hardly give, would have answered Garland's question best. How did Crane know about war? "There had been a boy who went confidently off to make war on a world and a city. He had been beaten to shelter and had lurched up a lane in darkness on the arm of some stranger. He had been praised for his daring while his novel, like a retreating army, lay in unsold heaps and the maker of images was sure of his own clay."

. . . .

*

The sensation of *The Red Badge of Courage* was made by the English critics. Crane's publisher Ripley Hitchcock, Thomas Beer, and others have denied this for fifty years, but the facts are simple. The book appeared in London two months later than here, and it was not until early in January that news of the British reviews came in: the *Pall Mall's*, George Wyndham's in the *New Review*, the *Saturday Review's*, others'. These were different from the American reviews. Wyndham, one of England's ablest critics, in a long article on "A Remarkable Book," said simply that "Mr. Stephen Crane, the author of *The Red Badge of Courage*, is a great artist," and "Mr. Crane's picture of war is more complete than Tolstoy's, more true than Zola's." The *Saturday Review* also thought Zola inferior to Crane, mentioned Tolstoy, Kipling, and Mérimée, thought Crane's irony Sophoclean, and in general seemed to lose its head: the book was "an inspired utterance that will reach the universal heart of man." "In the whole range of literature," said the *Daily Chronicle*, "we can call to mind nothing so searching in its analysis." They vied with each other. To *St. James's Gazette* it was "not merely a remarkable book: it is a revelation." "Most astonishing"—"no possibility of resistance"—and so on. But let us make sure of the dates. The issue in which the *Saturday Review* went overboard is dated January 11, 1896. Next day, Crane posted to a girl a clipping from the *Scranton Tribune: "The Red*

Badge of Courage has fascinated England. The critics are wild over it and the English edition has been purchased with avidity. Mr. Crane has letters from the most prominent English publishers asking for the English rights to all of his future productions; but the young author refuses to be hurried. . . ." In mid-January, as Beer says, New York began to buy the book; and these were the reasons. The advertisements quoted the British reviews (until 1896 the book went unmentioned or just listed in Appleton ads), people talked of them, American critics fell resentfully or eagerly into line and in ten months of 1896 *The Red Badge* went through thirteen editions in America.

The anomaly was pointed out repeatedly at the time, John D. Barry (the sponsor of Crane's "lines") being perhaps the first to do so. From New York for the Boston *Literary World*, also dated January 11th, he observed: "It is a satisfaction to note that the unique and promising work which Mr. Stephen Crane has done during the past three years has at last won distinguished recognition. I wish that this recognition came from Mr. Crane's own countrymen. . . . I cannot think of the case of another American writer who was accepted as a man of consequence in England before winning marked recognition in his own country, and I doubt if Mr. Crane's recent experience has a precedent. At any rate, now that the English critics are crying out his praises . . ." English fame had always helped, of course—a few years later Ezra Pound and Robert Frost were to have similar experiences. In February the New York *Bookman* took up the refrain ("Why is it . . . that in America critics are less sure and readers slower to discover a good book in spite of the genius in it?"), and on March 14th the *Literary Digest:* "It is scarcely to the credit of America that this book . . . was first pronounced a work of genius in England, where its success is great and growing. The story has now caught the attention of the American public, and it is said that during the first week in February the publishers were unable to supply the demand." By April 11th it was "now pretty generally admitted that Stephen Crane is a 'genius.' . . ." The English reception was less single-minded, naturally, than it has been represented; the *Academy* in a curt dismissal found the book funny (a discovery it laboriously repented), while the *Spectator* called it an essay in pathology. The American press had praised the book more highly than soon either it or the English press was recognizing; but the essential features of the success are unmistakable. It was inevitable that the truth should have got mislaid here since. More predisposition to hospitality existed than one might think. *Punch* in this December and January, despite the political crisis over Venezuela, was extolling *Huckleberry Finn* and extending a hand to Howells, while baiting Kipling, Meredith, and Hardy, with articles on "Dude the Diffuse" and rhymes:

> Hi, Kipple-Kipple!
> Your rhymes cease to ripple;
> Your prose too is turning abstruse . . .

There was a biographical misconception in England also, the author being assumed to be a man of some age and experience of war; this was to the book's credit as illusion. And the publisher was energetic and well-connected. But the intense excitement of the English critics, as well as their perspicacity, will be understood better when we remember that they did not see *The Red Badge of Courage* through a maze of imitations, which if they cloud for us its originality also incline to dignify it and above all lend it *plausibility*. The critics saw very well the work's main origins, but they saw its immense difference from these, and its value, and said so. Crane never forgot. Writing to an American editor shortly before his death, he came to the matter again, absolutely: "I have only one pride, and that is that the English edition of *The Red Badge of Courage* has been received with great praise by the English reviewers. I am proud of this simply because the remoter people would seem more just and harder to win."

Note

1 Chapter xxvi. "I had often had a curiosity to know how a green hand might feel. . . . So to me his story was valuable—it filled a gap for me which all histories had left till that time empty. . . . 'All through that fight I was scared nearly to death . . . but you see, nobody knew that but me. Next day General Polk sent for me, and praised me. . . . I never said anything, I let it go at that. I judged it wasn't so, but it was not for me to contradict a general officer.' "

William B. Dillingham

"Insensibility in *The Red Badge of Courage*"□

When Henry Fleming, the youth of Stephen Crane's *The Red Badge of Courage*, charges ahead of his comrades and fearlessly carries his flag into the very jaws of death, he seems to be a romantic hero rather than the protagonist of a naturalistic novel. But for Crane appearance was seldom reality. Bearing the symbol of his country's cause, Henry is unquestionably courageous, but the underlying causes of his deeds are neither noble nor humane. Throughout his life Crane deeply respected heroic action. His attitude was, as Daniel G. Hoffman has said, that it was "among the very few means man has of achieving magnificence";[1] nevertheless, he considered courage the product of a complex of non-rational drives. The difference between the external act of courage and the internal process that leads up to that act created for Crane one of the supreme ironies of life.

The Red Badge has frequently been read as the story of how a young soldier achieves some sort of spiritual salvation. One critic sees Henry Fleming's "growth toward moral maturity";[2] another, his "redemption" through "humility and loving-kindness."[3] His initiation has been called the successful search for "spiritual and psychological order,"

□ William B. Dillingham, "Insensibility in *The Red Badge of Courage*," *College English*, XXV (December, 1963), pp. 194–198. Reprinted with the permission of the National Council of Teachers of English and William B. Dillingham.

the discovery of a "vision of pattern."[4] Some readings emphasize Henry's new sense of brotherhood and call the book the story of a young man's developing awareness of social responsibility.[5] Such views as these offer more insight than may be indicated by a brief quotation and comment, but they also tend to obscure the central irony of the novel, that of the nature of courage, by making Henry Fleming as distinctive and as individually interesting a character as, say, Raskolnikov, Huckleberry Finn, or Isabel Archer. The young soldier whom Crane seldom calls by name is, as Alfred Kazin has suggested, Everyman—or at least every man who has the potentiality for courage.[6] The chief purpose of the novel is to objectify the nature of heroism through Henry Fleming. Through witnessing his actions and changing sensations we discover the emerging paradox of courage: human courage is by its nature subhuman; in order to be courageous, a man in time of physical strife must abandon the highest of his human facilities, reason and imagination, and act instinctively, even animalistically.[7]

In developing and illustrating this paradoxical definition of courage, Crane used a simple structural arrangement. The novel is divided into two parts of twelve chapters each. The first twelve chapters tell of Henry Fleming's early insecurities about himself; his first battle, where he fights and then runs; his various adventures during his retreat; and finally his encounter with the fleeing soldier and then his wound. Chapter 13 begins with Henry's coming back to his own camp to begin anew, and the remainder of the book takes the reader through the battles of the next day, in which Henry fights with great courage.

The first part of the book deals with the anatomy of cowardice, which is in Henry the result of an active imagination and a disposition to think too much. Until he receives the head wound in Chapter 12, he is characterized by a romantic and thoughtful self-consciousness. In his anxiety about how he will conduct himself in combat, he speculates constantly about himself and the nature of battle: "He tried to mathematically prove to himself that he would not run from a battle" (p. 30).[8] Trying to comfort himself through reason, he makes "ceaseless calculations" for days. Finally he has to admit that "he could not sit still and with a mental slate and pencil derive an answer" (p. 35). Henry's "own eternal debate" is frequently interrupted by the terrifying images of his imagination. In the darkness he sees "visions of a thousand-tongued fear that would babble at his back and cause him to flee" (p. 44). This constant activity of Henry's reason and imagination compels him to feel isolated until he experiences a vague sense of unity with his fellows during the first battle. Here he becomes suddenly caught up in the fight almost by accident. In contrast to his insensibility in later battles, "he strenuously tried to think," but he is luckily carried along by the momentary excitement of his comrades. The first encounter with the enemy is very brief, and his courage is not seriously tested. In the second engagement, his imagination is rampant: "He began to exaggerate the endurance, the skill, and the valour of those who were coming" (p. 73). He imagines the enemy as dragons and sees himself as being "gobbled." No longer feeling enclosed in the "moving box" of his first encounter and now stimulated by wild imaginings, Henry runs in terror from the battle.

In "The Veteran," a short story written as a sequel to *The Red Badge*, Henry, now an old man, reminisces about his war experience and tells how his imagination and his reliance on reason compelled him to run: "The trouble was . . . I thought they were all shooting at me. Yes, sir, I thought every man in the other army was aiming at me in particular, and only me. And it seemed so darned unreasonable, you know. I wanted to explain to 'em what an almighty good fellow I was, because I thought then they might quit all trying to hit me."[9]

After his retreat, he wanders behind the lines, still relying upon his reason and imagination, attempting to convince himself that he is the reasonable man, "the enlightened man," who "had fled because of his superior perceptions and knowledge" (p. 81). When he comes upon the group of wounded men, he is still debating his case. He then witnesses the death of his friend Jim Conklin. But even at this point he shows no significant change.[10] Shortly thereafter, his imagination still controls him as he magnifies "the dangers and

horrors of the engagement" from which he fled (p. 104). Until
he is wounded in Chapter 12, he is still rationalizing, still
trying mathematically to prove to himself that his cowardice
was "in truth a symmetrical act" (p. 104).

The episode in which Henry is struck by a retreating
Union soldier occurs at the center of the novel both physically
and thematically. The incident has frequently been called the
ironic peak of the story. A Union soldier, not the enemy,
gives Henry his wound, and unlike his comrades he is wounded
with the butt of a gun, not with a bullet. Upon this highly
ironic "red badge" Henry builds his courage. In addition to its
function as irony, the wound serves as the chief symbol of the
book. Significantly, the wound is inflicted on the *head*.
Almost from the moment he is struck, Henry starts to set aside
his fearful and potent imagination and his reason. Symbolically, the head wound is the damage the experience of war
gives to these highest human faculties. The chaos of war
teaches the necessity of insensibility. After the symbolic
wound, Henry finds his way back to his regiment, and the
last half of the book portrays a youth initiated into the ways
of courage. From here on, Henry runs from himself; he escapes his essential humanity in order to avoid running in
battle.

Henry's inner voices and visions, then, are obliterated
by the head wound. Through one half of the story, his mind has
been tried and found wanting. Henry's wound forces his
attention to his physical being. The only voices now heard are
those of the body. After he returns to camp, "he made vague
plans to go off into the deeper darkness and hide, but they were
all destroyed by the voices of exhaustion and pain from his
body" (p. 120). When he awakes, "it seemed to him that he
had been asleep for a thousand years, and he felt sure that he
opened his eyes upon an unexpected world" (p. 127). The Henry Fleming who before looked into the future, saw imagined
horrors, and speculated constantly about himself, now thinks
little of the future: "He did not give a good deal of thought to
these battles that lay directly before him. It was not essential
that he should plan his ways in regard to them" (p. 136). He
has become instinctively aware of a truth taught by intense

experience, that man can and must cultivate a dullness which
will serve as armor against the stings of fear and panic. The
totality of Henry's war experience thus far has helped to show
him that "retribution was a laggard and blind."

In contrast to the thoughtful and romantic boy of the
first part of the book, the young warrior of the last twelve
chapters is capable of unreason, even self-abandon. At the
first sight of the enemy, he "forgot many personal matters
and became greatly enraged" (p. 141). He becomes a prideful
animal, seeking the throat of the enemy with self-forgetful-
ness. The feelings of the imaginative young soldier, who once
thought of war as a glorious Greek-like struggle, now are
constantly described in terms of bestiality, unreason, and
even insanity. He "lost sense of everything but his hate"
(p. 148). Suspending all thought, he fights as a "barbarian, a
beast . . . a pagan" (p. 150). His actions are frequently described as "wild." He is "unconsciously" out in front of the
other troops, looking "to be an insane soldier." "There was
the delirium that encounters despair and death, and is heedless and blind to the odds. It is a temporary but sublime absence of selfishness" (p. 160). The selflessness implied here is
not self-sacrifice but insensibility, which enables Henry to
escape thoughts and suspend imagination, to get outside of
himself while the emotions of rage and hatred control his
actions. As he cultivates personal insensibility his mental
position as an observer becomes more and more pronounced:
"He was deeply absorbed as a spectator; . . . he did not know
that he breathed" (pp. 184–185). Henry's self-abandon spreads
to the others, who were "again grown suddenly wild with an
enthusiasm of unselfishness" (p. 189). Henry is no longer
aware of the personal element in the danger that he faces.
Now he does not think of the enemy as attempting to kill him
personally. He looks upon their bullets vaguely as "things
that could prevent him from reaching the place of his endeavour" (p. 189). So separated from meditation and imagination is Henry that he finds it difficult after the battle to become
himself again: "It took moments for it [his mind] to cast off
its battleful ways and resume its accustomed course of
thought. Gradually his brain emerged from the clogged

clouds, and at last he was enabled to more closely comprehend himself and circumstances" (pp. 196–197).

Henry's change is thus the result of intensely dangerous experience which reveals to him intuitively the impersonal nature of the forces that defeat men. After glimpsing the powers of "strange, squalling upheavals" he is able to control his fear. This ability comes to men not through intellectual or spiritual processes but through habit in being exposed to violence. As Henry becomes more accustomed to battle and the sight of death, he no longer thinks about the implication of these overwhelming experiences. He sinks into a subhuman dullness and is thereby able to act courageously. He does not learn to know himself, as one critic asserts,[11] but to escape himself—to make his mind blank, to become a "spectator."

Otherwise, Henry remains essentially unchanged during the course of the novel. It is a mistake to think of him as having become rejuvenated through humility or in any way changed into a better person morally. He has simply adapted himself through experience to a new and dangerous environment.[12] When the last battle is over, he is the same prideful youth, bragging on himself as he reviews his deeds of valor. The Christian references, which have so frequently been a subject of controversy, do not point to "rebirth" or "salvation" for Henry. The pattern of religious imagery built up through the use of such words as "sacrifice," "hymn," and "cathedral" is part of the pervasive irony of the book.[13] Just as Henry is not "selfless" in the usual sense of the word, neither is he "saved" in the Christian sense. It is his body that is saved, not his soul. He is trained by war to realize, in contradiction of Christian ideals, that he must desert the mind and spirit and allow his physical being—even his animal self—to dominate. Through Henry, Crane is saying with St. Matthew that whosoever will lose his life will find it. But the Christian paradox is in direct opposition to Crane's. Henry finds and retains his physical life by losing that sensibility characteristic of the highest forms of life.

The evidence for a "naturalistic" interpretation of *The Red Badge* is overwhelming.[14] Creating, chiefly through irony, a considerable degree of aesthetic distance, Crane studies the change in the behavior of a soldier. Through half the book this character is a sensitive youth. But sensitivity is incompatible with physical courage and the ability to kill. In the center of the story occurs the symbolic head wound, which damages the youth's sensibility and causes him to rely more on the physical and instinctive, less on the mental. For the rest of the book, Henry is brave in battle, having arrived at that state of self-discipline which makes one in danger resemble more an animal than a man. An iconoclast, Crane enjoyed laughing as he destroyed the illusions of a former tradition. He does not rejoice that Henry has found courage; he does not change him into a better person. Nor does he mourn as did Wilfred Owen for the tenderness and the innocence that war destroys in those who must kill.[15] With a keen sense of the incongruity of things, he simply shows that courage has been misunderstood. In order to be a Greek (in a Greek-like struggle), one must be a barbarian.

Notes

1 Daniel G. Hoffman, *The Poetry of Stephen Crane* (New York, 1957), p. 150.
2 James B. Colvert, "Structure and Theme in Stephen Crane's Fiction," *Modern Fiction Studies*, 5 (Autumn, 1959), p. 204.
3 Robert Wooster Stallman, introduction to *The Red Badge of Courage*, Modern Library (New York, 1951), p. xxxii.
4 Earle Labor, "Crane and Hemingway: Anatomy of Trauma," *Renascence*, 11 (Summer, 1959), p. 195.
5 John E. Hart, "*The Red Badge of Courage* as Myth and Symbol," *University of Kansas City Review*, 19 (Summer, 1953), pp. 249–256. See also M. Solomon, "Stephen Crane: A Critical Study," *Mainstream*, 9 (January, 1956), pp. 25–42.
6 Alfred Kazin, *On Native Grounds* (New York, 1956), p. 50.
7 Although the focus of his article is somewhat different from the present discussion, James Trammel Cox also states this central paradox of *The Red Badge:* ". . . the selfless behavior of heroism paradoxically emerges only from the grossest, most infantile, animalistic, fiery hatred born of the vanity of egocentrism." "The Imagery of *The Red Badge of Courage*," *Modern Fiction Studies*, 5 (Autumn, 1959), p. 219. Hoffman suggests the paradox in his treatment of Crane's indebtedness to Tolstoy: introduction to *The Red Badge of Courage and Other Stories* (New York, 1957), p. xii.
8 Page references are to *The Work of Stephen Crane*, ed. Wilson Follett (New York, 1925), I.
9 *Work*, I, p. 204.
10 For an opposite opinion, see Stallman, p. xxxiii.

11 Norman Friedman, "Criticism and the Novel," *Antioch Review*, 18 (Fall, 1958), pp. 356–361.

12 Crane never ceased to be interested in the molding influence of environment. His favorite situation shows man pitted against a new and quite different environment. In some cases, as in "The Blue Hotel" and "The Bride Comes to Yellow Sky," characters find it impossible to undergo the necessary change to survive and are either destroyed or disillusioned. In *The Red Badge* as in "The Open Boat," however, the chief characters manage to adapt to the dangerous new environment and thus to survive.

13 Two critics have made similar statements about the Christian imagery of the book: Bernard Weisbarger, *"The Red Badge of Courage,"* in *Twelve Original Essays on Great American Novels*, ed. Charles Shapiro (Detroit, 1958), pp. 104–105; and Cox, pp. 217–218.

14 Several naturalistic interpretations are available. See, for example, Winifred Lynskey, "Crane's *The Red Badge of Courage*," *Explicator*, 8 (Dec., 1949), 3; Richard Chase, introduction to Riverside Edition of *The Red Badge* (Boston, 1960); and Charles Child Walcutt, *American Literary Naturalism, A Divided Stream* (Minneapolis, 1956).

15 Owen's poem "Insensibility" is, however, a remarkably similar statement of the definition of courage:

> Dullness best solves
> The tease and doubt of shelling,
> And Chance's strange arithmetic
> Comes simpler than the reckoning of their
>   shilling.
> ....
> Happy are these who lose imagination:
> They have enough to carry with
>   ammunition.
> ....
> Having seen all things red,
> Their eyes are rid
> Of the hurt of the colour of blood for
>   ever.

Kermit Vanderbilt and Daniel Weiss

from *"Rifleman to Flagbearer: Henry Fleming's Separate Peace in The Red Badge of Courage"*□

The significance and to some extent the excellence of a literary work can be measured by the volume of critical debate which it has provoked. By this gauge, Stephen Crane's *The Red Badge of Courage* stands virtually unsurpassed among American novels. The critical issues have ranged from the meaning of Jim Conklin's death on the first day of battle to Crane's ironic or non-ironic intention on the second day when Henry Fleming presumably arrives at a quiet, unflinching manhood. Beyond these matters, a larger question of meaning has centered on whether Crane placed his youthful soldier in a world of naturalism, of Christian morality, or of primordial myth.

This wide disagreement over the intended meaning of an author who aimed to write "plainly and unmistakably" can be partly explained when one isolates a major frustration which critics of *The Red Badge of Courage* seem to have shared. It is this: after Henry, on the second day, has at last hurled himself into the cannon's mouth, and then only briefly (Chapter XVII), he abandons the role of rifleman and soon becomes a flagbearer. He gives up the psychic advantage

□ *Modern Fiction Studies*, XI (Winter, 1965–1966), pp. 371–380. © 1966, by the Purdue Research Foundation, Lafayette, Indiana.

of the soldier who can shoot back at the enemy and chooses, instead, this highly dangerous but auxiliary role in the final extended action of the second day. How does one account for Henry's self-election as standard-bearer in the final one-fourth of the novel (Chapters XVIII to XXIII)? Readings of *Red Badge* have consistently passed over these flagbearing chapters with, at most, a passage or two cited to provide a convenient transition from Chapter XVII to concluding Chapter XXIV.[1]

The present confusion over the unity of *The Red Badge of Courage* might have been partly avoided had Crane's later critics been more willing to accept his own stated intention, to present "a psychological portrayal of fear."[2] Cosmic issues aside, *Red Badge* is clearly what Crane said that it was, an extended dramatic portrayal of fear. He apparently intended to characterize a youth who is trying to maintain an equilibrium within himself and with relation to his own comrades and a fearsome enemy. The culmination of Henry Fleming's ordeal of fear, the point where Henry's essentially dependent, sensitive nature finally becomes reconciled to aggressive warfare, occurs not in his experience of Jim Conklin's death on the first day. Nor does it happen, again anticlimactically, during the initial charge of the second day, when Henry fights momentarily with blind and ferocious abandon. Rather, the climax of the novel occurs when Henry suddenly has a revelation later on the second day and elects to replace the slain flagbearer. This fourth and final act of the novel is a consistent, climactic, and in a qualified sense an ironic, culmination of Henry Fleming's ordeal as a soldier. In addition to illuminating Henry's psychological defenses against fear in the previous chapters of the novel, this final action also helps to reveal Crane's meaning in the final chapter of the book. By understanding Henry Fleming's self-appointed commission as flagbearer, we also discover the structural and psychological unity of Crane's novel.

I

Henry Fleming's major concern as a soldier is to cope with

his fear of death by discovering what his basic nature is and, in the process, to preserve his esteem within the regiment. His preliminary anxieties (Chapters I to III, to "one gray dawn," p. 247) are followed by a many-sided test of his fear during the first day of battle (Chapters III through XIII). Briefly summarized, this first day depicts Henry in an opening charge which reveals him to be neither courageous nor cowardly. He is borne along in a "battle-sleep." But an unexpected second wave of attack suddenly floods Henry with panic fear. He drops his rifle and runs. He next receives several grisly views of death close up, culminating in the death-ceremony of Jim Conklin. He invites his harmless "red badge of courage" by his annoying questions to a retreating Union soldier. So "wounded," he acts out in fancy several guilty and unsatisfactory daydreams of heroic courage, together with a death Jim-Conklin-fashion. He is finally reunited with his regiment through his childlike dependence on a magic helper, the "cheery soldier." And we see him at the close of the first day behaving with "doglike obedience" toward Wilson (p. 311), who protectively cares for the receptive Henry with "the bustling ways of an amateur nurse" (p. 310).

Before giving a somewhat more detailed account of Henry's fear on this first day of battle, we can first draw two tentative conclusions. One is that Henry's continuing defenses against fear after the death of Jim Conklin can dismiss the argument that Jim's death has produced any significant change in Henry. Second, Crane has given us no reason whatsoever to believe that his fearful youth is ready to awaken on the following morning the happy warrior. Henry's actions on the second day, with certain exceptions to be noted, will be, in fact, suspiciously like those of the first day. After his false bravado and one brief, demonic charge (Chapters XIV to XVII), Henry will again be threatened with overwhelming panic. But he will be rescued once more through the aid of a fantasied protector—this time the Union flag. In short, Henry experiences neither change nor regeneration in his two days of soldiering. Rather, he discovers the conduct proper to his native qualities as a man, which includes his relative unfitness as an aggressive rifleman.

Henry Fleming at the opening of the second day of battle does appear to be a new man, an aggressive, hell-for-leather fighting soldier. The main differences in Henry's attitude are two. First, he is encouraged by his "wound" to adopt an equally spurious pose of masculine aggressiveness— in returning Wilson's farewell letters of the previous day "with condescending pity" (p. 322); in constructing a private fantasy of being back home a hero recounting his war exploits to a worshipful audience; and in noisily criticizing the officers in authority. But a soldier unwittingly calls Henry's bluff, and "his mind shrank from going nearer to the danger, and thereafter he was silent. The significance of the sarcastic man's words took from him all loud moods that would make him appear prominent. He became suddenly a modest person" (p. 325). When Henry briefly returns to his criticism of the operational procedures, the "savage-minded lieutenant" quickly sets Henry down (p. 327). The second difference in Henry's behavior is more significant, the degree of anger which he now has been able to cultivate against the enemy. Gregory Zilboorg, writing about troop morale in World War Two, has described the sanction of anger:

It is a well-observed fact that "green" troops become "seasoned" as soon as they become angry—that is, as soon as they begin to convert their fear of death into hatred and aggression. This usually happens after the baptism of fire, not so much because the soldiers become accustomed to the fire of the enemy, but primarily because their anger begins to be aroused after they have lost some of their brothers in combat. It is the mechanism of revenge, of overcoming death by means of murder, that proves here too the most potent psychological force.[3]

But Henry's is a rage with a difference. The "mechanism of revenge" on behalf of comrades lost in battle plays no recognizable part at all. The anger which Henry feels when confronted by the relentlessly advancing enemy belongs to the passive, contemplative youth of the day before: "There was a maddening quality in this seeming resolution of the foe to give him no rest, to give him no time to sit down and think. Yesterday he had fought and had fled rapidly. There had been many adventures. For to-day he felt that he had earned opportunities for contemplative repose" (p. 328). Notice also that the cruel and saddening death of Jim Conklin has now become only one among the "many adventures" of the first day. So Henry is different on this second day because of anger, but it is an anger inspired directly by his continuing self-concern. It will, however, prove valuable as a temporary defense against overwhelming panic in his third charge.

One must conclude, then, that Henry's responses here are not substantially different from the first day. In the first charge of the second day, Henry's aggressive pose and "loud moods" are quickly supplanted by his old sense of personal impotence and of existing in a battle-sleep. He wishes that his rifle were "an engine of annihilating power. . . . When, in a dream, it occurred to the youth that his rifle was an impotent stick, he lost sense of everything but his hate . . ." (p. 329). Again, he returns to the delirium of his first-day battle experience: "The youth was not conscious that he was erect upon his feet. He did not know the direction of the ground. Indeed, once he even lost the habit of balance and fell heavily. He was up again immediately. One thought went through the chaos of his brain at the time. He wondered if he had fallen because he had been shot" (p. 330).

And again, this helplessness and delirium suggest the behavior of a young boy. What makes Crane's grasp of the psychology of soldiering a marvel of intuition throughout the novel lies in his recognition of what servicemen know from direct observation, that war invokes infantile responses, a primitive level of mind which is archaic to the uses of mature and peaceful culture. Army life decrees a moratorium on maturity in the mental lives of individual soldiers. The army becomes for the soldier a substitute family, an institutionalized version of both the protective and the punishing parents. In exchange for giving up his independence, the soldier entrusts his life and well-being to his superiors, fashioning the relationship out of its analogy with his earlier dependence on his parents. And so on the first day of battle, Henry finds his protective security not in the enveloping concern of his strong-minded mother for her only son, but in the collective activity of the army. When the battle forms, Henry is engulfed in the collective security of the "moving box" (p. 248), the "common personality . . . superior to circumstances . . . with a mighty power" (p. 261). He also appears both to be seeking and rebuking his lost father in the images of those officers whom Crane isolates, now here, now there, who represent aggression, authority, assurance, and an active omnipotence, but who also threaten to leave Henry to face his anxieties alone. Before battle, Henry feels that he can concern himself with "his personal comfort. For recreation he could twiddle his thumbs and speculate on the thoughts which must agitate the minds of the generals" (p. 233). He presently blames these paternal figures, however, for not protecting him against his anxiety: "In his great anxiety his heart was continually clamoring at what he considered the intolerable slowness of the generals" (p. 239; see again pp. 250, 251, 252). But when Henry conjures a fearful, impressionistic image of "the red eyes across the river . . . growing larger, as the orbs of a row of dragons advancing," he turns to the colonel on the horse and sees him, a looming, authoritarian, Kafkaesque figure, "lift his gigantic arm and calmly stroke his mustache" (p. 240). When this omnipotence seems to falter and Henry feels cast out on his own, he resents the officer who rebukes him and orders him to march ahead. To punish the officer, as well as to appease his own wounded conscience, Henry thinks like the dependent and angry small boy—he will die and then the unfeeling parent will be sorry: "He would die; he would go to some place where he would be understood. It was useless to expect appreciation of his profound and fine senses from such men as the lieutenant" (p. 253). The fantasy passes. The officer as Crane notes, is necessary to Henry's and the regiment's safety, and his voice speaks to a soldier with something of "divinity . . . stern, hard, with no reflection of fear in it" (p. 263).[4]

The first day of battle is replete with even more specific references to the regressive nature of soldiering in general, and of Henry Fleming in particular. Henry feels "like a babe" (p. 248) as he is carried along in the security of the moving box. Henry's perspiring face is "like that of a weeping urchin" (p. 260). He fights for air in the midst of the smoke "as a babe

being smothered attacks the deadly blankets" (p. 262), while
the soldier next to him is "babbling . . . like the monologue of
a babe" (p. 262). At the end of the first charge, Henry is filled
with the sensations of collective omnipotence and liberation
from the "red, formidable difficulties of war" (p. 265). In his
battle-sleep, he has been carried along to safety within the
family of his "subtle battle brotherhood" (p. 261), the
"mysterious fraternity" (p. 261) of the collective regiment.
And now, as "the youth awakened slowly" (p. 265), he "felt
the bonds of tied hearts" (p. 266). But he is also filled with the
sense of being something special within the brotherhood, of
being not only secure from danger but of being privately
"magnificent," and he goes into "an ecstasy of self-satisfac-
tion" (p. 266). But a few moments later, he is suddenly confronted by the Rebel Army in a second wave, and in a trance of
astonishment and helplessness, he suddenly grows numb with
fear and runs "like a rabbit" (p. 268).

Returning to the opening wave of attack on the second
day, one finds Henry still behaving like a fearful young boy.
What Crane suggests this time, in addition, is the essential
paradox of men at war who are most "heroic" when they have
become heedless, demonic children. Henry becomes the infantile berserker, shooting wildly at an enemy who seems more
like a swarm of "flies sucking insolently at his blood" (p.
329) than like men. He even continues to fire when the
retreating enemy is no longer there. Henry's flight to activity
on the second day, in short, leads him briefly to deny fear and
danger by the paradoxical strategy of exposing himself to the
very thing he fears. To prevent or forestall the terror of surprise and sudden annihilation, he plunges headlong into the
feared situation, preferring even destruction to the dread of
destruction. He is like Ovid's fear-crazed men in the plague-
ridden city who:

> Hung themselves
> Driving the fear of death away by death
> By going out to meet it.[5]

Henry Fleming's old need for reassurance of his own immunity
is bound up with his obsessive and very short-lived display
of fierceness in the first charge of the second day. He dimly

and ironically recognizes soon afterwards, when he has received the admiration of his comrades and the praises of his officer, that he has been a somnolent schoolboy commanding a phantom enemy to fall dead on command: "By this struggle he had overcome obstacles which he had admitted to be mountains. They had fallen like paper peaks, and he was now what he called a hero. And he had not been aware of the process. He had slept and, awakening, found himself a knight" (p. 331). What Henry senses here is that fear is a strictly personal emotion which may lie behind either cowardice or "courage." His central problem of mastering his fear has now taken the two extremes of adjustment—cowardice in flight from the dangerous object, and barbaric "courage" through flight toward the danger.

II

It is here, precisely, at what would seem to be the moment of his apotheosis as the soldier-hero that Henry Fleming makes his final adaptation, not only to his continuing fear of death but also to his basic nature as a man. After this third charge of his battle career, Henry, far from being the seasoned veteran who kills without scruple, now turns gradually to regain the softer emotional sensibilities of the non-combatant.

Henry's abdication from his brief role as the aggressive rifleman begins when he and Wilson go in search of water to fill their comrades' canteens. During the search, Henry once more resumes his earlier role of the curious spectator. He is again filled with anxiety over his helpless vulnerability: he has overheard the two officers of his division refer to his regiment as "a lot 'a mule drivers" (p. 335), and now "new eyes were given to him. And the most startling thing was to learn suddenly that he was very insignificant" (p. 335).

In the action of the fourth charge that follows, Henry's fear of death returns in its original form when he concurs with the fearful soldier who says "in a meek voice, 'We'll git swallowed' " (p. 337). The angry, reckless Henry of the previous charge, who had tried to swallow the enemy alone, has become again the passive fearful youth: "The youth stared at the land in front of him. Its foliages now seemed to veil powers and horrors" (p. 337). He is momentarily in the moving box, and then "directly he lunged ahead and began to run" (p. 337). He is again in a dazed condition until the young lieutenant "grappled with him as if for a wrestling bout" (p. 341). Henry is soon running "like a madman to reach the woods before a bullet could discover him. He ducked his head low, like a football player. In his haste his eyes almost closed, and the scene was a wild blur. Pulsating saliva stood at the corners of his mouth" (p. 342). More dazed and helpless than the day before, Henry suddenly has a revelation: he discovers a new source of immunity from the mounting terrors of death on the battlefield:

Within him as he hurled himself forward, was born a love, a despairing fondness for this flag which was near him. It was a creation of beauty and invulnerability. It was a goddess, radiant, that bended its form with an imperious gesture to him. It was a woman, red and white, hating and loving, that called him with the voice of his hopes. Because no harm could come to it he endowed it with power. He kept near, as if it could be a saver of lives, and an imploring cry went from his mind (p. 342).

That the color sergeant is suddenly struck dead does not alter Henry's belief in the efficacy which the flag will hold especially for him. In a brief rivalry over the flag with Wilson, Henry gains possession of his new magic helper. Just as the "cheery soldier" came along after Jim Conklin's death, seemingly with "a wand of a magic kind" (p. 306), to save the submissive Henry after the debacle of the first day, the flag serves Henry's need for a protector during the critical juncture of the second day. The flag, which he endows so obviously with intermingled trappings of invulnerability, maternity, and divinity, is, in effect, the protective Athena for this delicate young Achilles, and war becomes the "Homeric" game Henry had initially fancied it to be. He is clearly employing once more a delusional system linked to the reality of warfare as magic formulae are linked to the phenomena they control. In actuality, Henry has become the most conspicuous moving target on the battlefield. But the flag, in becoming his fantasied charm against danger, will allow Henry in the remaining charges of the second day to protect himself from fear and to maintain his self-respect within the regiment. To the young lieutenant rallying the troops, Henry becomes the helpmeet, not an identification this time but an independent, auxiliary relationship with the man of action. Henry can also charge along with his comrades and shout encouragement without incurring the risk of their vulnerability or their "misty-eyed" panic and confusion in the face of the aggressor: "He veiled a glance of disdain at his fellows who strewed the ground, choking with dust, red from perspiration, misty-eyed, disheveled" (p. 350). In short, the irony of Henry's final stance is that he is now praised by the colonel as the good soldier, a "jimhickey" (p. 353), and he has, in fact, returned to his original self-concern, his propensity for make-believe, and his preferred role of an absorbed spectator at a "great drama" (p. 357), at a "matched game" (p. 354).[6]

III

At the end of *The Red Badge of Courage*, Henry Fleming has constructed his own mental defenses against the "thousand-tongued fear," and so has learned how to control and master it. That he has gradually come to terms with "reality" through various fantasies, culminating with his being both a spectator at a controlled and ritualized "game" of war, and a nonaggressive participant divinely protected from danger through his magic helper, the flag—these are only a part of Crane's mild ironies at the end. Henry is also given to feel "a quiet manhood, nonassertive but of sturdy and strong blood. He knew that he would no more quail before his guides wherever they should point. He had been to touch the great death, and found that, after all, it was but the great death. He was a man" (p. 369). But this "manhood" does not include the aggressiveness which characterizes the good hard-boiled soldier, the primitive Fortinbras. Henry remains essentially the young Hamlet, the contemplative youth whose responses to danger could never be hammered into the merciless reflexes of the hardened veteran. Briefly at the opening of the second day, Henry's fear had driven him into aggressive activity; but it

was inevitably a spurious flight, a pantomime of the fierce
soldier from which he turned with a sense both of helplessness
and relief back to his old dependencies. As flagbearer, he
clearly has not thrown off the swaddling bands; instead, he
has extended their coverage. He has gained a female protec-
tress who will enclothe with total invulnerability her favored
and dependent only son. He has once again become someone
magnificent and special. (In the passage just quoted, Crane
had originally made unmistakable the irony of Henry's sense
of special immunity: Henry had discovered that the great
death "was for others" [p. 369].) Now feeling exalted within
the regiment, he discovers that he can put at a convenient
distance the haunting memory of his panic flight and his
shameful inability to help the tattered soldier on the previous
day. He has rid himself of the "red sickness of battle" (p.
370) without suffering the loss of self-esteem or social alienation from his fighting comrades. Henry has adopted his unique
and final role as bearer of the colors because it is entirely in
accord with his unconscious sense of himself.

Returning to the critical debate over *The Red Badge of
Courage*, one must conclude that the structure of Crane's
"psychological portrayal of fear" has been developed,
naturally enough, around Henry Fleming's instinct of fear.
The alternating rhythms of the novel on both days have been
defined by Henry's sleeps and wakings, his separations from
and reunions with some form of omnipotence, his alternating
flights (both real and imagined) into activity and then back
into passivity. In the flagbearing chapters, these rhythms have
been brought into unity and the discords of battle activity
privately resolved for Henry. Crane's final chapter fails to
support the reading of Henry either as a seasoned military
man or as a mythical hero dominated by altruistic concern for
his people. Nor does one discover here the concluding scene
in a Christian drama of spiritual growth and change: Henry's
private vision suggests the late nineteenth-century universe
not of Tolstoy but of Mark Twain. At the end, the novel and
its central character turn away from the problems of courage
and cowardice, from delirium, battle sleep, and the chaos of
human warfare.

He turned now with a lover's thirst to images of tranquil skies, fresh meadows, cool brooks—an existence of soft and eternal peace.

Over the river a golden ray of sun came through the hosts of leaden rain clouds (p. 370).

The landscape images the separate "golden" peace which Henry has arrived at through his fantasied election as flag-bearer, while the "leaden rain clouds" of war exist for Union soldiers less fortunate. Henry Fleming's final stance suggests both a return to himself and a farm boy's private reunion with a world of beneficent nature, a separate existence of security and peace in the midst of war.

Notes

1   A notable exception is John E. Hart's *"The Red Badge of Courage* as Myth and Symbol," *University of Kansas City Review*, XIX (Summer, 1953), pp. 249–256. Mr. Hart tries to give a total reading of the novel by interpreting Henry as a mythic hero whose arduous quest is fulfilled when he attains the "beautiful maiden," symbolized by the flag. Mr. Hart, however, overlooks Henry's basic self-concern and spectator-interest which are fully renewed during his second day's role as flagbearer.

2   Robert W. Stallman discounted Crane's statement and also criticized Thomas Beer's early study of Crane for its influential and misleading emphasis on fear in Crane. That Beer and later Crane critics failed to analyze in any detail the nature of fear in *Red Badge* might be more justly charged. Mr. Stallman's own "Notes Toward an Analysis of *The Red Badge of Courage*" which, not surprisingly, has been scored for being fragmentary, and thereby forced, insists that the novel "is about the self-combat of a youth who fears [sic] and stubbornly resists change, and the actual battle is symbolic of this spiritual warfare against change and growth" (*Stephen Crane: An Omnibus* [New York, 1952], pp. 582, 193).

All page numbers in the text of the present essay refer to Mr. Stallman's *Omnibus* edition.

3   "Fear of Death," *Psychoanalytic Quarterly*, XII (October, 1943), p. 474.

4   The omnipotent officer of *Red Badge* appears elsewhere in Crane. In "The Price of the Harness," written out of Crane's experience in the Spanish-American War, the unassailable officer returns in the following scene: "The whole scene would have spoken to the private soldiers of ambushes, sudden flank attacks, terrible disasters, if it were not for those cool gentlemen with shoulder-straps and swords who, the private soldiers knew, were of another world and omnipotent for the business" (*Stephen Crane: Twenty Stories*, ed. Carl Van Doren [New York, 1940], p. 436).

John Berryman's *Stephen Crane* (New York, 1950) first hypothesized Oedipal fixations in Crane's life and work. Maxwell Geismar, *Rebels and Ancestors: The American Novel, 1890–1915* (Cambridge, Mass., 1953), supported Berryman's thesis, and attempted also to give it social and religious significance. Whether or not Henry Fleming's conflicts within the military family are derived in part from Crane's own childhood is not crucial to the present analysis of the novel.

5 *Metamorphoses*, trans. Rolfe Humphries (Bloomington, 1955), Book Seven, lines 604–606.

6 Hemingway, who admired Crane and whose war career and writings about fear parallel Crane's in many respects, has Yogi Johnson in *The Torrents of Spring* liken war-combat to a football game; Crane has Henry Fleming, on the second day, race over the battlefield ducking "his head low like a football player." The similitude of the "matched game" in *Red Badge* recurs on the second day: the soldiers are like "sprinters before a signal" (pp. 336–337); the opposing armies exchange "blows in the manner of a pair of boxers" (p. 347). Suggested here is that Crane and Hemingway, both athletes, knew privately what psychologist Abram Kardiner has since verified: that fear generally and battle sickness in particular has a way of working themselves out through the spectator experience, actual or fantasied, of the ritualized sports event. (See *War Stress and Neurotic Illness* [New York, 1947], pp. 206 ff.)

IX

C Sister arrie (1900) by Theodore Dreiser

John Howard Lawson

from "Dreiser Discusses Sister Carrie"□

*I*n 1928, a young and forward-looking Broadway producer, H. S. Kraft, made contracts with Theodore Dreiser and myself for a dramatic presentation of Sister Carrie. I went to work on the play, in which Paul Muni was to perform the role of Hurstwood.

The plan fell through, largely because of my inability to provide an effective dramatization of Dreiser's massive and subtle novel. We discussed the use of a symbolic device—a series of interludes in which a tramp, a man destroyed by society and wandering in its lower depths, would give a poetic and prophetic sense of the fate awaiting Hurstwood. Looking back over the years, it seems obvious that the suggestion was artificial, and that it conflicted in mood and method with the naturalistic technique and profound psychological depth of the novel.

It seems to me that Dreiser's letters on the subject are of interest for two reasons: they illuminate aspects of the problem of translating a novel into dramatic terms. More importantly, they express the author's feeling concerning the social background and significance of one of his greatest stories.

JOHN HOWARD LAWSON

□ From *Masses & Mainstream*, vol. VIII (December, 1955), pp. 20, 21–22. Reprinted by permission of the publisher, American Dialog.

SISTER CARRIE (1900)
THEODORE DREISER

New York City, Oct. 10, 1928

My dear Lawson:

It does seem to me that you are getting much nearer the drama as well as the spirit of the book. And after a fashion I like the idea of the bum or down-and-out as suggesting what I emphasized—the need of presenting clearly the drama of Hurstwood's decay. But I think you will not get this straight, or be able to present it to the best advantage, until you ask yourself, as I asked myself a long time ago, what was it exactly that brought about Hurstwood's decline? What psychic thing in himself? for most certainly it could not have been just the commonplace knocks and errors out of which most people take their rise. It is not enough to say that he is not a strong man, or that he lacked a first class brain. Granted. And it is obvious from the book. But there is something more. A distillation not only of his lack of strength and his mediocre brain, but of the day and the city and the circumstances of which, at say forty odd, he found himself a part. And this is of a twofold character. First—a sense of folly or mistake in him because of his having taken the money of his employers and so having lost not only their friendship and confidence but the, for him, almost necessary milieu of Chicago—its significance as the center of his home, children, friends, connections —what you will. Next the ultimate folly of his hypnosis in regard to Carrie. For as the book shows her charm betrayed him. He erred, as he later saw it, in taking her, because she drifted from him—went her own mental way—did not sustain him. These two things, once he was out of Chicago and so away from all he had known and prized, concentrated to form a deep and cancerous sense of mistake which ate into his energy and force. It was no doubt finally the worm at the heart of his life. And without the power to destroy it he was doomed. And it is that *conviction* which is the thing that is stalking him and that is necessary to symbolize in some way. But how? By your bum who becomes a detective and then a bum again? In part, yes, I am inclined to think so, although I think it might be better if the bum never became a detective.

On the other hand, by some words of Hurstwood's here and there throughout the play—a Hamlet-like meditation, or phrase now and then—it is necessary to indicate the unchanging presence of this cancerous conviction of error— its almost psychic reality—a body and mind of defeat. For I do personally believe that in the super energies of all of us lie amazing powers. We can and do embody in the world without many things which fight or aid us. You, as you go along, will best see where and how the truth of this can be shadowed forth. But once it is in I think your listeners are likely to feel the essential awfulness of the man's fate. And so the real drama of the book. If so we are likely to have a successful play. I hope so. I like the spirit of your present outline very much and only wish I might read the completed play.

THEODORE DREISER

Malcolm Cowley

from "The Slow Triumph of Sister Carrie"□

Sister Carrie had the appearance of being a naturalistic novel and would be used as a model for the work of later naturalists. Yet it was, in a sense, naturalistic by default, naturalistic because Dreiser was writing about the life he knew best in the only style he had learned. There is a personal and compulsive quality in the novel that is not at all naturalistic. The book is felt rather than observed from the outside, like *McTeague*; and it is based on dreams rather than documents. Where *McTeague* had been a conducted tour of the depths, *Sister Carrie* was a cry from the depths, as if McTeague had uttered it.

It was a more frightening book to genteel readers than *McTeague* had been. They were repelled not only by the cheapness of the characters but even more by the fact that the author admired them. They read that Hurstwood, for example, was the manager of "A gorgeous saloon . . . with rich screens, fancy wines and a line of bar goods unsurpassed in the country." They found him an unctuous and offensive person, yet they also found that Dreiser described him as "altogether a very acceptable individual of our great American upper class —the first grade below the luxuriously rich." Genteel readers didn't know whether to be more offended by the judgement or

□ From *The New Republic*, vol. CXVI (23 June 1947), pp. 24–26. Copyright 1947 by Malcolm Cowley. Reprinted by permission of Malcolm Cowley.

by the language in which it was expressed, and they must have felt more than a premonition that Hurstwood and his creator belonged to a new class that threatened the older American culture. Most of all they resented Carrie Meeber. They had been taught that a woman's virtue is her only jewel, that the wages of sin are death; yet Carrie let herself be seduced without a struggle, yielding first to a traveling salesman, then to Hurstwood; and instead of dying in misery she became a famous actress. *McTeague* had offended the proprieties while respecting moral principles; every misdeed it mentioned had been punished in the end. *Sister Carrie*, on the other hand, was a direct affront to the standards by which respectable Americans had always claimed to live.

The battle over Carrie started even before the book was published. Dreiser had first given the manuscript to Henry Mills Alden, the editor of *Harper's Magazine*, who had already bought some of his articles. Alden said he liked the novel, but he doubted that any publisher would take it. He turned it over to the editorial readers for Harper and Brothers, who sent it back to the author without comment. Next the manuscript went to Doubleday, Page and Company, where it had the good fortune to be assigned to the man who could best appreciate what Dreiser was trying to do. "It *must* be published," Norris kept repeating to anyone who would listen. His enthusiasm for *Sister Carrie* won over two of the junior partners, Henry Lanier and Walter Hines Page, and with some misgivings they signed a contract to bring it out that fall. Then Frank Doubleday, the senior partner, came back from Europe and carried the proof sheets home with him to read over the weekend. Mrs. Doubleday read them too, and liked them not at all, but her part in the story is not essential. Her husband could and did form his own opinion of *Sister Carrie*. He detested the book and wanted nothing to do with it as a publisher.

There has been a prolonged argument over what happened afterwards, but chiefly it is an argument over words like "suppression"; most of the facts are on record. Doubleday spoke to his junior partners, who had great respect for his business judgment, and they summoned Dreiser to a conference. Norris managed to see him first. "Whatever happens," he said in effect, "make them publish *Sister Carrie*, it's your right." Dreiser then conferred with the junior partners, who tried to persuade him to surrender his contract. "Crushed and tragically pathetic," as Lanier remembers him, he kept insisting that the contract be observed.

It was a binding document and it was observed, to the letter. *Sister Carrie* was printed, if only in an edition of roughly a thousand copies. It was bound, in cheap red cloth with dull black lettering. It was listed in the Doubleday catalogue. It was even submitted to the press for review, if only, in most cases, through the intervention of Frank Norris. When orders came in for it, they were filled. It wasn't "suppressed" or "buried away in a cellar," as Dreiser's friends afterwards complained, but neither was it displayed or advertised or urged on the booksellers. I think it was in the travels of Ibn Batuta that I once read the account of some Buddhist fishermen whose religion forbade them to deprive any creature of life, even a sardine. Instead of killing fish, they merely caught them in nets and left them to live as best they could out of water. That is about what happened to *Sister Carrie*, which wasn't, incidentally, the first or the last book to receive such treatment from publishing houses that changed their collective minds. One couldn't quite say that it was killed; it was merely deprived of light and air and left to die.

Favorable reviews might have rescued it, but with two or three exceptions the reviews were violently adverse and even insulting. "The story leaves a very unpleasant impression," said the Minneapolis *Journal*. "You would never dream of recommending to another person to read it," said the *Post-Intelligencer* in Seattle. *Life*, the humorous weekly, was serious about Carrie and warned the girls who might think of following in her footsteps that they would "end their days on the Island or in the gutter." *Sister Carrie*, said the Chicago *Tribune*, "transgresses the literary morality of the average American novel to a point that is almost Zolaesque." The *Book Buyer* accused Dreiser of being "the chronicler of materialism in its basest forms. . . . But the leaven of the higher life remains," it added, "nowhere stronger than with us."

The book-buying public, most of which yearned for the leaven of the higher life, had no quarrel with the reviewers. The Doubleday records show that 1,008 copies of the book were bound, that 129 were sent out for review and that only 465 were sold. After five years the other 414 copies, with the plates from which they had been printed, were turned over to a firm that specialized in publishers' remainders. That was the end of the story for Doubleday, but not for Dreiser. As soon as he could scrape together $500, he bought the plates of his own novel. He succeeded in having it reprinted by the B. W. Dodge Company in 1907 and by Grosset and Dunlap in 1908. Later it would be reissued in successively larger editions by three other publishers—in 1911 by Harper and Brothers, the firm that had first rejected it, then in 1917 by Boni and Liveright, and in 1932 by the Modern Library—and it would also be translated into most of the European languages. For Dreiser the battle over *Sister Carrie* lasted for more than a quarter-century and ended with his triumph over the genteel critics.

Yet the first years were full of disasters, in spite of the help that Dreiser and his book received from Frank Norris. One English publisher remembered Norris as a man who was "more eager for Dreiser's *Carrie* to be read than for his own novels." Besides trying to get American reviews for the book, Norris kept writing about it to England. A London edition of *Sister Carrie* appeared in 1901 and was enthusiastically praised. "At last a really strong novel has come from America," exclaimed the *Daily Mail*; and there were echoes of the judgement in other English papers.

There was a different sort of echo in New York, a buzz of angry gossip about English critics and their fantastic notions of American fiction. Without the London edition, *Sister Carrie* might have been forgotten for years, but now it was arousing a quiet wave of condemnation among persons who had never seen a copy of the novel. Dreiser found that magazine editors were suddenly uninterested in his articles and stories, which had once been widely published; the new ones were coming back with rejection slips. One editor said, "You are a disgrace to America." The *Atlantic Monthly* wrote him that he was "morally bankrupt" and could not publish there. At the office of *Harper's Magazine* Dreiser happened to meet William Dean Howells, who had always been friendly since the day when Dreiser had interviewed him for another magazine. This time Howells was cold. "You know, I don't like *Sister Carrie*," he said as he hurried away. It was the first occasion on which he had failed to support a new work of honest American fiction.

Julian Markels

⌒ᘓᘓ⌒

from "Dreiser and the Plotting of Inarticulate Experience"□

If one thinks that such thoughts do not come to so common a type of mind—that such feelings require a higher mental development—I would urge for their consideration the fact that it is the higher mental development that does away with such thoughts. It is the higher mental development which induces philosophy and that fortitude which refuses to dwell upon such things—refuses to be made to suffer by their consideration. The common type of mind is exceedingly keen on all matters which relate to its physical welfare—exceedingly keen. It is the unintellectual miser who sweats blood at the loss of a hundred dollars. It is the Epictetus who smiles when the last vestige of physical welfare is removed.

SISTER CARRIE

By now the cataloguing of Dreiser's limitations has settled into a rather dry routine: his turgid and graceless style, which led F. R. Leavis to observe that Dreiser writes as if he hasn't a native language; his limited insight into the psychology of his characters; his wearisome attention to detail; and his editorial pretentiousness and inconsistency, in which he often seems bent on making metaphysical mountains out of mechanistic molehills. Such characteristics are not mere superfluous gimcrackery but part of Dreiser's substance, inseparable from his fictional method and from the conception of human experience that he attempts to shape in his fiction. Yet to pigeonhole Dreiser in this way is to obscure the fact that not all of his substance is composed of such defects. Equally the product of his method and conception, when he is at his best, is a powerful sense of the mystery underlying

□ Reprinted from *The Massachusetts Review*, II (Spring, 1961), © 1961 The Massachusetts Review, Inc. By permission of the publisher and Julian Markels.

human experience, of the fathomless processes which hold our lives in suspension, of the deep sources of pain and desire with which our human condition confronts us—in short, of what Dreiser himself called the wonder of life. Even if he is not a Balzac or a Dickens or a Dostoevsky, the whole of Dreiser's substance is frequently rich and moving and powerful. It is time finally to acknowledge him as our own and go on from there—to explore his quality and unravel his meaning for us. If we cannot afford to ignore his limitations, neither can we afford to let him lie bound in that literary dungeon to which he has been consigned for some years by the neoliberal Zeuses of contemporary criticism.

The greatest obstacle in the way of such an enterprise is not that Dreiser writes as if he hasn't a native language, but that as critics we are unprepared to pass beyond that fact. We are disconcerted to read a statement like Saul Bellow's in his review of F. O. Matthiessen's book on Dreiser: "But it is very odd that no one has thought to ask just what the 'bad writing' of a powerful novelist signifies." Such a remark suggests that in some significant way we are estranged from the novel as a literary form, that to recover Dreiser we must recover the suppleness of certain critical faculties which have been until recently the victims of atrophy.

The first, if indirect step, in such a recovery is to confront the fact that Dreiser's artistic purposes made no strenuous demands upon his style, which after all may be true of a novelist though not of a poet. Dreiser could on occasion produce a kind of "good writing," so that his characteristic style is the result not only of ineptness but of a choice of relevant means for communicating what he had to. At scattered moments in his writing there is a compactness and fluency which usually passes unnoticed. There is, for example, this paragraph from *An American Tragedy*:

The impact of this remark, a reflection of the exact truth, was not necessary to cause Clyde to gaze attentively, and even eagerly. For apart from her local position and means and taste in dress and manners, Sondra was of the exact order and spirit that most intrigued him—a somewhat refined (and because of means and position showered upon her) less savage, although scarcely less self-centered, Hortense Briggs. She was, in her small, intense way, a seeking Aphrodite, eager to prove to any who were sufficiently attractive the destroying power of her charm, while at the same time retaining her own personality and individuality free of any entangling alliance or compromise. However, for varying reasons which she could not quite explain to herself, Clyde appealed to her. He might not be anything socially or financially, but he was interesting to her.

Eliminate the flatulent next-to-last sentence, change the parenthetical into a subordinate clause, and you have in this passage a piece of smooth and deliberate prose such as might have been written by an imitator of Henry James. Just as it stands the passage has a liveliness and precision which, if more prevalent, would make Dreiser's style less vulnerable to attack. But such writing is not frequent and hence not memorable in Dreiser; and indeed, he writes in this way only when, as in the present instance, he is taking time out to summarize previously recounted information. When his eye is on his main business his ear goes flat, and he characteristically writes the thick prose by which we remember him.

The source of his power and his meaning for us lies elsewhere, then, and I think it is in his method of arranging the episodes of his plots in order to dramatize with perfect coherence that absence of foreordained purpose in the universe, and its corollary, the hegemony of chance, of which he speaks so awkwardly in his "philosophical" writings. Not consistently but in long and powerful sequences, Dreiser's plot construction results in a fully credible image of human experience as an amoral process; it implies the possibility of human purpose and dignity arising out of a necessary immersion in this process; and hence Dreiser's method excludes the deterministic pathos of the conventional naturalistic novel, which conceives of human experience as the closing of a trap rather than the unfolding of a process. Frequently in Dreiser's novels the moment-to-moment action gives us no reason to desire or expect either good or bad fortune for the characters, no reason to feel hopeful, fearful, sad, or angry on their behalf. We are convinced instead that for them whatever is, is right; and we are moved by the mystery of their experience being so coherently purposeless and yet possibly resulting for them in an enlargement of being. When we see Carrie Meeber respond to her experience directly in fear and desire, without imposing upon it any moral categories or expectations, when we see her enlarge her worldly status and her human identity by her unquestioning submission to the "whatever is" of her experience, then we know why Dreiser attributes to Carrie the quality of "emotional greatness." When we see Hurstwood and Clyde Griffiths ruined by an equally emotional and unquestioning submission, then perhaps we know in a glimmer what Dreiser must have meant by the mystery and terror and wonder of life.

Such knowledge arises from a rhythm in the sequence of Dreiser's episodes rather than from anything that can be communicated by a graceful style. It is the rhythm of inarticulate human experience, undifferentiated and hence by definition without style. Matthiessen suggested rightly that Dreiser's sea imagery, his symbol of the rocking chair, and his own fondness for a rocking chair, all point to "a physical basis for the rhythm of his thoughts." But where the imagery and symbols are only its symptoms, the "physical basis" itself is established by Dreiser's method of construction, which is his true source of strength. It is also the source of his weakness, as I will indicate later, in that his method of construction disables Dreiser from portraying the emergence in human experience of moral consciousness and its corollary, literary style.

.   .   .   .

[Parts I and II, here omitted, analyze examples of plot construction from *Sister Carrie* and *An American Tragedy*; they show how the characters typically are shuttled back and forth, "in a precisely elaborated pattern" of alternate hope and discouragement, so that their unquestioning immersion in life becomes credibly amoral.]

III

To fully perceive this weakness, first we must make what I

believe is a Dreiserian distinction between being articulate and being conscious. A person may be articulate in learning to recognize his desires, to name them, and to pursue their objects actively instead of passively. Consciousness requires further the ability to judge those desires, to anticipate the consequences of pursuing them for some larger system of values, and hence to become responsible for one's active choices. To grow from articulateness into consciousness is to step from an amoral into a moral world of experience; and it is precisely in portraying that step that Dreiser's method proves inadequate. The method works successfully only when the characters are, so to speak, below the threshold of consciousness. It works successfully to bring Clyde Griffiths to the murder at the end of Book Two of *An American Tragedy*. Then Book Three is devoted mainly to Clyde's debate with himself (and Dreiser's debate with us) whether he should become conscious of the implications of his act and accept responsibility for it. In *Sister Carrie* the method works successfully to the point where Carrie prefers Hurstwood to Drouet. And it is most significant that once Dreiser brings Carrie to that point, he does not know what to do with her, and shifts the entire focus of the novel from her rise to Hurstwood's decline, where again the method works successfully to record a fall below the threshold of consciousness into an undifferentiated state of being comparable to Carrie's at the beginning. Carrie's rise during the second half of the novel is so clearly directed toward the emergence of consciousness that we have no reason to doubt Dreiser's intention here. This crucial result of her immersion in the drift of experience is pointed at and argued. But it never acquires sufficient dramatic weight to balance Hurstwood's decline. The ultimate weakness of *Sister Carrie* is the thinness and lack of warmth, the pasteboard quality of the heroine during the last half of the novel. For Dreiser was unwilling, perhaps unable, to find a method for depicting the manifestations of Carrie's enhanced powers in conscious and morally responsible actions.

Dreiser's tenacity in clinging to his characteristic method forces him to give increasingly inconsistent accounts of Carrie once she begins reaping the fruits of her career.

The ripest fruit in her harvest is her relationship with Ames, who is introduced at Carrie's final stage of development as an unmistakable representative of the conscious life. She has only a few brief conversations with this shadowy young man, who "seemed wiser than Hurstwood, saner and brighter than Drouet," in his belief that self-aggrandizement is mere vanity, that one must read important books rather than sentimental novels, and that finally one must be selfless. In their last talk, after Carrie has become a successful comedienne, Ames urges her to give up comedy and try for serious parts, where her talents will be more valuable to others and will therefore endure:

. . . You have this quality in your eyes and mouth and in your nature. You can lose it, you know. If you turn away from it and live to satisfy yourself alone, it will go fast enough. The look will leave your eyes. Your mouth will change. Your power to act will disappear. You may think they won't, but they will. Nature takes care of that.

Here is Carrie's final attainment, the knowledge that if she lives only to satisfy herself she will lose herself. Her ceaseless drifting toward only what satisfies herself has led her to confront finally the demand of Nature that she consciously shape her experience to run in the channels of selflessness. Here more than anywhere in Dreiser is the justification for Eliseo Vivas' remark that "there is more to his own concrete dramatic picture of men and society than he finds room for in his mechanistic philosophy." But it is also true that at this moment Dreiser's dramatic picture is not very roomy either. In the sketchy characterization of Ames we have another instance of Dreiser's intention made perfectly clear but not rendered dramatically effective. And in his refusal to let Carrie take up the challenge of Ames' suggestion, he is squelching her arbitrarily. We have watched her ascend from the Hansons to Drouet and from Drouet to Hurstwood. Now, when Hurstwood is left behind and Ames appears, Dreiser becomes fussy and hesitant at the prospect of making Carrie as conscious and responsible as Ames challenges her to be.

Indeed, as if the record of Carrie's relation with Ames

were not already sufficiently thin and halting, in other
passages late in the novel Dreiser undermines Ames' position
and the resolution which Ames proposes to Carrie. Dreiser
allows Carrie brief glimmerings of consciousness, but only to
remember her early career in Chicago in terms that attribute
to it a rationale as thoroughly inconsistent with the facts as
Ames' challenge and the entire role he plays are consistent.
When Hurstwood stops looking for a job, Carrie remembers
scornfully that in her early struggle in Chicago she never
stopped trying; she decides that now, as in Chicago, she will
try to get an acting job "as a last resort in distress." The facts
are that although she did struggle valiantly in Chicago, she
also eventually stopped trying, and was ready to pack up and
go home when Drouet rescued her; and that her Chicago
venture as an amateur actress was not a last resort in distress
(though she had begun to tire of Drouet), but something ar-
ranged entirely by Drouet, signed, sealed and delivered on a
platter without Carrie's lifting a finger. Dreiser makes her
remember these things as if she had planned and pursued her
goals systematically. And this engrafted rationale leads him
into a damaging confusion in his final portrait of Carrie. Near
the end of the novel, long after her last interview with Ames,
and after her resounding success on the comic stage has
brought her a salary of $150 a week, we are told:

> It does not take money long to make plain its impotence,
> providing the desires are in the realm of affection. With her one
> hundred and fifty in hand, Carrie could think of nothing particular
> to do. . . . Her clothes had for some time been wholly satisfactory.
> Another day or two and she would receive another hundred and
> fifty. It began to appear as if this were not so startlingly necessary
> to maintain her present state. If she wanted to do anything better
> or move higher, she must have more—a great deal more.

For most of her life her desires were in fact in the realm of
money. But now that her experience with Ames has transformed them into desires for affection, now that money has
shown its impotence, she decides she must have more money.[1]
The whole paragraph until the last sentence is a confirmation
in her own experience of what Ames had told her. But instead
of letting her mind drift in characteristic fashion to memories

of Ames, as earlier it drifted to Drouet or Hurstwood in similar
situations, now Dreiser intervenes with a false explanation
which makes Carrie inaccessible to the wisdom derived from
her own immersion in the drift of experience. Dreiser increasingly stiffens to resist the deepest implications of his
own method as that method threatens to project Carrie across
the threshold of consciousness into the arms, so to speak, of
Ames.

Thus at the beginning of his career in *Sister Carrie* and
at its height in *An American Tragedy*, Dreiser balks at portraying the life of consciousness and responsibility which
arises logically out of his own conception of the inarticulate
drift of experience. He arbitrarily qualifies Carrie's emergence
into consciousness, and later he can do no more than make
Clyde Griffiths' similar emergence the subject of an essentially
unresolved debate. And without a dramatically rendered life
of moral consciousness there is no demand for style. There is
in fact an implicit denial of style, so that finally it is accurate
to say that Dreiser's style is the necessary defect of his virtue.
In its meandering syntax, its fuzzy diction, its jerky rhythms
and abrupt transitions, Dreiser's style is almost wholly
unarticulated. And in this respect it simply affirms the in-
articulateness of his characters. A coherently inflected style
would attribute to the characters a personal "style" appropriate only to a degree of consciousness that Dreiser does not
allow them; it would arrest the flow of experience created by
his method of plotting; it would embody the results of the
process rather than the process under way. Dreiser's own style
actually helps to articulate his vision of life as an amoral
process containing its own coherent rhythm, bearing us along
mysteriously and challenging us to become conscious of
ourselves.

The somehow unexpected power achieved despite his
style by Dreiser's method of plotting may serve to remind us
of the enormous resources of the novel as a genre. We often
hear nowadays that the novel is dead or dying, having exhausted its materials, with the possible exception of those
relating to the condition of the self. Dreiser's power is unexpected because he is not directly concerned with the self,

because in his gallery of characters there is so little of that "self-presence" which Ortega y Gasset told us is the sign of greatness in the novel and the one necessity for its continuance as a literary genre. Dreiser's novels do not bear the sign of greatness, but they show how various and new may be the novel's sources of life, for they derive their vitality precisely from Dreiser's ability to portray human experience before "self-presence" is achieved, to portray human beings in the process of becoming differentiated and conscious of themselves.

Dreiser's portrayal may remind us too that we still struggle to become conscious of ourselves and to locate the responsibilities that genuinely arise from our condition of life. It is traditional to compare Dreiser to James and find him parochial and thick-headed in his inability to portray the conscious life. But the social facts out of which James was able to imagine the conscious and moral life simply did not exist for Dreiser. And they do not exist for us. Dreiser's facts, which are our facts, are still largely inscrutable. And Dreiser's parochialism is simply part of a national phenomenon in our life and letters during this century, from the aloof clinical observation of the unconscious life in Stephen Crane's *Maggie* to the forced rejection of the conscious life in the novels of Ernest Hemingway. We smile nowadays to think how Dreiser's great contemporary Clarence Darrow made a monkey out of Bryan at the Scopes Trial. We too often forget the enormous waste of Darrow's granite courage and high intelligence engaged at the level of such monkeyshines. It is Dreiser's distinction that, despite his personal philosophy, as an artist he was often able to cut beneath the parochial oversimplifications of his time—from Social Darwinism and Zolaism to *nada* and Marxism and the honor of the South—to a core of substance that remains a central preoccupation of our best contemporary novelists. One might almost say that writers like Saul Bellow and Herbert Gold pick up where Dreiser left off, trying to discover by their art the point at which emerges from the amoral drift of experience a universal content for our proper consciousness of ourselves, the conditions under which we might honestly assume our responsibilities. Where

Dreiser was able to imagine coherently the processes of experience but not the self-presence of his characters, the younger writers create characters superbly endowed with self-presence but still searching to attune themselves to the fundamental processes of human experience. Such writers may be said to represent the conscience of America. And that is why, for this reader, to look back at the American novel in the twentieth century is to find Dreiser, with his stubborn yet hopeful challenge to immerse ourselves in the dark processes of life, standing at the center of the field of vision.

Note

1   There are objections to my reading here, on the grounds that "more" is ambiguous or even that it refers clearly to "affection" rather than "money." I can only rely on an ear which I hope is by now attuned to Dreiser's syntactical ambiguities, on other evidence for exactly the same kind of confusion in the later characterization of Carrie, and on the whole of the last sentence quoted. In that sentence, "better," "higher," and "more" all refer to "her present state." And Carrie's "present state" is founded on clothes and money, not affection.

Sheldon Norman Grebstein

"Dreiser's Victorian Vamp"□

Although the intrinsic merit of Theodore Dreiser's work is still under debate, Dreiser himself appears to have won a permanent place in our cultural history as a literary pioneer. Critics and scholars agree almost without dissent that Dreiser, rather than Crane or Norris, was chiefly responsible for establishing those attitudes—including the confrontation of the actual and the unpleasant, the candor and forthrightness, the refusal to be bound by the conventional, and the frankness in sexual matters—which have characterized and distinguished most of the best American fiction in this century. Even *The Literary History of the American People* (by Quinn, Ghodes, Murdock and Whicher), generally not sympathetic in its appraisal of realistic-naturalistic writing, offers this testimony to Dreiser's achievement: "If we can imagine an old-fashioned ladies' sewing-circle, decorously exchanging local gossip over cakes and tea, suddenly invaded by an ice-man in his working clothes, who enters without embarrassment, plants himself massively in the middle of the sofa, and begins to regale the company with anecdotes of the gashouse district, we may form some notion of the effect produced by Dreiser's first novels." And when Sinclair Lewis, the first American to receive the Nobel Prize for literature, made his acceptance speech in Stockholm on December 12, 1930, he paid tribute to the leadership of the man who had been his

□ *Midcontinent American Studies Journal*, IV (Spring, 1963), pp. 3–11. Reprinted by permission of the publisher and the author.

closest competitor for the award: "Dreiser's great first novel, *Sister Carrie*, which he dared to publish thirty long years ago and which I read twenty-five years ago, came to housebound and airless America like a great free Western wind, and to our stuffy domesticity gave us the first fresh air since Mark Twain and Whitman." Since there is little doubt that Dreiser was the trailblazer for modernity and that *Sister Carrie* marked a radical departure from what had been written before it, we may well inquire why it now seems such an old-fashioned book, virtually a period piece from the age it helped destroy.

But in order to understand in what specific ways *Sister Carrie* marked both the apogee of Victorian prudery and, simultaneously, the beginning of the modern American novel, we must first briefly reconstruct the official nineteenth century attitude toward women and toward the sexual relationship between men and women. William Dean Howells, in a book which is assuredly representative of the thought of its time, *The Rise of Silas Lapham*, expressed this sentiment early in the novel: "And, after all, that's [goodness] about the best thing in a woman. . . . If my wife wasn't good enough to keep both of us straight, I don't know what would become of me." Most readers would have profoundly agreed with this utterance by the book's hero; indeed, Silas' good wife serves to quicken his conscience throughout most of the novel, and supplies much of the impetus for his moral regeneration. To turn to quite another source, and to focus more sharply on the sexual (which is what the word "moral" has mainly signified in our culture) ethic of the age, we find this statement in a highly reputable manual of sexual instruction which still, even though it was published in 1916, perfectly delineated the authorized Victorian attitude: "It may be added here, that an occasional girl goes wrong through temperamental short-comings in herself . . . but the proportion of women who would willingly and deliberately sacrifice their virtue is vanishingly small as compared with the proportion of young men. . . . This is probably in part due to their training. . . . It is in part due to the instinctive and inherent purity of mind of the normal woman." Or, as Eric John Dingwall has put it in *The American Woman*: "Ladies merely submitted to the dictates of the

curious system of propagation apparently approved by God,
while only females were degraded enough to enjoy it."

As familiar as these principles are to us, and as much as
they continue to plague us, we sometimes fail to recognize in
them and in the entire Victorian attitude an interesting
ambiguity. Actually, this attitude represented a drastic
revision of a crucial concept which had long been promul-
gated by Christian tradition and which had thoroughly
saturated Christian culture: the Pauline hostility toward
women, and the conviction that woman's moral inferiority
had been demonstrated for once and for all by Eve's sin.
Although it is true that the concept of woman as a weak and
carnal Eve was counterposed by the ideal of feminine purity
and holiness, especially strong in the Virgin and Mother
figures of the Middle Ages, society's distrust of the female
remained active enough to keep her subjugated and under
constant suspicion. But in its journey through time and across
the sea to nineteenth-century America, a journey too long
and tortuous to log here, the notion had not only softened; it
had become veritably transformed. Woman was no longer
inferior to man because of Eve's sin and betrayal of Adam. She
had, somehow, become morally superior to man because of her
visibly greater physical delicacy, her seemingly lesser
animality, and her apparent freedom from most of his atavistic
and bestial passions. It was perhaps a classic example of the
American tendency to accept the surface appearance as the
total reality. This transformation became institutionalized in
the sexual practice we have named "the double standard of
morality," the code which somehow anticipates male frailty
and thus permits the man to sin because he is, after all, a man
(and everyone knows what men are like), yet which permits no
sin on the woman's part because she, as a woman, is too pure
to sin (but if she does, by god, she'll pay for it). Accordingly,
a woman's love and the state of marriage were something of
salvation for the man; it was what she offered in return for her
subsistence. For the male it was the willing surrender to
respectability and goodness—as in the Howells speech—and
the acknowledgement of his wife's moral superiority. By this
method, whatever the actualities of woman's nature, was the

once weak and fleshly Eve transformed into an angel of ice. The system was so beautifully ambiguous it could even be used to buttress all the arguments for not granting women the right to vote and the right to work, rights which they had begun to demand. After all, were they not delicate creatures who, for their own and society's good, had to be protected against debauchery by the coarsening experiences of politics and business? The orthodoxies of the age are manifest in this ringing declaration, which appeared in J. Richardson Parke's massive *Human Sexuality*, published in 1906: "If a woman's desires, aims, ambitions be abnormal, unseemly, or unwomanly; if they tend toward public speech-making, preaching, politics— pursuits primitively and naturally masculine—instead of the home, maternity, and the part which by her grace, beauty, and attractiveness, nature evidently intended her to play in society, she must be regarded as a sexual pervert, a monstrosity, and utterly unfitted for the serious duties of wifehood and mother- hood."

At this point it must be asked how these cultural facts apply to Dreiser's pivotal novel, *Sister Carrie*.

What has been portrayed in that book is an essentially Victorian heroine who comes very close to the stereotyped heroine of popular melodrama, but who is at the same time the first truly modern heroine in American fiction because her behavior operates within the sphere of naturalistic and iconoclastic pragmatism rather than Victorian moral dog- matism. As Claude Simpson, Kenneth Lynn and others have noted, this was the moral frankness which constituted the book's radicalism and which charted the path for the modern American novel. Grant Knight has aptly summed up the novel's narrative: "It introduced a pretty woman who twice stooped to folly and did so almost casually and without punishment, a salesman who entered almost as casually into a liaison and also went unpunished, a stronger man who went down to beggary and death, and a part of the American scene appallingly imbued with materialism and impoverished in culture." Not only does sin go unpunished in *Sister Carrie*, it usually goes unrecognized as sin. Such was Mrs. Double- day's realization when she demanded that her husband suppress the book that his firm had already printed, and such was the weight of Dreiser's influence on the fiction to follow. He had written the first American novel without moral bias, and for that deed he paid heavily, thrown by the book's withdrawal and by its scant critical notice into a depression so deep that his career as a novelist was nearly ended before it had fairly begun. We may see just how modern *Sister Carrie* was, in this sense, by recalling that its nearest relation was Crane's *Maggie: A Girl of the Streets*, and by momentarily comparing both the depiction and fate of the two heroines. Her virtue lost, Crane's character can suffer only disintegration and death, a fate expected and approved by the book's audience. How different is Dreiser's Carrie, who prospers in her appearance and her fortunes, finally achieving stardom on the Broadway stage.

Without this perspective the modern reader of *Sister Carrie* must suffer some puzzlement, for when we turn to the novel itself we are instantly aware that in the area where we expect it to be most bold, it is most reticent, and, indeed, acquiescent to the Victorian demand that the bedroom must not be opened onto the public square. Even in his description of the female form, the item which Dreiser never fails to give graphic treatment in his later novels, there are no details. We know only that Carrie is neat and attractive. Her sexual allure is completely that of the archetypal Victorian heroine, comprised of innocence, purity and helplessness. Although from the instant Carrie and the drummer Drouet meet on the train it is obvious something will happen between them, we are told only that there is magnetic energy in their gaze. (This is Dreiser's substitution for erotic appeal.) The same gaze recurs several weeks later in the restaurant, after Drouet has accidentally encountered and picked up the by-now destitute and defeated Carrie and given her money—a portentous sign to the Victorian reader—and predicts the seduction to follow.

Dreiser's handling of the seduction itself is the model of propriety and makes use of a number of the standard genteel clichés. As Drouet stands with Carrie at the door of her flat, having clothed her, wined and dined her, the scene shifts abruptly to Carrie's sister, who dreams, in this order, of

Carrie's descent into a coal mine pit, of Carrie perched on a
promontory of land, sinking, and at last of Carrie falling over
the edge of a rock. In his later books, Dreiser would resort to
Freudian terms to describe such matters, but here he creates a
transparent allegory in popular idiom of the stages of Carrie's
sexual and moral surrender. She has now become a "fallen"
woman in images which would have seemed both familiar and
appropriate to the nineteenth-century reader.

Even as Drouet and Carrie live in sin, there is no description of any physical contact between them. Drouet neither
kisses nor fondles her, except to touch her once on the waist—
to test the fit of a dress. For Carrie, the yielding to Drouet
comes not from passion but from need, and as the expression
of gratitude for his money and help; still, we cannot blame
him too bitterly as a foul seducer. Have we not been told that
although one of his main pursuits is the pursuit of women,
Drouet is fundamentally kind-hearted? And have we not been
repeatedly assured that Carrie is protected by a brute instinct
for survival, an instinct for her own safety? In other words,
Dreiser attempts to persuade the reader that Carrie's seduction will do her no harm; therefore, in his own but partially
successful pragmatic terms, Carrie's seduction is not evil. Nor
does Carrie herself accept her situation as a kept woman
without qualms. Her conscience, product of a religious home,
continues to trouble her. Thus we see, as Claude Simpson has
perceptively remarked, that Dreiser had not yet divorced
himself from the Christian morality he affected to renounce.
This underlying confusion and illogic is perhaps the source for
the peculiar nostalgia and bittersweetness which are almost
as characteristic of the novel as its naturalistic bluntness.

In any case, Carrie thrives. She fills out in form. She
becomes more aware. She learns delicacy and grace. What
better evidence that the wages of sin are not death? The scene
has also been prepared for the second seduction, for by the
time Hurstwood meets Carrie, she has become both attractive
and chic. A man of his experience, manager of a fashionable
cafe, would not have been smitten by the raw country girl
who had come to Chicago only a few months earlier.

In Hurstwood's brief courtship of Carrie there is much

more emotion on the part of both, including Dreiser's description of a kiss and Carrie's response to it—the erotic high
point of the novel—although even in this scene she does no
more than return the embrace and lay her head on his
shoulder. But as if to compensate for his boldness, Dreiser
now portrays Carrie as grown much more scrupulous in her
deportment. Despite her loss of virtue to Drouet, she will
permit Hurstwood no liberties before marriage and when
she learns Hurstwood is married, she is so shocked that she
breaks off their courtship. We observe the same reticence and
the same defence of Carrie's honor elsewhere in the book.
Contrary to the opinion of an earlier commentator, Carrie is
anything but casual in the bestowal of her affection.

In both instances where Carrie yields to the men,
Dreiser includes an emphatic statement about her helplessness, her need to surrender to the male's ardor for her own
protection against a cruel world. By so doing he has, I think,
attempted to excuse Carrie in the eyes of the contemporary
reader by again associating her with the pathetic heroine of
sentimental melodrama whose virtue is the price she must pay
either for her life or the mortgage. However, in this case
Dreiser permits no heroic intervention by Gallant Ned, nor
does he characterize the seducers as Villains. They are merely
doing what comes naturally. In other words, Dreiser combines
his own naturalistic convictions with the one extenuating or
modifying circumstance permitted by the age: Carrie must
become indecent in order to live decently. The fault has consequently been shifted away from the female to the male, as
the reader would expect, for in the first instance Drouet had
persuaded a worn and discouraged Carrie, and in the second
Hurstwood had first duped the confused girl into running
away with him and then promised her what she most longed
for—legal wifehood. Carrie's blind insistence that Hurstwood
marry her despite her knowledge that he is already married,
offers further evidence of Dreiser's strenuous attempts to
make his heroine conform to Victorian taboos. Ultimately, of
course, Dreiser places the blame for Carrie's fall upon his
favorite whipping boy, the social order which allows such
grim conditions to exist that survival, not moral precept or

decency, becomes the test of truth. So successful was Dreiser's modesty in the rendition of the novel's illicit sexuality, and so noble his social indignation, that it led one critic, writing in the *North American Review*, to overlook completely the book's underlying anarchy. He saw *Sister Carrie* as a timely warning to the errant: "The conditions under which she comes to live are not justified, nor excused, by any acceptable code. But they are not uncommon, and Mr. Dreiser handles them with such delicacy of treatment and in such a clean largeness of mental attitude, that they simply enforce an impressive moral lesson."

Dreiser suggests repeatedly that Carrie's seduction is not accomplished wholly by masculine lust and her own weakness. It is made amply clear that her seducer is also modern life, as symbolized in the big city, with its glamour and appeal. From the beginning of the novel Dreiser tells us, in a voice laden with the countryman's ambivalent fascination with Metropolis and fear of it, that a young girl who goes to the city is in grave danger. "The gleam of a thousand lights is often as effective as the persuasive light in a wooing and fascinating eye. Half the undoing of the unsophisticated and natural mind is accomplished by forces wholly superhuman," Dreiser writes. What happens to Carrie in Chicago could well have been predicted by any Victorian and many moderns; it is what happens to every innocent rural lass when she leaves home. The city was evil and only heaven could protect the working girl. Or, in larger terms, *Sister Carrie* could be seen as another version of one of our most compelling and pervasive literary themes, the destruction of innocence, in which youth encounters the world and is either disillusioned, depraved, damaged or destroyed by it. Considering the possibilities, Carrie is lucky to escape only with the loss of her virtue.

Perhaps the most remarkable aspect of the novel, at least in regard to its sexuality, is Dreiser's failure to demonstrate the operation and efficacy of those forces whose existence and power he asserts. Throughout *Sister Carrie* Dreiser comments on the power of romance, love, jealousy and passion, and he hints at but does not depict the sex act. Yet although he obviously believes in the "majesty of passion" as a determinant in man's fate (e.g., in *An American Tragedy* he calls the sexual urges "rearranging chemisms" fundamental to all human behavior), he offers no extended, frank or convincing description of their influence. Drouet and Hurstwood are moved by overriding sexual passion only at crucial moments, especially Hurstwood, who musters enough potency to persuade a reluctant Carrie to go with him and, in Montreal to become "his." However, while Dreiser is daring enough to depict Hurstwood's passion for Carrie as so great that it torments him and leads to a series of events which eventually produce his destruction, he also creates a situation in which both of the men who possess this desirable woman are afterwards able to resist her appeal. In fact, there is absolutely no evidence that she has any appeal, once conquered.

Now, while there is some justification for the lack of detail in the portrayal of the characters' sexual relationships, the absence of any suggestion of the *results* of such relationships—that is, Carrie's failure to hold her men once she has them—poses a question to which there are several answers.

We may find one answer in Dreiser's other books. Inevitably, once a man and woman have met and the sexual "chemism" has expressed itself in an initial mating, Dreiser begins to substitute other factors (such as class, status and money) in the place of the erotic in his descriptions of a romance or marriage. Consequently, in Dreiser's fictional world sex is never as strong after fulfillment as before. We see this in the behavior of Eugene Witla, in Frank Cowperwood, in Clyde Griffiths and perhaps in Dreiser himself, who avowed and practised a belief in sexual "varietism." To Dreiser's males the possessing is all. The mating once accomplished, man's sexual urge and the woman possessed seem relatively unimportant, to become important again only in some new conquest. It is a basic paradox in Dreiser that while he did more than any other American novelist of his generation to make sexual frankness possible, he probably did not succeed in convincing his readers of the power of sex. (That feat remained to be accomplished chiefly by such successors of Dreiser as Anderson and Hemingway.) The fault may lie in Dreiser's conception of sexuality, which was quantitative rather than qualitative. Each affair is as important as every other; each takes root instantly, grows at once, withers overnight; all are but slight variations of the same plant.

To return to *Sister Carrie*, it is perhaps necessitated by the special demands of the heroine's character delineation that Carrie be passive, both to reinforce Dreiser's conception of her moral blamelessness and to strengthen the reader's conviction that she has "class." She can sleep with two men but she must not enjoy it. If she were to take pleasure from sex and become adept and eager in its practice, she would lose that aura of innocence which she possesses in raw form from the beginning, which grows enough to captivate Hurstwood, and which later flames into the wistful beauty responsible for her Broadway stardom. Here Dreiser is also apparently working from the Victorian credo that only bad, low and evil women could find sex pleasurable. From this viewpoint, Carrie's short stay in the factory sweatshop has the aesthetic function of demonstrating her innate superiority to the other girls, who, in their bold manners, coarse speech and familiar ways with men, scream to us that they are crude creatures who know what sex is and like it. This is part of the fact which Carrie recognizes, and it is partly in revulsion at such a fate that she turns to Drouet. Indeed, in Dreiser's canon the proof and summation of a girl's lowness is her easy way with men. We find the same situation elsewhere in his books, notably in his portrayal of the unabashedly carnal, full-bosomed and thick-ankled working girls of the collar factory in *An American Tragedy*. The use of these stereotypes is a curious symptom of Dreiser's unresolved feelings toward his own class origin, an irresolution we must set beside Dreiser's own overt sympathies for the proletariat and his eventual identification with it.

The only passion or urge which Dreiser does grant Carrie is the urge, as much sublime as sensual, for nice things. Early in the narrative he sets forth Carrie's chief motivation: "She realized in a dim way how much the city held—wealth, fashion, ease—every adornment for women, and she longed for dress and beauty with a whole heart." This synthesis of aestheticism and materialism—the yearning for beauty, and the expression of the yearning largely in terms of elegant clothes, sumptuous houses and rich food—is integral to the novel as well as to Dreiser's total conception of character and *weltanschauung*. In Dreiser's men the yearning declares itself not solely but forcefully in the sexual: in their feeling for women. In Carrie, as in most of Dreiser's other feminine creations, the yearning is what she has in place of the sexual. This, too, would have conveyed the ring of truth to the nineteenth-century reader. Everyone knew that if women, those noble creatures, had a weakness (albeit one which might work to the advantage of a would be seducer), it was her fondness for the pretty and the decorative.

It may also be true that Dreiser's refusal to give Carrie passion stemmed from inability rather than unwillingness. Leslie Fiedler has put it this way in *Love and Death in the American Novel*: "He could never portray, for all his own later hectic career as a lover, any woman except the traditional seduced working girl of sentimental melodrama. . . . The deceived woman, the seduced virgin are for Dreiser the images through which he understands America and himself . . ." While Fiedler's statement will not endure too close a scrutiny, it is correct as it applies to *Sister Carrie*. We could further speculate that in this portrayal of Carrie, indeed in the very phrases used to describe her, "a half-equipped little knight," "a pilgrim," in the very characternym "Sister," Dreiser's intention is both to underscore Carrie's blamelessness and to soften and expiate the character of his own foolish sister, whose deeds had furnished the rough outline for the novel's plot. She had been living with an architect in Chicago, then met, become enamoured of and run away with a clerk at Chapin and Gore, only to discover that he had taken thirty-five hundred dollars of his employers' money with him. Although he returned most of the money and no charges were pressed, the whole affair became a noisy scandal. Eventually, the couple came to New York and operated a disreputable boarding house, later taking in another of Dreiser's sisters who had been made pregnant and then deserted by a rich man's son (a situation which in turn suggested the basis for Dreiser's second novel, *Jennie Gerhardt*).

Whatever the reasons for Carrie's depiction, they produce a heroine of curious flatness whose lack of dimension impresses most modern readers as the novel's greatest weakness. The flatness is also responsible for one of the larger holes in the book's fabric of realism. The author has given us the story of a beautiful and desirable woman surrendering to two attractive men, but has said nothing about the aftermath of the surrender or about its puissance in the lives of those involved. Had Dreiser given Carrie passion, womanly passion, or at least told us why she lacked.it, she would have assumed that depth and force as a character she now wants. As is, she is flat, or as Matthiessen has correctly noted, "She is never a woman in love." Consequently and inevitably the focus of the novel shifts to Hurstwood. There is no better evidence of Dreiser's commitment to some of the very taboos he shattered. He either could not, or dared not, portray his heroine with the same earthly lusts as the male. Women could fall, but they could not feel.

In short, we find that in *Sister Carrie*, the novel which began the literary revolution against prudery in America, Dreiser has created a Victorian Vamp: a woman who is precisely that mixture of strengths and weaknesses which the nineteenth century conceived her to be, but who is at the same time in her unrequited sexual sins the first modern heroine. Eve-like, she yields to the flesh, but in the strongest Victorian tradition she does so only out of the confusion and need engendered by woman's innate helplessness and man's predatory lustfulness. In accord with the highest fashion of the time she has no animality, no passion, no sexuality of her own. Her beauty attracts men, yes, but she is not responsible. Again, despite her fall, she is better than the men she lives with, and, in fact, better than anyone else in the novel except the shadowy Ames. The men and only the men have bestial urgings, and there is not the slightest hint that Carrie, even when possessed, abandons herself to them or responds in kind. Insofar as it is possible for Dreiser to make it so, Carrie sins chastely. Further, Carrie grows in refinement, in grace, in knowledge; she alone is capable of growth, while Drouet and Hurstwood her seducers, can only mark time or retrogress. The only male in the novel who shares Carrie's quest for betterment and beauty is Ames, who even in name is more symbolical than real. Finally, Carrie triumphs on the stage by becoming the image, the personification, of the Victorian ideal of womanhood; lovely, poised, demure, with a suggestion of refinement and a touch of pathos. She is, in retrospect, perhaps the first of the American love goddesses, those fabulous and yet ultimately familiar and wistful creatures who continue to fascinate us with their ambivalent sophistication and naiveté, simultaneously the embodiment of sexuality and innocence: at once the woman and the child, the wife and the daughter, the mistress and the sister.

X

The Ambassadors (1903) by Henry James

Henry James

from *The Notebooks of Henry James* □

Torquay, October 31st, 1895.

I was struck last evening with something that Jonathan Sturges, who has been staying here 10 days, mentioned to me: it was only 10 words, but I seemed, as usual, to catch a glimpse of a *sujet de nouvelle* in it. We were talking of W.D.H. and of his having seen him during a short and interrupted stay H. had made 18 months ago in Paris—called away—back to America, when he had just come—at the end of 10 days by the news of the death—or illness—of his father. He had scarcely been in Paris, ever, in former days, and he had come there to see his domiciled and initiated son, who was at the Beaux Arts. Virtually in the evening, as it were, of life, it was all new to him: all, all, all. Sturges said he seemed sad—rather brooding; and I asked him what gave him (Sturges) that impression. 'Oh—somewhere—I forget, when I was with him—he laid his hand on my shoulder and said *à propos* of some remark of mine: "Oh, you are young, you are young—be glad of it: be glad of it and *live*. Live all you can: it's a mistake not to. It doesn't so much matter what you do—but live. This place makes it all come over me. I see it now. I haven't done so—and now I'm old. It's too late. It has gone past me—I've lost it. You have time. You are young. Live!" ' I amplify and improve a little—but that was the tone. It touches me—I can see him—I can hear him. Immediately, of course—as

□ From *The Notebooks of Henry James*, edited by F. O. Matthiessen and Kenneth B. Murdock. Copyright 1947 by Oxford University Press Inc. Reprinted by permission, pp. 225–228.

everything, thank God, does—it suggests a little situation. I seem to see something, of a tiny kind, springing out of it, that would take its place in the little group I should like to do of *Les Vieux*—The Old. (What should I call it in English—*Old Fellows*? No, that's trivial and common.) At any rate, it gives me the little idea of the figure of an elderly man who hasn't 'lived,' hasn't at all, in the sense of sensations, passions, impulses, pleasures—and to whom, in the presence of some human spectacle, some great organization for the Immediate, the Agreeable, for curiosity, and experiment and perception, for Enjoyment, in a word, becomes, *sur la fin*, or toward it, sorrowfully aware. He has never really enjoyed—he has lived only for Duty and conscience—his conception of them; for pure appearances and daily tasks—lived for effort, for surrender, abstention, sacrifice. I seem to see his history, his temperament, his circumstances, his figure, his life. I don't see him as having battled with his passions—I don't see him as harassed by his temperament or as having, in the past, suspected, very much, what he was losing, what he was not doing. The alternative wasn't present to him. He may be an American—he might be an Englishman. I don't altogether like the *banal* side of the revelation of Paris—it's so obvious, so usual to make Paris the vision that opens his eyes, makes him feel his mistake. It might be London—it might be Italy— it might be the general impression of a summer in Europe— abroad. Also, it *may* be Paris. He has been a great worker, a local worker. But of what kind? I can't make him a novelist— too like W.D.H., and too generally *invraisemblable*. But I want him 'intellectual,' I want him *fine*, clever, literary almost: it deepens the irony, the tragedy. A clergyman is too obvious and *usé* and otherwise impossible. A journalist, a lawyer—these men WOULD in a manner have 'lived,' through their contact with life, with the complications and turpitudes and general vitality of mankind. A doctor—an artist too. A mere man of business—he's possible; but not of the intellectual grain that I mean. The Editor of a Magazine—that would come nearest: not at all of a newspaper. A Professor in a college would imply some knowledge of the lives of the young —though there might be a tragic effect in his seeing at the last that he hasn't even suspected what those lives might contain. (They had passed by him—he had passed them by.) He has married very young, and austerely. Happily enough, but charmlessly, and oh, so conscientiously: a wife replete with the New England conscience. But all this must be—oh, so light, so delicately summarized, so merely touched. What I seem to see is the possibility of some little illustrative action. The idea of the tale being the revolution that takes place in the poor man, the impression made on him by the particular experience, the incident in which this revolution and this impression embody themselves, is the point *à trouver*. They are determined by certain circumstances, and they produce a situation, his issue from which is the little drama. I am supposing him, I think, to have 'illustrated,' as I say, in the past, by his issue from some *other* situation, the opposite conditions, those that have determined him in the sense of the sort of life and feeling I have sketched and the memory, the consciousness of which roll over him now with force. He has sacrificed some one, some friend, some son, some younger brother, to his failure to feel, to understand, all that his new experience causes to come home to him in a wave of reaction, of compunction. He has not allowed for these things, the new things, new sources of emotion, new influences and appeals—didn't realize them at all. It was in communication with *them* that the spirit, the sense, the nature, the temperament of this victim (as now seems to him) of his old ignorance, struggled and suffered. He was wild—he was free—he was passionate; but there would have been a way of taking him. Our friend never saw it—never, never: he perceives that—ever so sadly, so bitterly, now. The young man is dead: it's all over. Was he a son, was he a ward, a younger brother—or an elder one? Points to settle: though I'm not quite sure I like the *son*. Well, my vague little fancy is that he 'comes out,' as it were (to London, to Paris—I'm afraid it *must* be Paris; if he's an American), to take some step, decide some question with regard to some one, in the sense of his old feelings and habits, and that the new influences, to state it roughly, make him act just in the opposite spirit—make him accept on the spot, with a *volte-face*, a wholly different inspiration. It is a case of some

other person or persons, it is some other young life in regard
to which it's a question of his interfering, rescuing, bringing
home. Say he 'goes out' (partly) to look after, to bring home,
some young man whom his family are anxious about, who
won't *come* home, etc.—and under the operation of the change
se range du côté du jeune homme, says to him: 'No; STAY:—
don't come home.' Say our friend is a widower, and that the
jeune homme is the son of a widow to whom he is engaged to
be married. *She* is of the strenuous pattern—she is the
reflection of his old self. She has money—she admires and
approves him: 5 years have elapsed since his 1st wife's death,
10 since his own son's. He is 55. He married at 20! Displeasing
the strenuous widow is a sacrifice—an injury to him. To marry
her means rest and security *pour ses vieux jours*. The 'revolution' endangers immensely his situation with her. But of
course my denouement is that it takes place—that he makes
the sacrifice, does the thing I have, vaguely, represented him,
supra, as doing, and loses the woman he was to marry and all
the advantages attaching to her. It is too late, too late *now*,
for HIM to live—but what stirs in him with a dumb passion of
desire, of I don't know what, is the sense that he may have a
little super-sensual hour in the vicarious freedom of another.
His little drama is the administration of the touch that contributes to—that prolongs—that freedom.

Joan Bennett

︿⚬︿

from "The Art of Henry James"□

Let us remind ourselves of *The Ambassadors*—what is this
novel about? We know from James' *Notebooks* as well as
from the Preface to the novel that the germ of *The Ambassadors* was an anecdote reported to James by Jonathan Sturges
in 1895. It told of a middle aged man who during his first long
stay in Paris was struck by all he had missed in life and advised a young friend "live all you can: it's a mistake not to.
This place makes it all come over me. I see it now. I haven't
done so—and now I'm old. It's too late. It has gone past me—
I've lost it. You have time. You are young. Live." The
anecdote remained in James' mind as the seed of a possible
subject for seven years before the novel began to take shape.
It is at once obvious that very many quite different fictions
might have sprung from such a seed. What a writer will discover in such a theme will depend upon what he has in his
mind—by temperament and by experience. What will the
words "life" and "live" give to him?

James evolved as his fable, or framework of the novel,
the story of a man called Strether, a widower. He is sent to
Paris to rescue (morally) one Chad Newsome, son of a wealthy
widow who will marry Strether when his mission is accomplished. He expects to find Chad ensnared by some French-
woman, and his mission is to persuade him to return to the
United States. At his home in Woollett he is to take over the

□ *Chicago Review*, IX (Winter, 1956), pp. 14–26. © *Chicago Review*.
Reprinted with permission.

management of a prosperous family business. The novel
reveals what happens to Strether and at the close he, like so
many of James' heroes, renounces happiness for himself.
Gradually we see him lose the power to enjoy what once
seemed good to him, marriage with the wealthy, morally-
complacent widow, Chad's mother. Another kind of happiness
is offered him. He could marry his good friend Maria Gostrey
(expatriate American) and remain with her in Paris. But he
returns to the States, certain that Chad will follow him and
his mission will be accomplished, though he now knows that
its failure is what he desires. He was sent to save Chad; by
the close of the novel he sees that he can only be saved if he
remains, faithful to Mme. de Vionnet. But although Strether
renounces his own happiness at the close of the novel and
knows that he has failed to influence Chad for his own good,
he has nevertheless profited by his experience. The drama we
witness and that (if we are susceptible to James' art) en-
thralls us from first to last is the conflict of values in Strether's
mind. I would like to indicate some aspects of that conflict
and to show how it reveals itself not only in the story but in
the form and language of the novel.

One aspect of the conflict of values (an aspect first
treated in English fiction by George Eliot) concerns the relation between absolute and relative morality. When Strether
arrives in Europe he is imbued with a morality derived from a
puritan tradition. It is a morality which assumes that what is
right or wrong in conduct is known and fixed. It does not depend on circumstances or on persons but on unalterable laws.
For instance, Chad has not married and settled down and taken
a job in Paris; if he had he would have deviated from his
tradition by settling abroad, but he would not have broken
with the moral code. As it is he has simply stayed there in
idleness; therefore it must be right for him to be lured back,
and if some woman is preventing him from coming she must be
a "bad influence" from whom he should be severed. From the
moment Strether first sees Chad he knows that this assumption is false since instead of finding Chad corrupted he finds
him enormously improved. The absolute moral laws don't
work as he expected; and the discovery that questions of right

and wrong depend upon all the actual circumstances of a case (including the nature, personal history, social environment, religious and cultural traditions of the persons involved) is one of the discoveries Strether is making throughout the book. Closely allied to this discovery of a gap between a fixed moral code and the moral values that count in actual human conditions, Strether finds also that there are two kinds of obligation, legal and moral—Mme. de Vionnet is bound to her husband by the laws of her church and state; for reasons which emerge she is not morally bound as she is to Chad; and Chad himself, who is in no way legally bound to her, is (it becomes increasingly clear to Strether) firmly bound by moral obligation. From another point of view we can see the conflict presented in the novel as that between the morality of self-denial and of self-fulfilment. Hitherto Strether has believed that the good life is one in which the senses are never indulged: his inherited puritan code of self-denial inculcates regular attendance to business (that is to say money-making), scant leisure, restrained appetites. All this is challenged as he discerns the value of discriminated sense-pleasures of eye, ear, and palate. He perceives values he has hitherto ignored as he observes the beauty of Mme. de Vionnet's dress or her room. He becomes aware of visual beauty as he looks at Paris or her environs; he becomes aware of social values in civilized conversation, and of aesthetic values in music, literature, architecture, pictures. According to Strether's puritan code the acquisition of wealth is good—it would be right for Chad to devote himself to the family business and improve it financially—no matter what the product of that business is. (Deliberately we are never told what it is.) To be idle—that is, not to be making money—is bad. Under the challenge of new impressions Strether becomes increasingly doubtful of all this.

Of course the conflict between absolute and relative morality or between denial and cultivation of the senses is never, in the novel, presented crudely as this analysis might suggest; but as the reader shares Strether's experiences he becomes, with Strether, more concerned with relative morals (morals in relation to individual persons and their circumstances), more concerned with cultivating than with repressing the senses, and more concerned with human values than with money values.

The Ambassadors is a novel not a treatise and not (as one modern critic has suggested) an allegory. In allegory the idea precedes and governs the fable; what James thought of this form is made clear in his book about Hawthorne where he writes:

> Hawthorne, in his metaphysical moods, is nothing if not allegorical, and allegory, to my sense, is quite one of the lighter exercises of the imagination . . . I frankly confess that I have as a general thing but little enjoyment of it and that it has never seemed to me a first rate literary form. . . . It is apt to spoil two good things—a story and a moral—a form and a meaning.

In *The Ambassadors* both are unspoiled; the moral content depends on a series of impressions arrived at because of what happens and the way in which happenings are presented. We experience the content of this novel through the consciousness of Strether. He is not always present; he does not narrate the story; he is, however present at every important scene (it is important because of its effect on him), and no character in the novel is better known to us than to him; we know them only as he knows them and because he knows them. But the "only" need not disturb us. When James decided that all the experience of the book should come to the reader through Strether he knew that Strether must be a man of perception— one capable of learning from experience. To see a character or a place as Strether sees them is to see them with penetration. As to the disposition and proportioning of the story it will perhaps be enough to say that the exposition is not (as it some-times is with James) too long. (By the end of the second book—there are twelve in all—we have all the data in our hands without having noticed any arrest in the action.) Every scene in the novel is relevant to Strether's central experience—his revaluation of all his values; everything leads up to and then on from the conversation with little Bilham in which the original germ of the story unfolds itself in the speech containing the words "Live all you can, its a mistake not to."

The word "life" is, naturally, a key word in this novel; and the main theme can be spot-lighted by isolating a number of points in the action where Strether considers and reconsiders the content of that word. It is worth while to look at four places in the novel where this happens. The first scene I shall quote from occurs at the end of the exposition, in the opening section of Book II. Strether is talking to Miss Gostrey (who is his confidante throughout) and explaining what he has come to Europe for. He tells her that if Chad goes home he will "come in for a particular chance—a chance that any properly constituted young man would jump at." An opening awaits him. It carries with it a large share of the profits of the expanding business, but it of course requires Chad's presence at Woollett.

"That's what I mean by his chance. . . . And to see that he doesn't miss it is, in a word, what I've come out for."

She let it all sink in. "What you've come out for then is simply to render him an immense service."

Well, poor Strether was willing to take it so.

"Ah, if you like."

"He stands, as they say, if you succeed with him to gain—"

"Oh a lot of advantages." Strether had them clearly at his fingers' ends.

"By which you mean of course a lot of money."

"Well, not only. I'm acting with a sense for him of other things too. Consideration and comfort and security—the general safety of being anchored by a strong chain. He wants, as I see him, to be protected. Protected, I mean, from life."

Miss Gostrey is quick to interpret this; evidently it is intended that Chad will marry as well as becoming a successful business man. Later in the novel we meet the intended young woman. But I want to arrest that scene on the important sentence "Protected, I mean, from life." From that let us turn to a scene from the second section of Book IV. Strether has met Chad and received his shock of surprise. Instead of finding the Chad he knew at Woollett or that same boy spoiled by a life of dissolute idleness in Paris, he has found him improved out of all recognition. Miss Gostrey has also been introduced to Chad.

His [i.e., Strether's] impression of Miss Gostrey after her
introduction to Chad was meanwhile an impression of a person
almost unnaturally on her guard. He struck himself as at first
unable to extract from her what he wished; though indeed *of* what
he wished at this special juncture he would doubtless have contrived to make but a crude statement. It sifted and settled nothing
to put to her, *tout bêtement*, as she often said, "Do you like him,
eh?"—thanks to his feeling it actually the least of his needs to
heap up the evidence in the young man's favour. He repeatedly
knocked at her door to let her have it afresh that Chad's case—
whatever else of minor interest it might yield—was first and foremost a miracle almost monstrous. It was the alteration of the entire
man and was so signal an instance that nothing else, for the
intelligent observer could—could it?—signify. "It's a plot!" he
declared—"There's more in it than meets the eye," he gave rein to
his fancy. "It's a plant." His fancy seemed to please her. "Whose
then?"

"Well, the party responsible is, I suppose, the fate that
waits for one, the dark doom that rides. What I mean is that with
such elements one can't count. I've but my poor individual, my
modest human means. It isn't playing the game to turn on the
uncanny. All one's energy goes to facing it, to tracking it. One
wants, confound it, don't you see?" he confessed with a queer
face—"One wants to enjoy anything so rare. Call it then life"—he
puzzled it out—"call it poor dear old life, simply, that springs the
surprise. Nothing alters the fact that the surprise is paralyzing, or
at any rate engrossing—all, practically, hang it, that one sees, that
one can see."

Strether's speech is humorous; it is fanciful; nevertheless it is
serious; he has advanced a long way since the time when he
could think of "life" simply as something against which Chad
must be protected. Life is now inscrutable, uncanny—it is
something one may enjoy, it can spring an engrossing surprise. Strether still hopes and believes that Chad will go home
with him: his judgement of what is right is not yet changed;
but what he most wants is to see more of Chad and to find out
how the change in him has been brought about. It is in Section
II of Book V that Strether gives his lecture on life to Chad's
friend, little Bilham. Again the tone of his talk is not solemn,
though it makes the young man momentarily so—"A contradiction," James comments, "of the innocent gaiety the

speaker had wished to promote." Yet it represents the serious reflections that have occurred to Strether during the action. He no longer thinks of life either as something to be protected against or as merely something to be observed:

"Live all you can; it's a mistake not to. It doesn't so much matter what you do in particular, so long as you have your life. If you haven't had that what *have* you had? This place and these impressions—mild as you find them to wind a man up so; all my impressions of Chad and of people I've seen at *his* place—well, have had their abundant message for me, have just dropped *that* into my head."

By this time Strether has shed the Woollett view of life (he had told Miss Gostrey at their first meeting "Woollett isn't sure it ought to enjoy.") but he has still much left to discover about "life."

I will quote from only one more scene in which the word "life" prominently figures. This is the last scene in the novel and Strether is saying goodbye to Miss Gostrey. We know already that he has renounced the possibility of remaining in Paris and of marrying this good friend of his. I quote only an image that occurs to Strether as he sits waiting for Miss Gostrey "in the cool shade of her little Dutch-looking dining room,"

To sit there was, as he had told his hostess before, to see life reflected for the time in ideally kept pewter, which was somehow becoming, improving to life, so that one's eyes were held and comforted.

But life can only "for the time" be so reflected. Its actual complexity and the difficult choices it offers is what, in the course of the action, Strether has learnt to appreciate.

When we isolate these four scenes which represent Strether's gradual discovery of new meanings in the word "life," we are following the main structure of the novel. What these scenes indicate is that aspect of the "buried bone" or "figure in the carpet" which James foresaw could be unfolded from the originating anecdote. Something more complex, rising up into the artist's consciousness only as he contemplated and explored his theme, reveals itself often in

his imagery. Here for example is the description of Miss
Gostrey's room as Strether first sees it (not the little Dutch-
looking dining room but her sitting room):

> Her compact and crowded little chambers, almost dusky, as
> they at first struck him, with accumulations, represented a supreme
> general adjustment to opportunities and conditions. Wherever he
> looked he saw an old ivory or an old brocade, and he scarce knew
> where to sit for fear of a misappliance. The life of the occupant
> struck him of a sudden as more charged with possession even than
> Chad's or Miss Barrace's; wide as his glimpse had lately become of
> the empire of "things," what was before him still enlarged it;
> the lust of the eyes and the pride of life had indeed thus their
> temple. It was the innermost nook of the shrine—as brown as a
> pirate's cave. In the brownness were glints of gold; patches of
> purple were in the gloom; objects all that caught, through the
> muslin, with their high rarity, the light of the low windows.
> Nothing was clear about them but that they were precious, and
> they brushed his ignorance with their contempt as a flower, in a
> liberty taken with him, might have been whisked under his nose.

From the language and imagery of that description
much of Strether's response to his environment emerges. We
are aware of his sense of bewilderment—the puritan conscience wincing at the pagan richness of Miss Gostrey's
taste and also recognizing the predatoriness that such trea-
sure-hunting represents. He is impressed but also dismayed.
He is intimidated but also critical. This "supreme general
adjustment to opportunities and conditions" is associated
with burdens—she is "charged with possessions" and her
possessions dominate her; he has been noticing the "empire
of *things*"—they represent that surrender to the world against
which the Bible warns us. "The lust of the eyes and the pride
of life had indeed thus their temple." Worship and piracy are
brought together in his mind. "It was the innermost nook of
the shrine—as brown as a pirate's cave." When, at the end of
the book, he renounces the happiness Miss Gostrey offers and
returns to the life of Woollett, about which he now has no
illusions, it is, among other things, this "lust of the eyes and
pride of life" he is renouncing. Also he has seen and seen
clearly another kind of empire. His impression of Mme. de

Vionnet's room is related to the impression of Miss Gostrey's. In Mme. de Vionnet's room he reflects that:

> He had never before, to his knowledge, had present to him relics, of any special dignity, of a private order—little old miniatures, medallions, pictures, books; books in leather bindings, pinkish and greenish, with gilt garlands on the back, ranged, together with other promiscuous properties, under the glass of brass-mounted cabinets. His attention took them all tenderly into account. They were among the matters that marked Mme. de Vionnet's apartment as something quite different from Miss Gostrey's little museum of bargains and from Chad's lovely home; he recognized it as founded much more on old accumulations that had possibly from time to time shrunken than on any contemporary method of acquisition or form of curiosity. Chad and Miss Gostrey had rummaged and purchased and picked up and exchanged, sifting, selecting, comparing, whereas the mistress of the scene before him, beautifully passive under the spell of transmission—transmission from her father's line he quite made up his mind—had only received, accepted and been quiet. When she hadn't been quiet she had been moved at the most to some occult charity to some fallen fortune. There had been objects she or her predecessors might even conceivably have parted with under need, but Strether couldn't suspect them of having sold old pieces to get "better" ones. They would have felt no difference as to better or worse. He could but imagine their having felt—perhaps in emigration, in proscription, for his sketch was slight and confused—the pressure of want or the obligation of sacrifice.

Thus Strether sees Mme. de Vionnet "passive under the spell of transmission." She is the inheritor of tradition and all that she does and is—including her relation to Chad and the marriage she arranges for her lovely, virginal, convent-bred daughter, belongs to the tradition of Catholic, aristocratic France. Strether fully responds to the beauty of that order as she represents it. Perhaps he responds also to Mme. de Vionnet's world with a sense that it is doomed. The scene from which I have quoted occurs in the first half of the novel when Strether first visits Mme. de Vionnet's room. It is on another visit, nearly at the end of the novel, that Strether seems to become aware of a menace surrounding his hostess' gracious way of living:

The windows were all open, their redundant hangings swaying a little, and he heard once more, from the empty court, the small plash of the fountain. From beyond this, and as from a great distance—beyond the court, beyond the *corps de logis* forming the front—came, as if excited and exciting, the vague voice of Paris. Strether had all along been subject to sudden gusts of fancy in connection with such matters as these—odd starts of the historic sense, suppositions and divinations with no warrant but their intensity. Thus and so, on the eve of the great recorded dates, the days and nights of revolution, the sounds had come in, the omens, the beginnings broken out. They were the smell of revolution, the smell of the public temper—or perhaps simply the smell of blood.

It was at present queer beyond words, "subtle" he would have risked saying, that such suggestions should keep crossing the scene; but it was doubtless the effect of thunder in the air, which had hung about all day without release. His hostess was dressed as for thunderous times, and it fell in with the kind of imagination we have just attributed to him that she should be in the simplest, coolest white, of a character so old-fashioned, if he were not mistaken, that Madame Roland must on the scaffold have worn something like it. This effect was enhanced by a small black fichu or scarf, of crêpe or gauze, disposed quaintly round her bosom and now completing as by a mystic touch the pathetic, the noble analogy.

It is perhaps in such a passage as this, with its memory of the revolution and its hint of a threatened social order, as also in the pirate imagery of the passage describing Miss Gostrey's room, that Mr. Spender detected an "indictment of society as fierce as that of Baudelaire, or indeed of a class-conscious Marxist." But here it is wise to tread warily. Primarily James' intention in the two passages is to contrast (through Strether's awareness) the acquisitiveness of the American emigré with the passiveness of the aristocrat who has inherited historic possessions. Moreover, when he associates Mme. de Vionnet with a particular victim of the guillotine, he does not choose an aristocrat but that Jacobin heroine, Mme. Roland. What he thereby suggests is not so much that Mme. de Vionnet represents a threatened social order as that she represents romantic courage and loyalty. She is a victim prepared for sacrifice. The passage is the prelude to a scene in which he discovers the full extent of her love for Chad and of her foresight that she will lose him. She tells him at the close: "There's not a grain of certainty in my future—for the only certainty is that I shall be the loser in the end." There is a danger (as there always is when a critic isolates imagery from the context) that he may mistake the overtones for the tune. The novel treats of a number of human beings in a particular situation. Through his intimate contact with them and his gradual discovery of the quality of each individual and all the bearings of their predicament, Strether grows in wisdom and understanding—not of society (except indirectly)—but of the individuals who compose it. It is his sense of moral values that changes, and the novel is not concerned with any political or economic theories.

It is, I think, possible in connection with another scene in which Mme. de Vionnet figures, both to illustrate further how James associates her in our minds with historic heroism and romance, and at the same time to encounter Mr. Grahame Greene's opinion that James was "fascinated, repelled and absorbent" of the Roman Catholic Church. At the beginning of the seventh book Strether wanders into *Notre Dame* driven by an impulse:

. . . the impulse to let things be, to give them time to justify themselves or at least to pass. He was aware of having no errand in such a place but the desire not to be, for the hour, in certain other places; a sense of safety, of simplification, which each time he yielded to it he amused himself by thinking of as a private concession to cowardice. The great Church had no altar for his worship, no direct voice for his soul; but it was none the less soothing even to sanctity; for he could feel there what he couldn't elsewhere, that he was a plain man taking the holiday he had earned.

Throughout the scene Strether is aware of himself as escaping temporarily, from the burden of human responsibilities; and he connects such an escape with cowardice. He can understand

. . . how, within the precinct, for the real refugee, the things of the world could fall into abeyance. That was the cowardice, probably, —to dodge them, to beg the question, not to deal with it in the hard outer light; but his own oblivions were too brief, too vain, to hurt any one but himself, and he had a vague and fanciful kindness for certain persons whom he met, figures of mystery and anxiety, and whom, with observation for his pastime, he ranked as those who were fleeing from justice. Justice was outside, in the hard light, and injustice too; but one was as absent as the other from the air of the long aisles and the brightness of the many altars.

This does not seem to me the language of one who is "fascinated and repelled" (and I think it is fair to identify Strether with his author to the extent of guessing that in this they are at one.) It is the language of secure detachment, sure enough of his own position to contemplate that of the believers with "a vague and fanciful kindness." Among those who have interested him is one in particular,

a lady whose supreme stillness, in the shade of one of the chapels, he had two or three times noticed. . . . She was not prostrate—not in any degree bowed, but she was strangely fixed, and her prolonged immobility showed her, while he passed and paused, as wholly given up to the need, whatever it was, that had brought her there. She only sat and gazed before her, as he himself often sat; but she had placed herself, as he never did, within the focus of the shrine, and she had lost herself, he could easily see, as he would only have liked to do. She was not a wandering alien, keeping back more than she gave, but one of the familiar, the intimate, the fortunate, for whom these dealings had a method and a meaning. She reminded our friend—since it was the way of nine tenths of his current impressions to act as recalls of things imagined—of some fine, firm, concentrated heroine of an old story, something he had heard, read, something that, had he had a hand for drama, he might himself have written, renewing her courage, renewing her clearness, in splendidly protected meditation.

She proves, of course, to be Mme. de Vionnet, and Mme. de Vionnet is a faithful child of the Roman Catholic Church. She is also a sinner, since she is a married woman enjoying intimate relations with one who is not her husband. She is clearsighted and courageously aware of the peril of her immortal soul. All this James' art communicates to us through his story and by means of his imagery. But I detect nothing in the presentation either of nostalgia for Roman Catholicism or of indignation against it, any more than I can detect a message about a doomed social order. In short, the novel seems to me to be about a particular human situation—though one sufficiently serious and sufficiently deeply explored, sufficiently amusing and ironical too, to be representative of universal human predicaments. The novel is not, in my opinion, concerned with either politics or religion except in so far as the selected human beings are molded by religious faiths and by economic and social conditions.

I must differ also from another distinguished critic and attempt to formulate an answer to him. Dr. Leavis writes of *The Ambassadors* in his book *The Great Tradition:*

> What, we ask, is this, symbolized by Paris, that Strether feels himself to have missed in his own life? Has James himself sufficiently inquired? Is it anything adequately realized? If we are to take the elaboration of the theme in the spirit in which we are meant to take it, haven't we to take the symbol too much at the glamorous face value it has for Strether? Isn't, that is, the energy of the "doing" (and the energy demanded for the reading) disproportionate to the issues—to any issues that are concretely held and presented?

It is characteristic of Leavis that he goes straight to the heart of the matter. Certainly these questions are the ones we should ask ourselves. The only adequate answers are contained in the novel itself—the work of art in which James unearths his buried bone. But some reader may be deterred from looking there by Leavis' implication that he will find nothing worth while. In case that should happen I will attempt to counterattack.

During the seven years that intervened between his hearing the anecdote and his writing *The Ambassadors* James was asking himself what it was "symbolized by Paris" that Strether felt himself to have missed. The answer is in the whole series of impressions we are made to share with him through the novel. Little more can be said, in other terms than James' own, except that he had missed those spontaneous joys that come from the contemplation of beauty, the culture of the mind and uncalculating love for a fellow-creature. It does not seem to James—and it does not seem to a reader who responds to his novel—that Paris has, by the end, a "glamorous face value" for Strether. It had something like that at the beginning of the book. But the Paris he renounces for himself contains cruelty, greed, and suffering as well as generosity, courage, and joy. The issues "concretely held and presented" are not, to my mind, disproportionate to the labor of writing or of reading because they are ever-relevant issues between true and false human values. Finally I should like to add that the "energy demanded for reading" is rewarded at every turn, not only because we share with James the discovery of important truths; but because we are continuously spell-bound by his story and amused by his irony, his wit, and his charm in presenting what he sees.

Christof Wegelin

"The Lesson of Social Beauty"□

lthough James never lost his deep moral bias, the special value of his vision derives ultimately from his detachment from any one local point of view. This detachment prevented him from the kind of simplification which sees the world in black and white and led him finally to see the contrast between America and Europe in certain fundamental qualities which, not in themselves good or bad, contain the potentials for both. Ultimately this contrast came for him to lie in the very sources of moral judgment: in the difference between idealism and empiricism, between the laws of conduct which the individual derives from the sense of his independent relation to God and, on the other hand, the rules derived from the needs of social life and formalized in certain institutions and conventions of society. If he had come to see dangers inherent in the moral self-reliance of Americans, Europe had taught him not merely the reality of moral corruption which may be hidden under the decor of art and social form, but also the moral significance of style, beauty, order.

There is an early essay which shows how long James' final point of view had been preparing. "If you have lived about," he wrote in 1878,

you have lost that sense of the absoluteness and the sanctity of the habits of your fellow-patriots which once made you so happy in the midst of them. You have seen that there are a great many *patriae* in

□ From *The Image of Europe in Henry James* (Dallas: Southern Methodist University Press, 1958). Reprinted by permission of the publisher.

the world, and that each of these is filled with excellent people for whom the local idiosyncrasies are the only thing that is not rather barbarous. There comes a time when one set of customs, wherever it may be found, grows to seem to you about as provincial as another.

"Compare then," he concluded, "as often as the occasion presents itself. The result as regards any particular people, and as regards the human race at large, may be pronounced agreeable, and the process is both instructive and entertaining."[1]

Occasion presented itself to James all his life, and the result of it is in his work. Finally he lost not only the smugness with which this early essay is touched, but his faith in the absoluteness of local values. Above all, international contrasts came to serve him as a means for exploring a more fundamental question—the nature of morality "as regards the human race at large." Yet, though the three climactic novels of his career—*The Wings of the Dove* (1902), *The Ambassadors* (1903), and *The Golden Bowl* (1904)—transcend what he called the "*emphasised* internationalism" of his early fiction, they nevertheless mark his return to the international scene. Though, as he said, a different setting might have served his thematic purpose in *The Ambassadors* if it could have represented "a place in which Strether's errand was likely to lie and his crisis to await him," Paris "had the great merit" of sparing him "preparations." Something like this is true of the other two novels of this period. Like *The Ambassadors*, they are concerned with a conflict between different moral sensibilities; and after years of expatriation James found such conflict most ready to his hand on the international scene. His sense of contrast—the kind of contrast on which, he felt, "any painter of life and manners inevitably much depends"—had been "rather oddly predetermined" for him by his "situation."[2] The consistency with which he arrayed various nationalities in his moral dramas is, therefore, neither incidental nor ephemeral. Taken together, the three novels form a trilogy exploring the possibilities of two radically different systems of morality represented by America and Europe. And coming just before his return to America in

1904, which led him to readjust his focus, they constitute a climax in his lifelong attempt to define his sense of the fundamental differences between the two worlds.

By this time, too, James had fully developed his late method: the author is abstracted from the text, and the story is wholly a story of individual consciousness—the characters' story of their story. Consequently, the international contrast has now ceased to be given in terms of an external conflict alone. Instead it is presented in terms of the growth of individual awareness—Strether's awareness of Parisian, Milly Theale's awareness of English, or Densher's of American modes of life. The novels, therefore, picture in the first place, not Europe and America, but the American experience of Europe, the European experience of America. They are novels of initiation and conversion and, in *The Golden Bowl*, finally, of fusion. Their very action consists in the apprehension of foreign modes of living, thinking, judging—a scheme which makes possible an analytical and comparative evaluation far more discriminating than anything in James' earlier work.

The first of James' novels to approach the international situation in this fashion was *The Ambassadors*.[3] Lambert Strether, the hero, is the one among all James' important characters one is most tempted to identify with his author.[4] The reason is not far to seek: *The Ambassadors* is a story of the making of an American cosmopolitan and in this sense may be regarded as a kind of spiritual autobiography. The action is of course fictitious; in fact it has something of the fable or fairy tale, the form which more and more became James' medium for projecting what he saw as psychological and moral realities.

Strether, through whom the story is seen entirely, is a "man of imagination,"[5] and has therefore some of Isabel Archer's American virtue. But this is not "his prime faculty," nor is he presumptuous like her. He is a middle-aged man, and James "rejoiced," as he says, "in the promise of a hero so mature"; for Strether's highly developed "analytic faculty" enabled him to do what in *The Portrait of a Lady* he had left undone: though Isabel Archer's story is eminently the story of her disillusionment, we never see the growth of that dis-

illusionment. At the end of Chapter XXXV we leave her engaged to Osmond; at the beginning of Chapter XXXVI she
has been married to him for more than three years and is
grimly undeceived. The break comes roughly in the middle of
the novel, the first half serving to establish her romantic
character and the second showing what the lesson of Europe
has made of it. Only in the twenty pages of internal monologue which constitute Chapter XLII do we get a summary survey of the intervening years. The structure of *The Ambassadors* differs radically from this. The whole book is a kind of
Chapter XLII, tracing the growth of the hero's perception step
by step. Analysis in *The Portrait of a Lady*, moreover, has
been primarily of the mind of the American heroine, of which
the "Europe" of the American imagination forms a part; we
have been interested primarily in what Isabel will *do*. In *The
Ambassadors*, analysis is largely of the European scene itself;
at the end Strether *sees*, and we are interested in *what* he
sees. "The business of my tale and the march of my action, not
to say the precious moral of everything," James says again,
"is just my demonstration of this process of vision," and his
emphasis falls both on *process* and on *vision*.

What is it that Strether sees? The answer to this question will show the relation between the themes of the lived
life and of the lesson of Europe. About the theme of no other
of his fictions did James commit himself so bluntly as about
that of *The Ambassadors*. "Nothing is more easy than to state
the subject"—thus his preface opens, and before the end of the
page he has quoted Strether's crucial speech in Gloriani's
garden in Chapter XI as an expression of "the essence" of the
novel: "Live all you can; it's a mistake not to. It doesn't so
much matter what you do in particular, so long as you have
your life." The speech is too well known to be here quoted at
length. This fragment, moreover, contains the essence of the
whole, which is much more startling in isolation than when
it is understood dramatically, as the speech must be understood. For James is of course far from advocating moral
anarchy. Strether's case is, in the words of the preface,
"comparative"—and comparative not merely with regard to
Europe and America but at the same time with regard to the

importance of doing and judging. What he comes to see is
that in too much judging he has missed life. It is what with
repeated emphasis he calls his past mistake, which is the
mistake of Woollett, Massachusetts, for Strether is a product of
"the very heart of New England." The crisis which leads to
his lucidity is the "false position" in which he finds himself
in Paris. He has come "primed with a moral scheme of the
most approved pattern," approved, that is, in New England
and hence "framed to break down on any approach to vivid
facts," at least "to any at all liberal appreciation of them."[6]

The capacity for liberal appreciation is what distinguishes Strether from the rest of the Woollett clan. James
calls *The Ambassadors* a "drama of discrimination," Strether's
discriminations of course since all is seen as it reflects itself
in his mind. But important among the things discriminated
are various American attitudes toward Paris, beside Strether's
own—whose changes constitute the action of the story—
most important those of Chad Newsome and his sister Sarah
Pocock, the latter representing Mrs. Newsome, their mother
and Strether's friend, who is never present in person but
throughout looms heavily as the purest and most potent source
of the Woollett spirit. This latter attitude is what has brought
Strether to Paris. He has come to rescue Chad, whom Woollett
believes to be in the clutches of a Parisian enchantress. This
view of Chad's imbroglio is very much what in the preface
James calls "the dreadful little old tradition, one of the plati-
tudes of the human comedy, that people's moral scheme *does*
break down in Paris." It is the image of Paris as the "consecrated scene of rash infatuations," which in *The American*
already he had felt to be a trap to be avoided by the novelist.
So in *The Ambassadors*, the initiation of Strether into a mode
of life radically different from that of Woollett "was to have
nothing to do with any *bêtise* of the imputably 'tempted'
state"—a fact which we shall have to remember when we
come to consider the much disputed end of the novel. Instead,
Strether was to be thrown "upon his lifelong trick of intense
reflexion," which was to lead him a wonderful dance through
winding passages of darkness and light to a realization of
"more things than had been dreamt of in the philosophy of

Woollett.''[7] What happens to Strether is that he is thoroughly emancipated from the "dreadful little old tradition." What in the end he sees with a new clarity and sharpness of vision is not only Paris but Woollett itself, represented by the human symbols of Madame de Vionnet and Mrs. Newsome.

The problem confronting Strether is the question whether Chad's attachment to Madame de Vionnet represents, as Woollett believes, the breakdown of his morals or whether, as one of Chad's young friends tells Strether, it is "virtuous." The "virtuous attachment" becomes the focal point in which the various themes meet: the question of morality, the question of the lived life, and the international contrast. Strether's *volte-face* is made in a succession of two or three appraisals of what is appearance and what reality.

To summarize the sequence of his adjustments briefly, what strikes him at his very first meeting with Chad is a tremendous improvement in the young man's appearance. Instead of being coarsened by the process of sowing his wild oats, he seems of unexceptionable taste and manners, even of a dignity which can momentarily affect the older man with a kind of awe. Chad has simply been "made over," and the fact prepares Strether to believe that the attachment to Madame de Vionnet is "virtuous." Nor does this lady's own appearance in any way serve to dispel the impression. It is important that Strether first meets her in the garden of Gloriani, the distinguished sculptor, during a party in which the place, the assembled company, and even the soft spring afternoon, all conspire in an "assault of images" which brings to a sudden focus what has been growing in him almost from the moment he set foot on European soil—a new sense of life, a sense of "ease" before which his past life shows up as poverty-stricken. This is what provokes his sudden and ardent outburst. Yet, Strether's Woollett conscience is not dead. In the very current of his passionate appeal he realizes that he is "a case of reaction against the mistake," and that "the voice of reaction" must always be taken with an "allowance." What he remains concerned with is the reality hidden behind the brilliant show. Do these people all show "for what they really are?" he asks, only to have his seriousness laughed off as Christopher Newman already had his moral seriousness laughed off by Parisian "frivolity": "Oh, I like your Boston 'reallys'!"

At any rate, Strether's conclusion is that Chad's attachment to Madame de Vionnet *is* "virtuous." It is a pragmatic conclusion drawn from Chad's "improvement" and from Madame de Vionnet's own charm and beauty: "Ah, she was neither Turk nor Pole!" She is a *femme du monde* at the same time that she impresses Strether with her "common humanity." And like other Americans before him—Isabel Archer, for instance—Strether is moved to trust by the presence of a young daughter, a perfect *jeune fille* whose exquisite innocence testifies to the "tone" of the mother. In a word, Madame de Vionnet is simply the most exquisite of women. This is the view which Strether stoutly adheres to in the face of Sarah Pocock, the second Woollett ambassador sent out because Strether, the first, seems to falter in his mission. Sarah is not open to the appeal of the show, of appearances. Like Henrietta Stackpole in *The Portrait of a Lady*, though much less appealingly, she knows perfectly in advance what she will find in Europe. To her, Paris *is* the "consecrated scene of rash infatuations"; to her an attachment of a young American to a French woman is "wicked" by definition, since it is what the Woollett image of Paris prescribes. And the irony of Strether's predicament is that Sarah's view turns out to have been right as far as the mere physical facts are concerned. For the second step in Strether's initiation is his sudden discovery of what Chad's relations to Madame de Vionnet really are.

This of course is the crisis in Strether's education. Up to this point he has been concerned only with the appearance of things. He has argued against Sarah Pocock's crude assumption of Chad's corruption on the grounds of Madame de Vionnet's amiability, her rarity, her distinction—all his own words for describing her. And he has explained that to take a woman "at once so charming and so beneficent" for anything but what she appears, characterizes merely the Woollett state of mind, which proceeds "from our queer ignorance, our queer misconceptions and confusions," whereas

he has found that "the proof of the pudding's in the eating"—
a repudiation, this, of moral absolutism which, as he realizes
immediately, cuts him off for good and all from Woollett.
Sarah breaks with him, and he is left to cope alone with his
last discovery that the particular "virtuousness" which he
has come to believe in does after all not exist. For it *is* a
discovery. Although to Sarah he has protested his right to
think highly of Madame de Vionnet without investigating her
actual "life," we find at the end that he has all along been
taking the beauty of the surface for a positive sign of "virtuousness" in the literal Woollett sense of the word. His
theory has been not only "that the facts were, specifically,
none of his business" but that they "were, over and above,
so far as one had to do with them, intrinsically beautiful."

His discovery that the relation of Chad and Madame de
Vionnet is not what he had assumed, that—although for the
wrong reasons—Woollett's estimate of the facts of this relationship has been accurate, comes therefore as a shock.
"A sharp fantastic crisis," he feels, has suddenly "popped up,"
and what above all makes him feel it "as quite horrible" is the
fact that Chad and Madame de Vionnet are clearly conscious
of having something "to put a face upon." He finds that all
along there has been "a *lie* in the charming affair," from the
very moment when he was told that Chad's attachment to
Madame de Vionnet was "virtuous." It is this "quantity of
make-believe" which, as he ruminates on the compromising
meeting he has had with the two lovers, most disagrees with
"his spiritual stomach." But it is just this, too, which in the
light of a new day ends by making the revolution in his moral
thinking complete.

The setting where Strether realizes this is again significant. All through his adventure he has been much under the
spell of the scenic frames of the people he has been concerned
with. He has first met Madame de Vionnet in Gloriani's old
garden among a company which has affected him like something of the "boundless menagerie" of which James speaks in
the preface[8]—creatures beautifully plumed and "magnificently marked." He has seen her next in the deep "mildness
and stillness" of her old house among her old possessions,

which have spoken to him of "her rare unlikeness to the
women he had known," of a beautiful passivity "under the
spell of transmission," of "a deep suspicion of the vulgar,"
and of an "air of supreme respectability, the consciousness,
small, still, reserved, but none the less distinct and diffused,
of private honor." And finally, he has his sudden revelation of
the facts of her relation to Chad in the French countryside, "a
land of fancy for him—the background of fiction, the medium
of art," and appealing quite particularly to him—thus James
emphasizes Strether's response to the pictorial and associa-
tional—by reminding him of "a certain small Lambinet that
had charmed him, long years before, at a Boston dealer's"—
all of which has made the conditions of his meeting with the
pair easy and natural and above all fundamentally different
from the conditions of Woollett.

But the moment of his full awareness of what has happened to his moral sense comes on the morning following his
night of lonely rumination. He is back in Paris, in the *Postes
et Télégraphes* sending a reply to Madame de Vionnet's
request to see him. And "the pressure of the place" again does
its work, deciding him to see her once more in her home, "in
her own best conditions." As he looks about himself at the
little people scribbling messages, he realizes suddenly that he
is "carrying on a correspondence, across the great city, quite
in the key of the *Postes et Télégraphes* in general," and that
accepting the fact as a matter of course, he is "mixed up with
the typical tale of Paris." The realization amounts to an
identification of himself with the Parisians: "they were no
worse than he," and he "no worse than they—if, queerly
enough, no better."

This last, that he should have arrived at a point where
his moral superiority has vanished, is hard to swallow. An
instinct in him still keeps him groping for some straw of
"discipline" in "the silver stream of impunity" in which he
feels himself floating with the rest of Paris. For a while he
keeps reverting to the tradition he has been brought up in,
which assumes that the "state" or at least the "happiness" of
the "wrongdoer," presents some "special difficulty." But
what strikes him above all now is the "ease" not only with

which Chad and his lover have managed their affair but also
with which he himself accepts the situation. The lesson of
this ease is what finally puts the period to his whole education.
"Their eminent 'lie,' Chad's and hers," this is where his
ruminations finally lead him, is after all simply "such an
inevitable tribute to good taste as he couldn't have wished
them not to render." And he finally makes his way to Madame
de Vionnet's house with the conviction that he can trust her
"to make deception right." "As she presented things," he
has learned, "the ugliness—goodness knew why—went out
of them."

This is a far cry from the moral absolutism of Woollett
—"to make deception right." Yet, it is what Strether comes
out with. Even the friend who described Chad's relation to
Madame de Vionnet as "virtuous" lied like a gentleman,
showed him, Strether in fact now feels—and this without
irony—"what's expected of a gentleman." For what has
finally changed for Strether are the very criteria by which he
determines what is "right" or "virtuous." That first lie was
only "technical" since the attachment, quite regardless of
certain facts, *is* virtuous because Madame de Vionnet is so.
What this amounts to is that Strether has abandoned the moral
"laws" of Woollett for some other criteria of what is "right,"
something which he can hardly name but which is represented
for him by Madame de Vionnet's distinction, her charm, her
amiability—qualities thrown vividly into relief by Sarah
Pocock's and, as Strether comes to see, Mrs. Newsome's
colder virtues. What has from the first acted as the wedge to
loosen Strether's old beliefs has been his sense of the outward
transformation of Chad. What makes him see virtue even in
the affair as it is finally revealed to him is the person of
Madame de Vionnet. Strether has quite simply become a
pragmatist.

Yet Strether has abandoned none of his moral seriousness. What he has come to see is that the precepts of Woollett
will not serve as guides for the moral evaluation of Paris,
since they are part of the localism of manners and therefore
subjective. The Woollett vision of Chad's imbroglio, from
which Strether emancipates himself, is naïve, is a manifesta-

tion of the old American "innocence," though what James emphasizes this time is its negative aspect. It is peculiarly exposed to corruption for the very reason that it lacks the awareness which comes from experience. Sarah Pocock and Waymarsh, another New Englander "in the real tradition," have their "romance" together, affected by the "charged, infectious air" of the "classic ground," the "great temple" of pleasure which Paris is to them. Not to mention Jim Pocock, Sarah's husband, who—full of "innuendo as vague," Strether feels, "as a nursery-rhyme, yet as aggressive as an elbow in his side"—slyly envies Strether for having one more "good time" before it is too late and who spends his days sniffing up what he "supposes" to be Paris. Jim has his New England "categories in hand" and, despite his chummy sympathy for what he thinks of as Strether's and Chad's philandering, is therefore no less blind than the others— "stupid or wilful," as they strike Strether, in their inability to see Madame de Vionnet's real qualities. In accord with the Woollett view of Paris as the playground of errant husbands, Jim leaves the "moral side" of their adventure to his wife to the extent even of calling on Madame de Vionnet "all alone" at a time when Sarah makes no bones about what she thinks of "this person" and of "*that* sort of thing." And Strether indeed realizes that "he would have been held less monstrous had he only been a little wilder."

What all this comes to is that the whole Woollett tribe indulge their own pleasure and their own preconceptions. They all exemplify in their various ways what in the preface to *The Reverberator* James calls the "passionless pilgrims" among the Americans, who regarded Europe as a toy to be used and discarded at will. "A hundred good instances," James writes, "confirmed this tradition that nothing in the new world was held accountable to anything in the old,"[9] and in *The Ambassadors* he adds another half dozen illustrations or so to his collection. Even Chad—and this is the last irony in Strether's developing lucidity—turns out to be among them. For it becomes more and more clear that in the end he will after all return to Woollett and the family business, so that Strether, who has originally come out to "save" him

from Madame de Vionnet, finds himself admonishing him:
"You'll be a brute, you know—you'll be guilty of the last
infamy—if you ever forsake her."

James' description of the "passionless pilgrims"
contains in fact one sentence which applies to none of his
characters as well as to Chad: "Europe," the "painted and
gilded holiday toy," serves "its purpose on the spot and for
the time" only "to be relinquished, sacrificed, broken and
cast away, at the dawn of any other convenience."¹⁰ What
could describe better the "infamy" which Strether feels Chad
subtly capable of? And what could be more ominous—
particularly if we remember James' feelings about the
vulgarity of modern publicity—than that the field in which
Chad's new "convenience" seems to be dawning is the
"science" of advertising? True, there are other suggestions:
young Mamie has been brought over as a bait for him; and
Strether half suspects "some other woman in London." But
the note on which we see Strether and Chad separate for the
last time, the fact that the latter has "encountered a revelation" in the "great new force of advertising"—in our "roar-
ing age," he tells Strether, "an art like another"—and that
this of all things is what finally kindles his interest in the
Woollett business serves as an ominous climax to the various
hints of vulgar insensitivity which Strether keeps hearing in
the cavalier manner of Chad's allusions to Madame de
Vionnet—a tone almost of street-corner swagger sometimes,
which makes Chad's professions of faithfulness to her suspect by a too-much of protestation.

If Chad is going to cast off *his* "gilded holiday toy,"
it is not because of any European corruption.¹¹ It is, quite on
the contrary, because in spite of all that Madame de Vionnet
may have done for him, he still is "none the less only Chad,"
"*our* little Chad," as Strether elsewhere says with significant
emphasis. The realization comes to him "with supreme
queerness," and well it might. All his battle with Woollett
has been an attempt to make them see that the Chad they
meet in Paris is *not* "the same old Chad" they've been
"glowering at across the sea," and now at the end he finds
that he has been mistaken after all. The Chad who threatens

to exchange Madame de Vionnet for the refinements of advertising, Strether realizes, is precisely the old Chad, and this last touch supplies the link which completes the chain of Strether's insights. For the last thing to which his eyes are opened is Woollett itself.

The most important symbol of Woollett is the distant figure of Mrs. Newsome, just as Madame de Vionnet is the most important symbol of Paris. And the transfer of Strether's allegiance from the one to the other is a token of his moral change of heart. His reassessment of Mrs. Newsome is pointed: *she* has not changed, she is "more than ever the same. But I do what I didn't before—I *see* her." The conversation in which this occurs points back explicitly to an earlier one, in which Strether's original vision of the lady is contained. There she rules over the family concern with "a delicacy and a discretion" beyond words, and after the fashion of the benevolent tycoon, she supports "as a tribute to the ideal" the green Review of which Strether is the editor. She is "a *moral* swell." At the end of his adventure Strether sees through all this. And though he does not formulate exactly what it is he sees, the accumulation of his thickening perceptions is clear enough.

Perhaps the most revealing of them comes half-way through the book. Strether has kept Mrs. Newsome religiously informed, has been in almost daily correspondence with her. But when he so obviously fails to return Chad to the bosom of Woollett, her letters stop, and it strikes him that he has "never so lived with her as during this period of her silence." This silence, more than anything else, expresses her to him—"so highly, so almost austerely, herself: pure and by the vulgar estimate 'cold,' but deep, devoted, delicate, sensitive, noble." Later, he himself is to judge her by the "vulgar estimate" when he realizes that the reason why Sarah can so effectively represent her is that "she's all cold thought" which can be served "cold without its really losing anything." That is, her virtues are not only ethereal, they are tenuous, to him who has come to see virtue more and more as a function of living. That her virtues—he comes to call them "idiosyncrasies"—should strike him most in her absence is symbolic of their divorce from the stuff of human contacts, a divorce which manifests itself in other ways, in what Strether comes to feel as "her want of tact" and above all in the moral obtuseness which makes her blind alike to Madame de Vionnet's beauty and to Jim Pocock's moral shabbiness. All this, as everything else in the novel, is Strether's point of view and merely indicates the change which has come over his sense of virtue. In his new vision, Mrs. Newsome's high idealism—for that is what it boils down to—takes on the color of the cold inhumanity which disturbs the reader in Euphemia de Mauves. Only, now the sense of the negative aspect is made more concrete—in those representatives of Woollett, Sarah and Jim and, after all, Chad.

The Ambassadors, then, is another version of the conflict between American and European manners, of American misapprehension of European conduct which had occupied James during his earlier career. Unlike The Portrait of a Lady, a story of disenchantment which invokes our sympathy for American idealism, it is a story of conversion. What we are asked to share is Strether's gradually growing awareness and finally his high sense of the moral sufficiency of Madame de Vionnet, even of the moral beauty which he comes to see in her despite her conflict with the moral regimen of Woollett. Strether's final position is to some extent deterministic as well as pragmatic, bound up as his judgment of Madame de Vionnet is with the forces of tradition that have shaped her. In Gloriani's garden he is explicit about this: "The affair of life," he says, is

at the best, a tin mould, either fluted and embossed, with ornamental excrescences, or else smooth and dreadfully plain, into which, a helpless jelly, one's consciousness is poured—so that one "takes" the form, as the great cook says, and is more or less compactly held by it: one lives, in fine, as one can.

Evidently out of such considerations, James did what he could to take the onus of what is technically adulterous from Madame de Vionnet's relation to Chad by giving her a background strikingly similar to that of Claire de Cintré in The American. Madame de Vionnet has "been married, out of hand," to a "polished, impertinent reprobate," whose brutality freed her entirely from the stigma of marital failure: luckily, "he was so impossible that she had the advantage of all her merits," she so amiable that "nobody had a word to say" against her when she was forced to live separately from him. All this is significant "history" to Strether and most significant the fact that Madame de Vionnet is part of an order "governed by such considerations as put divorce out of the question."[12] What this contributes to the moral content of the novel is to free Strether for the appreciation of Madame de Vionnet's virtues, which to him prove themselves in the beauty which she salvages from the wreck of her life.

It is significant that in quoting Strether's climactic speech in the preface James omitted the emphatically deterministic parts. In spite of his awareness of the limitations of human freedom, he had temperamentally not a trace of the naturalist in him. Indeed, Strether's outburst ends in an assertion: "Still, one has the illusion of freedom"; therefore, "don't make *my* mistake. For it was a mistake. Live!" It is an assertion strikingly similar in tone to William James' famous challenge to his own doubts, and like it the necessary beginning of a search for moral clarification: "I will assume," William James had told himself, that free will "is no illusion. My first act of free will shall be to believe in free will." Neither Strether nor his author is of course a philospher, yet one of William James' summaries of his own philosophy is a fit expression of their search for values: "My philosophy is what I call a radical empiricism," William James wrote in 1904, "which represents order as being gradually won and always in the making." It "rejects all doctrines of the Absolute." Similarly, Strether does not emancipate himself from his moral seriousness—any more than Emerson, for instance, in his revolt against dogmatism, denied the reality of moral distinctions. What his adventure teaches him is the fallibility of Woollett's "sacred rage" and, more important, the beauty of another mode of living—or, to borrow William James' words once more, the beauty of "the *attained* social character of European civilization."[13]

If Strether is no philosopher, he yet has the philosopher's love of truth. While the others are blinded by their preconceptions, while they make their beliefs subservient to their own desires, Strether's motives are quite impersonal. James emphasizes this by the question of Strether's marriage to Mrs. Newsome which constantly looms in the background as a potential motive. The task for which Strether has been sent to Paris resembles the traditional test which the fairy prince has to pass before he wins the hand of the princess. His returning Chad triumphantly to Woollett, he has more or less been given to understand, will be rewarded by the opening to him of the doors to Mrs. Newsome's heart. And as his moral exploration progresses, he comes to realize more and more that what it has been leading him away from is the safety not only of the Woollett creed but with it of an "opulent future" with Mrs. Newsome. But Strether scrupulously avoids being swayed by such personal considerations, and this precisely is part of his distinction. This is, as he realizes, "the refinement of his supreme scruple"—that he wishes to leave out of account what he himself may forfeit and to do everything for the sake of lucidity alone. It is why he leaves when Maria Gostrey, his mentor, falls in love with him and at the end all but offers herself as a substitute for the lady he has lost. Since it is his "only logic" not to have got anything for himself out of the whole affair, he must go "to be right."

The echo of Isabel Archer's final "as seems right" is striking, and Strether is indeed cousin-german to her. His vision was formed in Woollett, and he knows what inevitable cast that mold has given to the "helpless jelly" of his consciousness. Near the end, he sees himself under the likeness of "one of the figures of the old clock at Berne" which, when the hour strikes, come out to jig along "their little course in the public eye"—and the image, once more sounding the note of his determinism, has a part in what makes for his final decision. Once more, too, the temptation to speak of Strether's experience as a fable dramatizing James' own is great—not only because James could at times speak of his own situation as an accident imposed upon him. More important, if Strether despite his moral revolution retains an eye for what "makes" him right almost puritan in its "horrible" sharpness, James, too, despite expatriation, never lost the deep moral bias of his origins.

But the real reasons for Strether's tacit rejection of Maria Gostrey's tacit proposal are part of the dramatic structure of the novel. For one thing, his taking his ease at her inn would obfuscate the clear line between his impersonal motives and the Woollett conception of them, since Woollett, too, might conclude that "the proof of the pudding's in the eating." It would bring Strether dangerously close to the "*bêtise* of the imputably 'tempted' state," and this at a time when his unselfishness is more than ever important as a foil to Chad's egotism. Above all, however, Strether is more deeply moved by Madame de Vionnet than he quite realizes. To the end, she is to him "the finest and subtlest creature, the happiest apparition" it has been given him to meet. And it is this sense more than anything else that puts an end to Maria Gostrey's hopes. The contrast between these two women, too, is part of Strether's growing discrimination. Settling down to a comfortable old age among Maria Gostrey's "specimens" of crockery and silver and pewter would be a mere taking refuge from the fulness of his knowledge. For he has learned to distinguish between the items of her "little museum of bargains" and Madame de Vionnet's "quite different" relics, which speak to him not of the rummaging, exchanging, selecting of the "contemporary method of acquisition" but of the beautiful and quiet "spell of transmission" from one generation to the next and therefore of an order more private, more dignified and substantial than Maria's.

This contrast—similar to the one between Osmond and Warburton in *The Portrait of a Lady*—goes to the heart of the international theme of *The Ambassadors*. As the *Notebooks* show, James had found the germ of his story in a reported glimpse of Howells in Paris, "virtually in the evening" of his life and sadly aware of being too old to take advantage of what he saw for the first time.[14] But what the "little situation" turned into was a drama not merely of the loss of experience but of the gain of knowledge. And though Maria Gostrey has been Strether's mentor, he, the pupil, has out-distanced her.

"He has come so far through his total little experience that he has come out on the other side—on the other side, even, of a union with Miss Gostrey"—this is the way James put it in the long preliminary statement which he submitted to his publisher as a "project" of the novel. Strether's experience has made him "so quite other that, in comparison, marrying Miss Gostrey would be almost of the old order," and "their lingering, ripe separation" must therefore be "the last note."[15]

All this goes to say that if there is something tragic in Strether's life, it is not so much what he has missed as what he has learned. It is contained in his picture of Madame de Vionnet. For what he comes to see with a final shock is that the woman whose deep beauty is the main cause of his new vision is after all not proof against defeat and pain. He is amazed to find that *she* should be "down in the dust," and "put there by *our* little Chad." This is the only trace left here of James' earlier theme of the pretense of aristocracy, but how transformed it now is! What shocks Strether is not the artificiality of an institution which was the lesson of, say, Euphemia de Mauves' discovery of her husband's libertinism. It is the much profounder shock of seeing into the very depths of common human weakness. James avails himself of all the suggestive power of Shakespeare's Cleopatra when Strether can "think of nothing but the passion, mature, abysmal, pitiful" betrayed by the spectacle of the rare creature troubled as vulgarly "as a maidservant crying for her young man." Only, what distinguishes Madame de Vionnet in her prostration is that she judges herself as the maidservant would not, and the "weakness" of her "wisdom," Strether feels, seems but "to sink her lower"—which more than anything perhaps shows how far his experience has taken him from the moral thinking of Woollett.

Strether's new vision consists in the awareness that there is a virtue which cannot be measured by the bundle of moral "notions with which he started from home." One of the convictions which thicken for him in the course of his adventure is indeed a sense of the high value which the relation with a woman like Marie de Vionnet represents "for any young man." But if the revisions he has to make in his moral

assumptions are "almost grotesque," that is merely so because they land him in a fundamental contrast between
civilizations, between "the special phase of civilization"
embodied by the "bustling business at home, the mercantile
mandate, the counter, the ledger, the bank, the 'advertising
interest,' " and the civilization for whose "charm" Madame
de Vionnet comes to stand. This summary of the "core of the
subject" is James' own in his preliminary "project," and it
ends with the explicit statement that Strether's story amounts
to a moral reconsideration of civilization.[16]

But it must not be understood that *The Ambassadors*
represents James' last word on the subject, nor that *The
Wings of the Dove* and *The Golden Bowl*, which followed it,
constitute progressive revisions of his views. If the idealization of Madame de Vionnet is, in the light of his earlier
handling of the American girl, rather striking, the reason is
simply that here his emphasis falls on the possibilities of
social discipline and experience rather than on the promise
of innocence and spontaneity. In these novels, James was
much less interested in making final value judgments than in
exploring the origins and possibilities of contrasting modes of
moral life, and this precisely is his most important contribution to the American genre of international fiction. It is a
contribution inseparable from his concern with individual
consciousness. In these three novels, therefore, he analyzed
the awareness which the social conflict between America and
Europe brings to various representatives of either side. *The
Ambassadors* traces the growth of such awareness in the mind
of an American, *The Wings of the Dove* and *The Golden Bowl*,
as we shall see, in the representatives of the European order
as well. "The consequence of the cosmopolite spirit," he had
written in that early essay with which this chapter opens, "is
to initiate you into the merits of all peoples." And what stands
out in these late works is the idealization of different kinds of
merit: of social beauty in Madame de Vionnet, of a high
spiritual beauty in Milly Theale, and of their fusion in the
marriage of Maggie Verver and the Roman Prince in *The
Golden Bowl*.

Notes

1 *Portraits of Places*, pp. 115–118, *passim*.
2 James' words are to be found in the prefaces to Vols. XIV, XVIII, and XXI of the New York Edition; see *Art of the Novel*, pp. 198, 199, 280, 316.
3 Though published after *The Wings of the Dove*, *The Ambassadors* was written first.
4 See J. W. Beach, *The Method of Henry James* (New Haven, 1918), p. 269.
5 This and the other phrases from James' preface to the novel are to be found in *Art of the Novel*, pp. 308, 310, 316.
6 Again James' preface, *ibid.*, pp. 314, 315.
7 *Ibid.*, pp. 24, 316–317, *passim*, one of the formulations being from the preface to *The American*.
8 *Ibid.*, p. 315.
9 *Ibid.*, p. 189.
10 *Ibid.*
11 Randall Stewart has attributed Chad's anticipated defection to his European "corruption" ("The Moral Aspects of Henry James' 'International Situation,' " *University Review*, X [1943], 109–112), and Yvor Winters, in a generally excellent essay on James, speaks of Chad as the character in this novel "most profoundly affected by the contact with Europe" (*Maule's Curse*, p. 183)—misapprehensions both which seem due, and in Stewart's essay clearly are due, to the attempt to squeeze James into a pattern whose opposition of "cultural" and "moral" values entirely overlooks his most important contribution to the American analysis of international contrasts.
12 The parallels between Madame de Vionnet and Claire de Cintré of *The American* include further details. Both are the daughters of a French father and an English mother; both have in the marriage of their parents had "no example of comfort"; the fathers of both have died early but left them with "a memory all fondness." Such correspondence of details, some of which are hardly necessary to either story, sets one wondering, inevitably though perhaps vainly, about reasons. What they at any rate underline is the likeness of the two heroines in virtue.
13 The three formulations of William James are to be found in *The Letters of William James*, ed. Henry James (Boston, 1920), I, 147; II, 203–204; and in *The James Family*, ed. F. O. Matthiessen (New York, 1947), p. 313.
14 *Notebooks*, p. 226.
15 The "Project" is printed in the *Notebooks*; see p. 415. To Matthiessen, surprisingly, this last scene serves merely "to exaggerate the negative content of Strether's renunciation." Strether, he argues, "has awakened to a wholly new sense of life. Yet he does nothing at all to fulfill that sense. Therefore, fond as James is of him, we cannot help feeling his relative emptiness." And he sees this as an example of "the contrast in James between imputed and actual values" (*Henry James: The Major Phase*, pp. 38–39, *passim*). The answers to this view come tumbling out of the book thick and fast, and I have given some in the text. But the simplest answer is that Strether's separation from Maria Gostrey involves no renunciation at all on his part since—though for reasons of tact and kindness he cannot tell Maria—he is in love with Madame de Vionnet. And since *she* is in love

with Chad, it is hard to see how Strether could have found fulfilment of his love of *her*. Naturally, all this involves resignation on his part, but it is simply the resignation of a man who, at fifty-five, finds that he is too old to catch up on the mistakes of his youth, and who therefore wisely makes the most of that fulness of understanding which is the best "the great cook" has apportioned him.

16 *Notebooks*, pp. 395–396, *passim*.

John Paterson

"The Language of 'Adventure' in Henry James"□

Every inch the novelist, Henry James cultivated the near
rather than the far, preferred the ordinary in human experience to the extraordinary. Much has been made of the
rare refinement, even the preciosity, of his characters; but,
although he was himself to describe them as his "supersubtle
fry,"[1] he liked to think that they belonged in their essence to
the categories of the average and the normal. It was in fact
one of the chief articles of his artistic faith that in the ordinary
could be discovered the possibilities for the extraordinary.
The heroine of *The Portrait of a Lady* was to demonstrate
"what an 'exciting' inward life may do for the person leading
it even while it remains perfectly normal."[2] And though he
was to rejoice, in the hero of *The Ambassadors*, in "the
opportunity to 'do' a man of imagination," he was also to
rejoice in the assurance that Lambert Strether would not give
him "imagination in *predominance* or as his prime faculty.
. . ."[3] Hence his confidence in the psychological, the internal,
experience of character as a legitimate province of the artist
in prose fiction. To explore the unknown landscapes of the
mind was in effect to discover the extraordinary in the
ordinary, the heroic in the anti-heroic. Confronted by Walter
Besant's prescription "that a story must, under penalty of
not being a story, consist of 'adventures,' " James was sure

□ *American Literature*, XXXII (November, 1960), pp. 292–301. Reprinted
by permission of Duke University Press and John Paterson.

not only that "the moral consciousness of a child [was] as much a part of life as the islands of the Spanish Main," but also that "the one sort of geography [had] those 'surprises' of which Mr. Besant speaks quite as much as the other."[4]

I

In spite of his professional mistrust of the primitive novel of adventure, however, Henry James was as haunted as any Tom Sawyer by its crude and violent imagery. He appears to have delighted in memorializing and heightening, through images taken from those areas of experience conventional with the novel of adventure, the modest crises of his own singularly uneventful life. This imagery runs especially to hairbreadth escapes in heavy seas and savage jungles. If he has been "disgustingly silent," he explains to one correspondent, it is because "the waters of Rome have been closing over my head."[5] He describes his New Year's correspondence as a flood "which I've been till now buffeting and breasting"[6] and a letter to a friend as a "rude but affectionate signal from the desert-island of my shipwreck."[7] Invoking the predatory, the familiar image of the beast in the jungle, he reports that the subject of *The Ambassadors* "sprang at [him], one day, out of [his] notebook,"[8] that the inscription devised by his brother for his sister's urn has taken him "at the throat by its penetrating rightness. . . ."[9] Overcome by William's death, he finds the shadow of his memory "always of a sudden leap out of its lair."[10] He confesses elsewhere to "not being quick on the epistolary trigger."[11] If there is any hitch in the arrival of his brother's family, he will, he assures a correspondent, "bleed half to death."[12] "I will sound a horn," he writes, promising H.G. Wells not to visit him without adequate forewarning, "so that you yourself be not absent on the chase."[13]

To have seen in the portly priestly figure of Henry James the youthful lineaments of Tom Sawyer is not of course to have caught him redhanded. It is not to have found him the unwitting victim of his own fantasies. In its calculated extravagance, in the disparity between it and its reference, the heroic imagery pervasive in James' daily prose exposes, for one thing, a highly developed sense of the whimsical and the droll. When, furthermore, the relation between the heroic metaphor and its antiheroic subject involves not an ironic incongruity but a perfectly serious congruity, as is more generally the case, it is to publish his stubborn conviction that the moral and social emergencies of the human experience are every bit as spectacular as its physical emergencies, that the adventurer in the infinite realms of consciousness is just as heroic as the adventurer in the more palpable realms of the physical.

II

Hence the particular frequency of his heroic imagery in the prose of the prefaces and the essays in criticism. Conceiving the artist as the supreme example of the heroism of consciousness, James' imagination is especially susceptible to heroic visions when he is descanting on the artist's adventure, his failures and successes, on the high seas and bloody battlefields of prose fiction. "The intricate ins and outs of the compositional problem" he defines in fact as "adventure *transposed*";[14] and he confesses elsewhere to cherishing the record of his artistic difficulties "as some adventurer in another line may hug the sense of his inveterate habit of just saving in time the neck he ever undiscourageably risks."[15] The heroic commitment of the artist is perhaps most frequently imagined as a commitment to dangerous waters. "I don't still see . . .," James confides in the notebooks, "that by still clinging to the whole essence of the conception, I may not ride a wave that will yet float me through."[16] And it is the index of Balzac's courage that "it was up to his chin, constantly, that he sank in his illusion—not, as the weak and timid in this line do, only up to his ankles or his knees."[17] The artist's ordeal is elsewhere visualized in terms of ships exposed to all the hazards of the heaviest seas. Defining dialogue as "the fluid element" in prose fiction, James describes "its haunting and besetting penalty" as that "of springing, unless watched, a leak in its effect. It is as if the master of the ship"—and the reference here is to Balzac—"were keeping his eye on the pump . . .

that keeps the vessel free of too much water."[18] Later recalling the confident spirit in which he wrote *The American*, James wonders if, "recognizing after I was launched the danger of an inordinate leak—since the ship has truly a hole in its side sufficient to have sunk it—I may not have managed . . . to stop my ears against the noise of waters and *pretend* to myself I was afloat. . . ."[19] He fears elsewhere "going to smash on the rock of autobiography."[20]

The moving accidents of the creative experience elsewhere inspire images taken from the heroic world of the knight, the hunter, and the smuggler. Celebrating the example of Balzac, "the greatness of his intellectual adventure," he conceives him as "always astride of his imagination, always charging, with his heavy, his heroic lance in rest, at every object that sprang up in his path."[21] The great effects of Flaubert's celebrated style did not come, he insists, by themselves: "their arrival was determined only by . . . the arts of the chase, long waits and watches, figuratively speaking, among the peaks or by the waters."[22] Formed "to make the wary adventurer walk round and round it," the subject of *The Wings of the Dove* stood before him, he recalls, "with secrets and compartments, with possible treacheries and traps. . . ."[23] Justifying the element of the improbable in "The Aspern Papers," James represents the tone of "amusement" with which it is informed as "the current floating that precious influence home quite as one of those high tides watched by the smugglers of old might, in case of their boat's being boarded, be trusted to wash far up the strand the cask of foreign liquor expertly committed to it."[24]

III

It is, however, in the fiction itself that the imagery of violent and heroic physical adventure enters the prose of Henry James with the most telling purpose and effect. For if the psychological was to make the ordinary interesting, what, in its turn, was to make the psychological interesting? James' keen awareness of his problem and his purpose emerges in the preface to *The Portrait of a Lady*. Recognizing the mild-

ness of his heroine's adventures, "their independence of
flood and field, of the moving accident, of battle and murder
and sudden death," he sees the beauty and difficulty of his
task "just in showing their mystic conversion . . . into the
stuff . . . of 'story.' "[25] He describes "the long statement,
just beyond the middle of the book, of my young woman's
extraordinary meditative vigil," as an attempt "to make the
mere still lucidity of her act [of meditation] as 'interesting' as
the surprise of a caravan or the identification of a pirate."[26]
Hence the significance of James' heroic metaphors. How was
he more effectually to transform the domestic experience to
which he was committed as a novelist than by rendering it in
terms of caravans and pirates, in terms of the vocabulary and
imagery of the adventure novel? How was he otherwise to
show that the geography of the moral consciousness was as
full of adventures and surprises as the geography of the
Spanish Main?

He was, then, to conceive his often tubercular heroes
and heroines in the same flamboyant terms as his artist-
adventurers. If strict verisimilitude had been consulted, he
confesses, the preferred course of the Bellegardes in *The
American* "would have been to haul [Newman] and his fortune into their boat under cover of night perhaps, in any case
as quietly and with as little bumping and splashing as possible. . . ."[27] Milly Theale's very existence would create, he
thought, "that whirlpool movement of the waters produced by
the sinking of a big vessel . . ."[28] Into the central predicament
of *The Sense of the Past*, he remarks, his hero "emerges as
from below, after the fashion of a swimmer who has dived or
sunk or been dragged down for the minute and who comes up
to the surface, recovering breath with difficulty at first. . . ."[29]

This extravagant imagery is widely disseminated in
James' later novels, but it is nowhere more current than in
The Ambassadors, where he was, in the dramatic moral
development of Lambert Strether, to celebrate the bravery of
the human consciousness in action with unprecedented fullness and directness. Explicitly bearing witness to the argument, characteristically Jamesian, that "a human, a personal
'adventure' is no a priori, no positive and absolute and

inelastic thing . . . ."[30] *The Ambassadors* may in fact be read as a nearly direct repudiation of the objections raised by Besant to the psychological emphasis in fiction. For when the hero asks himself "what really *had* happened" at Gloriani's garden-party and finds that "the items made a meagre total," it is to suggest that such a man as Strether was, might have "an amount of experience out of any proportion to his adventures. . . ."[31] It is in the service and support of this germinal thesis that James invokes in the pages of this novel so many heroic images of emergencies at sea, in the jungle, and on the field of battle.

When the principals of the novel are represented as "ambassadors," for example, James visualizes them as members not of a diplomatic, but of a military, mission. Mistrusting the Babylonian temptations of the French capital, Strether decides to confront Chad immediately, "to advance, to overwhelm, with a rush" and thus to "anticipate—by a night-attack, as might be—any forced maturity that a crammed consciousness of Paris was likely . . . to assert on behalf of the boy" (p. 106). Called upon to defend his own unorthodox relations with Miss Gostrey, he will consider "carrying the war into the enemy's country by showing surprise at the enemy's ignorance" (p. 123). He is later confronted by a Mrs. Pocock who holds "her tall parasol-stick upright and at arm's length, quite as if she had struck the place to plant her flag" (p. 365). After "the retreat of the Pococks" (p. 404), Maria Gostrey marvels at his being asked to take Mrs. Newsome "at the point of the bayonet" (p. 385). When he is not advancing and retreating on the field of battle, Strether is being tossed violently and unceremoniously about. Overcome by his impression of Gloriani, he sees himself "as disorganized, as possibly floored" (p. 162). "The air of supreme respectability" which he unexpectedly encounters in the apartments of Mme. de Vionnet is described as "a strange blank wall for his adventure to have brought him to break his nose against" (p. 185). Tricked into committing himself to her cause, he feels "as if he had been tripped up and had a fall" (p. 208).

The fragile population of the novel is elsewhere exposed to dangers more deadly than falls, floorings, and broken noses. "You want to make a bonfire in fact," says Chad, accusing Strether of trying to bring him home in triumph, "and you pitch me on" (p. 114). To relieve the tension, Strether is prepared to meet with Mrs. Pocock even at the risk "of pulling down the roof on their heads" (p. 325). Sensing "that the situation was running away with him," he can "put his finger on the moment it had taken the bit in its teeth," breakfast with a French lady becoming, in James' dangerous world, "the smash in which a regular runaway properly ends" (p. 227).[32] Having interested Strether in her daughter, Mme. de Vionnet is said to have "driven in, by a single word, a little golden nail, the sharp intention of which he signally felt" (pp. 208–209). And it takes Strether a minute "to recover from the sense of being pierced" by the repudiation Mrs. Pocock "had let fly at him as from a stretched cord" (p. 372). The streets of the novel at times run red with the blood of the wounded. Chad administers a dig to Strether that "came nearer drawing blood" (p. 120) and in his fight with Mrs. Pocock is expected to use his elderly friend "to the last drop of [his] blood" (p. 321). Strether's tangled relations with people are later represented as bristling "with fine points . . . that pricked and drew blood" (p. 440).

The highly civilized folk of this dangerous universe are not always distinguishable in fact from man-eating predators. Accused of getting the ladies to work for him, Strether is imagined as "just preparing . . . to pounce—don't you see him?—on Mme. de Vionnet" (p. 153) while a guilt-ridden Waymarsh is later seen pacing and turning, "caged and leonine," before the friend he has betrayed (p. 263). Strether senses at Gloriani's garden-party "something in the great world covertly tigerish, which came to him, across the lawn . . . as a waft from the jungle." He sees Gloriani himself as "the glossy male tiger, magnificently marked" (p. 165). "They don't lash about and shake the cage," Jim Pocock says of his wife and formidable mother-in-law, "and it's at feeding-time that they're quietest" (pp. 280–281).[33]

On the whole, however, James' heroes and heroines are more likely to risk death and danger on the high seas of the novel than in its jungles and battlefields. If they—and above all Strether—discover darker and darker depths as their imaginations mature and develop, they fight to float and only go under in the expectation of coming up again. In the new-found freedom and leisure of the European experience, Strether sees himself as "washed up on the sunny strand, thankful for breathing-time, stiffening himself while he gasped, by the waves of a single day" (p. 61). Chad's charm becomes an eddy into which Waymarsh has been drawn in spite of himself: "there were days when Strether seemed to bump against him as a sinking swimmer might brush a submarine object" (p. 129). Denounced by Sarah Pocock at their final meeting, Strether tries "not to flounder in her grasp" (p. 368); but affronted by "his not clutching the pole she held out" (p. 369), Mrs. Pocock lets "him go on as if to sink and sink" (p. 371). When the principals of the novel are not being rescued, bloodied, from the field of battle, they are being rescued, drenched, from the perilous flood. Strether is sure that Mrs. Pocock "will take [Waymarsh] into her boat" (p. 264). Not long after, Strether himself, whose "sole license had been to cling, with intensity, to the brink, not to dip so much as a toe into the flood," will be taken into Mme. de Vionnet's boat: "he felt himself proceed to each of the proper offices, successively, for helping to keep the adventurous skiff afloat" (p. 286). To survive in the violent tides of *The Ambassadors* is indeed to be in possession of a watertight boat. Mme. de Vionnet has "settled in Paris, brought up her daughter, steered her boat" (pp. 173–174); but Chad is engaged, as Maria Gostrey has rightly guessed, in "the effort to sink her" (p. 129). Suddenly homesick in the presence of Mamie Pocock's charm, Strether could "have fancied himself stranded with her, on a far shore, during an ominous calm, in a quaint community of shipwreck" (p. 329).[34]

    If it is usually difficult to decide whether James' imagination is being exercised by the novel of adventure itself or simply by those fields of experience customarily exploited by that literature, there are occasions when little doubt is possible. Thus Maria Gostrey's apartments suggest to Strether's imagination "a pirate's cave" (p. 89), a "cave of treasures" (p. 315), while Gloriani's pavilion is "as striking

to the unprepared mind . . . as a treasure dug up" (p. 147).
The principals of the novel are elsewhere seen groping about
in the dark passages of Cretan labyrinths or Gothic castles.
Strether feels himself "moving in a maze of mystic, closed
allusions. Yet he kept hold of his thread" (p. 210); "I incline
to believe too you'll come out," Miss Barrace assures him.
"Only the question's about *where*" (pp. 348–349)—such
references as these are evidently to the labyrinth. Others,
however, vaguely recall the furniture of Gothic romance:
"Mme. de Vionnet had by her visit held up the torch to these
truths, and what now lingered in poor Maria's face was the
somewhat smoky light of the scene between them" (p. 443);
Chad leads the Pococks, at the party honoring their arrival,
"to the uttermost end of the passage accepted by them perforce as pleasant . . . they had come all the way without
discovering that it was really no passage at all. It was a brave
blind alley, where to pass was impossible . . ." (p. 338). Even
the horrendous melodrama of Edgar Allan Poe has been consulted at this point. "Mrs Pocock's built in, or built out . . . ,"
Miss Barrace exclaims; "she's packed so tight she can't
move." "She's bricked up," she cries, her imagination warm-
ing to its work, "she's buried alive!" (p. 349).

   Bearing witness to a bizarre sense of humor, James'
violent and heroic conceits produce comic effects ranging from
the ironic to the farcical. The sheer extravagance of the figure
renders character and action in terms of caricature as, for
example, when Sally Pocock is caught gathering her skirts
and her courage to leap from the runaway (p. 339) or as when
Chad is imagined as having "by a turn of the wrist and a jerk
of the far-flung noose, pulled up, in a bunch, Woollett brow-
sing in its pride" (p. 120). Not even Strether himself is spared.
Although his story has serious and even tragic undertones,
the lineaments of the familiar and unfailingly funny story of
the country bumpkin baffled by the ways of the big city are,
perhaps, recognizable under the sophistication of its surface.
In the process of his education out of the rough values of his
American heritage and into the finer values of the European
experience, Strether is required to assume a number of
ludicrously unheroic postures, as when he tumbles about with

Waymarsh, that other innocent abroad, in the submarine depths of Chad's charm or when Mme. de Vionnet's respectability is recognized as a wall against which he is called upon to break his nose. The function of the heroic imagery in such cases is to underline the comic antiheroism of character and action.

The congruities between James' metaphors and the subjects to which they refer are just as obvious and just as remarkable, however, as their incongruities. Notwithstanding the triviality of the action at the level of Besant's "adventures," issues of spiritual life and death *are* involved, and hence entirely justify the hyperbolical imagery they call into being. Maria Gostrey pledges herself to Strether's cause "till death" (p. 56). "You surely don't mean it will kill you," she asks him as he contemplates his impending disaster, "my real smash" as he calls it (p. 254). Strether foresees that, with his talent for self-sacrifice, "he should go to the scaffold yet for he wouldn't know quite whom" (p. 357). Eventually divining the urgency of Mme. de Vionnet's situation, "you're afraid," he exclaims, "for your life!" (p. 435). Here and elsewhere, the characters—and James himself—are in deadly earnest. Testifying to the grim realities beneath even the most smiling social appearances, to the extraordinary realities that underlie the most ordinary appearances, a nearly complete equivalence between the two halves of the analogy is asserted. In the perilous world of Henry James, there are indeed lions in the lobbies, tigers in the parlor, death by drowning in the dining rooms, and in the very boulevards of Paris armies locked in mortal combat.

IV

If James' comic exploitation of the imagery of violent action suggests his amusement and skepticism in the presence of the primitive novel of adventure, his entirely serious exploitation of it reveals what may sometimes suggest a mild infatuation. In *Ulysses*, that more worldly exercise in tragicomedy, Joyce would half transform, through the agency of myth and symbol, the commonplaces of the daily subjective human experience.

By diffusing through his prose the imagery inspired by the
novel of adventure, James earlier accomplishes—though his
transformations are less ambiguous, less ironical, than
Joyce's—the same essential result. Committed as a novelist to
the materials of the average and the commonplace, he demonstrates that the near is not less colorful, not less exciting, than
the far. Committed to developing the internal, the psychological, experience of character, he demonstrates that the territories of the mind are as fraught with perilous adventure as
the more rugged territories traversed by Scott, Stevenson,
and Kipling; that a moral and social geography provides as
eventful a field of operations for the swashbuckling hero as
the Scottish Highlands, the Spanish Main, and the Indian
frontier.

It may be difficult to imagine Huck Finn abroad in the
streets of London and Paris, but it is surely less difficult to
imagine Tom Sawyer there. Was Henry James not, in a sense,
all appearances to the contrary notwithstanding, his reincar-
nation?

Notes

1   Henry James, *The Art of the Novel: Critical Prefaces* (New York, 1934),
p. 221. (Hereinafter cited as *AN*.)
2   *Ibid.*, pp. 56–57.
3   *Ibid.*, p. 310.
4   James, "The Art of Fiction," *The Future of the Novel: Essays in the Art
of Fiction* (New York, 1956), pp. 22–23. (Hereinafter cited as *FN*.)
5   Percy Lubbock, ed., *The Letters of Henry James* (New York, 1920), II,
p. 74. (Hereinafter cited as *Letters*.)
6   *Letters*, I, p. 388.
7   *Letters*, II, pp. 173–174.
8   F. O. Matthiessen and Kenneth B. Murdock, eds., *The Notebooks of
Henry James* (New York, 1955), p. 228. Cited by the editors. (Hereinafter
cited as *NB*).
9   *Ibid.*, p. 321.
10   *Letters*, II, p. 330.
11   *Ibid.*, p. 184.
12   *Ibid.*, p. 97.
13   *Letters*, I, p. 298.
14   *AN*, p. 319. The italics are his.
15   *Ibid.*, p. 85.
16   *NB*, pp. 300–301.
17   "The Lesson of Balzac," *FN*, p. 112. Turgenev is approved on the
grounds, among others, that he saw character "in the general flood of life

. . . struggling or submerged, a hurried particle in the stream" ("Turgenev and Tolstoy," *FN*, p. 231).

18   "The Lesson of Balzac," *FN*, p. 123.

19   *AN*, p. 21.

20   *NB*, p. 321. He assures Mrs. Wharton that her novel "will gracefully ride the waves . . . long after every other temporarily floating object shall have sunk. . . ." (*Letters*, II, p. 281). "[A] scheme of fiction so conducted," he writes of Zola, "is in fact a capacious vessel. It can carry anything—with art and force in the stowage; nothing in this case will sink it. . . . [All other forms] have to confess . . . to the danger of distortion, explosion, combustion. The novel has nothing to fear but sailing too light" ("Emile Zola," *FN*, p. 164).

21   "The Lesson of Balzac," *FN*, p. 107.

22   "Gustave Flaubert," *FN*, p. 33.

23   *AN*, pp. 288–289.

24   *Ibid.*, p. 168. The complete seriousness of James's commitment to the artist's adventure is perhaps most forcibly betrayed by the sheer violence and cruelty—and the tone is not always whimsical—of much of his terminology. "What I said above about the 'rule' of presentation being . . . hard and fast," he writes Mrs. Humphrey Ward, "*that* I will go to the stake and burn with slow fire for—the slowest that will burn at all" (*Letters*, I, 326). *The Portrait of a Lady* is "all too faint and far away," he declares, ". . . and I have bloodier things *en téte*" (*ibid.*, p. 279). Translation is an effort "to *tear*"—and the italics are his own—"the hapless flesh" (cited by René Wellek, "Henry James's Literary Theory and Criticism," *American Literature*, XXX, 316, Nov., 1958).

25   *AN*, p. 56.

26   *Ibid.*, p. 57.

27   *Ibid.*, p. 36.

28   *Ibid.*, p. 293.

29   *NB*, p. 366.

30   Cited in *NB*, p. 277.

31   *The Ambassadors*, Doubleday Anchor Books (New York, 1958), p. 171. All page references hereinafter incorporated in the text are to this edition.

32   Strether will later find Mrs. Pocock in the same dire predicament: impressed in spite of herself by Chad's party, she will affect him "as a person seated in a runaway vehicle and turning over the question of a possible jump" (p. 339).

33   The social jungles of the novel are in fact as full of traps as of animals. Strether will thus interpret one social occasion as "the most baited, the most gilded of traps" (p. 84).

34   That the imagery of adventure was essential to James's conception of the novel is suggested by its frequency in the scenario which antedated its writing (see *The Notebooks of Henry James*). Learning that Strether is engaged to Mrs. Newsome, Maria Gostrey "has in fact . . . pointed the pistol at him" (*NB*, p. 385) while Chad will later recognize that, for Strether, "the assault is made, the charge sounded, too late" (*ibid.*, p. 396). The hero's mission is "to try to fish [Chad] out of his deep waters" (*ibid.*, p. 384), though he will contemplate a course as a result of which "Chad will be thrown overboard" (*ibid.*, p. 405).

XI

House

The
of Mirth
(1905) by
Edith
Wharton

Edith Wharton

⌒〰⌒

from *A Backward Glance* □

. . . **M**y problem was how to make use of a subject—
fashionable New York—which, of all others, seemed most
completely to fall within the condemned category. There it
was before me, in all its flatness and futility, asking to be
dealt with as the theme most available to my hand, since I had
been steeped in it from infancy, and should not have to get it
up out of note-books and encyclopaedias—and yet!

The problem was how to extract from such a subject
the typical human significance which is the story-teller's
reason for telling one story rather than another. In what aspect
could a society of irresponsible pleasure-seekers be said to
have, on the "old woe of the world," any deeper bearing
than the people composing such a society could guess? The
answer was that a frivolous society can acquire dramatic
significance only through what its frivolity destroys. Its
tragic implication lies in its power of debasing people and
ideals. The answer, in short, was my heroine, Lily Bart.

Once I had understood that, the tale rushed on toward
its climax. I already had definite ideas as to how any given
subject should be viewed, and from what angle approached;
my trouble was that the story kept drawing into its web so
many subordinate themes that to show their organic connection with the main issue, yet keep them from crowding to the

□ Reprinted with permission of Charles Scribner's sons from *A Backword
Glance*, pp. 206–208, by Edith Wharton. Copyright 1933, 1934 William R.
Tyler; renewal copyright © 1961, 1962.

front, was a heavy task for a beginner. The novel was already promised to "Scribner's Magazine," but no date had been fixed for its delivery, and between my critical dissatisfaction with the work, and the distractions of a busy and hospitable life, full of friends and travel, reading and gardening, I had let the months drift by without really tackling my subject. And then, one day, Mr. Burlingame came to my rescue by asking me to come to his. A novel which was to have preceded mine in the magazine could not be ready in time, and I was asked to replace it. The first chapters of my tale would have to appear almost at once, and it must be completed within four or five months! I have always been a slow worker, and was then a very inexperienced one, and I was to be put to the severest test to which a novelist can be subjected: my novel was to be exposed to public comment before I had worked it out to its climax! What that climax was to be I had known before I began. My last page is always latent in my first; but the intervening windings of the way become clear only as I write, and now I was asked to gallop over them before I had even traced them out! I had expected to devote another year or eighteen months to the task, instead of which I was asked to be ready within six months; and nothing short of "the hand of God" must be suffered to interrupt my labours, since my first chapters would already be in print!

I hesitated for a day, and then accepted, and buckled down to my job; and of all the friendly turns that Mr. Burlingame ever did me, his exacting this effort was undoubtedly the most helpful. Not only did it give me what I most lacked—self-confidence—but it bent me to the discipline of the daily task, that inscrutable "inspiration of the writing table" which Baudelaire, most untrammelled and nerveracked of geniuses, proclaimed as insistently as Trollope. When the first chapters appeared I had written hardly fifty thousand words; but I kept at it, and finished and delivered my novel on time.

N. Elizabeth Monroe

࿇

from *The Novel and Society*□

hus it is mainly because of the limitations of her subject matter that Mrs. Wharton's tragic vision of life was not fulfilled. This limitation and certain defects in her own point of view and understanding of life have kept her from taking her place with Balzac, Turgenev, Thackeray, and Jane Austen, who are her spiritual kin. Her subject matter forced her to concern herself only with negative values, and as a result even the technical brilliance of her work cannot give it a place with the great fiction of the world.

. . .

Mrs. Wharton brought to the delineation of manners a penetrating intelligence, a sense of the pervading irony of life, not inferior to that of the Greeks, solidity of observation and detachment of spirit, a flawless gift of phrase, and the unflagging invention and narrative gift of great art. It is doubtful whether any other novelist has ever said so many brilliant things about society as Mrs. Wharton has said, without becoming entangled in his or her own brilliance. Mrs. Wharton's irony, even in the form of epigram, rarely detaches itself from the page. Her ability to invent scenes and incidents that give the exact significance of the situation she

□ N. Elizabeth Monroe, *The Novel and Society: A Critical Study of the Modern Novel* (Chapel Hill: University of North Carolina Press, 1941), pp. 116, 118–119. By permission of the publisher.

has imagined is remarkable. Even where the story is concerned with trivial or somewhat typical characters, or with issues that seem unreal because cut off from their moral and spiritual bases, it never fails to absorb the reader's attention and to convince him of its truth to art.

In spite of her very great technical gifts, Mrs. Wharton suffers sometimes through defect of love. Many lesser novelists have had the gift of illuminating human experience through love or sympathy, the only means by which the secret recesses of the heart are opened, and all the great novelists have had it. Turgenev's *The House of Gentlefolk* is concerned with a trivial and disintegrated society which has no more significance than the society of *The House of Mirth*, but the moving depths below Turgenev's story have no counterpart in Mrs. Wharton. Lisa's renunciation is ennobled by the depth of her love, but Lily Bart's fate is to be swept out in the dust heap. Mrs. Wharton's story tells us everything about a parasitic and disillusioned society that supreme intelligence can see in it, but that leaves out of account the very soul of life.

Blake Nevius

from "Toward the Novel of Manners"□

It is to Edith Wharton's credit that she recognized the perilous transparency of the human nature she had to deal with—a human nature subject to no stresses that money could not alleviate, and therefore incapable of expressing itself with the greatest intensity. The characterization of Lily Bart was central to the problem; and since Lily, in order to satisfy her function in the novel, had to take her cue from the more worldly of her associates, she remains, so far as the moral significance of her actions is concerned, until almost the end of the novel an essentially lightweight and static protagonist. Nevertheless, she has, if only in embryo, certain qualities which raise her above her associates and make her distinctly worth saving, so that her fate, if not tragic according to any satisfactory definition of the term, at least impresses us with the sense of infinite and avoidable waste. Edith Wharton's own answer to her question was "that a frivolous society can acquire dramatic significance only through what its frivolity destroys. Its tragic implication lies in its power of debasing people and ideals." Change the word "frivolous" to "materialistic," and the story of Lily Bart assumes a larger significance. Edith Wharton was one of the first American novelists to develop the possibilities of a

□ From Blake Nevius, *Edith Wharton: A Study of Her Fiction* (Berkeley and Los Angeles: University of California Press, 1953), pp. 55–61. Reprinted by permission of the Regents of the University of California.

theme which since the turn of the century has permeated
our fiction: the waste of human and spiritual resources which
in America went hand in hand with the exploitation of the
land and forests. *The House of Mirth* belongs in the same
category with *Windy McPherson's Son*, *The Professor's House*,
Robert Herrick's *Clark's Field*, and countless other novels
which tried to calculate the expense of spirit that a program
of material self-conquest entailed.

There is some indication that Mrs. Wharton conceived
of her action, perhaps unconsciously, in terms of naturalistic tragedy. In *A Backward Glance* she recalls her introduction to "the wonder-world of nineteenth century science"
and the excitement of reading for the first time the works of
Darwin, Huxley, Spencer, Haeckel, and other evolutionists.
It is impossible, perhaps, to calculate their influence, but it
has never been considered. She was perfectly acquainted,
moreover, with the French naturalistic tradition beginning
with Flaubert, and it is not impossible that Emma Bovary is
the spiritual godmother of Lily Bart. But this is at best
circumstantial evidence, whereas the novel itself adequately
conveys the suggestion. Its theme is the victimizing effect of a
particular environment on one of its more helplessly characteristic products. It was the discovery of the nineteenth century,
as someone has said, that Society, rather than God or Satan,
is the tyrant of the universe; and the society into whose
narrow ideal Lily Bart is inducted at birth conspires with her
mother's example and training to defeat from the start any
chance of effective rebellion. In the naturalistic tradition,
the action of *The House of Mirth* is in a sense all denouement,
for Lily's conflict with her environment—no more than the
feeble and intermittent beating of her wings against the bars
of "the great gilt cage"—is mortgaged to defeat. Her vacil-
lation between the claims of the spirit represented by Selden
and the prospect of a wealthy marriage is never quite convincing. Beyond Selden's tentative solicitations there is
nothing in her life to encourage rebellion. And undermining
his influence is the symbolic figure of Gerty Farish, Lily's
cousin, embodying the "dinginess" which above everything
else Lily dreads.

Lily, in short, is as completely and typically the product of her heredity, environment, and the historical moment which found American materialism in the ascendant as the protagonist of any recognized naturalistic novel. Like any weak individual—like Clyde Griffiths or Carrie Meeber—she is at the mercy of every suggestion of her immediate environment; she responds to those influences which are most palpably present at a given moment. Although we are asked to believe that two sides of her personality are struggling for possession, there is no possibility of a genuine moral conflict until near the end of the action when as a result of suffering she experiences the self-realization which is the condition of any moral growth. Through no fault of her own, she has—*can* have—only the loosest theoretical grasp of the principles which enable Selden to preserve his weak idealism from the corroding atmosphere in which they are both immersed.

Inherited tendencies had combined with early training to make her the highly specialized product that she was: an organism as helpless out of its narrow range as the sea-anemone torn from the rock. She had been fashioned to adorn and delight; to what other end does nature round the rose-leaf and paint the humming-bird's breast? And was it her fault that the purely decorative mission is less easily and harmoniously fulfilled among social beings than in the world of nature? That it is apt to be hampered by material necessities or complicated by moral scruples?

The idea, much less happily expressed, might have been taken from Dreiser. It is all there: the deterministic view reinforced by analogies drawn from nature, even the rhetorical form of address. True to the logic imposed by her subject and theme, Mrs. Wharton seems to imply what Dreiser everywhere affirms: that in the struggle for survival the morally scrupulous individual has in effect disarmed himself. Lily's vagrant impulses of generosity and disinterestedness and her antique sense of honor are the weak but fatal grafts on her nature.

I do not want to press the point too far. The impact of the passage is after all still very different from what it would be in Dreiser, for Edith Wharton never rode determinism as a thesis. Her view was conditioned by a faith in moral values that collided head on with the implications of determinism, and it was impossible for her to present a situation without regard to its moral significance. But the day is past when we necessarily see a contradiction if the two views are embraced simultaneously. Naturalism allies itself conveniently—and, if need be, temporarily—with a personal mood of despair, and I think it likely that this is what happened in Mrs. Wharton's case. The mood renews itself periodically, but except in *Summer* (1917) it is never so strong again as in *The House of Mirth*. There is added support for this view, I believe, in the fact that both verbal and dramatic irony are usually active in this novel, helping to establish an unmistakably pessimistic tone.

It should be clear, at any rate, that we are deceiving ourselves if we try to account for the compelling interest of *The House of Mirth* by the nature or intensity of the moral conflict. Besides the reasons I have suggested, the alternatives proposed to Lily Bart in the persons of Selden and Gerty Farish are not at all attractively urged. It was beyond Edith Wharton's powers of sympathy and imagination, and at odds with her distrust of philanthropy, to make Gerty Farish, with her social work, her one-room flat, and the unrelieved dinginess of her life in general, an engaging figure. And what can we say of Selden, who maintains his integrity at the cost of any nourishing human relationship? Like Winterbourne in *Daisy Miller*, he is betrayed by his aloofness, his hesitations, his careful discriminations. He is the least attractive ambassador of his "republic of the spirit," and Mrs. Wharton knows this as well as her readers. In fact, the tragic effect of Lily Bart's fate is jeopardized by an irony directed principally at Selden, for she accidentally takes an overdose of sleeping pills while he is trying to make up his mind to marry her.

The quality in the novel that seizes and holds the reader, and that accounts more than any other for its persistent vitality, is the same which we find in the novels of Dreiser. In the spectacle of a lonely struggle with the hostile forces of environment, there is a particular kind of fascination which is not at all diminished by the certainty of defeat. The individual episodes in Lily Bart's story are moves in a game played against heavy odds, and the fact that the game is conducted according to an elaborate set of rules which are unfamiliar to the general reader gives it an added interest. After her initial success and unexpected reverses, the advantage moves back and forth, but always inclining toward the opponent's side, until Lily is maneuvering frantically to retrieve her position. On the whole, she plays like an amateur, but luck combined with flashes of skill keeps the game from going constantly against her. The episodic structure of the novel, which Mrs. Wharton labored vainly to control,[1] reinforces this impression: the individual moves and countermoves stand out prominently from the action as a whole. In contrast to *The Valley of Decision*, the author treats her subject for the most part scenically, letting the episodes speak for themselves. Moreover, if the interest were centered in the moral conflict instead of the external drama, it would be reasonable to expect a narrower aesthetic distance, as in *The Reef* or *The Fruit of the Tree*. Either that or we must agree with Mrs. Wharton's implication in *A Backward Glance* that she has learned very little from the later Henry James and is still inclined, as the master himself complained, to survey the psychological terrain from too great a height. But the fact seems to be that our attention is directed to a scene of life presented in its broader aspects rather than to a complicated moral dilemma.

For its contemporary interest, the novel relies less heavily than is sometimes assumed on the portrait of a particular society and on the value to the social historian of Mrs. Wharton's authentic delineation of manners. Lily Bart as a type has survived and multiplied, and the society in which she figured is still recognizable, although it has democratized itself to the point where it has lost some of the dramatic possibilities with which a complex gradation of manners once endowed it. Lily is what Justine Brent, in *The Fruit of the Tree*, lives in dread of becoming and what Sophy Viner, in *The Reef*, becomes—"one of those nomadic damsels who form the camp-followers of the great army of pleasure." In return for their hospitality, she serves her wealthy friends—or, rather, is used by them—as social secretary, chauffeur, auxiliary hostess, and, less agreeably, as go-between and scapegoat in their extramarital adventures. The personal freedom of Selden or Gerty Farish seems to her to be purchased at too great a cost. Her compromise is a familiar one in our society; her successors are legion.

Note

1 Letter to W. C. Brownell, Aug. 5, 1905 (before publication, Brownell evidently had praised the novel highly): "I was pleased with bits, myself; but as I go over the proofs the whole thing strikes me as so loosely built, with so many dangling threads, and cul-de-sacs, and long dusty stretches, that I had reached the point of wondering how I had ever dared to try my hand at a long thing— So your seeing a certain amount of architecture in it rejoiced me above everything."

Larry Rubin

"Aspects of Naturalism in *The House of Mirth*"□

The powerful strain of naturalism with which the art of Edith Wharton is suffused—a strain too often overlooked by critics—can be profitably studied by examining four representative novels: *The House of Mirth* (1905), *The Age of Innocence* (1920), *The Fruit of the Tree* (1907), and *The Custom of the Country* (1913). In these books we can trace certain broad aspects of naturalism as they are manifested in specific situations. The very theme of *The House of Mirth*, for example, has been defined as "the victimizing effect of a particular environment on one of its more helplessly characteristic products." This product is Lily Bart, a social parasite and perpetual bridesmaid, who finally proves a trifle too scrupulous to claim her place in the world of luxury and pleasure—a world for which she has long been groomed and a position to which she has always aspired. She is, to quote Blake Nevius, "as completely and typically the product of her heredity, environment and the historical moment which found American materialism in the ascendant as the protagonist of any recognized naturalistic novel." Having been made what she is by forces beyond her control, she eventually falls victim to those same forces. Dogged by poverty and hounded by scandal, she is "tossed as helplessly as a cork

□ From Larry Rubin, "Aspects of Naturalism in Four Novels by Edith Wharton," *Twentieth-Century Literature*, II (January, 1957), pp. 182–192. Reprinted by permission of the publisher and the author.

in the whirls and eddies of the social stream—tossed and buffeted and finally dragged under with her eyes wide open to her own helplessness."[1]

On the other hand, the critics who perceive marked restrictions in Mrs. Wharton's use of determinism refuse to view Lily herself as being entirely blameless. Miss Monroe, for instance, declares:

Lily Bart's environment has so fashioned her that she is almost bound to be a parasite. Yet every step in her downfall is occasioned by a mistake in her own judgment or the failure of her will to meet the challenge of poverty and hardship.

The moral implications of this verdict are stressed by Lovett: "Heredity and environment play a large part in her undoing. . . . Nevertheless, at the root of her case is a moral attitude which is fundamentally wrong, and Lily is real enough to suggest that she could have changed it. . . ." That Lily should have managed somehow to rise above the inexorable pressures beating her down to the ground is implied by P. H. Boynton, whose indictment of the heroine is that, instead of retaining a stoical control of self, she "succumbs to the circumstances that created her."[2]

Examining the text itself, however, one finds that Mrs. Wharton has placed such heavy emphasis upon the molding influence of environment that it seems as if Lily would have had to possess almost superhuman strength in order to withstand it. A strong hint of this influence appears in the very first chapter, when Selden, one of the few sensitive souls in the book, admires the heroine's beauty:

He was aware that the qualities distinguishing her from the herd of her sex were chiefly external: as though a fine glaze of beauty and fastidiousness had been applied to vulgar clay. Yet the analogy left him unsatisfied, for a coarse texture will not take a high finish; and was it not possible that the material was fine, but that circumstance had fashioned it into a futile shape?[3]

Tempted to advance her social position by setting aside a few scruples, she feels keenly the effect of her upbringing: "Her danger lay, as she knew, in her old incurable dread of discomfort and poverty; in the fear of that mounting tide of

dinginess against which her mother had so passionately
warned her" (page 478). Again, in answer to a friend's demand
to tell her "exactly what happened from the beginning,"
Lily gives her an answer which, though expressed in a
bantering tone, throws light on her problem:

"From the beginning?" Miss Bart gently mimicked her.
"Dear Gerty, how little imagination you good people have! Why,
the beginning was in my cradle, I suppose—in the way I was
brought up, and the things I was taught to care for. . . ." (page
363).

But the central statement of her heroine's dilemma
Mrs. Wharton chooses to issue herself:

Inherited tendencies had combined with early training to make her
the highly specialized product she was: an organism as helpless
out of its narrow range as the sea-anemone torn from the rock. She
had been fashioned to adorn and delight; to what other end does
nature round the rose-leaf and paint the humming-bird's breast?
And was it her fault that the purely decorative mission is less easily
and harmoniously fulfilled among social beings than in the world of
nature? That it is apt to be hampered by material necessities or
complicated by moral scruples? (pages 486–487).

Then, as if to make certain that no one has missed the point,
the author, shortly afterward, states the same idea in different
words:

But, after all, it was the life [the life of pleasure] she had been made
for; every dawning tendency in her had been carefully directed
toward it, all her interests and activities had been taught to center
around it. She was like some rare flower grown for exhibition, a
flower from which every bud had been nipped except the crowning
blossom of her beauty (pages 512–513).

Lily, then, as Pritchett notes, has been "fatally conditioned
from the first."[4] "There had been nothing in her training to
develop any continuity of moral strength," the author tells
us (page 422). In view of these facts, how can we, in all fair-
ness, ascribe moral culpability to such a person?

Actually, Lily Bart possesses a set of ethical principles
somewhat loftier than those displayed by most of her fellow-
hedonists in this elegant society; and it is part of the irony

of the book that the practice of these higher standards is what ultimately brings about her ruin. Scruples have no place in the world depicted in *The House of Mirth;* thus, in good naturalistic fashion, the environment becomes the force which crushes the protagonist.

Lily, in a word, is trapped. The idea of a lovely young woman, obviously meant for better things, completely hemmed in and cornered by the values and conventions of a frivolous society—this idea is conveyed by the author by means of a multitude of allusions, images, and direct statements, all suggesting a feeling of imprisonment. Selden, for example, thinks of Lily as "so evidently the victim of the civilization which had produced her, that the links of her bracelet seemed like manacles chaining her to her fate" (page 10). And the heroine herself feels as though she lives in a

great gilt cage in which they were all huddled for the mob to gape at. How alluring the world outside the cage appeared to Lily, as she heard its door clang on her! In reality, as she knew, the door never clanged: it stood always open; but most of the captives were like flies in a bottle, and having once flown in, could never regain their freedom (pages 86–87).

The sense of suffocation, which grows increasingly acute, is artistically suggested by a series of images in which the home of Lily's aunt, Mrs. Peniston (with whom the heroine lives), is seen as a tomb or prison:

The house, in its state of unnatural immaculateness and order, was as dreary as a tomb, and as Lily, turning from her brief repast between shrouded sideboards, wandered into the newly-uncovered glare of the drawing-room she felt as though she were buried alive in the stifling limits of Mrs. Peniston's existence (page 160).

Although her own room is spacious, "contrasted with the light tints and luxurious appointments of the guest-rooms where so many weeks of Lily's existence were spent, it seemed as dreary as a prison" (page 176). Again, after describing the furnishings of Mrs. Peniston's sitting-room, the novelist remarks: "Lily felt for these objects the same distaste which the prisoner may entertain for the fittings of the courtroom" (page 274). And, after Mrs. Peniston's death, when Lily learns that her aunt has virtually disinherited her, she sits "in the purple drawing-room, which more than ever, in its stuffy dimness, resembled a well-kept family vault, in which the last corpse had just been decently deposited" (page 360).

The concept of the trapped sensibility also finds expression in Lily's hopeless feeling of the empty life in store for her:

Lily seemed to watch her own figure retreating down vistas of neutral-tinted dullness. . . . When she ceased to amuse Judy Trenor and her friends she would have to fall back on amusing Mrs. Peniston; whichever way she looked she saw only a future of servitude to the whims of others, never the possibility of asserting her own eager individuality (page 162).

Even the physical environment helps to illustrate and re-inforce this sense of futility: "The future stretched before her dull and bare as the deserted length of Fifth Avenue, and opportunities showed as meagrely as the few cabs trailing in quest of fares that did not come" (page 372). This feeling pervades the book, and it is most painfully present on the last night of the heroine's life, just before she takes the overdose of sleeping medicine: ". . . the terrible silence and emptiness seemed to symbolize her future—she felt as though the house, the street, the world were all empty, and she alone left sentient in a lifeless universe" (page 519).

But I have not yet completely depicted the pathos of Lily's situation. In most books written from the naturalistic point of view, the trapped protagonist can expect no sympathy from the external world about him: nature and society seem simply not to care. And so it is with Lily Bart. This idea is succinctly stated early in the book, when the impecunious Lily, bemoaning her losses at cards, notes the large sums that several wealthy women in her party have won:

A world in which such things could be seemed a miserable place to Lily Bart; but then she had never been able to understand the laws of a universe which was so ready to leave her out of its calculations (page 42).

The indifference of society is typified by the impersonal

quality which Mrs. Wharton takes pains to impart to it.
"Society," she writes, "is a revolving body which is apt to
be judged according to its place in each man's heaven . . ."
(page 79). Carrying out the figure, she later refers to Lily as
"a star fallen from the sky" (page 461).

Even when "society" is reduced to living human beings,
Lily finds that she is up against a blank wall. She comes face
to face with this fact in a restaurant, for example:

> Her eyes sought the faces about her, craving a responsive
> glance, some sign of an intuition of her trouble. But the sallow,
> preoccupied women, with their bags and note-books and rolls of
> music, were all engrossed in their own affairs. . . . (pages 488–489).

The images with which the author implements her expression
of this view of life are manifold. In one place the heroine is
said to have "the doomed sense of the castaway who has
signalled in vain to fleeing sails" (page 368). In another,
Lily asserts sadly, "I was just a screw or cog in the great
machine I called life, and when I dropped out of it I found I
was of no use anywhere else" (page 498). On the last night
of her life she is possessed by "the feeling of being something
rootless and ephemeral, mere spin-drift of the whirling
surface of existence, without anything to which the poor little
tentacles of self could cling before the awful flood submerged
them" (page 515). Thus, the same force which first shaped
Lily and then trapped her now turns a cold and indifferent
shoulder to her despairing cries.

The amoral quality implied by such an impersonal
society is represented at one point by Mrs. Peniston: "That
lady's dread of a scene gave her an inexorableness which
the greatest strength of character could not have produced,
since it was independent of all considerations of right or
wrong" (page 274). Again, the businesslike matrimonial
proposition made to Lily by Sim Rosedale, the Jewish parvenu,
suggests the materialistic values of a society which seems to
operate on a level totally removed from the hampering,
tedious necessity of weighing moral alternatives:

It certainly simplified life to view it as a perpetual adjustment, a
play of party politics, in which every concession had its recognized

equivalent: Lily's tired mind was fascinated by this escape from fluctuating ethical estimates into a region of concrete weights and measures (page 417).

As for concrete details, in *The House of Mirth* the reader finds them to be legion. The social life of New York is recorded in this book with "an anthropologist's thoroughness";[5] and street addresses, *décor*, and costume are noted with laboratory precision. A single sentence from the book will suffice to indicate the particular care taken by Mrs. Wharton to be accurate and specific in these matters: "Mrs. Peniston seated herself in her black satin arm-chair tufted with yellow buttons, beside a beadwork table bearing a bronze box with a miniature of Beatrice Cenci on the lid" (pages 273–274). Often the minutiae of physical action are also faithfully recorded. Count the number of trivial details of bodily movement which appear in a few lines of one paragraph:

The pink-faced clock drummed out another hour, and Gerty rose with a start. She had an appointment early the next morning with a district visitor on the East Side. She put out her lamp, covered the fire, and went into her bedroom to undress. . . . laying aside her clothes with her habitual precision, setting everything in order for the next day. . . . Her servant did not come till eight o'clock, and she prepared her own tea-tray and placed it beside the bed. Then she locked the door of the flat, extinguished her light and lay down (page 262).

This is numbering the streaks of the tulip in earnest.

Here, then, is the evidence. The molding and determining forces of environment and heredity, the protagonist trapped and crushed by society, an indifferent, apparently amoral universe, and a host of specific details—such are the strains of naturalism which one finds deeply pervading *The House of Mirth*.

Notes

1 References, respectively, to Blake Nevius, *Edith Wharton: A Study of Her Fiction* (Los Angeles, 1953), p. 57; *Ibid.*, p. 57 and F. T. Cooper, *Some American Story Tellers* (New York, 1911), p. 174.
2 References, respectively, to N. Elizabeth Monroe, *The Novel and Society: A Critical Study of the Modern Novel* (Chapel Hill, North Carolina, 1941),

p. 117; Robert Morse Lovett, *Edith Wharton* (New York, 1925), pp. 18–19;
and P. H. Boynton, "American Authors of Today," *English Journal*, XII,
p. 30 (January, 1923).

3   Edith Wharton, *The House of Mirth* (New York, 1905), p. 7. All references
are to this edition.

4   V. S. Pritchett, "Books in General," *New Statesman and Nation*,
XLV, pp. 489 (April, 1953).

5   *Loc. cit.*

Irving Howe

"A Reading of The House of Mirth"□

I

The House of Mirth begins in a manner characteristic of Mrs.
Wharton, with a forthright attack on her material, hard and
direct, and without expository preparation. The elaborate
hovering over the imagined scene so habitual to Henry
James . . . is not at all her way of doing things, for she is a
blunt and often impatient writer. "My last page," she once
said, "is always latent in my first," and at least in *The
House of Mirth* the claim is true. At the very outset Mrs.
Wharton groups the main figures of her story—Lily Bart,
Lawrence Selden, Sim Rosedale—in several vignettes of
typical conduct. These comprise not so much a full novelistic
scene as a succession of compressed, scenic fragments, each
juxtaposed so as to yield quick information and stir immediate
concern. "The art of rendering life in fiction," Mrs. Wharton
wrote, "can never . . . be anything . . . but the disengaging of
crucial moments from the welter of experience."

That is precisely what she does in the opening chapters.
Lily is first seen through the eyes of Selden, the cultivated
lawyer who is to serve as a standard of moral refinement and
an instance of personal inadequacy. "Her discretions,"
writes Mrs. Wharton in one of those bristling sentences that
do their necessary damage to both Lily and Selden, "inter-

□ From "An Introduction to *The House of Mirth*" by Irving Howe, from
The House of Mirth by Edith Wharton, Rinehart Edition, edited by Irving
Howe. Introduction © 1962 by Irving Howe. Reprinted by permission of
Holt, Rinehart & Winston, Inc.

ested him almost as much as her imprudences: he was so sure
that both were part of the same carefully-elaborated plan."
Shrewd yet not sufficiently daring, Selden here begins to
enact that rhythm of involvement and withdrawal, advance
and retreat, which will mark his relations with Lily until the
very end of the book. He entices her with a vision of a life
better than the one she has chosen, yet fails to give her the
unquestioning masculine support which might enable her to
live by that vision.

We see Lily and Selden together, each a little uneasy
with the other, yet decidedly attractive as a pair and civilized
enough to take pleasure in knowing they are attractive—
Mrs. Wharton had a fine eye for the pictorial arrangements in
the social intercourse between the sexes. They amuse and test
each other with small talk—Mrs. Wharton had a fine ear for
the conversation that carries subtle burdens of meaning.
We see Lily and Selden taking each other's measure, Lily
admiring his quiet style yet aware of his handicaps and hesitations, Selden admiring her beauty yet aware that "she was
so evidently the victim of the civilization which had produced
her, that the links of her bracelet seemed like manacles
chaining her to her fate." This striking sentence is put to
several uses: it prepares us for the ordeal of a Lily Bart
neither at ease with nor in rebellion against her life as a
dependent of the rich; it provides a convincing example of
Selden's gift for superior observation; and because, ironically,
this gift is matched with his tendency to self-protection and
self-justification, it suggests that Mrs. Wharton will not
require nor allow Selden to serve as a voice of final judgment
in the novel. Given the caustic style of these opening pages, we
are entitled to suppose that Mrs. Wharton will reserve that
task for herself.

There quickly follows the encounter between Lily and
Rosedale. At this point Rosedale is mostly stock caricature,
the "pushy little Jew" taken from the imagery of social, that
is, polite, anti-Semitism; later Mrs. Wharton will do more
with him. Rosedale trips Lily in a lie and is not gentleman
enough to refrain from stressing his petty triumph, but the
main point is that Lily, usually so nimble at handling social

difficulties, has been caught off balance because she is still glowing with the pleasure of having met Selden. This too prefigures a major theme: the price, here in embarrassment and later in deprivation, that genuine emotion exacts from those who have chosen a life of steady calculation. Coming always at inconvenient moments—for it is Selden's presence which repeatedly causes her to falter—the spontaneous feelings Lily neither can nor wishes to suppress will lead to her social undoing.

Lovely as Lily Bart seems, Mrs. Wharton is careful to establish a firm dissociation between author and heroine, though never to the point of withdrawing her compassion. The similarity between Rosedale and Lily, each trying in a particular way to secure a foothold in the world of the rich, is faintly suggested by Mrs. Wharton as a cue for later elaboration. She also introduces the figure of Lily's cousin, Jack Stepney, who serves as Lily's Smerdyakov, the "double" grossly reflecting and disfiguring her ambitions. Lily, as Mrs. Wharton dryly remarks, "understood his motives, for her own course was guided by as nice calculations."

And then, to climax these introductory chapters, there come two moments of symbolic action, each isolating the central role of money in the life of Lily Bart. The first is Balzacian: Judy Trenor, the rich hostess and for a time Lily's friend, "who could have afforded to lose a thousand a night [at cards], had left the table clutching such a heap of bills that she had been unable to shake hands with her guests when they bade her good night." The second is probably beyond Balzac: Lily, having lost too much money at cards, retires to her room in the Trenor house and notices "two little lines near her mouth, faint flaws in the smooth curve of her cheek." Frightened, she thinks they may be caused by the electric light. She turns it off, leaving only the candles on her dressing-table. "The white oval of her face swam out waveringly from a background of shadows, the uncertain light blurring it like a haze; but the two lines about the mouth remained."

. . . At every point Lily's history is defined by her

journey from one social group to another, a journey both she
and her friends regard as a fall, a catastrophe. Only dimly,
and then after much pain and confusion, does she realize
that this social fall may have positive moral consequences.
For us, who have followed her story with that mixture of
ironic detachment and helpless compassion Mrs. Wharton
trains us to feel, it should be clear all the while that the
meanings of the book emerge through a series of contrasts
between a fixed scale of social place and an evolving measure
of moral value.

It is as if the world within which Lily moves consists of
a series of descending planes, somewhat like a modern stage,
and each part of the novel is devoted to showing the apparent
success with which Lily survives one drop after another but
also how each apparent success bears within itself the impetus
toward still another fall. As Mrs. Wharton remarks: "If
[Lily] slipped she recovered her footing, and it was only
afterward that she was aware of having recovered it each
time on a slightly lower level." There is, to be sure, much
more to *The House of Mirth* than these expert notations of
social status. There is a portrait of a young woman trapped
in her confusions of value, a story of love destroyed through
these confusions, and a harsh enactment of Mrs. Wharton's
sentiments about human loss and doom. But all of these take
on their particular cogency, their fictional shape, under the
pressures of the social milieu evoked in the novel.

Mrs. Wharton's great theme—the dispossession of the
old New York aristocracy by the vulgar new rich—is not quite
so visible in *The House of Mirth* as in *The Custom of the
Country* or *The Age of Innocence*. The action of *The House of
Mirth* occurs in the first years of the twentieth century,
several stages and a few decades beyond the dispossession of
old New York. We barely see any representatives of the faded
aristocracy; what we do see in the first half of the book are
several of its distant offshoots and descendants, most of them
already tainted by the vulgarity of the new bourgeoisie yet,
for no very good reasons, still contemptuous of it. The
standards of those characters who have any claim to the old
aristocracy are not so much guides to their own conduct as

strategies for the exclusion of outsiders. Like Gus Trenor, they have kept some pretense to social superiority but very little right to it, and even an exceptional figure like Lawrence Selden, who does try to live by cultivated standards, has been forced into a genteel bohemianism and an acceptance of his failure to act with manly decisiveness.

In no way is the old aristocracy, or even the *idea* of the old aristocracy, held up as a significant model for behavior. Indeed, in *The House of Mirth* the moral positives seem almost disembodied, hovering like ghosts over the figures of Lily Bart and Lawrence Selden. When the new rich make their assault upon the world of the established rich, there occurs a brief contest between an aspiring and an entrenched snobbism, and soon enough, as one might expect, a truce is struck. The victim of that truce is Lily Bart.

Each step in Lily's decline allows Mrs. Wharton to examine the moral ugliness of still another segment of the wealthy classes. In the novel Lily begins with

The Trenors, who maintain a pretense of loyalty to traditional styles and values, even while frequently violating them. That they feel obliged to keep up this pretense does, however, have a restraining influence upon their conduct. Gus Trenor may harass Lily, but she can still appeal successfully to his sense of being a gentleman ("old habits . . . the hand of inherited order . . ."). Once dropped by the Trenors—a major sign she is slipping—Lily finds a place with

The Dorsets, who are at least as rich and socially powerful as the Trenors but in Mrs. Wharton's hierarchy occupy a lower rung. They no longer pretend to care about traditional styles and values. Bertha Dorset is a ferocious bitch, her husband a limp dyspeptic. They ruthlessly abandon Lily and she, no longer able to stay afloat in her familiar element, must now turn to the new rich. She does this with the help of

Carrie Fisher, a brilliantly portrayed figure who acts as guide for those *arrivistes* willing to pay for their social acceptance. Frankly materialistic, yet likable for her candor, Mrs. Fisher is troubled neither by Lily's scruples nor her delusions, and for a time she arranges that Lily find refuge with

The Brys, very rich and feverishly on the make. Gus Trenor may sneer when the Brys give their expensive "crush," but he goes and thereby helps to seal the fusion between his set and all that the Brys represent. Unable or unwilling to remain with the Brys, Lily finds a haven of sorts with

The Gormers, who also have large amounts of money but care less for status than pleasure. Once, however, Mrs. Gormer is tempted socially by the poisonous Bertha Dorset, Lily finds herself displaced again and must take refuge with

Norma Hatch, the wealthy divorcee who lives in a chaos of indolence, forever a prey to sharpers and schemers. Lily finds this atmosphere intolerable, and nothing remains for her but the last fall into the abyss of poverty.

As Lily goes down step by step, two figures stand on the sidelines observing her and occasionally troubling to intervene, but never decisively, never with full heart or unqualified generosity. Selden feels an acute sympathy for her, but a sympathy marred by fastidiousness; he loves her, but except for the last moment, not with a love prepared to accept the full measure of its risks. Rosedale sees her as a possible asset for his social climb and later finds himself vaguely moved by her troubles, but at the end he turns away, convinced she has lost her market value. Selden's ethical perceptions are as superior to Lily's as Rosedale's are inferior, but Mrs. Wharton, with her corrosive and thrusting irony, places the two men in a relationship of symmetrical exposure. In Mrs. Wharton's world men are often weak, either too refined for action or too coarse for understanding: they fail one, they do not come through. . . . Lily ends her days alone.

II

The social setting of *The House of Mirth* is elaborated with complete assurance: one is always persuaded of the tangibility of Mrs. Wharton's milieu, the precision with which she observes nuances of status and place. But what finally draws and involves us is the personal drama enacted within this setting. Lily Bart is a victim of taste, both good and bad:

she has a natural taste for moral and esthetic refinements which causes her to be repelled by the world of the rich, and she has an acquired taste for luxury that can be satisfied only in that world. She is too fine in her perceptions to act ruthlessly enough to achieve her worldly aims, and too much the captive of those aims to be able to live by her perceptions. She has enough moral awareness to respect civilized structures of behavior, but not enough moral courage to abandon the environment in which they are violated. She is trapped in a heart struggle between the pleasures of this world, that is, to lure the dismal millionaire Gryce into marriage, and the refinements of personal relations, which means to drop Gryce for the privilege of walking with Lawrence Selden on a Sunday afternoon. She pays, in the words of Percy Lubbock, "for her fastidiousness by finding herself abandoned by the vivid crowd: and she pays for her courtship of the crowd, so carefully taught her by all the conditions of life, by discovering that her independence is only strong enough to destroy and not to remake her life."

Simply as an example of imaginative portraiture, Lily Bart is one of the triumphs of American writing. Mrs. Wharton has succeeded in that supremely difficult task of the novelist: to show a figure in plasticity and vibration while preserving the firm outlines of her conception. We soon grasp the nature of Lily's character, yet are repeatedly surprised and moved by its local shadings. Mrs. Wharton does not for a moment soften the judgments that Lily invites, nor does she hesitate to expose all of Lily's weakness and self-indulgence. Lily "was fond of pictures and flowers, and of sentimental fiction, and she could not help thinking that the possession of such tastes ennobled her desire for worldly advantage." And a still more biting sentence: "Selden's reputed civilization was generally regarded as a slight obstacle to easy intercourse, but Lily, who prided herself on her broad-minded recognition of literature, and always carried an Omar Khayam in her traveling-bag, was attracted by this attribute, which she felt would have had its distinction in an older society." Through a steady accumulation of incidents Mrs. Wharton makes it clear that Lily is pitifully lacking in any core of personal being. At home neither in the Trenor mansion nor Selden's book-lined rooms nor the shabby apartment of her cousin Gerty Farish, Lily is at the mercy of her restlessness, a strangely disabling kind of restlessness which marks an unfinished self. Yet all of these judgments are stated or implied by Mrs. Wharton with a profound compassion, a sense of the sadness that comes to one in observing a lovely human being dash herself against the rocks of her own bewilderment. If Lily cannot maintain those flashes of self-awareness that come to her in moments of failure, she is still a generous and warm-hearted woman, open, in Mrs. Wharton's magnificent phrase, to "one of those sudden shocks of pity that sometimes decentralize a life."

Lily's fall is treated partly as a naturalistic drama in which a victim of circumstance is slowly crushed. She admires Selden because

he had preserved . . . a happy air of viewing the show objectively, of having points of contact outside the great gilt cage. . . . How alluring the world outside the cage appeared to Lily, as she heard its door clang on her! In reality, as she knew, the door never clanged: it stood always open; but most of the captives were like flies in a bottle, and having once flown in, could never regain their freedom.

This sense of fatality in *The House of Mirth* is reinforced, step by step, as Lily confronts the social demarcations of her world. . . . The ordeal of Lily Bart continues to be a significant one, even if its terms and setting have come to seem historically dated. In one way or another, the problem of mediating between the expectations of a commercial society and the ideals of humane civilization is not exactly unknown to us; only on the surface is our society so very different from that of Lily Bart.

This view of the novel is not accepted, however, by certain critics who question whether Lily's fate is very important or deeply affecting, and who see in her story little more than the malaise of an idle woman unable to dispense with privileges. In a phrase of dismissal Henry Seidel Canby has written of *The House of Mirth* that "it reveals nothing in the history of Lily Bart which wealth would not cure." He is wrong; exactly the opposite is true. Mrs. Wharton goes to some pains to stress that wealth lies within Lily's grasp if only she will do what she cannot bring herself to do: make sacrifices of taste, forgo assumptions of honor, accept conditions of tedium. That Lily yearns for wealth is obvious; that anyone could suppose it to be a "cure" for her is astonishing. But apart from his inaccuracy, Mr. Canby's statement displays a somewhat comic complacence: he writes as if the pressures of financial need had nothing to do with human suffering in our time, as if true tragedy were something apart from the hustle of daily life, and as if literary critics never worked themselves into a moral corner through a conflict between desires and standards. Lily Bart, to be sure, is not a heroine in the grand style: she is a weak and lovely woman. Her life, torn apart by what Mrs. Wharton calls "the eternal struggle between man's contending impulses," may not satisfy the Aristotelian concept of tragedy. But to say this is perhaps nothing more than to suggest how limited a value there is in applying such concepts to modern literature.

In any case, our response to Lily can hardly be exhausted by the sum of moral judgments we make about her. Once all statements of discount have been entered against Lily, we remain concerned and stirred by her effort—who has not known or experienced similar ones?—to bring together irreconcilable ways of life. Before the pathos of her failure, judgment fades into love.

III

The House of Mirth is not written in the kind of prose, favored in many twentieth century novels, that aims to resemble a transparent glass, a clear window upon the action. Mrs. Wharton's prose solicits attention in its own right. It asks us constantly to be aware of an authorial voice speaking with a full readiness to provide comment and generalization. At various points in the novel we are allowed some entrance into Lily Bart's mind, but never to the point of forgetting that it is Mrs. Wharton who guides us there and will soon be guiding us away. We are always conscious that the narrative comes to us through a style of high polish, austere irony, epigrammatic conciseness. What Mrs. Wharton says in her own right is just as much a part of the texture of the novel as the action and the dialogue.

Her style impresses one by its capacity for severe qualifications. Here is Mrs. Wharton on Bertha Dorset:

She was smaller and thinner than Lily Bart, with a restless pliability of pose, as if she could have been crumpled up and run through a ring, like the sinuous draperies she affected. Her small pale face seemed the mere setting of a pair of dark exaggerated eyes, of which the visionary gaze contrasted curiously with her self-assertive tone and gestures; so that, as one of her friends observed, she was like a disembodied spirit who took up a great deal of room.

The writing here is extremely vivid, partly as a visual description of Bertha Dorset, but primarily as a generalized evocation of Mrs. Wharton's sense and judgment of her. There are numerous other examples that might be given for this power of concise and neat generalization. One remembers, as a comic instance, the sentence about Lily's dreary aunt: "Mrs. Peniston thought the country lonely and trees damp, and cherished a vague fear of meeting a bull." Or an instance of Mrs. Wharton's gift for dramatic summation: "It was success that dazzled [Lily]—she could distinguish facts plainly enough in the twilight of failure." Or Mrs. Wharton's capacity for a kind of statement that pertains both to the matter in hand and larger issues of human experience: Gerty Farish, pleased that Lily has contributed to a charity, "supposed her beautiful friend to be actuated by the same motive as herself—that sharpening of the moral vision which makes all human suffering so near and insistent that the other aspects of life fade into remoteness."

But even as one comes to savor the crispness of Mrs. Wharton's prose, there are passages in *The House of Mirth* that leave one uneasy. Usually these are passages in which she reveals the unfortunate tendency toward ladies'-magazine rhetoric that broke out in her later years. And usually they are passages in which she must confront a theme—the satisfactions of romantic love—she finds either too embarrassing or too upsetting to handle with ease. Writing about an encounter between Selden and Lily, she composes a sentence that, at least in its second clause, seems decidedly forced: "it was one of those moments when neither seemed to speak deliberately, when an indwelling voice in each called to the other across unsounded depths of feeling." Here is Mrs. Wharton's description of the last talk between Selden and Lily, utterly right in its first sentence and a purple lapse in the second:

Something in truth lay dead between them—the love she had killed in him and could no longer call to life. But something lived between them also, and leaped up in her like an imperishable flame: it was the love his love had kindled, the passion of her soul for his.

To notice this stylistic problem is to approach a central limitation of Mrs. Wharton's writing. . . . Her work overwhelms us with its harsh truths, but finally it seems incomplete and earth-bound. Mrs. Wharton believed firmly in the moral positives she had inherited, but she could seldom project them into her work; all too often they survive only in terms of their violation. Hence the grinding, unrelenting, impatient tone of her work as if she sensed some deficiency, perhaps in the very scheme of things or only in her own vision, and did not know how to fill the need. Mrs. Wharton was a thoroughly conservative writer but there are times one is inclined to say, a bit paradoxically, that she is too hard on the rich, too glacial in her contempt for their mediocrity, too willing to slash away at them because she does not know anyone else to turn toward or against.

Such difficulties occur to one mainly in retrospect. When one reads and submits to the urgencies of a novel like *The House of Mirth*, the effect is that of being held in a steady, inexorable enclosure. Mrs. Wharton's sense of the inescapability of waste—the waste of spirit, the waste of energy, the waste of beauty—comes to seem a root condition of human life. In her autobiography she wrote, "life is the saddest thing there is, next to death," and the best of her novels force us to entertain the possibility she is right.

XII

The Sun Also Rises (1926) by Ernest Hemingway

James T. Farrell

Ernest Hemingway's
The Sun Also Rises □

Ernest Hemingway's first novel, *The Sun Also Rises*, has been generally heralded as the definitive account of a war-wearied lost generation. In the light of this interpretation it is interesting to note that this novel was published in 1927, and that the time of its action is 1925. For these years fall within the most hopeful period of the post-Versailles world.

At that time there were many signs (at least in the eyes of superficial observers) to suggest that the world was returning to normalcy. After 1923, European capitalism seemed to have been restabilized, following the shocks of war, revolution, and dangers of revolution. At least to some, Germany looked like a going concern: the Weimar Republic was considered firmly secure. Hope was being revived in cartels as the means of achieving peaceable allocation of markets and equitable access to sources of raw materials. The epoch of disarmament talks, peace pacts, peace conferences had begun. America was in the full sweep of a tremendous economic boom, leading many to believe that this country was paving the way toward a new era of unprecedented world prosperity.

It may seem paradoxical that in such a period a novel

of war disillusionment, nihilistic in outlook, should have become an international success.

However, this paradox is only superficial. With signs of a return to world prosperity there were growing evidences of pacifism. In particular, the youth which had been too young to have been in the trenches was deeply pacifistic. Disillusionment with the war was more or less accepted. In addition, a re-examination of the character of disillusionment portrayed in *The Sun Also Rises* suggests that this mood had become a way of feeling and acting; in fact, a social habit. By 1925 those who had been morally unhinged or physically maimed during the war had had a number of years in which to make some kind of adjustment to the postwar world. The period of the first difficult readjustment had passed. Such, for instance, is the case of the chief protagonist in *The Sun Also Rises*. Jake Barnes, impotent as a result of wounds suffered on the Italian front, has more or less reconciled himself to his condition.

Whenever there is a widespread mood of disillusionment caused by an event as catastrophic as a world war, that mood is bound to be nihilistic and rather adolescent in character unless it serves as the basis for a radical and progressive political orientation that aims to change and better the world. This is illustrated in *The Sun Also Rises*.

The characters express their bitterness, their feelings of disenchantment, with calculated bravado. Their conversation is reduced to enthusiastic small talk about their escapades. And this talk, as well as their actions, is largely a matter of pose and gesture. They act like people who have not fully grown up and who lack the self-awareness to realize this; in fact, they possess no desire to grow up.

The Sun Also Rises influenced younger persons more widely than it did members of Hemingway's own generation. He may have reflected the feelings of many who fought in the war; but most of these men were finding some way of settling down and adjusting themselves in the nineteen-twenties. Some were doing creative writing, some finding editorial jobs, some launching themselves in careers that later won them Pulitzer prizes in poetry and so on. This novel struck deeper chords in the youth of the Twenties.

Hemingway's first books had hardly been published when he had imitators all over America; furthermore, boys and girls on campus after campus began to talk like Hemingway characters. One need not go into detail to describe certain features of the Twenties; these are too fresh in our minds. Suffice it to say that by and large younger people were revolting against the standards and conventions of their elders, against the accepted notions of middle-class society. At the same time they were nonpolitical in their revolt. Add to this the deep pacifism of the decade, and one can easily understand why this novel struck such chords of response among young people, why Hemingway suddenly became the influence he did become at the time.

His influence was not merely superficial. It played a liberating and salutary role on those who would become the next generation of writers, and, more so, numerically, on readers. The hopes of those days have now been proved a snare by history. The nihilistic character of Hemingway's writing helped to free younger people from these false hopes. And although this novel (and many of his early stories as well) is set against a European background, Hemingway helped focus the eyes of younger people sharply on American life.

His writing was exciting and possessed of an extraordinary power of suggestiveness; it won over the reader to the feeling that he was actually participating in the lives of very real men and women. His use of dialogue helped enormously to create this impression. Others, notably Ring Lardner, preceded Hemingway in exploring and revealing the literary possibilities of the use of American vernacular, but he used it with amazing skill and originality. Both his suggestiveness in conveying a sense of life and his use of dialogue tended to turn the attention of youth toward common American experiences and to the speech expressing them on city streets and farms.

But Hemingway's influence, though so widespread, at the same time has been one that seems quickly to have exhausted itself. For Hemingway is a writer of limited vision, one who has no broad and fertile perspective on life. Younger writers were influenced—even seduced—by his moods; and they could grasp from him a sense of the great possibilities to be discovered in the true and simple treatment of common subject matter and in the use of ordinary speech. But once they had learned these lessons, they could gain little more from Hemingway.

The Europe described in *The Sun Also Rises* is a tourist's Europe of the Twenties. Cafés, restaurants, hotels, particularly of the Left Bank, are the setting. When the action shifts to Spain, it is to permit a magnificent description of bull fights and a fiesta. The mood and attitude of the main characters is that of people on a vacation. They set out to do what people want to do on a vacation: they have love affairs, they drink, go fishing, and see new spectacles. Written in the first person, the book unfolds from the standpoint of a spectator's attitude. Jake, the narrator, is a newspaper man; his is an occupation that naturally tends to develop the point of view of the spectator. Jake is constantly looking at the other characters, at himself, at the scenery of Spain, at the bull fight, at everything that occurs or comes within his view.

The main characters have only a meager past. They are escaping from their past and usually do not wish even to talk or to think of it. They live for the present, constantly searching for new and fresh sensations. They do not really think; even Jake scarcely thinks about himself or about his own impotence. These people feel quite alike. They form a small clique, stoically accepting the ills of their life.

Robert Cohn, however, is an outsider. He is with them because of his doglike love for Lady Brett Ashley. Unlike the others, he is unable to drown his feelings in banalities, small talk, and new spectacles. Cohn's difference from the others is one of the central points of the novel. This contrast is stated overtly when Lady Brett says that Cohn is "not one of us," and when Jake thinks that Cohn has behaved badly by pursuing Lady Brett. Focused against Cohn, Jake's simple, stoical attitude is enforced more strongly. The attitude of Jake is one of the basic attitudes in Hemingway's writings.

Hemingway's realism is, by and large, one which deals with sensations—with shocks to the senses. He has tended to reduce life to the effect that sights, scenes, and experiences make upon the nervous system; and he has avoided complicated types of response. Herein we find one of the major factors revealing his limitations as a writer.

In his most representative work he has saved himself from the crudities of simple behaviorism because of his gift of suggestiveness and his developed skill of understatement. The moral outlook in his work is on a plane of equal simplicity with his characters and subject matter. It amounts to the attitude that an action is good if it makes one feel good. Such an outlook on characters and events suggests that a development of greater understanding—broader range of feeling and sympathy, greater depth of imagination—is practically precluded.

This has been the case in Hemingway's career. He arrived on the literary scene absolute master of the style he has made his own; his attitudes were firmly fixed at that time. And he said pretty much what he had to say with his first stories and his first two novels.

As a novelist, it is my opinion that the best of Ernest Hemingway is still to be found in *The Sun Also Rises*. Its freshness has not faded with time. It remains one of the very best American novels of the Twenties.

Philip Young

from "Death and Transfiguration"□

*T*he Sun Also Rises, which appeared later in 1926, re-
introduces us to the hero. In Hemingway's novels this man is
a slightly less personal hero than Nick was, and his adventures are to be less closely identified with Hemingway's, for
more events are changed, or even "made up." But he still
projects qualities of the man who created him, many of his
experiences are still literal or transformed autobiography,
and his wound is still the crucial fact about him. Even when
as Robert Jordan of *For Whom the Bell Tolls* he is somewhat
disguised, we have little or no trouble in recognizing him.

Recognition is immediate and unmistakable in *The
Sun Also Rises*. Here the wound, again with its literal and
symbolic meanings, is transferred from the spine to the
genitals: Jake Barnes was "emasculated," to speak very
loosely, in the war. But he is the same man, a grown Nick
Adams, and again the actual injury functions as concrete
evidence that the hero is a casualty. He is a writer living
in Paris in the Twenties, as, for example, Harry was; like Nick
he was transplanted from midwestern America to the Austro-
Italian front; when things are at their worst for him, like
Fraser he cries in the night. When he refuses the services of a
prostitute, and she asks, "What's the matter? You sick?" he

□ Reprinted from *Ernest Hemingway: A Reconsideration* (The Pennsylvania State University Press), pp. 82–88. Copyright 1966 by Philip
Young. By permission.

All excerpts from *The Sun Also Rises* by Ernest Hemingway in this
section reprinted with the permission of Charles Scribner's Sons.
Copyright 1926 by Charles Scribner's Sons; renewal copyright 1954
Ernest Hemingway.

is not thinking of his loss alone when he answers, "Yes."
He is the insomniac as before, and for the same reasons: "I
blew out the lamp. Perhaps I would be able to sleep. My
head started to work. The old grievance." And later he remembers that time, which we witnessed, when "for six months
I never slept with the light off." He is the man who is troubled
in the night, who leaves Brett alone in his sitting room and
lies face down on the bed, having "a bad time."

In addition, Jake like Nick is the protagonist who has
broken with society and with middle-class ways; again he
has made the break in connection with his wounding. He
has very little use for most people. At times he has little use
even for his friends; at times he has little use for himself.
He exists on a fringe of the society he has renounced; as a
newspaper reporter he works just enough to make enough
money to eat and drink well on, and spends the rest of his
time in cafés, or fishing, or watching bullfights. Though it is
not highly developed yet, he and those few he respects have a
code, too. Jake complains very little, although he suffers a
good deal; there are certain things that are "done" and many
that are "not done." Lady Brett Ashley also knows the code,
and distinguishes people according to it; a person is "one of
us," as she puts it, or is not—and most are not. The whole
trouble with Robert Cohn, the boxing, maladroit Jew of the
novel, is that he is not. He points up the code most clearly by
so lacking it: he will not go away when Brett is done with
him; he is "messy" in every way. After he has severely beaten
up Romero, the small young bullfighter, and Romero will not
give in, Cohn cries, wretchedly proclaims his love for Brett
in public, and tries to shake Romero's hand. He gets that
hand in the face, an act which is approved as appropriate
comment on his behavior.

Cohn does not like Romero because Brett does. She
finally goes off with the bullfighter, and it is when she leaves
him too that she makes a particularly clear statement of what
she and the other "right" people have salvaged from the
wreck of their compromised lives. She has decided that she
is ruining Romero's career, and besides she is too old for him.
She walks out, and says to Jake:

"It makes one feel rather good deciding not to be a bitch.
. . . It's sort of what we have instead of God."

In early editions, *The Sun Also Rises* had on its title
page, before the passage on futility in *Ecclesiastes* from which
the title is taken, Gertrude Stein's famous "You are all a
lost generation." The novel provides an explanation for this
observation, in addition to illustrating it in action. As in the
story called "In Another Country," the picture of the hero
wounded and embittered by his experience of violence is
broadened to include other people. Brett Ashley, for example,
and her fiancé Mike Campbell are both casualties from ordeals
similar to those which damaged Jake. Brett has behind her
the very unpleasant death of her first fiancé; Mike's whole
character was shattered by the war. *A Farewell to Arms* can
be read as background to the earlier novel: some of Brett's
past is filled in by Catherine Barkley, whose fiancé had
been blown to bits in the war, and most of Jake's by Frederic
Henry.

The fact that characters in *The Sun Also Rises* are
recognizable people, taken from "real life," does not contradict the fact that they are in this pattern. Various personages
known to Paris of the Twenties have thought that they
recognized without difficulty the originals—Donald Ogden
Stewart, Harold Stearns, Harold Loeb, Lady Duff-Twysden,
Ford Madox Ford, and Pat Guthrie—and even Jake had his
counterpart in actuality. But Hemingway, like most authors,
changed the characters to suit his purposes, and it is clear
that whatever his origins, Jake, for instance, owes most to
the man who created him, and is the hero.

He is the hero emasculated, however, and this must
primarily account for the fact that he does not always seem
entirely real. As he feels befits his status, he is largely a
passive arranger of things for others, who only wants to "play
it along and just not make trouble for people." But as
narrator, at least, he is convincing, and if there is something
blurred about him it helps to bring the participants into a
focus that is all the sharper. Hemingway had always been
good with secondary characters, finding them in a bright
flash that reveals all we need know. Here, as he somehow

managed to make similar people easily distinguishable, the revelations are brilliant. One remembers Brett and Cohn longest, for they get the fullest development, but Count Mippipopolous is wonderful, and wonderful too—save for their anti-Semitism, largely missing from an edition which advertised that "Not one word has been changed or omitted" —are Mike and Bill.

Chiefly it is Hemingway's ear, a trap that caught every mannerism of speech, that is responsible for the fact that these characters come so alive and distinct. That famous ear also caught a great many "swells" and "grands" that have dated— for slang is one thing almost certain to go bad with the passage of time—and some of the dialogue of camaraderie ("Old Bill!" "You bum!") is also embarrassing. But taken as a whole the talk is superb and, as a whole, so is the rest of the writing in the book. Hemingway's wide-awake senses fully evoke an American's Paris, a vacationer's Spain. Jake moves through these places with the awareness of a professional soldier reconnoitering new terrain. The action is always foremost, but it is supported by real country and real city. The conversational style, which gives us the illusion that Jake is just telling us the story of what he has been doing lately, gracefully hides the fact that the pace is carefully calculated and swift, the sentences and scenes hard and clean. This is true of the over-all structure, too: the book is informal and relaxed only on the surface, and beneath it lies a scrupulous and satisfying orchestration. It is not until nearly the end, for example, when Cohn becomes the center of what there is of action, that opening with him seems anything but a simply random way of getting started. This discussion of Cohn has eased us into Jake's life in Paris, and especially his situation with Brett. Suddenly the lines are all drawn. An interlude of trout fishing moves us smoothly into Spain and the bullfights. At Pamplona the tension which all try to ignore builds up, slowly, and breaks finally as the events come to their climax simultaneously with the fiesta's. Then, in an intensely muted coda, a solitary Jake, rehabilitating himself, washes away his hangovers in the ocean. Soon it is all gone, he is returned to Brett as before, and we discover that we have come full circle, like all the rivers, the winds, and the sun, to the place where we began.

This is motion which goes no place. Constant activity has brought us along with such pleasant, gentle insistence that not until the end do we realize that we have not been taken in, exactly, but taken nowhere; and that, finally, is the point.[1] This is structure as meaning, organization as content. And, as the enormous effect the book had on its generation proved, such a meaning or content was important to 1926. The book touched with delicate accuracy on something big, on things other people were feeling, but too dimly for articulation. Hemingway had deeply felt and understood what was in the wind. Like Brett, who was the kind of woman who sets styles, the book itself was profoundly creative, and had the kind of power that is prototypal.

Despite quite a lot of fun *The Sun Also Rises* is still Hemingway's *Waste Land*, and Jake is Hemingway's Fisher King. This may be just coincidence, though the novelist had read the poem, but once again here is the protagonist gone impotent, and his land gone sterile. Eliot's London is Hemingway's Paris, where spiritual life in general, and Jake's sexual life in particular, are alike impoverished. Prayer breaks down and fails, a knowledge of traditional distinctions between good and evil is largely lost, copulation is morally neutral and, cut off from the past chiefly by the spiritual disaster of the war, life has become mostly meaningless. "What shall we do?" is the same constant question, to which the answer must be, again, "Nothing." To hide it, instead of playing chess one drinks, mechanically and always. Love is a possibility only for the two who cannot love; once again homosexuality intensifies this atmosphere of sterility; once more the Fisher King is also a man who fishes. And again the author plays with quotations from the great of the past, as when in reply to Jake's remark that he is a taxidermist Bill objects, "That was in another country. And besides all the animals were dead."

To be sure, the liquor is good, and so are the food and the conversation. But in one way Hemingway's book is even more desperate than Eliot's. The lesson of an "asceticism" to

control the aimless expression of lust would be to Jake Barnes
only one more bad joke, and the fragments he has shored
against his ruins are few, and quite inadequate. In the poem
a message of salvation comes out of the life-giving rain which
falls on western civilization. In Hemingway's waste land there
is fun but no hope. No rain falls on Europe this time, and
when it does fall in *A Farewell to Arms* it brings not life but
death.

Note

1 It happens that this is not precisely the point Hemingway intended to
make. He once said that he regarded his first epigraph, "you are all a lost
generation," as a piece of "splendid bombast." (Later he devoted one of the
sketches, "Une Génération Perdue," of his *Moveable Feast* to an effective
attack on the phrase.) It was his idea that the second epigraph taken from
Ecclesiastes would "correct" the famous remark attributed to Miss Stein.
As far as he was concerned, he wrote his editor Maxwell Perkins, the point
of his novel is, as the Biblical lines say in part, that "the earth abideth
forever."
   Some support for this position can be found in the novel itself. Not
quite all the people in it are "lost"—surely Romero is not—and the beauty
of the eternal earth is now and then richly evoked. But most of the characters do seem a great deal of the time if not lost then terribly unsure of their
bearings, and few readers have felt the force of Hemingway's intention.
The strongest feeling in the book is that for the people in it (and one gets
the distinct impression that other people do not matter very much) life is
futile, and their motions like the motion of the sun of the title (as it appears
to our eyes): endless, circular, and unavailing. Further, for all who remember what the Preacher said in this well-known Biblical passage, the echo of
"Vanity of vanities; all is vanity" is rather loud. Thus what Hemingway
proposed to do and what he did again seem two things, but it is doubtful
that this hurts the book.

Mark Spilka

"The Death of Love in *The Sun Also Rises*" □

> She turns and looks a moment in the glass,
> Hardly aware of her departed lover;
> Her brain allows one half-formed thought to pass:
> "Well now that's done: and I'm glad it's over."
> When lovely woman stoops to folly and
> Paces about her room again, alone,
> She smoothes her hair with automatic hand,
> And puts a record on the gramophone.*
>
> T. S. Eliot, *The Waste Land*

O ne of the most persistent themes of the twenties was the death of love in World War I. All the major writers recorded it, often in piecemeal fashion, as part of the larger postwar scene; but only Hemingway seems to have caught it whole and delivered it in lasting fictional form. His intellectual grasp of the theme might account for this. Where D. H. Lawrence settles for the shock of war on the Phallic Consciousness, or where Eliot presents assorted glimpses of sterility, Hemingway seems to design an extensive parable. Thus, in *The Sun Also Rises*, his protagonists are deliberately shaped as allegorical figures: Jake Barnes and Brett Ashley are two lovers desexed by the war; Robert Cohn is the false knight who challenges their despair; while Romero, the stalwart bullfighter, personifies the good life which will survive their failure. Of course, these characters are not abstractions in the text; they are realized through the most

438

concrete style in American fiction, and their larger meaning is implied only by their response to immediate situations. But the implications are there, the parable is at work in every scene, and its presence lends unity and depth to the whole novel.

Barnes himself is a fine example of this technique. Cut off from love by a shell wound, he seems to suffer from an undeserved misfortune. But as most readers agree, his condition represents a peculiar form of emotional impotence. It does not involve distaste for the flesh, as with Lawrence's crippled veteran, Clifford Chatterley; instead Barnes lacks the power to control love's strength and durability. His sexual wound, the result of an unpreventable "accident" in the war, points to another realm where accidents can always happen and where Barnes is equally powerless to prevent them. In Book II of the novel he makes this same comparison while describing one of the dinners at Pamplona: "It was like certain dinners I remember from the war. There was much wine, an ignored tension, and a feeling of things coming that you could not prevent happening." This fear of emotional consequences is the key to Barnes' condition. Like so many Hemingway heroes, he has no way to handle subjective complications, and his wound is a token for this kind of impotence.

It serves the same purpose for the expatriate crowd in Paris. In some figurative manner these artists, writers, and derelicts have all been rendered impotent by the war. Thus, as Barnes presents them, they pass before us like a parade of sexual cripples, and we are able to measure them against his own forbearance in the face of a common problem. Whoever bears his sickness well is akin to Barnes; whoever adopts false postures, or willfully hurts others, falls short of his example. This is the organizing principle in Book I, this alignment of characters by their stoic qualities. But stoic or not, they are all incapable of love, and in their sober moments they seem to know it.

For this reason they feel especially upset whenever Robert Cohn appears. Cohn still upholds a romantic view of life, and since he affirms it with stubborn persistence, he acts like a goad upon his wiser contemporaries. As the narrator, Barnes must account for the challenge he presents them and the decisive turn it takes in later chapters. Accordingly, he begins the book with a review of Cohn's boxing career at Princeton. Though he has no taste for it, college boxing means a lot to Cohn. For one thing, it helps to compensate for anti-Semitic treatment from his classmates. More subtly, it turns him into an armed romantic, a man who can damage others in defense of his own beliefs. He also loves the pose of manhood which it affords him and seems strangely pleased when his nose is flattened in the ring. Soon other tokens of virility delight him, and he often confuses them with actual manliness. He likes the idea of a mistress more than he likes his actual mistress; or he likes the authority of editing and the prestige of writing, though he is a bad editor and a poor novelist. In other words, he always looks for internal strength in outward signs and sources. On leaving Princeton, he marries "on the rebound from the rotten time . . . in college." But in five years the marriage falls through, and he rebounds again to his present mistress, the forceful Frances Clyne. Then, to escape her dominance and his own disquiet, he begins to look for romance in far-off countries. As with most of his views, the source of this idea is an exotic book:

He had been reading W. H. Hudson. That sounds like an innocent occupation, but Cohn had read and reread "The Purple Land." "The Purple Land" is a very sinister book if read too late in life. It recounts splendid imaginary amorous adventures of a perfect English gentleman in an intensely romantic land, the scenery of which is very well described. For a man to take it at thirty-four as a guidebook to what life holds is about as safe as it would be for a man of the same age to enter Wall Street direct from a French convent, equipped with a complete set of the more practical Alger books. Cohn, I believe, took every word of "The Purple Land" as literally as though it had been an R. G. Dun report.

Cohn's romanticism explains his key position in the parable. He is the last chivalric hero, the last defender of an outworn faith, and his function is to illustrate its present folly—to show us, through the absurdity of his behavior, that romantic love is dead, that one of the great guiding codes of the past no longer operates. "You're getting damned romantic," says Brett to Jake at one point in the novel. "No, bored," he replies, because for this generation boredom has become more plausible than love. As a foil to his contemporaries, Cohn helps to reveal why this is so.

Of course, there is much that is traditional in the satire on Cohn. Like the many victims of romantic literature, from Don Quixote to Tom Sawyer, he lives by what he reads and neglects reality at his own and others' peril. But Barnes and his friends have no alternative to Cohn's beliefs. There is nothing here, for example, like the neat balance between sense and sensibility in Jane Austen's world. Granted that Barnes is sensible enough, that he sees life clearly and that we are meant to contrast his private grief with Cohn's public suffering, his self-restraint with Cohn's deliberate self-exposure. Yet, emasculation aside, Barnes has no way to measure or control the state of love; and though he recognizes this with his mind and tries to act accordingly, he seems no different from Cohn in his deepest feelings. When he is alone with Brett, he wants to live with her in the country, to go with her to San Sebastian, to go up to her room, to keep her in his own room, or to keep on kissing her—though he can never really act upon such sentiments. Nor are they merely the yearnings of a tragically impotent man, for eventually they will lead Barnes to betray his own principles and to abandon self-respect, all for the sake of Lady Ashley. No, at best he is a restrained romantic, a man who carries himself well in the face of love's impossibilities, but who seems to share with Cohn a common (if hidden) weakness.

The sexual parade continues through the early chapters. Besides Cohn and his possessive mistress, there is the prostitute Georgette, whom Barnes picks up one day "because of a vague sentimental idea that it would be nice to eat with some one." Barnes introduces her to his friends as his fiancée, and as his private joke affirms, the two have much in common. Georgette is sick and sterile, having reduced love to a simple monetary exchange; but like Barnes, she manages to be frank and forthright and to keep an even keel among the drifters of Paris. Together they form a pair of honest cripples, in contrast with the various pretenders whom they meet along the Left Bank. Among the latter are Cohn and Frances Clyne, the writer Braddocks and his wife, and Robert Prentiss, a rising young novelist who seems to verbalize their phoniness: "Oh, how charmingly you get angry," he tells Barnes. "I wish I had that faculty." Barnes' honest anger has been aroused by the appearance of a band of homosexuals, accompanied by Brett Ashley. When one of the band spies Georgette, he decides to dance with her; then one by one the rest follow suit, in deliberate parody of normal love. Brett herself provides a key to the dizzy sexual medley. With a man's felt hat on her boyish bob, and with her familiar reference to men as fellow "chaps," she completes the distortion of sexual roles which seems to characterize the period. For the war, which has unmanned Barnes and his contemporaries, has turned Brett into the freewheeling equal of any man. It has taken her first sweetheart's life through dysentery and has sent her present husband home in a dangerous state of shock. For Brett these blows are the equivalent of Jake's emasculation; they seem to release her from her womanly nature and expose her to the male prerogatives of drink and promiscuity. Once she claims these rights as her own, she becomes an early but more honest version of Catherine Barkley, the English nurse in Hemingway's next important novel, *A Farewell to Arms*. Like Catherine, Brett has been a nurse on the Italian front and has lost a sweetheart in the war; but for her there is no saving interlude of love with a wounded patient, no rigged and timely escape through death in childbirth. Instead she survives the colossal violence, the disruption of her personal life, and the exposure to mass promiscuity, to confront a moral and emotional vacuum among her postwar lovers. With this evidence of male default all around her, she steps off the romantic pedestal, moves freely through the bars of Paris, and stands confidently there beside her newfound equals. Ironically, her most recent conquest, Robert Cohn, fails to see the bearing of such changes on romantic love. He still believes that Brett is womanly and therefore deeply serious about intimate matters. After their first meeting, he describes her as "absolutely fine and straight" and nearly strikes Barnes for thinking otherwise; and a bit later, after their brief affair in the country, he remains unconvinced "that it didn't mean anything." But when men no longer command respect, and women replace their natural warmth with masculine freedom and mobility, there can be no serious love.

Brett does have some respect for Barnes, even a little tenderness, though her actions scarcely show abiding love. At best she can affirm his worth and share his standards and perceptions. When in public, she knows how to keep her essential misery to herself; when alone with Barnes, she will express her feelings, admit her faults, and even display good judgment. Thus her friend, Count Mippipopolous, is introduced to Barnes as "one of us." The count qualifies by virtue of his war wounds, his invariable calmness, and his curious system of values. He appreciates good food, good wine, and a quiet place in which to enjoy them. Love also has a place in his system, but since he is "always in love," the place seems rather shaky. Like Jake and Brett and perhaps Georgette, he simply bears himself well among the postwar ruins.

The count completes the list of cripples who appear in Book I. In a broader sense, they are all disaffiliates, all men and women who have cut themselves off from conventional society and who have made Paris their permanent playground. Jake Barnes has introduced them, and we have been able to test them against his stoic attitudes toward life in a moral wasteland. Yet such life is finally unbearable, as we have also seen whenever Jake and Brett are alone together, or whenever Jake is alone with his thoughts. He needs a healthier code to live by, and for this reason the movement in Book II is away from Paris to the trout stream at Burguete and the bull ring at Pamplona. Here a more vital testing process occurs, and with the appearance of Bill Gorton, we get our first inkling of its nature.

Gorton is a successful writer who shares with Barnes a love for boxing and other sports. In Vienna he has helped to rescue a splendid Negro boxer from an angry and intolerant crowd. The incident has spoiled Vienna for him, and as his reaction suggests, the sports world will provide the terms of moral judgment from this point onward in the novel. Or more accurately, Jake Barnes' feelings about sports will shape the rest of the novel. For with Hemingway, the great outdoors is chiefly a state of mind, a projection of moral and emotional attitudes onto physical arenas, so that a clear account of surface action will reproduce these attitudes in the reader. In "Big Two-Hearted River," for example, he describes Nick Adams' fishing and camping activities along a trout stream in Michigan. His descriptions run to considerable length, and they are all carefully detailed, almost as if they were meant for a fishing manual. Yet the details themselves have strong emotional connotations for Nick Adams. He thinks of his camp as "the good place," the place where none of his previous troubles can touch him. He has left society behind him, and as the story begins, there is even a burnt town at his back, to signify his disaffiliation. He has also walked miles to reach an arbitrary camp site, and this is one of the ways in which he sets his own conditions for happiness and then lives up to them. He finds extraordinary pleasure, moreover, in the techniques of making coffee and pitching camp, or in his responses to fishing and eating. In fact, his sensations have become so valuable that he doesn't want to rush them: they bring health, pleasure, beauty, and a sense of order which is sorely missing in his civilized experience; they are part of a healing process, a private and imaginative means of wiping out the damages of civilized life. When this process is described with elaborate attention to surface detail, the effect on the reader is decidedly subjective.

The same holds true, of course, for the fishing trip in *The Sun Also Rises*. As Barnes and Gorton approach "the good place," each item in the landscape is singled out and given its own importance. Later the techniques of fishing are treated with the same reverence for detail. For like Nick Adams, these men have left the wasteland for the green plains of health; they have traveled miles, by train and on foot, to reach a particular trout stream. The fishing there is

good, the talk free and easy, and even Barnes is able to sleep
well after lunch, though he is usually an insomniac. The
meal itself is handled like a mock religious ceremony: "Let
us rejoice in our blessings," says Gorton. "Let us utilize
the fowls of the air. Let us utilize the produce of the vine.
Will you utilize a little, brother?" A few days later, when
they visit the old monastery at Roncevalles, this combination
of fishing, drinking, and male camaraderie is given an edge
over religion itself. With their English friend, Harris, they
honor the monastery as a remarkable place, but decide that
"it isn't the same as fishing"; then all agree to "utilize" a
little pub across the way. At the trout stream, moreover,
romantic love is given the same comparative treatment and
seems sadly foolish before the immediate joys of fishing:

> It was a little past noon and there was not much shade, but I
> sat against the trunk of two of the trees that grew together, and
> read. The book was something by A. E. W. Mason, and I was read-
> ing a wonderful story about a man who had been frozen in the Alps
> and then fallen into a glacier and disappeared, and his bride was
> going to wait twenty-four years exactly for his body to come out on
> the moraine, while her true love waited too, and they were still
> waiting when Bill came up [with four trout in his bag]. . . . His
> face was sweaty and happy.

As these comparisons show, the fishing trip has been
invested with unique importance. By sticking closely to the
surface action, Barnes has evoked the deeper attitudes which
underly it and which make it a therapeutic process for him.
He describes himself now as a "rotten Catholic" and speaks
briefly of his thwarted love for Brett; but with religion
defunct and love no longer possible, he can at least find
happiness through private and imaginative means. Thus he
now constructs a more positive code to follow: as with
Nick Adams, it brings him health, pleasure, beauty and
order, and helps to wipe out the damage of his troubled life
in Paris.

Yet somehow the code lacks depth and substance. To
gain these advantages, Barnes must move to Pamplona,
which stands roughly to Burguete as the swamp in "Big
Two-Hearted River" stands to the trout stream. In the latter

story, Nick Adams prefers the clear portion of the river to its second and more congested heart:

In the swamp the banks were bare, the big cedars came together overhead, the sun did not come through, except in patches; in the fast deep water, in the half light, the fishing would be tragic. In the swamp fishing was a tragic adventure. Nick did not want it. . . . There were plenty of days coming when he could fish the swamp.

The fishing is tragic here because it involves the risk of death. Nick is not yet ready for that challenge, but plainly it will test his manhood when he comes to face it. In *The Sun Also Rises* Barnes makes no such demands upon himself; but he is strongly attracted to the young bullfighter, Pedro Romero, whose courage before death lends moral weight to the sportsman's code.[1]

So Pamplona is an extension of Burguete for Barnes: gayer and more festive on the surface, but essentially more serious. The spoilers from Paris have arrived, but (Cohn excepted) they are soon swept up by the fiesta: their mood is jubilant, they are surrounded by dancers, and they sing, drink and shout with the peasant crowd. Barnes himself is among fellow *aficionados*; he gains "real emotion" from the bullfights and feels truly elated afterwards. Even his friends seem like "such nice people," though he begins to feel uneasy when an argument breaks out between them. The tension is created by Brett's fiancé, Mike Campbell, who is aware of her numerous infidelities and who seems to accept them with amoral tolerance. Actually he resents them, so that Cohn (the perennial Jewish scapegoat) provides him with a convenient outlet for his feelings. He begins to bait him for following Brett around like a sick steer.

Mike's description is accurate enough. Cohn is always willing to suffer in public and to absorb insults for the sake of true love. On the other hand, he is also "ready to do battle for his lady," and when the chance finally comes, he knocks his rivals down like a genuine knight-errant. With Jake and Mike he has no trouble, but when he charges into Pedro's room to rescue Brett, the results are disastrous: Brett tells him off, the bullfighter refuses to stay knocked down, and no one will shake hands with him at the end, in accord with prep-school custom. When Brett remains with Pedro, Cohn retires to his room, alone and friendless.

This last encounter is the highpoint of the parable, for in the Code Hero, the Romantic Hero has finally met his match. As the clash between them shows, there is a difference between physical and moral victory, between chivalric stubbornness and real self-respect. Thus Pedro fights to repair an affront to his dignity; though he is badly beaten, his spirit is untouched by his opponent, whereas Cohn's spirit is completely smashed. From the beginning Cohn has based his manhood on skill at boxing, or upon a woman's love, never upon internal strength; but now, when neither skill nor love supports him, he has bludgeoned his way to his own emptiness. Compare his conduct with Romero's, on the following day, as the younger man performs for Brett in the bull ring:

Everything of which he could control the locality he did in front of her all that afternoon. Never once did he look up. . . . Because he did not look up to ask if it pleased he did it all for himself inside, and it strengthened him, and yet he did it for her, too. But he did not do it for her at any loss to himself. He gained by it all through the afternoon.

Thus, where Cohn expends and degrades himself for his beloved, Romero pays tribute without self-loss. His manhood is a thing independent of women, and for this reason he holds special attractions for Jake Barnes.

By now it seems apparent that Cohn and Pedro are extremes for which Barnes is the unhappy medium. His resemblance to Pedro is clear enough: they share the same code, they both believe that a man's dignity depends on his own resources. His resemblance to Cohn is more subtle, but at this stage of the book it becomes grossly evident. Appropriately enough, the exposure comes through the knockout blow from Cohn, which dredges up a strange pre-war experience:

Walking across the square to the hotel everything looked new and changed. . . . I felt as I felt once coming home from an out-of-town football game. I was carrying a suitcase with my football things in it, and I walked up the street from the station in the town I had lived in all my life and it was all new. They were raking the lawns and burning leaves in the road, and I stopped for a long time and watched. It was all strange. Then I went on, and my feet seemed to be a long way off, and everything seemed to come from a long way off, and I could hear my feet walking a great distance away. I had been kicked in the head early in the game. It was like that crossing the square. It was like that going up the stairs in the hotel. Going up the stairs took a long time, and I had the feeling that I was carrying my suitcase.

Barnes seems to have regressed here to his youthful football days. As he moves on up the stairs to see Cohn, who has been asking for him, he still carries his "phantom suitcase" with him; and when he enters Cohn's room, he even sets it down. Cohn himself has just returned from the fight with Romero: "There he was, face down on the bed, crying. He had on a white polo shirt, the kind he'd worn at Princeton." In other words, Cohn has also regressed to his abject college days: they are both emotional adolescents, about the same age as the nineteen-year-old Romero, who is the only real man among them. Of course, these facts are not spelled out for us, except through the polo shirt and the phantom suitcase, which remind us (inadvertently) of one of those dreamlike fantasies by the Czech genius, Franz Kafka, in which trunks and youthful clothes are symbols of arrested development. Yet there has already been some helpful spelling out in Book I, during a curious (and otherwise pointless) exchange between Cohn and another expatriate, the drunkard Harvey Stone. After first calling Cohn a moron, Harvey asks him to say, without thinking about it, what he would rather do if he could do anything he wanted. Cohn is again urged to say what comes into his head first, and soon replies, "I think I'd rather play football again with what I know about handling myself, now." To which Harvey responds: "I misjudged you. . . . You're not a moron. You're only a case of arrested development."

The first thought to enter Cohn's mind here has been suppressed by Barnes for a long time, but in Book II the knockout blow releases it: more than anything else, he too would like to "play football again," to prevent that kick to his head from happening, or that smash to the jaw from Cohn, or that sexual wound which explains either blow. For the truth about Barnes seems obvious now: he has always been an emotional adolescent. Like Nick Adams, he has grown up in a society which has little use for manliness; as an expression of that society, the war has robbed him of his dignity as a man and has thus exposed him to indignities with women. We must understand here that the war, the early football game, and the fight with Cohn have this in common: they all involve ugly, senseless, or impersonal forms of violence, in which a man has little chance to set the terms of his own integrity. Hence for Hemingway they represent the kinds of degradation which can occur at any point in modern society—and the violence at Pamplona is our current sample of such degradation. Indeed, the whole confluence of events now points to the social meaning of Jake's wound, for just as Cohn has reduced him to a dazed adolescent, so has Brett reduced him to a slavish pimp. When she asks for his help in her affair with Pedro, Barnes has no integrity to rely on; he can only serve her as Cohn has served her, like a sick romantic steer. Thus, for love's sake, he will allow her to use him as a go-between, to disgrace him with his friend, Montoya, to corrupt Romero, and so strip the whole fiesta of significance. In the next book he will even run to her rescue in Madrid, though by then he can at least recognize his folly and supply his own indictment: "That was it. Send a girl off with one man. Introduce her to another to go off with him. Now go and bring her back. And sign the wire with love. That was it all right." It seems plain, then, that Cohn and Brett have given us a peacetime demonstration, postwar style, of the meaning of Jake's shell wound.

At Pamplona the demonstration continues. Brett strolls through the fiesta with her head high, "as though [it] were being staged in her honor, and she found it pleasant and amusing." When Romero presents her with a bull's ear "cut by popular acclamation," she carries it off to her hotel, stuffs it far back in the drawer of the bed-table, and forgets about it. The ear was taken, however, from the same bull which had killed one of the crowd a few days before, during the dangerous bull-run through the streets; later the entire town attended the man's funeral, along with drinking and dancing societies from nearby communities. For the crowd, the death of this bull was a communal triumph and his ear a token of communal strength; for Brett the ear is a private trophy. In effect, she has robbed the community of its triumph, as she will now rob it of its hero. As an *aficionado*, Barnes understands this threat too well. These are decadent times in the bull ring, marred by false aesthetics; Romero alone has "the old thing," the old "purity of line through the maximum of exposure": his corruption by Brett will complete the decadence. But mainly the young fighter means something more personal to Barnes. In the bull ring he combines grace, control and sincerity with manliness; in the fight with Cohn he proves his integrity where skill is lacking. His values are exactly those of the hunter in "Francis Macomber," or of the fisherman in *The Old Man and the Sea*. As one of these few remaining images of independent manhood, he offers Barnes the comfort of vicarious redemption. Brett seems to smash this as she leaves with Pedro for Madrid. To ward off depression, Barnes can only get drunk and retire to bed; the fiesta goes on outside, but it means nothing now: the "good place" has been ruined.

As Book III begins, Barnes tries to reclaim his dignity and to cleanse himself of the damage at Pamplona. He goes to San Sebastian and sits quietly there in a cafe, listening to band concerts; or he goes swimming there alone, diving deep in the green waters. Then a telegram from Brett arrives, calling him to Madrid to help her out of trouble. At once he is like Cohn again, ready to serve his lady at the expense of self-respect. Yet in Madrid he learns to accept, emotionally, what he has always faintly understood. As he listens to Brett, he begins to drink heavily, as if her story has driven home a painful lesson. Brett herself feels "rather good" about sending Pedro away: she has at least been able to avoid being "one of these bitches that ruins children." This is a moral triumph for her, as Barnes agrees; but he can scarcely ignore its implications for himself. For when Brett refuses to let her hair grow long for Pedro, it means that her role in life is fixed: she can no longer reclaim her lost womanhood; she can no longer live with a fine man without destroying him. This seems to kill the illusion which is behind Jake's suffering throughout the novel: namely, that if he hadn't been wounded, if he had somehow survived the war with his manhood intact, then he and Brett would have become true lovers. The closing lines confirm his total disillusionment:

> "Oh, Jake," Brett said, "we could have had such a damned good time together."
>
> Ahead was a mounted policeman in khaki directing traffic. He raised his baton. The car slowed suddenly pressing Brett against me.
>
> "Yes," I said, "Isn't it pretty to think so?"

"Pretty" is a romantic word which means here "foolish to consider what could *never* have happened," and not "what can't happen now." The signal for this interpretation comes from the policeman who directs traffic between Brett's speech and Barnes reply. With his khaki clothes and his preventive baton, he stands for the war and the society which made it, for the force which stops the lovers' car, and which robs them of their normal sexual roles. As Barnes now sees, love itself is dead for their generation. Even without his wound, he would still be unmanly, and Brett unable to let her hair grow long.

Yet according to the opening epigraphs, if one generation is lost and another comes, the earth abides forever; and according to Hemingway himself, the abiding earth is the novel's hero. Perhaps he is wrong on this point, or at least misleading. There are no joyous hymns to the seasons in this novel, no celebrations of fertility and change. The scenic descriptions are accurate enough, but rather flat; there is no deep feeling in them, only fondness, for the author takes less delight in nature than in outdoor sports. He is more concerned, that is, with baiting hooks and catching trout than with the Irati River and more pleased with the grace and skill of the bull-fighter than with the bull's magnificence. In fact, it is the bullfighter who seems to abide in the novel, for surely the bulls are dead like the trout before them, having fulfilled their roles as beloved opponents. But Romero is very much alive as the novel ends. When he leaves the hotel in Madrid, he "pays the bill" for his affair with Brett, which means that he has earned all its benefits. He also dominates the final conversation between the lovers, and so dominates the closing section. We learn here that his sexual initiation has been completed and his independence assured. From now on, he can work out his life alone, moving again and again through his passes in the ring, gaining strength, order, and purpose as he meets his own conditions. He provides no literal prescription to follow here, no call to bullfighting as the answer to Barnes' problems; but he does provide an image of integrity, against which Barnes and his generation are weighed and found wanting. In this sense, Pedro is the real hero of the parable, the final moral touchstone, the man whose code gives meaning to a world where love and religion are defunct, where the proofs of manhood are difficult and scarce, and where every man must learn to define his own moral conditions and then live up to them.

Note

1 Hemingway's preoccupation with death has been explained in various ways: by his desire to write about simple, fundamental things; by his "sado-masochism"; or more fairly and accurately, by his need to efface an actual war wound, or to supplant the ugly, senseless violence of war with ordered, graceful violence. Yet chiefly the risk of death lends moral seriousness to a private code which lacks it. The risk is arbitrary; when a man elects to meet it, his beliefs take on subjective weight and he is able to give meaning to his private life. In this sense, he moves forever on a kind of imaginative frontier, where the opposition is always Nature, in some token form, where the stakes are always manliness and self-respect, and where death invests the scene with tragic implications. In *The Sun Also Rises*, Romero lives on such a frontier, and for Barnes and his friends he provides an example of just these values.

XIII

Absalom, Absalom! (1936) by William Faulkner

William Faulkner

Interviewed at the University of Virginia[□]

Q. Mr. Faulkner, in *Absalom, Absalom!* does any one
of the people who talks about Sutpen have the right view, or
is it more or less a case of thirteen ways of looking at a blackbird with none of them right?

A. That's it exactly. I think that no one individual can
look at truth. It blinds you. You look at it and you see one
phase of it. Someone else looks at it and sees a slightly
awry phase of it. But taken all together, the truth is in what
they saw though nobody saw the truth intact. So these are
true as far as Miss Rosa and as Quentin saw it. Quentin's
father saw what he believed was truth, that was all he saw.
But the old man was himself a little too big for people no
greater in stature than Quentin and Miss Rosa and Mr.
Compson to see all at once. It would have taken perhaps a
wiser or more tolerant or more sensitive or more thoughtful
person to see him as he was. It was, as you say, thirteen ways
of looking at a blackbird. But the truth, I would like to
think, comes out, that when the reader has read all these
thirteen different ways of looking at the blackbird, the reader
has his own fourteenth image of that blackbird which I
would like to think is the truth.

Q. Mr. Faulkner, Mr. Coldfield in *Absalom, Absalom!*
retreats into the attic when the War between the States starts.

□ Frederick L. Gwynn and Joseph L. Blotner, eds., *Faulkner in the University* (Charlottesville, Va.: The University of Virginia Press, 1959), pp. 273–275. Copyright 1959 by the University of Virginia Press. Reprinted by permission.

Now, why did he do that? Was it because he was a sort of conscientious objector, or was he all or part coward?

A. No, he was probably by religious scruples a conscientious objector. Also, he was very likely a Unionist. That he hated that threat to the dissolution of the Union. That he hadn't enough courage to do anything about it except to hide his head in the sand. But I think that he was probably a Unionist. He probably came from eastern Tennessee, where the people were Unionists at that time. His background was a tradition of fidelity to the United States as it was. He had no agrarian tradition behind him in which slavery was an important part of it.

Q. Sir, speaking of those two books, as you read *Absalom, Absalom!*, how much can a reader feel that this is the Quentin, the same Quentin, who appeared in *The Sound and the Fury*—that is, a man thinking about his own Compson family, his own sister?

A. To me he's consistent. That he approached the Sutpen family with the same ophthalmia that he approached his own troubles, that he probably never saw anything very clearly, that his was just one of the thirteen ways to look at Sutpen, and his may have been the—one of the most erroneous. Probably his friend McCannon had a much truer picture of Sutpen from what Quentin told him than Quentin himself did.

Q. But it's still Sutpen's story. It's not Quentin's story.

A. No it's Sutpen's story. But then, every time any character gets into a book, no matter how minor, he's actually telling his biography—that's all anyone ever does, he tells his own biography, talking about himself, in a thousand different terms, but himself. Quentin was still trying to get God to tell him why, in *Absalom, Absalom!* as he was in *The Sound and the Fury*.

Olga W. Vickery

⌒⌇⌒

"The Idols of the South:
Absalom, Absalom!"□

*A*bsalom, Absalom! continues Faulkner's attempt to make technique and structure focus the meaning of the novel. It is most closely linked to *The Sound and the Fury* whose structure it elaborates and enriches. Like Caddy Compson, Thomas Sutpen is never presented directly, and like her, he becomes a tremendously vital as well as an enigmatic figure by being the object of intense concern for a number of characters. The difference, and it is a large one, is that Sutpen, unlike Caddy, provides a dynamic rather than a static center. The perspectives are no longer self-contained and self-illuminating; as a result, we have a kaleidoscope instead of a juxtaposition of views. Each successive account of Sutpen is constantly being merged with its predecessors. At every moment, there falls into place yet another pattern which disavows some parts of the earlier interpretations but never discards them. Rosa's story of Sutpen makes its own impression and despite later qualifications and objections, it contributes to and influences Mr. Compson's narrative. Both of these are, in turn, caught up in Quentin's and Shreve's version. Rosa's "demonizing" is still evident in the final reconstruction, though altered considerably by Shreve's mocking tone. This means that our final picture of Sutpen

□ Reprinted from *The Novels of William Faulkner: a Critical Interpretation* by Olga W. Vickery. Reprinted with the permission of the author and the Louisiana State University Press.

results from a fusion of at least three accounts, each of which belongs to a different generation and reflects a different personal bias.

These successive accounts once more map out the relationship between truth and fact and between legend and history. For what we have in *Absalom, Absalom!* is the creation of the kind of legends that have already crystallized about the figure of Colonel John Sartoris in *Sartoris*. At the core are the facts of Sutpen's career—the dates of his birth, marriage, and death, the building of the plantation house, and so forth. This biographical data is inert and incapable of stirring either the imagination or the emotions. But there are also certain acts and gestures, such as Sutpen's arrival in Jefferson, Henry's and Bon's abrupt departure from the plantation, the shot echoing at the gates, each of which seems to contain within itself the whole meaning of the past, if only read aright. But to grasp this elusive meaning is rendered difficult, if not impossible, by the number of interpretations that any event can encompass. Conflicting voices, each claiming truth, converge upon every act of Sutpen. His refusal to reveal his reasons for coming to Jefferson or for leaving it provokes speculations about hidden loot, robbery, and even murder. And though these are later disproved, they are not entirely forgotten. Thus, not only do these submerged tales contribute to the legend of Sutpen, but they prevent any of the major narrators from circumscribing Sutpen for the reader. The element of ambiguity is sustained to the very end of the book.

This method of converging accounts and multiple perspectives reveals the creation of truth inherent in the attempt to find it. Whereas in *The Sound and the Fury* Faulkner's concern was with the relation of the individual to truth and reality, here he is interested in the contribution both of the individual and of time to a growing and expanding legend which may be called the public truth about Sutpen. Certain facts, as distinct from interpretations, are available from the beginning; others are either added by successive narrators or discovered by them. Mr. Compson, for example, reveals that Sutpen's wagonload of wild Negroes included a woman, a fact Miss Rosa either did not know or chose to ignore. Since there are not enough of these indisputable facts to "explain" Sutpen, the next step is to make facts out of convictions. Rosa feels that the only explanation needed for Sutpen's refusal to sanction Judith's marriage to Bon is his perverse, demonic nature. Mr. Compson offers as an alternative Sutpen's disapproval of Bon's New Orleans mistress. Quentin adds the "fact" of Eulalia Bon's Negro blood, and at this point, everything appears to fall into a logical and convincing pattern. But even this final revelation is open to question. There is no doubt that Quentin himself is convinced of the truth of his interpretation, but so is Miss Rosa of the truth of her "demonizing." Nor is there any doubt that in the light of it Sutpen's actions become more comprehensible, but the same is true of the disproved "fact" of his exploits as a highwayman.

The number of alternative explanations and unresolved ambiguities in the three accounts of Sutpen suggest the immense difficulties attendant upon the effort to arrive at truth. Adding to this difficulty is the fact that truth must eventually be fixed by words, which by their very nature falsify the things they are meant to represent. This distortion inherent in language is the reason for the tortuous style of *Absalom, Absalom!* The characters themselves are engaged in the frustrating attempt to capture truth and then to communicate it. Quentin tries to convey a look on Clytie's face and quickly eliminates "shock," "fear," and "triumph" without finding a word to satisfy him. The clearest example, however, is Miss Rosa's account of what was happening at the moment when Clytie stopped her at the head of the stairs. She qualifies, adds, masses analogies, similes, and metaphors, and goes over the same points incessantly as if the repetition would suddenly make everything comprehensible not only to Quentin but to herself. In the final effort to explain Clytie's action and her own reaction, she is forced to reiterate her entire history, her childhood, her dreams, and her disappointments. The qualities evident in Miss Rosa's description of a single incident are also found in the style as a whole. Whoever the speaker, the long sentences bristle with qualifications and alternatives beneath which the syntax is almost lost. And what is true of the sentence is true also of the paragraph, of the chapter, indeed of the total structure. Hence the style is more closely related to the creation of the legend of Sutpen and to the common effort to fix reality and formulate truth than it is to the characters who retell the story.

All the narrators are sincerely trying to be truthful, correcting and contradicting themselves as they reconstruct the past, and all have certain unique qualifications for the task. Miss Rosa obviously has the advantage of having lived through the events and of a close personal knowledge of Sutpen, while Mr. Compson has his carefully guarded objectivity, and Quentin and Shreve the uncluttered perspective afforded by the passage of time. Yet it is plain that the result of their efforts is not the truth about Sutpen but rather three quite distinct legends which reveal as much about the narrators as about Sutpen. The element of distortion most evident in Miss Rosa's version is, nevertheless, present in all three. For in accordance with his own experience and bias, each of them works the available facts into what is essentially an aesthetic form. Consequently, Sutpen takes the main role in Miss Rosa's Gothic thriller and in Mr. Compson's classical drama which is forever verging on satire. But in the story told by Quentin and Shreve, he recedes into the background as love becomes the dominant interest and chivalric romance the dominant form. Moreover, through the three successive accounts, history moves from the factual to the mythic, leaving Quentin and Shreve free to interpret, imagine, and invent so long as they remain true to what they believe is the spirit of the past.

Though Miss Rosa knew Sutpen most intimately, her account of him is the most distorted, revealing only her own obsession, the narrowness of her experience, and the grim inflexibility of her responses. Her "demonizing" is, however, natural and inevitable in view of her lifelong isolation. Born between two generations, the one destroyed by the Civil War and the other engaged in reconstruction, she can find no place for herself in either. Her youth with its ardent desire for experience is nullified by the old age of her parents, her culture, and her tradition with their insistence on living in memories of the past.

That isolation which leaves Miss Rosa forever watching other people's lives unfold while hers remains unchanged gives unlimited scope to her fantasies compounded of religion and romance. Without being put to the test of reality, the world becomes a matter of masks "interchangeable not only from scene to scene, but from actor to actor and behind which the events and occasions [take] place without chronology or sequence." (62) In her childhood Sutpen has been the demon-ogre who had carried Ellen to his "grim ogre-bourne" to produce "two half-phantom children." In her old age she merely adds a few new words and similes to embellish the childhood concept and to give it a religious overtone: "*He was the light-blinded bat-like image of his own torment cast by the fierce demoniac lantern up from beneath the earth's crust.*" (171) The other people she sees or even hears about are similarly drawn into her fantasies: Ellen becomes the captive maiden, Clytie is "*the cold Cerberus of his* [Sutpen's] *private hell,*" (136) while Judith and Charles Bon enact a fairy tale of love and courtship.

Only complete withdrawal from the world can preserve such fantasies as these from the impact of reality. Rosa, however, rushes forth in the conviction that her fantasies actually correspond to the people she encounters only to find, inevitably, her illusions of herself and others shattered. Her humble effort to provide Judith with a trousseau and so to share vicariously the role of bride is met with peals of laughter from Ellen, who has already betrayed her by acting like a lady of the manor rather than a captive in "Bluebeard's den." She rushes out to "save" Judith and Henry from Sutpen after Ellen's death only to find that neither of them will permit her to do any saving. Ready to weep with the widowed bride, she finds that Judith remains stone-faced and silent at the news of Bon's death. Perhaps her greatest surprise occurs in connection with Sutpen. The complete separation of her vision of Sutpen from the man himself is indicated by the ease with which she replaces the "*ogre of my childhood*" with "*a shape which rode away beneath a flag*". (167) The demon is slain by the hero who returns to claim a virgin bride. But this pleasant charade dissolves when Sutpen muffs his lines and destroys her image not only of him but of herself. His crude proposition forces Rosa to choose between her fantasy and an experience that is brutally shorn of all romantic illusion. The outrage to her sensibility as well as her moral principles simply intensifies her obsessions and completes her retreat into a world where nothing and no one can challenge her vision of Sutpen as the essence of all evil.

It is little wonder, then, that Miss Rosa's account of Sutpen and of the past in general is rank melodrama and that all the characters in it are exaggerated, distorted phantoms. The fine touch of the Civil War maiden-poetess, untouched by the brutalities of combat and so free to write of gallantry and honor and aesthetically placed wounds, is evident throughout. What she does is create a pattern which some have applied to the book as a whole—the Gothic novel with its gloomy castles, dark, evil villains, and innocent victims. As motive for and explanation of all the Gothic horror and violence that she evokes, she posits a mysterious curse, though she is curiously unable to decide whether it was incurred by Sutpen, her family, or the South. In any event, Sutpen is, for Miss Rosa, both curse and accursed. In the nightmare world of her imagination, his evil assumes such gigantic proportions that it threatens both social and cosmic orders.

The antithesis and antidote to Rosa's hallucinatory view of Sutpen is Mr. Compson's account. For him, Sutpen and the past provide scope for interesting speculations and a number of broad generalizations. His is the deliberately rational, impersonal approach which allows him not only to weave patterns and to posit hypotheses but also to doubt his own conclusions. The irony which pervades his section is as much directed at himself as raconteur as it is at the story he is telling. Yet in establishing his own impersonality, in attempting to abstract all emotional bias from his account, Mr. Compson also abstracts much of the human quality of the past. As a result, the pattern that he presents lacks even that artificial "demonic" vitality with which Rosa infuses her narrative. He is incapable of recreating the agony of a situation or of evoking the interplay of human emotions which give substance and reality to the words which he, like Miss Rosa, must use. The tension between Henry and Bon is explained as the meeting of the puritan provincial with the weary amoralist, each of whom has his own concept of honor and love. Judith's care of Etienne is pictured in terms of a conflict between her love for him and her awareness of his Negro blood. The rational has, in some way, submerged the imaginative power; deduction has taken the place of intuitive understanding. Accordingly, what he describes is a battle of ideas or concepts and not a conflict of people.

Mr. Compson's impersonality, however, enables him to make one contribution to the legend which is not in the power of either Rosa or Quentin. His age, experience, and temperament make him more aware of the characters in relation to society and time. The attention of Quentin and Shreve is directed toward the tensions of love rather than of society. For Rosa, Jefferson, like Sutpen's Hundred, is an "ogre-world" in which she has no place. So it is Mr. Compson who describes the interaction of Sutpen and Jefferson. He shows the town's curiosity, suspicion, indignation, and finally, its slow and unwilling acceptance of Sutpen. He shows Sutpen surrounded by his Negroes or by visitors from Jefferson during the building of the house. His account of Sutpen's courtship and wedding reveals the "intruder" in a better light than the town which seeks to reject him. Levelling his irony simultaneously at the follies of Sutpen and at the pettiness and cruelty of the old South, Mr. Compson is able to preserve his own detachment while exercising his bent for satire.

But the larger pattern in terms of which Mr. Compson reconstructs and evaluates the past is neither social nor ideological. Still less is it historical. If Miss Rosa's account of Sutpen can be described as Gothic thriller, then Mr. Compson's constitutes a classical tragedy. His habitual reading of the classics as well as his identification of Clytie with Cassandra indicate at least a predisposition to this particular literary form. Accordingly, his section of the narrative is filled with references to staging, to actors and the drama. It is he who presents the Sutpen family as actors each playing a role while "Fate, destiny, retribution, irony—the stage manager, call him what you will—was already striking the set and dragging on the synthetic and spurious shadows and shapes of the next one." (72–73) Miss Rosa's "ogre-world" is thus transformed into a heroic drama in which the characters are larger than life, not because they are demonic, but because their conflict is itself writ large and placed against the backdrop of eternity. They become " 'victims of a different circumstance, simpler and therefore, integer for integer, larger, more heroic and the figures therefore more heroic too, not dwarfed and involved but distinct, uncomplex who had the gift of loving once or dying once instead of being diffused and scattered creatures.' " (89) In this drama Sutpen is the protagonist, pitting himself not only against men and their society but against fate and eternity. Heroically he struggles against his own doom and his own extinction, trying to establish his dynasty in defiance of the gods. And like the heroes of Greek tragedy, he is doomed to defeat. Miss Rosa's vague unspecified curse becomes the family curse of the House of Sutpen working itself out in successive generations.

In contrast to Mr. Compson's and Miss Rosa's, the recreation of the past by Quentin and Shreve is the product of their youth and romantic imagination. These enable them to overcome geographical and cultural differences so that it is almost impossible to tell where the Southerner leaves off and the Canadian begins the reconstruction of the Sutpen legend. Both are able to anticipate the thoughts and words of the other and both are able to identify themselves with Henry Sutpen and Charles Bon simply because that identification is not one of individuals but of similar states of mind. It does not matter "what faces and what names they called themselves and were called by so long as the blood coursed—the blood, the immortal brief recent intransient blood which could hold honor above slothy unregret and love above fat and easy shame." (295)

The vividness with which they see and endow the past has its source in romantic rather than historical imagination. Thus, the eighty odd years which separate them from the events they seek to recreate allow them a kind of poetic license in arranging the scenes and characters. Charles carries a wounded Henry from the battlefield, knowing that Henry will prevent him from marrying Judith. Later he substitutes the octoroon's portrait for Judith's as a means of saving Judith tears and Henry her condemnation. Both these romantic gestures are contradicted by the earlier evidence of Miss Rosa and General Compson; nevertheless, they are true to the spirit of Shreve's account in a way that the prosaic "facts" could not be. Shreve can even insist that there must have been an embittered, vengeful mother living in dusty, baroque splendor and a Dickensian lawyer carefully entering Sutpen's assets in a ledger while he waited for Bon to grow up. All these creations or inventions are poetically true even as Mr. Compson's heroic simplifications and Miss Rosa's "demonizing" are true for their respective narratives. But in each case it is a truth far removed from the historian's concern with facts, evidence, and careful documentation.

Quentin and Shreve clearly remove from their actual social and historical context those parts of the Sutpen story which deal with love. Facts are preserved or discarded as they "fit the preconceived," revealing the moment of love, "where there might be paradox and inconsistency but nothing fault nor false." (316) This world of love is treated as pure legend and romance, possessing its own language and logic. As a result, the South becomes an atmospheric background providing even in the gloom of a Mississippi winter the correct mixture of magnolias and moonlight for the lovers, Judith and Charles. Miss Rosa's curse becomes "a glamorous fatality" which ennobles those it destroys. Against this background an intense drama of passion, courage, and self-sacrifice is played out.

Since it is a drama of love, it is understandable that it should evoke poetic echoes. Certainly it is in this final section that the greatest number of literary allusions occur. And in many instances it is impossible to determine whether poetry provides the pattern into which the events are fitted or whether the events recall the poetry. Henry's contemplation of incest, for example, is inextricably fused with the story of Duke

John of Lorraine. Charles is the "silken and tragic Lancelot nearing thirty," (320) Henry "an academic Hamlet waked from some trancement." (174) At times such allusions become ironic as when Rosa and Sutpen are likened first to Agamemnon and Cassandra and then to "an ancient stiff-jointed Pyramus" and an "eager though untried Thisbe." (177) Consistently Quentin and Shreve interpret the past and frame their narrative in terms of literature, for it is in it that they find those eternal values of youth which can be confined to no one place or time.

Yet only Shreve recognizes that the story they have jointly created is only poetically true and that its function is the symbolic one of embodying love, courage, and loyalty in a single form without exhausting them. Quentin, on the other hand, is unable to maintain aesthetic distance or to distinguish the symbolic from the literal. For he, like Henry Sutpen, is obsessed with the idea of incest and with his own responsibility for his sister. And since Henry's gesture in killing Bon is identified with "honor vindicated" and virginity protected, Quentin feels that only by repeating the gesture (which he attempts in *The Sound and the Fury*) can he defend Compson honor. Equally important to Quentin's confused and ambivalent reaction to the Sutpen story is the element of miscegenation he himself has introduced. That word, more terrible even than incest, alone has the power to destroy the world of love, to make Henry Sutpen kill the person he loved more than his father or sister. Quentin is thus forced into a decision the consequences of which have already been delineated in *The Sound and the Fury*. He has the choice of viewing the past symbolically or literally and of affirming or denying its "design." With his passionate reiteration that he does not hate the South, Quentin reveals his decision to perpetuate the design he has found in the past.

In this last respect, Quentin is related to the Sutpen story in which, shorn of the wealth of interpretive comment, one fact is clear. Each of the events discussed and rediscussed by the narrators represents a moment of decision for the characters in the story. Time is constantly weaving a pattern in opposition to the "design," whether inherited or self-created, that the individual seeks to live by. Even the most carefully considered act can have outrageous results simply because once committed, it becomes part of the sequence of natural events which no man can control. It is in these moments of crisis that the individual or the community is forced to re-examine its shibboleths. Since the Sutpen legend is part of the South, it follows that the conflict and the choice are rendered in Southern terms. The narrators see each of the characters in the legend as confronted by a human being who is also a Negro. This confrontation occurs, moreover, in a situation and at a moment in their lives when they feel compelled to deny either the man or the Negro. In essence, they are seen as being forced to choose between mutually exclusive alternatives, between personal and social relationships, between the individual and tradition.

Sutpen himself is a mirror image of the South, for his career in Jefferson merely repeats in a foreshortened form the rise of many families whose longer tenure of the land has given them respectability. Through his single-minded preoccupation with the "design," he effects consciously and in the span of a few years what other Southern families accomplished over a period of generations. But whereas he is far from being a special case, he is definitely an anachronism: he is the ruthless and purposeful founding father of a dynasty who lives in a time of consolidation rather than of expansion. Time proves his worst enemy, for not only has it established the social hierarchy of the Sartorises and Compsons, but it has limited the time he can devote to creating even the rudiments of a similar structure for his family. Because he lacks a past while recreating the past of the South, the townspeople regard him with distrust, then hatred, and finally with an exacted tolerance.

Nevertheless, Sutpen becomes the staunchest defender of the idols of the South at a time when they most need defending. At no point in any of the Yoknapatawpha novels or stories is Sutpen accused of failing the South during the four long years of agonizing combat. Not once does he place his property or the safety of himself or his family above that duty which he has assumed along with the Sartorises and Compsons. Even Rosa does not deny him courage and gallantry on the battlefield. Like the South as a whole, Sutpen refuses to admit defeat or the changes that it inevitably brought about. He attempts to rebuild his plantation and to set his family in order as if the war had never occurred, an attempt that is very much like Colonel Sartoris' defiant rebuilding of his mansion on a grander scale than before. For better or worse, Sutpen does reflect both the virtues and the vices of the South, but he does it without any of the social graces, the courtly gestures of the Sartorises.

It is through a deliberate choice involving the repudiation of his past that Sutpen becomes an image of the South. However lacking in elegance, his mountain home had stressed certain fundamental human values—the man rather than his possessions—"Because where he lived the land belonged to anybody and everybody and so the man who would go to the trouble and work to fence off a piece of it and say 'This is mine' was crazy." (221) But as he and his family journey into the valley, all the familiar and comprehensible beliefs and manners give way to a strange, nightmare world which has no place for them. As they pass from hamlet to hamlet, the Negroes become the focus of their bewilderment. That bewilderment is channelled into resentment by the poor whites who find relief in hating the Negro as a symbol of and foundation for an economic and social system in which the land is "all divided and fixed and neat with a people living on it all divided and fixed and neat because of what color their skins happened to be and what they happened to own." (221)

Sutpen feels the full force of this pattern of exclusion and its application to himself when the "monkey-nigger" orders him to the back door of the plantation house. In that brief moment the central symbol of *Absalom, Absalom!* is established—the boy seeking admittance and being turned away in the name of the social code. What makes it even more disastrous for the young Sutpen is that nothing in his past has prepared him for such a moment. Nothing or no one can help him either to understand or to accept it. The rifle analogy will not hold, and so there is no way that he can integrate this new experience into the old. Consequently, for the first time, he is forced to think, to employ a logic which culminates in his formulation and adoption of the "design." His instinctive reaction is to believe that the behavior of the plantation owner as expressed through the Negro is wrong and inhuman. Yet his final decision betrays that instinctive reaction and he exchanges individual integrity for a handful of social concepts and conventions. His acceptance of circumstance or "luck" as the controlling factor in man's life is replaced by his worship of a man-made pattern; his primitive mountain ethics give way to what he believes to be the code of the South.

The germ of Sutpen's design is simply his determination to create by his own shrewdness, courage, and will that pattern which he sees, rightly or wrongly, in Southern society and to conduct his life strictly in terms of its ethical code. Both designs, Sutpen's and the South's, are based on concepts which deny human values in a large area of conduct and on social rather than natural definitions of the individual. The security of a long family line and of an undisputed position allows a Bayard Sartoris to chat with Will Falls on terms of intimacy and to permit his old Negro servant certain liberties. Sutpen, on the other hand, never deviates from the design, never allows himself to forget the letter of that law by which he has chosen to regulate his own behavior. Since his position must be achieved rather than simply maintained, he cannot afford any such relaxation of principle.

Nor does this rigid attitude provoke any tensions or conflicts in his own mind. During his agonizing stay in the cave, Sutpen had made an irrevocable decision; consequently, his succeeding choices involve no apparent agonies on either a personal or a moral level. He is presumably bound to Eulalia Bon by ties of marriage, children, and daily companionship. Yet in the "just" divorce that follows, he gives up all these without hesitation in order to conform to the South's worship of pure blood and its horror of miscegenation, though as Quentin points out, " 'he could have closed his eyes and, if not fooled the rest of the world as they had fooled him, at least have frightened any man out of speaking the secret aloud.' " (266) Sutpen's "innocence" is manifest: it consists not only of his unquestioning belief in the value of all the idols of the South but in his belief that the structure, the design, is itself the secret of its strength and its perpetuation, that he need only follow its ritual to grasp its substance and that he can do so with the same blunt honesty which was part of his mountain heritage. On the contrary, it quickly becomes evident that each betrayal of humanity betrays its agent as well as the victim. Sutpen's rejection of his wife and son constitutes a rejection of himself as husband and father.

A new attempt to create his counterpart of the South's design takes Sutpen to Jefferson. He is once more the outsider, but at least he knows the passwords—wealth and power. Lack of a respectable past remains a disadvantage, but the grandest mansion with the most magnificent furnishings in Jefferson helps to compensate. Moreover, Ellen Coldfield is bought to complete the picture and to provide him with those roots in Jefferson which he can never obtain through his own efforts. Despite her tears at the wedding, interpreted in quite different ways by Miss Rosa and Mr. Compson, Ellen rapidly learns to play the lady of the manor to Sutpen's lord. She develops into the social butterfly, "gracious and assured and talking the most complete nonsense, speaking her bright set meaningless phrases out of the part which she had written for herself, of the duchess peripatetic with property, soups and medicines among a soilless and uncompelled peasantry." (69) Ultimately she becomes not only the instrument of Sutpen's design by bearing his children but his partner, for she it is who seeks to acquire the elegant Charles Bon as the final, graceful complement to the manor.

In the complex tensions existing between Sutpen and his children, particularly Charles Bon, the boy symbol and the rejection are repeated under different circumstances. The most striking instance, of course, is Charles's arrival at Sutpen's Hundred and his unspoken demand for recognition. The boy is no longer barefoot and tattered, but he too is seeking acceptance on his own merit. It is denied him, as it was to his father, for the sake of the design. Time has once more produced a situation in which Sutpen must choose between his adherence to the concept of pure blood and his own and his son's humanity. His refusal to acknowledge Charles goes far toward destroying the very design it was intended to protect. Just as the unconscious action of his boyhood insulter had driven Sutpen to violate the *status quo*, so his own rejection of Charles marks the beginning of another eruption in which Charles challenges the moral *status quo*. Like his father, Charles eventually forces an indirect recognition, though at the cost of his own life.

The death of Charles, the subsequent flight of Henry, and the self-imposed withdrawal of Judith forces Sutpen to one more effort at coercing circumstance to fit his design. Judith cannot give him the grandchildren he needs, and even if she were to do so, they would still be on the distaff side and hence a compromise with the Southern notion of male hierarchy and primogeniture. Henry, unfortunately, has negated his own potential contributions at the moment of destroying his brother and friend. And Sutpen's own ability to put matters right through a new wife and a new heir is limited, if not rendered impossible, by the approach of old age. He turns, therefore, to Rosa, the poor dependent relation, and with the same simple logic that permitted him to disown his first wife, proposes that Rosa prove her ability to further his design. The crudeness of the proposal shocks "the little dream woman" completely out of her fairy tale world in which a Sutpen in love becomes softened and mellowed by her presence. With a single phrase Sutpen destroys her illusion both of him and of herself. It is an insult she cannot forgive, if only because it denies her the opportunity of either saving or annihilating the demon of her childhood in some fittingly dramatic fashion.

Only one more trial faces Sutpen and with it he comes full circle. In denying Milly, he once more rejects the claims of a wife and a child because they do not conform to his pattern. The fact that Milly is the granddaughter of his own retainer, that she is probably both ignorant and inelegant, shows the extent to which Sutpen has been forced to compromise. But he still holds firm to the central core of his design—the male heir who will possess and perpetuate his name and property through all time. In rejecting Milly, Sutpen also destroys the admiration, which is almost hero-worship, of Wash Jones. In a sense, the aging Jones is closely akin to the young Sutpen, for he too stands bewildered before a world that posits and flaunts inequality. But he seeks to enter the privileged circle through Milly's marriage and Sutpen's benevolence rather than his own efforts. And though he had been able to countenance Milly's seduction and even to see in it a mark of favor, the brutality of Sutpen's rejection of her and her child rouses him to an awareness of his own humanity. His violent and fatal attack on Sutpen is but the most extreme protest against the design in that series which begins with Sutpen's own hurt bewilderment.

The necessity of choosing between social patterns and the individual is not restricted to Sutpen alone. Each new generation and every individual in it faces the same problem. The only difference is that Charles Bon, Henry, and Judith go through an emotional struggle which is rendered in vividly dramatic terms by the sympathy of Quentin and Shreve. In contrast, all of Sutpen's agony is compressed into the single incident of his lonely vigil in the cave and even that is lacking in the kind of dramatic immediacy that would make it imaginatively compelling. Sutpen's children all learn that the demands of circumstance frequently run counter to the dictates of their heredity, training, and principles. Temporarily, Judith and Henry both become rebels for the sake of love: the former is willing to marry Charles Bon without parental consent, the latter actually gives the lie to his father and renounces his patrimony in order to accompany his friend. For them, the conflict at first is simply between love and filial duty with its implicit obedience to authority. Their youth and idealism prompt them to choose the former.

The crucial test, however, is one that neither Judith nor Henry nor Bon can meet. At the core of Sutpen's design and of the social structure of the South is the concept of the "Negro" as an inferior being or social pariah. The drop of black blood effectively prevents the recognition of certain individuals as human beings with human needs and desires.

To accept the man behind the mask of the Negro simply as a man would necessitate a denial of the precepts rendered sacred by years of unquestioning obedience. Bon, believing himself to be white, treats his octoroon wife with more courtesy and perhaps more kindness than is attributed to Sutpen's treatment of Eulalia, if only because the octoroon represents a costly investment. There is even a certain kind of honor evident in his behavior since he assumes responsibilities toward her that he has no intention of abrogating. But one thing he cannot give her is a place in society equal to his own. Neither he nor the octoroon question the "justice" of this, nor is it questioned by any other member of his class. There is no moral stigma attached to Bon's treatment of his mistress as there would have been had he actually claimed her as his wife. Consequently, there is no conflict; that comes when Bon is himself forced to battle for the recognition denied him, ironically enough, on the grounds of blood.

The choice Henry has to make is a much more agonizing one. For him, Bon represents all that is admirable, fine, and noble in a man. The faint suggestion of homosexuality and Henry's ardent hero-worship create unusually strong bonds of love and affection, so strong indeed that Henry does not hesitate in choosing between father and friend. So compelling is his emotional commitment that, after a self-torturing struggle, Henry is even willing to countenance Bon's incestuous marriage with Judith. Such a sin, involving, as it would, "*the irrevocable repudiation of the old heredity and training and the acceptance of eternal damnation,*" (347) would only be a further proof and affirmation of a love which will not be restricted. But there is still one more test, one more aspect of his heredity and training which is stronger than love itself. It is "*the miscegenation, not the incest, which [he] can't bear.*" (356) The shadow of the Negro effectively separates brother from brother, son from father, lover from beloved. The emotional pressure exerted on Henry is revealed by the juxtaposition of the two short sentences which state the nature of the choice he is faced with: "*—You are my brother.—No I'm not. I'm the nigger that's going to sleep with your sister. Unless you stop me, Henry.*" (357–58) By his shot at the gate of Sutpen's Hundred, Henry commits himself and his sister to an affirmation of Sutpen's design. The lives of Charles Bon, of Judith, and of Henry are sacrificed to an abstract principle and a social tradition that proves stronger than the moral or religious.

Although Judith is not a party to Henry's decision, she, nevertheless, condones it by her own subsequent action. Charles Etienne, the white-skinned Negro, the nephew to both her and Clytie, is brought to Sutpen's Hundred by her direction. Whether the two women ever realize that he is their nephew is one of the unresolved ambiguities of *Absalom, Absalom!* but that they know him to be the son of an octoroon is beyond dispute. With his appearance the boy symbol recurs in the third generation. Etienne's youth, his dependence, his complete vulnerability arouse a certain maternal love and affection in both Judith and Clytie, but in neither of them is it allowed to express itself freely and naturally. His claims on their love are balanced by his Negro blood, a situation that is dramatically rendered by the sleeping arrangements made for him midway between Judith's bed and Clytie's pallet.

Judith finally makes her decision, the one already made by her father, brother, lover, and the whole South. The frail youth is not allowed to be simply Charles Etienne St. Velery Bon. To the name must be added the label and the stigma of "Negro." Thus, in her relation with Etienne, Judith repeats almost exactly the action of her father in connection with Eulalia Bon. She too need only have closed her eyes to have "fooled the rest of the world"; she too chooses to assert principle at whatever cost to her own and the boy's emotions. But having revealed the taint of Negro blood, Judith is herself horrified by what she has done and urges him to hide the very thing she has impressed upon his consciousness: "What ever you are, once you are among strangers, people who don't know you, you can be whatever you will." (204) No change of scene can, however, restore Etienne's world of innocence "where pigmentation had no more moral value than the silk walls and the scent" (199) or erase his own awareness of that concept of Negro which can he neither ignore, accept, nor reject. Judith's subsequent behavior, nursing the stricken

Etienne and scrimping to pay for his tombstone, is her way of expressing penitence, a penitence that is perhaps also implied in Henry's painful return to and concealment in Sutpen's Hundred.

Within the design, whether Sutpen's or the South's, only the Jim Bonds have the possibility of surviving. This half-mocking conclusion of Shreve's refers to Bond's survival both as "Negro" and as idiot. Lacking reason, this last descendant of Sutpen is incapable of realizing that he is colored or that there are social conventions which define his position with respect to other men. The information that he was a Negro's son would have "vanished from what you (not he) would have had to call his mind long before it could have set up any reaction at all, either of pride or pleasure, anger or grief." (215) Whatever feelings and emotions he may have arise out of his needs for the essentials of human existence rather than for social status. It is because the South cannot control him that he can outlast the South. The full irony of Shreve's remark thus becomes apparent: the only one who is not forced to decide between the claims of humanity and society, the only one who is not destroyed by the very necessity of choosing is the idiot who possesses nothing which can be destroyed. He alone escapes all social categories, he alone has perfect freedom and scope to be himself, and all he can be is an idiot.

But insofar as Shreve's statement also implies the survival of Jim Bond as Negro, another factor is involved. It is the Negroes who are fighting to be recognized as human beings, and it is a fight in which victory must ultimately be theirs, if only because the whites destroy their own integrity and humanity each time they succeed in reasserting their position. In this respect, Bond's projected triumph constitutes a warning of the possibility of a doom which may yet be avoided. The choice confronting the Sutpens is a recurrent one and therefore there is always the hope that someone, some time will open the doors of the plantation, thus reversing Sutpen's decision, ignoring all categories, racial and economic, and altering the course of history itself.

The fact that the Sutpen story is framed in terms of a

choice between one's responsibility to man and to social tradition suggests that the narrators are related to the story they tell in yet another way. Miss Rosa, Mr. Compson, and Quentin, each exemplify, though in different ways, the abdication of responsibility to man. Each is free to interpret the past and to accept it or to modify it according to his own emotions and his awareness of the demands of a living present. Rosa, however, uses the past to justify her moral judgments, which have been formulated in advance of the situations she feels called upon to judge. More important, she uses it as the justification for her withdrawal from the world of present experience. With the grim air of a vengeful Cassandra, she waits for all those who have provoked her censure to " 'prove not only to themselves but to everybody else that she had been right.' " (176) She is, in a sense, the perfect defender of the idols of the South, for she is never tempted either to question or to deny them.

While Rosa's attitude is explained by her self-delusion, Mr. Compson has no such excuse. He appears to see the nature of man's struggle with himself and with time; he formulates the conflict between instinct and precept with commendable clarity; and he even recognizes the responsibility of the individual. But, whatever his reason, he has rejected the gambit of life for the sake of sitting on the sidelines and playing the role of ironic commentator. His refusal to concern himself with the Sutpen legend, his careful avoidance of choosing sides makes his section a quiet interlude between Rosa's fury and Quentin's passion, but it also makes him less of a man. His intellectualism may be a little more refined, a little more subtle than Sutpen's halting logic, but it serves just as efficiently to isolate him from humanity. In so doing, it replaces a " 'single simple Yes and a single simple No as instantaneous and complete and unthinking as the snapping on and off of electricity' " (272) with a deliberate weighing of ideas which precludes any action. By default, Mr. Compson contributes to the perpetuation of a system whose vices and follies he sees all too clearly.

The intense absorption of Quentin in the Sutpen story is accounted for by the fact that his decision is yet to be made;

meanwhile, his relation to Caddy adds urgency to the problem. In *The Sound and the Fury* Caddy's promiscuity challenges his identification of "virginity" with Compson "honor" by placing her immersion in life and the present against his abstractions and preoccupation with the past. His despairing cry at the end of *Absalom, Absalom!* reveals Quentin's decision and his solution to the problem of his dual self. He commits himself to the past, denying the Quentin preparing to enter Harvard and to participate in life for the sake of the Quentin "who was still too young to deserve yet to be a ghost, but nevertheless having to be one for all that." (9) He insists on the reality of his concepts and on the validity of the past the character of which he himself has helped to establish. And when he cannot recreate in his own life the principles and gestures which he admires in Henry, he commits suicide.

Absalom, Absalom! is an extension not only of the structure but also of the theme of *The Sound and the Fury*. The relation of the narrators to the center once more points out the essential ambiguity of fact and the multiplicity of "subjective" truths to which it can give rise. The later novel also examines the relation of time to the center: with successive generations the diverse versions coalesce, the inconsistencies are ironed out, and the legend assumes an independent existence. The legend, in its turn, becomes a motivating factor for those individuals who inherit it. Once the contributions of individual narrators, their deductions, speculations, and inventions, are forgotten, the legend, which embodies a poetic truth, tends once more to become identified with fact. Accordingly, it becomes a motivating force for those who inherit it. Quentin, whose "very body was an empty hall echoing with sonorous defeated names," (12) represents all those who are dedicated to serving the past, to preserving and perpetuating in their own lives those myths and rituals enshrined by their tradition. Neither the tradition nor the dedication is necessarily bad; but when they are used simply for self-perpetuation, and when they resist all change and alteration demanded by the exigencies of the present, they become a destructive or at best a stultifying force. The Golden

Age of necessity exists in the past, while its return can be envisaged only as of the future. And just as necessarily man's position is confined essentially to the present. To recognize this is to accept the truth of the legend without becoming helplessly paralyzed by its form.

As in *The Sound and the Fury*, inherited traditional concepts of the Old South are contrasted with the eternal virtues and truth which cannot be confined to a single historical period. In *Absalom, Absalom!* the choice between them is not only rendered dramatically in each of the Sutpens but is extended to the present in the figure of Quentin. Consequently, the decision is formulated in terms of the whole South rather than a single family. Sutpen's design is and can be no other than a microcosm of the South; his values are its values. To make Sutpen the scapegoat as Rosa does or to isolate him from Jefferson in a kind of moral quarantine as Quentin tends to do distorts the meaning of what is perhaps Faulkner's finest novel. For it is when a Sutpen makes a travesty of "principles" by a too meticulous observance, when a Charles Etienne destroys his life, or a Henry his love, that a re-examination of the tradition and the past becomes imperative for characters and readers alike.

Richard B. Sewall

from *The Vision of Tragedy* □

Although a sense of doom pervades the story of the rise and fall of Thomas Sutpen and his "design" in *Absalom, Absalom!* (a doom that is sealed in the final scene of the smoking ruins of his once proud mansion), more than one escaped to tell of it. In the telling, many meanings are revealed that help explain, partly illuminate, and transcend the ugly surface facts of the saga of Sutpen; his ambition; his two wives, two daughters, and two sons; miscegenation; fratricide; his own dismal end and the end of his line: "and there was only the sound of the idiot negro left." "Violence is just a tool I use," said Faulkner; and here the surface facts are merely the occasion of a long, anguished, "tragic" search for their meaning: like Hawthorne searching out the full meaning of the "certain affair of fine red cloth." "It's just incredible [says Mr. Compson, trying to explain one phase of the story—the fratricide—to his son Quentin]. It just does not explain. . . . We have a few old mouth-to-mouth tales; we exhume from old trunks and boxes and drawers letters without salutation or signature . . . we see dimly people, the people in whose living blood and seed we ourselves lay dormant and waiting, in this shadowy attenuation of time possessing now heroic proportions, performing their acts of simple passion and simple violence, impervious to time and inexplicable— Yes, Judith, Bon, Henry, Sutpen: all of them. They are

□ Richard B. Sewall, *The Vision of Tragedy* (New Haven: Yale University Press), pp. 135–147. Copyright © 1959 by Yale University Press.

there, yet something is missing . . . you re-read, tedious
and intent, poring, making sure you have forgotten nothing,
made no miscalculation; you bring them together again and
again nothing happens: just the words, the symbols, the
shapes themselves, shadowy inscrutable and serene . . ."

Mr. Compson, who had heard the story from his father,
the General, moves as best he can through its intricacies,
sees the heroic side of Sutpen, sees his ambition (the "design")
as rooted in his boyish sense of injustice and hence "innocence," and, a fatalist himself, tells the story with a fatalist's
detachment. Miss Rosa Coldfield, a victim of the "design,"
tells her side of the story to young Quentin ("Maybe some
day you will remember this and write about it")—of Sutpen as
"the evil's source and head," of his goal as mere "respectability" and "vain magnificence," of the "accelerating circle's
fatal curving course" which brought him to his violent—and
(to her) just—end.

But then there is Quentin's version—Quentin a more
sensitive and vulnerable Ishmael, for whom the telling (in
his cold Harvard study, to his roommate Shreve McCannon)
is itself a tragic experience. He cannot enjoy the security
of his father's detachment nor the single-minded certainty
of Miss Rosa's bitter moral verdict. The story, as he pieces
it together from a lifetime of listening to his elders ("his
very body was an empty hall echoing with sonorous defeated
names; he was not a being, an entity, he was a common-
wealth") and as he himself recreates its later scenes in a
passionate attempt to bore into its meaning, has a peculiarly
intimate, shocking effect on him, testing to the limit his
deepest loyalties and beliefs. It is as if the whole burden of
the South's (and mankind's) tragic dilemma is suddenly
placed on his young shoulders. After the telling, he lies
sleepless and anguished in his dormitory room. "I am older
at twenty than a lot of people who have died," he says to
Shreve at the end.

Indeed, the moment (in Faulkner's term) for which,
going back eighty years and three generations, the whole
story would account is this full and tragic realization by
Quentin of the paradox of his Southern heritage, and the

dilemma of man, with which he must somehow come to terms and cannot. ("Nevermore of peace. Nevermore of peace," he thinks to himself on his dormitory cot.) It is as if a son of a lesser Hamlet or of an untutored Faustus were telling his father's story and finding himself unable to live with it. Quentin is no tragic hero; he neither initiates nor is involved in an action of magnitude; he is helpless to do anything about his tragic perceptions except tell about them. The real actors and in this sense the "heroes" of the story are Thomas Sutpen and his son Henry. They initiate the actions but never understand, as Quentin does, their full tragic meaning, nor feel their full tragic impact. They are the furious or possessed or committed ones; they are not (in Dmitri's sense) "philosophers"; they are both "innocent." But their "acts of simple passion and simple violence" provide the impulse, or the first phase, of tragedy—its final phases (the deep spiritual upheaval and knowledge gained) to be realized in Quentin's sensitive and brooding consciousness.

Thomas Sutpen, the son of a migrant, alcoholic hillman, himself descended from the first Sutpen who had probably come to America direct from the Old Bailey, had been reared, barely literate, in a cabin in a mountain cove where "the land belonged to anybody" and "the only colored people were Indians." "So he didn't even know [Mr. Compson told Quentin] there was a country all divided and fixed and neat because of what color their skins happened to be and what they happened to own . . ." At fourteen he had his first brush with property and power. Delivering a message for his father, he was told by a Negro servant at the big house "never to come to that front door again but to go around to the back." It was as simple as that; but his goal from then on was fixed— "which most men [said Mr. Compson] do not begin to set up until the blood begins to slow at thirty or more and then only because the image represents peace and indolence or at least a crowning of vanity." It was not that he was angry, or wanted riches (here Miss Coldfield was wrong) or vengeance—he could have shot the plantation owner, but that was not it. He had to "do something about it [said Mr. Compson] in order to live with himself for the rest of his life . . ." He must "combat

them"—and to combat them he had to have what they had—
"land and niggers and a fine house."

So he conceived his purpose of "doing something"
about it, of achieving through his own courage and shrewdness the values from which he had been excluded, of one day
admitting at his own front door "a little boy without any
shoes on and with his pap's cut-down pants for clothes" (at
least this is the way Quentin imagines it), and thereby
righting the injustice he had suffered. He proceeded with
Ahab's mono-maniac intentness and a kind of Faustian wager
with destiny: first to the West Indies to make the money to
do it with; then (twelve years later) back to America and
Yoknapatawpha County, where he arrived looking as if he
had been through "some solitary furnace experience which
was more than just fever," with a French architect and a
handful of West Indian slaves—his "twenty subsidiary
demons." A sense of something a little less than justice seemed to compel him as he tore from the wilderness what was to
be the crowning symbol of his design, the largest and finest
mansion in the county. He connived, enslaved, brutalized
whenever he found it necessary to the design. He had abandoned his Haitian wife and child when he saw them as fatal
to it. He took another wife and got other children to fulfill it,
with the same shrewdness with which Ahab manipulated the
crew of the *Pequod* to his purpose. When they too failed him,
he tried a third time to found a line. He proposed to Miss
Rosa Coldfield, his dead wife's sister and thirty-eight years his
junior, that "they try it; and if it's a boy, we'll get married."
And he finally perished at the hands of a poor white underling
and drinking partner (Wash Jones) who hacked him to death
with a rusty scythe for getting Jones' sixteen-year-old
granddaughter with a child who Sutpen hoped would be his
son and heir (Miss Rosa having refused his offer). But the
child turned out to be a girl.

Sutpen comes to us, for all his dreary end, with some of
the qualities and many of the trappings of a tragic hero.
Even Miss Rosa admitted his extraordinary power of will and
his bravery ("I have never gainsaid that"), though she denied
him (wrongly) pity and honor. He had impressive qualities of

leadership—like the "authority" that Kent recognized in Lear. In Haiti, on the eighth night of the rebelling sugar-workers' siege of the plantation house, when all seemed lost, Sutpen put down his musket, "had someone unbar the door and then bar it behind him, and walked out into the darkness and subdued them"—how, Mr. Compson is not sure: "maybe by yelling louder, maybe by standing, bearing more than they believed any bones and flesh could or should . . ." Rearing his mansion in the Mississippi wilderness, he led his "twenty demons" with the same mysterious (and this time quiet) power; General Compson told Quentin's father that, "while the negroes were working Sutpen never raised his voice at them, that instead he led them, caught them at the psychological instant by example, by some ascendancy of forbearance rather than by brute fear." It is by this same curious ascendancy that he enlisted into his design Mr. Coldfield, Rosa's father, the Methodist steward of "immaculate morality," first by getting him to sign his very dubious bond and then by persuading him (again, no one knew how) to let him marry Ellen, Rosa's older sister, by whom he intended to become respectable and found his line. ("He had marked down Miss Coldfield's father with the same cold and ruthless deliberation with which he had probably marked down the French architect" who had been essential to the building of the house itself.) In the same way he subdued the town which he had "marked down" for his purpose. He outfaced the crowd of townspeople. (by this time restless as well as suspicious) who came to disrupt his wedding—"standing there motionless, with an expression almost of smiling where his teeth showed through the beard, holding his wild negroes with that one word," leading his bride to the carriage, while the crowd "vanished back into the region from which they had emerged for this one occasion like rats." In the War he became a colonel, and returned with a citation for bravery signed by Lee himself. He set about restoring his house and plantation with the same "fierce constant will" with which he originally built it—and from which nothing could deflect him, not even the deputation of Klansmen whom he refused to join when they put to him the "friend or enemy" question. "This may be war," they told him; and he answered, "I am used to it."

But he is more than a strong and determined man, of whom (said Quentin's grandfather) "anyone could look at him and say, *Given the occasion and the need, this man can and will do anything.*" To many, he seemed something more (or less) than human—to Miss Rosa "fiend, blackguard and devil," "the evil's source and head"; to Shreve as he listened, a "Faustus . . . demon . . . Beelzebub"; to Wash Jones, whose idol he was for long, "*A fine proud man. If God himself was to come down and ride the natural earth, that's what He would aim to look like.*" Shreve, when he had heard more, imagined him (had the design succeeded) an Abraham, who, full of years, could say, " 'Praise the Lord, I have raised about me sons to bear the burden of mine iniquities . . .' " Or (as Faulkner suggests by the title of the book) he was David, the favored one of God, lamenting his son Absalom. If to Miss Rosa, his face was "like the mask in a Greek tragedy," always ogre-like, he had another and more important affinity with the classic heroes. "His wild braggart dream," as she saw it, provoked "the very dark forces of fate" and spelled his inevitable doom: death at the hands of poor, forlorn Wash Jones, "brute instrument [as Miss Rosa described him] of that justice which presides over human events . . . which, by man or woman flouted, drives on like fiery steel and overrides both weakly just and unjust strong . . ." Quentin's father spoke of "that entire fecundity of dragons' teeth" Sutpen had sewn, and of the irony, suggesting something more than mere coincidence, of Charles Bon's appearing after twenty-seven years at Sutpen's Hundred—his own son to court his own daughter—and bringing the collapse of all that he had hoped and worked for.

Thus there is at once a whiff of sulphur about him and a touch of the superhuman, a man out of the ordinary in whom the Fates themselves seemed concerned. The dimension lacking, of course, is what made Oedipus suffer twice—"once in the body and once in the soul"; the fearful echoes that thundered in Faustus' ears; that which in Job and in Lear made them long for "instruction"; which made Ahab see himself as "a forty years' fool"; and what Dmitri meant when he called the Karamazovs philosophers. "Sutpen's trouble was innocence," Quentin tells Shreve, summarizing the judgment handed down from his grandfather. But it was more than the innocence of the evil of property and caste and exploitation—the innocence with which in Haiti (that "theatre for violence and injustice and bloodshed and all the satanic lusts of human greed and cruelty") he believed the earth to be "kind and gentle and that darkness was merely something you saw," not knowing that "what he rode upon was a volcano . . ." It was more even than his naively innocent view of morality whose ingredients were "like the ingredients of pie or cake and once you had measured them and balanced them and mixed them and put them into the oven it was all finished and nothing but pie or cake could come out." It was an innocence which overlooked the moral relationship of means and ends and with which he could view the collapse of his design, not as retribution, not as "fated," not even as bad luck, but simply the result of a "mistake." "You see [he told Quentin's grandfather], I had a design in mind. Whether it was a good or a bad design is beside the point; the question is, Where did I make the mistake in it . . . "

"According to the old dame," said Shreve, meaning Miss Rosa, "he never had had a soul" to begin with; and the question implicit in the narrations of the others (especially Quentin's) is the extent to which he ever developed one. Doctor Faustus knew he had a soul but thought it was his own to bargain with, until experience changed his mind. Sutpen's innocence never comprehended "soul." At least, we are not shown that it did. He is described as a man in action, "on the way," in the sureness of his cause not harassed by the tragic hero's doubts or self-doubts. And yet there is sufficient ambiguity about him to pause, as it did, agonizingly, to Quentin. To be sure, he saw nothing wrong in his design or his methods, and had scarcely a twinge of conscience about abandoning his first wife and child. By concealing the fact of her Negro blood, she had cancelled, so he thought, whatever responsibility he might have had for her; and even then he made generous provisions for her welfare. "Grandfather [Quentin told Shreve] said there was no conscience about that." Then for nearly thirty years the course of his design ran smooth. Only Bon's arrival at Sutpen's Hundred threatened it and presented him with a moral problem not to be settled by the swift Yes or No of an unclouded purpose. It brought him as near an actual spiritual struggle as he ever came.

His question was whether to keep Bon's identity undisclosed and (he told Quentin's grandfather) "let matters take the course which I know they will take and see my design complete itself quite normally and naturally and successfully to the public eye, yet to my own in such fashion as to be a mockery and a betrayal of that little boy who approached that door fifty years ago and was turned away, for whose vindication the whole plan was conceived and carried forward to the moment of this choice . . ." How real he felt his dilemma to be, to what extent it opened up for him those dark areas of the soul which tragic heroes know, we are not told. "He left for Virginia that night," and for the War. Quentin and Shreve (now caught up in the narrative), as they dramatize between them the meeting of father and son at night in a tent in a Carolina bivouac, throw Sutpen's renunciation in a suddenly tragic light—Sutpen's fatherly embrace, his "Henry—My son . . . I have seen Charles Bon . . . You are not going to let him marry Judith, Henry" and his final revelation of the Negro blood. "So he got his choice made, after all," Shreve said. "He played that trump after all."

What it cost him in spiritual anguish, what he learned, is not dramatized. He returns from the War a hero, still furious in his determination to try for his design once more, but this time in corrupted innocence. He ages rapidly, gets fat, fraternizes with Wash Jones, and bullies his women. Miss Rosa quits the place after his preposterous proposal; and his betrayal of Wash's granddaughter, Milly, leads to his swift (and to Miss Rosa) just end. Miss Rosa, forty years later, watches the decaying symbol of his design, the mansion, go up in smoke, taking the last survivors (except one) with it: "and there was only the sound of the idiot negro left." The spiritual ordeal of this hero, the "war in the cave" from which Job (and Oedipus and Faustus and Hester Prynne) emerged

with calmer mind and deepened insight, is only hinted at
and its results never articulated. It is not that Sutpen had
"forgotten the infinite"; he never knew it. His downfall is a
reminder of whatever is grave and constant in human suffering; but, in spite of Miss Rosa's ready-made notions of doom
and fate (part Greek and part Old Testament) there is nothing
secret about its cause. His fall, like Agamemnon's, was moral,
not tragic.

The tragedy is Quentin's. The action he is involved in
extends through four months. It begins when Miss Rosa
summons him, one September afternoon a few days before he
is to leave for Harvard, to listen to her story and thus get him
to escort her, that same night, to Sutpen's Hundred to find
out if her suspicion is true that Henry (now in his sixty-first
year) is in hiding there—still a murderer in the eyes of the
law. After supper that night, while waiting for the time to go
with Miss Rosa, his father fills out the story, recounting what
his father, the General, had told him, and showing Quentin
the letter of proposal that Bon had written Judith from the
front. Later, when it is quite dark, Quentin and Miss Rosa
make the trip and find Henry in the stripped and crumbling
mansion, wasting with fever on his deathbed, tended by old
Clytie, Sutpen's daughter by a Negro slave. Three months
later, Miss Rosa brings ambulance and attendants to the
mansion to rescue Henry, only to have Clytie mistake them
for the police and touch off the blaze which, by prearrange-
ment with Henry, had been prepared for three months. In
mid-January Quentin hears from his father of Miss Rosa's
death and that night tells the story to Shreve.

The course of Quentin's four-month action shows him
becoming ever more deeply involved. At first he had been a
little bored with those "stubborn back-looking ghosts,"
his elders, who seemed obsessed with the past and curiously
insistent on imposing their memories on him. "But why tell
me about it?" he asked his father after the first session with
Miss Rosa. "What is it to me that the land . . . the earth or
whatever it was got tired of him at last and turned and
destroyed him? What if it did destroy her family too? It's
going to turn and destroy us all some day, whether our name

happens to be Sutpen or Coldfield or not." During that sultry September afternoon, he had listened politely, with an occasional "Yes-sum" or "No'me" to prove his attention; but in spite of himself the story soon penetrates his youthful indifference and easy fatalism—reminiscent of Ishmael's before he saw horrors he could not be social with. During his "day of listening," first to Miss Rosa and then to his father, he not only becomes caught up in the story but finds himself visualizing its scenes with almost painful reality. Of the fratricide, for instance, "it seemed to Quentin that he could actually see them [Henry and Bon], facing one another at the gate," young, gaunt, on two gaunt horses, the pistol lying across the saddle bow, the quiet command and the refusal; and then the shot and "the running feet on the stairs . . ." Often his mind leaps beyond the narrator's version (his father's or Miss Rosa's) to speculate or build upon it, living it through more fully in his imagination, trying it out on his pulses.

Following this first sense of involvement, which is a kind of commitment, comes the increasing pressure of the story's meaning. It is Shreve who touched off the final phase, that January evening at Harvard, when, wondering at Quentin's curious concern over the news of Miss Rosa's death—an "old dame" and no kin to him—he puts his flippant request: *"Tell about the South. What's it like there. What do they do there. Why do they live there. Why do they live at all—"* As Quentin tells the story, Shreve himself goes through something of a transformation, though not a permanent one. He tends to vulgarize and simplify (the architect, he suggests, fled because he wanted a woman; Sutpen "chose lechery" or —a little higher level— "So he just wanted a grandson. That was all he was after"). Halfway through the narrative Shreve explodes, "Jesus, the South is fine, isn't it. It's better than the theatre isn't it. It's better than Ben Hur, isn't it. No wonder you have to come away from it now and then, isn't it." But he himself is drawn in, though never as Quentin is, and the two boys together, now one talking, now the other, re-create for themselves the final scenes of the story. Shreve never comes out from "that protective coloring of levity behind which the youthful shame of being moved hid itself"; but, coming to Henry's part of the story, both boys talk themselves, as it were, out of themselves, out of their cold room: "Because now neither of them were there. They were both in Carolina and the time was forty-six years ago . . . and both of them were Henry and both of them were Bon, compounded each of both and yet either neither, smelling the very smoke which had blown and faded away forty-six years ago . . ."

Although, the story told, Shreve could return to his detachment—interested, perplexed, honestly (not flippantly) trying to understand, Quentin had lost his forever. During the narrative he had grown increasingly tense and morose. Shreve becomes more voluble as the night wears on, taking more part in the narrative— "Now let me play awhile," he says at one turn in the story. Shreve bundles up in the growing chill of the room (though he forgets his breathing exercises), while Quentin sits huddled, wan, "brooding," his overcoat forgotten on the floor. He answers Shreve's questions tersely, as if deep in a personal anguish he cannot share with his friend. "Wait. Listen," says Shreve. "I'm not trying to be funny, smart. I just want to understand it if I can . . . What is it? something you live and breathe in like air?" "You can't understand it," replies Quentin. "You would have to be born there." To Shreve, the South, and this story of the South, had presented little more than a problem, as Hamlet's situation was a problem to Horatio. To Quentin it had become a matter almost of survival—a test of the most vital kind. We witness his increasing tension, the growing "tomb-like" chill of the room, his irrepressible trembling, his long, long thoughts as he broods over the enigma of the tale just told: " 'And she waited three months before she went back to get him,' Shreve said. 'Why did she do that?' Quentin didn't answer. He lay still and rigid on his back with the cold New England night on his face and the blood running warm in his rigid body and limbs, breathing hard but slow, his eyes wide open upon the window, thinking, 'Nevermore of peace. Nevermore of peace. Nevermore Nevermore Nevermore.' "

It is as if Quentin, through this saga of Sutpen and his son, had, like Ishmael, looked in the face of fire. These acts of simple passion and simple violence—Sutpen knowing no

restraints (but one) to the fulfillment of his design, Henry
acting out the role of the Southern chevalier in killing his
friend to save his sister's honor—proved not so simple after
all. To Quentin they were dragon's teeth. "What is it to me
. . ." he had asked his father after the talk with Miss Rosa;
and four months later in far-off Massachusetts he began to
find out. It was partly the move to the North, with the sudden,
sharp change of perspective; partly Shreve's prodding,
which made him retell (and relive) the story all but against
his will: "*Am I going to have to hear it all again* he thought
. . . *I shall have to never listen to anything else but this again
forever* . . .", as if he dreaded confronting face-to-face the
hidden and desperate meanings which he had begun to sense
on the September afternoon with Miss Rosa. He feels the
"cursed spite" of Hamlet's fated involvement, is irritated
at Shreve's insistence, and talks often as if to himself, staring
down at the letter (about Miss Rosa's death) on his desk.
Unlike Hamlet, he never speaks of his shattered illusions nor
passes judgment. All we know is that the story in some way
found him out, laid a question on his plate that he could not
live with in peace. Was it Sutpen's ambition, furiously
ambiguous, symbolic of an era and of all eras? Was it Henry's
fatal predicament? Miss Rosa's wasted life? Was it the South's
tragic dilemma, seen by him clearly for the first time—and,
since the South's, his own? Perhaps it was all these questions
and many more, plus the image of a certain kind of heroism
against which he could not help measuring himself, that
made him feel suddenly older "than a lot of people that have
died." He has found unacceptable what he once accepted on
boyish faith, and yet he cannot wholly reject it; these very
living ghosts are his and he cannot renounce them. " 'The
South,' Shreve said. 'The South. Jesus. No wonder you folks
all outlive yourself by years and years and years.' " At the
very end, Shreve, "the child of blizzards and cold," had one
more question: " 'Now I want you to tell me just one thing
more. Why do you hate the South?' 'I don't hate it,' Quentin
said. . . . *I dont hate it* he thought, panting in the cold air, the
iron New England dark; *I dont. I dont! I dont hate it! I dont
hate it!*' "

This is as far in the tragic course as Quentin goes—

that is, barely through initiation. He is like young Kalganov after witnessing the first shocking revelation of the Karamazov tragedy: "What are these people? What can mankind be after this?" In *Absalom, Absalom!* we never see what happens to Quentin after the first shock. He is never called upon, as Hamlet was, to act, and so we never know what he might become. Though heavy with a past, the situation in this sense lacks a future; and we are left, as after the sinking of the *Pequod*, in doom and despair. But, as with *Moby-Dick*, the very shock sends us back to the full story, to all that has been recounted and revealed about the possibilities in humankind for good and evil; and again we see that life has been presented as neither trivial nor base nor unlovely. Both Sutpen and Henry had great capacities, though not for self-analysis and self-knowledge. They had crude but vital principles for which they were prepared to take the ultimate risk—each swore, in his own way, "a pact with mankind." Even Miss Rosa, cherishing her hate for forty-three years, insisting "out of some bitter and implacable reserve of undefeat" that her story be told, had heroic qualities. Shreve suggests that in the end she even conquered her hate and went with ambulance and doctors to save Henry—or at least, knowing what might happen, was willing to risk losing "for his sake" this object of hate which like a drug had kept her going all these years. As the various narrators recount their versions of the story, or, like Quentin and Shreve, re-create its scenes in their own imaginings and become vicarious participants in it, the ugly surface facts are distanced and transcended. They are brought into the perspective of a whole community of values and shown to be rooted deep not only in time but in the timeless, in the ancient feud of man with his own nature and his destiny. The truth of Sutpen's story comes to us not as One but as Many—many-faceted, ambiguous, a sum of irreconcilables. This is the source of its terror for Quentin, the glimpse it gives him into the abyss. The novel never specifies his future, or ours, but it leaves open many possibilities, for evil and for good. The total vision is neither of doom nor redemption, but of something tantalizingly, precariously in between. We have no hope, yet we hope. It is tragic.

Melvin Backman

꙳

from *"Absalom, Absalom!"* □

S
even years after the publication of *The Sound and the Fury* came *Absalom, Absalom!* (1936). *The Sound and the Fury* dealt with the fall of a family, *Absalom* deals with the fall of a society. The Quentin Compson of *Absalom* is not quite the same as the earlier Quentin: his concern is social rather than personal and his role is identified for the most part with a central quest in the novel—the quest to discover the truth about the rise and fall of his South. In its search for the truth about a whole society, the novel circles and shuttles back and forth in time, its sentences twist and strain, and its narrators attempt to re-create a past on the basis of some fact and much conjecture. Sometimes the narrators mislead unintentionally, sometimes they contradict one another, and often they are carried away by their own bias, preoccupation, or imagination. Admittedly, it is hard to come by truth, but still one might question whether a novel whose pitch is too shrill, whose approach is emotional and poetic, whose perspective seems unclear and shifting—one might question whether such a work presents the best way of getting at historical truth. The method of narration apparently mirrors not only the difficulty in getting at truth but the struggle to face truth. For all its straining, its complexities and obscurities, *Absalom*, I would conclude, is Faulkner's most historical novel.

□ From *Faulkner: The Major Years* by Melvin Backman. Copyright © 1966 by Indiana University Press. Reprinted by permission.

All excerpts from *The Mind of the South* by W. J. Cash in this section reprinted with permission of Alfred A. Knopf, Inc. Copyright 1941 by Alfred A. Knopf, Inc. Renewed 1969 by Mary R. Maury.

Its intention, Ilse Dusoir Lind has said,

is to create, through the utilization of all the resources of fiction,
a grand tragic vision of historic dimensions. As in the tragedies
of the ancients and in the great myths of the Old Testament, the
action represents issues of timeless moral significance. That
Faulkner here links the decline of a social order to an infraction
of fundamental morality cannot be doubted. Sutpen falls through
innate deficiency of moral insight, but the error which he commits
is also socially derived and thus illustrates the flaw which dooms
with equal finality the aspirations of a whole culture.[1]

For Mrs. Lind and most other critics, Sutpen is the South.[2]
Yet some influential critics have qualified or contradicted
this interpretation. Both Malcolm Cowley and Robert Penn
Warren have stated in effect that "the Deep South was
settled partly by aristocrats like the Sartoris clan and partly
by new men like Colonel Sutpen."[3] Whereas they see Sutpen
as only partly representative of the Deep South, Cleanth
Brooks would question whether Sutpen is a Southerner at all.
For Brooks, Sutpen is in many ways a Yankee: he "is a
'planner' who works by blueprint and on a schedule. He is
rationalistic and scientific, not traditional, not religious, not
even superstitious." "Indeed, Sutpen is at some points more
nearly allied to Flem [Snopes] than he is to the Compsons and
the Sartorises. Like Flem, he is a new man with no concern
for the past and has a boundless energy with which to carry
out his aggressive plans."[4] In seeing Sutpen as basically
different from the other Yoknapatawpha planters and in
associating him with the Snopeses, Brooks is making use of
certain stereotypes that have been best described by George
Marion O'Donnell:

In Mr. Faulkner's mythology there are two kinds of characters;
they are Sartorises or Snopeses, whatever the family names may
be. And in the spiritual geography of Mr. Faulkner's work there
are two worlds: the Sartoris world and the Snopes world. In all of
his successful books, he is exploring the two worlds in detail,
dramatizing the inevitable conflict between them.
        It is a universal conflict. The Sartorises act traditionally;
that is to say, they act always with an ethically responsible will.
They represent vital morality, humanism. Being anti-traditional,

the Snopeses are immoral from the Sartoris point of view. But the
Snopeses do not recognize this point of view; acting only for self-
interest, they acknowledge no ethical duty. Really, then, they are
amoral; they represent naturalism or animalism. And the Sartoris-
Snopes conflict is fundamentally a struggle between humanism
and naturalism.[5]

Such a view—with its simplistic division of the South into
Sartorises and Snopeses, its blindness to the guilt and tension
and ambivalence which beset its Quentin Compsons—maps
the reality neither of the historical South nor of Yoknapatawpha. It would, in fact, shut out reality and substitute
legend; it would reduce the complexity of human life and
character to a single abstraction. Contrary to the Sartoris-
Snopes thesis, the antebellum South, though once ruled by
the planter class, did not consist only of planter aristocracy
and poor whites; the great majority of its people have always
been hard-working small farmers,[6] like the Tulls and Bun-
drens and Houstons and Quicks and Armstids of Yoknapatawpha. Moreover, to attribute the decline of the South to
the Snopeses is to compound legend with fantasy, for not
only does such a view assume the existence of an aristocratic
South based on a benevolent system of slavery and characterized by humanistic values but it finds a ready scapegoat for
its ills in a tribe of Southern "Yankees," the Snopeses. It is
more logical and just to assign the major responsibility for
the fortunes of the South to its rulers—the Thomas Sutpens.
And it is essential, if we are to understand *Absalom*, to know
(1) the fact and legend of Southern history and (2) how
Sutpen's life and career mirror the history and heritage of
the South, moral as well as social and political.

Northern Mississippi was settled in the 1830's and
1840's. Mississippi did not become a state until 1817, and the
town of Oxford, generally accepted as the prototype for
Jefferson, was still an Indian trading post in 1835.[7] De
Tocqueville, who travelled through America in the 1830's,
described Southwestern society as "only an agglomeration
of adventurers and speculators,"[8] and Baldwin's *The Flush
Times of Alabama and Mississippi* (1853) confirms de Tocqueville's appraisal. Historians generally agree that the Deep

South, right up to the Civil War, was largely frontier country.[9]
W. J. Cash, for example, describes the making of the great
or Deep South in this manner:

1810 came and went, the battle of New Orleans was fought and
won, and it was actually 1820 before the plantation was fully on
the march, striding over the hills of Carolina to Mississippi—
1820 before the tide of immigration was in full sweep about the
base of the Appalachians.

From 1820 to 1860 is but forty years—a little more than the
span of a single generation. The whole period from the invention
of the cotton gin to the outbreak of the Civil War is less than
seventy years—the lifetime of a single man. Yet it was wholly
within the longer of these periods, and mainly within the shorter,
that the development and growth of the great South took place.
Men who, as children, had heard the war-whoop of the Cherokee
in the Carolina backwoods lived to hear the guns at Vicksburg.
And thousands of other men who had looked upon Alabama when
it was still a wilderness and upon Mississippi when it was still a
stubborn jungle, lived to fight—and to fight well, too—in the ranks
of the Confederate armies.

The inference is plain. It is impossible to conceive the great
South as being, on the whole, more than a few steps removed
from the frontier stage at the beginning of the Civil War. It is
imperative, indeed, to conceive it as having remained more or less
fully in the frontier stage for a great part—maybe the greater
part—of its antebellum history.[13]

If this is so, who were the aristocrats of the Deep South?
For the great part, they were "but the natural flower of the
backcountry grown prosperous."[11] In Mississippi before
1860, a white man could lay claim to the title of gentry if he
acquired the land and the slaves. The importance of the
established gentry of the Carolina, Tidewater, and Natchez
plantations lay not in their migration to the undeveloped
South but in the potency of their influence upon the South's
lower classes. Although some planters or their sons did come
to the lower South, most of the men pushing into the Mississippi wilderness were from the backwoods. The plantation
aristocracy served them as a symbol and goal, as the crown
of a Southerner's achievement; it provided the more successful and ambitious with a manner and tradition which they

put on, so to speak, like a new cloak. But after the Civil War the South, "beset by the specters of defeat, of shame, of guilt," submerged the fact and romanticized the claim of the planter.[12] Hence was spread the legend of the Old South:

the legend of which the backbone is, of course, precisely the assumption that every planter was in the most rigid sense of the word a gentleman.

Enabling the South to wrap itself in a contemptuous superiority, to sneer down the Yankee as low-bred, crass, and money-grubbing, and even to beget in his bourgeois soul a kind of secret and envious awe, it was a nearly perfect defense-mechanism.[13]

Under the spur of the Civil War defeat, the Southerner's need to believe in the aristocracy of his ancestors and in the superiority of his tradition hastened the spread of the Southern legend. The legend affected the whole South, not just the Deep South. The force of its need and conviction submerged the fact that almost no members of the Cavalier aristocracy ever left England for America, that the Southern aristocracy derived from the low and middle classes, and that the aristocracy of the Deep South was made in one generation.[14] Scratch the veneer of the aristocrat of the Deep South and you would find a frontiersman. It was these new planters who took over the leadership of the Old South. The Natchez and Virginia gentry, longer exposed and hence more susceptible to the opinion of the rest of the Western world, were less able to conceive of slavery as a "positive good." But the new men brought to their position the frontier's aggressiveness, the strength and ruthlessness of self-made men, and a fierce faith in the righteousness of their cause and their interests. Nine-tenths of the men who directed the affairs of the Confederate government, like nine-tenths of the men who officered its armies, says Cash, were not Colonial aristocrats but new people.[15]

With the possible exception of Sartoris, all the founders of the ruling clans in Yoknapatawpha were new men. Sutpen, McCaslin, and Compson got their land by hook or by crook. Compson acquired his by swapping a mare to the Indians, Sutpen got his with a little Spanish gold, and McCaslin "bought the land, took the land, got the land no matter how."[16] Faulkner has not told us how Sartoris got his land, but Sartoris possessed the "violent and ruthless dictatorialness and will to dominate"[17] which generally characterize the founders of the Yoknapatawpha ruling clans. The getting of the land, the hacking of a plantation out of the wilderness, and the establishment of a family dynasty would naturally promote violence, ruthlessness, and strength of character, and not "vital morality and humanism."

Nevertheless, Faulkner does make a distinction between Sartoris and Sutpen. They are different, not in the sense that Sartoris was an established Yoknapatawpha planter when Sutpen arrived at Jefferson in 1833—Sartoris did not arrive until a few years after Sutpen[18]—but in the sense that Sartoris' origin was "aristocratic" whereas Sutpen's was plebeian. Colonel Sartoris, as we see him in *Sartoris* and later in *The Unvanquished*, is a much more traditionally romantic figure than Sutpen. Sartoris, it is generally acknowledged, is modeled in part on the character and life of the author's great-grandfather, Colonel William C. Falkner. Yet Falkner's origin more closely approximates that of Sutpen than of Sartoris: Sartoris came to Mississippi "with slaves and gear and money"[19] from a Carolina plantation, but Falkner came out of Tennessee as a poor boy. The inference is plain: Sartoris represents in part a projection of the legend, but Sutpen represents the reality.

To get at the reality, however, would be difficult for Faulkner, difficult because he would not only have to work his way out of the distortions wrought by Southern legend and pride but he would have to repudiate the uncritical allegiance and assent demanded by a closed society even though it was still his home and native land. Yet the story, he said, "wouldn't let me alone"; he had to write it.[20] Next to *The Sound and the Fury*, *Absalom* was, admittedly, the novel that gave him the most trouble, the novel that apparently sprang out of compulsion and reluctance, out of pride and guilt, out of love and hate. The character in *Absalom* that expresses these ambivalent feelings is of course Quentin Compson. Without Quentin the story would never be told. He brings together all the facts and conjectures about Sutpen, he is the story's compelled listener and narrator, and he cares most about what Sutpen signifies.[21] "Out of the rag-tag and bob-ends of old tales and talking,"[22] out of Miss Rosa's "demonizing" and his father's speculating, he must reconstruct a past that might have been, a man that apparently was. He must because the man in a sense was his ancestor, the past his past and present too.

Notes

1 Ilse Dusoir Lind, "The Design and Meaning of *Absalom, Absalom!*," in Frederick J. Hoffman and Olga W. Vickery (eds.), *William Faulkner: Three Decades of Criticism*, p. 278.

2 For example, Mrs. Vickery treats Sutpen as "a mirror image of the South," O'Connor as "the essence of the history of the South"; Howe regards *Absalom* as the "story of the fall of the homeland," Sullivan as the "complete statement of Southern ambition, execution and success, guilt, doom and destruction in one novel," Hoffman as "the vision of the South as a whole (or of human society itself) as a creation of this selfish and impulsive drive," and Waggoner as both "a lyric evocation of the Southern past" and "a search for the truth about human life as that truth may be discovered by understanding the past." See Olga W. Vickery, *The Novels of William Faulkner*, pp. 92–95; William Van O'Connor, *The Tangled Fire of William Faulkner*, pp. 94–96; Irving Howe, *William Faulkner: A Critical Study*, p. 161; Walter Sullivan, "The Tragic Design of *Absalom, Absalom!*," *South Atlantic Quarterly*, 50 (Oct., 1951), p. 560; Frederick J. Hoffman, *William Faulkner*, pp. 74–79; and Hyatt H. Waggoner, *William Faulkner: From Jefferson to the World*, pp. 149–153.

3 This is Cowley's statement, which Warren paraphrases. See Malcolm Cowley, "Introduction to *The Portable Faulkner*," and Robert Penn Warren "William Faulkner" in *William Faulkner: Three Decades of Criticism*, pp. 102 and 111 respectively.

4 Cleanth Brooks, *William Faulkner: The Yoknapatawpha Country*, pp. 306, 307.

5 George Marion O'Donnell, "Faulkner's Mythology," in *Three Decades of Criticism*, pp. 83–84.

6 Avery Craven, *The Growth of Southern Nationalism, 1848–1861* (Baton Rouge, Louisiana State University, 1953), p. 11; Avery Craven, *The Coming of the Civil War* (New York, Scribners, 1950), pp. 26–29; and Herbert Weaver, *Mississippi Farmers, 1850–1860* (Nashville, Tenn., Vanderbilt University, 1945), pp. 11–13, 28–29, 41, 48 and 57.

7 Charles Sackett Sydnor, *Slavery in Mississippi* (New York, Appleton-Century, 1933), pp. 41, 247–248; and Ward L. Miner, *The World of William Faulkner* (Durham, N.C., Duke University, 1952), pp. 18–36.

8 Alexis de Tocqueville, *Democracy in America*, ed. Phillips Bradley (New York, Knopf, 1946), I, p. 204.

9 See, for example, Howard W. Odum, *The Way of the South* (New York, Macmillan, 1947), p. 23; Vernon Lane Wharton, *The Negro in Mississippi, 1865–1890* (Chapel Hill, University of North Carolina, 1947), p. 216; and Avery Craven, *The Coming of the Civil War*, pp. 25–27.

10 W. J. Cash, *The Mind of the South* (New York, Alfred A. Knopf, Inc. 1941) p. 24

11 Ibid., p. 33. See also Frank Lawrence Owsley, *Plain Folk of the Old South* (Baton Rouge, Louisiana State University, 1949), p. 90.

12 Cash, p. 73. See also Craven, *The Coming of the Civil War*, pp. 17–18; and Sydnor, *Slavery in Mississippi*, p. 248.

13 Cash, p. 73.

14 Historians have long recognized that the Cavalier and planter legends derive from wishful thinking rather than fact. For early research on the subject, see Thomas Jefferson Wertenbaker, *Patrician and Plebeian in Virginia* (Charlottesville, privately printed, 1910), Preface and pp. 1–21 [Recent editions of his works have been published by Russell & Russell]; and G. W. Dyer, *Democracy in the South Before the Civil War* (Nashville, Methodist Episcopal Church, South, 1905), pp. 30–34. Although Wertenbaker established convincingly the non-aristocratic origins of the Virginia gentry, W. J. Cash, writing a generation later, had to explode the myth again. For other historical commentary, see Avery Craven, *The Coming of the Civil War*, pp. 17–34; C. Vann Woodward, *The Burden of Southern History* (Baton Rouge, Louisiana State University, 1960), pp. 12–13; and William R. Taylor, *Cavalier and Yankee* (New York, Braziller, 1961), pp. 17–18, 67, 96, 146–148, 203–205 and 334–341.
The general acceptance of the Sartoris-Snopes interpretation of Faulkner's works suggests that the myth, in another form, still lives with us.

15 Cash, p. 71. Avery Craven states: "A careful study of biographical materials and facts revealed in the manuscript census shows that only some 7.73 per cent of the men who represented Virginia, the Carolinas, Alabama, Mississippi, Louisiana, Georgia, and Tennessee in the House and Senate from 1850 to 1860 were plantation owners or had come from families of plantation owners." Craven, *The Growth of Southern Nationalism*, p. 163.

16 William Faulkner, *Go Down, Moses, and Other Stories* (New York, Random House, 1942), p. 256.

17 William Faulkner, *The Unvanquished* (New York, Random House, 1938), p. 258. These words are voiced silently by Colonel Sartoris' son as he broods over his father's character.

18 William Faulkner, *Requiem for a Nun* (New York, Random House, 1951), p. 44.

19 Ibid.

20 *Faulkner in the University*, ed. by Frederick L. Gwynn and Joseph L. Blotner, p. 281.

21 Many critics have recognized that the Sutpen story is Quentin's story too, that its full meaning does not make itself felt until the story has impacted upon Quentin's brooding, Hamlet-like conscience. The very tension between Quentin and what he is hearing and telling gives the novel its peculiar shading and significance. Faulkner himself has said that *Absalom* is both the story of Sutpen and "the story of Quentin Compson's hatred of the bad qualities in the country he loves" (*Faulkner in the University*, p. 71). A good analysis of this aspect of *Absalom* may be found in an essay by Richard B. Sewall, *The Vision of Tragedy* (New Haven, Conn., Yale, 1959), pp. 133–147.

22 *Absalom, Absalom!* (New York, Modern Library, 1951), p. 303. All quotations from *Absalom* are from this edition.

XIV

Invisible Man (1952) by Ralph Ellison

Alfred Chester and Vilma Howard

⌒〰⌒

from "Ralph Ellison: An Interview"□

INTERVIEWERS: Can you give us an example of the use of folklore in your own novel?

ELLISON: Well, there are certain themes, symbols, and images which are based on folk material. For example, there is the old saying among Negroes: If you're black, stay back; if you're brown, stick around; if you're white, you're right. And there is the joke Negroes tell on themselves about their being so black they can't be seen in the dark. In my book this sort of thing was merged with the meanings which blackness and light have long had in Western mythology: evil and goodness, ignorance and knowledge, and so on. In my novel the narrator's development is one through blackness to light; that is, from ignorance to enlightenment: invisibility to visibility. He leaves the South and goes North; this, as you will notice in reading Negro folk tales, is always the road to freedom—the movement upward. You have the same thing again when he leaves his underground cave for the open.

It took me a long time to learn how to adapt such examples of myth into my work—also ritual. The use of ritual is equally a vital part of the creative process. I learned a few things from Eliot, Joyce and Hemingway, but not how to adapt them. When I started writing, I knew that in both *The Waste Land* and *Ulysses* ancient myth and ritual were used to give form and significance to the material; but it took me a few years to realize that the myths and rites which we find functioning in our everyday lives could be used in the same way. In my first attempt at a novel—which I was unable to complete—I began by trying to manipulate the simple structural unities of *beginning, middle,* and *end,* but when I attempted to deal with the psychological strata—the images, symbols, and emotional configurations—of the experience at hand, I discovered that the unities were simply cool points of stability on which one could suspend the narrative line— but beneath the surface of apparently rational human relationships there seethed a chaos before which I was helpless. People rationalize what they shun or are incapable of dealing with; these superstitions and their rationalizations become ritual as they govern behavior. The rituals become social forms, and it is one of the functions of the artist to recognize them and raise them to the level of art.

I don't know whether I'm getting this over or not. Let's put it this way: Take the "Battle Royal" passage in my novel, where the boys are blindfolded and forced to fight each other for the amusement of the white observers. This is a vital part of behavior pattern in the South, which both Negroes and whites thoughtlessly accept. It is a ritual in preservation of caste lines, a keeping of taboo to appease the gods and ward off bad luck. It is also the initiation ritual to which all greenhorns are subjected. This passage states what Negroes will see I did not have to invent: the patterns were already there in society so that all I had to do was present them in a broader context of meaning. In any society there are many rituals of situation which, for the most part, go unquestioned. They can be simple or elaborate, but they are the connective tissue between the work of art and the audience.

INTERVIEWERS: Do you think a reader unacquainted with this folklore can properly understand your work?

ELLISON: Yes, I think so. It's like jazz; there's no inherent problem which prohibits understanding but the assumptions brought to it. We don't all dig Shakespeare uniformly, or even "Little Red Riding Hood." The understanding of art depends finally upon one's willingness to extend one's humanity and one's knowledge of human life. I noticed, incidentally, that the Germans, having no special caste assumptions concerning American Negroes, dealt with my work simply as a novel. I think the Americans will come to view it that way in twenty years—if it's around that long.

INTERVIEWERS: Don't you think it will be?

ELLISON: I doubt it. It's not an important novel. I failed of eloquence and many of the immediate issues are rapidly fading away. If it does last, it will simply be because there are things going on in its depth that are of more permanent interest than on its surface. I hope so, anyway.

INTERVIEWERS: Have the critics given you any constructive help in your writing, or changed in any way your aims in fiction?

ELLISON: No, except that I have a better idea of how the critics react, of what they see and fail to see, of how their sense of life differs with mine and mine with theirs. In some instances they were nice for the wrong reasons. In the U.S. —and I don't want this to sound like an apology for my own failures—some reviewers did not see what was before them because of this nonsense about protest.

INTERVIEWERS: Did the critics change your view of yourself as a writer?

ELLISON: I can't say that they did. I've been seeing by my own candle too long for that. The critics did give me a sharper sense of a larger audience, yes; and some convinced me that they were willing to judge me in terms of my writing rather than in terms of my racial identity. But there is one widely syndicated critical bankrupt who made liberal noises during the thirties and has been frightened ever since. He attacked my book as a "literary race riot." By and large, the critics and readers gave me an affirmed sense of my identity as a writer. You might know this within yourself, but to have it affirmed by others is of utmost importance. Writing is, after all, a form of communication.

INTERVIEWERS: When did you begin *Invisible Man?*

ELLISON: In the summer of 1945. I had returned from the sea, ill, with advice to get some rest. Part of my illness was due, no doubt, to the fact that I had not been able to write a novel for which I'd received a Rosenwald Fellowship the previous winter. So on a farm in Vermont where I was reading *The Hero* by Lord Raglan and speculating on the nature of Negro leadership in the U.S., I wrote the first paragraph of *Invisible Man*, and was soon involved in the struggle of creating the novel.

INTERVIEWERS: How long did it take you to write it?

ELLISON: Five years with one year out for a short novel which was unsatisfactory, ill-conceived, and never submitted for publication.

INTERVIEWERS: Did you have everything thought out before you began to write *Invisible Man?*

ELLISON: The symbols and their connections were known to me. I began it with a chart of the three-part division. It was a conceptual frame with most of the ideas and some incidents indicated. The three parts represent the narrator's movement from, using Kenneth Burke's terms, purpose to passion to perception. These three major sections are built up of smaller units of three which mark the course of the action and which depend for their development upon what I hoped was a consistent and developing motivation. However, you'll note that the maximum insight on the hero's part isn't reached until the final section. After all, it's a novel about innocence and human error, a struggle through illusion to reality. Each section begins with a sheet of paper; each piece of paper is exchanged for another and contains a definition of his identity, or the social role he is to play as defined for him by others. But all say essentially the same thing: "Keep this nigger boy running." Before he could have some voice in his own destiny he had to discard these old identities and illusions; his enlightenment couldn't come until then. Once he recognizes the hole of darkness into which these papers put him, he has to burn them. That's the plan and the intention; whether I achieved this is something else.

INTERVIEWERS: Would you say that the search for identity is primarily an American theme?

ELLISON: It is *the* American theme. The nature of our society is such that we are prevented from knowing who we are. It is still a young society, and this is an integral part of its development.

INTERVIEWERS: A common criticism of "first novels" is that the central incident is either omitted or weak. *Invisible Man* seems to suffer here; shouldn't we have been present at the scenes which are the dividing lines in the book—namely, when the Brotherhood organization moves the narrator downtown, then back uptown?

ELLISON: I think you missed the point. The major flaw in the hero's character is his unquestioning willingness to do what is required of him by others as a way to success, and this was the specific form of his "innocence." He goes where he is told to go; he does what he is told to do; he does not even choose his Brotherhood name. It is chosen for him and he accepts it. He has accepted party discipline and thus cannot be present at the scene since it is not the will of the Brotherhood leaders. What is important is not the scene but his failure to question their decision. There is also the fact that no single person can be everywhere at once, nor can a single consciousness be aware of all the nuances of a large social action. What happens uptown while he is downtown is part of his darkness, both symbolic and actual. No; I don't feel that any vital scenes have been left out.

INTERVIEWERS: Why did you find it necessary to shift styles throughout the book; particularly in the Prologue and Epilogue?

ELLISON: The Prologue was written afterwards, really —in terms of a shift in the hero's point of view. I wanted to throw the reader off balance—make him accept certain non-naturalistic effects. It was really a memoir written underground, and I wanted a foreshadowing through which I hoped the reader would view the actions which took place in the main body of the book. For another thing, the styles of life presented are different. In the South, where he was trying to fit into a traditional pattern and where his sense of certainty had not yet been challenged, I felt a more naturalistic treatment was adequate. The college trustee's speech to the students is really an echo of a certain kind of Southern rhetoric and I enjoyed trying to re-create it. As the hero passes from the South to the North, from the relatively stable to the swiftly changing, his sense of certainty is lost and the style becomes expressionistic. Later on during his fall from grace in the Brotherhood it becomes somewhat surrealistic. The styles try to express both his state of consciousness and the state of society. The Epilogue was necessary to complete the action begun when he set out to write his memoirs.

INTERVIEWERS: After four hundred pages you still felt the Epilogue was necessary?

ELLISON: Yes. Look at it this way. The book is a series of reversals. It is the portrait of the artist as a rabble-rouser, thus the various mediums of expression. In the Epilogue the hero discovers what he had not discovered throughout the book: you have to make your own decisions; you have to think for yourself. The hero comes up from underground because the act of writing and thinking necessitated it. He could not stay down there.

INTERVIEWERS: You say that the book is "a series of reversals." It seemed to us that this was a weakness, that it was built on a series of provocative situations which were canceled by the calling up of conventional emotions.

ELLISON: I don't quite see what you mean.

INTERVIEWERS: Well, for one thing, you begin with a provocative situation of the American Negro's status in society. The responsibility for this is that of the white American citizen; that's where the guilt lies. Then you cancel it by introducing the Communist Party, or the Brotherhood, so that the reader tends to say to himself, "Ah, they're the guilty ones. They're the ones who mistreat him; not us."

ELLISON: I think that's a case of misreading. And I didn't identify the Brotherhood as the C.P., but since you do I'll remind you that they too are white. The hero's invisibility is not a matter of being seen, but a refusal to run the risk of his own humanity, which involves guilt. This is not an attack upon white society! It is what the hero refuses to do in each section which leads to further action. He must assert and achieve his own humanity; he cannot run with the pack and do this—this is the reason for all the reversals. The Epilogue is the most final reversal of all; therefore it is a necessary statement.

INTERVIEWERS: And the love affairs—or almost-love-affairs—

ELLISON: [*Laughing*] I'm glad you put it that way. The point is that when thrown into a situation which he thinks he wants, the hero is sometimes thrown at a loss; he doesn't know how to act. After he had made this speech about the Place of the Woman in Our Society, for example, and was approached by one of the women in the audience, he thought she wanted to talk about the Brotherhood and found that she wanted to talk about brother-*and-sisterhood*. Look, didn't you find the book at all *funny?* I felt that such a man as this character would have been incapable of a love affair; it would have been inconsistent with his personality.

INTERVIEWERS: Do you have any difficulty controlling your characters? E. M. Forster says that he sometimes finds a character running away with him.

ELLISON: No, because I find that a sense of the ritual understructure of the fiction helps to guide the creation of characters. Action is the thing. We are what we do and do not do. The problem for me is to get from A to B to C. My anxiety about transitions greatly prolonged the writing of my book. The naturalists stick to case histories and sociology and are willing to compete with the camera and the tape recorder. I despise concreteness in writing, but when reality is deranged in fiction, one must worry about the seams.

INTERVIEWERS: Do you have difficulty turning real characters into fiction?

ELLISON: Real characters are just a limitation. It's like turning your own life into fiction: you have to be hindered by chronology and fact. A number of the characters just jumped out, like Rinehart and Ras.

INTERVIEWERS: Isn't Ras based on Marcus Garvey?[1]

ELLISON: No. In 1950 my wife and I were staying at a vacation spot where we met some white liberals who thought the best way to be friendly was to tell us what it was like to be Negro. I got mad at hearing this from people who otherwise seemed very intelligent. I had already sketched Ras, but the passion of his statement came out after I went upstairs that night feeling that we needed to have this thing out once and for all and get it done with; then we could go on living like people and individuals. No conscious reference to Garvey is intended.

INTERVIEWERS: What about Rinehart? Is he related to Rinehart in the blues tradition, or Django Rheinhardt, the jazz musician?

ELLISON: There is a peculiar set of circumstances connected with my choice of that name. My old Oklahoma friend, Jimmy Rushing, the blues singer, used to sing one with a refrain that went:

> Rinehart, Rinehart,
> It's so lonesome up here
> On Beacon Hill,

which haunted me, and as I was thinking of a character who was a master of disguise, of coincidence, this name with its suggestion of inner and outer came to my mind. Later I learned that it was a call used by Harvard students when they prepared to riot, a call to chaos. Which is very interesting, because it is not long after Rinehart appears in my novel that the riot breaks out in Harlem. Rinehart is my name for the personification of chaos. He is also intended to represent America and change. He has lived so long with chaos that he knows how to manipulate it. It is the old theme of *The Confidence Man*. He is a figure in a country with no solid past or stable class lines; therefore he is able to move about easily from one to the other. . . .

You know, I'm still thinking of your question about the use of Negro experience as material for fiction. One function of serious literature is to deal with the moral core of a given society. Well, in the United States the Negro and his status have always stood for that moral concern. He symbolizes among other things the human and social possibility of equality. This is the moral question raised in our two great nineteenth-century novels, *Moby Dick* and *Huckleberry Finn*. The very center of Twain's book revolves finally around the boy's relations with Nigger Jim and the question of what Huck should do about getting Jim free after the two scoundrels had sold him. There is a magic here worth conjuring, and that reaches to the very nerve of the American consciousness—so why should I abandon it? Our so-called race problem has now lined up with the world problems of colonialism and the struggle of the West to gain the allegiance of the remaining non-white people who have thus far remained outside the Communist sphere; thus its possibilities for art have increased rather than lessened. Looking at the novelist as manipulator and depicter of moral problems, I ask myself how much of the achievement of democratic ideals in the U.S. has been affected by the steady pressure of Negroes and those whites who were sensitive to the implications of our condition; and I know that without that pressure the position of our country before the world would be much more serious than it is even now. Here is part of the social dynamics of a great society. Perhaps the discomfort about protest in books by Negro authors comes because since the nineteenth century American literature has avoided profound moral searching. It was too painful and besides there were specific problems of language and form to which the writers could address themselves. They did wonderful things, but perhaps they left the real problems untouched. There are exceptions, of course, like Faulkner who has been working the great moral theme all along, taking it up where Mark Twain put it down.

I feel that with my decision to devote myself to the novel I took on one of the responsibilities inherited by those who practice the craft in the U.S.: that of describing for all that fragment of the huge diverse American experience which I know best, and which offers me the possibility of contributing not only to the growth of the literature but to the shaping of the culture as I should like it to be. The American novel is in this sense a conquest of the frontier; as it describes our experience, it creates it.

Note

1   Marcus Garvey: Negro nationalist and founder of a "Back to Africa" movement in the United States during the early 1900s.

Barbara Christian

"Ralph Ellison: A Critical Study"□

In 1952, reviewers across the country in both black and white periodicals hailed the then newly published book, *Invisible Man*, as a most impressive work of fiction. In that same year, Ralph Ellison's first novel was given collective critical acclaim for it was called the best novel of the last twenty years. There is no doubt that Ellison, although not very prolific (*Invisible Man* is his only completed creative work), is a skilled, impressive and lyrical writer. But he is not only a novelist; Ellison is also a critic with a particular point of view. His point of view can be seen in almost any paragraph in his collected essays, *Shadow and Act* (1966). Ellison's speech when he received the National Book Award reveals his particular slant:

Thus to see America with an awareness of its rich diversity and its almost magical fluidity and freedom, I was forced to conceive of a novel unburdened by the narrow naturalism which has led, after so many triumphs, to the final and unrelieved despair which marks so much of our current fiction. I was to dream of a prose which was flexible and swift as American change is swift, confronting the inequalities, but yet thrusting forth its images of hope, human fraternity and individual self-realization. It would use the richness of our speech, the idiomatic expression and the rhetorical flourishes

□ City College Lecture on Ralph Ellison's *Invisible Man*, May, 1967. Reprinted from *Black Expression: Essays By and About Black Americans in the Creative Arts*, edited by Addison Gayle, Jr. Copyright © 1969 by Weybright & Talley, Inc. Reprinted by permission of Weybright & Talley, Inc. and David McKay Co., Inc.
All excerpts from *Invisible Man* by Ralph Ellison in this section reprinted with the permission of Random House, Inc.

from past periods which are still alive among us. And despite my personal failures, there must be possible a fiction, which, leaving sociology to the scientists, can arrive at the truth about the human condition, here and now, with all the bright magic of a fairy tale.

The emphasis in this acceptance speech is without a doubt on the aesthetic problems of the artist. Unlike Wright and other notable black writers, Ellison is the spokesman for the "infinite possibilities" that he feels is inherent in the condition of being an artist rather than a Negro artist. He repeatedly states in his essays that his primary concern is not the social but rather the aesthetic responsibilities of the writer.

As we shall see, Ellison's positions in many of his essays do not always coincide with the ideas expressed in *Invisible Man*. Nonetheless, the essays, such as "Richard Wright's Blues," his interview with *Partisan Review*, and many of his essays on music are worth our attention for they reveal his interests and philosophy as they have developed and in this sense are a means of clarifying certain sections of *Invisible Man*.

There is one word that crops up repeatedly in both the essays and *Invisible Man* and which is at the base of Ellison's aesthetic beliefs. That word is *myth*, the magical transformer of life. Influenced by T. S. Eliot whom he calls his literary ancestor, Ellison combines the literary past and the memory and culture of the individual with the present, thus placing the contemporary writer alongside the other men who have written in the English language. Baldwin stresses the fact that the writer creates out of his own experience. Ellison would add that one writes out of one's experience as understood through one's knowledge of self, culture, and literature. Self, in Ellison's case, refers to his own past and background, culture to the American culture and more specifically to Negro American culture, and literature to the entire range of works in European literature that help to make up Western sensibility.

Even Ellison's name itself is steeped in myth as he points out in the essay, "Hidden Names and Complex Fate." His father had named him after Ralph Waldo Emerson and

Ellison recalls that "much later after I began to write and work with words, I came to suspect that my father had been aware of the suggestive powers of names and the magic involved in naming." The name *Ralph Waldo* indeed had magic for it enabled Ellison to see the power of the myth and to envision the role that myth could play in achieving his aim which was, as he put it, "to add to literature the wonderful American speech and idiom and to bring into range as fully as possible the complex reality of American experience as it shaped and was shaped by the lives of my own people." Myths in order to be preserved and appreciated must be written down, and Ellison, in his comments on Hemingway and Faulkner, is constantly aware that one element of the American past is sorely missing from most American literature. As Ralph Waldo Emerson could merge the myths and attitudes of New England into his philosophy of Transcendentalism, Ralph Waldo Ellison would merge that essential element, the nature of blacklore and life style, into American literature—and myth could be the carrier.

The past, especially the American past, is also a magical word for Ellison. Perhaps the impact of this concept on Ellison can be seen only when one looks at this writer's individual history. He was born and grew up in Oklahoma City in the 20's; he was raised in a virtual frontier town which had been a state only seven years when he was born. The newness of the state, the lack of a tradition of slavery allowed the boy to believe that nothing was hopelessly beyond the reach of the black world really, "because if you worked and you fought for your rights, and so on, you could finally achieve it." By early adolescence, Ellison remembers that "the idea of the Renaissance Man had drifted down to him and his friends and that they discussed mastering themselves and everything in sight as though no such thing as racial discrimination existed." No doubt, Ellison's background, with its illusion of personal freedom, is a strong determinant in his philosophy of "infinite possibilities."

In addition to the belief that he could be a Renaissance man, Ellison wanted to be a great musician. His youth and dreams were obsessed by his love of music both in the classical field which he studied at school and in the blues and jazz that he heard in the black community around him. The sense of timing, the flow of lyricism developed through this first love comes to fruition in *Invisible Man* and is one of the most beautiful aspects of the book. Music, too, gave Ellison an insight into the life around him. He tells us:

The blues speak to us simultaneously of the tragic and comic aspects of the human condition and they express a profound sense of life shared by many Negro Americans precisely because their lives have combined these modes. This has been the heritage of a people who for hundreds of years could not celebrate birth or dignify death and whose need to live despite the dehumanizing pressures of slavery developed an endless capacity for laughter at their painful experience.

This analysis of the blues as a tragic-comic form was to contribute a great deal to *Invisible Man*, for this is precisely the stance that the hero takes when he explains his invisibility to us. But more important for Ellison, the craftsman, music taught him that "technique was that which transforms the individual before he is able to transform it. The artist discovers that he has taken on certain obligations; that he must not embarrass his chosen form, and that in order to avoid this he must develop taste." The meditation on form led Ellison to one of his basic tenets:

He (the artist) learns—and this is most discouraging—that he is involved with values which turn in their own way, and not in the way of politics, upon the central issues affecting his nation and his time.

The aesthetic, rather than the political, was to be Ellison's concern; his grand social gesture was to be his creative work.

After graduating from high school, Ellison's love of music took him to Tuskegee where he planned to study under a famous musician. But like the hero in *Invisible Man*, he left the shelter of the dream-like college to work in New York for the summer, and never came back. Unable to find work, and disappointed with the sculpture he had come to study, the young man began to write. In his travels through Harlem he met Richard Wright who was then writing *Native Son* and who got Ellison's first piece, a book review, published. Wright encouraged the young musician in the art of writing, stressing not so much a mystical process but emphasizing craft, hard work, and thought. He guided Ellison to such writers as Henry James, and discussed the literary effects of Conrad, Joyce, and Dostoevsky with his new student. Although Ellison was overwhelmed by the towering personality of Richard Wright and though he learned a great deal about writing from him, he, even at that time, found Wright's novels disturbing. His comment on *Native Son* was that "Bigger Thomas had none of the fine qualities of Richard Wright, none of the imagination, none of the sense of poetry, the sense of gaiety," and Ellison summarily preferred Wright to Bigger Thomas. The younger writer always thought of himself as an artist taken up with the magical quality of writing and the poetry of it, while Richard Wright, he felt, was overcommitted to ideology.

By 1945, Ellison had devised a plan for a book which would incorporate the myth and literature of the Western world into the experience of the American black man. This book would reveal the travelings of the mind as it escaped from the darkness of illusion into the light of reality. Just as Dante had summarized the whole of medieval myth in his passing from the dark circles of Hell to the light of the Paradiso, Ellison would use the literature and legends of American society, both black and white, as a means of clarifying and transforming the meaning of twentieth century existence. This was a grand aim and it took Ellison seven years, from 1945 to 1952, to create and revise the book.

Like Joyce's *Portrait of an Artist as a Young Man*, a book which has greatly influenced Ellison's work, *Invisible Man* has been called the story of a young man's search for his identity. Both heroes must escape from the illusions and limitations of their environments in order to find themselves. Joyce's Stephen has to confront his Irish, Catholic, and family traditions. Ellison's hero has to penetrate the illusions built around the fact that he is black, not only in others, but more importantly in himself. As he moves from darkness to light,

a basic motif in the book, the hero must encounter variations
of deception which attempt to blind him to his image, that as a
black man in America, he does not in relation to the rest of
his world really exist.

This is the substance of the book but actually the hero
has found his identity before the book opens. His first statement is to assure us that he knows who he is. "I am an invisible man," he proclaims with mingled pride and fear. Rather
than searching for his identity, he is more interested in clarifying for himself his reasons for descending into his hell-like
hole, and possibly for rising out of it, if and when he decides
to do so. His goal in telling us his story is to separate the pride
from the fear to make sense out of his experience. He is forced
to explain himself not because it is necessary in that hole of
his, but because he needs to face the world outside: "What did I
do to be so black and blue?" Just as hibernation could not work
for Dostoevsky's hero in his underground, so it cannot work for
Ellison's hero. It is impossible for both of these intellectuals
to protest their situation silently (hibernation is nothing less
than passive protest) because of the nature of their minds.

So I took to the cellar; I hibernated, I got away from it all. But that
wasn't enough. I couldn't be still in hibernation. Because, damn it,
there's the mind, the mind. It wouldn't let me rest.

It is the mind that puts these heroes in hell and it is the pain
of consciousness that forces them to murder an old self and
create a new one.

Actually the invisible man's mind hadn't been at rest
since his grandfather had uttered that loathsome curse on his
deathbed. The old man, usually meek and gentle, turned
violent on his deathbed and hissed out his last words of advice:

Live with your head in the lion's mouth. I want you to overcome
'em with yeses, undermine 'em with grins, agree 'em to death and
destruction, let them swoller you till they vomit or bust wide open.

The snake had crawled into the garden of Paradise. These
words were to haunt the life and dreams of the hero throughout the book not so much because he does not understand them
but because he senses the irony that lies beneath them.

It is with this mental assault, rather than with a

physical attack, that Ellison begins the book (contrast this with the beginning of *Native Son*); it is with his first disturbance of a child's mind. The narrator's grandfather had simply accepted the fact that Negroes survived by lying to white people and he suggests that the lie is not only the tool for survival but a means of victory as well. But the narrator does not want to believe this and it is precisely by telling the truth, accidentally sometimes, as in the speech he makes at the Battle Royale, that he continues to get into trouble. His grandfather's warnings, though, held another meaning—that a person, a race, a people must not fool itself into believing its own lies. Our narrator does believe in his own deceptive speech at the Battle Royale, in his own behavior at the college; he believes the actions that are meant to fool white people. But in spite of his resistance to the truth, his grandfather's swan song is harsh enough to unsettle him for the rest of his life.

The power of the lie, the fact that it is at the base of the relations between whites and blacks in this country, is forced home traumatically to the hero in the junior year at his dream-world college which had been built on and had survived exactly by those very lies. And Ellison, anxious to show the complexity and attractiveness of the illusion, literally flushes this section with pseudo myth and ritual The college is the hero's religion, its ceremonies, his act of worship. Presiding over this universe, untouchable and benevolent, are the great white fathers, like Mr. Norton who had created this world through the mediation of the Christ-like Negro teacher and leader of his people. Barbee, the blind minister, gives us the full impact of the Founder who could effectively mediate between the gods and the people, since he was brother racially to the people and understood mentally the wishes of the gods. The religious overtones in this section are heightened even more by the hero's encounter with one of these white gods, Mr. Norton. Such words as *destiny*, *fate*, *salvation* regularly flow out of Norton's lips just as sums of money for the benefit of the college flow out of his pocketbook. In exchange for creating this dream-world, Mr. Norton expects, kindly it is true, adoration and power.

In this setting, Ellison then introduces Jim Trueblood and the vet, two demoniac characters, companions no doubt of the hissing grandfather. Both are blasphemers, for Jim Trueblood (the pun is marvellous) commits the unforgivable sin and lives, despite the pronouncement of the gods, while the vet deliberately attacks the supremacy and benevolence of the gods who had supposedly given him so much. During Norton's talk with Trueblood and the vet, the narrator shows signs of increasing disturbance and fear, for these men were talking to white men as if they were simply other men, not gods. These men were speaking the truth. The vet, protected by his status as an insane man, says ironically:

You don't have to be a complete fool to succeed. Play the game but don't believe in it.

Bledsoe, president of the college, tells the narrator the whole truth, puts his finger exactly on what was wrong with the Golden-Day episode, why it was actual treason, and why the hero must be expelled from the college:

You're dangerous, boy, why the dumbest black bastard in the cotton patch knows that the only way to please a white man is to tell him a lie. What kind of education are you getting around here?

So much for the American Dream. The dream-world college is built on a lie, Bledsoe knows it, he assumes every Negro does; but our narrator naively believes that he is telling the truth when in fact he has not even found it. Bledsoe lives the doctrine of the grandfather. He is the first of the long line of yes-ers in the book, of people who are used by and use white people and who know exactly where it's at. He represents for the invisible man his first concrete glimpse into the real world and the narrator never forgives him for it.

The trip North, archetypal for the black man in this country, precipitates the hero's search for work and then for his own identity. Cast out from the dream-world college, both physically and spiritually, he descends into *Mister* Brockway's underground hole where Optic White paint is made. The irony of this scene is hilarious as Ellison juxtaposes the supreme lie of the Negro "white is right" with the slogan of the company, "If it's Optic White, it's the right white." Why not whitewash everything? Just as Negroes had conveniently told whites that they were right when in fact they knew they weren't, Lucius Brockway improves on the saying by turning it into a slogan which gives him prestige in the eyes of the man upstairs. The whole nightmarish experience, underlined by the hero's first attempt at violence and by the serious injury he receives, his first literal blow on the head, is a preparation for one of Ellison's most impressive pieces, the surrealistic hospital dream of castration and loss of identity that the narrator suffers. Dreams had been used before in the book. "Keep that nigger running," the dream caused by his grandfather's words, is a father to the horrifying dream sequence that the hero now experiences. Music, too, plays an essential part in dramatizing the trauma of the nightmare. Beethoven's Fifth becomes unbearable and is pitted against the hero's childhood songs now magnified in horrifying proportions in his dream. Although the Invisible Man knows who Brer Rabbit is, he hasn't learned what this cunning fellow, essential to Negro folklore, really represents. Brer Rabbit, the symbol of the yes-er who destroys through yessing, knows when he is conning and when he is not. The hero is still trapped by his wish to believe that in fact he can survive by deceiving himself.

The nightmare with all its grotesque images of the hero's past indicates that he does know unconsciously the truth but that the mind with its affinity for rationality cannot stand for the absurdity that is implied in the truth. How can his mind grasp the fact that he does not really exist? The dream does rid the narrator of one fear though. When he is released from the factory hospital he reflects:

Leaving him and going out into the paint-fuming air I had the feeling that I had been talking beyond myself, had used words and expressed attitudes not my own, that I was in the grip of some alien personality lodged deep within me. It was as though I were acting out a scene from some crazy movie. Or perhaps I was catching up with myself and had put into words feelings which I had hitherto suppressed. Or was it I thought that I was no longer afraid? I was no longer afraid. Not of important men, not of trustees and such; for knowing now that there was nothing which I could expect from them, there was no reason to be afraid.

At this point in the story, the intensity of the action subsides; the narrator becomes "cool" as he withdraws from society for the first time. This time it is not into the hole but into the warm generous arms of Mary, Mary Rambo, whom he does not think of as a friend but as a force, familiar and stabilizing. And during this hibernation with Mary, we see the hero wrestle with his benefactor. Mary belongs to his past for she insists that he do something, that he be one of those men who will save his people. But he becomes more and more convinced that anything he could do would only be futile.

This time the feeling of futility lasts only for a little while. The voice of the past wins out. The hero returns to society as he is reminded by those hot juicy yams as to who he is and that he had tried to suppress his past in his dream-world college. It is no accident, I think, that Ellison follows up the eating of yams with the eviction scene in which the hero speaks his mind. But this time he speaks an accepted lie, "We are a law-abiding people," in order to provoke and arouse the crowd to action. For the first time in the book he feels potent and alive. Just as Bigger Thomas becomes aware of his own life through the murder he had unintentionally committed, so too Ellison's hero comes to life as he destroys the false myth that Negroes can and will suffer anything.

But another obstacle is placed in the hero's path before he can see it like it is. Intrigued by the power and stability which the brotherhood represents, he becomes a part of their group. Again, he feels, as he had at college, that he is engaged in discovering and promoting the truth, that he has gained recognition, that he is living a significant life. However, just as Barbee, the blind minister, had perpetuated the myth of the great Christlike Founder, so Jack, the one-eyed leader of the Brotherhood, worships the myth of history. As patronizing as Norton, Jack leads the hero into another deception, that in history, there is salvation and that salvation can be attained through subordinating the individual to a cause bigger than himself. Thus, in dealing with Christianity and Communism, and in relating them to each other, Ellison presents two important paths by which black people have tried to find themselves.

That Ellison calls his organization the Brotherhood rather than the Communist Party, which it obviously is, is significant, I believe. For what he might be suggesting is that the essence of any such *ism* is an abstraction such as "history saves." And that when push comes to shove, this abstraction rules and controls the living entities within it. Harlem is only a political entity to Jack. He doesn't know nor want to know

the gin mills, and the barber shops and the juke joints and the churches and the beauty parlors on Saturday when they're frying hair, the whole of unrecorded history called reality.

History, as Jack sees it, is a means of imposing order on chaos. It is not the reality itself; it is an ideal which is imposed on the real. Thus, the problem of scientific objectivity, the ritual of this organization, is the first obstacle that the hero now turned orator faces when he joins the Brotherhood. Many brothers protest that although his speeches are effective, they are not scientific. And when the narrator, angered by the fact that the organization will not avenge the death of Tod Clifton, accuses Brother Hambro of being mechanical, communication between him and the organization falls apart. The organization called for the sacrifice of Harlem, but the narrator sees that "for them it was simple, but hell, I was both sacrificer and victim. *That was reality*. They did not have to put the knives to their own throats."

Enraged by the brotherhood's betrayal, the hero looks for another alternative. Ras and Rinehart, the two powerful figures who dominate the rest of the book, represent other means of existence. The narrator's introduction to Ras is worth looking at closely since Ras represents a complete departure from the other characters in the book. He is definitely visible (perhaps the only completely visible person in the book) in the most dangerous fashion imaginable. Tod Clifton acknowledges after his street brawl with Ras: "But it's on the inside that Ras is strong. On the inside he's dangerous." The narrator misreads Clifton's comment as he believes the inside that Tod is talking about to be the inside of the Brotherhood. Tod's tragic end itself, though, is a testimony to the truth of Ras's philosophy. The narrator, helpless, looks on as Tod,

months later, goes nuts, peddling Sambo dolls on Times
Square, and is finally gunned down by the police. "I don't
know," Tod had said, "I suppose sometimes a man has to
plunge outside history . . . otherwise he might kill somebody,
go nuts." And Ras is nuts to those who do not understand his
logic, his existence, his visibility. The narrator obviously does
not understand that the militant Ras is an alternative to his
present existence, as can be seen in their encounter during
the riots.

Rinehart, however, is an alternative to our nameless
hero—Rinehart, numbers runner, preacher, lover, conman,
whose invisibility gives him the potential to live more than
one life at the same time —who indulges in the infinite possibilities of life. Rinehart is an urban Brer Rabbit; he yesses
everybody. This multiple personality knows that the people
around him recognize him only by his outer trappings, that
the people are blind and that he can take advantage of their
blindness. Rinehart is a boldface liar, but he has flair and is
effective precisely because he knows that he does not really
exist. The hero's one night transformation into Rinehart brings
him to the realization that "the people who define him are
blind, bat blind, hearing only the echoes of their own voices.
And because they were blind, they would destroy themselves
and he would help them." In a Rinehart fashion, the hero sees
that "it was a joke, an absurd joke." Once the narrator's
mind accepts the absurdity of his world, he is able to see
himself as he really is:

And now I looked around a corner in my mind and saw Jack and
Norton and Emerson merge into one single white figure. They were
very much the same, each attempting to force his picture of reality
upon me and neither giving a hoot in hell for how things looked to
me. I was simply a material, a natural resource to be used. I had
switched from the arrogant absurdity of Norton and Emerson to
that of Jack and the Brotherhood, and it all came out the same—
except that now I recognize my invisibility.

Now that he knows he is invisible, what should he do? Well,
he could be a Rinehart, "he could overcome them with yesses,
undermine them with grins, he could agree them to death and
destruction."

But it is too late to become Brer Rabbit. The truth will out and it bursts out violently in the riots, a scene which is packed full of the swift American idiom that Ellison delights in. Rinehartism eventually is bound to fail for the acrobatics that one has to perform to keep it up tries the nerves. As the hero says at the beginning of the book:

You often doubt if you really exist. You wonder whether you aren't simply a phantom in other people's minds. Shy, a figure in a nightmare which the sleeper tries with all his strength to destroy. It's when when you feel like this that out of resentment, you begin to bump people back. And let me confess, you feel that way most of the time. You ache with the need to convince yourself that you do exist in the real world, that you're a part of all the sound and anguish, and you strike out with your fists, you curse and you swear to make them recognize you. And alas, it's seldom successful.

Alas it is seldom successful. The hero, buried alive in his hole at the end of the riots, is most painfully aware of that fact. The horror of that realization calls up the maddening, powerful, and tortuous dream that keeps him in this hole. Accosted by the grotesque figures of Jack, Norton, Bledsoe, and the rest, tortured by their question: "How does it feel to be free of illusions?", the crushed invisible man can only scream with intense ferocity, "Painful and empty, painful and empty." What is an invisible man but a man who doesn't exist?

If Ellison's novel had ended with that dream, it would fall into the well-known category of the absurd along with the French existentialists of the '40's and the American playwrights of today. But that mind won't leave the hero be. He has progressed from being blind to being invisible. He has traveled a long way. Nonetheless he must deal with invisibility as a concept which is still an unknown quality to him, a concept that eludes even his imagination, far less his rational mind.

The epilogue reasserts his need to make his past rational. By reliving his experience he sees that many false ideas have been cleared away. Still, he is left with his will to transcend invisibility. Pushed by his instinct for survival, the narrator stumbles into the efficacy of diversity, the inevitability of necessity. "Life," he says, "is to be lived not controlled and humanity is won by continuing to play in the face of certain defeat.'' A worthy and noble ideal but not very convincing. As the invisible man prepares (perhaps) to leave his hole, he gives us a more credible reason for doing so. Could it be that we're all invisible men? That white men could blind themselves to their own invisibility, but black men could not? And he settles on this point with a howl, a sense of triumph as well as a sense of terror,

> *Who knows that on the lower frequencies*
> *I speak for you.*

Robert A. Bone

༾ེ

from "The Contemporary Negro Novel"□

*I*nvisible Man, which won the National Book Award as the best American novel of 1952, provides a fitting note on which to conclude the present chapter. Ellison is a writer of the first magnitude—one of those original talents who has created a personal idiom to convey his personal vision. It is an idiom compounded of fantasy, distortion, and burlesque, highly imaginative and generally surrealistic in effect. It possesses at bottom a certain mythic quality, to which Ellison alludes in his acceptance speech. He was striving, he recounts, for a prose medium "with all the bright magic of the fairy tale."

Though not in the narrow sense a political novel, *Invisible Man* is based on a cultivated political understanding of the modern world. The first half of the novel portrays the disillusionment of the protagonist with the shibboleths of American capitalism—a social system which he apprehends through the institutional structure of the Southern Negro college. The latter half treats of his disillusionment with Stalinism, which he encounters through a revolutionary organization known as the Brotherhood. By means of this carefully controlled parallel development, Ellison penetrates to the heart of the two great illusions of his time.

John Aldridge once remarked that "the quality and in-

□ Robert A. Bone, *The Negro Novel in America*. Revised Edition (New Haven: Yale University Press, 1965), pp. 196–212. Copyright © 1958, 1965 by Yale University Press. Reprinted by permission.

tensity of a literary work will depend upon the success with which the writer can find and communicate his private truth in the public truth of his age." Ellison's private truth is that his color threatens constantly to deprive him of individuality; the public truth to which this corresponds is that all men have been deprived of individuality in the machine age. Invisibility is Ellison's symbol for this loss of self. *Invisible Man*, then, is a stubborn affirmation of the worth and dignity of the individual in the face of forces which conspire to render him invisible. The novel is dedicated in spirit to the suffering, mangled, helpless, plucked victim of Authority, whose only defense against power is his own humanity.

Although the author denies that *Invisible Man* is auto-biographical, it is clear that in main outline, if not in detail, the novel is rooted in personal experience. Ralph Ellison (1914-) was born in Oklahoma City and educated in its public schools. With the help of a scholarship from the State of Oklahoma, he attended Tuskegee Institute as a music major from 1933 to 1936. Leaving for New York with the aim of becoming a composer, he struck up a friendship with Richard Wright and was soon drawn into the orbit of the Federal Writers' Project and the Communist party. He worked with Wright on *New Challenge*, and then branched out in the *New Masses* with stories, articles, and reviews. In the mid-forties, and more recently, he published in *Horizon, Tomorrow, Common Ground*, the *Reporter*, the *Saturday Review*, etc. His fugitive pieces have recently been collected in *Shadow and Act* (New York, Random House, 1964).

Ellison's early apprenticeship was dominated by Richard Wright, and the stories of this period yield to none in bitterness and stridency. Violent, brutal, and full of mutilation fantasies which reveal an intense fear of a hostile environment, they anticipate much of the emotional content but little of the overmastering form of *Invisible Man*. Ellison's break with the Wright School is all the more interesting because of this background, and not least of all because it illustrates so strikingly the historic shift described in the last Chapter. For in this instance the revolt against protest was extended to include a revolt against the naturalistic novel as such.

In accepting the National Book Award, Ellison states his reasons for avoiding the "hard-boiled" Hemingway idiom.[1] There is first the problem of understatement, which "depends, after all, upon commonly held assumptions, and my minority status rendered all such assumptions questionable." Then there is the problem of the clipped, monosyllabic prose: "I found that, when compared to the rich babble of idiomatic expression around me, a language full of imagery and gesture and rhetorical canniness, it was embarrassingly austere." Finally, he feels compelled to reject "the rather rigid concepts of reality" which inform these works in favor of a more fluid, more mysterious, more uncertain conception: "Thus to see America with an awareness of its rich diversity and its almost magical fluidity and freedom, I was forced to conceive of a novel unburdened by the narrow naturalism which has led after so many triumphs to the final and unrelieved despair which marks so much of our current fiction."

In repudiating naturalism, Ellison turns to the broad tradition established by Joyce, Kafka, and Faulkner. Like them, he finds the shattered forms of postimpressionism most effective in portraying the chaos of the modern world. But Ellison apprehends this chaos through a particular cultural screen. It is precisely his vision of the possibilities of Negro life that has burst the bonds of the naturalistic novel. His style, like that of any good writer, flows from his view of reality, but this in turn flows from his experience as a Negro. His unique experience, Ellison insists, requires unique literary forms, and these he tries to provide from the raw material of Negro culture. It is a major contribution to the evolution of the Negro novel.

What stylistic resources can a folk culture offer the creative writer? To begin with, there is the rhetorical skill of the American Negro, whose verbal expression, under slavery, was necessarily oral. The revival meeting, the funeral sermon, the graduation address, the political speech are used to good account in *Invisible Man*. Then there are the sonorous biblical phrases which season the dialogue, along with the spicier ingredients of jive. To freshen up a jaded diction, a whole new vocabulary is available—terms evocative of the numbers racket, of voodoo charms, of racing sheets, of spiritualist cure-alls, of the jazz world, the boxing ring, the ball park, the bar-room—in a word, of Harlem.

One of the nuances of Negro speech exploited by Ellison is the sheer delight in verbal play, in pure *sound*, which might be experienced by a child—or a transplanted people—in learning a new language. This is more readily sampled than described: "Then came the squad of drum majorettes . . . who pranced and twirled and just plain girled in the enthu-siastic interest of Brotherhood." Closer to its folk origin is this bit of dialogue: "I'll verse you but I won't curse you—My name is Peter Wheatstraw, I'm the Devil's only son-in-law, so roll 'em! You a southern boy ain't you?" Intellectualized once more: a college professor, lecturing on Joyce, remarks, "Stephen's problem, like ours, was not actually one of creating the uncreated conscience of his race, but of creating the uncreated features of his face."

In their spoken idiom a people may unwittingly betray their innermost thoughts and feelings. The things that they laugh at are equally revealing of their deepest values, and Ellison's treatment of in-group humor is masterful. He dis-plays a true comic genius, ranging from his sly description of a belligerent colored bartender ("He sliced the white heads off a couple of beers with an ivory paddle") to the raucous comedy of the riot scene (in which one looter asks indignantly, "With all them hats in there and I'm going to come out with anything but a *Dobbs*?"). With his heritage of laughter-to-keep-from-crying, Ellison balances adroitly on the thin line which divides comedy from tragedy, and this double vision, this ability to perceive events as at once poignant and faintly ridiculous, introduces a subtle emotional tension into the novel. The solvent for this tension is a pervasive irony, through which the author achieves a satisfactory distance from his experience.

Jazz and the blues form an important part of Ellison's consciousness (he has played jazz trumpet since high school) and consequently of his style. The tone of the novel, for example, is established in the prologue by Louis Armstrong's not-so-innocent question,

> What did I do
> To be so black
> And blue?

The blue note is sustained by occasional snatches of blues lyrics, and by such passages as this: "I strode along, hearing the cartman's song become a lonesome, broad-toned whistle now that flowered at the end of each phrase into a tremulous, blue-toned chord. And in its flutter and swoop I heard the sound of a railroad train highballing it, lonely across the lonely night" (p. 135).

Jazz forms have also influenced what might be called the composition of the novel. Something is always going on in the background of Ellison's prose—something not quite heard at first, but nevertheless insistent, which produces a feeling of depth and resonance when finally perceived. The circling, diving, plummeting pigeons which hover in the background during the shooting of Tod Clifton will serve to illustrate the point. It is a passage thoroughly characteristic of Ellison's technique: he writes a "melody" (thematic line) and then orchestrates it.

Not to overstate the case for a distinctive Negro style, some general literary influences should be acknowledged. At farthest remove is Flaubert, to whom can be traced a tightness of style in which no detail is superfluous, no word or phrase without its place in the design. In sifting through his American tradition for evidence of a usable past, Ellison discovered our classical novelists of the 19th century, and especially Melville and Twain. In them, he notes, he found a greater sense of responsibility for the future of democracy than among his own contemporaries. But above all, he found a sense of the unknown and mysterious frontiers of American life which corresponded to his experience as a Negro. "In their imaginative economy," he writes, "the Negro symbolized both the man lowest down and the mysterious, underground aspect of human personality."

Closer at hand is his debt to Faulkner and Eliot. To the extent that Ellison's style is directly imitative, it is Faulknerian. The lengthy sentences, the rapid flow of consciousness conveyed by a string of participles, the series of abstract

nouns joined together by an overworked conjunction—these
are familiar trademarks. From Faulkner, too, comes a sense
of the grotesque, the monstrous, the outrageous in Southern
life. The incest scene in *Invisible Man*, for example, is unimaginable without the precedent of Popeye. On the whole, it
is more the symbolist of *The Sound and the Fury* than the
local colorist of *The Hamlet* to whom Ellison pays the supreme
compliment, but both elements are present in his style to a
degree.

There are direct echoes of Eliot, too, in *Invisible Man*,
and one of the epigraphs (the other is from Melville's *Benito
Cereno*) is from *Family Reunion*. But Ellison's real debt stems
from Eliot's insistence upon the importance of tradition. It
was this reassurance from a major contemporary that forti-
fied him in his determination to anchor his fiction firmly in his
Negro heritage. It was Eliot who taught him to value a past
which was both painful and precious and, flinching neither
from slavery nor incest nor prostitution nor chaos itself, to
assimilate even his negative heritage, conquering it, transforming it into an asset, a weapon.

But if one were to pinpoint the influence of a particular
literary work on this novel, it would be Dostoevsky's *Notes
from Underground*. This book, as a matter of fact, stirred the
imaginations of both Ellison and Wright, inspiring not only
Invisible Man but a powerful short story of Wright's called
"The Man Who Lived Underground."[2] The story preceded the
final publication of the novel by several years, and without a
doubt Ellison was familiar with it. It would be a mistake, however, to conclude that the germinal idea of the novel was
borrowed from Wright. The debt still goes back to Dostoevsky,
even though Richard Wright may well hold a first mortgage
on the property. In any event, Ellison succeeds in developing
on a full scale themes which Wright treats only sketchily.

It is not very difficult to understand why Wright and
Ellison were fascinated by this extraordinary book. Dostoevsky's protagonist is a man of morbid sensitivity, prone to
resentment and offense and consumed with self-hatred. Convinced that he excites aversion, his constant fate is humiliation and his constant study is revenge. Yet on this score he

feels quite helpless: "The mouse distrusts alike its right to wreak vengeance and the ultimate success of its scheme, since it knows in advance that its poor attempts at retribution will bring upon its own head a hundred times more suffering than will fall to the lot of the person against whom the vengeance is aimed."[3] Against the historical backdrop of 19th-century Russia, Dostoevsky is describing a socially patterned neurosis which has an obvious parallel in the psychic life of the American Negro.

But beyond this matter of insult and revenge, there are vaster themes in *Notes from Underground* which commanded Ellison's attention. In exploring the lower depths of human personality, Dostoevsky poses questions about the nature of reality, the meaning of social responsibility, and the limits of human possibility, all of which are pursued with lively interest in *Invisible Man*. Both authors, moreover, share a central concern with individuality, with that which enables man to insist upon himself in the face of all rational systems. Dostoevsky's attack upon science, his profound antirationalism, is likewise shared by Ellison, though it rests on Freudian rather than Christian premises.

Given these common philosophical concerns, some borrowing of literary forms was perhaps inevitable. The basic image of the novel—withdrawal from humanity into an underground den—is a case in point. So, too, is its basic strategy: the presentation of an abstract spiritual state (invisibility), followed by a flashback (the main body of the novel) which provides the concrete experience from which the psychic state evolved. The two protagonists, moreover, have much in common: both are anonymous victims (*non*heroes), and both address the reader in the first person with a certain ironic familiarity. Both are dealers in paradox and ambiguity, and both have known a shame so intense that in recalling it their venom turns to jest.

Neither the underworld of Dostoevsky nor that of Ellison is a pleasant place. Both authors are invading those cavernous recesses of human consciousness which the civilized world has preferred to ignore. Yet below in those murky depths, unknown or unacknowledged by respectable society, they discover the healing power of love and of human fraternity. That Ellison undertakes this descent to the particular underworld of his time and circumstances is sufficient testimony to his creative powers. Whatever his debt to Dostoevsky, no one who reads *Invisible Man* will challenge his claim to originality.

The prologue of the novel finds the protagonist ensconced below ground in the basement of a building rented strictly to whites, in a section "shut off and forgotten during the nineteenth century." Here he lives in the glare of 1369 light bulbs, whose current is supplied from a tapped line of Monopolated Light and Power. Light, he explains, gives form to his invisibility, and this is quintessential to a man whose fellows refuse to see him as he really is. And so he remains for the present in a state of contemplative hibernation, summoning from the past events which have led to his invisibility.

The first of these is an episode from his adolescence, about the time of his graduation from high school. He is invited by the superintendent of schools to address a white businessmen's smoker, but once there he is forced to participate in an obscene ritual symbolic of the Negro's status in American society. A group of colored boys are confronted with a naked blonde and threatened equally if they look and if they avert their eyes. This scene, which expresses in sexual terms the basic ambivalence of Negro life, is followed by a battle royal in which the boys are thrust blindfolded into a boxing ring and forced to fight one another (rather than, symbolically, their real enemy). Then they are compelled to retrieve their prize money from an electrified rug. All of the prizes of white society (money, women) are thus held out to them, only to be denied.

In spite of this degradation, and swallowing his own blood, the boy, who thinks of himself as a potential Booker T. Washington, delivers his prepared address. As a reward he receives a scholarship to a Negro college, along with a gleaming new calfskin briefcase. In a dream which closes this nightmarish episode, the boy imagines that he opens the briefcase and finds an inscription which reads, "To Whom it May Concern: Keep this Nigger-Boy Running."

The next few chapters concern an incident which occurs in his junior year and results in his expulsion from college. Assigned as a driver to one of the visiting white trustees, he commits the unpardonable sin of taking him away from the "whitewashed" campus into the back country. Through the figure of Mr. Norton, the trustee, Ellison traces "the unseen lines that run from North to South," converging on the Southern Negro college. He is a banker, a Bostonian, a bearer of the white man's burden, who feels that the destiny of the Negro people is somehow bound up with his own. Viewed historically, he is emblematic of those enlightened Northern capitalists who, looking ahead to the industrialization of the South, joined with the Southern gentry and the conservative Negro leaders in founding such centers of technical training as Tuskegee Institute.

What Mr. Norton (Northern) discovers back in the quarters is chaos, in the form of a colored sharecropper who has had incestuous relations with his daughter. Trueblood (*pur sang*) is the full-blooded, half-assimilated African in whom historic circumstances of the past three centuries have neither encouraged nor indeed permitted the civilized amenities to develop. His story, which is rendered with an altogether convincing combination of humor, delicacy, and horror, is a narrative tour de force. The crucial point is that, far from becoming a pariah, Trueblood is treated by his white neighbors as something of a local celebrity. They lavish upon his infamy material benefits which they have always denied to his industry. Norton, moreover, whose Oedipal attachment to his own daughter has been subtly touched upon, acknowledges his kinship with chaos by a gift of a hundred dollars.

Severely shaken, Mr. Norton requests a stimulant, and the youth reluctantly drives him to the nearest source of supply—a colored roadhouse called the Golden Day. Unfortunately, it is the day when the inmates of a nearby veterans' hospital pay their weekly visit to the local prostitutes. Once more Mr. Norton encounters chaos.

The theme of this episode is repression: the hospital attendant Supercargo (Superego) is responsible for maintaining order, and *double* order with white folks present. But Supercargo is symbolically drunk upstairs, and "when he was upstairs they had absolutely no inhibitions." A wild brawl ensues, with the attendant the main target of its fury. He represents the internalization of white values (order as against chaos), and it is no accident that the hapless veterans whom he supervises have been doctors, lawyers, and teachers in civilian life. They are emblematic of the repressed Negro middle class; their spokesman is a former surgeon who was dragged from his home and beaten with whips for saving a human life. It is thus (Trueblood-in-reverse) that the white South rewards genuine accomplishment.

In the light—or perhaps one should say the darkness—of Trueblood and the Golden Day, the irony of the Southern Negro college, the irony of its very existence, is revealed. Its function is not to educate but to indoctrinate with a myth. This is why the vet calls Norton "a trustee of consciousness," "a lyncher of souls." Yet Ellison presents the myth in all its splendor in the Chapel address of the Reverend Homer Barbee, not wishing to minimize the power of the system to provide dreams. It is "the black rite of Horatio Alger" which is enacted from the podium, and its slogan is "We are a humble, but a fast-rising people." To the hope which the speaker holds out to the race, if only they will adopt the white man's success formula, the protagonist responds with a desperate conviction, for the alternative of bitterness, of revenge, of racial conflict seems hopelessly destructive. It is only toward the end of this magnificent speech that he realizes that Homer Barbee is blind.

In taking Norton behind the scenes, the protagonist has betrayed the myth, and the president of the college swiftly administers discipline. Dr. Bledsoe is a harsh but essentially accurate portrait of the Southern Negro educator—a pragmatist who holds his own in a ruthless power struggle by hard and cynical methods. He possesses power without dignity, though the trappings of dignity are in ample evidence. It is the only kind of power available to the black man in the Deep South. Bledsoe suspends the youth but endorses his proposal that he seek employment in the North, in hopes of being reinstated in the fall. As a gesture of reconciliation he furnishes the youth with letters of introduction to several wealthy patrons of the school.

The youth leaves for New York, his success ideology still intact, and he makes the rounds with his impressive-looking letters. But somehow the formula doesn't work, and he receives only evasive answers from his prospective employers. At last he learns the truth from a disillusioned younger son who finds himself incapable of his wealthy father's cynicism. The contents of the Bledsoe letters are revealed, and the youth discovers that he has been not suspended but expelled. The letters contain instructions, in effect, to "keep this nigger-boy running."

Two densely symbolic chapters follow, which conclude Ellison's portrait of the status quo. The first of these embraces the experience of the protagonist with modern industry, as he hires out as an unskilled laborer to Liberty Paint. It is a large concern which thrives on government contracts; its trademark is a screaming eagle, and its slogan "Keep America Pure with Liberty Paints." The youth is put to work on a batch of paint which is headed for a national monument, and his task is a puzzling one. He is asked to measure ten drops of dead black liquid into each bucket of "Optic White," and stir until the black becomes invisible. It is a famous national formula, of which the company is justly proud: "That's paint that'll cover just about anything!" his foreman remarks. Unfortunately, the youth takes his refill from the wrong tank and dopes the paint with concentrated remover. By rendering visible that which is black (compare the Norton episode), he unwittingly sabotages the national whitewash.

On another level, this chapter recapitulates the Negro's historic experience in American industry. The youth is hired in the first place so that the company will not have to pay regular union wages. He goes to work for a "slave driver" named Kimbro, who introduces him to the regimentation and fundamental irresponsibility of factory life. Shortly he is sent to the basement to work for a colored foreman named Lucius Brockway, who represents the skilled stratum of Negro labor which has been entrenched in American industry from the beginning—the black base on which our industrial pyramid is reared. Brockway has made himself indispensable, for it is he who mixes the base of the paint, and yet he lives in constant dread of being replaced by skilled whites. For this reason he is an Uncle Tom, a loyal worker who is fanatically anti-union.

The bewildered protagonist is caught in a crossfire between Brockway and the union, for each party suspects him of harboring sympathies for the enemy. His first act of rebellion against the system occurs in this context, and significantly he strikes out at the Negro underling. In the course of a quarrel with Brockway they forget to check their pressure gauges. An explosion occurs (not to be taken too literally), and the youth finds himself in the factory hospital, a part of his personality blasted away.

The hospital scene is primarily symbolic of the protagonist's rebirth; it is a transitional chapter which prepares us for his new life in the Brotherhood. At the same time, the machine age begins to emerge as his true antagonist. Only half conscious, he is strapped into a strange machine and subjected to a painful shock therapy, whose purpose is "to produce the results of a prefrontal lobotomy without the negative effects of the knife." The atmosphere of antiseptic efficiency, of coldness and impersonality, of helplessness and passivity which one associates with a modern hospital is brilliantly evoked as a symbol of contemporary life. The diction, which is abstract and scientific throughout, contributes powerfully to this effect. The identity theme is sounded as he is asked to think of his name, and of his mother. When he fails to remember, thus relinquishing all claims to individuality, he is pronounced cured. The machine is opened, the electric cord to the stomach node is cut, and he is born again.

Part II of *Invisible Man* is at bottom a projection of the author's involvement with the Communist party. Ellison, more than most writers who have felt the party's branding iron, has survived the experience and mastered it artistically. And yet this section of the novel tends to slip back into the naturalistic mode, as if the author's imagination were stumbling over the rugged terrain of his political past. On the other hand, Ellison's satirical portrait of a movement not famous for its humor is as trenchant as it is amusing. In a more serious vein, he succeeds in drawing a pointed parallel between the protagonist's new life and his former existence as a victim of capitalist society. To their victims, after all, the two power systems look remarkably alike. This perception gives the novel a better balance and a sharper cutting edge than most of the current fiction of political disillusionment.

The protagonist's personal fate in the Brotherhood is representative of a whole generation of Negro intellectuals. Deeply wounded by society, he becomes aware of "a painful, contradictory, inner voice" which calls insistently for revenge. After leading a spontaneous demonstration against a sidewalk eviction, he is recruited by the Brotherhood and thereby catapulted into history. In the Brotherhood he finds a new identity, a new outlet for his ambition, and a new myth. He is initiated into the mysteries of the dialectic by Brother Jack, and assigned to agitational work in Harlem. Just as a mass movement begins to develop, the "line" shifts in emphasis from local to international issues, and the Harlem organization is left stranded. The protagonist now faces a dilemma well known to the captives of Stalinist ideology: to remain historically relevant, he must betray the Negro masses; to retain his integrity, he must break with the Brotherhood and consign himself to political limbo.

In the end he rejects the Brotherhood more on philosophical than racial or political grounds. Brother Jack's glass eye (he is half blind) cannot penetrate the dark waters of Harlem. His peculiar brand of unreality ignores the unpredictable element at the core of our humanity which transcends politics and science and history and is at once more fundamental and mysterious than these. In an organization which is proud of its willingness to sacrifice the individual on the altar of history, the protagonist remains as invisible as ever. His loss of individuality is felt most keenly when his sense of responsibility collides with the iron discipline of the Brotherhood. Eventually he realizes that behind the façade of party discipline Brother Jack has been "running" him no less cynically than Norton or Bledsoe. It is then that he takes to the cellar, in order to renew his sense of self.

His sense of self has in fact been threatened all along, by the ambiguous position of the Negro in the Communist movement. On the one hand, he is constantly reminded of his Negro heritage and encouraged to embrace it; on the other, he is warned against the dangers of black chauvinism and offered all the inducements of universal brotherhood. This conflict between assimilationism and Negro nationalism is not new to the protagonist: he has passed through a phase of "white" (bourgeois) assimilationism in which he regards the renunciation of pork chops and grits as some sort of moral victory. But this particular form of self-effacement is discarded early in Part II, together with the success formula which inspired it. Confronted by a steaming tray of baked yams, he surrenders to its pleasures with a new sense of freedom and self-acceptance.

The Brotherhood, however, upsets his equilibrium with an irresistible hope: "For the first time . . . I could glimpse the possibility of being more than a member of a race." He now enters a period of "red" (revolutionary) assimilationism, in which his racial ties are subtly weakened through identification with a broader cause. This phase is symbolized by his abandonment of Mary, his landlady-mother, and his acceptance of new "living quarters" provided by the Brotherhood. But he cannot shed his old skin so easily. The grinning statuette which he tries unsuccessfully to discard and the leg chain presented to him by Brother Tarp are symbolic links to his racial past.

The inner doubts and reservations of the colored Brothers are strikingly projected in the magnificent figure of Ras the Destroyer. Ras (race) is a black nationalist, a West Indian agitator modeled upon Marcus Garvey, who would ban the sale of chicken breasts in Harlem if he could. In an attempt to drive the Brotherhood out of Harlem, he engages the protagonist and his chief lieutenant, Tod Clifton, in a savage street fight. Winning the upper hand over Clifton, Ras is unable to kill him because they are blood brothers: "We sons of Mama Africa, you done forgot?" Pleading the case for Negro nationalism with great eloquence, he accuses them of selling out for white women and a good job (the fight takes place beneath a sign which reads "Checks Cashed Here"). Ras' strength lies in the fact that he is not far from the mark in his appraisal of the white race, and not least of the Brotherhood. It is his all-important margin of error, his black vengeance and unrelenting hatred, which makes him a Destroyer.

Tod Clifton now comes to the fore as Ellison's symbol of a tragically divided personality. When, as Ras predicted, the Brotherhood betrays the Negro struggle, Clifton cracks under the strain and takes "the plunge outside of history." The protagonist discovers him on a downtown sidewalk, peddling an obscene, self-mocking image called "Sambo the the Dancing Doll." This spiritual death (*Tod*) is quickly objectified when Clifton is brutally shot down by a policeman while resisting arrest for a minor misdemeanor. Stunned by the murder, the protagonist stumbles into a subway station, where he notices two nuns, one colored and the other white. The rhyme which spins through his dazed consciousness expresses his final attitude toward even the most sincere of his white allies:

> Bread and Wine
> Bread and Wine
>   Your cross ain't nearly so
> Heavy as mine.

Like Clifton, the protagonist is threatened by destruction from his own nationalist impulses; but in running from them, he discovers invisibility. Pursued one evening by Ras' thugs, he slips into a drugstore and, improvising a hasty disguise, buys a pair of dark glasses and a wide-brimmed hat. The disguise is an unqualified success; everyone takes him for a certain Mr. Rinehart, and he decides to play along as the instances of mistaken identity proliferate. Hipsters and zoot-suiters greet him; an old woman inquires about today's number; a cop tries to shake him down; a married woman makes a date and slips money into his pocket. Obviously Rinehart is a man of parts, but this is only the beginning. On the other side of town, the protagonist picks up a handbill which invites him to the store-front church of "Rev. B. P.

Rinehart, Spiritual Technologist." Sensing that he is on the brink of a great discovery, he asks excitedly, "Could he be all of them: Rine the runner and Rine the gambler and Rine the briber and Rine the lover and Rinehart the Reverend?" As he pursues the implications of his discovery, the metaphysical depths of the novel are sounded.

The dark glasses provide a point of departure for his speculations. Through their murky green, the world appears as a merging fluidity of forms. "What on earth was hiding behind the face of things?" he wonders. How can one distinguish the outer from the inner, the rind from the heart? Rinehart's multiple personality seems to suggest an answer: "His world was possibility and he knew it. He was years ahead of me and I was a fool. I must have been crazy and blind. The world in which we lived was without boundaries. A vast, seething, hot world of fluidity, [where] Rine the rascal was at home" (p. 376). This fluid conception of reality, the protagonist now perceives, is far more accurate than the rigid categories of the Brotherhood. Here, he reflects, is the crux of his quarrel with the Communists. In a fluid universe nothing is impossible; freedom is the recognition not only of necessity but of possibility.

The final chapter of *Invisible Man* is a freely distorted version of the Harlem riot of August 1943. Against a surrealistic background of looting and shooting, the major conflicts of the novel are resolved. Rinehartism, to begin with, is discarded for a less manipulative form of invisibility. For a time the protagonist has toyed with the idea of sabotaging the Brotherhood from within, but during the riot, when he discovers the full extent of their perfidy, he abandons any attempt to beat power at its own game. Authentically enough, he withdraws not merely from Stalinist politics but from politics as such. His retreat from politics, however, is somewhat mitigated by the episode of the tenement fire. When a well-organized group of tenants deliberately burns down the filthy tenement in which they have lived and suffered, his faith in the masses, if not their self-appointed leaders, is restored.

Meanwhile Ras appears astride a great black horse, dressed in the costume of an Abyssianian warrior, complete with shield and spear. He is out to spear him a white cop, as one of the bystanders observes, and to convert the riot into a race war. In a symbolic encounter the protagonist effectively silences his inner Ras, but in fleeing the scene he meets a gang of white hoodlums armed with baseball bats. Running for his life, he plunges through an open manhole into a coal cellar, where he can at last enjoy the safety of invisibility. He falls asleep and dreams of being surrounded by his enemies—all those who in one way or another have run his life. When he announces grimly that he is through running, they reply collectively, "Not quite." They advance upon him with a knife, and at last they leave him in command of his own destiny—castrated, but free of illusion.

In the end, Ellison succeeds brilliantly in rendering blackness visible. By far the best novel yet written by an American Negro, *Invisible Man* is quite possibly the best American novel since World War II. In any event, Ellison has set a high standard for contemporary Negro fiction. There was a period in the history of the Negro novel when a simple literacy was to be marveled at. Now, a century after Brown's *Clotel*, historical relativity is no longer a valid attitude. With the appearance of such novels as *Cane, Native Son*, and *Invisible Man*, the reading public has a right to expect no less than the best from the serious Negro artist.

Notes

1   All quotations are from *Crisis*, *60* (1953), pp. 157–58.
2   *Cross Section*, ed. Edwin Seaver (New York, 1944), pp. 58–102.
3   *Notes from Underground* (Everyman Edition, New York, Dutton, 1953), p. 15.

XV

Go Tell It On The Mountain (1953) by James Baldwin

James Baldwin

"Autobiographical Notes"

I was born in Harlem thirty-one years ago. I began plotting novels at about the time I learned to read. The story of my childhood is the usual bleak fantasy, and we can dismiss it with the restrained observation that I certainly would not consider living it again. In those days my mother was given to the exasperating and mysterious habit of having babies. As they were born, I took them over with one hand and held a book with the other. The children probably suffered, though they have since been kind enough to deny it, and in this way I read *Uncle Tom's Cabin* and *A Tale of Two Cities* over and over and over again; in this way, in fact, I read just about everything I could get my hands on—except the Bible, probably because it was the only book I was encouraged to read. I must also confess that I wrote—a great deal—and my first professional triumph, in any case, the first effort of mine to be seen in print, occurred at the age of twelve or thereabouts, when a short story I had written about the Spanish revolution won some sort of prize in an extremely short-lived church newspaper. I remember the story was censored by the lady editor, though I don't remember why, and I was outraged.

□ Reprinted from *Notes of a Native Son* by James Baldwin, "Autobiographical Notes" (pp. 3–9). Reprinted by permission of the Beacon Press, copyright © 1955 by James Baldwin.
□ All excerpts from *Go Tell It On The Mountain*, by James Baldwin in this section reprinted with permission of the publisher, The Dial Press.

Also wrote plays, and songs, for one of which I received a letter of congratulations from Mayor La Guardia, and poetry about which the less said, the better. My mother was delighted by all these goings-on, but my father wasn't; he wanted me to be a preacher. When I was fourteen I became a preacher, and when I was seventeen I stopped. Very shortly thereafter I left home. For God knows how long I struggled with the world of commerce and industry—I guess they would say they struggled with *me*—and when I was about twenty-one I had enough done of a novel to get a Saxton Fellowship. When I was twenty-two the fellowship was over, the novel turned out to be unsalable, and I started waiting on tables in a Village restaurant and writing book reviews—mostly, as it turned out, about the Negro problem, concerning which the color of my skin made me automatically an expert. Did another book, in company with photographer Theodore Pelatowski, about the store-front churches in Harlem. This book met exactly the same fate as my first—fellowship, but no sale. (It was a Rosenwald Fellowship.) By the time I was twenty-four I had decided to stop reviewing books about the Negro problem—which, by this time, was only slightly less horrible in print than it was in life—and I packed my bags and went to France, where I finished, God knows how, *Go Tell It on the Mountain.*

Any writer, I suppose, feels that the world into which he was born is nothing less than a conspiracy against the cultivation of his talent—which attitude certainly has a great deal to support it. On the other hand, it is only because the world looks on his talent with such a frightening indifference that the artist is compelled to make his talent important. So that any writer, looking back over even so short a span of time as I am here forced to assess, finds that the things which hurt him and the things which helped him cannot be divorced from each other; he could be helped in a certain way only because he was hurt in a certain way; and his help is simply to be enabled to move from one conundrum to the next—one is tempted to say that he moves from one disaster to the next. When one begins looking for influences one finds them by the score. I haven't thought much about my own, not enough anyway; I hazard that the King James Bible, the rhetoric of the store-front church, something ironic and violent and perpetually understated in Negro speech—and something of Dickens' love for bravura—have something to do with me today; but I wouldn't stake my life on it. Likewise, innumerable people have helped me in many ways; but finally, I suppose, the most difficult (and most rewarding) thing in my life has been the fact that I was born a Negro and was forced, therefore, to effect some kind of truce with this reality. (Truce, by the way, is the best one can hope for.)

One of the difficulties about being a Negro writer (and this is not special pleading, since I don't mean to suggest that he has it worse than anybody else) is that the Negro problem is written about so widely. The bookshelves groan under the weight of information, and everyone therefore considers himself informed. And this information, furthermore, operates usually (generally, popularly) to reinforce traditional attitudes. Of traditional attitudes there are only two—For or Against—and I, personally, find it difficult to say which attitude has caused me the most pain. I am speaking as a writer; from a social point of view I am perfectly aware that the change from ill-will to good-will, however motivated, however imperfect, however expressed, is better than no change at all.

But it is part of the business of the writer—as I see it —to examine attitudes, to go beneath the surface, to tap the source. From this point of view the Negro problem is nearly inaccessible. It is not only written about so widely; it is written about so badly. It is quite possible to say that the price a Negro pays for becoming articulate is to find himself, at length, with nothing to be articulate about. ("You taught me language," says Caliban to Prospero, "and my profit on't is I know how to curse.") Consider: the tremendous social activity that this problem generates imposes on whites and Negroes alike the necessity of looking forward, of working to bring about a better day. This is fine, it keeps the waters troubled; it is all, indeed, that has made possible the Negro's progress. Nevertheless, social affairs are not generally speaking the writer's prime concern, whether they ought to be or not; it is absolutely necessary that he establish between himself and these affairs a distance which will allow, at least, for clarity, so that before he can look forward in any meaningful sense, he must first be allowed to take a long look back. In the context of the Negro problem neither whites nor blacks, for excellent reasons of their own, have the faintest desire to look back; but I think that the past is all that makes the present coherent, and further, that the past will remain horrible for exactly as long as we refuse to assess it honestly.

I know, in any case, that the most crucial time in my own development came when I was forced to recognize that I was a kind of bastard of the West; when I followed the line of my past I did not find myself in Europe but in Africa. And this meant that in some subtle way, in a really profound way, I brought to Shakespeare, Bach, Rembrandt, to the stones of Paris, to the cathedral at Chartres, and to the Empire State Building, a special attitude. These were not really my creations, they did not contain my history; I might search in them in vain forever for any reflection of myself. I was an interloper; this was not my heritage. At the same time I had no other heritage which I could possibly hope to use—I had certainly been unfitted for the jungle or the tribe. I would have to appropriate these white centuries, I would have to make them mine—I would have to accept my special attitude, my special place in this scheme—otherwise I would have no place in *any* scheme. What was the most difficult was the fact that I was forced to admit something I had always hidden from myself, which the American Negro has had to hide from himself as the price of his public progress; that I hated and feared white people. This did not mean that I loved black people; on the contrary, I despised them, possibly because they failed to produce Rembrandt. In effect, I hated and feared the world. And this meant, not only that I thus gave the world an altogether murderous power over me, but also that in such a self-destroying limbo I could never hope to write.

One writes out of one thing only—one's own experience. Everything depends on how relentlessly one forces from this experience the last drop, sweet or bitter, it can possibly give. This is the only real concern of the artist, to recreate out of the disorder of life that order which is art. The difficulty then, for me, of being a Negro writer was the fact that I was, in effect, prohibited from examining my own experience too closely by the tremendous demands and the very real dangers of my social situation.

I don't think the dilemma outlined above is uncommon. I do think, since writers work in the disastrously explicit medium of language, that it goes a little way towards explaining why, out of the enormous resources of Negro speech and life, and despite the example of Negro music, prose written by Negroes has been generally speaking so pallid and so harsh. I have not written about being a Negro at such length because I expect that to be my only subject, but only because it was the gate I had to unlock before I could hope to write about anything else. I don't think that the Negro problem in America can be even discussed coherently without bearing in mind its context; its context being the history, traditions, customs, the moral assumptions and preoccupations of the country; in short, the general social fabric. Appearances to the contrary, no one in America escapes its effects and everyone in America bears some responsibility for it. I believe this the more firmly because it is the overwhelming tendency to speak of this problem as though it were a thing apart. But in the work of Faulkner, in the general attitude and certain specific passages in Robert Penn Warren, and, most significantly, in the advent of Ralph Ellison, one sees the beginnings—at least—of a more genuinely penetrating search. Mr. Ellison, by the way, is the first Negro novelist I have ever read to utilize in language, and brilliantly, some of the ambiguity and irony of Negro life.

About my interests: I don't know if I have any, unless the morbid desire to own a sixteen-millimeter camera and make experimental movies can be so classified. Otherwise, I love to eat and drink—it's my melancholy conviction that I've scarcely ever had enough to eat (this is because it's *impossible* to eat enough if you're worried about the next meal)—and I love to argue with people who do not disagree with me too profoundly, and I love to laugh. I do *not* like bohemia, or bohemians, I do not like people whose principal aim is pleasure, and I do not like people who are *earnest* about anything. I don't like people who like me because I'm a Negro; neither do I like people who find in the same accident grounds for contempt. I love America more than any other country in the world, and, exactly for this reason, I insist on the right to criticize her perpetually. I think all theories are suspect, that the finest principles may have to be modified, or may even be pulverized by the demands of life, and that one must find, therefore, one's own moral center and move through the world hoping that this center will guide one aright. I consider that I have many responsibilities, but none greater than this: to last, as Hemingway says, and get my work done.

I want to be an honest man and a good writer.

Howard M. Harper, Jr.

from "James Baldwin— Art or Propaganda"□

Baldwin's first novel, *Go Tell It on the Mountain* (1953), is a powerful account of the bleak physical environment and the lacerating emotional tensions of Negroes in the Harlem ghetto. It is focused upon the religious experience of a fourteen-year-old boy, John Grimes, whose life resembles Baldwin's in many details, as readers of *The Fire Next Time* will recognize. But the name John Grimes suggests that his story is intended to have a much broader social relevance.

The novel is very carefully constructed; it even has a Table of Contents. Epigraphs are used extensively to heighten the meaning of the sections. Part One, "The Seventh Day," is an account of the day in March, 1935, which is John's fourteenth birthday. The day culminates in the Saturday night service (which extends into the seventh day) at the Temple of the Fire Baptized, a storefront church. Part Two, "The Prayers of the Saints," enters the minds and memories of the three adult members of the Grimes family who attend the service: Florence, John's aunt; Gabriel, his stepfather; and Elizabeth, John's mother. Part Three, "The Threshing Floor," is the story of the religious experience which overwhelms John with its intensity.

The novel quickly documents the shabbiness and de-

□ Reprinted from *Desperate Faith* (1967) by Howard M. Harper, by permission of the publisher, the University of North Carolina Press.

spair of life in the ghetto. More appalling than the physical
details, however, are the psychological and spiritual dimensions of the prison. Gabriel is a bitter and sadistic religious
zealot. His favorite text, "Set thine house in order," is ironic;
he refuses to see or understand the frustrations and feelings of
his family. His son Roy, though younger than John, is already
driven by hatred, and on this Saturday is knifed in a gang fight
in a white neighborhood. When Gabriel's wife tries to tell him
what is happening to Roy, he slaps her, and he beats Roy
viciously when Roy tries to protect her. Gabriel feels that his
position as deacon of the Temple invests him with infallibility
and absolute power, and he regards the nonelect not with
Christian love, but with thinly veiled contempt. He has told
John that his face bears the mark of the devil, and John is
vulnerable enough to believe him.

But the book reveals evidences of love too, especially in
the relationship between John and his mother. Her favorite
Biblical text, amazingly optimistic in view of what Part Two
reveals about her past, is in direct contrast to Gabriel's:
"Everything works together for them that love the Lord." For
John, his mother represents "patience . . . endurance . . .
long suffering." She reminds us, in fact, of Faulkner's Dilsey.
Her love is all that keeps the family together.

The isolation of the people of the ghetto, simply a given
fact in Part One, is made more explicit in the stories of Part
Two. Florence and Elizabeth had worked as cleaning women
in Wall Street, and Gabriel had worked in a menial position
for a white family in the Deep South; but the two races are
almost unaware of each other's existence in any real, human
sense. This is made most evident in Elizabeth's story. Her
lover Richard, a sensitive and proud young Negro, had been
picked up for a crime he did not commit, and had been
savagely beaten by the police. Identified by a white man who
later said that all Negroes look alike, Richard had despaired
of living in a world where color is a standard of value, and had
committed suicide, not knowing that Elizabeth was pregnant
with the child who would be John.

The names Elizabeth and Gabriel suggest that this John
is to be identified with John the Baptist. As Isaiah had prophe-

sied, John had appeared in the wilderness to proclaim the coming of Christ and to preach "a baptism of repentance for the forgiveness of sins" (Mark 1:4). The Negro spiritual "Go Tell It on the Mountain" reinforces this identification. The epigraph to Part One suggests a further association with the John in Revelation, who had seen the Holy City in an apocalyptic vision, and who comforted the early Christians who were suffering persecution.

Much of the power of *Go Tell It on the Mountain* comes from the integrity of Baldwin's attitude toward his material. Although the book is a savage indictment of the white world, which has radically limited the lives and hopes of Negroes, the implications of the novel go far beyond that. It is also a searching examination of the meaning of the Negroes' own attitudes. In *The Fire Next Time* Baldwin says that "the principles governing the rites and customs of the churches in which I grew up . . . were Blindness, Loneliness, and Terror. . . ." The imprisoned Negroes sublimate their anger and their sense of injustice in the hysterical rites of the Temple of the Fire Baptized. And ironically, they are seeking a God they do not really believe in, an illusion which becomes finally, in *Another Country* and in *Blues for Mister Charlie*, an even more horrifying reality—a white God.

The consequences of illusory belief are shown most fully in Gabriel. Like his namesake who visited Elizabeth and Mary in the Bible, he is a messenger. But inside Baldwin's Gabriel the message of hope is translated into despair. Unable to see the truth in himself, he cannot see it in others, and this failure has crippled him. His darkest secret is his failure to acknowledge Royal, his illegitimate son, whose death was at least an indirect result of that failure. Although he had felt the "holy fire" leave him, he has continued to preach, and his whole life is now a lie. His fanatical belief is an elaborate rationalization, an evasion of his responsibilities as a human being.

In John we see the process beginning all over again. The force which causes him to fall to the threshing floor of judgment is not God, but an obscure sense of sexual guilt.[1] And there are other causes, less immediate, but equally powerful. Unable to please his father, who hates him as the living evidence of Elizabeth's sin, John is unconsciously trying, through his religious experience, to win the approval he needs and to exorcise the hatred and resentment he feels. He also has a need for revelation—about himself and about his race—and a need for purpose. The reconciliation with the stepfather never comes about; Gabriel's hatred is implacable. And though John assumes an identity through his religious experience, it is to some extent a false identity; no longer John Grimes, he is now just another "saint."

Walking home from the church, John feels that "the avenue, like any landscape that has endured a storm, lay changed under Heaven, exhausted and clean, and new." The experience has had a cleansing effect, similar to the one which Baldwin's later protagonists feel in the physical experience of love. But as John reaches home, "he felt the March wind rise, striking through his damp clothes, against his salty body. He turned to face his father—he found himself smiling, but his father did not smile." The wind, symbolic throughout Baldwin's work of fatal inevitability, suggests what the father's response makes more explicit: that John's experience, dramatic and inevitable as it has been, has not really changed anything. In the Temple he symbolically joins his people, but his mission of revelation will involve the later rejection of their religion of despair.

Go Tell It on the Mountain is a remarkable first novel, and a considerable achievement by any standards. The most successful parts of the book are those dealing with John himself, where the prose, like Joyce's in *A Portrait of the Artist*, is a subtle reflection of the protagonist's awareness. Baldwin very skillfully re-creates his adolescent consciousness, and shows the events through that consciousness rather than from the perspective of maturity. The view of the Temple of the Fire Baptized and its saints, for example, is not the view of *The Fire Next Time*, in which the escapism of that religion is denounced. Instead, Baldwin provides the raw materials from which the later denunciation grew, but along with it, he reveals the awe and innocence and idealism which motivate the boy's acceptance of the illusions of the Temple.

And through the creation of this very subtle double vision Baldwin achieves powerful dramatic irony.

Part Two, which constitutes slightly over half of the book, lacks the subtlety of John's story, but serves to give it broader and deeper significance. The stories of Florence, Gabriel, and Elizabeth help to explain the racial heritage which John must both accept and reject; they make the experience on the threshing floor inevitable. In the emphasis upon Richard, however, the novel slips out of focus, as several critics have noted. Because Richard is not given enough motivation or credibility, his story becomes something of a tract, and its length disturbs the balance of emphasis in the novel. Part Two as a whole is far too long in relation to the others, so much so that John's story, with its subtlety, economy, and powerful sense of felt experience, is in danger of being lost in this panorama of Negro history.

But Part Three, with its magnificent prose and powerful evocation of the mysteries of religious experience, brings Baldwin through. In the calm of the final paragraphs he has brought the reader through, also, like John Grimes, to a feeling for which *catharsis* seems to be the only right word. Part Three, by returning the story to the deeply felt experience of John, makes it clear that the importance of the story transcends the argument of Part Two. *Go Tell It on the Mountain* becomes once again something more than a tract: a record and a revelation of universal human experience.

Notes

1 Marcus Klein, *After Alienation: American Novels in Mid-Century* (Cleveland: World, 1964), points out that the object of John's sexuality is his mother and that this is the reason that John turns first to masturbation and then to homosexuality, which is hinted at in the relationship with Elisha but specified in a short story called "The Outing" in which John Grimes appears. John's relationship in "The Outing," however, is with David Jackson rather than with Brother Elisha, who also appears in the story.

Robert A. Bone

from "James Baldwin"

The best of Baldwin's novels is *Go Tell It on the Mountain* (1953), and his best is very good indeed. It ranks with Jean Toomer's *Cane*, Richard Wright's *Native Son*, and Ralph Ellison's *Invisible Man* as a major contribution to American fiction. For this novel cuts through the walls of the storefront church to the essence of Negro experience in America. This is Baldwin's earliest world, his bright and morning star, and it glows with metaphorical intensity. Its emotions are his emotions; its language, his native tongue. The result is a prose of unusual power and authority. One senses in Baldwin's first novel a confidence, control, and mastery of style that he has not attained again in the novel form.

The central event of *Go Tell It on the Mountain* is the religious conversion of an adolescent boy. In a long autobiographical essay, which forms a part of *The Fire Next Time*,[1] Baldwin leaves no doubt that he was writing of his own experience. During the summer of his fourteenth year, he tells us, he succumbed to the spiritual seduction of a woman evangelist. On the night of his conversion, he suddenly found himself lying on the floor before the altar. He describes his trancelike state, the singing and clapping of the saints, and the all-night prayer vigil which helped to bring him "through." He then recalls the circumstances of his life that

☐ Robert A. Bone, *The Negro Novel in America*. Revised Edition (New Haven: Yale University Press, 1965), pp. 218–225. Copyright © 1958, 1965 by Yale University Press. Reprinted by permission.

prompted so pagan and desperate a journey to the throne of Grace.

The overwhelming fact of Baldwin's childhood was his victimization by the white power structure. At first he experienced white power only indirectly, as refracted through the brutality and degradation of the Harlem ghetto. The world beyond the ghetto seemed remote, and scarcely could be linked in a child's imagination to the harrowing conditions of his daily life. And yet a vague terror, transmitted through his parents to the ghetto child, attested to the power of the white world. Meanwhile, in the forefront of his consciousness was a set of fears by no means vague.

To a young boy growing up in the Harlem ghetto, damnation was a clear and present danger: "For the wages of sin were visible everywhere, in every wine-stained and urine-splashed hallway, in every clanging ambulance bell, in every scar on the faces of the pimps and their whores, in every helpless, newborn baby being brought into this danger, in every knife and pistol fight on the Avenue."[2] To such a boy, the store-front church offered a refuge and a sanctuary from the terrors of the street. God and safety became synonymous, and the church, a part of his survival strategy.

Fear, then, was the principal motive of Baldwin's conversion: "I became, during my fourteenth year, for the first time in my life afraid—afraid of the evil within me and afraid of the evil without."[3] As the twin pressures of sex and race began to mount, the adolescent boy struck a desperate bargain with God. In exchange for sanctuary, he surrendered his sexuality, and abandoned any aspirations that might bring him into conflict with white power. He was safe, but walled off from the world; saved, but isolated from experience. This, to Baldwin, is the historical betrayal of the Negro Church. In exchange for the power of the Word, the Negro trades away the personal power of his sex and the social power of his people.

Life on these terms was unacceptable to Baldwin; he did not care to settle for less than his potential as a man. If his deepest longings were thwarted in the church, he would pursue them through his art. Sexual and racial freedom thus became his constant theme. And yet, even in breaking with the church, he pays tribute to its power: "In spite of everything, there was in the life I fled a zest and a joy and a capacity for facing and surviving disaster that are very moving and very rare."[4] We shall confront, then, in *Go Tell It on the Mountain*, a certain complexity of tone. Baldwin maintains an ironic distance from his material, even as he portrays the spiritual force and emotional appeal of store-front Christianity.

So much for the biographical foundations of the novel. The present action commences on the morning of John Grimes' fourteenth birthday, and before the night is out, he is born again in Christ. Part I, "The Seventh Day," introduces us to the boy and his family, his fears and aspirations, and the Temple of the Fire Baptized that is the centre of his life. Part II, "The Prayers of the Saints," contains a series of flashbacks in which we share the inmost thoughts and private histories of his Aunt Florence, his mother Elizabeth, and his putative father, Gabriel. Part III, "The Threshing-Floor," returns us to the present and completes the story of the boy's conversion.

Parts I and III are set in Harlem in the spring of 1935. The action of Part II, however, takes place for the most part down home. Florence, Elizabeth, and Gabriel belong to a transitional generation, born roughly between 1875 and 1900. *Go Tell It on the Mountain* is thus a novel of the Great Migration. It traces the process of secularization that occurred when the Negro left the land for the Northern ghettos. This theme, to be sure, is handled ironically. Baldwin's protagonist "gets religion," but he is too young, too frightened, and too innocent to grasp the implications of his choice.

It is through the lives of the adults that we achieve perspective on the boy's conversion. His Aunt Florence has been brought to the evening prayer meeting by her fear of death. She is dying of cancer, and in her extremity humbles herself before God, asking forgiveness of her sins. These have consisted of a driving ambition and a ruthless hardening of heart. Early in her adult life, she left her dying mother to come North, in hopes of bettering her lot. Later, she drove from her side a husband whom she loved: "It had not been her fault that Frank was the way he was, determined to live and die a common nigger'' (p. 92).[5] All her deeper feelings have been sacrificed to a futile striving for ''whiteness'' and respectability. Now she contemplates the wages of her virtue: an agonizing death in a lonely furnished room.

Elizabeth, as she conceives her life, has experienced both the fall and the redemption. Through Richard, she has brought an illegitimate child into the world, but through Gabriel, her error is retrieved. She fell in love with Richard during the last summer of her childhood, and followed him North to Harlem. There they took jobs as chambermaid and elevator boy, hoping to be married soon. Richard is sensitive intelligent, and determined to educate himself. Late one evening, however, he is arrested and accused of armed robbery. When he protests his innocence, he is beaten savagely by the police. Ultimately he is released, but half hysterical with rage and shame, he commits suicide. Under the impact of this blow, Elizabeth retreats from life. Her subsequent marriage to Gabriel represents safety, timidity, and atonement for her sin.

As Gabriel prays on the night of John's conversion his thoughts revert to the events of his twenty-first year: his own conversion and beginning ministry, his joyless marriage to Deborah, and his brief affair with Esther. Deborah had been raped by white men at the age of sixteen. Thin, ugly, sexless, she is treated by the Negroes as a kind of holy fool. Gabriel, who had been a wild and reckless youth, marries her precisely to mortify the flesh. But he cannot master his desire. He commits adultery with Esther, and, informed that she is pregnant, refuses all emotional support. Esther dies in childbirth, and her son, Royal, who grows to manhood unacknowledged by his father, is killed in a Chicago dive.

Soon after the death of Royal, Deborah dies childless, and Gabriel is left without an heir. When he moves North, however, the Lord sends him a sign in the form of an unwed mother and her fatherless child. He marries Elizabeth and promises to raise Johnny as his own son. In the course of time the second Royal is born, and Gabriel rejoices in the fulfillment of God's promise. But John's half brother, the fruit of the

prophet's seed, has turned his back on God. Tonight he lies at
home with a knife wound, inflicted in a street fight with some
whites. To Gabriel, therefore, John's conversion is a bitter
irony: "Only the son of the bondwoman stood where the
rightful heir should stand" (p. 128).

Through this allusion, Baldwin alerts us to the metaphorical possibilities of his plot. Gabriel's phrase is from
Genesis 21: 9-10, "And Sarah saw the son of Hagar the
Egyptian, which she had born unto Abraham, mocking.
Wherefore she said unto Abraham, Cast out this bondwoman
and her son: for the son of the bondwoman shall not be heir
with my son, even with Isaac." Hagar's bastard son is of
course Ishmael, the archetypal outcast. Apparently Baldwin
wants us to view Gabriel and Johnny in metaphorical relation
to Abraham and Ishmael. This tableau of guilty father and
rejected son will serve him as an emblem of race relations in
America.

Baldwin sees the Negro quite literally as the bastard
child of American civilization. In Gabriel's double involvement with bastardy we have a re-enactment of the white man's
historic crime. In Johnny, the innocent victim of Gabriel's
hatred, we have an archetypal image of the Negro child.
Obliquely, by means of an extended metaphor, Baldwin
approaches the very essence of Negro experience. That
essence is rejection, and its most destructive consequence is
shame. But God, the Heavenly Father, does not reject the
Negro utterly. He casts down only to raise up. This is the
psychic drama that occurs beneath the surface of John's
conversion.

The Negro child, rejected by the whites for reasons that
he cannot understand, is afflicted by an overwhelming sense of
shame. Something mysterious, he feels, must be wrong with
him, that he should be so cruelly ostracized. In time he comes
to associate these feelings with the color of his skin—the basis,
after all, of his rejection. He feels, and is made to feel, perpetually dirty and unclean:

John hated sweeping this carpet, for dust arose, clogging his nose
and sticking to his sweaty skin, and he felt that should he sweep it
forever, the clouds of dust would not diminish, the rug would not be

clean. It became in his imagination his impossible, lifelong task, his hard trial, like that of a man he had read about somewhere, whose curse it was to push a boulder up a steep hill.   [p. 27]

This quality of Negro life, unending struggle with one's own blackness, is symbolized by Baldwin in the family name, Grimes. One can readily understand how such a sense of personal shame might have been inflamed by contact with the Christian tradition and transformed into an obsession with original sin. Gabriel's sermons take off from such texts as "I am a man of unclean lips," or "He which is filthy, let him be filthy still." The Negro's religious ritual, as Baldwin points out in an early essay, is permeated with color symbolism: "Wash me, cried the slave to his Maker, and I shall be whiter, whiter than snow! For black is the color of evil; only the robes of the saved are white."[6]

Given this attack on the core of the self, how can the Negro respond? If he accepts the white man's equation of blackness with evil, he is lost. Hating his true self, he will undertake the construction of a counter-self along the line that everything "black" he now disowns. To such a man, Christ is a kind of spiritual bleaching cream. Only if the Negro challenges the white man's moral categories can he hope to survive on honorable terms. This involves the sentiment that everything "black" he now embraces, however painfully, as his. There is, in short, the path of self-hatred and the path of self-acceptance. Both are available to Johnny within the framework of the Church, but he is deterred from one by the negative example of his father.

Consider Gabriel. The substance of his life is moral evasion. A preacher of the gospel and secretly the father of an illegitimate child, he cannot face the evil in himself. In order to preserve his image as the Lord's anointed, he has sacrificed the lives of those around him. His principal victim is Johnny, who is not his natural child. In disowning the bastard, he disowns the "blackness" in himself. Gabriel's psychological mechanisms are, so to say, white. Throughout his work Baldwin has described the scapegoat mechanism that is fundamental to the white man's sense of self. To the question, Who am I? the white man answers: I am *white*, that is immaculate, without stain. I am the purified, the saved, the saintly, the elect. It is the *black* who is the embodiment of evil. Let him, the son of the bondwoman, pay the price of my sins.

From self-hatred flows not only self-righteousness but self-glorification as well. From the time of his conversion Gabriel has been living in a world of compensatory fantasy. He sees the Negro race as a chosen people and himself as prophet and founder of a royal line. But if Old Testament materials can be appropriated to buttress such a fantasy world, they also offer a powerful means of grappling with reality. When the Negro preacher compares the lot of his people to that of the children of Israel, he provides his flock with a series of meta-phors corresponding to their deepest experience. The Church thus offers to the Negro masses a ritual enactment of their daily pain. It is with this poetry of suffering, which Baldwin calls the power of the Word, that the final section of the novel is concerned.

The first fifteen pages of Part III contain some of Bald-win's most effective writing. As John Grimes lies before the altar, a series of visionary states passes through his soul. Dream fragments and Freudian sequences, lively fantasies and Aesopian allegories, combine to produce a generally surrealis-tic effect. Images of darkness and chaos, silence and empti-ness, mist and cold—cumulative patterns developed early in the novel—function now at maximum intensity. These images of damnation express the state of the soul when thrust into outer darkness by a rejecting, punishing, castrating father figure who is the surrogate of a hostile society. The dominant emotions are shame, despair, guilt, and fear.

At the depth of John's despair, a sound emerges to assuage his pain:

He had heard it all his life, but it was only now that his ears were opened to this sound that came from the darkness, that could only come from darkness, that yet bore such sure witness to the glory of the light. And now in his moaning, and so far from any help, he heard it in himself—it rose from his bleeding, his cracked-open heart. It was a sound of rage and weeping which filled the grave, rage and weeping from time set free, but bound now in eternity;

rage that had no language, weeping with no voice—which yet
spoke now, to John's startled soul, of boundless melancholy, of
the bitterest patience, and the longest night; of the deepest water,
the strongest chains, the most cruel lash; of humility most wretched
the dungeon most absolute, of love's bed defiled, and birth dis-
honored, and most bloody, unspeakable, sudden death. Yes, the
darkness hummed with murder: the body in the water, the body in
the fire, the body on the tree. John looked down the line of these
armies of darkness, army upon army, and his soul whispered,
Who are these? [p. 228]

This is the sound, though John Grimes doesn't know it,
of the blues. It is the sound of Bessie Smith, to which James
Baldwin listened as he wrote *Go Tell It to the Mountain*. It is
the sound of all Negro art and all Negro religion, for its flows
from the cracked-open heart.

On these harsh terms, Baldwin's protagonist discovers
his identity. He belongs to those armies of darkness and must
forever share their pain. To the question, Who am I? he can
now reply, I am he who suffers, and yet whose suffering on
occasion is "from time set free." And thereby he discovers his
humanity, for only man can ritualize his pain. We are now very
close to that plane of human experience where art and religion
intersect. What Baldwin wants us to feel is the emotional
pressure exerted on the Negro's cultural forms by his exposure
to white oppression. And finally to comprehend that these
forms alone, through their power of transforming suffering,
have enabled him to survive his terrible ordeal.

Notes

1 *The Fire Next Time* (New York, Dial Press, 1963), pp. 29–61.
2 *Ibid.*, p. 34.
3 *Ibid.*, p. 30.
4 *Ibid.*, p. 55.
5 All page references are to the Dial Press editions of the novels.
6 *Notes of a Native Son*, p. 21.

XVI

A The Assistant (1957) by Bernard Malamud

Ihab Hassan

ༀ

from *Radial Innocence* □

*T*he *Assistant*, presumably, is a love story, a domestic romance, a grocery store idyll of unwarranted poverty and harsh spiritual deprivation. It is a tale of loneliness, of life-long frustrations and delicate, budding hopes. It is a "human" story albeit deeply ironic. For irony is indeed the key to Malamud's attitude toward man, to his estimate of him. The irony is not "dry," not scathing; it is best described by Earl Rovit when he says, "The affectionate insult and the wry self-deprecation are parts of the same ironic vision which values one's self and mankind as both less and more than they seem to be worth, at one and the same time."[1] This is the ambivalence of vision which qualifies, sometimes even under-cuts, the affirmative power of Malamud's fiction.

The world revealed by *The Assistant* is, materially speaking, bleak; morally, it glows with a faint, constant light. Morris Bober and his wife, Ida, toil sixteen hours a day in a grocery store, barely eking out a living. They are well past middle age, and have given up their lives, their illusions, even the promise of a richer future which comes with education for their single daughter, Helen. The store, as we are told many times, is an open tomb. Twenty-one years are spent in it, and in the end Bober dies of double pneumonia, leaving his family

□ Reprinted from *Radical Innocence: Studies in the Contemporary American Novel*, Princeton University Press, 1961. All excerpts from *The Assistant* in this section have been reprinted with the permission of Farrar, Straus & Giroux, Inc. From *The Assistant* by Bernard Malamud, copyright © 1957 by Bernard Malamud.

penniless; he has to be buried in one of those huge anonymous
cemeteries in Queens. America! "He had hoped for much in
America and got little. And because of him Helen and Ida had
less. He had defrauded them, he and the blood-sucking store."[2]
This is what Bober thinks as one of two men who hold up his
store slugs him on the head, because he is a Jew, and Bober falls
to the ground without a cry. An appropriate ending to his weary,
profitless day. Others may have luck, like the affluent Karp
who owns a liquor store across the street, or the Earls whose
son, Nat, attends law school—and takes Helen's virginity.
But the Bobers live on stolidly, honestly, in squalor and
sickening destitution. They are, like the grocery "assistant,"
Frank Alpine, victims of circumstance. What, then, gives these
characters the measure of spiritual freedom they still possess?

The nature of the characters themselves holds the
answer. Morris Bober, to be sure, is another example of the
eiron, the humble man. He is more. He has endurance, the
power to accept suffering without yielding to the hebetude
which years of pain induce. He is acquainted with the tragic
qualities of life—"The world suffers. *He* felt every schmerz"—
and he defines the Jew as a suffering man with a good heart,
one who reconciles himself to agony, not because he wants to
be agonized, as Frank suggests, but for the sake of the Law—the
Hebraic ideal of virtue.[3] Yet this is only one source of Bober's
strength. His other source is charity, which in his case
becomes nearly quixotic. Bober, though close to starvation
himself, extends credit to his poor customers. He wakes up
every day before dawn so that he may sell a three-cent roll to a
Polish woman on her way to work. He takes in Frank Alpine,
feeds him, and gives him an opportunity to redeem himself,
though Frank begins by stealing the grocer's bread and milk.
Nor can he bring himself, in the extremity of despair, to burn
down his property in order to collect insurance. Inured to
failure, Bober still strives to give suffering the dignity of men
who may trust one another in their common woe. But Karp
calls him a "schlimozel."

The central action of the novel, however, develops from
Bober's relation to Frank Alpine, and from the latter's relation to Helen. Frank, as the title suggests, is probably the

hero of the book. He, too, is an *eiron*, a collector of injustices —with a difference. The regeneration of Frank—his literal and symbolic conversion to the Jewish faith—is the true theme of the book. His regeneration, at best, is a strange and mixed thing. When Frank first appears, he is a wanderer, an anti-Semite, even a thief. Yet one of his idols is St. Francis, and his hardened face conceals a hungry soul. "With me one wrong thing leads to another and it ends in a trap. I want the moon so all I get is cheese," he tells Bober.[4] The grocery store, which is Bober's grave, becomes a cave or haven for Alpine. It also becomes the dreary locus of his painful rebirth. Impelled by his gratitude to the grocer, and motivated by his guilt at having robbed him, with the aid of tough Ward Minogue, Frank puts all his energies into the store and ends by pumping some of his own obstinate life into the dying business. Meanwhile, he falls in love with Helen Bober.

From here on, ambiguities prevail. The racial prejudices of Frank are matched by those of Ida Bober, and to some extent, of her daughter Helen, against Gentiles. (The store improves, it is suggested, precisely because Frank is not a Jew.) Frank's gratitude to Morris does not prevent him from continuing to steal petty cash from the register— which he keeps account of and intends to return. Yet when Bober is incapacitated by sickness, Frank takes a night job, in addition to his grocery chores, and secretly puts his pay in the cash box. And his gnawing love for Helen, which she is slow to return, finally ends, ironically, with an act of near-rape as he rescues her from the clutches of Ward Minogue, only to force her himself, right there and then in the park, at the very moment in their relationship when she is at last ready to surrender herself freely to him. "Dog," she cries "—uncircumcised dog!"[5] Guilt, gratitude, love—perhaps even the hope of a life he could glimpse but never attain—combine to sustain Frank Alpine, Bober's strange, saintly, pilfering assistant, in his impossible struggle against poverty, against hopelessness itself.

He wanted her but the facts made a terrible construction. They were Jews and he was not. If he started going out with Helen her mother would throw a double fit and Morris another. And Helen made him feel, from the way she carried herself, even when she seemed most lonely, that she had plans for something big in her life—nobody like F. Alpine. He had nothing, a backbreaking past, had committed a crime against her old man, and in spite of his touchy conscience, was stealing from him too. How complicated could impossible get?

He saw only one way of squeezing through the stone knot; start by shoveling out the load he was carrying around in his mind. . . .

So the confession had to come first. . . . He felt he had known this, in some frightful way, a long time before he went into the store, before he had met Minogue, or even come east; that he had really known all his life he would sometime, through throat blistered with shame, his eyes in the dirt, have to tell some poor son of a bitch that he was the one who had hurt or betrayed him. This thought had lived in him with claws; or like a thirst he could never spit out, a repulsive need to get out of his system all that had happened—for whatever had happened had happened wrong; to clean it out of his self and bring in a little peace, a little order; to change the beginning, beginning with the past that always stupendously stank up the now—to change his life before the smell of it suffocated him.[6]

Purgation in humility, rebirth through love—this is Frank's inchoate purpose, the reason for his willing acceptance of a backbreaking burden others—Minogue, Karp—find easy to reject. Yet it is in consonance with the character of the novel that purgation and rebirth both should appear ironic, awkward, and inconclusive. Frank tells Bober about his complicity in the robbery only to discover that the latter already knows. Bober catches his assistant rifling his till just when Frank had resolved never to steal again. And Frank's attempt to make a clean breast of it all to Helen merely serves to confirm her revulsion. His dogged and desperate love expresses itself in the form of a physical outrage. The savior of the Bobers is, in a sense, their archenemy. (The symbolic inversion of this relation may be discovered in the burial scene in which Frank topples accidentally into Bober's open grave.) But enemies suffer too, according to their conscience. Frank Alpine, it seems, can only expend the last vestige of his money, energy, or hope in agonized silence, a prey to the ironies which rip and twist his purpose. In the end, the value of confession is to the soul that makes it. And even love is a kind of realized solitude. Like Frank, Helen goes her lonely way, carrying the broken dreams of the Bobers to some distant and uncompromising end.

It is obvious that if the world of *The Assistant* is not drained of values, it is nevertheless saturated with pain, flooded with contradictions. Its two major characters find their identity in humiliation, an extreme and quixotic sense of obligation. They are not tragic heroes but merely heroes of irony. They retreat before the ultimate tragic ordeal: the fullness of tragic awareness itself. This is a fact the form of the novel supports.

Time, we know, leaves the characters suspended in the void which their failures create; the hints of regeneration are barely audible. Morris Bober dies in bankruptcy; Helen continues at her dreary job, dreaming of a better life; Frank slaves at the store, trying to provide for the Bobers, send Helen to college, and win back her love. The fate of each remains less than what it could be in heroic tragedy, less even than what it usually amounts to in realistic fiction. Thus, for instance, does Helen evaluate the life of her father: "People liked him, but who can admire a man passing his life in such a store? He buried himself in it; he didn't have the imagination to know what he was missing. He made himself a victim. He could, with a little more courage, have been more than he was."[7] And thus does Frank reflect upon his incessant labors: " 'Jesus,' he said 'why am I killing myself so? He gave himself many unhappy answers, the best being that while he was doing this he was doing nothing worse.' "[8] Whatever awareness time brings to the characters, whatever qualified dignity it confers upon their failures, every act in the novel is whittled by irony, every motive is mixed with its opposite.

Because time cannot unravel the knotted relations of the characters—what could be more gnarled than the relation of Gentile to Jew, of savior, seducer, and thief to those upon whom he preys, those from whom he gains an identity—the point of view of *The Assistant* dissociates itself from the protagonists, veering toward one then the other in friendly detachment. The characters are simply there, and they criticize each other's behavior; the point of view encourages us to perceive how ludicrous pain can be, and how unhappy virtue. The subtle, incredible twists of the plot, the reversals and accidents which affect the fortunes of the Bobers, are finally envisioned in a moral as well as dramatic perspective which acknowledges no certainties except the fact of suffering. (It is appropriate that Morris Bober should be an unorthodox Jew, and that at his funeral the rabbi should say, "Yes, Morris Bober was to me a true Jew because he lived in the Jewish experience, and with the Jewish heart. . . . He suffered, he endured, but with hope.")[9]

Notes

1   Earl H. Rovit, "Bernard Malamud and the Jewish Literary Tradition," *Critique* (Winter-Spring, 1960), p. 5.
2   Bernard Malamud, *The Assistant* (New York, 1958), p. 25.
3   *Ibid.*, p. 10.
4   *Ibid.*, p. 32.
5   *Ibid.*, p. 133.
6   *Ibid.*, pp. 72f.
7   *Ibid.*, p. 181.
8   *Ibid.*, p. 189.
9   *Ibid.*, p. 180.

Jonathan Baumbach

from "All Men Are Jews: *The Assistant* by Bernard Malamud"□

The most Dostoevskian of Malamud's novels, *The Assistant*, is about an ambivalent saint, a man who in seeking expiation for a crime succeeds only in increasing and intensifying the burden of his guilt. The hero Frank Alpine is congenitally and circumstantially unable to translate his good intentions into moral acts. In the end, however, racked by anguish and suffering, he finds the occasion to redeem his sins, electing to live the saint's life of the old man he has sinned against. *The Assistant* has two central biographies: the life and death of Morris Bober, unwitting saint, and the guilt and retribution of Frank Alpine, saint-elect, the first life creating the pattern and possiblity of the second. At the end, as if by metamorphosis, the young Italian thief replaces the old Jewish storekeeper, the reborn son replacing the father.

Morris Bober, the luckless owner of an impoverished grocery store, is the center of the first half of the novel. That he is a Jew in a non-Jewish area, a commercial failure surrounded by success, an honorable man among thieves, indicates his inescapable isolation—his exemplary role. Early in the novel, in a passage which has a gnarled eloquence, Malamud defines the terms of Bober's existence:

The early November street was dark though night had ended, but

□ Jonathan Baumbach, *The Landscape of Nightmare: Studies in the Contemporary Novel* (New York University Press, © 1965), pp. 111–116, 117–121.

the wind, to the grocer's surprise, already clawed. It flung his
apron into his face as he bent for the two milk cases at the curb.
Morris Bober dragged the heavy boxes to the door, panting. A large
brown bag of hard rolls stood in the doorway along with the sour-
faced, grayed-haired Polisheh huddled there, who wanted one.

"What's the matter so late?"

"Ten after six," said the grocer.

"Is cold," she complained.

Turning the key in the lock he let her in. Usually he lugged
the milk and lit the gas radiators, but the Polish woman was impatient. Morris poured the bag of rolls into the wire basket on the
counter and found an unseeded one for her. Slicing it in halves, he
wrapped it in white store paper. She tucked the roll into her cord
market bag and left three pennies on the counter.[1]

It is autumn on the calendar but already winter in Bober's
world. The writing is empathic, evoking the unrelieved burden
of Morris' day-to-day existence. The old Polish woman is seen
as Morris sees her, "a sour-faced, gray-haired Polisheh." She
has no other identity because she has no other existence in the
novel except as one of Morris' private ghosts. The details of
his morning, performed every morning for all the waking-
suffering days of his life, are ritualistic—attrition enacted by
rote. To sell a three-cent roll, he must wake up and go out into
the cold an hour earlier than he would otherwise. Though he is
an old man and needs his rest more than the three pennies, he
feels constrained to serve the dour old Polisheh out of an uncompromising sense of the responsibilities of his office. That
he continues to serve her thanklessly despite her chronic dis-
content is a part of his burden, his anonymous decency in an
indecent and abusive world. Like the grocer in Malamud's
short story "The Bill," Morris, despite his practical resolves,
extends credit indiscriminately, even in cases where he
knows payment is unimaginable. If it is in his power to satisfy
them, he will not ignore the needs of another human being. It
is the least one man can do for another. He is, therefore, an
easy mark, a victim of his own undiscriminating kindness.
Like Roy Hobbs, he does not learn from the past; he continues
to believe human beings are better than their actions; he continues, in spite of all the evidence of his suffering, to extend

the grace of trust. Before the action of the novel begins, he has been thoroughly cheated by a man whom he has trusted as his partner; he has had his livelihood diminished by his "friend" Karp who rents a store across the way to a rival grocer. His victimization is not limited to man's inhumanity but is compounded by the fates; he is a predestined, inexorable sufferer. His daughter Helen, who is a sufferer in her own right, contrasts her father's low estate to that of his successful neighbor Karp:

The grocer, on the other hand, had never altered his fortune, unless degrees of poverty meant alteration, for luck and he were, if not natural enemies, not good friends. He labored long hours, was the soul of honesty—he could not escape his honesty, it was bedrock; to cheat would cause an explosion in him, yet he trusted cheaters— coveted nobody's nothing and always got poorer. The harder he worked—his toil was a form of devouring time—the less he seemed to have. He was Morris Bober and could be nobody more fortunate. With that name you had no sense of property, as if it were in your blood and history not to possess, or if by some miracle to own something, to do so on the verge of loss. At the end you were sixty and had less than at thirty. It was, she thought, surely a talent.
[p. 17]

Karp's luck, as if parasitic, seems to improve only when someones else's (usually Morris') gets worse. If Karp has a golden touch, Morris has a leaden one, the two like counter-weights on a universal balance. When two men come to hold up Karp's plush liquor store, they end up (as Morris' "talent" would have it) robbing and beating the impoverished grocer. Morris accepts even this unutterable indignity, as he has the long line of lesser ones preceding and anticipating it, with hopeless resignation and a sense of renewed guilt for his failure. As he sees the gun irrevocably descend, Morris

felt sick of himself, of soured expectations, endless frustration, the years gone up in smoke, he could not begin to count how many. He had hoped for much in America and got little. And because of him Helen and Ida had less. He had defrauded them, he and the blood-sucking store.

He fell without a cry. The end fitted the day. It was his luck, others had better.
[p. 25]

Morris, even on the verge of destruction, has faith in God's justice, accepts the responsibility for his lot. Though he continues to suffer until death brings him relief, after the robbery he is no longer the center of the novel's focus; he is replaced by Frank Alpine, one of the men who robbed his store. The old grocer's Jobean existence defined early in the novel provides an anticipatory parallel and exemplar to Frank's penitential suffering and final conversion to Judaism.

I suggested earlier the significance of the symbolic father-son conjunction between Morris and Frank—Jew and non-Jew. There are four pairs of fathers and sons dealt with in the novel, Detective Minogue and Ward, Julius Karp and Louis, Sam Pearl and Nat, Morris and Frank; in each the son inherits and fulfills the possibilities of the father. Detective Minogue's merciless rigidity, his inability to give love or pity, make his son Ward into a viciously degraded criminal. When Minogue discovers that Ward has broken into Karp's liquor store, the policeman hunts him down and beats him viciously, with the malic of his own failed responsibility. Ward dies some hours afterward, trapped in a fire from which he is too enfeebled to escape; his father's beating, in effect, is the cause of his death. Earlier in the novel, Minogue, nominally investigating the daily pilfering of a quart of milk and two rolls from the front of Morris' store, asks the grocer if he would recognize Ward if he saw him:

> "I don't know," said Morris. "Maybe yes or maybe no. I didn't see him for years."
> "If I ever meet up with him," said the detective, "I might bring him into you for identification."
> "What for?"
> "I don't know myself—just for possible identification."
> [p. 42]

The detective knows, if only by knowing his own impulses, that his son is the enemy, his enemy and consequently society's. Ward commits crimes—only in his father's area of authority—seeking punishment, the only recognition his father can give him. That the father has to have a stranger "identify" his son ironically suggests the extent of Minogue's spiritual blindness. The ironic parallels in the scene are extensive, Morris, whose own son has died, pities the detective for having the burden of a son he is unable to recognize. Yet Frank, whom Morris later in a sense adopts as a son, permitting him to work in the family grocery without pay, is the very thief the grocer has been hunting. When Frank disillusions Morris, the universally forgiving grocer is unable to forgive him. Morris has become too fond of Frank to risk further ill use at his hands. The failure of the boy to live up to Morris' ideal of him results in the final disillusionment of the old man; in him, as Malamud puts it in one of his short stories, "breaks what breaks." Blinded by the maze of deceit and ingratitude he has suffered all his life, Morris misjudges Frank, banishes him from the store for stealing when Frank, attempting to undo his wrong, has actually been putting his own money in the cash register. In a sense, Morris, like the detective, becomes unable to recognize his own son.

Frank Alpine, the gentile-Jew, the victimizer and victim, is, until the end of the novel, a mass of internal ambivalences. Despite his intense (actually religious) desire to do good, he is unable to resist the least admirable of his instincts. Out of acquiescence, he accompanies the degraded Ward Minogue when he robs "the Jew's" grocery store. Guilt-ridden for his complicity in Ward's vicious treatment of the grocer, he haunts the area of Morris' store, looking for an opportunity to redeem himself. He makes the occasion, insinuating himself as Morris' assistant without pay. Not only does he run the store for Morris while the injured grocer recuperates but he manages through a conspiracy of salesmanship and circumstance to increase the grocer's income. Disturbed by his own apparent selflessness (a loss of identity), Frank begins to steal small amounts from the grocer—negating one impulse by the other. He is not bad; it is only that he finds it prohibitively difficult to be as good as he would wish— a saint's good. This is the essential paradox of Frank's existence; he means to do good, yet he compulsively continues to do harm. Early in the novel, before we really know Frank, Malamud introduces us to his romantic admiration for St. Francis, whose pattern of life Frank unsuccessfully imitates. Over a cup of coffee, he passionately explains the saint's concerns to the indifferent candy store owner Sam Pearl.

"For instance, he gave everything away that he owned, every cent, all his clothes off his back. He enjoyed to be poor. He said poverty was a queen and he loved her like she was a beautiful woman."

Sam shook his head. "It ain't beautiful, kiddo. To be poor is dirty work."

. . . .

"Everytime I read about somebody like him I get a feeling inside of me I have to fight to keep from crying. He was born good, which is a talent if you have it."   [p. 28]

Like Saint Francis, Morris has a talent for goodness, and in the grocer's abiding gentleness of spirit Frank senses an essential likeness to his patron saint. Though Frank's devotion to Saint Francis as fable is wholehearted, he is ambivalent toward the same qualities in the here-and-now impoverished and suffering grocer: ("His pity leaks out of his pants, he thought, but he would get used to it.") Though repelled by Morris' indiscriminate compassion, Frank is attracted to the grocer's martyred existence. His motive for staying on to help the old man long after his debt of conscience has been repaid is to discover the mystery of Morris' virtue. He feels that the fact of Morris' Jewishness has something to do with the grocer's capacity for self-immolation.

. . . . . .

Frank's relationship to Morris is as significant to the development of the novel's theme as his unfulfilled love affair with Helen is to the development of its melodramatic action. Frank's attraction to Helen is an uneasy fusion of the sensual and the spiritual: at one moment he rages with lust for her; at another, he is filled with profound tenderness for her suffering. Yet even after he comes to know her, she remains unreal to him, a personification of the beauty of the world from which the conditions of existence have shut him off. Since he believes that this beauty is justifiably inaccessible to him, he compulsively destroys the relationship at the very moment its

realization becomes possible. While they are still strangers,
Frank's unrequited desire for Helen impels him to climb an
elevator shaft to spy on her in the bathroom, to make love to
her inaccessible nakedness with his desperate eyes. In a
powerful scene, an evocation worthy of Dostoevsky, Malamud
describes the self-induced torments of Frank's shame:

Holding his breath, he crouched motionless, clinging to the swaying ropes. Then the bathroom window was shut with a bang. For a
while he couldn't move, the strength gone out of him. He thought
he might lose his grip and fall, and he thought of her opening the
bathroom window and seeing him lying at the bottom of the shaft
in a broken, filthy heap.

It was a mistake to do it, he thought.

But she might be in the shower before he could get a look at
her, so, trembling, he began to pull himself up. In a few minutes he
was straddling the ledge, holding onto the ropes to steady himself
yet keep his full weight off the wood. . . .

He felt a throb of pain at her nakedness, an overwhelming
desire to love her, at the same time an awareness of loss, of never
having had what he wanted most, and other such memories he
didn't care to recall.

Her body was young, soft, lovely, the breasts like small
birds in flight, her ass like a flower. Yet it was a lonely body in spite
of its lovely form, lonelier. Bodies are lonely, he thought, but in
bed she wouldn't be. She seemed realer to him now than she had
been, revealed without clothes, personal, possible. He felt greedy
as he gazed, all eyes at a banquet, hungry so long as he must look.
But in looking he was forcing her out of reach, making her into a
thing only of his seeing, her eyes reflecting his sins, rotten past,
spoiled ideals, his passion poisoned by his shame.   [pp. 61–62]

This scene, in which Frank symbolically violates Helen,
anticipates his actual violation of her later in the novel. The
same self-destructive instinct that permits the first act compels the second. Frank peeps through the bathroom window,
not so much to gratify his lusts as to torture himself with the
impossibility of their fulfillment. It is at least partly an act of
debasement and self-punishment.

All of the sons in the novel, Nat Pearl, Louis Karp,
Ward Minogue, and Frank Alpine, court Helen's love in one

way or another. Helen, the least convincing of Malamud's characters, is both practical and idealistic, less ordinary than her surroundings though not extraordinary enough to surmount them. Her dream of bettering herself is an admixture of Bovarism, and genuine sensitivity. What she wants, as she puts it, is "the return of her possibilities," though she is only vaguely aware of what her possibilities include. While the unambitious liquor clerk Louis Karp is not good enough for her, she is more than willing to settle for the equally shallow Nat Pearl, an ambitious law student who has apparently risen above his surroundings. It is part of her tragedy that the real Nat is not the dream hero she has romantically envisioned. Insensitive to her, he devalues the gift of her love, taking it as his due, and irreparably wounds the giver. Despite the difference in their situations, Nat is the spiritual heir of his father, a good but materialistic man, whose livelihood comes from selling penny candy. That Helen's dream of a better life might be satisfied by marriage to Nat Pearl suggests the inadequacy of her aspirations. Whereas she loses the possibility of marrying Nat by yielding herself too readily, she loses the possibility of a real relationship with Frank by witholding herself too long. Inhibited by the pain of the first experience, she is unwilling to risk the second until her last nagging self-doubt is assuaged. When Helen is finally sure that she loves Frank, it has become, for a conspiracy of reasons, too late.

Melodramatic circumstances (fate as authorial prerogative) conspire against the ill-fated lovers. While Helen is waiting for Frank in the park to tell him that she loves him, Ward Minogue, also looking for Frank, appears in his place and attempts to rape her. When, after saving her from Ward, Frank forcibly makes love to her, she feels disgraced, as if Ward had actually consummated his attempt; in the merging of the acts, the two identities seem as one. Though circumstances contrive against them, Helen and Frank are in themselves responsible (fate as character) for the failure of their relationship. A Malamudian irony: Helen is able to love Frank only until he makes love to her; the fact debauches the illusion.

Having lost Helen through his lust, Frank, waking

from a guilt-ridden nightmare, has a revelation about himself:

> Frank got up to run but he had run everywhere. There was no place left to escape to. The room shrank. The bed was flying up at him. He felt trapped—sick, wanted to cry but couldn't. He planned to kill himself, at the same minute had a terrifying insight: that all the while he was acting like he wasn't, he was really a man of stern morality. [p. 139]

Like S. Levin, Frank discovers (in a comparable illumination) that he is a man of principle, but unlike Levin, he is at the same time a compulsive sinner. His own most merciless judge, Frank continually sets up occasions in which he can test his actual self against his ideal of himself. Guilty of imperfection (the presumption of the romantic hero), he debases himself as penance; he destroys his relationship with Helen and continues to steal gratuitously from the grocery store. Since he wants more than anything else to be a good man, his crimes are a means of self-punishment; each time he pockets money from Morris' register, he torments himself with guilt. Moreover, he increases his debt, psychologically and financially, to the grocer, which means he must punish himself still further to make requital. As penitent he must fall deeper and deeper into his interior hell before he can allow himself salvation. This is the pattern of his life and a central concern of the novel.

Malamud uses the changing of the seasons and the seasons themselves as physical symbols, providing his timeless and placeless New York landscape with a kind of metaphysical climate. The novel starts in early November and ends in mid-April, symbolically covering the Fall, the Death, and the Redemption of Man. The seasons mirror the inner condition of the central characters. Winter is the longest season in Malamud's bleak world. Throughout the almost endless winter, Frank, Morris, and Helen suffer their wounds in isolation, waiting for the spring as if it were some sort of relief-bringing god. The February day on which Helen decides to accept Frank's love is a warm, prematurely spring day which carries with it an illusory sense of flowering, of awakened love. She discovers, however, after her nightmarish experience in the park, that she has been victimized by her romantic illusions, that it is still winter, the season of death, the destroyer of love.

Morris too is destroyed by the conspiracy of a protracted winter and an illusory spring. Winter reasserts itself late in March with a heavy snowfall. Morris, refusing to acknowledge the winter cold ("tempting fate"), goes out to shovel snow without a coat. As a direct consequence ("every move he made seemed to turn into an inevitable thing"), he gets pneumonia and dies. Among the ravages of a protracted winter, Morris' death, like his life, goes unnoticed, soundless as the falling of the snow which covers the path he has sacrificed his life to clear. Yet spring ultimately does come, and with its coming Frank, almost triumphantly, renews Morris' existence.

At Morris' burial, Helen tosses a rose into the grave and Frank falls in after it, landing feet first on the coffin. It is an absurd accident, embarrassing the solemnity of the occasion; yet it is also a kind of spiritual communion between son and father. In entering the grave, Frank achieves final identification with Morris, which is the ultimate act of self-sacrifice. His rising from the grave as Morris is a symbolic resurrection; the season aptly enough is spring, shortly before Passover and Easter.

Ironically, Frank's rebirth leads him only to the assumption of Morris' living death in the tomb of the grocery store. In a hauntingly bitter passage, Ida and Helen console each other.

> " 'Your father is better off dead,' said Ida. As they toiled up the stairs they heard the dull cling of the register in the store and knew the grocer was the one who had danced on the grocer's coffin."   [p. 182]

Like Morris, Frank becomes wholly committed to the store, sacrificing his energies to support Ida and Helen. Totally committed, he even gets up an hour earlier, as Morris had, to sell the three-cent roll to the "Polisheh." In continuing Morris' life, Frank fulfills the possibilities of the grocer's actual son, the son who died while still a child. (Symbolically, the son becomes the father, continues his life by continuing his identity.) It is the least Frank can do for the man he has wronged, and the most. In suffering for Morris and, in Morris' role for all of us, Frank achieves his own redemption, becoming at last a wholly honest and good man. In Frank's purification through pain and suffering, Malamud unites the disparate concerns of mythic ritual and conventional realism. *The Assistant* ends on a transcendent note. As a consequence of Morris' death, Frank finds the occasion to fulfill his no longer self-conscious quest for sainthood.

Notes

1   Bernard Malamud, *The Assistant* (New York: New American Library, 1958), p 7. All quotations are from this edition.

Ruth B. Mandel

from "Ironic Affirmation"□

Malamud piles irony upon irony to achieve the tremendously oppressive and suffocating atmosphere of *The Assistant*. It is the disparity between the hopes, dreams, and aspiration of the characters in the novel and the horrible reality that is insisted upon over and over again as it denies the fulfillment of their dreams that produces the overwhelming pathos. This shocking and repeated juxtaposition of hope and reality is an essential part of the ironic technique in *The Assistant*.

There is another significant juxtaposition in many of *The Magic Barrel* stories and in *The Assistant* which explains part of the artistic achievement. This is found in the idiom in which the Yiddish characters think and in the dialogue; it refers to the antithesis between the *way* that characters like Morris and Ida Bober speak and *what* they say. Here Malamud treads a precarious line between humor and desperation in order, again, to produce overwhelming pathos. Taken out of context, the immigrants' distortion of the English language into Yiddish-American sometimes sounds comic. Remarks such as " 'A buyer will come next Purim,' " and " 'Also helps a little the new apartment house that it opened in December,' " if inserted into the script of a Molly Goldberg television program would provoke laughter. The mixture of

□ From Ruth B. Mandel, "Bernard Malamud's *The Assistant* and *A New Life:* Ironic Affirmation," *Critique: Studies in Modern Fiction*, VII (Winter, 1964–1965), pp. 114–117.

Yiddish and English, the distorted syntax, characteristic figures of speech, ellipsis, and the intonation of Yiddish-American tend to be comic. Yet in Bernard Malamud's work the breath is sucked out of the laugh. As it is used in *The Assistant*, this seemingly humorous language cannot be funny in the right sense of that word. The whole weight of the novel crushes laughter. It is unlaughable comedy about the funny little man who is not funny at all.

This is the artistic achievement—the grotesque mixture of high seriousness with what seems funny and yet is not. All of which heightens the pathos. During the most somber moments in *The Assistant* this technique is applied. Just before two thieves enter the grocery shop, Karp and Morris are referring to them as "holdupniks," a term which, because of the diminutive's effect, makes these public menaces seem like children playing cops and robbers. But of course they are not playing. And when Morris has exposed himself to the pneumonia which will kill him, he describes, in broken English, his need for a moment of freedom: " 'For twenty-two years stinks in my nose this store. I wanted to smell in my lungs some fresh air.' " There is pathos and desperation here—not humor.

The rabbi who delivers the eulogy at Morris' funeral is depicted as a semi-ludicrous figure in his manner of speaking. Again Malamud treads a fine line between the ludicrous and the serious, and again it results in a heightening of pathos. The rabbi makes a futile attempt to describe Morris, a man he never knew. That he never knew Morris is clear when we examine his speech, for in his remarks is an implicit denial of all the ironies Malamud has so devastatingly presented in *The Assistant*:

"Who runs in winter time without hat or coat, without rubbers to protect his feet, two blocks in the snow to give back five cents that a customer forgot? Couldn't he wait till she comes in tomorrow? Not Morris Bober. . . . This is why the grocer had so many friends who admired him. . . . He was also a very hard worker, a man that never stopped working. . . . And for this reason that he worked so hard and bitter, in his house, on his table, was always something to eat. So besides honest he was a good provider."[1]

THE ASSISTANT (1957)
BERNARD MALAMUD

Here the rabbi draws two conclusions about Morris Bober: because he was an honest man everyone admired him; and because he worked so hard, he was a good provider. Who admired Morris? Karp called him a *schlimozel* and betrayed him; Sobeloff embezzeled from him; his wife disapproved of everything he did; and the customers to whom he was kind left him and patronized the new supermarket. Was he a good provider? His store was almost bankrupt; he could not find a job when he visited the agencies; Helen had to get a job with a ladies undergarment manufacturer so that Morris could continue making payments on the house; and he could not provide for Helen what she wanted most—a college education. Obviously, then, the rabbi's conclusions are all wrong and Morris has been misrepresented. For the rabbi believes what we would all like to believe and what Malamud will not allow us to even hope in *The Assistant*: that honest, selfless men are rewarded with people's admiration, and that hard work is rewarded with material success. Just as Frank Alpine cannot recognize the real Morris when he looks at the body in the coffin, so the Jewish clergyman cannot recreate Malamud's Jew—Morris Bober.

Malamud's treatment of Ida Bober, Morris's wife, once more denies the possibility of real laughter. Ida has all the stereotyped characteristics of a perpetually worried, nagging Yiddish wife. She has the typical fears and aspirations. She wants to move into a Jewish neighborhood, be blessed with a Jewish son-in-law (a professional of course), and warn her husband about being too kind to penniless customers and stray *goyim* in search of a job. Given these characteristics, one could imagine a satirical portrait of the woman who pounds on the floorboards every time her husband smokes a cigarette and who follows her daughter to see if she is dating a non-Jewish man. But Ida slaves in a worthless store despite her sick legs. Within a period of months her husband is wounded by robbers, almost dies in a gas-filled apartment, roams the streets searching for a counterman's job, suffers from lung ailments, get pneumonia, and finally dies just when things look good for a moment. She has one hope: a buyer will come and purchase the store. This is the one event in the book for which she dresses up. The buyer does not come, and when he finally appears, he leaves without buying the store. She fears everything; yet this cannot be a humorous caricature of the woman who is unnecessarily perpetually worried and afraid, for all Ida's fears are realized. Her life is miserable, her suffering unalleviated.

Thus, in *The Assistant* Malamud offers moral affirmation while, at the same time, employing an ironic technique and laughless humor which function thematically to dramatize his world of hopeless hope.

Notes

1   *The Assistant* (New York: Signet, 1958), pp. 179–180.

Tony Tanner

~~~

from "Bernard Malamud and the New Life"□

Just what a man can learn from his experience and suffering, and what are the possibilities for a second life may be said to be the main preoccupation of Malamud's novels. In *The Assistant* Malamud seems to have moved towards realism. The economic facts of Morris Bober's fading attempts to keep his little grocer's shop running are made depressingly accurate. Morris is a poor Jew, a consistently good man who has unfailingly bad luck. History has very much happened *to* him. Even his newspaper is 'yesterday's'—he is floundering and sinking in Time. He is effectively 'entombed' in his store, which is just one of the many dark constricted spaces in which so many of Malamud's characters have to live out their suffering. But although the plight of the Bober family is real enough, the novel moves effortlessly towards fable. Morris Bober is the dying father who has already lost his only son. Frank Alpine, who stumbles so strangely into his life, replaces that lost son. First of all he joins in a squalid hold-up of Bober's shop in which Morris is literally felled—a ritual 'killing,' followed quite shortly afterwards by actual death. Out of remorse, and some more complicated feelings, Frank returns to the shop and gradually takes over all the work. In view of the fading energies of the

□ *Critical Quarterly*, X (Spring-Summer, 1968), pp. 155–157. Reprinted by permission of Tony Tanner.

sick old man he becomes the indispensable 'assistant.' When Morris is being buried, Frank accidentally slips into the grave, thus inadvertently dancing on the dead father's coffin. From now on he takes on the role and responsiblities of the father—provider, protector, living for others where he had previously lived only for himself.

This transformation of Frank does not happen easily. Like Roy Hobbs he has a lot of selfish hungers in him; but he also has a quality of moral aspiration revealed by his growing desire 'to change his life before the smell of it suffocated him.' 'He stared at the window, thinking thoughts about his past, and wanting a new life. Would he ever get what he wanted?' What kind of 'new life' does he want? Is it to help himself to more of the goods of life, as he helps himself to the cash register even while working for the store, and as, in a moment of desperate frustration, he helps himself to the daughter Helen? But that would not be a 'new' life, only an extension of the old. A really new life involves a radical change of attitude towards the self and other people. The painful emergence of selflessness from selfishness is the real drama of the book. We learn that he has always been attracted to St. Francis of Assisi since he heard about him in the orphanage where he was brought up; and since he likes to feed birds, and has a talent for carving wooden flowers, we are not surprised to find certain saintly inclinations in Francis Alpine which finally prove stronger than his merely appetitive self. In particular his attitude to the Jews changes. At first he is often disgusted with what seems to be Morris Bober's cowed resignation. 'What kind of man did you have to be born to shut yourself up in an overgrown coffin? . . . The answer wasn't hard to say—you had to be a Jew. They were born prisoners.' Yet he is increasingly drawn towards something in the Jewish attitude to life. He asks Morris for his definition of a Jew. Dismissing details of orthodoxy Morris says that the only important thing for a Jew is that he believes in 'the Law.' ' "This means to do what is right, to be honest, to be good." ' Frank complains that Jews seem to 'suffer more than they have to'. Morris answers: ' "If you live you suffer. Some people suffer more, but not because they want. But I think if a

THE ASSISTANT (1957)
BERNARD MALAMUD

Jew don't suffer for the Law, he will suffer for nothing. . . ." '
Frank asks Morris what he suffers for and receives the answer:
' "I suffer for you"'. Asked for more clarification Morris only
adds ' "I mean you suffer for me"'.

It sounds like a simple lesson, but it is one which
Malamud's characters learn only through pain and anguish,
and after much resistance to commitments and responsibilities
which override the clamouring hungers of the self. Morris
Bober is a Jew because, as the rabbi says at his funeral:
' "he lived in the Jewish experience . . . He followed the
Law . . . He suffered, he endured, but with hope . . . He
asked for himself little—nothing . . ." ' It is this kind of Jew
which Frank Alpine finally becomes. Paradoxically it is by
identifying himself with these figures of imprisonment and
suffering that he finds the 'better life' he sought. Helen
recognises the change in him when she discovers that he
works all night to keep the family fed and her at school. He is
not the hungry man who once raped her. 'It came to her that
he had changed. It's true, he's not the same man, she said to
herself . . . It was a strange thing about people—they could
look the same but be different. He had been one thing, low,
dirty, but because of something in himself . . . he had changed
into somebody else, no longer what he had been.' The main
focus of the novel is not on the economic misery of the Bobers,
but on the moral transformation of Frank Alpine. In taking on
the shop, replacing the father, and becoming a Jew, he is
really coming to man's estate and putting away childish
things. He suffers for others now, not simply for self: in this
sense he is the 'new man' he wanted to be. He has learned
what Roy Hobbs failed to learn, and he has won his 'new life.'
Thus realism becomes parable in Malamud's imagination
and vision.

Bibliographical Appendix

The following bibliographies will supply further criticism of American novels:

Donna Gerstenberger and George Hendrick, *The American Novel 1789-1959: A Checklist of Twentieth-Century Criticism*. Denver: Alan Swallow, c. 1961.

C. Hugh Holman, [comp.], *The American Novel Through Henry James*. Golden Tree Bibliographies. New York: Appleton-Century-Crofts, c. 1966.

Lewis Leary, [comp.], *Articles on American Literature 1900-1950*. Durham, N.C.: Duke University Press, 1954.

Blake Nevius, [comp.], *The American Novel: Sinclair Lewis to the Present*. Golden Tree Bibliographies. New York: Appleton-Century-Crofts, c. 1970.

Robert E. Spiller et al., eds., *Literary History of the United States: Bibliography*. New York: The Macmillan Company, 1948. Vol. III. *Bibliography Supplement*, edited by Richard M. Ludwig. New York: The Macmillan Co., c. 1959.

Floyd Stovall, ed., *Eight American Authors: A Review of Research and Criticism*. Bibliographical Supplement by J. Chesley Mathews. The Norton Library. New York: W. W. Norton & Co., Inc., c. 1963.

James Woodress, ed., *American Literary Scholarship: An Annual.* Durham, N.C.: Duke University Press. Appearing annually for the years 1963 et. seq. from 1965 on.

Furthermore, the following journals publish bibliographies:

American Literature, published quarterly by the Duke University Press, "Articles on American Literature Appearing in Current Periodicals."

Modern Fiction Studies, published quarterly by the Purdue University Department of English, "Selected Checklists" of Criticism in issues devoted to individual writers.

Publications of the Modern Language Association of America (PMLA), annual bibliographies.

Twentieth-Century Literature: A Scholarly and Critical Journal, published quarterly at Immaculate Heart College, Los Angeles, "Current Bibliography."